CELEBRATED CRIMINAL CASES OF AMERICA

BY

THOMAS S. DUKE

CAPTAIN OF POLICE. SAN FRANCISCO

PUBLISHED WITH APPROVAL OF THE HONORABLE BOARD OF POLICE
COMMISSIONERS OF SAN FRANCISCO

SAN FRANCISCO, CAL.

1910

PREFACE.

This volume, which is the first history published of the celebrated criminal cases in America, includes the most important cases during the past eighty years.

They have been collected after years of systematic investigation and verified with the assistance of police officials throughout America, without whose co-operation an authentic history would be impossible.

The hundred and ten cases presented in this volume should prove interesting to the general reader because of the psychological and, in many cases, the historical interest which attaches to them.

This book also contains a brief history of the San Francisco Police Department from the date of its organization; an accurate history of the far-famed Vigilance Committee; the Kearney riots; the life of Chief Justice Terry, including the famous duel in which he killed United States Senator Broderick and his tragic death while assaulting Justice Field of the United States Supreme Court; also a synopsis of the police and municipal history of the great earthquake and fire, which contains much information which has not heretofore been published.

While this volume will show that in some instances fabulous amounts of money have been unlawfully obtained, it will also show that retribution invariably overtakes the professional criminal and brings with it untold misery and degradation.

Although there are isolated cases where the perpetrator of an atrocious crime succeeds in escaping the iron hand of the law, there is one court he cannot escape, and that is the one "whose findings are incontrovertible and whose sessions are held in the chambers of his own breast."

The dread of discovery is constantly with him by day and by night, and who can doubt but that he finally concludes that even an ignominious death on a scaffold would be preferable to such a miserable existence.

A perusal of this volume will show that, while many of the most desperate characters have inherited their criminal tendencies, environment frequently transforms an ideal youth into a veritable fiend.

To the police officials and others who have supplied me with valuable information and photographs of criminals, I hereby acknowledge my gratitude, especially to the following named gentlemen:

Assistant Superintendent of Police Schuettler of Chicago, Mr. William Pinkerton, Detective Frank Geyer of Philadelphia (who investigated the case of Holmes, the "Criminal of the Century"), Mr. James McParland of Mollie Maguire fame, Captain Harry Morse, Theodore Kytka, the handwriting expert; Sergeant John Moffitt and Photographer George Blum of the San Francisco police. Captain of Detectives Walter Peterson of Oakland, and last but not least, to the affable Mr. J. H. Deering of the San Francisco Law Library.

THOMAS DUKE,

Captain of Police, San Francisco.

October 2, 1910.

PART I.

SAN FRANCISCO CASES.

BRIEF HISTORY OF SAN FRANCISCO POLICE DEPARTMENT.

(From "Annals of San Francisco" and Police Records.)

Under the laws of Mexico, an *Alcalde* had entire control of municipal affairs and administered justice pretty much according to his own ideas without being tied down entirely to precedents and formal principles of law.

Lieutenant W. Bartlett, U. S. N., was the first Alcalde of San Francisco under the American flag.

When the Americans seized this part of the country from the Mexicans, the old order of things prevailed until peace was declared and a constitution was adopted.

On January 30, 1847, the following "Ordinance" appeared in the "California Star":

"An Ordinance.

"Whereas, the local name of Yerba Buena, as applied to the settlement or town of San Francisco, is unknown beyond the district; and has been applied from the local name of the cove on which the town is built: Therefore, to prevent confusion and mistakes in public documents, and that the town may have the advantage of the name given on the public map, "It is hereby ordained, that the name of San Francisco shall hereafter be used in all official communications and public documents, or records appertaining to the town.

"Wash'n a. Bartlett,
"Chief Magistrate. "

Published by order.
"J. G. T. Dunleavy, Municipal Clerk."

The population of the town at that time was 459.

On February 22, 1847, Alcalde Bartlett was succeeded by Edwin Bryant, who held office only a few months, when he resigned and Military Governor Mason appointed Mr. George Hyde to fill the vacancy.

On August 15, 1847, the Governor issued an order to Alcalde Hyde as follows:

"There is wanted in San Francisco an efficient town government, more so than is in the power of an Alcalde to put in force. There may be soon expected a large number of whalers in your bay, and a large increase of your population by the arrival of immigrants. It is therefore highly necessary that you should at an early day have an efficient town police, proper town laws, town officers, etc., for enforcement of the laws, for the preservation of order, and for the proper protection of persons and property.

"I therefore desire that you call a town meeting for the election of six persons, who when elected shall constitute the town council, and who in conjunction with the Alcalde shall constitute the town authorities until the end of the year 1848.

"All the municipal laws and regulations will be framed by the council, but executed by the Alcalde in his judicial capacity as at present.

"The first Alcalde will preside at all meetings of the council, but shall have no vote, except in cases where the votes are equally divided.

"The town council (not less than four of whom shall constitute a quorum for the transaction of business), to appoint all the town officers, such as treasurer, constables, watchmen, etc., and to determine their pay, fees, etc.

"No soldier, sailor or marine, nor any person who is not a bona fide resident of the town shall be allowed to vote for a member of the town council."

On September 13 the election was held. As soon as the result was known, the newly elected councilmen entered upon the duties of their office. Six constables were appointed to preserve the peace.

On January 11, 1848, a law was passed providing that "all money found on a gambling table shall be seized for the benefit of the town," but this was repealed shortly afterward and for several years gambling games were permitted to run openly and were licensed. In 1853 there were 537 places in San Francisco where liquor was sold, 46 of which had gambling houses attached. The leading gambling-places at that time were the "El Dorado," located at the present Hall of Justice site opposite Portsmouth Square, and "The Arcade" and "Poker" Clubs on Commercial Street. Women were permitted to play and refreshments were served. Coin was scarce, but bags of gold dust furnished a circulating medium which answered all purposes. Many of the smaller games were conducted in tents.

In the early part of 1849 the population had increased to 5,000 inhabitants, but the only police protection consisted of six undisciplined constables. About this time an organization of ruffians known as the "Hounds" terrorized the whole community. They assisted each other in sickness or peril and elected one Sam Roberts as their leader. They committed all the crimes on the calendar with impunity and met with their woman associates in a tent called "Tammany Hall."

On Sunday, July 15, 1849, their conduct became unbearable. On the following Monday a mass meeting of law-abiding citizens was called by Alcalde Leavenworth at Portsmouth Square. Subscriptions were taken to buy rifles. Two hundred and thirty citizens became volunteer policemen, and W. E. Spofford was elected leader.

That same day twenty "Hounds" were arrested, and Sam Roberts was captured while attempting to escape to Stockton. The prisoners were taken on board the U. S. S. "Warren," as there was no suitable jail on shore.

A second meeting was called for Monday night and Dr. William Gwin and James Ward were elected Judges to try the prisoners. Horace Hawes was elected District Attorney and Hall McAllister assistant.

A "Grand Jury" was appointed and "indictments" were found. The trials were conducted with dignity and impartiality. All were convicted, and Roberts, the leader, was sentenced to serve 10 years in any prison the Governor selected.

This put an end to the "Hounds" and to lawlessness for about one year and the volunteer police force disbanded.

On April 1, 1849, Colonel John W. Geary, of Mexican war fame, arrived in San Francisco on the steamship "Oregon," which was the second steamship to arrive in San Francisco harbor. He had been appointed Postmaster of San Francisco by President Polk and given power to create post offices and establish mail routes.

On August 1 of the same year he was nominated for Alcalde and received 1,516 votes, being the entire number cast. No candidate could be found to run against him.

Having a lively recollection of the outrages committed by the "Hounds" some months previous, Alcalde Geary and the town council proceeded to organize a police force, and on August 10, 1849, Malachi Fallon was appointed City Marshal and placed in command of a force consisting of twelve men.*

Fallon was born in Ireland in 1814. When a child he moved to New

York City and in 1839 he was made Keeper of the famous "Tombs," where many celebrated criminals have been incarcerated. He held this position until 1848 when he started west. On February 28th, 1849, Fallon and about four hundred others, including D. W. C. Thompson, who also served as City Marshal, entered San Francisco bay on the Pacific Mail steamship "California." This side-wheeler was the first steamship to enter the harbor, and the citizens gathered at the wharf to give her a "California" welcome.

In 1850 the population of San Francisco increased to about 15.000. The New Charter was adopted in that year and on May 1 an election for City officers was held.

Colonel Geary was elected the first Mayor of the City and Malachi Fallon was elected City Marshal.

On April 28, 1851, Robert G. Crozier was elected to succeed Marshal Fallon. The summary methods employed to subdue the "Hounds" kept that element within bounds for about a year.

In 1850, immigrants swarmed into the town and by 1851 it was estimated that the population had reached 30.000 people. Among these immigrants were many of the most desperate criminals in the country, and the result was that a series of depredations were committed which struck terror to the hearts of the law-abiding citizens.

The police force, consisting of twelve men, was regarded with contempt by the criminal class and conditions were growing worse daily.

On December 24, 1849, and on May 4 and June 14, 1850, great conflagrations swept over large portions of the territory bounded by Jackson, DuPont and California Streets and the waters of the bay, which resulted in an aggregate loss approximately estimated at $4,000,000.

As the criminal class began to plunder simultaneously with the breaking out of the flames, it was strongly suspected that they had set the fires to give them this opportunity. A reward of $5,000 was offered for the apprehension and conviction of any of the incendiaries, and although several arrests were made no convictions were obtained.

Finally on June 18, 1851, a great number of the leading citizens determined to take the law into their own hands and as a result, the far-famed Vigilance Committee was organized. (See History Vigilance Committee.)

Marshal Crozier, realizing his utter helplessness with the inadequate force at his command, demanded that the department be reorganized and strengthened.

His demand was heeded and on July 26, 1851, the department was reorganized and increased to fifty men, including Hampton North and John McKenzie, both of whom afterward served as City Marshal. The department was also provided with two Captains and two assistant Captains. In 1852 Hampton North was made assistant Captain.

A few months after the election in April, 1851, a dispute arose regarding the wording of the New Charter. Those opposed to the officers in power contended that the law required that another election be held for City officers in September, five months after the last election, but those in office disregarded the claim and refused to place a ticket in the field. The result was that a new set of officers were "elected," including D. W. Thompson, who ran for City Marshal. The courts subsequently decided, however, that this last election was illegal.

On November 2, 1852, Crozier was again elected City Marshal. On September 14, 1853, Brandt Seguine was elected to succeed Crozier. As Seguine was sick from July 19 to August 1, 1854, Assistant Captain Hampton North acted as Marshal.

On October 28, 1853, the Board of Aldermen passed Ordinance No. 466, which provided for the reorganization of the police department.

Sections one and two provided as follows:

"The People of the City of San Francisco do ordain as follows:

"Sec. 1. The Police Department of the City of San Francisco, shall be composed of a day and night police, consisting of 56 men (including a Captain and assistant Captain), each to be recommended by at least ten tax-paying citizens.

"Sec. 2. There shall be one Captain and one assistant Captain of Police, who shall be elected in joint convention of the Board of Aldermen and assistant Aldermen. The remainder of the force, viz., 54 men, shall be appointed as follows:

"By the Mayor, 2; by the City Marshal, 2; by the City Recorder, 2; and by the Aldermen and assistant Aldermen, 3 each."

Among the three men appointed by Alderman John Nightengale was Isaiah W. Lees, who came to San Francisco with Nightengale and for nearly half a century after joining the department was recognized at home and abroad as one of the greatest detectives in America.

In September, 1854, Officer John W. McKenzie was elected City Marshal. Twelve months later Hampton North was nominated on the "Know Nothing" party ticket and was elected to succeed McKenzie.

In May, 1856, the Vigilantes again became dissatisfied with the manner in which justice was being administered, especially after the jury disagreed in the case of Cora, who killed United States Marshal Richardson, and the cowardly murder of James King of William by Supervisor James Casey. The committee therefore resolved to resume operations. (See History of Vigilance Committee.)

Marshal North was bitterly opposed to the methods of the Vigilantes, so that organization formed a private police force of which James Curtis was made Chief.

In July, 1856, the "Consolidation Act" went into effect. This act abolished the office of City Marshal and created in its stead the office of Chief of Police.

Under this law the force was increased to 150 men, and the Chief (whose office was elective), the Mayor and Police Judge constituted the Police Commission, which had full power to appoint, promote, disrate or dismiss members of the department.

Immediately after the Consolidation Act went into effect. Marshal North's office being abolished, J. McElroy was appointed to act as Chief until the election in the following November.

About the time that North became a private citizen, the Vigilantes received information that as City Marshal, North had permitted certain violations of the law, and it was suggested that he lose no time in leaving San Francisco. North acted on the suggestion and was never seen in San Francisco again.

On November 4, 1856, the first election was held under the Consolidation Act and James Curtis, Chief of the Vigilantes' force, was elected the first Chief of Police.

He held office until 1858, when he was succeeded by Martin Burke, who held office until 1865, after which he became identified with the real estate firm of Madison & Burke.

Patrick Crowley, who was a constable in 1859, followed Burke and held office until 1874, when he was succeeded by Theodore Cockrill. In 1876 Cockrill gave way to H. H. Ellis, who had served for many years as a detective with Captain Lees.*

On the morning of September 12, 1859, Lees and Ellis learned that the duel between United States Senator David Broderick and Chief Justice of the Supreme Court David Terry was to be fought near Lake Merced. They arrived on the ground just as the weapons were being handed to the men and placed them under arrest. The case was dismissed by Judge Coon that day and on the following day the duel was fought in the same neighborhood and Broderick was killed. These same officers afterward arrested Terry. (See history of Broderick-Terry duel.)

On April 3, 1876, the Legislature passed "An Act to create a City Criminal Court in San Francisco." All cases where persons charged with misdemeanors demanded jury trials, and all persons indicted for misdemeanors, were assigned to this court. Section 7 of this act provided that:

"The Judge of the City Criminal Court and the County Judge of San Francisco are hereby made ex-officio Police Commissioners of said City and County and said Commission shall, from and after the passage of this act, consist of the Mayor, Police Judge, Chief of Police, Judge of City Criminal Court and County Judge, and shall receive no compensation as such Commissioners."

The last Commission under this law consisted of Mayor A. J. Bryant, County Judge Selden S. Wright, City Criminal Judge Robert Ferral, Chief Kirkpatrick and Police Judge Davis Louderback.

In 1878 John Kirkpatrick was elected Chief. Although San Francisco had developed into a large city, the Consolidation Act provided that the police force should not exceed one hundred and fifty officers. While Kirkpatrick was Chief the so-called "Kearney riots" occurred, and it soon became evident that the police force was entirely too small to handle the situation. (See History of Kearney Riots.)

Frank McCoppin, who was formerly the superintendent of the steam road which ran out Market and Hayes Streets, and who afterward served as Supervisor and Mayor of the City, was a State Senator at the time of these riots and he introduced a bill which provided:

1st: *"That the Board of Supervisors of San Francisco be granted power to increase the police force from 150 to 400 men."*

2nd: *"That the Judges of the Fourth, Twelfth and Fifteenth Judicial Districts be empowered to choose three reputable citizens of San Francisco who, together with the Chief of Police, shall constitute the Police Commission."*

3rd: *"That this Board shall have all the powers and supersede the Board provided for in 'An act to create a City Criminal Court in San Francisco.'"* And

4th: *"That at the expiration of the official term of the present Chief of Police, said office shall cease to be elective but shall be filled by the Police Commissioners."*

This act went into effect in April, 1878.

As Chief Kirkpatrick's term did not expire until twenty months after the so-called McCoppin Act became effective, he continued to serve as Chief for that period.

The Commissioners selected by the three Judges were Robert Tobin of the Hibernia Bank, ex-Mayor William Alvord of the Bank of California, and Major Hammond.

Kirkpatrick's term expired on December 31, 1879, and ex-Chief P. Crowley was appointed Chief of Police. He held this office until April 7, 1897, when he retired and was succeeded by the veteran Captain of Detectives, I. W. Lees.

Immediately after Lees' promotion was announced, the venerable John Nightengale, who appointed Lees on the force forty-five years before, called on the new Chief and insisted upon going on his official bond.

After forty-seven years of brilliant work in the department. Chief Lees was retired on a pension on January 2, 1900. His loyalty to his friends, and the manner in which he frequently antagonized powerful influences by battling for his men when he believed them to be in the right, won for him the admiration of the entire department.

The Police Commission, having in mind the fact that the New Charter, which gave the Mayor full power to appoint Police Commissioners, would go into effect on January 8, 1900, it was decided to leave the position of Chief of Police vacant and appoint Captain George Wittman as acting Chief until the new Commission organized and selected a Chief of Police.

The first Commission under the new Charter was appointed by Mayor James D. Phelan and consisted of George Newhall, William J. Biggy, Dr. W. F. McNutt and Attorney William Thomas.

Immediately after their appointment they met and decided to delay the appointment of a Chief, but Commissioner Biggy, who had formerly served as a State Senator and Registrar of Voters, was appointed acting Chief. He served in this capacity until February 13, of the same year, when he was removed from the department by Mayor Phelan, and Colonel Wm. P. Sullivan, the Mayor's private secretary, was appointed Chief.

Sullivan died on November 11, 1901, and Captain of Police George Wittman was appointed Chief on November 21, 1901.

During the month of November, 1904, Police Commissioner Harry Hutton was informed that a Chinese gambling game was being conducted at 820 Washington Street. On the night of November 29, 1904, Hutton telephoned to the Central Station and requested that a policeman be sent to his office at once. Officer William Minehan was sent and upon arriving at the office was instructed to enter a hack with Attorney Grant Carpenter and Hutton. They were driven to 820 Washington Street, where several Chinese, who were said to have been secretly assisting Hutton and Carpenter, and who had access to the gambling places, were stationed.

When they saw the carriage approach, the Chinese made a pretense at passing through the several heavy doors, which were ordinarily bolted against the police. Instead of passing the doors, a Chinaman stopped by each one leading toward the gambling room, and held the same ajar, so that the party had an unobstructed passage to the gambling tables when the games were in full operation.

Thomas Ellis was appointed a member of the department on April 1, 1886, because, as a citizen, he came to the rescue of Captain Lees when the latter was about to be overpowered by a desperate criminal he was attempting to arrest. Lees, who never forgot a friend, was also instrumental in promoting Ellis to the rank of Sergeant.

At the time of the Hutton raid, Ellis was in charge of Chinatown and he was charged with neglect of duty for failing to suppress gambling. He was subsequently interrogated by the "Andrews" Grand Jury and confessed that he had permitted gambling in Chinatown for a monetary consideration and to corroborate his statement he produced $1100 which he had. accepted as bribe money. He was found guilty on February 15, 1905, and subsequently dismissed from the department.

On the night Ellis was found guilty. Chief Wittman was suspended from duty and the Secretary of the Police Commission was instructed to file charges of incompetence against him for failing to suppress gambling in Chinatown. After a lengthy trial he was dismissed from the department on March 24, 1905.

Captain John Spillane acted as Chief from the date of Wittman's suspension until April 5, 1905, when Detective Jerry Dinan was appointed

Chief.

While Dinan was Chief, Attorney Francis J. Heney, and Detective Wm. J. Bums, formerly of the United States Secret Service, began what was commonly known as the "Graft" investigation in San Francisco.

On November 22, 1906, Dinan was called as a witness before the so-called "Oliver" Grand Jury and interrogated by Heney in regard to questionable resorts then located at 620 Jackson Street and 714 Pacific Street. Because of alleged false testimony given on that occasion, Dinan was indicted for perjury.

On November 15, 1906, Mayor E. E. Schmitz was indicted on a charge of having extorted money from the French restaurant keepers and on June 13, 1907, he was found guilty. On March 9, 1908, the Supreme Court decided that the indictment did not show that a crime had been committed, thereby sustaining the opinion rendered by the Court of Appeals on January 9, 1908.

Schmitz was removed from office shortly after his conviction and Edward Robeson Taylor was appointed in his stead.

On August 22, 1907, the Schmitz Board of Police Commissioners retired and were replaced by a Board appointed by Taylor.

Dinan immediately resigned as Chief but retained his position as detective. He was subsequently suspended pending the outcome of the perjury charge, but as the court failed to set a date for the trial, Francis J. Heney filed charges of unofficerlike conduct against Dinan before the Police Commission because of the alleged perjured testimony. After hearing the evidence the Commission rendered a verdict of not guilty and Dinan was restored to duty in the detective office on November 17, 1909.

On September 13, 1907, former Commissioner William J. Biggy was appointed Chief of Police to succeed Dinan.

On the evening of November 30, 1908, he telephoned to Police Commissioner Hugo Keil, who lived across the bay at Belvedere, and informed him that he intended to cross the bay that night to confer with him (Keil) in relation to important police matters. Shortly afterward, the police boat "Patrol" hove in sight of Keil's home, which was at the water's edge, and Biggy entered Keil's house.

After a lengthy conference, the Chief returned to the "Patrol" and started home; he and Engineer Murphy being the only persons on board.

About 1 1:20 p. m. the boat passed Alcatraz Island, and Biggy left the cabin in the rear and came forward to chat with Murphy, who was running the launch. After a few words, Biggy returned toward the cabin.

When the boat neared the wharf, Murphy called to the Chief to inform him that they were nearing land. Receiving no response, he instituted a search, but all in vain, for Biggy was never seen alive again.

As he was being subjected to very severe criticism about this time by those opposed to his policy, it was hinted that he committed suicide by jumping overboard, but an inspection of the boat showed very clearly that death could have been and probably was, accidental. On December 14th, his body was found floating near Goat Island.

On December 26, 1908, Sergeant Jesse B. Cook, commonly called "Captain" Cook because of his position as Property Clerk of the department, was appointed Chief.

On the evening of January 27, 1910, Mayor P. H. McCarthy removed the three remaining Commissioners appointed by Mayor Taylor and appointed I. Spiro, Walter O'Connell and Percy Henderson in their stead, H. P. Flannery having been appointed to succeed Charles Sweigert on January 8.

Chief Cook handed in his resignation on the same evening and Retired Captain John B. Martin was immediately restored to active duty and then appointed Chief of Police.

HISTORY OF THE FAMOUS VIGILANCE COMMITTEE AND BATTLES WITH SQUATTERS.

(From "Annals of San Francisco" and Hittel's "History of California.")

While the discovery of gold brought thousands of desirable citizens to San Francisco it also brought an army of the most daring thugs that ever operated in a civilized community.

In 1851 the population of San Francisco was estimated at 30,000 inhabitants, and there were over 500 saloons and nearly fifty gambling places. The police force, however, consisted of only twelve men. These officers were absolutely powerless to enforce the law and the criminal element was quick to take advantage of the situation.

On February 19, 1851, two men entered the store of C. J. Jansen, apparently to buy blankets, but they assaulted and almost killed the proprietor and took $2,000.

Thomas Burden was arrested the next day and positively identified, as was also one Windred, as being the two assailants. On Saturday, February 22, the defendants were in court and a mob of 5,000 people attempted to seize and lynch them, but were repulsed by the "Washington Guards." Mayor John W. Geary delivered an address in which he advised that the law be permitted to take its course.

Finally it was decided that William T. Coleman and eleven other citizens should try the men according to their own methods. These men could not agree on their guilt, and it was subsequently proven that the defendants were innocent, and Burden, who was mistaken for James Stuart, the real criminal, was presented with a sum of money by the citizens to compensate him in part for the injustice done him.

About March, 1851, the criminal element became bolder than ever, their headquarters being in the vicinity of "Clark's Point," at the lower end of Broadway and Pacific Streets. They set fires to buildings for the purpose of looting them, and about 100 murders were committed in five months. In June, 1851, the famous "Vigilance Committee" was organized and adopted the following constitution:

"Whereas, it has become apparent to the citizens of San Francisco

that there is no security for life and property, either under the regulations of society as it at present exists, or under the law as now administered; therefore, the citizens, whose names are hereunto attached, do unite themselves into an association for the maintenance of the peace and good order of society, and the preservation of the lives and property of the citizens of San Francisco, and do bind ourselves, each unto the other, to do and perform every lawful act for the maintenance of law and order, and to sustain the laws when faithfully and properly administered; but we are determined that no thief, burglar, incendiary or assassin, shall escape punishment, either by the quibbles of the law, the insecurity of prisons, or a laxity of those who pretend to administer justice. And to secure the objects of this association we do hereby agree:

"1. That the name and style of the association shall be the Committee of Vigilance, for the protection of the lives and property of the citizens and residents of the city of San Francisco.

"2. That there shall be a room selected for the meeting and deliberation of this committee, at which there shall be one or more members of the committee, appointed for that purpose, in constant attendance, at all hours of the day and night, to receive the report of any member of the association, or of any other person or persons whatsoever, of any act of violence done to the person or property of any citizen of San Francisco; and if in the judgment of the member or members of the committee present, it be such an act as justifies the interference of the committee, either in aiding in the execution of the laws, or the prompt and summary punishment of the offender, the committee shall be at once assembled for the purpose of taking such action as a majority of the committee when assembled shall determine upon.

"3. That it shall be the duty of any member or members of the committee on duty at the committee room, whenever a general assemblage of the committee is deemed necessary, to cause a call to be made by two strokes upon a bell, which shall be repeated with a pause of one minute, between each alarm. The alarm to be struck until ordered to be stopped.

"4. That when the committee have assembled for action, the decision of a majority present shall be binding upon the whole committee, and that those members of the committee whose names are hereunto attached, do pledge their honor, and hereby bind themselves, to defend and sustain each other in carrying out the determined action of this committee at the hazard of their lives and their fortunes.

"5. That there shall be chosen monthly a president, secretary and treasurer, and it shall be the duty of the secretary to detail the members required to be in daily attendance at the committee room.

"A sergeant-at-arms shall be appointed, whose duty it shall be to *notify such members of their details for duty. The sergeant-at-arms shall reside at and be in constant attendance at the committee room.*

"There shall be a standing committee of finance, and qualification, consisting of five each, and no person shall be admitted a member of this association unless he be a respectable citizen, and approved of by the committee on qualification before admission."

An occasion soon happened to test the character and uses of this most extraordinary association. On the evening of June 10, 1851, a person named John Jenkins feloniously entered a store on Long Wharf and stole a safe. He was subsequently seen with a large burden slung across his back, and an alarm being raised, was pursued. He then got into a boat, and sculled out into the bay, followed by a dozen other boats in keen pursuit.

The fugitive was soon overtaken; but before his captors reached him he was seen to throw the burden into the water. This was soon drawn up, and proved to be the stolen safe. The prisoner was next taken to the rooms of the Vigilance Committee, in Battery Street, near the corner of Pine Street.

About 10 o'clock of the same night a signal was given on the bell of the Monumental Engine Company, and shortly afterwards about eighty members of the committee hurried to the appointed place, and on giving the secret password were admitted. Meanwhile knots of people, some of whom knew and all suspected what was going on, gathered about the premises, and impatiently awaited the further progress of events.

For two hours the committee was closely occupied in examining evidence. At midnight the bell of the California Engine House was tolled, as sentence of death by hanging was passed upon the wretched man. The solemn sounds at that unusual hour filled the anxious crowds with awe. The condemned at this time was asked if he had anything to say for himself, when he answered: "No, I have nothing to say, only I wish to have a cigar." This was handed to him, and afterwards, at his request, a little brandy and water. He was perfectly cool, and seemingly careless, confidently expecting, it was believed, a rescue, up to the last moment.

A little before 1 o'clock, Mr. S. Brannan came out of the committee rooms, and ascending a mound of sand to the east of the Rasette House, addressed the people. He had been deputed, he said, by the committee to inform them that the prisoner's case had been fairly tried, that he had been proved guilty, and was condemned to be hanged, and that the sentence would be executed within one hour upon the plaza. He then asked the people if they approved of the action of the committee, when great shouts of "Aye, Aye," burst forth, mingled with a few cries of "No." In the interval a clergyman had been sent for, who administered the last consolations of religion to the condemned.

Shortly before 2 o'clock the committee issued from the building, bearing the prisoner (who had his arms tightly pinioned) along with them. The committee were all armed and closely clustered around the culprit to prevent any possible chance of rescue. A procession was formed, and the whole party, followed by the crowd, proceeded to the plaza. Arrived at the flagstaff, some thoughtlessly suggested that it might serve to hang the condemned upon, but the proposal was indignantly overruled as desecrating the liberty pole. Those in charge of the execution proceeded to the south end of the adobe building, which stood on the northwest corner of the plaza. The opposite end of the rope, which was already about the neck of the victim, was hastily thrown over a projecting beam. Some of the authorities attempted at this stage of affairs to interfere, but their efforts were unavailing. They were civilly desired to stand back and not delay what was still to be done. The crowd, which numbered upwards of a thousand, was perfectly quiescent, or only applauded by look, gesture and subdued voice the action of the committee. Before the prisoner had reached the building, a score of persons seized the loose end of the rope and ran backwards, dragging the wretch along the ground and raising him to the beam. Thus they held him till he was dead.

The hanging of Jenkins had a salutary effect on the criminal class and many left the city. As there was a tendency to ignore the demands of the committee the following notice was issued on July 5, 1851:

"Vigilance Committee Room. — It having become necessary to the peace and quiet of this community that all criminals and abettors in crime should be driven from among us, no good citizen, having the welfare of San Francisco at heart, will deny the Committee of Vigilance such information as will enable them to carry out the above object. Nor will they interfere with said committee when they may deem it best to search any premises for suspicious characters or stolen property. Therefore,

"Resolved, That we, the Vigilance Committee, do claim to ourselves the right to enter any person or persons' premises where we have good reason to believe that we shall find evidence to substantiate and carry out the object of this body; and further, deeming ourselves engaged in a good and just cause, WE intend to maintain it. By order of

"The Committee of Vigilance,

"No. 67, Secretary. "San Francisco, July 5, 1851."

At 9 a. m., July 11, the bell was rung, and when the Committee had assembled, Joseph Stuart, for whom Berdeu was mistaken in the Jansen robbery, and an all-around criminal, was tried and confessed to all his crimes. Colonel J. D. Stevenson addressed the citizens gathered, and after relating 'what had transpired, asked if it was the wish of the citizens I that Stuart be executed. The citizens cried "Yes," and he was hanged at the end of Market Street Wharf.

In August, 1851, Sam Whitaker and Robert McKenzie were tried for several crimes and confessed. They were sentenced to be hanged on August 20. Before the execution Governor John McDougall issued a proclamation to the citizens of San Francisco, in which he protested against the acts of the Vigilance Committee, but the committee answered by reminding him that he had privately expressed his approval of their method of procedure.

On August 21, before sunrise, Sheriff John Hayes, accompanied by a squad of police, entered the room of the Vigilance Committee where Whitaker and McKenzie were awaiting execution, seized the prisoners and took them to jail.

On Sunday, August 24, 1851, thirty-six members of the committee broke into jail during religious services which the two men sought were attending, and took them to Battery Street and hanged them. This was the last active work done for the time being by this committee.

On September 16, 1851, the committee decided to suspend operations and thereafter render financial assistance to enable the authorities to apprehend and properly prosecute criminals.

During the first two years after the Vigilance Committee ceased operations, the criminal element was conspicuous by their absence, but about 1854 a financial storm could be seen approaching, which was accompanied by political and social corruption. The better element, in their feverish rush for gold, neglected their duties as citizens and voters, and the result was that the lawless class gradually gained great power.

Over 1,000 homicides were committed between 1849 and 1856, and the only legal hanging was that of Jose Formi, who, on December 10, 1852, murdered Jose Rodriguez, for which he was hanged on Russian Hill on July 20, 1853.

On the evening of November 15, 1855, Charles Cora, a notorious gambler, accompanied a beautiful woman known as Belle Cora to the theater. This woman, who conducted a brothel, was undoubtedly infatuated with Cora, whose name she took.

On this evening their seats in the theater were next to those occupied by United States Marshal William R. Richardson and wife. Between acts the Marshal met Cora in the barroom, and it is said Richardson took Cora to task for allowing Belle Cora to sit beside his (Richardson's) wife.

About two days afterward Richardson met Cora on Leidesdorff Street, and Cora shot Richardson in the breast, producing a wound which caused almost instant death. Cora claimed that he shot in self-defense, as he claimed Richardson was about to attack him with a knife.

Belle Cora employed Colonel E. D. Baker, one of the ablest lawyers in the city, to defend her lover. Baker made a hard fight for his client, and attacked the private life of Richardson in his closing argument. On January 17, 1856, the jury disagreed.

On July 26, 1848, James King of William arrived in San Francisco. On December 5, 1849, he opened a banking house at Montgomery and Washington Streets, but failed in his enterprise, and on October 5, 1855, began publishing the San Francisco Bulletin.

He was as courageous as he was able, and as he denounced the lawless element in most bitter terms he naturally had numerous enemies. After the Cora jury disagreed King denounced the lawless element more than ever, and on May 14, 1856, published an article in which he stated that Supervisor James P. Casey had served a term for burglary at Sing Sing Prison. Immediately upon reading the article Casey proceeded to the Bulletin office, which was located on Merchant near Sansome Street, denounced King for exposing his past life, and then left the office in a great rage. About 5 p. m. King left his office to walk to his home at Pacific and Mason Streets.

At Montgomery and Washington Streets Casey intercepted him, and without any warning shot King through the chest. Casey surrendered and was taken by Marshal Hampton North and Officer I. W. Lees (afterward Chief of Police)   to the jail on Broadway Street. Great difficulty was experienced in preventing Casey from being lynched by the indignant citizens while en route to jail.

Mayor Van Ness finally succeeded in persuading the people to disperse. On May 15, 1856, the day after the shooting of King, the Vigilantes met to reorganize, and selected William T. Coleman as leader.

A great many members of the militia also joined the Vigilance Committee. All the members, which included such men as John Parrott and William Ralston, were designated by numbers. The membership increased to about thirty-five hundred. The meeting place was changed from Turn Verein Hall on Bush Street, between Stockton and Powell Streets, to the building on Sacramento Street, between Davis and Front, which was subsequently known as "Fort Gunny Bags," because gunny bags filled with sand were piled about ten feet high around the building as an additional protection. The activities of the Vigilance Committee caused a feeble attempt to be made toward fortifying the Broadway jail. Governor Johnson came to San Francisco, and it is claimed that after learning the facts, he privately approved of the methods employed by the Vigilantes. On Sunday, May 18,

King was sinking rapidly, and the Vigilantes decided to act at once. They had been secretly drilled in military tactics, and the several companies armed with rifles formed in all four directions from the jail and marched in columns to the jail, all companies arriving simultaneously.

The Vigilantes' artillery then advanced and set a cannon in front of the jail and very deliberately loaded it. At this point a written notice was served on Sheriff Dave Scannell to surrender Casey and Cora. When the leader, William T. Coleman, appeared, his forces saluted in true military style by presenting arms. Scannell seeing that resistance was useless admitted Coleman and his immediate aids. They proceeded to Casey's cell and found him defiantly brandishing a knife, Coleman assured him of a fair trial, and he surrendered, and he and Cora were marched from the jail. The proceeding was conducted with the greatest solemnity. They were taken to the Vigilance Committee headquarters, and their trials were set for the following Tuesday. Both men were provided with attorneys and allowed to produce witnesses.

King died on the same day the trials began. The defendants were found guilty and sentenced to be hanged on Friday, May 23, at the same time as King's funeral. The executions took place in front of the Vigilantes' building. The condemned men were permitted to consult spiritual and legal advisers, and shortly before they went to the gallows Belle Cora, who had spent a fortune trying to save her lover, entered the jail, and she and Cora were married by Father Accotti. The remains of Cora and Casey are buried at the Mission Dolores Cemetery, where the headstones are still standing.

On May 26, 1856, Billy Mulligan,* Yankee Sullivan and numerous others of their ilk, were arrested. They were the leaders of the gang of ballot box stuffers who were making elections a farce.

*Before coming to San Francisco Billy Mulligan was the Beau Brummel of the New York gamblers and as desperate a character as could be found in New York. He came to San Francisco during the gold excitement and took a prominent part in local politics. He served as keeper of the County Jail under Sheriff Scanlan, who subsequently became Chief of the Fire Derp'artment.

When the Vigilantes drove Mulligan from San Francisco he returned to New York and to his former haunts. One night he attempted to kill a man in a fashionable gambling-place, and for this crime he was sentenced to serve two years at Sing Sing.

While awaiting trial at the Tombs a beautifully gowned young woman visited the prison and fell desperately in love with Mulligan. She sacrificed her diamonds and jewelry to meet the expenses of his trial. On the evening preceding his departure for Sing

Sing she offered to marry him and he consented. The ceremony was immediately performed by Judge Brennan, and the bride accompanied the convict to Sing Sing on the following day.

Believing that he was sincere in his promise to reform and lead an upright life she worked night and day in his behalf, and at the expiration of two months procured his pardon. In spite of the devotion manifested by his loyal wife, Mulligan deserted her almost immediately after being released and returned to San Francisco in January, 1864.

On the afternoon of July 7, 1865, while suffering from delirium tremens he imagined that the Vigilantes were going to hang him. . He had a room facing the Street at the St. Francis Hotel, located at the southeast corner of DuPont and Clay Streets. He fired a pistol from his window and seriously wounded a Chinese laundryman who lived across the Street.

John McNabb, a friend of Mulligan's, attempted to approach his room with a glass of whisky, at the same time attempting to pacify him. Mulligan shot him dead.

In attempting to shoot the officers on the Street he shot and killed John Hart, of Eureka Hose Company No. 4. Officers with rifles were stationed in windows in the neighborhood and finally Mulligan again appeared at the window and was shot dead by Officer Hopkins.

After a trial they were sentenced to leave San Francisco, and warned that if they returned they would be hanged. While in jail Sullivan confessed to participating in election frauds and became extremely melancholy. He labored under the hallucination that he was to be hanged. On May 30 he was found dead in his cell with a knife wound on his left arm, from which he bled to death. Rumors were circulated that he had been murdered by a guard stabbing him with a bayonet, but the charge was never proved. A table knife covered with blood was found in his cell.

Notwithstanding the fact that Governor Johnson was alleged to have uttered words of encouragement to William Coleman in the work he had undertaken, he addressed a communication to General John Wool on June 10, 1856, in which he requested the latter, as Commander of the United States Army forces at Benicia, to proceed to San Francisco and stop the activities of the Vigilantes. Wool declined to interfere. A great many prominent citizens opposed the actions of the Vigilance Committee, and they formed an organization known as the "Law and Order Committee," and evidently intended to oppose the Vigilantes with force, as they began to gather arms.

On June 21, 1856, positive information was received that Reuben Maloney was assisting the "Law and Order Committee" to procure arms. S. A. Hopkins, a Vigilante policeman, was detailed to locate and arrest Maloney. Hopkins located him in company with Justice David S. Terry, of the State Supreme Court. Terry was opposed to the Vigilantes and ordered Hopkins not to make an illegal arrest in his presence.

Hopkins withdrew temporarily, but returned with several Vigilante policemen and again attempted to arrest Maloney. Terry drew a pistol and Hopkins grabbed it, whereupon Terry drew a dagger and stabbed Hopkins in the neck, inflicting a wound which was feared would result fatally.

Terry was at once arrested by the Vigilantes, but his trial was delayed until July 24 in order to ascertain definitely the extent of Hopkins' wounds. He was found guilty, and after being confined in a cell for forty-seven days was released on August 7, 1856.

On July 24, 1856, Joseph Hetherington shot and killed Dr. Andrew Randall in the latter's office at Sansome and Commercial Streets. When Hetherington entered the office he renewed a quarrel over money which he alleged Randall owed him. He finally grappled with Randall, when they drew pistols almost simultaneously. Hetherington fired, inflicting a wound from which Randall died on July 26.

Captain of Detectives I. W. Lees arrested Hetherington, but the Vigilantes, knowing that Hetherington had, on August 1, 1853, shot and killed Dr. John Baldwin, because of a dispute over property, and was subsequently acquitted, decided that this case required their personal attention. Accordingly they surrounded Lees and took his prisoner from him.

On June 3, 1856, Philander Brace killed Joseph B. West, a deputy police officer and Captain in the National Guards. The shooting took place on San Miguel Rancho. Thereafter Brace committed numerous robberies, but always managed to escape justice. The Vigilance Committee arrested him and he and Hetherington were tried about the same time.

They were found guilty and on July 29, 1856, were hanged from a scaffold on Davis Street, near Commercial. They were the last men hanged by the Vigilance Committee. The moral atmosphere had then cleared perceptibly, and on August 18, 1856, the Vigilance Committee held their final parade. They paraded with their arms and in military formation. The city was decorated in their honor and they were constantly cheered along the line of march. Shortly afterward they organized the People's party and selected a committee of twenty-one men, who had absolute power to select candidates for the various offices. Neither politics nor religion were considered. James F. Curtis, who had served as Chief of the Vigilantes' private police force, was their candidate for regular Chief of Police.

The office of Chief of Police was created to supersede the City

Marshal by the Consolidation Act, which was drafted by Assemblyman Horace Hawes and adopted by the Legislature on April 19, 1856. The election was held on November 14, 1856, and the People's party elected nearly all their candidates. For many years this party remained a power in politics, and the municipal government was all that could be desired.

In October, 1856, William T. Coleman visited New York, and Reuben Maloney, then residing in that city, and whom Officer Hopkins attempted to arrest in the presence of Judge Terry, entered a suit for damages against him. The Vigilantes voluntarily assessed themselves to render financial assistance to Coleman. This case and others of a similar nature were dismissed for lack of jurisdiction.

From 1849 until the Act of Congress in 1864 the laws in relation to property rights were so conflicting, so far as they applied to San Francisco, that it was shown that "possession was nine-tenths of the law." "Squatting" on property became an occupation, and after the fire of 1851, claimants of property were forced to fence in their land, over the hot ashes, to preserve their rights, and many lives were lost in battles growing out of disputes over ownership.

On June 4, 1854, squatters took possession of a lot at Mission and Third Streets, which belonged to Captain James Folsom, and they erected a heavy wooden fort. So strongly fortified were they that Folsom decided that the best policy would be to compromise the matter, and for a monetary consideration the squatters vacated. Believing they had intimidated Folsom they proceeded immediately to another lot at Howard and First Streets, which also belonged to Folsom, and a battle with pistols followed, which resulted in George Smith, of the Folsom party, being killed and two squatters named John Larkin and James McNabb being wounded.

On June 5, 1854, rival squatters attempted to gain possession of a lot belonging to James Lick, which was located near Green and Powell Streets. John Murphy and Thomas Mooney were opposed by John Murphy and wife. A pistol fight followed, during which Mrs. Murphy was killed.

On June 6, 1854, prominent citizens formed "The AntiSquatter's League" and organized a special police force to assist the regulars.

SAN FRANCISCO POLICE OFFICERS KILLED IN THE DISCHARGE OF THEIR DUTY.

Murder of Substitute Officer John Coots.

On the midnight watch on June 12, 1878, Substitute Officer John Coots was patrolling Pike Street, now known as Waverly place, instead of the regular officer, Chas. Coleman.

About 1:30 a. m., two young hoodlums named John Runk and Chas. Wilson passed through the alley, which was lined on either side by houses of ill repute.

At that time the women were permitted to sit at their windows and these ruffians began abusing them without any provocation.

Coots cautioned them to behave in a gentlemanly manner, but as they acted defiantly, he followed them to Sacramento Street. At this point the men began to abuse the officer, and defied him to arrest them.

Wilson was an ex-convict and Coots placed him under arrest, while Runk followed a few feet in the rear. They proceeded toward the police station at the old City Hall, located at Merchant and Kearny Streets, and upon reaching DuPont and Clay Streets. Officer Joe Kelly, who was standing at that corner, asked Coots if he needed any help.

Coots replied: "No, this fellow thought I couldn't take him down."

Kelly remained at the corner and when the party had proceeded down Clay as far as Brenham place, which is about one hundred feet from where Kelly was standing, a shot was heard and Kelly saw Coots fall and the other two men ran through Brenham place, thence through Washington and Bartlett alleys. Kelly followed closely behind them, blowing his whistle the while, and Officers Tom Price and Eaton, who were on Pacific Street at the time, ran to Bartlett alley and the fleeing men ran into their arms. Runk still had the pistol in his hand.

Coots was shot in the back of the head by Runk and died instantly. As it was not proven that Wilson aided or encouraged in the killing, he escaped punishment, but Runk was tried, convicted and hanged on November 12, 1879.

The Murder of Police Officer John Nicholson,

John Nicholson was born in Canada in 1843 and on April 13, 1880, he was appointed a member of the San Francisco Police Department.

At 1:45 a. m., February 16, 1884, Officer J. H. Callahan, who had reported off duty at midnight, was in his home at the southeast corner of Jones and Pacific Streets, when, above the noise of the rain and wind, he heard the sounds of pistol shots.

He hastened to the window and observed two men running down Jones Street toward Pacific; the tall man in the rear, evidently Officer Nicholson, was apparently pursuing the shorter man in the lead.

Callahan ran out of his house and shortly afterward found the body of Officer Nicholson lying on the sidewalk near the fire house of Truck Company No. 4 on Pacific Street, above Jones.

In the dead officer's right hand a pistol was clutched, all the chambers being empty, and in his pocket a chisel was found which had evidently been taken from his assailant.

Over his left eye and on his left cheek, long, deep gashes were found and the third and fatal wound consisted of a deep knife wound in the neck which severed the jugular vein.

When G. W. Reid, who slept in the rear of his grocery store located at 1131 Pacific Street, near Jones, arose that morning, he found that the store had been burglarized during the night and that the entrance had been effected by climbing over the transom of the front door.

On the drawer of the desk a chisel mark was found which corresponded exactly, as regards width, with the chisel found in the dead officer's pocket.

The only article missing was a cheap clock which was afterward found near a Chinaman's cap on Jackson Street nearby.

A further search of the store resulted in the finding of a pair of Chinaman's slippers.

It is presumed that the officer observed the burglar, evidently a Chinaman, as he was leaving this store and that he overtook him and removed the chisel from his possession at the point where the cap and clock were found. The prisoner then broke away and was overtaken at the point where the murder was committed.

The assassin was never apprehended.

At the time of the tragedy an estimable young lady was en route from New York to San Francisco, where all arrangements had been made for her marriage to Nicholson.

The Murder of Officer E. J. Osgood.

E. J. Osgood was born on June 26, 1832, and was appointed a member of the San Francisco Police Department on April 24, 1878.

At 3:50 a. m., December 13, 1886, Osgood was standing at the corner of Pacific and DuPont Streets, where he was observed by Tillie Mullin, a woman of the lower world, who was sitting in her window nearby.

At this time a roughly dressed young man approached Osgood and in a loud tone of voice complained to the officer that his watch had been stolen from him in a brothel some hours before.

As the man could not state definitely which brothel he visited and as the majority of such resorts were closed for the night and the inmates had left, the officer informed him that nothing could be accomplished then, but advised him to report the theft at headquarters at 10 a. m.

The man crossed the Street, but returned to the officer and began to abuse him for not making a search at once. The officer threatened to arrest him if he did not keep still. The enraged man then whipped out a knife, stabbed Osgood in the neck and fled down Pacific Street. Osgood attempted to follow and at the same time pulled out his police whistle which he attempted to blow. He then staggered and fell.

Officers Burges and Tennis soon appeared on the scene and conveyed the wounded officer to the Receiving Hospital, where he died on December 17.

Until October 15, 1888, nothing was learned as to the identity of the murderer.

On that date the ship Childwall, Captain Watson, arrived in San

Francisco from Bombay, India.

The captain proceeded at once to Police Headquarters to ascertain if any man named Osgood had been murdered in San Francisco.

Upon receiving an affirmative answer he made the following statement:

"In 1886 I left San Francisco for the British Isles in command of the ship James M. Blaikie.

"Two sailors named Frank Norman and Thomas Long shipped with me. They were good sailors, but Norman was quarrelsome and when we had been out about six weeks I had a violent quarrel with him.

"He was entirely in the wrong and his friend Long told him so in my presence.

"That night while Long and Norman were on watch I passed along the deck and I overheard the two men quarreling. I approached without being observed and heard Norman say to Long:

"'You coward, you sided with the skipper to-day.

It looks as if you're going back on me.'

"Long replied: 'I guess you have forgotten what I did for you when you cut Osgood's throat in San Francisco.'"

Norman's reply could not be heard by the Captain and the conversation thereafter was in an undertone.

The Captain never intimated to the sailors that he had overheard their conversation. Norman was never apprehended.

The Trials of the Prominent Actor, Maurice Curtis,

Alias Sam'l o' Posen, for the Murder of Police Officer Alexander Grant.

Maurice Bertram Strelinger was born in London, England, in 1851.

When a boy he came to this country and procured employment as a porter in a store in New York City.

He next worked at cheap theaters in the Bowery and finally appeared in minor parts. While thus employed he became enamored of a ballet girl, a French Jewess who had adopted the stage name of Albina Del Mer. They were married and both obtained employment with a traveling show, Strelinger then assuming the name of Curtis. They finally drifted to San Francisco.

As Curtis at that time was an uncouth individual, and apparently had no ability as an actor, he practically lived on charity. His wife became disgusted with him and suddenly left for New York.

Curtis finally obtained employment at the Grand Opera House in San Francisco, and after accumulating enough money to buy a ticket he left for New York for the purpose of importuning his wife to return.

At first she turned a deaf ear to his pleadings and the despondent Curtis sought employment at the Star Theater in New York. He was engaged at fifteen dollars per week to play the character of "Sam'l of Posen," a Hebrew peddler. He made such a success of the character that the play was rewritten and "Sam'l of Posen" was the leading character. The play met with wonderful success and in four years Curtis accumulated $250,000, a large portion of which was invested in real estate in Berkeley, Cal.

About 1886, Curtis retired from the stage and became a prominent citizen of Berkeley, being a director of one of the leading banks.

Alexander Grant was born in Nova Scotia in 1851, and came to Bodie, California, in 1874, where he obtained employment as a carpenter.

He was appointed a police officer on August 19, 1897, and was assigned to Sixth Street, where he earned the repudiation of being a most efficient officer.

At 12:45 a. m., September 11, 1891, a jeweler named Horace Badgely was walking down Fifth Street near Folsom when he heard three shots on Folsom Street quite near him.

He ran to the corner, arriving within a few seconds after the firing and observed only two men, one lying prostrate on the sidewalk and the other running toward Fifth Street.

The Southern Police Station was then on Folsom Street near the scene of the tragedy and Officer J. J. Allen, upon hearing the shots, ran out of the station and up the Street in the direction of the shooting. He also observed the man running and saw him turn into Fifth Street. Allen apprehended the fleeing man at Shipley and Fifth Street just as Officer Bodie intercepted him.

The man was Curtis and his first exclamation was: "My God! I'd give the world to get back the last four hours." He then became reticent and declined to make any further statement.

On his right wrist was a police officer's nipper and an abrasion on the wrist clearly indicating that he had been struggling with the man who held the other end of the nippers.

The officers then returned to the prostrate form on the sidewalk and found Officer Grant unconscious and dying from a pistol shot wound through the forehead.

Near-by a 38-calibre Smith and Wesson hammerless revolver was found containing three empty shells. Officer Grant's revolver was found in his pocket fully loaded but the nipper which he was known to carry was not in his pocket.

James Creighton, a bartender at Fifth and Folsom, Thomas Mullins of 56 Shipley Street, and E. Toomey of 252 Perry Street, all stated, and subsequently testified, that they saw Grant with one prisoner just before he turned around the corner from Fifth on to Folsom Street and that he said to the prisoner, who was resisting: "Come along now," and that almost immediately after the two men passed out of their sight around the corner, three shots rang out. These three witnesses hurried to the corner and saw a man running away. They stated that with the exception of the wounded officer no other person was on the Street in that block on Folsom Street at that time.

Augustine Marcoval, a tamale peddler, stated that he saw Grant with one prisoner of Curtis' description at 6th and Folsom a few moments before the shots were fired.

Mrs. Annie Johnson, who resided at 846 Folsom Street, was sitting near her window with her sick baby and saw the prisoner trying to pull away from the officer and then three shots were fired whereupon the officer fell and the prisoner escaped. She was positive only two men were present.

John Schultheis, a machinist employed at the Phoenix Iron Works on First Street, identified the nippers found on Curtis' wrist as a pair he had repaired for Officer Grant.

Upon hearing the evidence, the Coroner's Jury charged Curtis with murder, and on October 12, 1891, Police Judge Rix held him to answer before the Superior Court.

Three of the leading attorneys of San Francisco, George Knight, W. W. Foote and Colonel Kowalsky were engaged to defend Curtis.

The trial commenced on January 25, 1892, and Attorney Knight referred to it as an "unholy persecution of an innocent man by the police."

Captain of Detectives Lees, who handled the case, stated that he had reliable information that Curtis was a degenerate and it was Lees' theory that Grant had caught him in a compromising position and Curtis, becoming frantic when he realized that exposure would follow his arrest, decided to forever seal the lips of the officer and then escape.

The witnesses for the prosecution testified according to the statements previously made and on February 15th Curtis took the stand in his own behalf and testified as follows:

> "I came to San Francisco from my home in Berkeley on the evening of September 10 and met my wife by appointment in her box at the Grand Opera House during the Sarah Bernhardt performance. I left during the play and went to the Tivoli Opera House where I remained with Mark Thall until 11:45 p. m., when I started for the Grand Opera House to escort my wife home. On Mission Street I noticed a strange man following me so I continued to Howard Street, when I was struck on the back of the head and fell. An officer then appeared, and placed us both under arrest. A nipper was placed on my wrist and when we had proceeded a short distance I heard three shots and fearing that I was being shot at, I ran.

> "I could not remember anything else. I never carried a pistol and I did not shoot the officer."

Curtis could give no satisfactory explanation as to why he did not continue to the theater which was close at hand on Mission Street if he feared an assault, instead of going out of his way to walk down a comparatively dark Street, thus inviting attack.

Attorney Kowalsky testified that Toomey and Mullins, witnesses for the prosecution, called upon him and intimated that they were "ready to do business" and inquired "how much is in it?"

Mrs. M. Abbott and B. E. Harrington, who resided at Fifth and Folsom Streets, gave testimony tending to corroborate Curtis' testimony regarding the presence of a third man.

In rebuttal, George Alpers, a saloonkeeper at Fifth and Folsom, and afterward a Supervisor, Henry Teaman and James Kernan all testified that they were in Alpers' saloon when the shots were fired and that they ran out immediately and saw only one man running away.

Henry Faust, a gardener formerly in the employ of Curtis, testified that he had seen Curtis carry a pistol on numerous occasions.

In surrebuttal Mrs. J. McMillan and her daughter, Mrs. Lacy, testified that a second man ran away from the scene after the shooting.

The case was submitted to the jury on February 24 and after forty-eight hours' deliberation they failed to agree and were discharged.

On the next trial Curtis was acquitted, but as he was then financially ruined, he returned to the vaudeville stage where he has for years eked out a living by producing a sketch from the play which had once made him famous and wealthy.

William J. Hurley, who conducted a saloon at 1201 Steiner Street, was a juror in the first trial and was one of the two jurors who held out for acquittal. Shortly afterward he was indicted for accepting a bribe for his part in "hanging" the jury. He was acquitted but was again arrested on January 28, 1895, for attempting to bribe Chauncey M. Johnson, a juryman in the case of Richard McDonald who was charged with perjury because of his sworn statement regarding the financial condition of the Pacific Bank which had recently failed.

During this trial. Hurley admitted that the charge was true and claimed that he had received $500 to hang the jury. He also admitted that he had been promised $5,000 to "hang" the Curtis jury but received nothing for his services.

During his trial Hurley made two attempts to commit suicide.

On March 29, 1895, he was found guilty and sentenced to five years' imprisonment.

He died in San Francisco on July 13, 1909.

Horace Badgely, an eye-witness to the murder of Grant, disappeared before his testimony could be procured.

On April 8, 1895, he was interviewed in Stockton, Cal., and stated that the reason he disappeared was because a man called at his home and paid him $3,000 for a cheap picture which hung on the wall, at the same time suggesting that a change of climate would be beneficial to Badgely's health.

Captain Lees expressed the opinion that Badgely's statement was correct.

The Murder of Lieutenant of Police Burke by Theodore Park Haynes.

William Burke was born in County Galway, Ireland, on March 3, 1852.

He was appointed a member of the San Francisco police department on September 12, 1878, and for years afterward he and Officer William Price were specially detailed to subdue the criminal element which had the Mission district terrorized.

The brilliant detective work and courageous deeds of these officers resulted in their promotion until they reached the rank of Lieutenants.

On the morning of March 23, 1898, Theodore Park Haynes, an eccentric old tinsmith residing at Montcalm Street and Peralta Avenue, in the Mission district, had a controversy with his neighbor, Alfred Hopkinson, in regard to the boundary lines of their respective properties.

Suddenly Haynes drew a revolver and fired two shots at Hopkinson. The latter retreated and meeting Officers T. Kennedy and James Wilkinson, related his experience with the "old tinker," as Haynes was known.

Hopkinson then accompanied the officers to the scene of the disturbance. Haynes was standing at the door of his cabin, pistol in hand. The officers advanced toward him but Haynes raised his weapon and commanded them to halt or be shot.

The officers stopped and finally retreated for the purpose of conferring as to the best course to pursue. They telephoned to the Seventeenth-Street Police Station and notified Corporal Heney of the situation and he in turn sent Patrol Driver George Cashil to notify Lieutenant Burke, who was at his home nearby. The Lieutenant instructed Cashil to convey him in the patrol wagon to the scene of the shooting. When they reached Twenty-sixth Street Officer G. Marlowe joined the Lieutenant. The wagon was stopped about a block from Haynes' house and after learning the details from Wilkinson, the Lieutenant, who was in civilian dress, ordered the uniformed officers to follow him. As Burke approached the cabin he observed Haynes, who was still standing by his door, pistol in hand.

The Lieutenant showed his star and in a mild manner said to Haynes: "I am an officer. I won't harm you; I just want to talk to you."

The words had scarcely left Burke's lips when Haynes raised his pistol and fired two shots. The Lieutenant staggered, placed his left hand to his groin, drew his own pistol and after firing two shots, neither of which was effective, fell to the ground.

In the meantime Officer Merchant appeared on the scene. There were many conflicting statements as to the conduct of the officers after Burke was shot, but the majority of the witnesses agreed that Merchant and Kennedy emptied their revolvers at Haynes, who was using a heavy barrel full of water which was near his door, as a shield, and that they left the scene temporarily for the sole purpose of procuring more ammunition.

A majority of the witnesses also agreed that Marlowe and Wilkinson displayed cowardice in their manner of retreat. At any rate, when the "coast was clear," Haynes ran out to Burke, who was writhing in agony on the ground, and wrenching the pistol from his hand, fired two more shots into the body of the prostrate man and then ran back to the cabin.

Almost immediately after this, Patrol Driver George Cashil rushed up to Burke, carried him down the hill to the patrol wagon and hastened to the hospital where the wounded man died shortly afterward.

Officer Kennedy returned to the scene with a shotgun. By this time a posse from the Central Station, consisting of Sergeant George Baldwin, who in 1910 was Chief of the Census Bureau of San Francisco, Sergeant Christiansen, Officer Steve Bunner, afterwards distinguished for his detective ability, Maurice Duane and many other officers, arrived upon the scene.

A few moments later Haynes looked out the door and Kennedy shot him in the face with his shotgun. The wound, although not serious, almost blinded the "tinker" with his own blood. He closed the door and shortly afterward opened it again. Officer Bunner, who was standing in an exposed position about sixty feet in front of the cabin, dared Haynes to come out of the door.

While the murderer's attention was attracted to Bunner's defy, Sergeant Baldwin and Officer Duane crept upon him from the left and overpowered him.

When taken into custody Haynes began to feign insanity but prominent alienists pronounced him perfectly rational.

His preliminary examination began before Judge Conlan on March 31 and on April 11 he was held to answer before the Superior Court, where he was found guilty by a jury.

On June 18, 1898, he was sent to Folsom State Prison for life.

Wilkinson and Marlowe were charged with cowardice and after a trial were dismissed from the police department on October 7, 1898.

Patrol Driver Cashil was appointed a regular police officer for his courageous work on the day of Burke's murder.

The Murder of Officer Eugene Robinson and the Clever Capture of the Assassins — The Mysterious Murder of the Conspirator Who Turned Informer.

On the evening of January 20, 1902, six thugs named Frank Woods, William Kaufman, alias St. Louis Fat, John Courtney, alias Leadville Jimmy, William Kennedy, alias Yellow and Allen, alias "Kid" Goucher, who was a son of State Senator Goucher of Fresno, assembled in their room at 203 Turk Street, in San Francisco, and entered into a conspiracy to visit Cypress Lawn Cemetery in San Mateo county and blow open the safe in the office.

They took the paraphernalia necessary for the work at hand and leaving the room in two groups of three each, repaired to the cemetery.

Upon arriving there they discovered a man with a rifle on guard in the office, so they reluctantly abandoned the attempt and again dividing into two parties, boarded the same car bound for San Francisco. It was then about midnight and as the car went no further into the city than Twenty-ninth and Mission Streets, they were compelled to continue the journey on foot. They walked down Valencia Street; Henderson, Woods and Kaufman in the lead and Kennedy, Courtney and Goucher in the rear.

When they reached Twenty-fifth and Valencia, a signal was given and the gang assembled for the purpose of discussing the advisability of breaking into the office of a coal yard there located with the intention of blowing open the safe.

The majority were opposed to the proposition on the ground that the contents would probably not justify the risk taken of being discovered.

They then separated as before and proceeded cityward, but when they reached a point on Valencia Street between Sixteenth and Seventeenth, the three men in the rear, Kennedy, Courtney and Goucher, met a Japanese named G. R. Aikyo, who was subsequently appointed a commissioner to represent the Japanese Government at the St. Louis Exposition.

They placed pistols to Aikyo's head and commanded him to throw up his hands, but he managed to escape and ran into his home a few doors away. As he did so Kennedy fired a shot which missed its mark. He and Courtney then scaled a fence and disappeared while Goucher ran up and joined the trio in the lead.

Officer Eugene C. Robinson was patrolling Valencia Street that night. He was a handsome, athletic young man, and the sole support of a widowed mother.

On hearing the shot, Robinson ran up to the four men and asked who had fired it.

Henderson and Kaufman moved away but Woods and Goucher closed in on the officer, and then a shot was fired, closely followed by a volley of shots.

Robinson fell and died within a few hours.

Woods and Goucher then joined Henderson and they fled from the scene, Woods exclaiming that the officer had shot him twice.

Officer Charles Taylor, whose beat was on Sixteenth Street, heard the shots and was hastening to the scene when he observed the three men running.

He called upon them to halt but their only reply was to fire a volley of shots at him. He knelt and taking deliberate aim, responded with three shots, but as they had no apparent effect, he continued the pursuit. The trio then turned and fired another volley.

Taylor fired again and the largest of the three men staggered. The officer then ran up to him and told him he would kill him if he did not throw up his hands.

The fellow complied and was taken into custody and upon examination it was found that he was only slightly wounded.

He stated that his name was Henderson and after several days he made a complete confession to Detectives Dinan, Wren and Taylor, and gave the names of his accomplices.

A remarkable piece of work was done in capturing every one of the gang.

Courtney was arrested a few days afterward while riding the brakebeams of a train near Benicia.

Kennedy was arrested at Grants Pass, Oregon, for burglarizing a post office and was identified and brought here for trial.

Kaufman and Woods fled to Portland, Oregon, and Woods, being wounded by one of Robinson's bullets, Kaufman had him concealed in a lodging-house and was acting as his nurse.

The Portland police were informed of this fact and they visited the room while Kaufman was at a neighboring drugstore procuring bandages. Woods was captured, but Kaufman, learning that the officers were in the building, escaped temporarily and fled to Canada.

Detective Murray of Victoria, B. C, saw him posing as a cripple on a train and begging from passengers. Murray knew he had seen his picture but did not recall the circumstances, but on leaving the train his mind was refreshed as to who the man was and what he was charged with.

He telegraphed ahead to the Constable at Calagar, Canada, but Kaufman evidently saw Murray observing him very closely and fearing he had been recognized, he left the train at Calagar and went into the railroad tank house.

The station telegraph operator saw this move and as Constable Dodge had confided to the operator who he was waiting at the station for, the operator closed the tank house door on Kaufman, thus making him a prisoner until Dodge came to his assistance and Kaufman was arrested.

Goucher went to St. Paul, Minn., where he committed a burglary and under the name of Roy Williams he was sentenced to serve three years in the Stillwater Penitentiary, where the notorious Younger brothers were once confined.

At the expiration of this term he was returned to San Francisco.

On January 31, 1903, Kaufman was sentenced to serve 15 years at San Quentin.

On April 2, 1904, after a long legal battle, the charge against Kennedy was dismissed on the ground that sufficient evidence had not been produced to corroborate the testimony of the accomplice Henderson, but in the next year he was arrested at Woodland, Yolo County, for burglary and on March 22, 1905, he was sentenced to serve 45 years at Folsom.

Woods was executed on October 6, 1905, as it was shown that it was he who fired the fatal shot.

Goucher was sentenced to serve 25 years at San Quentin, but would probably have been hanged had not his father, the aged and respected Senator Goucher, made a personal and eloquent plea to the jury, which brought tears to nearly every eye in the court-room, except those of his fiendish son, who was absolutely devoid of feeling.

The charge against Courtney was reduced to manslaughter and on May 12, 1903, he was sentenced to serve six years at San Quentin.

In consideration of the services rendered to the prosecution by Henderson, he was on April 3, 1905, given his freedom on probation.

The criminal class had the bitterest feeling toward him for turning informer and it was commonly known that his life was in danger.

When he was released from the prison he was afraid to venture on to the Street without police protection and he immediately left San Francisco.

That availed him nothing, however, for his body, with a knife-wound in the back, was found shortly afterward on a road leading into Montreal, Canada.

The Murder of Officer James S. Cook.

James S. Cook was born in San Francisco on November 19, 1874.

As a young man, he followed the occupation of a teamster until December 9, 1902, when he joined the Police Department.

For many months after the earthquake and fire officers were detailed at the several banks in the burned district. Cook was assigned to the bank at Seventh and Market Streets, and upon reporting off duty at midnight on August 29, 1906, he walked down Seventh Street toward the Southern Pacific Railroad yards, intending to catch a freight train to Ocean View where he and his family resided.

At Seventh and Brannan Streets he observed four men who were in the act of unreeling from a large spool, some cable which belonged to the Home Telephone Company and which workmen had left there preparatory to running it down through the manhole nearby.

Cook approached these men and began to interrogate them.

Suddenly one of the group drew a pistol and fired three shots into the officer's stomach in rapid succession.

Cook fell to the ground but he managed to draw his own pistol and discharge its contents in the direction of the fleeing men.

The man who shot the officer then turned and fired two more shots in the direction of the prostrate man and then disappeared in the darkness.

Cook was removed to the Emergency Hospital. From the description he furnished of his assailants, four men were arrested, one of them being a laborer named John Dunnigan. Cook's identification of this man was not entirely satisfactory.

On September 5 the officer died and Dunnigan was charged with murder, but the case was finally dismissed.

————————

The Murder of Police Officer George O'Connell

(Retired)

George P. O'Connell was born in Waterford County, Ireland, on April 1, 1851. He was appointed a member of the San Francisco Police Department on May 11, 1878, and was retired because of disability on April 4, 1904.

About 9 p. m. on the evening of November 16, 1906, O'Connell, Steve Lynch, Louis Delatour and several others were chatting at the bar in a saloon located at the northeast corner of Sixth and Brannan Streets.

Presently the front and side doors were opened simultaneously and two men wearing blue handkerchiefs as masks appeared, one at each door.

They instantly raised large, black revolvers and commanded all present to hold up their hands.

With the exception of O'Connell, all complied with the request, but the retired officer exclaimed:

"No can make me throw up my hands," and he instantly drew his own revolver and fired at the robber at the front door.

Both robbers opened fire simultaneously, the one at the side door firing two shots. The first shot fired by the robber at the side door passed through O'Connell's arm and thence through his lungs. Lynch was shot in the abdomen and Delatour's jaw was shot away.

The robbers then fled. Lynch and O'Connell died shortly afterward.

Captain of Detectives Duke and Detectives Reagan, O'Connell, O'Dea and B. Wren were on the ground shortly after the shooting.

About sixty feet south of this saloon the dead body of one of the robbers was found, one of O'Connell's bullets having pierced his chest. He still wore his blue handkerchief as a mask and an empty, black, 38-calibre revolver was in his hand.

The remains were soon identified as those of Frank Burke, an ex-convict who was an habitué of Sullivan's saloon, a rendezvous for thieves and cutthroats, which was located on the opposite side of Sixth Street about 300 feet south of the scene of the tragedy.

As several witnesses saw the other robber run towards Sullivan's resort the officers proceeded there forthwith.

This saloon was closed unusually early that night and after gaining an entrance, the officers found the hangers-on apparently asleep on the floors in the rear rooms.

There were two men there whose general physique and clothing answered the description of the robber who fired the shot that killed O'Connell. One proved an alibi but the other was so extremely pale and nervous that it was decided to take him to the scene of the tragedy.

Arriving there, a young man named Clarence Pool immediately identified the prisoner, whose name was John Byrne, as the man who had on the previous evening, in company with the dead robber, acted in such a mysterious manner in front of a saloon across the Street from the scene of the tragedy that it was suspected that they intended to rob that place.

A search was made of the prisoner's pockets and a blue handkerchief of identically the same description as the one worn by the other robber was found in his coat pocket. The handkerchief was somewhat damp and one corner was still twisted in a manner to indicate that it had recently been tied in a knot.

A search was then made for the second weapon. Byrne was with the searching party and as the officers drew near the spot where the pistol was concealed, the prisoner began trembling so violently that Detective O'Dea asked him what he was shaking about.

The gun was found under the back steps of Sullivan's saloon. It was a 45-calibre army revolver which had been stolen from the Presidio some months previously. Two 44calibre shells were discharged and the bullet subsequently removed from O'Connell's body was found to be of the same calibre. The man who conducted the saloon where this tragedy occurred was also named O'Connell and on the night preceding the tragedy, his wife sat in her darkened front window directly over the saloon and observed the mysterious actions of two men in front of the saloon across the Street.

Presently these men came across the Street and appeared to be looking between the doors of her husband's saloon. She observed them closely and became so nervous that she sent her little boy down stairs to warn her husband, but in the meantime the fellows disappeared. Mrs. O'Connell positively identified the dead robber as one of the men and Byrne as the other.

A few moments before the tragedy, a brakeman named Heffernan saw Burke and Byrne together across the Street from O'Connell's saloon.

Nearly all the men in the saloon at the time of the tragedy stated that the robber who fired from the side door was the same size and dressed the same as Byrne, but owing to the mask they could not see his face.

On January 15, 1907, Police Judge Shortall held Byrne to answer before the Superior Court for the murder of O'Connell.

When the case was called before Judge Lawlor of the Superior Court, Byrne testified that he knew absolutely nothing in regard to the killing of O'Connell, but after so testifying he made a statement to Assistant District Attorney O'Gara and Captain Duke which was substantially as follows:

"That part of my testimony wherein I stated I knew nothing in regard to the murder of O'Connell was false.

"I was in the barroom of Sullivan's saloon on the night of the tragedy and we heard several shots. A couple of minutes later, Tom Hogan, a young blacksmith employed on Brannan near Third Street, ran in the back way of Sullivan's place. He cried: 'They got Burke and pretty near got me.'

"There was blood on Hogan's jaw and a bullet was sticking in his chin. I pulled it out and threw it out the back door. Two of the gang then led Hogan out the back door."

Byrne was recalled for further cross-examination and repeated this story before the jury.

Hogan was at once apprehended and there was a noticeable scar at the point indicated by Byrne.

It was proven, however, that this scar was the result of a wound caused by a kick during a Street fight two weeks before the tragedy.

Byrne evidently saw the wound, and decided to invent this story to save his own neck.

Several of Byrne's friends, who were in Sullivan's saloon throughout the evening of the shooting and perjured themselves in an effort to prove an alibi for the defendant, denounced Byrne for inventing the Hogan story. Hogan proved by several witnesses that he was attending a birthday party miles from the scene of the shooting at the time it occurred.

Experts testified that the wound on Hogan's chin was not caused by a bullet and explained the improbability of a bullet remaining in the position described by Byrne.

On April 13, 1907, the defendant was found guilty of murder and sentenced to be hanged, but Attorney Theodore Roche, who ably handled the defense, has appealed to the Supreme Court for a new trial.

The Killing of Policeman Edward J. McCartney.

McCartney was born in Seneca County, New York, on November 10, 1879. He joined the Police Department on May 9, 1907, and was assigned to the Mission Station.

In May, 1907, the entire Street-car system in San Francisco was temporarily tied up owing to differences between the Carmen's Union and the railroad companies, but within a few days the cars were again operated by non-union men.

On Labor Day, September 2, 1907, no settlement had been reached and the non-union men were still operating the cars.

About 3 o'clock on the following morning. Officers P. J. Mitchell and Edward McCartney were standing at the corner of Twenty-fourth and Folsom Streets when they heard an unusual noise at Crowley's saloon, located at Twenty-fourth and Howard Streets. They proceeded in that direction when four men came out of the saloon whom the officers intercepted at Shotwell Street. Just then two of the men turned down Shotwell Street but the officers accosted the other two and after warning them to cease raising a disturbance at that hour, ordered them to go home.

Neither man showed any disposition to move, and one who was a physical giant, said: "I guess the Streets are free." The officers then shoved both men violently and told them to move on or be locked up.

The two men then walked down Twenty-fourth Street and disappeared in the darkness.

The officers crossed the Street to a restaurant for the purpose of getting a cup of coffee but as none was prepared they returned to the Street. They walked down Twenty-fourth Street and stopped under an awning. They had been there but a few moments when they saw the two men they had ordered away coming back on the same side of the Street that the officers were on but which was the opposite side from where the first conversation was had. As it was quite dark where the officers were standing it is probable that these two men did not observe them until the officers came out upon them from under the awning.

According to the statement subsequently made by Officer (now Corporal) Mitchell, he seized the small man while McCartney advanced toward the large man.

Just then the large man suddenly drew a revolver and fired two shots, one of which struck McCartney in the neck inflicting a wound which caused almost instant death.

McCartney fell into Mitchell's arms and by the time he had laid the dying officer on the sidewalk, the two men had disappeared in the darkness.

Acting Lieutenant Arthur Layne of the Mission Station was notified of the tragedy and after procuring good descriptions of the two men he proceeded to the car barn at Twenty-fourth and Utah Streets as he suspected that the assassin was a railroad man. As the man wanted was unusually large and wore his hair in a peculiar manner, the railroad inspector stated that the description fitted but two railroad men at that barn; one being a man named Nickol and the other a striking car man named John Tansey. Nickol was located and interrogated but he easily proved an alibi and Mitchell said he was not the man.

Tansey was then located in his bed at 1025 Vermont Street, where he claimed he had been since midnight. But Mitchell positively identified him as the man who had fired the shot and he was arrested.

The next day Acting Lieutenant Layne learned that a man named

Bell was Tansey's companion on the night of the tragedy and he was at once apprehended. He unhesitatingly admitted that he was with Tansey and that it was Tansey who killed the police officer. Bell was released but was subpoenaed as a witness. He disappeared, however, and has never been seen since.

When the case came to trial, Tansey admitted that he was present when the shot was fired but claimed that it was Bell who fired it.

Tansey was convicted of manslaughter and sentenced to ten years' imprisonment, but was paroled* on May 10, 1909, as he had become a victim of consumption.

*Tansey was not paroled but bailed out pending appeal. A new trial being denied, he was sent to San Quentin on January 5, 1910.

The Murder of Police Officer William Heins.

William Heins was born in San Francisco on August 11, 1870. He was a lithographer by trade and followed that occupation until he was appointed a member of the Police Department on September 4, 1896.

On the watch beginning at midnight June 4, 1908, he was assigned to patrol Pacific Street from Battery to Stockton.

About 12:30 a. m. of that date, Thomas O'Young and James O'Young, 19 years old, twin brothers, who looked exactly alike, entered the O. K. saloon located on the south side of Pacific Street near Montgomery and shortly afterward engaged in a dispute with a waiter named Robert Pacheco, in regard to the payment for a bottle of beer.

During the controversy Tom O'Young drew a pistol which he pointed at the waiter, but a waitress named Lucile Sharpe pulled the ruffian's arm down to his side. While in this position the weapon was discharged, the bullet entering the floor and the flash setting fire to O'Young's trousers. Some sailors then disarmed him and upon being informed that the police were coming, he proceeded to leave the place. He was closely followed by his brother James who passed him another pistol, at the same time saying: "Take this, Tom, you may need it." Tom placed the weapon in the waistband of his trousers.

He then started to run east on the south side of Pacific Street.

Officer Heins being attracted by the shot, started in pursuit and ordered Young to halt, at the same time firing a shot into a vacant building nearby.

At that instant Young fell to the sidewalk. Heins immediately came upon him and said: "Get up, you're not hurt," at the same time endeavoring to assist the man to his feet. While still lying on the sidewalk. Young drew his pistol and shot Heins, the bullet passing through his left arm and then into his chest, producing a wound which resulted fatally shortly afterward.

Tom then jumped to his feet and was joined by his brother James, who was on the opposite side of the Street when the shot was fired.

The latter was heard to say: "Did you get him?" to which Tom replied: "You bet I did."

The two brothers then ran down Montgomery Street toward Jackson, Tom passing the pistol back to James.

Tom stumbled and fell and upon getting up, ran down into an excavated lot on Jackson near Montgomery. James ran to the International saloon at Kearny and Jackson, and proceeded directly to the toilet where he hid the pistol behind an ash can. He was immediately apprehended by citizens and turned over to the police.

Officers J. B. O'Connor and John Evatt were informed by S. H. Vansyckel of Morse's Patrol that one of the brothers was secreted in the excavated lot, but it was so dark that the officers surrounded the lot and sent for lanterns.

These two brothers not only looked alike but dressed alike, except that Tom wore a red necktie.

When the lanterns arrived, Evatt and O'Connor proceeded down into the lot and found Young. As the tie was missing, a further search was made immediately and it was found where Young attempted to conceal it.

When James O'Young was interrogated at the prison by Chief Biggy and Captain Duke he admitted that he saw his brother Tom kill the officer and he signed a statement to that effect.

Both men were held to answer before the Superior Court. Tom O'Young had two trials, the jury disagreeing the first time.

Attorney Joseph Dunne was engaged as special prosecutor during the next trial. In an effort to save his brother, James testified that he fired the fatal shot. The jury found Tom guilty on May 1, 1909, and he was sentenced to life imprisonment.

On August 21 James was found guilty of manslaughter and sentenced to ten years' imprisonment.

The Murder of Sergeant Anton Nolting and His

Remarkable Presentiment.

Anton J. F. Nolting was born in San Francisco on February 9, 1860.

He was of a studious disposition and acquired a high education.

As a young man he was in comfortable circumstances financially but meeting with reverses, he joined the police force on December 2, 1895.

On March 29, 1905, he was made a Corporal and on July 9, 1907, was advanced to the rank of Sergeant.

Because of his quiet, unassuming and kindly manner, he was one of the most popular men in the department and was also generally admired because of his devotion to his invalid wife.

On October 2, 1907, he was assigned as a Patrol Sergeant to the Central Station.

He reported for duty on the watch beginning at midnight January 8, 1909, and it was noted that he was in an extremely melancholy mood.

As a storm was raging, all patrol officers wore regulation rain coats throughout this watch.

About 1 a. m., Nolting met Officer William Cavanaugh at Kearny and Bush Streets. The Sergeant said that he felt that something terrible had happened or was about to happen.

After some meditation he said: "Perhaps something has happened to my poor wife."

Nolting complained of dizziness and at Cavanaugh's suggestion he went into the saloon at the southeast corner of Kearny and California Streets and ordered a bromo-seltzer. The Sergeant then said he did not want to be alone and requested Cavanaugh to accompany him down California to Montgomery Street. Upon reaching that corner Nolting thought he saw the Montgomery Street officer at Sacramento Street and proceeded alone in that direction, Cavanaugh returning toward Kearny Street.*

* Subsequent discoveries proved that Nolting had evidently mistaken a civilian, who was also wearing a rain coat, for the officer.

About the time Nolting reached Sacramento Street he heard a shot fired on Washington Street near Montgomery.

He proceeded in that direction, but when he reached Clay Street he observed a soldier with a drawn pistol who was in the act of forcing two other soldiers to march ahead of him. Nolting approached the trio and began to expostulate with the soldier with the drawn revolver. At this instant the other two soldiers fled down Clay Street toward the ferry. Seeing that he could accomplish nothing by argument, the Sergeant closed in on the soldier and began grappling for the pistol. Nolting slipped and fell and while his back was partially turned, the soldier fired into his body, inflicting a wound which caused almost instant death. After firing three more shots at the officer, the soldier attempted to escape. He ran into a vacant lot which was almost immediately surrounded by Officers Brady, Teutenberg, Cavanaugh and Sheble, who were attracted to the scene by the shots. These officers closed in on the assassin shortly after he stumbled and fell and they found the empty revolver by his side.

When taken before Captains Anderson and Duke at the Central Station, he disclaimed all knowledge of the shooting and claimed that his mind was a complete blank regarding his actions during the preceding hour.

He stated that his name was Thomas Jordan and that he belonged to the Coast Artillery stationed at Fort Baker. Shortly afterward, the two other soldiers were apprehended at the water front.

One of the two made a statement substantially as follows:

"My name is Charles Nibarger and my companion's name is John Kralikouski. We are soldiers stationed at Fort Baker. I had been sent out as a provost guard and was armed with a revolver. I was in the New Western saloon at Kearny and Washington about midnight with Jordan and Kralikouski. In some manner Jordan got possession of my gun and pointing it at Kralikouski and me, he ordered us to march ahead of him. When we were going down Washington Street he said we were not moving fast enough and he fired a shot in the air. When we reached Montgomery Street he ordered us to turn toward Clay. When we reached the last named Street, the police Sergeant approached and asked who fired the shot.

"While he and Jordan were arguing we ran down Clay Street. We had only traveled about forty feet when we heard the shots."

On Sunday, January 10, Sergeant Nolting's funeral took place. The Mayor, Police Commissioners and about 300 officers attended. The largest floral piece around the casket was one sent by the soldiers from Fort Baker.

Jordan was held to answer in the Superior Court. The defendant claimed that he was in an "alcoholic trance" when the deed was done.

Hiram Johnson was retained as special prosecutor.

On March 12, 1909, Jordan was found guilty and sentenced to life imprisonment.

After the death of her husband, Mrs. Nolting failed rapidly and she was found dead in her bathtub on October 24 of the same year.

THE STRENUOUS LIVES OF SENATOR BRODERICK AND JUDGE TERRY AND THEIR FAMOUS DUEL.

(From A. E. Wagstaff's History.)

David C. Broderick was born in the District of Columbia on February 4, 1820, and as a boy worked with his father as a stonecutter on the United States Capitol building. He afterwards joined the New York Volunteer Fire Department and conducted a saloon; at the same time becoming a politician. He left for San Francisco, arriving on June 13, 1849. He was a leader in organizing the volunteer fire department here, "Broderick No. 1" being the name given one of the fire companies in his honor.

On January 8, 1850, Broderick was elected a State Senator and was subsequently elected president of the Senate. He innocently made a false accusation against ex-Governor Smith of Virginia, which caused the latter's son, Judge Caleb Smith, to challenge him to fight a duel. The challenge was accepted and the duel occurred on March 17, 1852, near Oakland Point. No injuries were inflicted but Smith's bullet struck Broderick's watch. Broderick subsequently apologized before the Senate for his offensive remarks.

After a long and bitter fight, lasting for years, Broderick was elected United States Senator on January 9, 1857.

David S. Terry was born in Todd County, Kentucky, on March 8, 1823. He came from a family of warriors, his grandfather commanding a regiment during the Revolution. His older brother was killed while commanding a regiment of Confederates, and his youngest brother, a prominent Southern attorney, while not actually participating in that war, asked for and was granted permission to witness the battle of Shiloh and was killed the first day.

Terry's father contracted habits which forced his wife to procure a divorce, and in 1833 she moved to Texas with her children, where she purchased a large cotton plantation. In 1836 Mrs. Terry died, and in the same year, David, then in his thirteenth year, participated in the battle of San Jacinto, and on the achievement of Texan independence returned to his home.

In 1841 he began studying law and in 1843 was admitted to the bar, shortly afterward opening an office in Galveston, Texas. In 1846, when the war between the United States and Mexico was inaugurated, he enlisted as a lieutenant.

In December, 1849, Terry came to California, and after mining in Calaveras County for a few months, he began the practice of law in Stockton. Shortly after this he was induced to accept the nomination for Mayor of Stockton on the Whig ticket, but he was defeated by Samuel Purdy.

In September, 1855, Terry was the Know-Nothing party's candidate for Chief Justice of the State Supreme Court. He was elected and took office the next month.

On June 20, 1856, he was arrested by the Vigilance Committee for stabbing Officer Hopkins, and was held in custody until August 7. (See history of Vigilance Committee.) During Terry's incarceration Broderick did all in his power to assist him and they were close friends.

When the Lecompton convention was held in 1859, Broderick was in control and Terry sought to be renominated, but it was decided by Broderick that it would not be good policy to give him the nomination. This caused Terry to deliver a speech in Sacramento in June, 1859, in which he stated that the convention which refused to nominate him was owned by a man whom they were ashamed to acknowledge as their master.

Two days afterward Broderick was seated at the breakfast table in the International Hotel in San Francisco, and on reading this speech called the attention of D. W. Perley, a former law partner of Terry's, to its contents. Broderick then referred to Terry as a "damned miserable ingrate" for failing to appreciate what he (Broderick) had done for him while he was in the custody of the Vigilantes. He further stated that he had changed his mind in regard to Terry's honesty.

Perley took the matter personally and challenged Broderick to fight a duel, but Broderick declined to accept the challenge because he was about to enter into a bitter political campaign, and for the further reason that Perley did not occupy an equally elevated or responsible position. But he added that when the campaign was concluded he would be prepared to answer for any statement made by him.

Terry, learning of this significant statement, decided to wait until after the election, which occurred on September 7 and resulted in the defeat of Broderick by U. S. Senator William T. Guinn, who had the distinction of being one of the two first United States Senators from California in 1850, John C. Fremont being his colleague. Terry then addressed the following letter to Broderick:

"Oakland, September 8, 1859.

"Hon. D. C. Broderick — Sir: Some two months since, at the public table of the International Hotel, in San Francisco, you saw fit to indulge in certain remarks concerning me, which were offensive in their nature. Before I had heard of the circumstance, your note of 20th of June, addressed to Mr. D. W. Perley, in which you declared that you would not respond to any call of a personal character during the political canvass just concluded, had been published.

"I have, therefore, not been permitted to take any notice of those remarks until the expiration of the limit fixed by yourself. I now take the earliest opportunity to require of you a retraction of those remarks. This note will be handed to you by my friend, Calhoun Benham, Esq., who is acquainted with its contents, and will receive your reply.

"D, S, Terry,"

Broderick requested Terry to designate what remarks were considered offensive, Terry did so and the Senator replied that he had made the statements attributed to him and that it was for him (Terry) to judge whether they afforded good grounds for offense.

Terry then stated that he was left no alternative but to demand the satisfaction usual among gentlemen, and appointed Calhoun Benham, former district attorney in San Francisco, to arrange the details. Terry then resigned as Chief Justice of the Supreme Court.

The seconds met, decided that pistols should be the weapons used, and that the time and place of the meeting would be at sunrise, September

11, 1859, near Lake Merced, San Mateo County.

Captain of Detectives I. W. Lees and Detective H. H. Ellis procured warrants for their arrest from Judge Coon and followed the carriages to the dueling ground. When the distance had been measured off and Terry and Broderick were handed their weapons, they were placed under arrest, but the cases were dismissed by Judge Coon the next day.

On the following morning, September 13, they met again near the same place. It was agreed that the combatants should fire at the count of three, but at the count of one Broderick accidentally discharged his pistol, the ball striking the ground nine feet from him, but in the direction of Terry. Just at the count of "two" Terry fired, the ball striking Broderick in the chest. His frame trembled like a ship that had struck a rock. He gradually released his hold on his weapon, and after a heavy convulsion, sank to the ground. The gigantic Terry stood like a statue with his arms folded, closely watching Broderick.

When the condition of Broderick was announced, Terry left the field with his seconds, ex-District Attorney Calhoun Benham and Thomas Hayes, after whom "Hayes Valley" was named, and they proceeded to Terry's home near Stockton.

On the 16th inst. Broderick died, and Lees and Ellis procured warrants for Terry's arrest. Mr. Ellis, who subsequently served as Chief of Police, related to the author his experience in attempting to serve the warrant, in the following language:

> "Lees and I procured a warrant against Terry and had it properly endorsed. We then proceeded to Terry's home. When we arrived within about one hundred feet of the house, a window was thrown open and Calhoun Benham, Tom Hayes, Sheriff O'Neill and Terry leveled shotguns at us and told us to 'halt.'

> "We did so and announced that we were officers with a warrant for Terry. He stated that he was certain that he would not receive a fair trial and feared violence at that time, but agreed to surrender three days afterwards at Oakland. Knowing that he would keep his word in this, as we also knew he would do when he told us that if we came nearer to his house they would all shoot, we decided to allow him to dictate terms. He surrendered as per agreement, and the case was heard by Judge James Hardy in Marin County, a change of venue having been granted because of the alleged prejudice against Terry in San Francisco. This case was dismissed but Terry was subsequently indicted by the Grand Jury in San Mateo County. The point was then raised that he had been once in jeopardy, and being well taken, that case was also dismissed."

After his acquittal Terry was practically ostracized. He went to the mines in Virginia City, but in 1862 returned to Stockton, where he resumed the practice of law. In 1863 he joined the Confederate Army as a Colonel. He rose to the rank of Brigadier-General and was placed in command of a brigade from Texas.

Disgruntled at the outcome of the Rebellion he returned to Texas and engaged in the wool and cotton industries, but failing in this, he again returned to Stockton, where he resumed the practice of law.

In 1878 he was elected a delegate to the convention to revise the State Constitution, and in 1880 he was selected as a presidential elector on the Democratic ticket.

Judge Terry's wife died on December 24, 1884.

Sarah Althea Hill was born in Missouri in 1848. In 1854 her parents died, leaving her and her brother Morgan an estate valued at $40,000.00. Sarah received a good education and developed into a beautiful young woman.

In 1870 she came to California with her uncle, who provided her with a suite of rooms in the Palace Hotel. Here she met the owner of the hotel, United States Senator William Sharon, from Nevada, a multi-millionaire.

In 1883 Sarah Althea produced a document claiming that it was a marriage contract entered into between Sharon and herself on August 25, 1880. On October 3 Sharon began proceedings to have the marriage contract, alleged to have been entered into by Miss Hill and himself, declared null and void. A long and bitter fight ensued, at the outset of which Miss Hill was represented by Attorney W. B. Tyler.

On August 3, 1885, S. C. Houghton, acting as Examiner in Chancery of the United States Circuit Court, had a witness named R. U. Piper on the witness stand undergoing examination in reference to this case. At this hearing William M. Stewart was representing the Sharon interests. While Piper was testifying. Miss Hill became enraged at Attorney Stewart and cried out: "I feel like taking that man Stewart out and cowhiding him. I will shoot him yet; that very man sitting there."

The Master in Chancery attempted to pacify her and succeeded for the moment, but shortly afterward she opened a satchel and drawing out a revolver, pointed it at Judge O. P. Evans, also of opposing counsel. He remained cool and asked her if she wanted to shoot anybody. She replied: "I am not going to shoot you now unless you would like to be shot and think you deserve it." He assured her that he had no desire to undergo any such experience, and after considerable persuasion she handed the revolver to the Master in Chancery and the examination immediately adjourned.

On August 5 this incident was reported to Judges Field and Sawyer, who were then Judges of the United States Circuit Court, but no action was taken, other than the issuance of an order that the Marshal of the Court should take all such measures as might be deemed necessary to keep the defendant disarmed and under strict surveillance while attending the examination.

Judge Terry finally took charge of Miss Hill's case, but on the death of Senator Sharon at the Palace Hotel on November 14, 1885, a new fight began for the estate. On January 7, 1886, Judge Terry married his fair client.

The fight for the estate was continued until September 24, 1888, when Stephen Field, who at this time was a Justice of the United States Supreme Court, rendered a decision against the Terry's. At this point Mrs. Terry jumped up and cried out to the Justice: "How much money did you get for that decision?" The Court ordered United States Marshal Franks to put her out of the courtroom, whereupon Terry sprang to his feet and dared any one to lay a hand on his wife. The Marshal ignored Terry's remark and forcibly ejected Mrs. Terry. Her husband then drew a bowie knife and attempted to follow Franks, but was overpowered.

As a result of this outbreak, Terry was found guilty of contempt of court and was sentenced to six months' imprisonment in the Alameda County Jail and his wife was sentenced to thirty days' imprisonment.

While in jail Terry swore he would have revenge, and as a result David Neagle was appointed Deputy United States Marshal and assigned as bodyguard to Justice Field. Neagle was born and raised in San Francisco, where he took an active part in politics. He afterward went to Tombstone, Arizona, where he served as City Marshal. One day, one of Neagle's officers was shot by a Mexican desperado, who then rode away to the hills. Neagle pursued him, and the next day came into town on horseback with the Mexican's body thrown over the saddle in front of him. He then went to Butte, Montana, but returned to San Francisco in 1883. He was employed in the Tax Collector's office when appointed to guard Justice Field, whom he accompanied to Los Angeles.

On August 13, 1889, the court adjourned in Los Angeles, and Field and Neagle started for San Francisco. On reaching Fresno, Terry and his wife boarded the same train, but did not see Justice Field then.

At 8:15 a. m., August 14, the train arrived at Lathrop and stopped to allow the passengers to partake of breakfast in the dining-room in the depot. Justice Field and Neagle preceded Terry and his wife to the dining-room. Immediately after Judge Terry and his wife took their seats, Mrs. Terry observed Justice Field, and, after informing her husband of his presence, she arose and left the dining-room hurriedly.

T. W. Stackpole, who conducted the dining-room, recognized his guests, and being familiar with their past differences, and feeling somewhat uneasy at Mrs. Terry's actions, he approached her husband and asked if she contemplated doing anything rash. Terry gave an evasive answer, and immediately arose, walked over to Justice Field, and slapped his face. Neagle jumped to his feet with his revolver drawn, and, as Terry was about to continue the assault, Neagle placed the revolver to Terry's chest and fired. The latter sank to the floor and died instantly.

His wife heard the shot, and rushed to the dining-room with an open satchel in her hand. She was stopped by Stackpole, who removed a revolver from the satchel. Mrs. Terry then became hysterical and cried for vengeance.

Field and Neagle returned to their stateroom, where they were joined by Constable Walker, who placed Neagle under arrest and took him to the jail in Stockton.

Justice Field was arrested on August 16 in San Francisco on a warrant sworn to by Mrs. Terry, charging him with complicity in the "murder."

The case against Justice Field was dismissed in the Circuit Court on August 27, 1889. He presented Neagle with a gold watch and chain as a token of his appreciation for services rendered.

Neagle's case was finally dismissed in the United States Circuit Court on September 16, 1889, where it was taken on a writ of habeas corpus.

Since his acquittal, Neagle has acted as a bodyguard for different prominent men in San Francisco.

Mrs. Terry became a physical and mental wreck after the death of her husband, and on March 10, 1892, she was committed to the Stockton Insane Asylum.

DENNIS KEARNEY RIOTS.

In February, 1848, the brig "Eagle" arrived in San Francisco harbor with the first Chinese to enter this city. The party consisted of two men and one woman. There was no demonstration against this race at first, but by 1852 it is estimated that at least 8,000 Chinese had arrived in this State, and as their frugality made it impossible for white laborers to compete with them, considerable apprehension was entertained to the effect their presence would have on the white population. In 1877 many of the white men had grown to abhor the Chinese, and numerous acts of violence were committed.

About this time, Dennis Kearney, a drayman, belonged to a debating club which met at Dashaway Hall, near Grant Avenue and Post Streets. Topics of the day were discussed, but as the feeling was strong against the Chinese, Kearney decided to devote his "eloquence" to that subject. As his following grew rapidly, he was forced to hold his meetings out of doors and the sandlot in front of the City Hall dome, opposite Eighth and Market Streets became his meeting-place. At that time Kearney enjoyed the complete confidence of his following, who were wrought up to a high pitch of excitement by his incendiary speeches.

Because of numerous strikes in the East at the time, a mass meeting was held in San Francisco on July 23, 1877. Alleged orators took advantage of the occasion and prophesied that similar conditions would soon exist in San Francisco if the Chinese were not driven out.

After the meeting adjourned a gang of hoodlums proceeded to several Chinese washhouses and wrecked them and assaulted the Chinese. They concluded their work by setting fire to a washhouse at Leavenworth and Turk Streets.

On the following day a Committee of Safety was organized, as the police force, consisting of 150 men, was unable to cope with the situation. William T. Coleman, of Vigilante fame, was selected as a leader. Five thousand citizens joined the organization and they met at Horticultural Hall, on Stockton, near Post Street.

On July 25 a mob burned a large lumber yard near the mail dock, located at First and Brannan Streets, and attempted to burn the dock because the Chinese were landed there, but were repulsed by the safety committee and police. In this battle the committee was armed with rifles and pick handles. Several men were shot and otherwise wounded on this occasion.

On July 27 a James Smith was arrested for setting the lumber yard fire and held on $20,000 bail.

On July 30, 1877, the Citizens' Committee disbanded.

On January 3, 1878, Kearney formed a parade of fifteen hundred of his followers and marched to the City Hall and demanded that Mayor A. J. Bryant provide them with work. The Mayor explained that he was powerless to furnish employment, whereupon they returned to the sandlot, where

Kearney made a speech which resulted in an indictment being found against him on January 5, charging him with uttering language with intent to incite riot.

About January 17, 1878, the McCoppin bill increasing the San Francisco police force from 150 to 400 men was passed because of these riots.

Congressman Tom Geary presented a bill before Congress known as the "Chinese Exclusion Act." This bill became a law on May 6, 1882. Kearney went to Washington in the interest of the bill, and when he returned to San Francisco his followers carried him through the Streets amid great enthusiasm.

On May 5, 1892, a law went into effect which provided that all Chinese laborers must procure certificates of residence before May 6, 1893, and by affirmative proof show their right to remain in the country.

The first Chinaman to be deported under this law was Ming Lee Twe. He was shipped on the Rio de Janeiro, and the United States Government paid his fare, amounting to $30.

THE MURDER OF GEORGE HILL FOR A WORTHLESS

CLUSTER OF IMITATION DIAMONDS.

In 1865 there resided in San Francisco a young man named George Hill, who had inherited a comfortable fortune, which he had almost entirely dissipated in the gambling games. He was a flashy dresser and constantly wore a scarf pin, said to contain a cluster of diamonds valued at $1,500.

Hill had a room in the Mansion House, on DuPont, near Sacramento Street, and on February 15, 1865, he disappeared. Being of a somewhat wild and roving disposition, no significance was attached to this, either by his landlady or associates.

Some weeks after his disappearance, a gardener named Mr. McGloin was walking through the sand out near his home in San Souci Valley, which is now better designated as the vicinity of Fulton and Baker Streets. A dog he had with him began pulling and tugging at a piece of hay rope, which appeared to be securely fastened to something buried under the sand.

Curiosity prompted Mr. McGloin to investigate, and to his horror he found that the rope was tied around the badly decomposed body of a man. He immediately informed the police of his discovery and the body was brought into town for identification. There was a hole in the side of the head made by some blunt instrument which had evidently caused his death. All valuables had been removed from the body.

Owing to the advanced state of decomposition, it was very difficult to identify the body and the authorities were about to bury the remains when a newspaper reporter who knew Hill well, identified the body.

The police then proceeded to Hill's room, and the landlady stated that the day after his disappearance, a young man whom she described accurately had come to her house and stated that Hill was about to go to Contra Costa County to procure some money, but that he had met with an accident.

The stranger produced a shirt which had some blood on it and stated that Hill had instructed him to exchange it for a clean one. He was admitted to Hill's room and, after putting the bloody shirt in the trunk and removing some other articles, he departed, but returned shortly afterward to regain possession of the shirt. The landlady's suspicions becoming aroused she refused to admit him to Hill's room.

One of the officers who heard the landlady describe this man recalled that a man then in custody on a charge of forgery answered that description perfectly. Upon being brought before the landlady he was positively identified as the man she referred to and it was learned that his name was Thomas Byrnes, a butcher by trade and the son of the keeper of a roadhouse near Calvary Cemetery.

Mr. McGloin, who discovered Hill's body, was a warm friend of the family of the murderer.

It was ascertained that on the evening of February 15, 1865, Hill procured a two-horse buggy from Wright & Roden's livery stable on Kearny Street, near Pine, and in company with Byrnes started for the Cliff House.

About midnight the horses returned alone to the stable, causing the stable-keeper to conclude that there had been a runaway and that the horses had broken away from the vehicle. After a while Byrnes came in and stated that they had met with an accident and that his partner being injured, had sent him for another team.

Before starting away with his second rig, Byrnes asked for a shovel, stating that he wanted to dig the wheels of the other buggy out of the sand. It was observed by the stable man that Byrnes threw a piece of hay-rope into the buggy.

When Hill and Byrnes started the first time, Byrnes insisted on taking a monkey-wrench along, stating that it might be needed.

When they arrived at a spot near where the body was found, Brynes crushed Hill's skull with the monkey-wrench, the end of which fitted into the wound perfectly. He then cut the harness and scared the horses away, to make it appear that Hill met his death in a runaway accident. He reconsidered, however, and decided that the runaway would not account for the loss of Hill's property, so the idea of burying the body came to his mind. The rope was used to drag it into the sand, and of course the shovel was used to dig the grave.

It was afterwards learned that Byrnes attempted to pawn Hill's jewelry and was greatly chagrined to learn that "diamonds" which he thought were worth nearly two thousand dollars, were in reality worth less than three dollars.

Byrnes was found guilty of murder and after a futile appeal to the Supreme Court was executed on September 3, 1866.

THE SENSATIONAL KILLING OF THE PROMINENT ATTORNEY, ALEXANDER CRITTENDEN, BY LAURA D. FAIR.

Alexander Crittenden was born in Lexington, Ky., on January 14, 1816. Andrew Jackson was a close friend of his family, and it was through Jackson's influence that Alexander was sent to West Point. He graduated from this military college with Sherman and remained in the army about one year. At the age of twenty-two he married and went to Texas, where he was admitted to the bar. In 1852 he came to San Francisco and associated himself with S. M. Wilson. Under the firm name of Crittenden & Wilson, they became one of the most prominent law firms in San Francisco.

Laura D. Fair was a native of Mississippi, and at the age of sixteen she married a man named Stone, who died about one year afterward. She then married a Thomas Gracien of New Orleans, but a divorce was obtained six months afterward. In 1859 she married Colonel W. B. Fair, who was at that time Sheriff of Shasta County, California, but who subsequently moved to San Francisco with his wife. Owing to family troubles he committed suicide in December, 1861. After the death of her husband, Mrs. Fair conducted the Tahoe House in Virginia City.

During the war her sympathies were with the South to such an extent that she took a shot at a Northern soldier, but as her aim was very bad she was never punished for her action. On another occasion she shot a man at the Russ House in San Francisco, whom she claimed had made a disparaging remark concerning her, but again her aim was bad and again she escaped prosecution.

Mrs. Fair had some ability as an actress and appeared at the Metropolitan Theatre in Sacramento on March 5, 1863, as Lady Teazle in the "School for Scandal." In August, 1870, a young man named Jesse Snyder married her, but on October 8 of the same year they were divorced.

In September, 1870, Crittenden sent his wife and seven children East for a pleasure trip, and on the afternoon of November 3 he went to Oakland to greet them on their return. He met his family at the Oakland pier and accompanied them aboard the ferry El Capitan. From the time of the family reunion, Mr. Crittenden's son, Parker, noticed a woman dressed in black and heavily veiled, who seemed to be watching their actions very closely, and when the family were seated on the boat she hurried toward them and, suddenly whipping out a pistol, shot Crittenden Senior in the chest. The wounded man fell unconscious and the woman hurried away and took a seat, but Captain Kentzel of the Harbor Police, who was on the boat at the time, disarmed her and placed her under arrest. It was subsequently learned that she was Mrs. Laura D. Fair. Immediately after being arrested she began to act in a peculiar manner, and when a stimulant was handed to her in a glass of water, she bit a piece out of the glass.

At 6 p. m., November 5, Crittenden died, and on the day of his funeral the Federal, State and municipal courts adjourned. His funeral was one of the largest ever held in San Francisco up to that time.

Mrs. Fair was charged with murder, and during the trial, which occurred in San Francisco, she testified that she and Crittenden had been intimate for seven years past. The defense offered was that Crittenden's perfidities had wrought havoc with Mrs. Fair's mind and that she was in a blind frenzy when she shot him.

On April 26, 1871, the jury after a short deliberation brought in a verdict of guilty of murder, and on June 3, 1871, Mrs. Fair was sentenced to be hanged on July 28.

On July 11 the Supreme Court granted her a stay of execution and finally granted her a new trial, at which she was acquitted, because of her attorney's plea to the jury that the defendant was a victim of emotional insanity.

For many years after her acquittal Mrs. Fair made a living as a book agent in San Francisco.

BANKER J. C. DUNCAN, CHARGED WITH EMBEZZLEMENT—HIS SENSATIONAL ATTEMPTS TO EVADE ARREST.

On October 8, 1877, J. C. Duncan, president of Duncan's Bank, located at Montgomery and California Streets, disappeared, and the bank failed for $1,213,000, alleged to have been caused by Duncan's unfortunate investments made with depositors' money.

A warrant was issued for Duncan's arrest on a charge of embezzlement, and Captain Lees received information that Duncan was about to take passage on a schooner bound for Callao, Peru. This schooner was lying far out in the bay opposite "Hathaway's wharf," which was near Steuart and Folsom Streets. It was also learned that a red stack tug would take Duncan outside the heads at nighttime, and that he would board the schooner at sea.

Captain Lees with a posse had the tug "Elaine" in readiness at North Point dock. At this time Steuart Street was in such shape that a vehicle could make but little progress on it, so Officer John McGreevy, who then held the Coast championship for long-distance running, was detailed to watch the schooner from Hathaway's wharf. About 3 a. m. he heard the sailors heaving anchor, so he ran all the way to North Point, and, after imparting this information to Captain Lees, fell from exhaustion. Lees ordered his tug out in the stream, and seeing another tug, gave chase, but lost it temporarily. The schooner then hove in sight, and, upon overtaking it, Lees sent a posse aboard, where they found a part of Duncan's wardrobe.

With the remainder of his posse he again located the other tug and followed it to Mission-Street wharf, where they saw a man go ashore and disappear among the lumber piles.

Shortly afterward Captain Lees learned that a lady, who conducted a dressmaking parlor at California and Kearny Streets, was a friend of Duncan's, and on positive information being received that she was harboring him, a search was made of her apartments on February 24, 1878. Duncan was found concealed in what was apparently a bureau, but which had all drawers and internal framework removed. Throughout the four trials, in all of which the juries disagreed, Mrs. Duncan remained loyal to her husband, and lived in the cell with him until he was finally discharged. It was reported that Duncan was drowned at sea three years afterward.

"WHEELER, THE STRANGLER."

At 11:55 p. m., October 20, 1880, a heavy-set, middle-aged man entered the Central Police Station at Washington and Kearny Streets, and addressing Sergeant John Shields, spoke as follows:

> *"My name is George Wheeler and I wish to surrender, as I have just strangled my sister-in-law, Delia Tillson. Here is a key to a trunk in room 14 at 23 Kearny Street. Go there and you will find her body."*

As this statement was made with the greatest nonchalance, the officers were somewhat skeptical. The man was taken into custody, however, and officers were sent to the room, where they found the trunk as described, and on opening it they found that the body of a good-looking and well-proportioned young woman had been crowded into it. The body was fully dressed. Upon interrogating people who resided in the house, the officers learned that this woman was known as Wheeler's wife instead of his sister-in-law, and that another woman, who was out at the time, was known as the sister-in-law.

The officers then returned to the station, where Wheeler voluntarily made an additional statement, as follows:

> *"Delia Tillson, the girl whose body you found, is my sister-in-law, regardless of any statement made to the contrary, and she was 21 years old a few months ago. I married her sister Mary in Massachusetts eleven years ago.*
>
> *"Six years later I became intimate with Delia, who lived in the same house with us. About a year afterward Delia confessed to my wife*

that she was in a delicate condition and that I was responsible for it. Their folks were highly respected, and to avoid a scandal Mary protected Delia and the child was born in our house, but it died a few weeks afterward.

"Shortly after this the three of us came to San Francisco, but failing to obtain employment, I took both women to Cisco, Placer County, where I was employed as an engineer. At this place Delia met a man named George Peckham, with whom she became intimate, according to her confessions to me. By this time I had grown to love Delia as much as I did Mary, my wife, and the three of us occupied one room.

"When Delia made this admission I became furious, but I forgave her with the understanding that she should cease her relations with Peckham and accompany me to San Francisco, where we engaged the rooms in which I strangled her to-night, and where we were known as man and wife. We came here about five months ago. About one month ago my wife located us and came to live with us, she posing as my sister-in-law.

"Tonight I went out to see Officer Moorehouse on business, and when I returned Delia was in the rooms and had on her hat and gloves. I asked her where she had been. She sat on my knee and confessed that she had been in constant communication with Peckham ever since we left Cisco and that it was he who told my wife where we were located.

"Delia furthermore told me that she and Peckham had met that night, and had agreed to go to Sacramento and live as man and wife. This admission crazed me, and as she sat on my knee I strangled her. I then crowded the body into the trunk. My wife was out at the time."

Mrs. Wheeler was located, and she reluctantly admitted that her husband's statements were substantially correct.

Notwithstanding his confession, Wheeler made a hard fight for his life, and it was only after four trials that he was found guilty. He was hanged on January 23, 1884.

THE MURDER OF CAPITALIST NICHOLAS SKERRITT BY ATTORNEY WRIGHT LE ROY.

Nicholas Skerritt arrived in San Francisco in March, 1849, and almost immediately afterward engaged in the dry goods business on Montgomery Street near Bush.

Skerritt could never have been traced through life by the money he threw away, and after conducting his dry goods store for fifteen years he retired with a fortune of $120,000, which he invested in real estate.

He was an eccentric old bachelor, and resided at 503 Bush Street with a Mr. Sam Dixon, a stock broker, who was one of the few people in whom Skerritt confided his business affairs.

On August 5, 1883, Skerritt came home and informed Mr. and Mrs. Dixon that he had met a man named La Rue, who had just made considerable money in the Colorado mines. He stated that La Rue had a prepossessing appearance and that he (Skerritt) had that day consummated a deal whereby La Rue was to rent all of his property, with the right to sublet it.

On Sunday afternoon, August 12, La Rue called at Dixon's home and had a conversation with Skerritt. On Monday, Skerritt left home and never returned. On Wednesday, Dixon received the following dispatch from Sacramento:

"Have made a clean sweep of my real and personal property to parties from Colorado. Going there to complete sale. Have one-half in hand. La Rue will take charge; favor him; he is solid and reliable.

"N. Skerritt."

This telegram aroused suspicion in the mind of Dixon, as it was not worded in the language ordinarily used by Skerritt. He took the telegram to Donald McLea, another friend of Skerritt, and McLea stated that he had received a similar dispatch.

Knowing that the Donohoe-Kelly Bank transacted considerable business for the missing man, these two men repaired to that institution and learned that they also had received a similar message.

On that same day La Rue called at the home of the Dixons and stated that he came to take charge of Skerritt's effects, and took away all that he could carry conveniently.

By this time Dixon's suspicions were fully aroused and he notified the police authorities. The case was assigned to Detective Robert Hogan, who ascertained that deeds had been filed with the Recorder showing the alleged transfer of nearly all of Skerritt's property to La Rue.

On August 27, 1878, a lawyer named Wright Le Roy was sent to State Prison for a forgery committed in Alameda County, and, although he committed no physical violence, the circumstances in connection with the forgery were very similar to this case. Le Roy was liberated on May 27, 1883. These circumstances, and the similarity of names, caused Hogan to suspect that La Rue was in reality Le Roy, and that he could explain Skerritt's disappearance.

It was learned that La Rue had made an appointment to call at Mr. McLea's home, and Chief Crowley, Captain Lees and Detective Byram were there to receive him. When he appeared, the officers covered him with revolvers and ordered him to throw up his hands. It was then seen that the man who assumed the name of La Rue was the ex-convict, Le Roy.

Captain Lees asked him why he sent the three telegrams from Sacramento, but he denied all knowledge of them, and he also denied removing Skerritt's personal property from his home. Le Roy was taken into custody pending further investigation.

Captain Lees sent to the telegraph office at Sacramento and had the original messages forwarded to him, and it was apparent that they were in Le Roy's handwriting. It was also proven by experts that it was Le Roy who forged the deeds filed with the Recorder.

When interrogated as to Skerritt's whereabouts, Le Roy stated that Skerritt went to Sacramento on the Monday previous with two men named Townsend and Miller and that the three intended to go to Denver, where Skerritt was to be paid for the property which he had sold to these two men.

He was then sent back to his cell and, after realizing that his statement must have sounded ridiculous in view of the evidence already obtained, he entangled himself still more hopelessly by sending for Captain Lees and admitting that his statement regarding Skerritt was false, but that he was prepared to tell the facts. He then said:

> "I met Townsend three weeks ago at Geary and DuPont Streets, and he told me he was going to make a raise in some manner. At this time Miller joined us and shortly after Skerritt passed, and I remarked that if Townsend had his (Skerritt's) money he would not

have to make a raise. I then introduced Townsend to Skerritt, and afterwards Townsend told me that he would capture Skerritt's person and then his money. The next time I saw Townsend and Miller, they told me that they had accomplished their object. I told them that Skerritt's friends would institute a search for him, so at my suggestion they wrote the three telegrams which I sent from Sacramento. When I asked where Skerritt was, they laughed and said that he was O. K. in Contra Costa County."

When a thorough search was made of Skerritt's room, fifty dollars, two diamond studs and other jewelry were found which had been overlooked by Le Roy, but which proved conclusively to those who knew Skerritt that he would never willingly depart and leave such valuables behind.

It was then ascertained that Le Roy had been seen in Union Square with two ex-convicts named Jas. Dollar and Thomas McDonald and it was furthermore learned that Dollar went with Le Roy to a second-hand store on Fourth near Market Street and purchased a mattress and blankets. But it was not clear what use these persons would make of them or where they would be taken.

Feeling confident that a murder had been committed, Detective Hogan requested Mr. Chichester, a handy-man in Skerritt's employ, to accompany him to the different vacant buildings owned by the missing man.

The first place they went to was 1129 Ellis Street, and upon opening the door both men were sickened by the odor of decomposed flesh which confronted them. They found Skerritt's body, black, swollen and decomposed, in a sitting position against the wall in a closet, with a blanket thrown over it.

When Le Roy was arrested he had several keys in his possession, all of which were accounted for, except a key for a Yale lock. He roomed at a lodging-house conducted by a Mr. Perkins at California and Powell Streets, and underneath the mattress several of Skerritt's papers were found, but, as other articles were still missing which Le Roy took from Skerritt's home, it was decided that the suspect must have another room and that the mysterious key for the Yale lock was the pass-key to the house where that room was located. A great number of duplicates were made and officers were looking all over the city for a lock to fit this key, when one evening Captain Lees asked Detective Hogan to accompany him to the Grand Hotel. After remaining there a short time they left, but when they had crossed Market Street. Lees excused himself for a few moments and returned to the hotel.

Having nothing to do in the meantime, Hogan got out his duplicate key, and he can attribute his movements immediately afterward to nothing except his intuitive powers, for he went to the door of a lodging-house a few feet away, No. 620 Market Street, and there found that his key opened the lock of the Street door. When Lees returned, Hogan reported his discovery, but owing to the late hour they decided to investigate further on the following morning. When they returned they located Le Roy's room, and in it they found the remainder of the property stolen from Skerritt's room, which Le Roy denied having taken. They also found twelve large cans of chloride of lime, in which he probably intended to consume Skerritt's body at the first opportunity.

It will be recalled that Le Roy purchased a mattress and blankets on Fourth Street and in addition to that he purchased carpets at another place.

A lady living next door to 1129 Ellis Street identified Le Roy as the man who called on her shortly after Skerritt disappeared and inquired if she had seen a wagon call with any furniture for the next flat.

When the officers arrived at 1129 Ellis Street, they found the articles purchased on Fourth Street, and afterward Dollar and McDonald testified that they assisted in bringing them there for Le Roy. This house was one of the buildings for which Le Roy filed a forged deed with the Recorder.

On August 27, 1883, the Coroner's jury returned a verdict, in which they found that Skerritt was strangled to death by Le Roy.

He was tried in Judge Ferral's court and convicted of murder in the first degree. He endeavored to persuade Governor Stoneman to interfere but failed, and on January 18, 1885, he was hanged by Sheriff Hopkins.

THE CELEBRATED TRIAL OF DR. MILTON BOWERS FOR THE MURDER OF HIS WIFE, AND THE TRIAL OF JOHN DIMMIG FOR THE MURDER OF HENRY BENHAYON, MRS. BOWERS' BROTHER.

J. Milton Bowers was born in Baltimore, Maryland, in 1843 and at the age of sixteen he went to Berlin to study medicine, but not as a matriculated student.

In 1863, he returned to America and served in the Civil War. In 1865 he settled in Chicago, where he married Miss Fannie Hammet, who died very mysteriously in 1873.

Shortly after her death. Bowers proceeded to Brooklyn, N. Y., where he married Thresa Shirk, a remarkably clever and beautiful actress who had been his patient in Chicago. As Bowers was in poor health, the couple came to San Francisco by steamer, arriving in July, 1874.

On January 29, 1881, Thresa Shirk Bowers died at the Palace Hotel and there were many circumstances in connection with her death which were never satisfactorily explained.

In 1852 a wedding between J. Benhayon and a widow was celebrated in Germany. The widow had a little baby girl named Cecelia. In 1854 a boy was born and was named Henry Benhayon. The family then came to San Francisco and after several unsuccessful business ventures, Benhayon finally became a traveling salesman.

Cecelia married a man named Sylvian Levy, and a little daughter was born and named Tillie. Shortly afterward Levy procured a divorce from his wife, who bore an unenviable reputation.

On July 19, 1881, less than six months after his second wife died, Bowers married Cecelia Benhayon Levy. In public Bowers was most assiduous in his attentions to each of his wives, but in his home life it was claimed that he was brutal. Knowing his reputation in this respect, Mrs. Benhayon was bitterly opposed to the marriage, and it resulted in an estrangement between the bride and her relatives, which continued until a few months previous to Mrs. Bowers' death.

In July, 1885, Mrs. Bowers' face and body began to swell until she assumed such an extraordinary aspect that her own mother hardly recognized her, and she suffered excruciating pains, especially during frequent convulsions.

Mrs. Bowers took out life insurance policies in favor of her husband amounting to $17,000, among which was a policy for $5,000 from the American Legion of Honor. On October 28, 1885, a stranger entered the office of this order and inquired of Grand Secretary Burton if he could inspect the membership list of the various local councils of the order. Upon being informed that such a list could not be procured, he stated, after much hesitation, that a woman was sick who was a member of the order; that foul play was going on and that she would die in a few days. He then departed without disclosing his identity.

On November 2 another mysterious man hastily entered the

Coroner's office and announced that Mrs. Dr. J. Milton Bowers had just died at the "Arcade House," 930 Market Street, and that there were suspicious circumstances surrounding her death, which should be officially investigated. After imparting this information he vanished as though the earth had swallowed him.

The Coroner, Dr. C. C. O'Donnell, proceeded at once to the place and found Mrs. Bowers' body in the same room with Dr. Bowers. He informed Bowers of the rumors afloat and the latter, with characteristic coolness, stated that the funeral would take place on the following afternoon, and that if an investigation was decided upon it should be made immediately so as not to interfere with the services. As Bowers claimed his wife died from abscess of the liver, six physicians performed an autopsy, and they decided that she had not died from that ailment. Other physicians made an examination, some of whom stated that some of the symptoms and conditions usually present in cases of phosphorus poisoning, were present in this case.

The dead woman's stomach was removed and traces of phosphorus were found by Dr. W. D. Johnson, professor of chemistry at Cooper Medical College. It was said that Bowers received this poison in the form of samples from manufacturing chemists, but all these samples, which Bowers admitted having received, disappeared mysteriously from his office shortly after the investigation began.

Mrs. Benhayon, the mother of the dead woman, stated that when she first visited her daughter after their estrangement, it was apparent that she could not live, and she expressed this opinion to Dr. Bowers, who informed her that Cecelia was recovering and he added that he had so much confidence in his judgment that he had made preliminary arrangements to take her on a nice trip to the country. As the days passed by, Mrs. Benhayon lost faith in Bowers' ability as a physician and she stated that it was only after repeated solicitations that he consented to call in Dr. W. H. Bruner.

After a month's experience, Mrs. Bowers' relatives lost faith in Bruner and Dr. Martin of Oakland was substituted. After Martin was called in the only noticeable change in the patient was in her complexion, which assumed a beautiful and clear appearance. As her sufferings seemed to increase rather than diminish, it was suspected that arsenic had been administered. Mrs. Benhayon furthermore said:

"On the Sunday before Cecelia died, her aunt and cousin called at Mrs. Bowers' request. I admitted them into the sick chamber, unknown to the doctor, but he rushed in and excitedly exclaimed: 'You must get out of here; I allow no one to see my wife,' and he almost forcibly put them out. Although Bowers has $17,000

insurance on his wife's life, he has refused to have any policy made out in favor of her daughter by her first husband, and when medicines were brought to the house, he usually examined them privately and then administered them himself."

Drs. Bruner and Martin, who treated Mrs. Bowers, stated that from what Dr. Bowers had told them of the history of the case, and from their own observations, they also believed that she was suffering from abscess of the liver and treated her accordingly.

On November 12, 1885, the coroner's jury found that Mrs. Bowers came to her death by phosphorus poisoning, and Bowers was at once taken into custody by Detective Robert Hogan, and charged with the murder of his wife.

On March 8, 1886, Bowers' trial began before Judge Murphy of the Superior Court. Eugene Duprey, who afterwards defended Durrant, acted as special prosecutor. In his opening statement to the jury he stated that he expected to prove that Mrs. Zeissing, who nursed Mrs. Bowers, had shown unmistakable indications of being in collusion with the prisoner, and he accused Theresa Farrell, Bowers' housekeeper, who afterward married John Dimmig, of attempting to shield Bowers. He claimed that before the death of his wife, Bowers had made arrangements to marry a woman from San Jose, and that she had already prepared her trousseau. He furthermore stated that Bowers had courted his last wife before the death of the second one.

Bowers' record in Chicago had been obtained from the Chief of Police of that city, and the prosecuting attorney asked permission to read it to the jury, but an objection from Bowers' attorney was, of course, sustained. The defendant was also charged with being a professional abortionist.

The case was finally submitted to the jury at 4:15 p. m., April 23, 1886, and at 9 p. m. the jury returned a verdict of guilty of murder in the first degree.

On June 2, 1886, Bowers was sentenced to be hanged, but the case was appealed to the Supreme Court. This Court was not entirely satisfied with the sufficiency of the evidence against Bowers and handed down a decision ordering a new trial. Shortly before this decision was handed down the most remarkable feature of the case occurred.

The Mysterious Death of Henry Benhayon.

Henry Benhayon, Mrs. Bowers' half-brother, was apprenticed to a stone cutter in Sacramento when he was about fifteen years of age, and although he became an expert at an early age, he tired of the work and accompanied his family to San Francisco. He then became "stage struck" and took lessons in elocution. He recited at lodge meetings and amateur entertainments and showed a predilection for the powerful, villain type of recitation. He once appeared in "Richard III," but realizing that he was an utter failure, he made no further attempts in that direction. After this he sought no permanent employment, but lived off of Mrs. Bowers and his mother a great deal of the time.

On Sunday, October 23, 1887, the Coroner was notified that the body of a dead man had been found in room 21 of a lodging-house located at 22 Geary Street. The officials proceeded at once to the place and the landlady, Mrs. Higgson, conducted them to the room and on the bed the body of a young man apparently about 27 years old was found. He was laid out as though prepared for a coffin, and the bed clothing was in no manner disturbed. The landlady said that she had never seen the man before.

Shortly afterward the remains were identified as those of Henry Benhayon, the brother of the late Mrs. Bowers. Three bottles were found in the room, one containing whisky, one chloroform liniment and a third cyanide of potassium with the label removed; all bottles being corked.

Three letters were also found in the room, one being addressed to the San Francisco Chronicle, which read as follows:

"To the Editor of the Chronicle:

"Sir: Enclosed find $1.00 to pay for this advertisement and the balance as a reward. I will call in a few days. "Yours truly,

"Oct. 21, 1887. Henry Benhayon."

The advertisement read as follows:

"Lost, Oct. 20th, near the City Hall, a memorandum book with a letter. A liberal reward will be paid if left at this office."

The second letter was addressed to Dr. Bowers, who was still confined in the County Jail awaiting the decision of the Supreme Court on his appeal for a new trial. It read as follows:

"City, Oct. 22, 1887.

"Dr. J. Milton Bowers:

"I only ask that you do not molest my mother. Tillie is not responsible for my acts and I have made all reparation in my power.

"I likewise caution you against some of your friends, who knew Cecelia only as a husband should.

"Among them are C. M. McLennan and others whose names I cannot think of now, but you will find some more when the memorandum book is found. Farewell.

"Yours,

"H. Benhayon."

The third letter, addressed to the Coroner and headed "Confession," created a sensation. It read as follows:

"The history of the tragedy commenced after my sister married Dr. Bowers.

"I had reasons to believe that he would leave her soon, as they always quarreled, and on one occasion she told me that she would poison him before she would permit him to leave her.

"I said in jest, 'Have him insured.'

"She said 'alright,' but Bowers objected for a long time, but finally said: 'If it will keep you out of mischief, alright, go ahead.'

"They both joined several lodges and I got the stuff ready to dispose of him, but my sister would not listen to the proposition and threatened to expose me.

"After my sister got sick I felt an irresistible impulse to use the stuff on her and finish him afterward. I would then become administrator for my little niece, Tillie, and would then have the benefit of the insurance.

"I think it was on Friday, November 24, 1885, that I took one capsule

out of her pill-box and filled it with two kinds of poison. I didn't think Bowers could get into any trouble as the person who gave me the poison told me it would leave no trace in the stomach. This person committed suicide before the trial, and as it might implicate others if I mention his name I will close the tragedy.

"H. Benhayon.

"P. S. I took Dr. Bowers' money out of his desk when my sister died."

Handwriting experts were at once put to work on the letters and they were divided in opinion as to whether they were genuine or forgeries.

Mrs. Higgson stated that on October 18 a young man called at her house and signified his desire to rent room 21, in which Benhayon's body was found, but the landlady stated that the room was occupied, and although she offered him other rooms, he desired only this particular one.

On the following day another man called and asked for the same room, but Mrs. Higgson informed him that while it was at that time occupied it would be vacated Saturday. He would not look at any other room, but offered to pay a deposit of $5 on that room with the understanding that he could occupy it Saturday. She accepted the money and gave him a key. On Sunday she entered the room with the pass key and found Benhayon's body.

An autopsy showed that his death was caused by being poisoned with cyanide of potassium.

The identity of the person who engaged the room was never learned, but the man who called on the 18th inst. was positively identified as John Dimmig, who married Bowers' housekeeper, Theresa Farrell, who was accused by the prosecution in the Bowers case with committing perjury in the defendant's behalf.

Mrs. Dimmig, accompanied by Mrs. Zeissing, Mrs. Bowers' former nurse, frequently visited Bowers at the County Jail.

Dimmig was born in Ohio, where he learned the drug business, but later he moved to Texas and worked as a cattle herder. Later he came to San Francisco and obtained employment at a drug store at Eleventh and Mission Streets, but finally became a book agent.

When Captain of Detectives Lees and Detective Robert Hogan asked Dimmig if he had made inquiry for room 21 at 22 Geary Street, he admitted that he had, although he had a home on Minna Street. When asked why he tried to engage the room he replied: "Well, it was a stall. I was trying to sell books." But when Captain Lees told him that he did not believe his story, Dimmig said that he wanted the room for the purpose of meeting a woman from San Jose there. He stated that he only knew the woman by the name of "Timkins," and that she wrote to him asking that he engage a room for Saturday night, but he added that he had destroyed the letter. He denied delegating any one to procure the room for him and did not explain why he wanted that particular room. He stated that he was under the influence of liquor on the night following the day he attempted to procure this room, and that he probably met Benhayon and incidentally mentioned the room.

Dimmig stated that he did not meet the "Timkins" woman at any place on Saturday evening, and claimed that he could not understand how Benhayon gained admission to the room which he, Dimmig, was so anxious to rent.

Dimmig then handed Captain Lees a letter which was addressed to him (Dimmig) at The Western Perfumery Co., 26 Second Street, and which read as follows:

"City, Oct. 22, 1887.

"J. A. Dimmig,

"Sir: — Call on me at once. I am in a devilish fix. I don't want your money but your advice. I think it is all up with me. You will find me at Room 21, No. 22 Geary Street.

"Henry Benhayon."

Notwithstanding the remarkable coincidence that this letter indicated that Benhayon was occupying the same room Dimmig inquired for, the latter stated that he paid no attention to it and when it was submitted to the handwriting experts they disagreed as to its genuineness.

Although Dimmig was not in the habit of having his mail sent to the Western Perfumery Company, he called at this establishment shortly after this letter arrived to learn if there was any mail there for him.

Captain Lees stated that Dimmig had obtained twenty-five grains of cyanide of potassium at the drug store of Dr. Lacy and tried to procure it at several other drug stores but failed.

Detective Hogan stated that when first questioned on the subject, Dimmig denied having purchased any of this poison.

Another singular coincidence in connection with the location of the room where Benhayon's body was found, was that Mrs. Zeissing roomed at Morton and Grant Avenue, and the back entrance to the scene of the tragedy was only a few feet away. The Benhayon's stated that there was an intense hatred between her and the dead man.

Louis Goldburg stated that some weeks previous he met Benhayon and accompanied him to a room at 873 1/2 Market Street, where Benhayon stated he was doing some writing for a book agent. As Benhayon was a slow and poor writer it seemed singular that he should be employed in that line of work, unless it might be for the purpose of obtaining specimens of his handwriting. Dimmig admitted having a room on Market Street but he stated that he forgot the number.

On the Saturday afternoon preceding his death, Benhayon made arrangements to visit a dentist on the following Monday, and he had also purchased tickets to take his little niece, Tillie, to the theater on Sunday night.

No one was produced who could show that Benhayon had even attempted to purchase any deadly poison. Assuming that he did commit suicide his reason for so doing was never made clear.

If the alleged confession was genuine, his voluntary statement regarding Mrs. Bowers' character would indicate that it was not done through a desire to expiate that crime, and in speaking confidentially to friends shortly before his death, Benhayon expressed a firm belief in Bowers' guilt and also expressed the greatest hatred for him.

It was not apparent that he had any reason to believe that his guilt would be discovered, nor is it probable that the lost memorandum book contained anything of an incriminating nature when he contemplated offering such a trivial reward for its return.

Benhayon was last seen alive at 11 p. m. on Saturday night when he appeared to be in an intoxicated or drugged condition. He was accompanied by a man and woman, yet these two persons never appeared to explain where or under what circumstances they left him.

Four witnesses testified that on the Friday evening preceding the death of Benhayon, Dimmig entered Dewing's Bush Street book store to purchase some books for Mrs. Zeissing, and that he then had a flask of whisky similar to that found by Benhayon's body.

On November 12 Captain Lees charged Dimmig with the murder of Benhayon. The defendant made repeated efforts to be released on a writ of habeas corpus, but failed.

During this trial a prosecution was begun for criminal libel against Loring Pickering, of the San Francisco Call, because of an editorial published on November 13 in regard to Dimmig's wife.

On December 10 Judge Hornblower held Dimmig to answer before the Superior Court. In doing so, Hornblower attached considerable importance to the fact that the testimony showed that Dimmig called at the Western Perfumery Company to learn if any message had been left for him, and upon being handed the letter with a special delivery stamp on it, which was alleged to have been sent by Benhayon, he took no further action, although he carefully preserved it, contrary to his usual custom, but did not notify the police of having received it until they called to interrogate him regarding his efforts to procure the room in which Benhayon's body was found.

On February 20, 1888, Dimmig's trial in the Superior Court began before Judge Murphy, and on March 14 the jury disagreed after deliberating sixteen hours.

His second trial began before the same judge on December 10, 1888 and after deliberating twenty-three hours the jury acquitted him.

As some of the handwriting experts swore that the Benhayon "confession" was genuine, so far as the handwriting was concerned, the District Attorney, believing that it would be impossible to convict Bowers again, consented to his discharge. He resumed his practice in San Francisco and shortly afterward married Miss Bird of San Jose. They apparently lived happily together until his death in 1905.

ALEXANDER GOLDENSON, MURDERER.

During the year of 1886 Alexander Goldenson, a nineteen-year-old youth, lived with his folks at 24 Hayes Street. In the adjoining house lived a thirteen-year-old girl named Mamie Kelly, who attended the John Swett Grammar School. She had a childish infatuation for Goldenson, which she concealed from her mother. About November 9, 1886, the girl wrote a note to Goldenson in which she complained of his indifference toward her.*

*This note was found in his pocket when arrested.

On November 11, 1886, Goldenson waited at Ash Avenue and Polk Street, which place the girl usually passed on her way home from school. On this day she was accompanied by a classmate who continued on her way when Mamie Kelly stopped to talk to Goldenson. They conversed for a few moments when Goldenson whipped out a revolver and shot her over the right eye. She immediately sank to the ground and expired.

He then ran to the police station in the New City Hall at McAllister and Larkin Streets and surrendered, throwing his pistol into the grass plat as he passed into the building. He was immediately transferred to the city prison in the old hall at Kearny and Washington Streets, but the news of his atrocious crime spread through the city like wildfire and the feeling toward the murderer became so bitter that it was deemed advisable to secretly transfer him to the Broadway jail, which was more secure. Early in the evening a mob began to assemble in front of the Broadway jail and people were coming from all directions.

Cries of "lynch him" were frequent. By 9 p. m. a crowd of several thousand people had gathered and they were becoming more desperate every minute.

Chief Crowley and Captain Douglass had sent in a riot call and every available policeman in the city was present. Finally a man on a balcony threw a brick at an officer. The officer made a rush for the balcony, got hold of the post which was supporting the part of the balcony where he was perched, and pulled the post away, which caused him to drop to the ground with the balcony. After a little rough usage he was taken into custody and then a general charge on the mob with clubs was ordered. The officers went at them like tigers and in five minutes policemen were very much in the majority in that neighborhood, and those of the mob who remained were in the custody of officers en route to the Receiving Hospital.

Goldenson was immediately indicted by the Grand Jury and on April 14, 1887, was sentenced to be hanged. The case was appealed to the Supreme Court, which affirmed the decision of the lower Court, and on September 14, 1888, he was executed.

THE MURDER OF SAMUEL JACOBSON BY SYDNEY BELL, WHO CONFESSED TO PARTICIPATING IN SIXTY-FIVE ROBBERIES.

About 1 o'clock Sunday morning, August 17, 1890, Samuel Jacobson, of the trunk dealers' firm of Steele & Jacobson, located at No. 222 Bush

Street, staggered into his home at No. 2300 California Street, where he resided with his parents and sisters, and stated that he had just been shot in the abdomen.

He said that as he alighted from a westbound California Street car at Webster Street, a few steps from his home, two men approached him, and that the smaller of the pair, who wore a mask, pressed a pistol against his body and commanded him to throw up his hands. He stated that he grappled with this man, who shot him, and then both of the robbers fled down Webster Street.

A Chinatown guide named John Shaw said that he was in the immediate vicinity when the shot was fired, but that he saw no one on the Street.

In addition to this statement, the conductor on the westbound car, which passed at the time, stated that the only passenger to leave his car at Webster Street was a Chinaman.

This caused many to suspect that Jacobson was equivocating, and it was rumored that a big scandal would be unearthed if the true facts were known. It was even hinted that the reason that Shaw saw no one on the Street was because the shooting occurred in Jacobson's own home. On August 18 he died, and when the autopsy was performed a 32-calibre bullet was found near his heart.

At the time of the shooting Jacobson was keeping company with a milliner named Miss Courtney, and it was said that they would have been married had it not been that they disagreed regarding religion. This circumstance caused another rumor to be circulated that Jacobson had been murdered by some rival for the young lady's hand.

At this time two footpads were operating in this city, and as they usually wore masks, the only description given was that one was tall and that the other was short.

A few weeks after the death of Jacobson, a tall young man named Edward Campbell, who was employed as a solicitor for the Singer Sewing Machine Company, became particularly friendly toward Detectives Hogan and Silvey, who were detailed to apprehend the two footpads. He was "too sweet to be wholesome" and it was suspected that he aimed to creep into favor with the detectives because he feared that he would need their friendship at some future date.

Upon investigation, it was found that under the name of Harry Weston he was arrested by Sheriff Cunningham, of Stockton, Cal., for horse stealing in 1885 and was sentenced to seven years' imprisonment, but was pardoned in 1888.

To prove that he could be of service, Campbell informed these officers that a thief named Charles Schmidt had shipped a number of stolen articles from San Jose to San Francisco. A watch was set and when Schmidt called for the property he was detained and it was found that some of the articles had been stolen from citizens in San Francisco, by the "tall man and the short man."

Schmidt, who was very tall, then confessed that he had been implicated with a short man named Sydney Bell in seven robberies.

Shortly after Schmidt's capture, Campbell put a very significant hypothetical question to Detective Hogan. He asked: "If A. and B. started out to commit a robbery, but after starting B. refused to participate in any crime and insisted on going home, and then, without warning of his intentions, A. suddenly whips out a revolver and holds up a citizen who offered resistance and is killed by A., would B. be guilty of any offense?"

Hogan gave an evasive answer, but it was then understood why Campbell sought the friendship of the police.

After this conversation, Campbell was kept under constant surveillance, as it was expected that he would be seen talking to the short man who murdered Jacobson, Campbell being almost as tall as Schmidt.

As they did not meet, Captain Lees finally told Campbell that he was positive that he (Campbell) knew the facts regarding the Jacobson murder.

As evidence had already been obtained showing that he was the other tall man who operated with the short man, he, Campbell, stated that he was willing to confess if granted immunity. This being satisfactorily arranged, Campbell made the following confession:

"In May, 1890, I was sent out with Sydney Bell to canvass for the Singer sewing machine.

"We became confidential and Bell suggested that I assist him in robbing belated pedestrians. After some hesitancy I consented and we executed several 'jobs' successfully.

"On the night of August 17, I met Bell at my home, 235 Clara Street, and we traveled out through the Western Addition. Bell showed me a .32-calibre revolver and a policeman's club loaded with lead.

"Throughout the entire evening I protested against robbing anyone and Bell became provoked at me. We arrived at Webster and California Streets after midnight and I told him that I intended to take the next eastbound California-Street car and go home.

"Before it arrived, a westbound car passed and a man whom I have since learned was Samuel Jacobson, alighted, and, without consulting me, Bell went up to him and commanded him to throw up his hands.

"Jacobson grabbed Bell, who fired a shot, and then Bell and I ran along Webster Street and started for town. When we separated Bell said that he would get someone that night.

"He came to my house the next night and stated that he had robbed a fellow of $240 after we parted that morning."

In addition to the crime just related, Campbell admitted that he assisted Bell in a great number of robberies, but that Bell frequently operated alone.

It was then ascertained that Bell resided on Stockton Street, near Bush, but as he had an appointment to call on Campbell, whose home was on Prospect place, it was decided to allow Campbell to go to his home, closely followed by detectives.

Campbell was anxious that the arrest should not occur in his house, so it was arranged that he and Bell should leave the house together and the arrest was made on the Street.

When taken into custody Bell had the loaded club and 32-calibre pistol described by Campbell, in his possession. He would not admit that he had participated in the Jacobson murder, but he confessed to sixty-five robberies.

Three of his victims, Edward Crome, J. H. Curley, the tailor, and Peter Robertson, the well-known newspaper man, positively identified Bell and he chatted with them in regard to the details of the crimes.

He told Robertson that he was one of the most belligerent persons he had ever dealt with, and when Curley informed him that he (Curley) wore a magnificent diamond ring on the night he was robbed, Bell stated that if he had known that at the time, he would have bitten Curley's finger off.

Schmidt was Bell's companion during these three robberies.

When a visit was made to Bell's room, a little sixteen year-old girl was found there who posed as his wife, but who afterward admitted that she ran away from her home in the East, where her parents had surrounded her with every comfort, and that her meeting with Bell in San Francisco was purely accidental. She was sent home, and as her parents were prominent people her name was never made public.

On January 19, 1891, Bell's preliminary examination for the murder of Jacobson began before Judge Rix. He was held to answer on that charge and was subsequently held to answer for the three robberies already referred to.

On April 22 the trial for murder began in the Superior Court and on May 7 he was found guilty of murder in the first degree.

This case was appealed to the Supreme Court and a new trial was granted, but as the evidence in the robbery cases was so strong that Bell saw that it would be useless to fight the charges, it was decided to abandon the murder case and proceed with three robbery charges. He pleaded guilty to each charge on September 15.

On September 17 he was sentenced to serve forty years for robbing Edward Crone, ten years for robbing Peter Robertson and ten years for robbing J. H. Curley.

Schmidt was found guilty of the robberies in which he assisted Sydney Bell, and was sentenced to serve a term in San Quentin Prison. He stated that he would never have committed a crime had he not been swindled out of all of his earthly possessions, and he added that notwithstanding the fact that he had been convicted and sentenced, he had a presentiment that he would never go to a State Prison.

He fully realized his disgrace, and on the day that he was being taken to San Quentin, it was evident that he was laboring under an intense but suppressed excitement.

As he reached the prison gate he placed his hand to his mouth and then turned deathly pale and staggered and fell dead in the arms of the deputy sheriff. An autopsy showed that he died from cyanide of potassium poisoning.

Campbell was given his freedom in recognition of the service he had rendered to the prosecution, but he never amounted to anything afterward, being frequently arrested for vagrancy. Bell was paroled in May, 1909.

THE MURDER OF ADDIE GILMOUR, THE MILLINER

WHOSE SKULL WAS FOUND IN THE BAY.

On September 12, 1893, some Italian fishermen found a head encased in a wire netting, floating in the bay and fastened with a rope to the shore near Lime Point.

The ears and all the flesh from the face had disappeared, but a few hairs from the head were found in the netting, and judging from their length it was decided that it was the head of a woman.

A few days afterward, a boy named Stephenson discovered the trunk of a woman's body floating in the bay near Oakland.

Two different theories were advanced, both of which found ready supporters.

One was that a foul murder had been committed, but this was laughed at by those who theorized that the remains were those of some unfortunate whose body had found its way to the dissecting-room and was afterward placed in the bay by students in an effort to create a sensation.

As the body was badly decomposed it was impossible to ascertain from its appearance which theory was correct.

In August, 1893, Miss Addie Gilmour, who with Miss Laura Allen, conducted a millinery store in the little town of Colusa, Cal., came to San Francisco to purchase a supply of goods for the fall trade, but in order to acquire a knowledge of the latest styles, she procured employment with F. Toplitz, a Market Street milliner. She resided at the Elmer House, 314 Bush Street.

About the first of September, her partner came to the city, but on hearing that Miss Gilmour had left her temporary residence and place of employment without any previous notice, Miss Allen returned at once to Colusa. On learning that Miss Gilmour was not at home she became thoroughly alarmed.

As Miss Gilmour was a quiet, industrious young lady, whose mind seemed to be entirely absorbed in her business affairs, the mystery became greater until at last her twin sister reluctantly came forward and stated that Addie had written to her on September 4 that she was in trouble and about to submit to an operation at the hands of Dr. Eugene West, who was located at 132 Turk Street.

It was then ascertained that she had moved to this address on September 1.

Miss Allen and Miss Gilmour's brother-in-law, W. K. de Jarnett, proceeded to San Francisco and demanded of West information as to Miss Gilmour's whereabouts. They were joined shortly afterward by the parents of the missing girl.

According to the statements of the parents, West admitted that he had performed an operation on Miss Gilmour on September 4, and that she died on the 9th inst. He stated that he gave the body to medical students.

The family dreaded the publicity of a prosecution, but finally made known the facts to the police.

Detective Chas. Cody was sent to arrest West, but he had suddenly left his home, and after some difficulty was located at the home of W. Voorhies at 525 Turk Street.

West had an unenviable reputation among reputable physicians, who spoke in most disparaging terms of him. Upon being taken to police headquarters he was accused of having been responsible for Miss Gilmour's death, but he denied the accusation.

Working on the theory that the skull and portion of a body found in the bay were a part of the remains of Addie Gilmour, Richard Stewart, a dentist from Chico, examined the teeth and positively identified some gold fillings as work that he had done for Miss Gilmour on February 9 of the same year. Shortly after this a thigh and portion of a woman's breast were found which had been cut from that portion of the body previously recovered.

After that, small portions of the body were found in different parts of the bay.

On September 26, two Oakland boys saw a coal oil can floating in Oakland creek, which they brought ashore, and it was found to contain two arms and hands, and a foot. It also contained a lady's purse, hat pins and hair combs, which were identified as the property of Miss Gilmour.

A Miss Annie Staley, who was in the employ of Dr. Eugene West, was suspected by the police of knowing considerable that would be very damaging to the prisoner if told, but she remained loyal to him, and on September 28 a contract marriage was entered into between her and West, which prevented the prosecution from putting her on the witness stand and also enabled her to visit West in the prison.

Miss Gilmour confided her troubles to a young medical student named D. B. Plymire, who was studying in the office of Dr. Harvey at 1126 Market Street. The only male acquaintance to whom Miss Gilmour appeared to give more than a passing thought was a young man known as "Jack." She did all in her power to conceal his identity and as Plymire visited her on one occasion when she probably realized that she was about to die, she handed him a letter which she was too weak to tear up, and requested him to do so. He immediately complied with the request, but seeing no suitable place to throw the pieces, he placed them in his pocket.

After leaving her he realized that in case the unfortunate young woman should die, he might appear in a peculiar light, as he was her only visitor. He thought of the torn letter in his pocket, and with the instinct of self-preservation, he arranged the fragments in their proper order and pasted them on a paper. It was then learned that "Jack" was J. C. McGrury, who flirted with Miss Gilmour in June, 1892, while he was a railroad brakeman. After that they became friendly and finally she stayed all of one night in his room on Kearny Street.

Mrs. Lee Austin, who was employed in the millinery store where Miss Gilmour was last employed, called on Dr. West as soon as she learned the contents of the note Miss Gilmour sent to her twin sister, Emma. She there met a young lady named Miss May Howard, who resided at 815 Clay Street, Oakland. This lady informed Mrs. Austin that she had met Miss Gilmour three times; that two of the meetings took place in West's office and the third on an Oakland ferry boat.

She stated that on the occasion of the meeting on the ferry boat, Miss Gilmour appeared to be despondent and hinted that she intended to drown herself. She also said that Miss Gilmour entered the ladies' retiring room, but as she did not come out for a considerable length of time, she, Miss Howard, went into the room and found it vacant and the window open, causing her to believe that Miss Gilmour had jumped into the bay.

Afterward Miss Howard testified that her statement in regard to meeting Miss Gilmour on the boat was false, but that she did see her twice at West's office. She claimed that West persuaded her to make this statement.

It was the theory of the prosecution that West intended to convey the impression that Miss Gilmour had committed suicide, believing that it would be impossible to identify the skull found in the bay.

West was held to answer, and on February 5, 1894, his trial began in the Superior Court, Judge Wallace presiding. On February 16 he was found guilty of murder in the second degree. On February 23 West was sentenced to twenty-five years' imprisonment.

The case was appealed to the Supreme Court and a new trial was granted to the defendant.

In December, 1895, the second trial began. The evidence for the prosecution was substantially the same as at the previous trial, but in the second trial West testified that Dr. W. A. Harvey had turned Miss Gilmour over to him and that she was at that time suffering from the effects of malpractice and died on the following morning, but he did not testify that Harvey had performed the operation.

He furthermore claimed that he turned the body over to Dr. Tuchler, who, he stated, intended to use it in the interest of science. He added that Tuchler had subsequently admitted to him that the head found at Lime Point was the head of Miss Gilmour and that he (Tuchler) had placed it there for the purpose of cleansing it.

West also testified that the reason he had previously made conflicting statements regarding the case and failed to testify during the first trial regarding Tuchler and Harvey, was because they were his friends and he desired to protect them.

Dr. Harvey followed West in rebuttal, and testified that there was not one word of truth in West's testimony regarding him.

After the arguments, the case was submitted to the jury and after deliberating for one hour a verdict of not guilty was returned.

THE MIDNIGHT MURDER ON THE HIGH SEAS ON

BOARD THE BARK HESPER.

On December 22, 1892, the bark *Hesper*, carrying a valuable cargo, sailed from Newcastle, N. S. W., for this port. On January 13, 1893, Second Mate Maurice Fitzgerald took command of the midnight watch, which consisted of three sailors, named Thomas St. Clair, Herman Sparf and Hans Hansen. It was a black, wild night, the seas were running high and the wind howled through the rigging. But above this noise, the captain's wife heard a shriek; the dog on the deck began to bark, and then all was silent. The sullen conduct of the sailors above mentioned had already aroused suspicion, and it was at once decided that something was amiss.

The officers of the ship armed themselves and went aft with lanterns, A search was made for Mate Fitzgerald, but, instead of finding him, a considerable amount of blood was found on the deck near the ship's side. An attempt had been made to wash it away, but the job was poorly done because of the blackness of the night. A hatchet was then found, upon which was blood and some of Fitzgerald's hair.

The three sailors were then overpowered, placed in irons and brought to San Francisco. Sparf confessed that, when at sea a few days, Hansen, St. Clair and himself entered into a conspiracy to kill the officers, seize the ship and dispose of the cargo in Chile. He then made the following statement:

> "On the night in question, we inveigled Fitzgerald to the side of the ship and then split his head open with a hatchet. He uttered one cry and fell. Then the dog began to bark. We threw the mate overboard, and, realizing that there must be considerable blood on the deck, although it was too dark to see, we washed it off as best we could, and then the officers appeared on deck."

St. Clair and Hansen were tried in the Federal Courts and found guilty. On October 18, 1895, they were hanged at San Quentin.

KILLING OF HARRY POOLE BY JANE SHATTUCK.

During the month of November, 1892, Miss Truly Shattuck was employed in a store called the "Vienna Bazaar," at 1132 Market Street. She was a girl of striking appearance and had admirers galore, but her favorite seemed to be a young man named Harry Poole, who, on the death of his grandfather, Mr. Gerlack, expected to inherit $100,000.00.

In 1893 Truly secured an engagement as a chorus girl in the Tivoli Opera House. She and Poole gradually became more intimate and on June 4, 1894, Mrs. Jane Shattuck, the mother of Truly, addressed a note to Poole, in which she requested him to declare his intentions toward Truly. This note resulted in a bitter quarrel between Poole and Mrs. Shattuck.

On Sunday morning, July 7, 1894, Truly Shattuck returned to her home at 413 Stevenson Street. She admitted to her mother that she had spent the night with Harry Poole, but attempted to pacify her by saying that they were to be married on the following Monday.

Mrs. Shattuck then ordered Truly to write a note to Poole, which the mother dictated as follows:

> "Dear Harry: — For God's sake come down at once for Mama is dying and wants to see you. My darling, if you love me, come quickly, or

you may not see her alive.

"With love, Truly.

"P. S. — Harry, you can afford to forgive her, and for love of heaven come quickly."

This note was sent by a messenger and Poole called immediately. He found Mrs. Shattuck propped up on pillows in her bed. She told Poole that he and Truly had done wrong. Poole began stroking her left hand, which was outside of the bed covers, and admitted that the accusation was true, but stated that on the following day he would make amends for the evil he had done by making Truly his wife.

Truly left the room at this moment, and the next instant a pistol shot rang out. She rushed back to the room and found Poole lying on the floor dying, with a bullet hole in his temple, while Mrs. Shattuck had a revolver in her right hand which she had previously concealed in the bed. She was hysterical and declared she had killed Poole because he had taken her "baby girl."

She was tried before Judge E. A. Belcher, and was found guilty of murder. On June 4, 1894, she was sentenced to life imprisonment.

Her defense was insanity and a new trial was subsequently granted by the Supreme Court, with the result that on December 15, 1895, she was acquitted.

Truly took advantage of the notoriety she gained following this tragedy and procured an engagement as a singer on the vaudeville stage. Her beautiful face and figure, and fairly good voice, made her quite an attraction both in America and Europe, but a critic has recently referred to her as "Truly Shattuck, with a voice truly shattered."

THE FIENDISH MURDER OF THE AGED MRS. LANGFELDT BY THE FORMER AUSTRIAN ARMY

OFFICER, JOSEPH BLANTHER.

Joseph Blanther was born in Rankerburg Steirmart, Austria, in 1859. When nineteen years of age he was made a Lieutenant in the Austrian army, and a few months later, on December 12, 1878, was knighted and decorated by Emperor Franz Josef for distinguished services in battle.

Because of some peculiar transaction he retired from the army and left his native land. He arrived in San Francisco on February 2, 1896, and took up lodgings at the residence of Mr. Hogan, at 222 Haight Street. He was a liberal spender among the fair-weather friends he chanced to meet, and delighted to maintain a show of wealth.

He had been living at the Hogan residence only a short while when he borrowed $15 from Miss Hogan, at the same time obtaining $9.70 from a Mrs. Gilbert, who lived in the same house. For security he gave both ladies worthless checks on the Columbia Bank.

About this time he met Mr. C. H. Tebbs, a newspaper artist. Blanther, who had done some writing for Harper's and the Argonaut, and Tebbs, became quite friendly, and Blanther borrowed Tebbs' camera. When the artist asked him to return it, Blanther made so many excuses that the Harry Morse detective agency was finally employed to recover it. Captain Cullenden was assigned to the case, and obtained a confession from Blanther to the effect that he had pawned the camera to a broker on Kearney Street, where it was subsequently recovered.

As Blanther claimed that he was actually starving and was forced to raise the money, Tebbs declined to prosecute him.

In 1896 an aged and decrepit old lady named Mrs. Philipini Langfeldt occupied a room at the residence of Dr. Kleineburg, at 1225 Geary Street. She loved to create the impression that she possessed much wealth, and almost constantly wore five very valuable rings set with diamonds and pearls.

Blanther remained at the Hogan home but a short time, and after a brief trip to Portland took up his residence at the home of the widow of Detective James Handley, at 828 Geary Street, four blocks from the Langfeldt home.

He learned of the "wealthy" old lady and obtained an introduction. Notwithstanding the great differences in their ages, he paid her marked attention and made a great display of his decorations, never missing an opportunity to tell of his hairbreadth escapes on the bloody battlefield, and incidentally to refer to the honors bestowed upon him by the Emperor.

On Friday, May 15, 1896, Mrs. Langfeldt told Mrs. Kleineburg that she expected Mr. Blanther to call that evening.

While no one saw Blanther enter the house, different members of the household heard some man laughing and talking with Mrs. Langfeldt in her apartments. This person arrived about 9 p. m., and Dr. Kleineburg heard him leave at ll:10 p. m.

At 9 a. m. on the following morning a domestic in the house named Susie Miller took a cup of coffee to Mrs. Langfeldt's room, but as she received no response to her knocks at the door she notified Dr. Kleineburg.

Officer Thomas Atchison was called, and he broke in the door. In the middle of the floor was the body of the old lady, her head almost severed from the body, evidently by a razor. As might be imagined, everything near the body was saturated with blood.

Captain of Detectives Lees was called and he found drops of blood in remote corners of the room, which convinced him that the assassin had probably cut one of his hands in cutting the old lady's throat. The five rings which she wore were stripped from her fingers, and the apartments were rifled. Suspicion at once fell on Blanther.

Mrs. Handley, his landlady, was visited, and she stated that Blanther arrived home on the preceding evening at 11:20, ten minutes after Dr. Kleineburg heard Mrs. Langfeldt's visitor leave. She stated that he went to the bathroom, and while she heard him leave the house on the following morning at 6 o'clock, an unusually early hour, he did not sleep in his bed during the night.

J. E. Lynch, a roomer in the same house, stated that he saw Blanther leave the bathroom about 11:30 on the preceding night, just as he entered it, and noticing crimsoned water in the bottom and on the sides of the basin he concluded that Blanther had a "nose bleed" or had cut his hand.

Architect George Dodge came forward and made a statement substantially as follows:

"I became acquainted with Blanther when he resided at Mr. Hogan's home on Haight Street. I saw him on Friday evening, the night of the murder, and he was despondent. He informed me that he had just pawned his overcoat, and if he did not get some money somewhere he would commit suicide.

"When he left me at 8:15 p. m. he told me that he was going to visit a friend on Geary Street.

"On the following morning he appeared at my office at 9 o'clock, an unusually early hour, and pretended to be in high spirits. He seldom wore gloves, but on this morning he wore a maroon colored glove on his left hand, even while rolling a cigarette.

"Many weeks ago Blanther told me that while at the racetrack one day he met a lady named Mrs. Genevieve Marks, who resided with a Mrs. King, at 427 O'Farrell Street. He said that this lady had valuable diamonds upon which she desired to borrow some money, and he asked me if I could procure a loan on them. I replied that I thought I could, but that I would require a written authorization from Mrs. Marks.

"On Saturday morning he delivered two unset diamonds to me with the following note:

"'Mr. J. Blanther: I hereby authorize you to borrow money on collateral security given to you by me, consisting of diamonds. GENEVIEVE MARKS.'

"After reading the letter of authorization I felt reassured and returned it to Blanther. I then went with Blanther to a money lender named Henry Lacey, who loaned me $100 on the stones.

"Blanther did not enter Lacey's office, but remained outside. As I had business in Alameda, and as Blanther told me that he was going to Oakland, thence to San Jose to meet Mrs. Marks, we rode across the bay together.

"As he pulled out several cigars during the morning I playfully opened his coat and looking at the pocket where the cigars were kept, I laughingly said: 'You must have beat the slot machines.' When I opened his coat I noticed a razor in the pocket with the cigars. I now recall that Blanther did not appreciate my little joke.

"He left the local train at Seventh and Broadway Streets, and said he would see me the next evening."

Mrs. Marks made a statement substantially as follows:

"It is true that I know Blanther, and he called at my home many times. I have several diamonds, and Blanther annoyed me with the interest he took in them and the questions he asked regarding their value.

"The man became obnoxious to me, so I suggested to him that it would be better if he ceased to call, and I notified Mrs. King, my landlady, that thereafter I was not at home if Mr. Blanther called.

"I have not seen him for weeks, and yesterday, the day I was alleged *to have made an appointment for a meeting at San Jose, I was sick in bed at home.*

"I never asked Blanther to hypothecate any diamonds for me nor did he ever have any of my jewelry in his possession."

Mrs. King, when questioned, corroborated Mrs. Marks' statement.

Henry Lacey, the money lender, was interrogated, and he produced the diamonds received by him from Mr. Dodge.

Mrs. Kleineburg identified them as being exactly the same as those in Mrs. Langfeldt's rings.

Francis Korbel, the Austrian Consul, was called in to examine Blanther's medals, decorations and papers, and he stated that they were undoubtedly genuine and added that Blanther was not only an officer in the Austrian army, but a Knight in several imperial orders.

Captain Lees had positive information that Blanther boarded train No. 19, bound for Los Angeles, which left Sixteenth Street, Oakland, at 5:30 p. m., on the day the body was found. Blanther purchased a ticket to Martinez on the train, but when he reached Port Costa he purchased a ticket to Los Angeles, and continued his journey on the same train. He attracted general attention because of the fact that he wore maroon colored gloves at all times, even when eating his meals.

Captain Lees telegraphed to the Los Angeles authorities to apprehend him at the train, but through some misunderstanding the officer arrived ten minutes too late.

It was subsequently learned that Blanther procured the ticket under the name of Forbes.

Captain Lees then decided to flood the country with circulars containing a picture of Blanther, but only two pictures of the fugitive could be found. One was taken in his military regalia when he was scarcely a man, and while the other picture, which was unmounted, had been a good likeness, it had faded so that it was useless for copying purposes. It was turned over to Theodore Kytka, the handwriting expert, who observed that it was printed on solio paper. As this kind of paper had only been in use for this purpose for two years, it was easy to conclude that the picture had been taken within that time. Because of the modeling of the shadows on the face, Kytka concluded that it was printed in some well-equipped gallery. He obtained Captain Lees' consent to communicate with the police departments and the Pinkerton agencies throughout America, who were requested to visit all photograph galleries and ascertain if Blanther or

"Forbes" had within the last two years sat for a picture, and if so to procure the negative.

The Pinkerton agency located the negative in Brand's gallery in Chicago, and it was forwarded to Kytka, who removed the retouching, to make the picture look as natural as possible.

A good picture and description of the fugitive was then sent to the Chicago Detective, a paper of wide circulation, with instructions to publish the same.

On March 2, 1898, the county assessor came into the sheriff's office in a little town in Texas and saw Blanther's picture, taken from the Chicago Detective, pasted on the wall.

He said: "Hello, who is this?" The sheriff gave him the desired information. The assessor then said: "Well, if that ain't the picture of Archibald Forbes our schoolmaster over at Koppearl, I am very much mistaken."

The more he studied the picture the more convinced he became. Finally he persuaded the sheriff to accompany him to the school.

After interrogating "Forbes" the sheriff decided to take him into custody. As he did so the schoolmaster attempted to draw a pistol, but he was overpowered and placed in the jail at Meridian, Texas, pending a further examination, which proved conclusively that he was Blanther.

Detective Ed. Gibson was sent after him, but Blanther had probably been prepared for nearly two years for such an occasion, as he had cyanide of potassium concealed under the band of his hat, and the jailers found him dead in his cell.

WILLIAM M. FREDERICKS, MURDERER, BANK AND STAGE ROBBER.

William M. Fredericks came to California in 1890. He worked for a short while as a barber in Shasta County. In the spring of 1890 he robbed a stage in Mariposa County and was sentenced to three years' imprisonment at Folsom. While incarcerated he became friendly with convicts Frank

Williams and Anthony Dalton, and shortly after being discharged, he furnished the weapons with which the jail break, headed by George Sontag, of the Sontag and Evans gang, was attempted on June 27, 1893, in which three prisoners were killed and several wounded. (See history of Sontag and Evans for particulars.) A few days after this he shot and seriously wounded J. T. Bruce, a brakeman at Gold Run, Placer County, and two days later he slew Sheriff Pasco of Nevada County, at Grass Valley, as he was under the false impression that the sheriff was about to arrest him,

A circular was issued giving a description of Fredericks, and offering a reward for his capture.

On March 14, 1894, Fredericks arrived in San Francisco, and on the same night went out to Golden Gate Park and there held up and robbed a young man from Truckee named Martin Smith. After procuring $150.00 and a gold watch and chain, he struck his victim over the head with his pistol. Smith uttered a cry of pain and started to run, when Fredericks fired at his head, but Smith had placed his hand to his wounded head and the bullet penetrated his wrist.

On March 23 Fredericks entered the San Francisco Savings Union Bank at Market and Fell Streets, about the noon hour, and drawing a revolver he commanded the cashier, William A. Herrick, to hand out the money. Instead of doing so, Herrick reached for a pistol, but as he did so Fredericks shot him dead. At this instant another clerk fired at Fredericks, and although the bullet missed him it shattered a pane of glass, a splinter of which flew into Fredericks' eye, permanently ruining it. The robber then fled up Market Street to Twelfth and crawled under a building.

Police Officer W. J. Shields gave chase, and as he started to crawl under the building Fredericks aimed his revolver at him and told him to stop or he would be killed. The brave officer did not hesitate, but continued and placed the desperado under arrest. When his picture appeared in the paper, Martin Smith at once recognized it as the likeness of the man who assaulted and robbed him in Golden Gate Park.

On March 24 he called at the jail and positively identified him. Fredericks then made a complete confession to Detective John Seymour of his whole criminal career.

He was convicted on the charge of murdering Cashier Herrick and was hanged in San Quentin on July 26, 1895.

THE CHINESE "HIGHBINDERS," OR "HATCHET MEN."

THE CELEBRATED LEE CHUCK AND "LITTLE PETE"

MURDER CASES AND THE RACE TRACK FRAUD.

The word "Highbinder" is a phrase once used by a New York policeman in referring to a certain Chinese hoodlum, and ever since that time it has been applied to that class of Chinese.

In recent years nearly all of the "bad men" among the Chinese have joined different "tongs," or societies, which are organized for the sole purpose of blackmail and extortion and to protect their own members.

The fact that they do protect their members has caused a great number of reputable merchants to join and submit to heavy assessments for the purpose of being protected from extortionate demands from opposing tongs, and some merchants belong to several tongs for this reason.

The fighting is always done by the "bad men" of the organization, who seldom follow any legitimate vocation. They were formerly called "hatchet men," because their favorite weapon was a lather's hatchet, with which they would split open their victim's skull. A hatchet has often been found partially buried in the head of the victim. In later years they have discarded the hatchet, as there were several instances where the prospective victim overpowered the would-be assassin before the fatal blow was struck. They now use large revolvers, and usually aim at the small of the back, with the expectation that if the wound does not prove fatal immediately, the bullet will cut the intestines and death will eventually follow from blood-poisoning.

The assassin is always accompanied by a confederate. They aim to commit the deed when no white witnesses are present, and as the Chinese witnesses are afraid to testify, it is difficult to obtain convictions.

Fong Ching, alias Little Pete, was born in Kow Gong, Canton, China, in 1864, and came to San Francisco ten years later. He attended the Sunday school of the Methodist Chinese mission and learned to speak the English language fluently.

Two of the largest associations in Chinatown are the Sam Yups and the See Yups, and a great deal of rivalry has existed between them in the past.

Pete joined the Sam Yups, and became the society's interpreter and conducted all of their business, so far as their dealings with Americans were concerned. He was really quite a handsome appearing fellow and was always immaculate in appearance. He took excellent care of his health, was bright eyed and clear skinned, and indulged in none of the vices common to his race. While he had the Oriental cunning to a rare degree and combined with it the ability to adapt it to Occidental conditions, still he had many redeeming qualities. He was extremely ambitious, and even when he was receiving but $10 per month, while employed in a shoe store, he contributed toward the support of his relatives.

When Pete had acquired a sufficient knowledge of the shoe business he borrowed a few hundred dollars and established himself in that business under the name of "F. C. Peters & Co." He rapidly built up a big wholesale business and paid his white drummers and other employees as high salaries as they could obtain anywhere in that line.

The object in using the American name was to prevent the patrons of the retailers, who might be prejudiced against Chinese, from knowing that their footwear was manufactured in the heart of Chinatown. The enterprise flourished up to the time of Pete's death, and he also conducted several gambling clubs.

Pete also found time to woo and win a Chinese maiden, and he had a happy little family, consisting of a wife and three bright little children.

Before he was of age he organized the "Gi Sin Seer" society or "tong," and a large proportion of its members were of the criminal class and principally highbinders. Pete was unscrupulous, audacious and resourceful, and backed up by this organization of hatchet men he levied tribute on all classes, and if the demand was not complied with the obstinate one's "head's assurance was but frail."

This "tong" was so successful that another faction of the same class of criminals organized, naming their "tong" the "Bo Sin Seer."

The bitterest enmity existed between these rival organizations, as Pete constantly outwitted the opposition.

It was decided that the only way to conquer him was to kill him, and Pete, learning of this, immediately employed a Chinaman named Lee Chuck to act as his bodyguard.

About July 23, 1886, Detective Glennon told Lee Chuck to be on his guard, as a conspiracy was afoot to kill him. Accordingly Lee procured a heavy coat of mail, which weighed thirty-five pounds. It was shaped like a vest and was a mass of small steel chains.

On October 28 he met Yen Yuen, a highbinder of the rival tong, at the corner of Spofford alley and Washington Street. After an exchange of words Lee Chuck pulled a pistol and shot his opponent five times, killing him instantly.

Officers J. B. Martin (afterward Chief of Police) and M. O. Sullivan rushed to the scene. Martin pursued Lee Chuck, and was rapidly overtaking him when the Chinaman turned and snapped his pistol twice as Martin came upon him. Fortunately the cartridges did not explode, and the officer had about overpowered him when the Chinaman drew another revolver; but Sullivan arrived at this moment, and between the two the murderous heathen was disarmed. When he was searched at the prison he was wearing the coat of mail above described.

Shortly after the arrest of Lee Chuck, Little Pete approached Officer Martin and offered him a bribe of $400 if he would perjure himself and give testimony favorable to the defendant. Martin took Little Pete into custody, and on August 5, 1886, he was indicted by the Grand Jury for attempting to bribe an officer.

On August 23 Lee Chuck was held to answer before the Superior Court by Judge Rix, and on January 26, 1887, the trial began before Superior Judge Toohy.

In the early part of the trial Pete, who was out on bail, was ordered from the courtroom for attempting to prompt witnesses. The next sensation was the arrest of one Dick Williams for attempting to bribe one of the jurymen, but he was acquitted.

On February 4, 1887, Lee Chuck was found guilty, and on March 29 he was sentenced to be hanged. The case was appealed to the Supreme Court, and a new trial was granted, but with the same result. The case was again appealed and again a new trial was granted, and on this occasion he was sentenced to fifty years imprisonment.

On February 10, 1892, he was adjudged insane and committed to the Agnews Asylum, where he remained until May 30, 1904, when Governor Pardee agreed to pardon him provided he was deported.

He was reported as having recovered, but the steamship companies refused to carry him, fearing that the Chinese Government would not permit him to land. He was taken back to San Quentin on June 17, 1904, but on April 13, 1905, he was again sent to Agnews.

We now return to the trials and tribulations of "Little Pete," who was held to answer for the attempted bribery, and on January 7, 1887, his trial began, which resulted in the jury disagreeing on January 18. On May 16 the second trial began, and on the 27th inst. the jury again disagreed.

On August 16 the third trial began, but was far more sensational than those preceding, as numerous efforts were made to bribe jurymen. A. Mayfield was the first juror to report that he had been approached by a mysterious white man, who offered him $250 "to look after Pete's interests." The next day a similar proposition was made to Juror Feder by a Chinaman. Then Juror Blanchard swore out a warrant of arrest for J. T. Emerson, charging him with offering a bribe. This was the same Emerson who testified in behalf of Williams, who was charged with a similar offense in the Lee Chuck case.

Assistant District Attorney Dunne afterward stated that but for the untimely publicity given to the attempts to corrupt this jury, he would have trapped the leaders, and when the facts were known it would have caused one of the greatest sensations in the criminal history of San Francisco.

On August 24, 1887, this jury returned a verdict of guilty, after thirty minutes' deliberation, and on September 7 Pete was sent to Folsom for five years.

At the expiration of Pete's term he was liberated, but the only effect that his imprisonment had was to make him more cautious.

In the early part of March, 1896, the bookmakers and the public who attended the races at the Bay District track realized that they were being systematically victimized, but the conspiracy was too deep for them to fathom, and their bankrolls were diminishing at an alarming rate. It was impossible to say what would have happened if a jockey named A. Hinricks, who was one of the conspirators, had not become disgruntled and confessed. It was then shown by his statement, which was substantiated by confessions subsequently obtained from others, that Little Pete had told Dow Williams, a colored trainer employed by Lucky Baldwin, Jockey Chevalier, Jockey Chorn of Barney Schreiber's stable, and Hinricks, that if they would follow his directions they would all become rich and no one would be the wiser.

He explained that as Chevalier, Chorn and Hinricks usually rode the fastest horses, it could be arranged in advance which one of the three should win the race, and then Pete would play heavily on that horse and share his winnings with the four.

Suspicion would be at once aroused if any of these jockeys were seen talking confidentially to such a notorious character as Pete, so the colored trainer, Williams, was to perform his little part by ascertaining the horse selected to win and whisper the word to Pete.

After a few weeks Hinricks began to suspect that he was not getting his share, so he confessed everything to Tom Williams, the President of the California Jockey Club.

Pete was known to have bet as much as $6,000 in one day, and it is estimated that the conspirators cleared up about $100,000 in a few weeks. Pete also gave tips to his close friends, many of whom profited by the fraud.

After hearing all the evidence the Board of Stewards made public the following findings:

"To the Board of Directors, California Jockey Club:

"Gentlemen: The Stewards having become cognizant that a conspiracy existed between certain jockeys riding at the Bay District track and a Chinaman known as 'Little Pete,' in the placing of horses in the races or the purpose of fraud, have instituted a most thorough investigation, and their findings warrant the expulsion of Jerry Chorn, Hippolyte Chevalier, and 'Little Pete' for conspiracy and fraud, and the ordering off of Dow Williams and his horses, and the refusal of permission to ride to A. Hinricks.

"(Signed) THOS. WILLIAMS, JR.

"J. J. BURKE. "J. W. BROOKS. "EDWIN T. SMITH."

After his return from State prison, Pete employed a white man named Ed. Murray to act as his bodyguard, and on the evening of January 24, 1897, Pete left his home, located at 821 Washington Street, and went downstairs to the barber shop to get shaved.

Believing that he would not be attacked in that place he sent his bodyguard down to the New Western Hotel, two blocks distant, to learn the result of the horse races.

This was the first time that Pete had been unguarded for months. The assassins had probably trailed him all of that time, and like a flash they took advantage of this opportunity. Two Chinese rushed into the shop and began firing at Pete as he sat in the barber chair. He was virtually shot to pieces, two bullets passing through his head.

The two highbinders then fled around the corner into Waverley Place, threw their guns in the Street, so as to be rid of all incriminating evidence, entered a building, passed out the back way and were never seen again.

Two Chinese named Wing Sing and Chin Poy were arrested as suspects, but were released because of insufficient evidence.

The news of the murder spread like wildfire through the Chinese quarter, and Pete's adherents flocked to the scene of the crime. They saw the brains of their organization oozing out on the barber-shop floor, and the sight transformed them into wild-eyed fiends.

A Chinaman known as "Big Jim," because of his gigantic proportions, was the leader of the See Yup Society, and as this organization was said to be antagonistic to Pete's society, the Sam Yups, it was suspected that he was the chief conspirator, especially as he was near the scene of the killing when it occurred.

Jim was a millionaire and undoubtedly the richest Chinaman in America, with the possible exception of some of the officials at Washington.

Pete, because of his resourcefulness, was a constant thorn in the side of Jim, as he was continually upsetting his best laid plans, and it was in view of these facts that Jim was suspected and a price put upon his head.

Jim then demonstrated that he had none of Pete's fighting qualities in his composition, for he immediately went into seclusion, and after hurriedly arranging his business affairs, he fled to China with his white wife and family. Pete's loyalty to Lee Chuck even commanded the respect of his adversaries and caused him to be worshiped by his adherents, many of whom would have gladly fought and died for him.

On the day of the funeral they came by the thousands from adjoining towns to pay their last respects, and it was estimated that there were at least 30,000 Mongolians in the Chinese quarters while the services were being conducted.

All factions suspended business, and the feeling between the See Yups and Sam Yups was so intense that one overt act would have instantly started a battle whereby hundreds of lives might have been lost.

Although Pete received his religious training in the Methodist Chinese Mission, the moment he died his relatives took all the precautions in vogue among the heathen Chinese to bribe any evil spirits which might be hovering near.

Little slips of paper, supposed to have intrinsic value because they were "blessed" by the priest, were burned in front of the door to appease the wrath of the evil spirits, and while en route to the graveyard a Chinaman sat on the hearse, which was drawn by six magnificent black horses, and scattered similar slips to the four winds of heaven.

A roasted pig, surrounded by Chinese delicacies and burning punks, was placed at the head of the casket for the purpose of preventing Pete's spirit from suffering from hunger. By placing small cups of tea near the other delicacies, the spirit's thirst was also provided for.

The funeral was conducted with all the barbaric splendor known to the Chinese race, with a mixture of Occidental customs. The services at the home were conducted by a long, lean and hungry-looking priest, who was attired in his gaudiest array. The widow and children were seated on the floor, and whenever the paid mourners, who were on their hands and knees, with their heads down to the floor, ceased their "weeping and wailing and gnashing of teeth," the priest would ring a little bell and begin "chanting" a prayer until again interrupted by the wail from his leather-lunged brethren on the floor. He would then salaam and patiently await another opportunity.

In strange contrast with the general surroundings were the magnificent floral pieces sent by American friends. The funeral procession was headed by an American military band, followed by the Chinese band.

After the American band finished playing a dirge, the Chinese would make an attack with their tom-toms, cymbals and screeching flutes, which certainly must have created a panic among the evil spirits thereabout.

The immense tinsel-covered image of a dragon, the head of which was at least eight feet across and the body at least seventy feet long, was carried by about two dozen Chinese, who had it propped up in the air by means of sticks. About one hundred carriages escorted the remains to the receiving vault, where they reposed until his widow had them shipped to China.

HISTORY OF WM. HENRY THEODORE DURRANT, MURDERER OF BLANCHE LAMONT AND MINNIE WILLIAMS.

Theodore Durrant was born in Toronto, Canada, in 1871, and while a child came to San Francisco with his parents, who gave him a good education. In 1895 he was a medical student at Cooper Medical College. He pretended to be a devout Christian and was one of the most active members of Emanuel Baptist Church, which is located on Bartlett, near Twenty-third Street. The younger members of this church organized a society for social purposes, and Durrant was elected Secretary, and was also a Superintendent in the Sunday-school. In 1894 a most estimable young lady, named Blanche Lamont, left her home in Dillon, Mont., because of poor health and came to San Francisco to continue her studies for the purpose of eventually following the vocation of a school-teacher.

She made her home with her uncle and aunt, Mr. and Mrs. C. G. Noble, at 209 Twenty-first Street, where her sister, Maud, also resided. Blanche was a very religious girl and seldom went to places of amusement, but when she did she was usually accompanied by her relatives. She always attended the Emanuel Baptist Church and was a member of the Christian

Endeavor, where she was a great favorite, because of her lovable disposition and good qualities.

On the morning of April 3, 1895, Miss Lamont left home as usual to attend the Boys' High School, in which building she was taking a course at that time. While en route to this school she was accompanied by Durrant, who, after leaving her, went to the Cooper Medical College. After Miss Lamont finished her studies at this school she repaired to the Normal School on Powell Street, between Clay and Sacramento, where she was to take instructions in cooking, between 2 and 3 p. m. Shortly after 2 o'clock Durrant appeared in front of this school and waited impatiently until nearly 3 p. m., when Miss Lament came out of the building accompanied by a classmate named Minnie Edwards. Durrant approached and engaged Miss Lamont in conversation. Miss Edwards continued to the corner and got inside of the next southbound Powell Street car and saw Durrant and Miss Lamont take seats on the dummy, Miss Lamont having her school books with her.

Two other classmates of Miss Lamont, Miss Lanagan and Miss Pleasant, who were walking home, also saw her sitting on the dummy with Durrant.

On this day some Street-pavers were re-laying some old-fashioned paving at Twenty-second and Bartlett Streets, and as Attorney Martin Quinlan was passing this place curiosity prompted him to stop and watch the re-laying of this almost obsolete style of paving. While so doing, Theodore Durrant, whom he knew well, passed with a young lady of the same general appearance of Miss Lamont.

They were then walking in the direction of the Emanuel Baptist Church, a few hundred feet distant. Quinlan fixed the time as about 4:15 p. m., because of an appointment he was about to keep with a Mr. Clark on Mission Street.

Diagonally across the Street from this church, at 124 Bartlett Street, lived a Mrs. Leake, who had a married daughter named Mrs. Maguire, whose home was in San Mateo. On this date the daughter came to San Francisco, called on her mother and then went downtown to do some shopping, informing her mother that she would be back in the early afternoon.

As it was growing late the mother became uneasy about her daughter and sat in the window eagerly awaiting her return. At seventeen minutes past four she looked at the clock and then returned to the window, but instead of seeing her daughter approach she saw Durrant, whom she knew well as a member of her church, and a young lady of Miss Lamont's general appearance walk up to the church, where Durrant opened the side gate and followed the young lady inside. This was the last seen of Blanche Lamont.

About 5 p. m. George King, the church organist, came to the church for the purpose of practicing for the next service. He had hardly begun his practice when Durrant opened the door leading down from the belfry. Durrant and King had been close friends, and King stated that when Durrant opened this door he was very pale, nervous and weak and was without a coat and hat. He stated that Durrant explained his weakened condition by saying that he had been up near the roof, trying to locate a leak in the gas pipe and had been overcome by gas. King ran to a drug store near Valencia and Twenty-second Streets and returned with a bottle of bromo-seltzer, which Durrant drank.

When he claimed that he had recovered, King asked him to assist in carrying a small organ from the auditorium upstairs down to the main floor. Durrant consented, but King stated that he detected no odor of gas whatever while upstairs, and furthermore that all the gas fixtures had been inspected by plumbers just previous to this time and were in good condition. Shortly after removing the organ the two men left the church, Durrant walking to King's home with him, although Durrant's home was in an opposite direction and he claimed to be feeling weak because of his alleged narrow escape from gas asphyxiation.

That night a prayer meeting was held at the church. Blanche Lamont, not having returned home, caused her aunt, Mrs. Noble, to worry greatly. Thinking Blanche might possibly have gone to the home of some friend, and would, as usual, attend the prayer meeting, Mrs. Noble also attended the meeting in hopes of seeing her niece. The lady was almost distracted, but refrained from telling of Blanche's disappearance, believing that the girl would return. Durrant had a seat just in the rear of Mrs. Noble, and during the services said to her: "Is Blanche here tonight?" Mrs. Noble replied: "No, she did not come."

Durrant then said: "Well, I regret that she is not with us to-night, as I have a book called The Newcombs,' for her, but I will send it to the house."

After a few days of suspense Mrs. Noble could stand the strain no longer and she communicated the mysterious disappearance of her niece to the police and the press. As Durrant was "above suspicion," no one considered it worthwhile to mention the fact that they had seen her in his company on the day of her disappearance. Durrant called on Mrs. Noble and offered his services in the search for the lost girl, and subsequently intimated to Mrs. Noble and a fellow student named Herman Slagater that he had received information which caused him to arrive at the conclusion that Blanche Lamont had not departed from this life, but worse: she had departed from the life of morality, and was even then in a house of ill repute from which he would endeavor to persuade her to return to the path of righteousness. A few days after making this statement, the church janitor saw Durrant at the Oakland Ferry landing and asked him what he was doing there. Durrant replied that he was working on a clew he had obtained as to

Blanche Lamont's whereabouts.

At the time of Miss Lamont's disappearance she had three rings in her possession, and on April 13 the postman delivered to Mrs. Noble an Examiner, wrapped in the usual fashion for the mail, and upon opening it, the three rings which Blanche Lamont wore fell out.

Subsequently, Adolph Oppenheimer, who conducted a pawn shop at 405 DuPont Street, identified Durrant as the man who attempted to sell one of these rings to him, between the 4th and 10th of April.

On April 12, an estimable young lady named Minnie Williams, left the home of C. H. Morgan in Alameda, and as she was about to leave his employ she had her trunk sent to the residence of Mrs. Amelia Voy at 1707 Howard Street, in this city. Miss Williams was also a member of the Emanuel Baptist Church, and on this very day she announced to the Morgan's that she contemplated attending a meeting of young church members to be held at the home of a dentist named Dr. T. A. Vogel, at 7:30 that evening.

The girl never appeared there, and Durrant, who was secretary of the society and should have been prompt in attendance, did not arrive until 9:30 p. m., and his excited and overheated appearance was a matter of general comment among those present. The meeting adjourned at 11:25 p. m. and the young folks repaired to their homes with the exception of Durrant, who, for reasons best known to himself, went to Emanuel Baptist Church at this midnight hour.

April 13, the day Mrs. Noble received her niece's rings, was the Saturday preceding Easter Sunday, and the Christian ladies proceeded to this church laden with flowers to suitably decorate in honor of the greatest anniversary of the Christian year.

Mrs. Nolt, of 910 Twenty-first Street, accompanied by Misses Minnie Lord and Katie Stevens, were among the first to arrive, and in the library they found the horribly mutilated remains of Minnie Williams. Her clothing was partially torn from her body and she had been repeatedly stabbed, then gagged and outraged. Some of her torn clothing had been stuffed down her throat so tightly that it required considerable effort to remove it. A broken knife blade was still in her breast.

The police immediately instituted an investigation and Captain Lees, who was at the time in Los Angeles, proceeded to San Francisco to take charge of the case, assisted by Detectives John Seymour, Ed. Gibson and others.

Charles Hill, of 203 1/2 Bartlett Street, stated that about 8 o'clock on the preceding night he had observed a young lady of Miss Williams' appearance enter the church in company with a young man whom he thought was Theodore Durrant. This caused a search to be made for Durrant at his home, but it was learned that early on the morning of the discovery of Minnie Williams' body, he had left the city with the Signal Corps of the State Militia. A search was made of his clothing in his room, and Minnie Williams' purse was found in his overcoat. Detective A. Anthony was detailed to trail Durrant and arrest him, and on Sunday, April 14, Anthony and Constable Palmer arrested him near Walnut Creek, notwithstanding the indignant protest made by Lieutenant Perkins against this "outrageous accusation."

While Anthony was engaged in apprehending Durrant, the remainder of the detective force began a systematic search of the church, with the result that they found even a more blood-curdling sight in the belfry than that beheld by the ladies in the library.

This belfry was in semi-darkness, but enough light entered for the detectives to behold what appeared like a marble carving of an absolutely nude girl lying on the floor, with a block of wood under her head. She was laid out on her back after death with her hands carefully crossed over her breast, in a position similar to that of bodies used by medical students in the dissecting room. A far more thorough search was necessary to locate her clothes and school-books, but they were eventually found poked in between the studdings and the lath and plaster of the building. Blanche Lamont's name appeared in the books.

An autopsy disclosed the fact that she died from strangulation but decomposition had reached such a state that it was impossible to determine if an outrage had been committed. While the body was as white as marble as it lay in the cool belfry, when it was removed to the body of the church, where the air was much warmer, it turned almost jet black.

Notwithstanding the overwhelming amount of evidence, which proved conclusively that Durrant accompanied Miss Lamont from the school to Emanuel Baptist Church, he denied having seen her that day and attempted to prove an alibi by swearing that he was at Cooper Medical College at the time it was alleged he was in the very act of murdering this girl. While it is true that the records showed that some one answered his name at roll call at the conclusion of Dr. Cheney's lecture, it was shown that it was customary for the students to answer for each other in case of absence, and no one would swear that Durrant was present at this lecture. As proof that he was not present, it was shown that several days afterward he persuaded a fellow student, Mr. Glaser, to give him the notes that he, Glaser, had taken at the lecture. As soon as the finger of suspicion was pointed toward Durrant, information poured in to Captain Lees, proving that the prisoner was a degenerate of the most depraved class. For obvious reasons, names cannot be given of young ladies to whom he made the most disgusting propositions, and the wonder of it is that he was not killed, or at least exposed before. But in most instances the nature of his insults were such that the young ladies offended feared to inform their relatives, lest they would take the law in their own hands. One young lady told her mother that some time previous to these murders, Durrant had inveigled her into this same library and excusing himself for a moment, returned stark naked and she ran screaming from the church.

Although Minnie Williams was frightfully butchered and the room resembled a slaughter-house, not one drop of blood could be found on Durrant's clothes, and there is no doubt but that he was naked when he committed this crime. He probably strangled Blanche Lamont in the library and then dragged her body up to the belfry, head first. That this was the manner in which he got her body to the place where it was found was proven by the finding of hairs from her head which caught in splinters on the steps.

Durrant also attempted to inveigle Miss Lucille Turner into this library for the purpose of making a "physical examination."

The preliminary examination of Durrant began before Police Judge Charles Conlon on April 22, 1895. He was defended by General John Dickenson, and later by Eugene Duprey. On May 22 he was held to answer before the Superior Court for both murders. Captain Lees and District Attorney William Barnes decided to try him for the murder of Blanche Lamont, as that appeared at the time to be the strongest case, but subsequently additional evidence was gathered which made the Minnie Williams case even stronger than the one on which he was tried.

His trial began before Judge Murphy on July 22, 1895, and over one month was occupied in selecting a jury, during which time over one thousand prospective jurors appeared in court.

During the trial the Alcazar Theater Company produced a play called the "Criminal of the Century," which was a dramatization of the Durrant murders. This was produced in defiance of an order of court prohibiting its production, and as a result W. R. Daily, the manager, was sent to jail for three days for contempt of court.

During Durrant's trial fifty witnesses testified for the prosecution alone. On September 24 the case was finally submitted to the jury, and after deliberating five minutes, brought in a verdict of guilty with the death penalty attached.

The case was appealed to the Supreme Court, which affirmed the decision of the lower court on April 3, 1897. The day of execution was then set for June 11, 1897.

At this stage of the proceedings, Governor James Budd was appealed to, and after making an extensive personal investigation, he concluded that Durrant was guilty and refused to interfere.

On April 10, 1897, he was taken to San Quentin, and another appeal taken which was denied.

On January 7, 1898, he was hanged.

He protested his innocence to the last and was one of the coolest murderers who ever mounted the scaffold. When Warden Hale started to read the death warrant to him he said: "I will waive that right and spare you an unpleasant duty."

The parents took charge of the body immediately after the execution, and as they feared grave-robbers, they attempted to have the body cremated, but no crematory in San Francisco would accept the corpse, so strong was the public sentiment. A Los Angeles firm accepted it, however, and it was cremated in that city on January 13, 1898.

In nearly all cases when a celebrated criminal is captured, certain classes of women take advantage of the opportunity to leap into the lime-light by showering him with attentions, and the more atrocious and depraved the criminal, the more these women appear in evidence. This case was no exception to the rule, and as soon as the trial began a young woman of prepossessing appearance became a constant attendant and almost daily presented Durrant with testimonials of her sympathy in the shape of small bunches of sweet peas, which accounted for her being known as the "Sweet Pea Girl." Durrant did not know the girl, but with characteristic mendacity, he claimed that she was a friend who had positive knowledge of his innocence, but he was too "chivalrous" to divulge her identity. It subsequently transpired that she was Mrs. Rosalind Bowers, and was even then neglecting her young husband to worship at the shrine of this degenerate. She afterwards lived in a Sutter-Street house under the name of "Grace King," and was accused of inveigling a wealthy clubman named Edward Clarke into a marriage while he was under the influence of liquor.

The author has a photograph taken of Durrant at a picnic when he was only sixteen years of age, and the position in which he posed proves conclusively that he was a degenerate even as a child.

Shortly before these crimes were committed, Durrant's sister Maude went to Europe to study music. Fourteen years later it was learned that "Maude Allen," who was creating a sensation in Europe with the "Vision of Salome" dance, was in reality Maude Durrant.

HISTORY OF CHARLES BECKER, PRINCE OF FORGERS.

Charles Becker was admitted to be the cleverest forger of modern times, and the work of Chief Lees and the Pinkertons Agency in capturing and convicting him attracted world-wide attention, as will be seen by the following clipping from the Chicago Detective, one of the leading police journals in the United States:

> "The recent conviction in San Francisco of Charles Becker, alias 'The Prince of Forgers,' and James Creegan, charged with raising a check on the Crocker-Woolworth Bank from $12.00 to . $22,000.00 and obtaining the money from the Nevada Bank of the same city, has brought a sigh of relief to the thousands of bankers of the United States and Europe.

> "The imprisonment of Becker disposes effectually of the cleverest bank swindler of modern times, as he is undoubtedly the ablest man intellectually who ever adopted forgery as a profession.

> "The Pinkerton agency were employed by the bankers, but they were ably assisted by I. W. Lees, the veteran Chief of Police of San Francisco, who had entire charge of the San Francisco end of the case and whose knowledge of criminals and crime is second to none in the United States."

The first record we have of Becker is when Joseph Chapman, "Little Joe" Elliott and he burglarized the Third National Bank in Baltimore in 1872. The "Chapman & Elliott Brokerage Office" was opened on the floor over the bank and they tunneled through the floor and drilled the vault. They then fled to Europe and committed forgeries throughout that country, obtaining about $50,000.00. They were captured in Smyrna, Turkey, tried before the English Consular Court and sentenced to three years. They escaped, Elliott and Becker fleeing to London and deserting Chapman.

Chapman's wife was the custodian of the savings of the trio, and suspecting that his companions would endeavor to obtain money from her, he telegraphed, instructing her to give them nothing. It then became necessary to procure the money by strategy, so on April 13, 1873, they drugged her, but she, having heart disease, died, and they fled to New York, where Becker and Joe Riley passed a counterfeit check on the Union Trust Company for $64,000.00. They were arrested, but Becker was granted immunity for turning State's evidence, and Riley served a term in prison.

Becker and his father-in-law, Clement Hearing, then forged an enormous amount of scrip of the Philadelphia and Reading Railroad.

At this time they were conducting a lithograph business in New York. Becker was convicted and served a term for this crime. In 1881 Becker was again arrested with his father-in-law for counterfeiting 1,000 franc notes on the Bank of France and served ten years at Kings County Prison.

When released he took James Creegan as a middle man. They invaded every city in the country and left a long list of victims behind them.

In Omaha they defrauded five banks in one day.

In 1894 Becker, Creegan and Frank Seaver, alias Dean, made a trip to the Pacific Coast, and it is estimated that they cleared $100,000.00.

They returned East and in 1895, Becker, Ed Mullady, the financial backer; Creegan, the middleman, and Frank Seaver and Joe McCluskey came to San Francisco, taking different routes.

Becker confided in none but Creegan, and the others did not even see him. They lodged in different parts of the city. Seaver rented an office in the Chronicle Building under the name of A. H. Dean, commission merchant, and deposited $2,500.00 in the Nevada Bank, and either drew or deposited almost daily to make it appear that he was a business man. At the Bank of Woodland, Cal., he obtained a draft for $12.00 on the Crocker-Woolworth Bank and gave it to Creegan, who delivered it to Becker. The figure $ "12" $ being perforated on the draft he filled the holes with paper pulp and punched $22,000.00$ instead. He erased and altered the draft to correspond. It was then returned to Seaver, who deposited it to his own credit at the Nevada Bank on December 18, 1895. It passed this bank and also the Clearing House.

The next day Seaver procured a horse and buggy and a messenger boy and went to the bank and drew the $22,000.00 in gold and drove out Mission Street. He stopped in front of a house where he said he lived and bade the boy take the buggy to the stable. After the boy got out of sight, Seaver went several blocks to his room, where McCluskey and Creegan awaited him. They divided the spoils, Creegan taking his own share, also Becker's.

Becker and Creegan left that night for New York, Seaver and McCluskey following a few days later. The fraud was discovered on January 4, 1896, when the accounts of the Crocker-Woolworth and Woodland Banks were balanced. All bankers throughout the country were at once notified of the methods employed by the forgers and a description of Seaver furnished.

Chief Lees handled the San Francisco end of the case and Pinkertons attended to the East. Shortly afterward A. A. Anderson of the St. Paul National Bank stated that a man of the appearance of Seaver, alias Dean, had opened an account, and about the same time a man of McCluskey's appearance did the same thing in Minneapolis. Both men were arrested and brought to San Francisco in March, 1896.

In the meantime Becker and Creegan were under constant police surveillance in the East. McCluskey was released because of insufficiency of evidence and went East to Becker and Creegan and demanded that they render financial assistance to Seaver, which they refused to do.

Seaver then confessed and on his testimony, with other evidence already gathered, indictments were found against the other three, and they were returned to San Francisco. Then McCluskey confessed.

Creegan and Becker not only protested their innocence, but claimed that they were not in California at the time the crime was committed.

By the testimony of porters, conductors, hotel men and others Chief Lees and Pinkerton showed the jury the movements of these men from the time they left New York until they returned.

They were found guilty on August 28, 1896, and sentenced to life imprisonment, but the Supreme Court granted a new trial because of an alleged error in the instructions to the jury. The new trial was set for December 3, 1896, but in the meantime Creegan broke down and confessed, and then Becker did likewise and was sentenced to seven years' imprisonment.

Creegan was sentenced to serve two years at Folsom, and McCluskey died shortly afterward.

———————

ALBERT FREDERICK GEORGE

VERENESENECKOCKOCKHOFF (ALIAS HOFF),

MURDERER OF MRS. MARY CLUTE.

In the latter part of 1897, Mrs. Mary Clute, wife of a prominent commercial traveler, resided at 230 Page Street, San Francisco.

She was a lady of attractive appearance and had a host of friends because of her kindly disposition.

Albert F. G. Vereneseneckockockhoff, commonly known as "Hoff," was a short, chunky, middle-aged German, with a heavy, ill-kept beard and a coarse, brutal face, which took on a fiendish expression when he was angered. He resided at the Lindell House, No. 262 Sixth Street, and made a living by working as a handy man about different homes.

On December 12, 1897, Mrs. Clute decided to move from 230 Page Street to 803 Guerrero Street. Having previously employed Hoff to do some upholstering, she sent a note to the Lindell House, requesting him to call the next day. She then went to a store to purchase some carpet lining, but the upholsterer informed her that he would not sell her the lining unless he was given the work of laying the carpet. This was the work she intended to give to Hoff, but having no assurance that he would respond promptly, she accepted the upholsterer's terms.

Hoff called on her the next morning, and she explained her predicament and expressed regret that she had inconvenienced him. Hoff's manner plainly indicated his displeasure, but to compensate him for his loss of time, Mrs. Clute told him to come the next afternoon and she would give him a job hanging her pictures. The next day, December 15, Hoff called at 803 Guerrero Street shortly after noon, but as Mrs. Clute was not at the house, he rang the doorbell of the lower flat and one of the occupants, Mrs. L. A. Legg, came to the door. Hoff announced his business and made inquiry as to the whereabouts of Mrs. Clute. Upon learning that she was not in, he proceeded to 230 Page Street, arriving about 4 p. m. There he met Mrs. Clute who informed him that she was exceedingly sorry, but her express man had disappointed her, and that she would surely be moved the next day, and requested Hoff to call at 803 Guerrero Street at 1 p. m. December 16.

At this time Hoff was slightly intoxicated; his breath was foul; his whiskers were besmeared with liquor, and he was in an ugly mood because of his loss of time. Mrs. Clute then announced to Mrs. Uchold, a neighbor, in the presence of Hoff, that she was going over to her new home, and left Hoff talking with Mrs. Uchold regarding some work the latter contemplated giving him. When they had finished their conversation, Hoff announced that he was going to see Mrs. Clute, to which Mrs. Uchold replied: "Why are you going there, she does not want you until to-morrow?"

Hoff apparently disregarded this remark, and proceeded to 803 Guerrero Street.

A few moments after 4 p. m., Mrs. Legg, who lived in the flat below Mrs. Clute's new home, saw this man return, ring Mrs. Clute's bell and go upstairs. At this time Mrs. Clute was in her new flat with Jos. Foley, who was laying the carpets. At 4:45 p. m. Foley left and at that time Hoff was walking aimlessly about the flat while Mrs. Clute was engaged with some housework.

Mrs. Legg's aged father-in-law resided with her and her husband in the lower flat, and about 5 p. m. he rushed into the kitchen and exclaimed excitedly to his daughter-in-law, who was preparing dinner: "I thought I heard you scream." They listened a second and then they heard something heavy fall in the upper flat. Mrs. Legg started upstairs and seeing Hoff passing from one room to another called out: "What is the matter up there?" Hoff made no reply and the lady, becoming alarmed, returned to her father-in-law. Presently they saw Hoff sneak away from the house with a small bag on his shoulder, in which he carried his tools. They called out to him to learn the cause of the disturbance upstairs, but he pretended not to hear them and hurried away. An investigation was then instituted and Mrs. Clute's horribly mutilated body was found in a back room. Her head was lying in a pool of blood; her face was beaten beyond recognition; there were eight different fractures of the skull, and near the body was found a railroad coupling pin covered with blood.

Mrs. Clute wore valuable jewelry and also had a well-filled purse with her at the time she was killed. As none of these valuables were taken the motive for the crime has never been proven, although it is probable that Mrs. Legg's unexpected appearance on the scene caused the murderer to abandon his original plans and consider nothing but the possibility of being discovered.

The next day the papers devoted considerable space to this crime and dwelt at length on Mrs. Legg's observations. Hoff read this, and realizing that there would be no difficulty in locating him, he called on Chief Lees and trembling with suppressed excitement, announced that he was the man Mrs. Legg probably referred to, but denied all knowledge of the crime. He stated that Mrs. Clute was alive and well when he left the house and that Mrs. Legg did not come upon the stairs and inquire as to the cause of any noise, nor did any one call to him regarding anything of the kind when he left the house. He disclaimed all knowledge of any coupling pin and laughingly inquired as to what use a carpet-layer would have for such a cumbersome thing.

The laugh ceased however when J. G. Zimbleman and Mayer May stated positively that they had seen the same pin with Hoff's tools on previous occasions.

While being interrogated by Chief Lees and Detective John Seymour, Hoff studiously held his hat in one position in his left hand and it attracted the attention of Detective Seymour, who asked: "What is the matter with your left hand?" "Nothing," replied Hoff. But upon being examined, a deep cut was found in the palm. He told two different stories as to how this happened. On one occasion he stated that it was caused by handling a board with a nail in it and on another occasion he said it was caused by coming in contact with a tack which was in some carpet he handled at Mrs. Clute's house.

The theory was advanced that Mrs. Clute inflicted this wound with a dust pan while trying to defend herself.

Hoff was charged with the murder. On March 15, 1898, his trial began, and on April 2 he was found guilty and was subsequently sentenced to be hanged.

His attorney, Wm. Schooler, appealed to the Supreme Court on the grounds that the trial judge had erred in the instructions given to the jury. The prosecution in this case depended entirely on circumstantial evidence and in delivering his instructions to the jury the trial judge said:

> *"Circumstantial evidence has this great advantage, that various circumstances from various sources are not likely to be fabricated."*

It was held that whether it is entitled to such credit or not, is a question to be determined by the jury from the evidence, and that therefore the charge was plainly an argument for the prosecution, and in violation of Section 19, Article VI, of the Constitution, which provides that: "Judges shall not charge juries with respect to matters of fact, but may state the testimony and declare the law."

Hoff was granted a new trial, which began on December 3, 1900, before Judge Carroll Cook, and on December 15, exactly three years after the commission of the crime, he was again found guilty of murder with the penalty fixed at life imprisonment.

(The decision of the Supreme Court in this case also resulted in Mrs. Botkin being granted a new trial. See history of Mrs. Botkin.)

On the night after Hoff committed this murder he slept with a shoemaker named Robert Goepel, at 524 Post Street, and he attempted to prove an alibi by this man, who on September 16, 1898, committed suicide by shooting himself in the head.

JOHN BUTLER, AUSTRALIAN MURDERER.

In the early part of 1897, a man named John Butler advertised in the Sydney, Australia, papers for partners to accompany him on prospecting trips in the Blue Mountain district, adjacent to Sydney.

A man named Conroy answered the advertisement and made preliminary arrangements to accompany Butler, but before his plans were completed, he was appointed a Constable in Sydney and abandoned the trip.

A man named Captain Lee Weller took his place and the journey began.

When walking, several miles out of the city, Butler shot Weller in the back of the head, killing him instantly.

Shortly after the shot was fired a boy met Butler in the road and asked him who fired the shot. Butler replied: "It was me shooting at some game." The boy remarked that he had never seen any game in that neighborhood.

When the body of Weller was discovered the boy related his experience to the Sydney police.

Conroy, the newly appointed Constable, who contemplated accompanying Butler, recognized the description of the "hunter" as that of Butler. A search was instituted and he was traced to the British ship "Swanhilde," bound for San Francisco. In the meantime the bodies of three other men were found in the Blue Mountains and all of the circumstances indicated that they had met death in the same manner.

Constable Conroy was sent to San Francisco on the first steamer. He arrived some days in advance of the "Swanhilde," and was in the party headed by Captain of Detectives Lees, which went outside the heads, intercepted the ship and located and arrested Butler.

He was returned to Australia. It was proven that he killed all four of the persons whose bodies were found in the mountains, and that his motive was to rob them of all money in their possession. As he would not accept a partner who would not take along a stipulated sum of money, it is estimated that he secured considerable money before being discovered. He was hanged for his crimes six weeks after his return to Australia.

FRANK MILLER, ALIAS HEIFLER, WHO INVEIGLED A

TRAMP INTO THE HOUSE WHERE HE WAS EMPLOYED AND, CLAIMING HE WAS A BURGLAR, KILLED HIM TO GAIN A REWARD FROM HIS EMPLOYER.

About 3 a. m., February 14, 1895, Mr. Samuel Salomon, who was residing in the residence of Julius L. Franklin at 2930 California Street, San Francisco, heard pistol shots in the basement. He ran down stairs and found the side door open and the butler, Frank Miller, lying on the floor.

Miller was apparently suffering great pain in the region of the abdomen. He stated, between gasps, that he had heard someone at the side door, and upon opening it was struck on the head with some blunt instrument and kicked in the stomach.

He claimed that he then fired his pistol in self-protection and his assailant fled.

Mr. Franklin, his employer, had full confidence in Miller's honesty, and to show his appreciation of his butler's "bravery," presented him with a watch valued at $75.00 and $200.00 cash.

Miller then pretended to have a desire to leave Mr. Franklin's employ, as he expressed a fear that the "robbers" would return, but the family was exceedingly kind to him and finally persuaded him to remain.

Exactly one year afterward, about 5 a. m., shots were again heard in the basement, and upon making an investigation, a man who was afterward identified as Billy Murray, of Butte City, Mont., was found dying in the back part of the basement with a bullet hole in his head. Miller was lying on the floor, apparently unconscious, with a bullet wound in his neck.

When he was "sufficiently revived" he told a weird tale in regard to hearing Murray enter the house, after breaking a small piece of glass out of the back door, and that he shot in self-defense, killing the alleged burglar.

Captain Lees investigated the case, and in addition to proving the impossibility of Miller's story, it was shown that he met Murray near Portsmouth square and inveigled him out to Franklin's house, evidently claiming that he was lonesome, and Murray, being out of work and penniless, was glad to partake of his "hospitality."

Miller no doubt had in mind the generous manner in which Mr. Franklin had rewarded his "bravery" on a previous occasion, and undoubtedly thought the time was ripe to reap further golden rewards.

The wound in Miller's neck was probably made by grasping the loose skin under the jaw and pulling it away from the neck as far as possible, at the same time raising the pistol with the other hand and shooting through the skin. Powder marks on the left hand also tended to bear out this theory.

Mr. Franklin at first declined to believe the police theory and refused to assist in a prosecution, but he subsequently changed his mind regarding Miller's innocence.

Miller, who was never prosecuted, left San Francisco, and went to Santa Barbara, where he committed a fiendish assault on a young girl, for which he was sent to State Prison on December 9, 1896, for five years.

MRS. CORDELIA BOTKIN, MURDERESS.

On February 12, 1891, John P. Dunning, who became famous as a war correspondent, married Miss Mary Pennington, daughter of ex-Congressman John Pennington, in Dover, Delaware, and the couple came to San Francisco to reside.

The next year a little daughter was born. The family then moved to 2529 California Street, and while living at this address. Dunning took a stroll in Golden Gate Park one afternoon and flirted with a woman sitting on a bench. They entered into a conversation, during which the woman said her name was "Curtis," and that her husband was in England. After they became more familiar the woman admitted that she was the wife of Welcome A. Botkin, whom she married in Kansas City on September 26, 1872, and that she had a grown son named Beverly. Her maiden name was Cordelia Brown, and the town of Brownsville, Neb., was named after her father. Botkin was for many years connected with the Missouri Valley Bank in Kansas City, but lived in Stockton, Cal., with his son, Beverly, at the time his wife met Dunning. While his wife remained in San Francisco Dunning met Mrs. Botkin clandestinely, but Mrs. Dunning took her baby to her father's home in Dover, Delaware, and thereafter her husband and Mrs. Botkin were constant companions at the races and cafes.

Mrs. Botkin moved to 927 Geary Street and Dunning took a room in the same building. In the course of conversation he told Mrs. Botkin that his wife was passionately fond of candy and that she had a very dear friend in San Francisco named Mrs. Corbaley.

On March 8, 1898, Dunning accepted a position as war

correspondent with the Associated Press, which made it necessary for him to depart immediately for Porto Rico. When he told Mrs. Botkin his plans, she pleaded with him to remain with her. He turned a deaf ear to her pleadings and told her bluntly that he would never return to San Francisco.

She accompanied him across the bay and wept bitterly when they parted.

On August 9, 1898, a small package arrived in Dover, Delaware, addressed to Mrs. John P. Dunning, That package was placed in the mail box belonging to her father, and was called for by Mr. Pennington's little grandson and taken home.

The family consisted of Mr. and Mrs. Pennington, their two daughters, Mrs. Dunning and Mrs. Joshua Deane; their son-in-law, Mr. Deane, and the two little children of Mr. and Mrs. Deane,

After supper the family repaired to the veranda, and Mrs. Dunning opened the package, which proved to be a fancy candy box containing a handkerchief, chocolate creams and a small slip of paper on which were the following words:

"With love to yourself and baby. — Mrs. C."

Mrs. Dunning could not imagine who had sent the package, but being a noble woman, with friends galore, she did not suspect that she had an enemy in the world, and therefore her suspicion was not aroused,

Mrs. Dunning and Mrs. Deane and the latter's two children partook of the candy, as did also two young ladies. Miss Millington and Miss Bateman, who chanced to pass the Pennington residence while the family were seated on the veranda. During that night all who partook of the candy were taken with retching pains in the stomach and vomited freely.

All recovered with the exception of Mrs. Dunning, who died on August 12, and Mrs. Deane, who died on August 11. Autopsies disclosed the fact that these ladies died from arsenic poisoning.

Mr. Pennington examined the handwriting on the box and on the slip of paper and discovered that it corresponded with the handwriting of an unknown person who had written an anonymous communication from San Francisco to Mrs. Dunning many months previously, in which it was alleged that Mr. Dunning was on intimate terms with a woman in San Francisco. Dr. Wood, a chemist, examined the candy which had not been eaten, and discovered a large amount of arsenic present.

John P. Dunning was advised by telegraph of what had transpired and he proceeded at once to Dover. He immediately recognized the handwriting as that of Mrs. Botkin and recalled his remark to her regarding his wife's fondness for candy, and also that his wife had a friend in San Francisco named Mrs. Corbaley, which accounted for the initial "C." signed to the note.

Detective B. J. McVey was sent to San Francisco with the candy, handkerchief, candy box and the note found in the box. Chief of Police I. W. Lees took charge of the case. Mrs. Botkin was located in Stockton, Cal., where she was living with her husband and son. Detective Ed. Gibson brought her to San Francisco, and in a few days an overwhelming amount of circumstantial evidence was piled up against her.

She was positively identified by Miss Sylvia Heney and Miss Kittie Dittmer as the woman who, on July 31, bought candy in the candy store of George Haas under the Phelan block on Market Street. Miss Heney furthermore swore that this woman requested that the candy be placed in a fancy box which did not have the firm's name on it, and also instructed that the box be not filled completely as she had another article to place in the box.

John P. Dunning produced love letters written to him by Mrs. Botkin, and handwriting expert Theodore Kytka testified to what was obvious to all, namely, that the person who wrote the love letters wrote the address on the candy box and the note therein.

Mrs. Botkin even neglected to remove the store tag from the handkerchief which she purchased in the "City of Paris" store from Mrs. Grace Harris, who even recalled the conversation she held with Mrs. Botkin. When asked why she recalled this so clearly, she stated that Mrs. Botkin's resemblance to her dead mother startled her. She subsequently produced a photograph of her mother to show the striking resemblance.

Frank Grey, a druggist employed at the "Owl" drug store, positively identified Mrs. Botkin as the woman who had purchased two ounces of arsenic for the alleged purpose of bleaching a straw hat, and insisted upon getting this drug even when the druggist informed her that there were other preparations better adapted for the purpose.

On August 4 the package of candy was mailed at the Ferry Post Office and was particularly noticed by a postal clerk named John Dunnigan because the address, "Mrs. John Dunning," reminded him of his own name. On this same day Mrs. Botkin left San Francisco for St. Helena.

Mrs. Almura Ruoff related a conversation she had with Mrs. Botkin in Stockton on July 27, 1898, in which the latter made inquiries as to the effect of different poisons on the human system, and asked if it was necessary to sign one's name when sending a registered package through the mail.

After Mrs. Botkin left the Hotel Victoria at Hyde and California Streets, where she had been stopping some months, W. P. Rossello, a porter, and W. W. Barnes, a clerk, found a torn piece of a gilded seal, similar to those pasted on candy boxes, on the floor of room 26, which Mrs. Botkin vacated. It was proved that the seal came from Haas' store and the wrapping on the candy box clearly showed where it had been removed.

Extradition papers were forwarded from Delaware as it was planned to take her there for trial, but her attorney, George Knight, attempted to procure her release on the grounds that the evidence was insufficient, and furthermore, that the jurisdiction for the trial was in California and not Delaware.

Superior Judges Cook, Borden, Wallace, Troutt and Seawell, sitting *en banc*, rendered a decision on October 23 to the effect that the jurisdiction for the trial was in California, as Mrs. Botkin's flight from Delaware was not actual but constructive. This decision was upheld by the Supreme Court.

The evidence was presented to the Grand Jury and on October 28, 1898, Mrs. Botkin was indicted. On December 9, 1898, the trial for the murder of Mrs. Dunning began.

On December 19, while testifying in the case, John P. Dunning refused to mention the names of other women he had been intimate with, and he was adjudged guilty of contempt and sent to jail, where he remained for several days until the question was withdrawn.

On December 30, 1898, Mrs. Botkin was found guilty and on February 4, 1899, she was sentenced to life imprisonment.

On March 9 Mrs. Botkin's husband, Welcome A. Botkin, sued her for a divorce on the grounds that she had been convicted of a felony.

Before Mrs. Botkin could be sent to State prison, a decision was rendered by the State Supreme Court in the case of "Hoff," who murdered Mrs. Clute on Guerrero Street, wherein it was decided that the trial Judge erred when, in his charge to the jury, he stated that "circumstantial evidence has the advantage over direct evidence, because it is not likely to be fabricated." It was held that by so doing he expressed to the jury his opinion upon the force and effect of the testimony and intimated his views of its sufficiency. As the same form of charge was delivered in the Botkin and numerous other cases, she experienced no difficulty in obtaining a new trial.

This necessitated the bringing of all the Delaware witnesses back to San Francisco. The second trial also resulted in a verdict of guilty and on August 2, 1904, she was again sentenced to life imprisonment, which judgment was affirmed by the State Supreme Court on October 29, 1908.

After the conviction of Mrs. Botkin she was confined in the Branch County Jail, pending the decision from the higher court.

About this time Superior Judge Cook lost his wife and each Sunday he visited her grave, riding out on a car which passed the jail. On one Sunday he was astonished at seeing Cordelia Botkin in the same car and apparently unguarded. The murderess signaled the car to stop at the county jail and she proceeded in the direction of that institution, but was lost to the Judge's view, as he remained on the car.

The next day he instituted an investigation. It was charged that the voluptuous woman was on intimate terms with one or more of the guards, which accounted for the fact that she was surrounded with every comfort at the jail. It was also charged that she was probably accompanied on the pleasure trip by a friendly guard who was on another part of the car.

Judge Cook failed to find anyone connected with the jail who would admit that the prisoner had been away from the building on Sunday, and the woman attempted to take advantage of the situation by claiming that the person who resembled her so much that the trial judge was mistaken, was probably the person who purchased the arsenic, candy and handkerchief, but the claim was not seriously considered.

After the great earthquake and fire the branch county jail, where Mrs. Botkin was confined, became crowded because of the destruction of the main jail, and as a result this woman lost the comfortable quarters she had enjoyed for years.

Although the Supreme Court had not yet reached a decision in her case, she made application to be transferred to San Quentin State Prison, and the request was complied with on May 16, 1906.

After her conviction her erstwhile lover, her mother, sister, son, and also her former husband, died within a short time.

The prisoner became a victim of nervous prostration and was soon a physical wreck. During the latter part of 1909 she began to suffer from melancholy. In February, 1910, she applied for parole because of her health, but it was decided that she was not eligible.

On March 7, 1910, she became unconscious and died. The death certificate shows that she died from "softening of the brain, due to melancholy."

She was 56 years old at the time of her death.

THE MURDER OF NORA FULLER.

Eleanor Parline, better known as Nora Fuller, was born in China in 1886.

In 1890 her father was an engineer on the Steamer Tai Wo. One night he was sitting asleep in a steamer chair on the deck of the vessel while at sea. Shortly after he was seen in this position his services were required in the engine room, but when a helper was sent after him the chair was vacant, and Parline was never seen again. A year later Mrs. Parline married a man named W. W. Fuller, in San Francisco, but seven years later she obtained a divorce.

As she had four small children, Mrs. Fuller experienced much trouble in getting along. In 1902 she lived at 1747 Fulton Street. At that time Nora, who was then fifteen years of age, decided to quit school and seek employment.

On January 6 she wrote to a theatrical agency, and after stating that she had a fairly good soprano voice, asked for employment. Two days later the following advertisement appeared in the Chronicle and Examiner:

"Wanted — Young white girl to take care of baby; good home and good wages."

At the foot of the advertisement was a note directing anyone answering to address the communication in care of the paper the advertisement was found in. Nora Fuller answered it, and on Saturday, January 11, she received the following postal:

'"Miss Fuller: In answer to yours in response to my advertisement, kindly call at the Popular restaurant, 55 Geary Street, and inquire for Mr. John Bennett, at 1 o'clock. If you can't come at 1, come at 6.

JOHN BENNETT."

Mrs. Fuller sent Nora to the rendezvous, and the girl took the postal card with her. About one hour later Mrs. Fuller's telephone bell rang, and her twelve-year-old son answered.

A nervous, irritable voice, which sounded some like Nora's, told him that the speaker was at the home of Mr. Bennett, at 1500 Geary Street, and her employer wanted her to go to work at once.*

*It was subsequently learned that 1500 Geary Street was a vacant lot.

The boy called out the message to his mother, who instructed him to tell Nora to come home and go to work Monday. The boy repeated the message, and the person at the other end said: "All right"; but before any more could be said by the boy the receiver at the other end was hung up. Nora Fuller never came home. A few days later the distracted mother notified the police.

F. W. Krone, proprietor of the Popular restaurant, was questioned and he stated that about 5:30 o'clock on the evening of January 11, a man who had been a patron of his place at different times during the past fifteen years, but whose name he had not up to that time heard, came to the counter and stated that he expected a young girl to inquire for John Bennett, and if she did to send her to the table where he was seated.

The girl did not appear, and Bennett, after waiting one-half hour, became restless and walked up and down the sidewalk in front of the restaurant for several moments. He then disappeared.

This man was described as being about forty years of age, five feet nine inches high, weighing about 170 pounds, wearing a brown mustache, well dressed and refined appearing.

A waiter employed at the Popular restaurant, who frequently waited on "Bennett," stated that the much-wanted man was a great lover of porterhouse steaks, but the fact that he only ate the tenderloin part of the steak earned for him the sobriquet of "Tenderloin."

On January 16 lengthy articles were published in the papers in regard to the mysterious disappearance of the girl.

On January 8 a man giving the name of C. B. Hawkins called at Umbsen & Co.'s real estate office, and, addressing a clerk named C. S. Lahenier, inquired for particulars regarding a two-story frame building for rent at 2211 Sutter Street. The terms were satisfactory to Hawkins, but Lahenier asked the prospective tenant for references. He replied that he could give none, as he was a stranger in the city, but as he had a prepossessing appearance the clerk let him have the key after paying one month's rent in advance. The man then signed the name "C. B. Hawkins" to a contract.

He stated that he was then stopping at the Golden West Hotel with his wife. The description of Hawkins was identically the same as the description of Bennett.

On the following day the real estate firm sent E. F. Bertrand, a locksmith and "handy man" in their employ, to the Sutter-Street house to clean it up.

Many days after this a collector for the firm named Fred Crawford reported that the house was still vacant — judging from outside appearances. He went to the Golden West Hotel to inquire for Hawkins, but he was not known there.

On February 8 the month's rent was up, and a collector and inspector named H. E. Dean was sent to the house.

Using a pass key he entered, but finding no furniture on the lower floor, he went upstairs, where he found the door to a back room closed. This he opened, but as the shade was down the room was in semi-darkness. He discerned a bright-colored garment on the floor, but as he seemed to know by intuition that something was wrong, he hurriedly left the building, and meeting Officer Gill requested him to accompany him back to the house. The officer entered the room, and upon raising the shade found the dead body of a young girl lying as if asleep in a bed. On the bed were two new sheets, which had never been laundered, a blanket and quilt. An old chair was the only other furniture in the house. Neither food nor dishes could be found. Nor was there any means of heating or lighting the house, as the gas was not connected.

The girl's clothing was in the bedroom, also her purse, which contained no money, but a card with the following inscription thereon:

"Mr. M. A. Severbrinik, of Port Arthur."

(It was subsequently learned that this man sailed for China on the Peking three hours before Nora Fuller left home on January 11.)

On the floor was the butt of a cigar, and on the mantelpiece in the front room was an almost empty whisky bottle. There were no toilet articles in the house except one towel.

Many letters were found addressed to Mrs. C. B. Hawkins, 2211 Sutter Street. They were from furniture houses and contained either advertisements or solicitations for trade. A circular letter addressed to

Mrs. Hawkins and bearing a postmark of January 21, 11 p. m., or ten days after the disappearance of Nora Fuller, had been opened by someone and then placed in the girl's jacket, which was found in the room. Mrs. Fuller identified the clothing as belonging to her daughter, and subsequently identified the body as the remains of Nora. No trace was ever found of the postal card Nora received from Bennett.

Dr. Charles Morgan, the city toxicologist, examined the stomach and found no traces of drugs or poisons. Save for an apple, which the deceased had evidently eaten about one or two hours before death, the stomach was empty.

There was a slight congestion of the stomach, possibly due' to partaking of some alcoholic drink when the stomach was not accustomed to it. Mrs. Fuller stated that Nora ate an apple shortly before she left home on January 11.

Dr. Bacigalupi, the autopsy surgeon, found two black marks on the throat, one on each side of the larynx, and as there was a slight congestion of the lungs, he concluded that death was due to strangulation. But the child had been otherwise assaulted and her body frightfully mutilated, evidently by a degenerate. Captain of Detectives John Seymour took charge of the case.

B. T. Schell, a salesman at J. C. Cavanaugh's furniture store, located at 848 Mission Street, stated that at 5 p. m., January 9, a man of the same description as "Hawkins" or "Bennett," and wearing a high silk hat, called and said that he wanted to furnish a room temporarily. He purchased two second-hand pillows, a pair of blankets, a comforter and top mattress. He insisted that the goods be delivered at night or not at all. This Schell promised to do. The customer then wanted to know what assurance he had that the salesman would not substitute another mattress, and Schell suggested that he put his initials on the mattress as a means of identification. Acting on this suggestion Hawkins used a large heavy pencil and wrote the letters "C. B. H." on the mattress. After leaving word to deliver the articles that night to 2211 Sutter Street the man departed.

Lawrence C. Gillen, the delivery boy for this firm, stated that he had to work overtime in order to take the articles to the Sutter Street house that night.

When he arrived the house was in darkness. He rang the bell and a man came to the door, and from what he could see with the lights from the Street lamps he was of the same description as the man who made the purchases, and he wore a silk hat. Gillen asked him to light up so he could see, but he said, "Never mind, leave the things in the hall."

Richard Fitzgerald, a salesman employed at the Standard Furniture Company, 745 Mission Street, stated that a man of "Bennett's" description bought a bed and an old chair from him on January 10, and that he engaged an express man, Tom Tobin, to deliver the same to 2211 Sutter Street.

Tobin stated that this man was present when he arrived, and requested him to set up the bed in the room where it was found. This man he described as being of Bennett's appearance.

It is probable that the sheets, towel and pillow cases were purchased at Mrs. Mahoney's dry goods store, 92 Third Street, which was just around the corner from the Standard Furniture Company. These articles were carried away by the purchaser.

On the floor of the room where the girl's body was found was a small piece of the Denver Post of January 9, upon which was a mailing label addressed to the office of the Railroad Employees' Journal, 210 Parrott building.

When this paper arrived at the Parrott building it was given by Exchange Editor Scott to a Mr. Hurlburt, a delegate from Denver to a railroadmen's convention then in session in the assembly room in the Parrott building. After glancing at it he threw it on a large table, and some other delegate picked it up and took it to Dennett's restaurant, where he left it on the dining table. The steward of the restaurant, Mr. Helbish, picked it up, and after taking it to the counter began to read it, believing it was the San Francisco Post. He laid it down, and Miss Drysdale, the cashier, glanced over it. She laid it down, and how it got to 2211 Sutter Street remains a mystery.

A seventeen-year-old girl named Madge Graham met Nora Fuller in June, 1901, and they became very friendly. Madge boarded at Nora's house for a while until her guardian. Attorney Edward Steams, requested her to move away, because a lawyer named Hugh Grant was a frequent visitor at the Fuller home.

She claimed that Nora Fuller frequently spoke to her of having a friend named Bennett, also she believed that the advertisement was a trick concocted by Nora and "Bennett" to deceive Mrs. Fuller.

She furthermore stated that Nora often telephoned to some man, and that one day Nora requested her to tell Mrs. Fuller that she and Nora were going to the theater that night. Madge did as requested, but she stated that instead of going with her, Nora went with some man. It was also claimed that someone gave Nora complimentary press tickets to the theaters.

A. Menke, who conducted a grocery at Golden Gate and Central Avenues, stated that Nora Fuller frequently used his telephone to call up someone at a hotel, although she had a telephone in her own home a few blocks away.

Theodore Kytka, the handwriting expert, made an examination of the original slips filled out by "Bennett" for his advertisement for a young girl, and also the signature of "C. B. Hawkins" to the contract when he rented the house, and found both were written by the same person.

On February 19 the Coroner's jury rendered the following verdict:

"That the said Nora Fuller, aged fifteen, nativity China, residence 1747 Fulton Street, came to her death at 2211 Sutter Street in the City and County of San Francisco, through asphyxiation by strangling on a day subsequent to January 11 and before February 4, 1902, at the hands of parties unknown. Furthermore we believe that she died within twenty-four hours after 12 m., January 11. In view of the heinousness of the crime, we recommend that the Governor offer a reward of $5,000 for the discovery and apprehension of the criminal.

"ACHILLE ROSS, Foreman."

Believing that the person who committed this crime might have changed his address and sent a written notification to that effect to the postal authorities, Theodore Kytka examined 32,000 notifications of changes of address. Of this number he found three signatures that bore considerable resemblance to the Bennett-Hawkins style of penmanship, and one of these three was almost identically the same.

This proved to be the signature of a man in Kansas City, Mo., and Captain Seymour went east to make a personal investigation. It was found, however, that the man had nothing to do with the crime.

On January 16, five days after the disappearance of Nora Fuller, but three weeks before her fate was known, the papers of San Francisco gave considerable space to the mysterious case. Two days later a gentleman connected with a local paper notified the police department that a clerk in their employ named Charles B. Hadley had disappeared. It was afterward said that he was short in his accounts with his employers.

Detective Charles Cody was detailed to locate the man, and he found that he had lived at 647 Ellis Street with a girl born and raised in San Francisco, who had assumed the name of Ollie Blasier, because of her infatuation for a notorious character known as "Kid" Blasier.

No trace of Hadley was found. Finally the body of Nora Fuller was discovered, and photographs of the signature of "C. B. Hawkins" on the contract with Umbsen & Co., and the "C. B. H." on the mattress, were published in all the papers.

The Blasier woman had a photograph of Hadley in her room, upon the back of which he had written his name, "C. B.   Hadley." Seeing the great similarity in the handwriting she delivered this to Detective Cody, who in turn delivered it to Theodore Kytka for investigation.

Kytka determined at once that the person who wrote "C. B. Hadley" on the photograph also wrote "C. B. H." on the mattress, and "C. B. Hawkins" on the contract.

While Hadley had the same general physique as "Hawkins," it was known that he was always clean shaven. Miss Blasier stated, however, that she had seen Hadley wear a false brown mustache about the house, and it was subsequently learned that he purchased one at a Japanese store on Larkin Street.

In addition to this, Chief of Police Langley, of Victoria, B. C, made an affidavit to the effect that a Mr. Marsden, a storekeeper in Victoria, B. C, had stated that he had been a companion of Hadley's, and that while out on a "lark" he had seen Hadley wear a false mustache. Miss Blasier made a further statement substantially as follows:

"I now recall that after the disappearance of Nora Fuller Hadley made a practice of getting up early in the morning and taking the morning paper to the toilet to read.

"On the day of his final disappearance he followed this practice, and after he left the house I found the morning paper in the toilet, and I noticed a long article about the disappearance of Nora Fuller. It was evident that his mind was greatly disturbed on this morning.

"The next day I was making up my laundry, and at the very bottom of the pile of soiled clothing I found some of his garments which had blood on them. I burned them and also his plug hat.

"It is well known that Hadley is partial to porterhouse steaks and that he eats only the tenderloin.

"On the evening of January 16, Hadley telephoned to me that he would not be home. I confess that I suspect he committed this murder."

Theodore Kytka obtained Hadley's photograph and altered it by giving him the appearance of wearing a mustache and plug hat. This was shown to different persons who had dealings with "Hawkins," with the following results:

Tobin, the express man, said it looked very much like him; Lahenier, the real estate man, said it bore a marked resemblance. Ray Zertanna, who had seen Nora in the park with a man, stated that the picture was a good likeness of this man. Schell, who suggested that "Hawkins" place his initials on the mattress, said it was an exact likeness of Hawkins. Fred Krone, the restaurant man, who had the conversation with "Bennett" on the evening Nora left home, said it was not a likeness of Bennett.

Hadley left his money in a certain bank in this city, where it remains even now.

An investigation was then made as to his past, and it developed that he was an habitué of the tenderloin district, and that he was on the road to degeneracy. His true name was Charlie Start, and his respected mother resided in Chicago.

On May 6, 1889, Superintendent of Police Brackett, of Minneapolis, issued a circular letter offering $100 reward for the arrest of Charles Start for embezzlement.

About two years before the murder of Nora Fuller, Hadley enticed a fifteen-year-old girl into a room and outraged her. He then purchased diamonds and jewelry from a certain large jewelry store in San Francisco and gave them to the girl, who is now a respectable married woman residing in the neighborhood of San Francisco.

The country was flooded with circulars accusing Hadley of this murder and calling for his apprehension, but he was never located.

Many believe that he committed suicide.

MURDERS AND OTHER CRIMES COMMITTED BY LEON SOEDER.

In 1882 Leon Soeder came to America from Germany. He was by occupation a cook. Under the name of Leon Seter, he committed a burglary in Alameda County, for which he was sentenced to serve three years in San Quentin in October, 1884.

On January 29, 1894, Officer Martin Tannian arrested him for burglarizing Johnson's Restaurant in San Francisco, for which he was sent to San Quentin for three years.

About 1901, he married Miss Pilar Mirander, of Petaluma. They went to Tesla, Cal., where he procured employment as a cook, and his wife worked as a waitress. Several dogs died from poison in the town while Soeder was there and it was afterwards learned that Soeder had been using the dogs in experimental work.

Soeder and his wife left Tesla in December, 1902, and returned to Petaluma where Soeder had his wife's life insured for $2000.00. She died shortly afterward under the most suspicious circumstances, but for some reason no investigation was made.

A few days after his wife's death, Soeder proposed marriage to Miss Lillian Justi of the same town. Shortly after this the restaurant which he was conducting in Petaluma burned down. On this property he had $2000.00 insurance, being far more than its value.

In March, 1903, Soeder met Miss Katherine Flatley at her home, 251 Marshall Street, San Francisco. She was a young woman of attractive appearance, and Soeder presented jewelry to her valued at several hundred dollars.

On April 18, 1903, he left for Alaska, returning to San Francisco on September 15 of the same year. On October 16 he left for Germany, telling Miss Flatley that the object of his visit was to obtain $10,000.00 as a part of his interest in an estate.

On October 24, he sent her a telegram from New York stating that he had been robbed, and requesting that she forward $100.00, which was done. He proceeded to Germany, and after much persuasion, induced his sister's husband, Jos. Blaise, a lumberman, to accompany him to this country, and he also endeavored to induce his own brother to make the trip.

When they reached New York, about December 1, Soeder at once attempted to procure an insurance policy on Blaise's life for $5000.00, but as there seemed to be considerable delay, he lost patience and brought Blaise to San Francisco, arriving here on December 13. On December 26, Soeder wrote to Miss Flatley announcing his arrival in San Francisco, and informing her that he was sick and desired her to call. He concluded the letter by promising to make her additional presents as soon as his "fortune" arrived.

She ignored this letter, and on December 29 he again wrote, reprimanding her for not calling.

On January 11, 1904, Wm. Hogan, a laborer, was passing along Taylor Street, between Green and Vallejo, where he found a man lying at the bottom of a cliff, and on close inspection it was found that the man was dead. There was a cut on the back of his head and on the right side of the throat was a deep knife wound. His pockets were turned inside out, but this had been so thoroughly done, that it was suspected the object of doing so was to create the false impression that the motive for the crime was robbery. Soeder and Blaise roomed together at the residence of Jos. Neibias at 827 Jackson Street, and on the following morning Soeder told the landlord that Blaise had not been home that night and as he had $90.00 in his pockets, he feared foul play.

Soeder reported the matter at police headquarters, where he was advised to visit the morgue to view the body of the murdered man. He immediately identified the body as that of his brother-in-law, and affected much grief.

Shortly afterward, when it was learned that Soeder was an ex-convict and had a heavy insurance on his brother-in-law's life, he was taken into custody.

Detective Tom Gibson was assigned to the case and in Soeder's rooms he found a knife, on which was human blood.

Gripman Chas. Vose, on the Union Street line, stated that he had carried Blaise on his car about 8:30 p. m. January 10, and that he left the car at Union and Taylor Streets, where Blaise met a man standing by the Street lamp who resembled Soeder.

Three policies issued by the Pacific Life Insurance Co. were found in Soeder's possession. Each was for three thousand dollars.

One was a policy taken out by Blaise in which his wife was made beneficiary, in the second Soeder was the beneficiary, and the third was taken out by Soeder and made payable to Blaise. Subsequent investigation showed that Soeder had taken advantage of Blaise's ignorance of the English language and had his name inserted as beneficiary when Blaise understood that both policies were made payable to his wife. On December 23, Soeder attempted to procure a $10,000.00 accident policy for Blaise, but was informed that as Blaise represented himself to be a cook, he could only procure $3000.00. Soeder showed outward signs of displeasure. He then attempted to procure a $10,000.00 life insurance policy from the Pacific Mutual Life Insurance Co. on Blaise, but as J. M. Kilgarif, the manager, doubted his ability to keep up payments, he would only write a $3000.00 policy. Soeder wanted to pay up for only three months, but the company forced him to pay for one year.

On December 16, 1903, Soeder pawned a watch and diamond ring for $130.00 in order to obtain sufficient money to pay the premiums on

Blaise's policies.

Soeder afterward asked Dr. W. G. Mizner, who was connected with the company, why he was questioned so closely by the officials, to which the doctor replied: "Oh, they thought you wanted to do away with Blaise." Soeder replied: "Oh, no; we were schoolmates and he married my sister." While awaiting trial in the Superior Court, his cellmate was John Cooper, who was in custody on a charge of forgery.

Cooper subsequently testified that Soeder told him that he expected $1000.00 from Germany, and that he would give Cooper one-half if he could procure witnesses who could swear that he, Soeder, was in another part of the city at the time the crime was committed. Cooper produced a piece of the San Francisco Examiner upon which Soeder drew a diagram indicating the spot where the murder was committed.

On the diagram he wrote names of Streets, etc. Soeder had previously stated that he had never been near the scene of the killing, but this diagram was drawn with such accuracy that it would have been impossible for a stranger to the surroundings to have drawn it.

After drawing the diagram, Soeder, according to Cooper, admitted that he had committed the murder and that he first struck Blaise with a shovel.

Theodore Kytka, the handwriting expert, proved that the writing on the diagram was done by Soeder.

The defendant also confessed to the murder of his wife. The case was submitted to the jury on May 23, 1904. After deliberating for twenty minutes, they returned a verdict of guilty.

Soeder was hanged on March 29, 1907.

THE MURDEROUS CAREER OF MILTON FRANKLIN ANDREWS, ALIAS CURTIS, BRUSH, ETC, WHICH WAS BROUGHT TO A TRAGIC END IN SAN FRANCISCO.

On the night of October 11, 1905, a man was found in a semiconscious condition in the neighborhood of 2214 Ellsworth Street, Berkeley, Cal. His head and face were covered with blood. It was soon learned that he was a man known as "Friday" Ellis, formerly a famous steeplechase rider in England and Australia, who earned his sobriquet because of a sensational ride he made on a horse called "Friday." Ellis was afterward suspended from the track for "pulling" horses, but he finally became a bookmaker on the Kensington racetrack in Australia.

In August, 1905, he "welched" (refused to pay off bets) and took the next steamer for America. On that trip he was accompanied by a man and woman known as Mr. and Mrs. Brush, also known as Curtis, whom he met at the race-track. Brush was an expert poker-player.

When Ellis recovered he made the following statement regarding his experience with Brush:

"We arrived in San Francisco on October 2, 1905, and a few days later we moved to a cottage at 2214 Ellsworth Street, Berkeley.

"The first night I spent in the house convinced me that something was wrong, as I noticed Brush and his wife holding whispered conversations when they imagined they were not observed. So uneasy did I become that I spent a sleepless night, and the next day I moved away.

"After much persuasion, Brush induced me to call on October 11. While sitting at the table eating marmalade, he struck me on the head with a hammer. I fell and he robbed me of $500. I recovered slightly while he was robbing me and, struggling to my feet, I gave him battle. At this moment the woman presented a pistol at my head and I staggered out of the house, but after traveling a short distance I fell from loss of blood."

The officers made a search of the premises which plainly showed where the assault was committed, but no trace could be found of Brush or his "wife."

Ellis gave a good description of his assailants and added that Brush had told him that he once had a row with a woman near Colorado Springs but that he fixed her all right.

Officer W. E. Atchison of Berkeley then looked up the records and learned the following facts:

*On December 16, 1904, two men found the badly decomposed body
of a young woman on Mount Cutler, Colorado. A bullet wound in the
back of the head showed that murder had been committed and, to
prevent identification, the assassin had built a bonfire and thrown
the body into it, but the fire went out after the face had been burned
so that identification was impossible. All the jewelry was removed
from the body.*

*The young woman had evidently been dead for months, and as
there was no report of any missing woman in that locality it was
concluded that the victim was probably one of the thousands of
tourists from all over the world who visit the neighborhood of
Colorado Springs.*

*An examination of the mouth showed that a great amount of
dental work had been done, including bridge work, gold teeth, etc.
An elaborate diagram of this work was drawn by a dentist and a
photograph of the diagram placed on circulars, which were sent
to every Chief of Police in the country with the request that every
dentist in each city or town be shown the diagram.*

*Finally the dentist who did the work was located and he stated
that it was done for a Mrs. Bessie Bouton, wife of an electrician in
Syracuse, New York, named George Bouton, It was said that she
had traveled about the country as the wife of Milton F. Andrews,
a professional gambler, who had a wife living in Holyoke, Mass.,
whom he deserted after stealing her money and jewelry. Andrews
was seen with Mrs. Bouton near where the body was found and he
suddenly disappeared on October 5, 1904.*

Upon getting this evidence Chief Reynolds of Colorado Springs
procured a good photograph of Andrews, a copy of which appeared on
circulars which were sent to all police departments.

Andrews, who was 6 feet 3 inches high, had a very narrow,
deformed chest, and because of stomach trouble was compelled to subsist
almost entirely on malted milk.

Officer Atchison found this circular and when he read the
description and showed the picture to Ellis, the latter exclaimed: "That's the
man who tried to kill me."

Great publicity was given to the case, especially to the fact that
the desperate fugitive consumed large quantities of malted milk. The
description of both Brush and his wife were also published.

In October, 1905, Mrs. M. Hornbeck conducted a little grocery and bakery at No. 743 McAllister Street, San Francisco. She gained the patronage of a dark-haired and mysterious-acting young woman, who purchased large quantities of malted milk. Suddenly this woman bleached her hair and began wearing smoked glasses. Mrs. Hornbeck had not followed the papers closely and therefore did not realize the significance of these circumstances.

The mysterious woman continued to trade at the store, and three weeks later Mrs. Hornbeck casually mentioned the circumstance to Detectives M. V. Burke and Fred Smith. They trailed the woman to the residence of Jas. Meagher, No. 748 McAllister Street. As it was learned that Meagher could be trusted, the officers confided their suspicions to him and asked about the woman. He laughed at them and said that she was a Miss Eda Little from Sacramento and that he could almost swear that she alone occupied her room, as no one in his house, which was a private home, had ever seen or heard anyone else there. Mr. Meagher's family were equally positive on this point.

But the officers were not satisfied and Detectives Tom Gibson and John Freel were detailed on the case.

Detective Burke posed as the owner of the property, and Meagher, who rendered every assistance, went to Miss Little's room and told her the landlord wanted to look at the gas fixtures.

After some hesitation the girl opened the door. The officer looked at the gas fixtures and also looked around the room. Seeing nothing to indicate that the woman had a companion, he stepped outside, but when he did so the woman seemed to be so anxious to get the door closed and bolted that it aroused the officer's suspicions. He conferred with his brother officers, who were concealed in the hallway, and they immediately asked her to open the door again. This she refused to do. The officers then told her who they were and warned her that if she did not open the door, they would break it. She replied: "If you do I will kill you."

Just then two shots rang out. The officers burst in the door and found the dead bodies of a young man and woman, each having a bullet wound in the forehead. It was evident that the man had fired both shots and that he was concealed in a clothes-closet when the officer first entered.

It was seen at a glance that they answered the description of Andrews and his companion, who proved to be Nulda Olivia.

In the girl's stocking was a lengthy confession written by Andrews. In reference to his assault on Ellis he said:

"I sat him at the dinner-table and tried to comb some of the treachery out of his brain with a hammer. I did not know at the time

that he had a gorilla's skull or I would have used a pile-driver."

Afterward the detectives obtained evidence amounting almost to proof that on August 2, 1904, Andrews murdered Eugene J. Bosworth at New Britain, Conn., crushing his victim's skull and robbing him of several hundred dollars and a diamond ring.

Jewelry found in the room was subsequently identified as the property of Mrs. Bouton, who was murdered on Mount Cutler.

———————

THE MURDER OF BIAGGIO VILARDO BY PIETRO TORTORICI.

At 10:30 p. m. on April 5, 1905, George J. Oliva of 3 1/2 August place was standing at the corner of Mason and Vallejo Streets, when a man passed him who was carrying a heavy and bulky bundle done up in a woman's shawl. When about one hundred feet past Oliva, the man dropped the bundle and hastened away.

More curious than suspicious, Oliva leisurely strolled to where the package was thrown, and upon opening it he was horrified to find the trunk of a man, the head, arms and legs having been amputated. His cry for help caused Charles Torre of 1821 DuPont Street and John Copertini of 730 Vallejo Street to respond. They in turn called Officer William Minihan, who discovered that the body was still warm and that the blood had not as yet congealed. Appearances indicated that the body had probably been mutilated with an ax. It was taken to the Morgue and a search was instituted for the head and limbs.

At 4:30 p. m. on April 6, Joseph Lanteri and three other small boys were playing at the water's edge near Fisherman's wharf at the foot of Mason Street, when they noticed a barley sack floating in the water. They pulled it ashore and untied a blue sock which was fastened around the mouth of the sack. When the boys found that the sack contained the head, evidently of a young Italian, and both arms and legs, they uttered a cry of horror.

The sack and its contents were removed to the Morgue, where it was seen at a glance that the head and limbs belonged to the trunk found on the preceding day.

On the following evening, at 8:45 o'clock, Crispino Vilardo of 1762 Harrison Street called at the Morgue and identified the remains as those of his half-brother, Biaggio Vilardo, a native of Palermo, Sicily, who had been in America twenty-three months. Crispino stated that the murdered man was an intimate friend of one Brogardo, who was murdered on January 21, 1905, and that he was extremely active in the prosecution of Brogardo's assassins. Crispino appeared to be so terror-stricken that he hesitated some time before stating positively that the mutilated remains were those of his brother, and after doing so he became hysterical. When he regained his composure, he stated that Biaggio had lived at 736 1/2 Green Street, with Pietro Tortorici and his wife and baby.

The detectives went to the house, where the Tortorici family had rooms in the basement. A casual glance convinced them that the kitchen was the scene of the butchery. The floor, walls and ceiling were bespattered with blood, and under the sink was found a blood-stained cleaver upon which were some small particles of bone that were broken in the uncouth dissecting process.

The detectives concealed themselves in the house, in the hope that the occupants would return. About daylight on the following morning, Mrs. Rose Tortorici came in with her baby. She was immediately taken to headquarters, and after a long cross-examination made the following statement:

"I have known Biaggio Vilardo for about one year. I believe he was murdered by my husband, but not through jealousy, as I was not friendly with Vilardo, and if my husband suspected I was not true he would have killed me. On Wednesday evening (the night of the murder) I cooked dinner and then took my baby into the garden (Washington Square). When I returned about 9:30 p. m., something told me that all was not well, and I asked my husband where Vilardo was, and he replied: 'Woman, mind your own business.' He then went out and I went to bed. He did not come home that night, so the next morning I was afraid to stay in the house and I went to some friends at 1611 Powell Street, where I remained until I returned to my home and was arrested. I have not seen my husband since the night of the murder."

An examination of the dead man's stomach showed that he had been murdered almost immediately after he ate a meal. Several Italians were arrested on suspicion, but were subsequently released without being charged.

Although there was very little evidence against Mrs. Tortorici she was indicted, as an attorney had attempted to procure her release on a writ of habeas corpus. On May 29 her case was called in the Superior Court, but owing to the insufficiency of the evidence the case never came to trial and she was permitted to go to the home of her mother in New Orleans. Tortorici was never apprehended.

————————

MARTHA BOWERS, WHO MURDERED HER HUSBAND

WITH ARSENIC.

In 1889, Miss Martha Byers, daughter of Mrs. Elizabeth Byers, a highly esteemed lady residing in Portland, Oregon, married an elderly man named Dale. After being married one year she procured a divorce and shortly afterward married Alfred Allen. She only remained with him a short time when she procured a divorce, and in 1902 she married Martin L. Bowers, a bridge builder, residing in San Francisco. They lived at 370 Clementina Street, and on June 5, 1903, Dr. Carl Von Tiedemann was called in to prescribe for Bowers. Mrs. Bowers gave him a history of the case, and stated that she attributed his sickness to ptomaine poisoning caused by eating some ham. The doctor made a diagnosis and treated the patient for that affliction, but because of a misunderstanding with Mrs. Bowers over financial matters, he dropped the case. Dr. J. F. Dillon was the next physician called, and from information received he also concluded that the patient was suffering from ptomaine poisoning, and prescribed accordingly. After a few visits the patient apparently improved and he ceased to call.

A few days afterward Bowers became very weak and Dr. A. McLaughlin was called in. After hearing Mrs. Bowers' statements, he agreed with the other physicians, but insisted that the patient be removed to the Waldeck Sanitarium forthwith. Although the doctor was greatly puzzled by some of the peculiar symptoms of his patient, still his suspicions were not aroused as Bowers, after a month's treatment, was convalescent, and at the earnest solicitation of his wife, he was removed to his home. The doctor instructed Mrs. Bowers to give her husband massage treatments daily, and about a week afterward he called at their home and learned that his instructions had not been obeyed. On examining Bowers, he became alarmed at his condition and ordered him removed to the German Hospital forthwith. Bowers sank rapidly and passed away on August 25, 1903. As soon as he was pronounced dead, the widow threw herself on his body and became "hysterical."

Harry Bowers, who was the brother of the dead man, and who knew something of Mrs. Bowers' character, concluded that "something was wrong." He therefore communicated with the coroner and demanded an investigation, with the result that the dead man's stomach was turned over to City Chemist Frank Green and Dr. Chas. Morgan, a toxicologist, for analysis. In their report they stated that they found four grains of arsenic undissolved and they furthermore ridiculed the theory that Bowers died from ptomaine poison through eating ham, for the reason that the ham would not carry ptomaine because of the fact the salt and creosote used in curing it would tend to destroy the poison.

This report was given great publicity and the question arose as to who administered the poison and where and how it was procured.

The answer, in part at least, was furnished by a druggist named J. C. Peterson, who was employed at Fifth and Clementina Streets. He described a woman who called at his store on the afternoon of August 20 with a prescription purporting to be signed by Dr. A. McLaughlin, which simply called for "arsenic." As it was not written on a physician's blank and as the amount of arsenic to be furnished was not specified, it naturally caused the clerk to ask the woman several questions and pay particular attention to her appearance.

The description did not fit Mrs. Bowers, but it did fit her sister, Mrs. Zylpha Sutton, and upon being brought before her, the druggist immediately identified her.

The prescription was then procured and it showed where the druggist had written on the original the amount of arsenic delivered.

Upon searching Mrs. Bowers' home, a composition book belonging to a school boy named John Baptiste was discovered, and the page was found from which the paper used in writing the prescription was torn.

In the same book were indited a number of songs, admitted to be in the chirography of Mrs. Bowers. Theodore Kytka, the handwriting expert, swore that the person who wrote the songs also wrote the prescription on which Dr. McLaughlin's name was forged. It was also proven that her mourning robes were prepared before her husband died and to prove that her heart was "bursting with grief" when she threw herself on her husband's corpse immediately after death, she was afterwards forced to admit that she proceeded to her home within two hours after he died and then began a two-day carousal with one Patrick Leary.

Notwithstanding the fact that this man was illiterate and of repulsive appearance, Mrs. Bowers was undoubtedly infatuated with him and it was the theory of the prosecution that her motive for killing her husband was to free herself from a man who had become obnoxious because of his strenuous objections to Leary's attentions to her.

Detective Sergeant Thos. Ryan and District Attorney Byington had charge of the case, and as soon as the evidence began to accumulate against Mrs. Bowers, she and her sister, Mrs. Sutton, were placed under police surveillance. On August 28 they were arrested and subsequently charged with the murder of Bowers. At the conclusion of the preliminary examination Mrs. Sutton was released because of insufficiency of evidence, but Mrs. Bowers' trial began on January 14, and she was found guilty of murder on January 20, 1904. On February 14 she was sentenced to life imprisonment.

———————

ATTORNEY GEORGE D. COLLINS, THE BRILLIANT ATTORNEY, WHO COMMITTED BIGAMY AND PERJURY— A REMARKABLE CASE.

An article appeared in the San Francisco papers of April 24, 1905, to the effect that George D. Collins, the brilliant attorney from San Francisco, had on the day previous married Miss Clarice McCurdy at a hotel in Chicago. Miss McCurdy was the daughter of Mrs. S. A. McCurdy, a wealthy widow residing in Stockton. A few days afterward, Collins returned to San Francisco with his bride and mother-in-law and secured apartments at the Palace Hotel.

William Newman, a member of the Fire Department, appeared before the Grand Jury about this time, and stated that if Collins had actually married Clarice McCurdy he was guilty of bigamy, as he had married his sister, Charlotta Newman, on May 15, 1889, and that Father M. D. Connelly performed the ceremony.

Attorney Thomas E. Curran and Florence Newman, who were present at the ceremony, corroborated this statement. On May 13, 1905, Collins was indicted for bigamy. In his defense, Collins replied that he had married Agnes Newman on the day in question, but that through a clerical error the license was made in the name of Charlotte Newman, the sister. Agnes died in May, 1901, and Collins had a plate put on her casket bearing the name of "Agnes Collins." He claimed that he had left his three children in the care of his sister-in-law, Charlotte Newman, who was merely his housekeeper.

In answer to this, Charlotte laid bare the remarkable story of her life, which is as follows:

"I was married to George D. Collins on May 15, 1889, and five children were born to us. On April 8, 1890, our son George was born; on September 28, 1892, Consuela was born; on September 28, 1897, May was born. In 1893 a child was born which died two days afterward, and on April 1, 1895, another child was born which lived only two days. My sister Agnes lived in the same house with us. In the early part of 1891, Agnes confessed to me that she expected to become a mother and that my husband was responsible for her condition. She furthermore said that if I turned her from the house she would commit suicide. I protected her, and she went into seclusion and none of our relatives knew of her condition. In May, 1891, she gave birth to a little girl at St. Mary's Hospital. To protect my sister's name, I represented myself to be the mother of the child and Agnes continued to live with us.

"This child was named Susan, and in May, 1901, she contracted diphtheria, from which she died on the 13th inst. Agnes was again in a delicate condition, and she was stricken with the ailment from which Susan died. While in bed suffering from this disease she gave birth to another child, and both died.

"It is true that the words 'Agnes Collins' were engraved on the plate of the casket, but Mr. Collins claimed the mistake was due to the stupidity of the engraver and that it was too late to have it rectified.

"Mr. Collins has lived at our home, 2519 Pierce Street, right up to the time that he went East to marry Miss McCurdy, and since his return he spent one night with me and assured me that there was no truth in the report that he had again married."

After the death of Agnes Newman, Collins obtained the money she had deposited in the Hibernia Bank, on the representation that he was her husband. The attorneys for the bank began disbarment proceedings against him for this act and there was some talk of charging him with obtaining money by false pretenses.

The McCurdy's believed Collins innocent and rendered him every assistance. Collins conducted his own defense, and endeavored to prove that the San Francisco courts lacked jurisdiction and that the trial should properly take place in Illinois. This point being decided against him, he endeavored to prove that the Grand Jury which indicted him was not a legalized inquisitorial organization. Neither was this point well taken.

While in the midst of his battle, Charlotta Collins sued him on May 26, 1905, for $200 per month for the support of herself and children. In answer to this suit, Collins swore that he had never married Charlotta.

His trial began in June, 1905, and the work of impaneling a jury was in progress when, on the morning of June 12, he failed to appear.

An investigation disclosed the fact that a character known as "Bogie O'Donnell," who had a contract for carrying morning newspapers across the bay on a launch, had also taken Collins across. He was subsequently traced to Victoria, B. C. Under the treaty of extradition between this country and Canada, bigamy is not an extraditable offense, which undoubtedly accounted for Collins' actions. But as he swore in the civil suit that he was not the husband of Charlotta Newman, he was indicted for perjury and extradition papers were issued.

Detective Tom Gibson was sent after him, and after a legal battle lasting over three months, Collins was returned on October 24, 1905, and was placed on trial for perjury. During this trial he testified that he had never married Charlotta Newman, and for this he was again indicted for perjury on December 29, 1905.

The charge of bigamy and the former charge of perjury were then dropped, and he was tried on the last indictment, found guilty, and on March 10, 1906, he was sentenced to serve fourteen years in State Prison.

As Collins contended that he could not legally be tried for any crime other than the one for which he was extradited, he appealed to the State Supreme Court and to the Federal Circuit Court, but the trial court was sustained in both instances.

Collins was undoubtedly one of the most resourceful lawyers in California and while in the County Jail he devoted all his time to a study of the law and decisions on extradition and perjury. He prepared a lengthy appeal to the United States Supreme Court, but on May 17, 1909, Justice Peckham handed down a decision sustaining the lower courts. In this decision the Justice said:

> "It is impossible to conceive of representatives of two civilized
> countries solemnly entering into a treaty of extradition and therein
> providing that a criminal surrendered according to demand for a
> crime that he has committed if subsequent to his surrender he is

equally guilty of murder or treason or other crime, is, nevertheless, to have the right granted to him to return unmolested to the country which surrendered him. We can imagine no country, by treaty, as desirous of exacting such a condition of surrender or any country as willing to accept it."

On June 5 Collins applied to Governor Gillett for a pardon, which was denied, and on June 17 he was removed to San Quentin Prison, where he was immediately put to work in the jute mill.

SYNOPSIS OF THE SAN FRANCISCO POLICE AND MUNICIPAL RECORDS OF THE GREATEST CATASTROPHE IN AMERICAN HISTORY.— THE ADOPTION AND RIGID ENFORCEMENT OF THE "LAW OF NECESSITY" BY THE POLICE AND SOLDIERS.— HOW A FAMINE WAS PREVENTED PREVIOUS TO THE ARRIVAL OF PROVISIONS FROM OUTSIDE CITIES.— THE KILLING OF HERBERT TILDEN, FRANK RIORDAN AND JOSEPH MEYER, AND THE TRIAL OF ERNEST DENIKE FOR KILLING AN UNKNOWN MAN.— THE ACCIDENTAL DEATH OF FIRE CHIEF SULLIVAN, AND THE TRAGIC END OF OFFICER MAX FENNER WHILE TRYING TO

SAVE A WOMAN.— NOVEL AND HEROIC METHODS EMPLOYED TO SAVE THE POLICE RECORDS FROM THE CONFLAGRATION.

As this great disaster has been the theme of numerous able historians, the main events will be but briefly dealt with, and we will then pass to the events known only to those who for three days and nights battled "amid the crash and roar of the burning city," constantly risking their lives to rescue others and to procure provisions from burning stores in order to prevent a famine.

The great earthquake occurred at 5:14 a. m., April 18, 1906. As the shock shattered the principal water mains, the fire department was practically helpless and as a result, the fires which were started by the overturning of stoves, crossing of electric wires, the liberation of chemicals by breakage of containers, etc., rapidly spread until a territory of 4.7 square miles in the heart of the city was burned, and a loss approximately estimated at $275,000,000 was incurred.

The City Hall was a mass of ruins after the earthquake, so Mayor E. E. Schmitz proceeded to the Hall of Justice, where his first orders were issued.

As the earthquake rendered the jails unsafe, he ordered that all petty offenders be released, while those charged with more serious offenses were sent to San Quentin State Prison.

Reports reached headquarters that thieves were burglarizing wrecked stores and deserted homes, and it was also learned that in the Mission district the body of a woman was found, the finger upon which she wore several valuable rings having been amputated, evidently by some thief.

The next report was to the effect that rowdies were breaking into saloons and helping themselves to liquor.

As the police were busy conveying the wounded to the temporary hospitals and had no time to arrest thieves even if caught in the act, and no place to incarcerate them if arrested, the Mayor issued his first order to Chief Dinan under the "law of necessity," which was substantially as follows:

> "Apr. 18, 1906. "As it has come to my notice that thieves are taking advantage of the present deplorable conditions and are plying their nefarious vocations among the ruins in our city, all peace officers are ordered to instantly kill anyone caught looting or committing any other serious crimes.

"E. E. Schmitz, Mayor."

About 8 a. m. Brigadier General Frederick Funston, U. S. A., called at the Hall of Justice, and after a conference with Mayor Schmitz, he placed his troops at the disposal of the Mayor. From that time until conditions became normal, the soldiers worked in conjunction with the police, either in preserving order or distributing provisions.

Shortly after the troops began patrolling the Streets the first looter was caught while he was making an attempt to burglarize Shreve's jewelry store at Post and Grant Avenue. He was turned over to a soldier who killed him and left his body to be consumed by the fire.

The Morgue, which was only constructed for ordinary occasions, was soon filled to overflowing with the bodies of victims of falling walls, etc., so the target range of the Central Police Station was turned into an emergency Morgue for the time being. But as the fire was rapidly approaching that building, the twenty-eight bodies placed there were temporarily buried in Portsmouth Square.

Of the 478 bodies finally recovered a great number were unrecognizable because of their mangled condition. It will never be known how many were killed, as the heat of the fire was so intense that the bodies were reduced to ashes in many instances, but judging from reports of persons missing and other circumstances, the number has been estimated at between 1,000 and 1,500.

On Third Street near Mission, a building collapsed in such a manner as to pinion an unknown man to the ground. His cries attracted people on the Street, who attempted to rescue him, but at that time the fire had reached the rear end of the building. Realizing that he would soon be burned to death he begged the bystanders to kill him. After some hesitancy, a large, middle-aged man stepped forward, and after a few words with the unfortunate prisoner, he whipped out a revolver and shot him through the head, killing him instantly. He then requested the witnesses to accompany him to the Hall of Justice, where the Mayor, who after hearing the circumstances and seeing the man's distressed appearance, commended him for his humane act.

Among those killed was Dennis Sullivan, the able Chief of the Fire Department, who was asleep in his room at the Engine House adjoining the California Hotel on Bush Street.

The engine house was a two-story structure and a massive brick chimney fell from the top of the eight-story hotel, crashed through the engine house roof and struck the Chief. He was removed to the Presidio Hospital, where he died on April 22.

The greatest damage done by the fire was in the Harbor Police district, commanded by Captain John Martin; the Southern district, commanded by Captain Henry Colby; the Central Police district, commanded by Captain Thomas Duke, and the Mission district, commanded by Captain M. O. Anderson.

As it seemed that the fire would sweep the entire city, about 200,000 panic stricken people took advantage of the free transportation furnished by President Harriman of the Southern Pacific Railroad and left the city. Another hundred thousand, who lost their homes, camped in the public parks and graveyards, many gladly taking advantage of the shelter afforded by the vaults for the dead, especially during the rainstorm beginning on April 23. Because of this storm the police took possession of all vacant buildings and placed as many families in each as the building could comfortably hold. It is estimated that about 2,000 families were provided for in this manner.

On the morning of the earthquake it became apparent that steps must be taken to prevent a famine. Police officers were therefore detailed to seize all suitable conveyances and remove the contents of all grocery stores which were in danger of being burned. This work was kept up for three days and nights, and as a result the contents of 390 grocery stores were delivered to the refugees.

On April 19 it was learned that several large ships, which had been heavily loaded with provisions previous to the disaster, were about to leave for foreign ports. To prevent this a police guard was placed on board the vessels, and as an extra precaution Lieutenant Frederick Green was instructed to procure the tug "*Sea Rover.*" With a squad of eight officers on board this vessel, the exit from the harbor was blockaded from April 19 to 24 inclusive. By this time provisions were arriving by the trainload and the danger of a famine had passed.

For many weeks after the earthquake all saloons in the unburned district were kept closed by order of the Mayor. In some instances a disposition was shown to ignore this order, and the result was that every ounce of liquor in the establishment was turned into the sewer.

When it became apparent that the Hall of Justice would be destroyed by fire, all valuable police records were removed to Portsmouth Square and left in charge of a detail of officers, consisting of Detectives Charles Taylor, George McMahon and others. These officers were provided with provisions but no water was obtainable. The fire rapidly surrounded the square and the officers became prisoners. The heat was terrific and the cinders, which were falling like hail, were constantly igniting the canvas spread over the records. As there was a saloon across the Street which had not at that time caught fire, a raid was made on the place, and for the next twenty-four hours bottled beer was used to keep the canvas from igniting, and thus the records were saved.

Several insane patients were confined in the Receiving Hospital in the City Hall building on the morning of the earthquake, and when the building began to rock and the walls began to fall, their condition can be better imagined than described. Officer Frank Parquette made his way through the wreckage to their rescue, and by the use of much tact succeeded in getting them into the Mechanics' Pavilion, which was utilized as a general hospital until the fire drew near.

Patrolman Max Fenner, known as the Hercules of the Police Department, was standing opposite the Essex Lodging House, a seven-story brick building on Mason near Ellis Street, when the earthquake occurred. He observed that the front wall of the building was tottering and at the same time he saw a woman run out of the building onto the sidewalk. He tried to warn her of her danger, but as she did not move he rushed over toward her. Just then the whole front of the building fell out, and while the woman ran inside the doorway and was unharmed, Fenner was instantly killed and his mangled body was buried in Portsmouth Square until the fire subsided.

As has been previously stated, no water was available for fire-fighting purposes, so dynamiting squads were operating near the fire line under the supervision of the army and police officials. By the use of this explosive, great structures were leveled to the ground for the purpose of checking the fire. Captain of Police Henry Gleeson and Lieutenant Charles C. Pulis, U. S. A., were in command of a detail on Sixth Street. They had placed a heavy charge in a building located on Sixth Street near Market and lit the fuse. This burned much more rapidly than expected, and before the officers could escape the explosion occurred and they were blown out into the Street, where considerable wreckage from the building fell upon them. Both men were rendered unconscious. They were removed to the temporary hospital at the Mechanics Pavilion, thence to the Presidio Hospital, where they eventually recovered.

During the height of the conflagration. Officer Edward Leonard, accompanied Deputy L. K. Jones into the City Tax Collector's office in the ruins of the City Hall, and records were saved which enabled Tax Collector J. F. Nichols to collect over $1,000,000 in taxes.

A volume would be required to record the many heroic deeds performed by the firemen and police during those three eventful days and nights. And it must be remembered that the majority of them labored with little nourishment and no sleep, and with the knowledge that their homes were destroyed and the fate of their families unknown. Officer James Connolly had concluded that his entire family had been killed, but a week later he located them in Vallejo, Cal.

On the evening of April 19, Officer T. Flood was about to enter his home at 1722 Hyde Street with the intention of saving some articles from the fire which was fast approaching. The officer's uniform was burned and he was in civilian clothes. Just as he was about to go up his front stairs, two men came out of the front door. Flood demanded that the strangers state what business they had there, but the only answer he received was a blow on the jaw which knocked him down. Flood's assailant then kicked him on the side of the head, splitting his ear. The officer drew his revolver and killed him but the other man escaped. The body was taken to Portsmouth Square for temporary burial, but the dead man's identity was never learned.

As there were only a very few pipes in the city from which water could be obtained for many days after the fire, it was distributed for cooking purposes by means of the Street sprinkling wagons.

For several days after the earthquake the city was in absolute darkness at night time, as no lights were permitted in houses; but on April 22 Mayor Schmitz issued the following order:

> "Lights are permitted in houses between sunset and 10 p. m. only, unless sentinels are convinced that some latitude should be allowed in case of sickness.

> "As all chimneys were more or less injured by the earthquake, no fires will be permitted in houses in grates, stoves or fireplaces unless the occupants hold a certificate issued by an authorized chimney inspector. Said certificate to be posted in a conspicuous place in front of the building.

> "The importance of this provision is emphasized by the fact that no effective means are at hand for stopping fires.

> "Our greatest danger in the immediate future may be expected from unavoidable unsanitary conditions and every person is cautioned that to violate in the slightest degree the instructions from the officers will be a crime that cannot be adequately punished.

> "All persons, except suspicious characters, will be permitted to pass sentinels without interruption.

> "E. E. Schmitz, Mayor."

The order prohibiting persons from building fires in houses resulted in all kitchen stoves being moved into the Street, where cooking was done for many weeks.

After the fire the Streets in the burned district were covered with debris, and instructions were issued to force all idle and dissolute men to assist in clearing the Streets.

On April 26, Major-General Greely, U. S. A., General Koster, of the National Guard, and Mayor Schmitz entered into an agreement to the effect that the regular soldiers should police one-third of the city, the National Guard one-third and the regular police one-third. This continued for some weeks until the police took complete control. The regular army also had charge of the distribution of all food and clothing shipped to San Francisco for relief purposes.

In addition to the police service already mentioned, several men organized what was known as a "Citizens' patrol" of watchmen, and they were armed with rifles and pistols. On May 26 the Mayor ordered the patrol to disband.

The Unfortunate Killing of Herbert Tilden by

"Volunteer Police."

After the great catastrophe, one of the first citizens to volunteer his services to the Red Cross Society was Mr. Herbert Tilden, a prominent merchant and a man of great popularity because of his kindly disposition. He worked night and day with his large automobile, carrying invalids to places of shelter from the storm then raging.

On the evening of April 22 he tore himself away from this work for the purpose of visiting his own family in the neighborhood of San Mateo, a few miles from San Francisco. He used his automobile for this purpose, and was accompanied by Acting Lieutenant Seamans of the Signal Corps.

After leaving his family he and Seamans returned to San Francisco, reaching Twenty-fourth and Guerrero Streets about midnight. A large Red Cross flag was flying from the machine at the time, and Tilden was acting as his own chauffeur. At this point some men in civilians' clothes called "halt," but as the machine drew nearer and they observed the flag it was permitted to pass. At Twenty-second Street three other men called out "halt," but Tilden, believing that they would see his flag as he drew nearer, paid no attention to the command and passed on. Someone on the corner then began firing a revolver and Seamans responded, emptying his revolver.

While Seamans was firing, Tilden 'fell forward, mortally wounded, and Seamans was also wounded. The machine was stopped and the men on the corner hurried up to it and then learned the result of the shooting.

Three of these men were arrested and charged with murder. Their names were Edward Boynton, Vance Malcolm and G. W. Simmons. It was shown that they were members of the so-called "Citizens' Police," an organization formed for the purpose of assisting the police, but having no authority as peace officers. Their preliminary examination was held before Judge Shortall, who on May 24 held them to answer before the Superior Court.

On September 20 the trials of Boynton and Simmons began before Superior Judge Cook. Mayor E. E. Schmitz testified that he issued an order on April 18 for all guardians of the peace to kill thieves or persons committing any serious crime.

Boynton testified that he had been detailed at Twenty-second and Guerrero Streets, and that he had received orders to halt all persons and ascertain the nature of their business. He also stated that he was under the impression that martial law had been declared. He testified further as follows:

"At about midnight two men came along on foot, and upon halting them I learned that they were fellow guards named Malcolm and Simmons. At that instant I observed an automobile coming down Guerrero Street at a high rate of speed, and I also noticed that the driver ignored the command to halt given by my fellow guards two blocks away. Believing that the machine had been stolen I cried 'halt,' but as the chauffeur only increased his speed, I fired a shot in the air as they passed. A man in the machine began firing, so in self-defense I fired directly toward the machine, emptying my revolver. Simmons also fired one shot from his rifle."

Judge Cook's instructions to the jury were in part as follows:

"This is in many respects an extraordinary case, arising under extraordinary conditions.

"I charge you as a matter of law that at the time in question, martial law did not prevail. The State law was supreme and mere proclamations could not make laws.

"No soldier or police had any right to stop citizens without legal cause, and ignorance of the law is no excuse.

"But the Penal Code expressly excepts from among persons capable of committing crime, those who commit an act or omission under a mistake of fact that disproves criminal intent.

"It is a matter of history that the entire community believed that martial law prevailed during the great fire.

"Therefore, if the defendants honestly believed and the circumstances were such as to lead them to believe that they were acting under martial law, and the evidence proves that that mistake removes any criminal intent, then the defendants were incapable of committing this alleged crime.

"The question to be decided is: Did the defendants honestly believe at the time of the firing of the shots that the automobile was stolen and that they were preventing the further commission of a felony? If so they were justified under the law."

After a few moments' deliberation the jury returned a verdict of not guilty, and on motion of the District Attorney, the charge against Malcolm was also dismissed.

The Killing of Frank Riordan by L. Betchel, N. G. C.

On the evening of April 20, Randolph Merriwether, a member of the National Guard of California, was stationed at Cedar Avenue and Post Street, when Frank Riordan, a veteran of the Philippine war, approached him and is alleged to have referred to Merriwether as a "tin soldier." This resulted in a fight, during which Lawrence Betchel, of the National Guard, appeared upon the scene and advanced toward Riordan with drawn bayonet. The latter grasped the rifle, whereupon Betchel fired, killing Riordan almost instantly.

Betchel claimed that the act was in self-defense and that he was justified in approaching Riordan with a drawn bayonet, as the latter was in the act of disarming a soldier on duty.

On June 12, Betchel was held to answer and the case was set for trial before Judge Cook on December 4, but in view of the instructions to the jury in the Tilden case, the District Attorney moved that the case be dismissed, and it was so ordered by the Court.

———————

The Killing of Joseph Meyers, Superintendent of the Children's Playgrounds, by Corporal Jacob Steinman, of the National Guard.

On the night of April 19, Columbia Square, located at Eighth and Harrison Streets, was filled with refugees who were surrounded by the great fire, which spread from one to two miles in all directions. A detachment of National Guardsmen was assigned to preserve the peace in the square, and in this detachment was a Corporal named Jacob Steinman.

About 9 p. m., on this date, Steinman, accompanied by one Bush, approached Joseph Meyers, the Superintendent of the Children's Playgrounds, which was located in the vicinity. At the time, Meyers was conversing with a Miss Kessel, who gave the following version of what transpired:

> *"Bush and Meyers became engaged in an altercation and finally Meyers called to Steinman, who was standing a few feet away, and said, 'You know me,' to which Steinman replied, 'No, I don't know you and don't want to.'*

> *"Meyers and Bush then grappled with each other. At that instant I attempted to lead Meyers away, but Steinman pulled out a revolver and shot Meyers, killing him almost instantly."*

Steinman was arrested on May 2 and his preliminary examination was held before Superior Judge Graham, who sat as a committing magistrate. The defendant was held to answer on May 15.

On September 4 his trial began before Judge Lawlor, Hiram Johnson appearing for the defendant, and S. Shortridge appearing as special prosecutor.

Steinman produced witnesses who swore that Meyers assumed the attitude of a man who was about to draw a pistol when Steinman shot him. It was also claimed that immediately after the shooting the defendant exclaimed: "Well, this is pretty rough work, but it is an act of martial law."

In charging the jury Judge Lawlor said in part:

"Mayor Schmitz's proclamation was void and illegal and therefore cannot legally justify the defendant in the commission of the act upon which the charge before the court is based.

"In stating the law there is no disposition to criticize the Mayor in meeting the extraordinary conditions prevailing at the time and which involved the highest interests of the community."

On September 13 the cause was finally submitted to the jury, and after deliberating fifty minutes a verdict of not guilty was returned.

The Killing of an Unknown Man by Captain Ernest Denicke.

Ernest Denicke came from a highly respected family, his father being Colonel E. Denicke, a prominent capitalist. Young Denicke was a graduate of the State University and a retired captain of the National Guard. He was a civil engineer by profession. Immediately after the earthquake he donned a khaki uniform of Captain's rank and stationed himself with the soldiers detailed at the water front near East and Lombard Streets.

On the afternoon of April 20 Horace Hudson, of the San Francisco Chronicle, and Andrew Sbarboro, the well-known capitalist, saw some soldiers in an intoxicated condition at Battery and East Streets. They immediately proceeded to the officers' headquarters at East and Lombard Streets and reported their observations to Ernest Denicke, who started to return with them to East and Battery Streets.

When the trio neared this point, according to the statements of Sbarboro and Hudson, they observed a man carrying some fowls.

Denicke evidently suspected that they were stolen, and he ordered a sailor who was acting as a sentinel to instruct the man to drop the fowls and get out and fight the fire.

The man dropped the fowls and started away, when Denicke is alleged to have ordered the sailor to prod him with a bayonet. The sailor attempted to do so, but the stranger grappled with him, and after disarming the sailor it is claimed he started toward the bay with the rifle.

At that instant Denicke fired several shots at the man, who fell mortally wounded. The stranger died shortly afterward, and that night Lieutenant Charles Herring, U. S. A., weighted the body with iron and had it thrown into the bay. It was afterward claimed that the fowls were given to this man at the distribution car.

On May 24 Denicke was arrested, and he made a statement substantially as follows:

"I saw the man with the chickens, and believing he had stolen them I ordered the sentry to take them from him, and after he did so the man robbed him of his rifle and turned toward me. I believed that he was about to shoot at me, and as a matter of self-defense I shot him.

"At the time I was under the impression that martial law prevailed, and I had in mind the order to kill all persons caught stealing."

As the body of the unknown was never recovered, Denicke was charged with the murder of John Doe.

Ex-Governor James Budd and Abraham Ruef were engaged by the defense and the preliminary examination began before Police Judge Shortall on May 27.

After hearing the evidence the Judge dismissed the charge against the defendant. As there was a belief in some quarters that Denicke should be punished, he was again arrested, and Superior Judge Lawlor sat as a committing magistrate.

After hearing the evidence the Judge held the defendant to answer before the Superior Court. The trial took place before a jury in Judge Cook's court, and the defendant was found not guilty, on November 28, 1906.

At the time these trials were being conducted the great fire had made the Hall of Justice but a memory of the past, so the sessions of the different courts were held in basements of private buildings, in halls and churches throughout the city.

Judge Cook's court was first held in the basement of Calvary Church, at Washington and Fillmore Streets, and later at the Salvation Army Hall, at Fillmore and Post Streets, where Seimsen and Dabner, the gas-pipe thugs, received their death sentence.

Judge Lawlor's court was held in the magnificent Jewish Synagogue, at California and Webster Streets, where John Byrne, the murderer of Police Officer George O'Connoll, was sentenced to be hanged.

————————

DABNER AND SEIMSEN, THE "GAS-PIPE" MURDERERS.

Never since the days of the famous Vigilance Committee in 1852-56 were the citizens of San Francisco more terror-stricken by the criminal element than during the five months following the great earthquake and fire in April, 1906.

Because of the vast amount of taxable property destroyed it was decided that all branches of the municipal government must economize, and the police force was temporarily reduced about one-fifth by forcing members to take a leave of absence. The criminal element was quick to take advantage of the situation, and the result was that a series of most atrocious crimes were committed.

Some of our most prominent citizens were beaten and robbed on the Streets, and finally the desperadoes became more bloodthirsty and murdered merchants and bankers in their places of business in broad daylight.

On the night of July 10, 1906, Coroner Leland was assaulted and robbed by two thugs at the corner of Laguna and Vallejo Streets.

Owing to a remarkable chain of circumstantial evidence an ex-convict named James Dowdall was arrested for this crime, partially identified by Dr. Leland, and convicted. He was sentenced to fifty years' imprisonment.

Johannes Pfitzner was the son of Adolph Pfitzner, the Chief Architect to Emperor William of Germany. The son left home to make his own way in the world, and immediately after the big fire opened a small shoe store at 964 McAllister Street.

On the afternoon of August 20, 1906, he was found on the floor of his store in a dying condition, his head having been crushed in by a window weight, which was found near the body. About $140 and his gold watch was missing. It was evident that he was in the act of trying a pair of No. 8 shoes on some man when the fatal blow was struck.

At 3:10 p. m. on September 14, 1906, a little boy named Robert Anderson and his sister, Thelma, entered the clothing store conducted by William Friede, at 1386 Market Street.

Seeing no one in the front part of the store the children went to the rear, which was Friede's workshop and where customers tried on clothing. Here they found Friede lying in a pool of blood, his head being battered to a pulp. His tape measure lay beside him, his pockets were turned inside out; his watch, containing a picture of his family, was missing, and the money drawer was empty. The wounded man died the next day without having recovered consciousness.

There was no evidence to show what instrument was used in committing this assault. On the following day Friede's watch was found on Market Street, near Dolores.

At 12:30 p. m., October 3, 1906, a Japanese named Yazo Kitashima entered the Japanese bank, known as the "Kimmon Ginko," located at 1588 O'Farrell Street, but failing to receive any response to his calls he proceeded to President M. Munekato's office in the rear. Here he found the President and A. Sasaki, a clerk, lying on the floor, their heads having been beaten almost to a pulp.

Nearby was a piece of one and one-quarter inch gas-pipe about fourteen inches in length and wrapped in a piece of ordinary wrapping paper. It was covered with blood and evidently was the weapon used in committing the assault.

After rendering the bank attaches helpless, the assailants took all the money in sight, about $2,800. Munakato died two hours after the assault, but Sasaki, after months of suffering, finally recovered, but his mind always remained a blank regarding the circumstances leading up to the assault.

Governor Pardee took cognizance of the unprecedented number of atrocious crimes being committed in San Francisco, and on October 12, 1906, he offered a reward of $1,500 for the arrest and conviction of the murderers of Pfitzner, Friede and Munakato.

On Saturday evening, November 3, 1906, three men entered the jewelry store conducted by Henry Behrend, at 1323 Steiner Street, and after making a pretense at purchasing jewelry assaulted him. One man took about $75 from the till, another held Behrend, while the third rained blows on his head with an iron bar.

Behrend resisted and dodged the blows. This caused the man who was holding him to place one hand on the side of his head to hold it still so that the third man's blows would be effective. The next blow struck one of the fingers of the man who was holding Behrend and almost cut it off. The robbers became alarmed and fled, with the exception of the man who was wielding the iron.

Notwithstanding the fact that Behrend's face and head were covered with his own blood, he bravely held on to this man until Officers John T. Conlon, William Lambert, James Welch and W. F. Brown, a fireman, appeared and took the assailant into custody. The cry that one of the "gas-pipe" men had been captured spread like wildfire, and the great crowd which assembled in front of the jewelry store were continually uttering cries of "Lynch him," and considerable difficulty was experienced in dispersing the indignant citizens. The robber was taken before Chief Dinan and Captain of Detectives Duke. He at first refused to discuss his identity, but upon being told that he would be shown at midnight to every policeman in the city for identification he admitted that his name was Louis Dabner and that he resided at 1786 Union Street. He also admitted that his roommate was John Seimsen, whose father was at one time a very wealthy citizen in Honolulu. Dabner claimed that Seimsen had nothing to do with the assault just committed. Upon making an investigation it was learned that the description of Seimsen tallied with that given by Behrend of the man who held him, and Behrend furthermore stated that the man who held him had a wounded finger.

Some days previous, Seimsen, who had posed as the heir to a vast estate in Honolulu, secretly married Miss Hulda Von Hoffen, whose father conducted a jewelry store on Union Street near Buchanan. Seimsen had an appointment that evening with his wife, who was still living at her father's home.

Subsequent developments proved that Seimsen was actually the assailant whom Behrend described as having a wounded finger. As it was necessary for Seimsen to explain this injury to his wife, he stated that he had been "held up" and that because his diamond ring could not be readily removed the highwayman attempted to cut his finger off.

His wife telephoned the details of the alleged robbery to her father, against the wishes of Seimsen. Shortly after receiving the message Mr. Von Hoffen met Chief Dinan and Captain Duke, who were en route to Dabner and Seimsen's room, and informed them of his daughter's message.

The officers pretended that they had heard all about the "robbery" of Mr. Seimsen, and stated that they had located the robbers and were looking for Mr. Seimsen to identify them. Mr. Von Hoffen was highly elated, and bade them wait at his door, as his daughter had telephoned that they were on the way home. Presently Seimsen arrived with his wife, and the officers said: "Well, Mr. Seimsen, we have the men who robbed you and we want you to accompany us to the station to identify them." Seimsen stated that he would call the next day. As he moved his hand toward his hip pocket the officers closed upon him and removed a big pistol from his possession. He then said: "Well, I guess it's all up," and confessed to participating in the robbery that night, but denied having taken part in any other crime. He was at once identified by Chief Dinan as an ex-convict who had served four years for stealing some instruments from a Hawaiian musician.

Within a few days the police gathered an abundance of evidence against the pair, even ascertaining where the $2,800 taken from the Japanese bank was spent. Dabner's father was a highly respected citizen of Petaluma, Cal., and on November 6, 1906, in company with Captain of Detectives Duke and Detective Wren, he visited his son. At this time he demanded proof that his son had committed murder, and the evidence was laid before him. Being convinced of his own son's guilt he begged him to tell the truth. The boy still professed to be innocent, but when additional evidence was disclosed, he finally weakened and made the following remarkable confession:

"On the night of July 10, Seimsen and I held up Coroner Leland at the corner of Vallejo and Laguna Streets. I know it was Dr. Leland because we got papers and checks from his person giving his name. We sent the check, gunmetal watch, chain and Masonic emblem back to him in a pasteboard box, by mail. We got the pasteboard box at the candy store at the corner of Union and Octavia Streets. I enclosed a note to Dr. Leland in my own handwriting, and wrote the address on the box.

"Seimsen said to Leland: 'Throw up your hands,' and pointed a gun at him. Leland attempted to wrestle, and he got hold of the gun. Seimsen held the gun with one hand and used the other to go through him, and I went through him on the other side. We got over a hundred dollars. I am almost sure we took either a five or a one dollar greenback. Seimsen ordered him to walk down the Street. Seimsen and I ran across the lot where the refugees built their fires.

"We jumped the fence and went through a private yard and out the front way. We saw a fellow stand and look at us, but we kept running. We left two old black overcoats, three-quarter size, two slouch hats and a few of Leland's keys in a chicken house back of an empty house on Filbert or Greenwich Street, between Buchanan and Laguna. We stayed in the chicken house about half an hour and then went home.

"We were in court as spectators when James Dowdall was convicted *for this crime and also when he was sentenced to life imprisonment.*

"On the night of August 18, myself, Seimsen and Harry Sutton, an ex-convict, went out on Pacific Avenue and Buchanan Street. We saw a tall, stout man, with sandy mustache, coming east on Pacific Avenue. He had some parcels in his hand. Seimsen jumped out and told him to throw up his hands. Harry Sutton went through one side of him and I went through the other side. Seimsen hit him with a black jack, but the lead flew off and it did not hurt him. We got $5 from him. We each took $1, and drank up the remainder. This man, whom we learned through the papers was J. H. Dockweiler, a civil engineer, ran to a house, rang the bell and yelled 'Police.'

"One Saturday night in the month of May, Seimsen and I went into E. E. Gillon's hardware store, on Point Lobos Avenue, on the north side. I pretended to want to purchase a knife. He showed me one and I threw out $20, and he threw back the change. Seimsen then threw the gun up at him and ordered him to throw up his hands and throw up the money and face about. I took $38 of his money. Seimsen then ordered him to the back part of the store. Seimsen watched him awhile and we then walked away. We laid low for a while and then took the car and went home.

"On the day of the Pfitzner murder, Seimsen and I looked in the showcase of the store and went down the Street and then came back to the store. Seimsen tried on a pair of shoes the first time, but complained that they were too dear, and we went out. We walked around the block and came back. We both went in the store and I tried on a pair. When he was trying on my shoes Seimsen hit Pfitzner on the head with a window weight and he fell to the floor. I then put on my own shoes and held the door at the same time, while Seimsen went through Pfitzner. Seimsen got about $100, which we divided at our home on Union Street. We threw Pfitzner's watch in the water at the foot of Fillmore Street.

"Seimsen and I passed Friede's place on Market Street the day of the murder. At this time there was a 'run' on the Hibernia Bank, so we watched the depositors leaving, intending to follow up any one who looked to be worth the while, but not seeing anything that looked 'good' we passed back by Friede's. We were looking into the store, and Seimsen said he thought this was an easy place. We went in and Seimsen told me to try on a suit. Friede was measuring me for a pair of pants when Seimsen hit him on the head and knocked him unconscious with a gas-pipe that I picked up. Seimsen then went through his pockets and I went through the till. I took all the money I found in the till, which I divided with Seimsen at our home on Union Street, where we went immediately after the assault.

"Immediately after we killed Friede in the back part of his store a customer came in the front part, and fearing that he would come to the rear and discover our deed, I pulled the shop tag off the new coat which I then had on, took off my hat, and pretending to be a clerk, walked out behind the counter and asked him what he wanted. He said he wanted some 'canvas for lining.' I informed him that I was a new clerk and was not familiar with the stock, and asked him to please call later, which he agreed to.

"Friede's money was evidently in an old-fashioned money drawer which slid under the counter and could only be opened by someone having a knowledge of the combination under the drawer which were manipulated with the fingers.

"I realized that if I pressed the wrong keys and attempted to open the drawer the bell would ring, which would probably be heard in the next store, as it was only a temporary building with thin board partitions, and we were forced to operate very quietly. I reasoned that Friede, being familiar with the combination and using it many times a day would press only on the proper key, and that the key would show the effects of constant usage, whereas the others would probably be dusty. I therefore lit a match and getting under the counter it was apparent at a glance which keys of the combination had been used, so I pressed them and the drawer containing the money flew open,

"On the morning of the Japanese bank robbery, Seimsen and I left home together. We had planned the day before to rob the Japanese bank on the following day at noon. Seimsen went into the bank on the day previous to the murder. When he came out he told me that he had represented himself to be a man of business and that he intended to deposit money there.

"On the day of the robbery we hung around the bank for a while, and after we saw the clerks go away to lunch we went in. Seimsen stepped in front and told the Japanese in the front part that he wanted to see the manager. Then Seimsen and I went back to the manager's office. Seimsen saw the manager was writing, and as the other Jap was not looking, he (Seimsen) hit the manager over the head with a gas-pipe which I got at Convey's store on Union Street, near our house, and which I wrapped in a piece of paper I got in the same store. I got this pipe the night before the assault.

"After Seimsen knocked the manager out I called the other Jap back to the rear office, according to our original plan. When he came back, Seimsen hit him over the head several times and he fell.

"The Jap who was called from the front started to get up, and I hit *him myself with the pipe on the head, and he fell again. Seimsen then went through the till and we got about $2,800, partly in silver and partly in gold, which we put in a satchel. Not being able to find anything else but checks we left.*

"We then went to Seimsen's horse and buggy, which we left standing on Webster Street, between O'Farrell and Geary, and drove to Van Ness Avenue, where we met Seimsen's wife.

"We separated, as he said he was going to take his wife out for a drive. I then took one of the Von Hoffen children in my buggy out to the Presidio, and I brought her home in about two hours.

"During the time I had the Von Hoifen child out riding and until 7 o'clock that night I left the satchel containing the money in a sack of oats where we kept our rig. About 7 p. m. I came and got the satchel containing the money and took it to the room occupied by myself and Seimsen. We counted it that evening and left it in our closet. On this evening I took the horse and rig to Conlan's stable, on Greenwich Street, near Laguna, and stabled it there. It was a sorrel horse with a white face and legs, and the buggy is now at Worst's paint store.

"Seimsen and I spent $246 of the silver which we took from the Japanese bank at Macey's Jewelry Company, 1700 Fillmore Street. We also spent about $200 in silver at Paul Garen's jewelry store, 1558 Fillmore Street. We spent $165 at the Hub clothing store, on Fillmore Street. At Heller's, on Van Ness Avenue, Seimsen spent $95 and I spent $50. Seimsen also spent $75 at Alexandra's, on Van Ness Avenue, near Sutter Street. Seimsen spent $150 at Alexandra's for a locket, watch and diamond engagement ring for his wife. All of the money above mentioned was taken from the Japanese bank.

"This and all statements and confessions made by me this date (November 6, 1906), to Captain Duke, in the presence of my father, are free and voluntary and without threats or promise of reward.

"(Signed), LOUIS DABNER."

Seimsen, on being confronted by Dabner after the confession, at first denied that the statements were true, but he finally weakened and admitted that it was the truth and signed his name to it. Seimsen then explained how Friede's watch was found at Market and Dolores Streets.

He stated that Dabner and he boarded a Market Street car

immediately after the assault and stood on the rear end. When they reached Dolores Street he noticed a watch hanging to a button on his vest. He opened it, and seeing that it contained a picture of a group consisting of his latest victim, a lady and baby, he concluded that the ring of the watch became caught on the button in some inexplicable manner while searching the body. He then threw it into the Street.

Detective Gus Harper was immediately detailed to substantiate the confession in relation to the robbery of Dr. Leland, and as it was proved beyond all doubt that the confession was true, the matter was laid before Governor Pardee, who granted a pardon to Dowdall.

Seimsen and Dabner were tried for the murder of Munakato. Dabner pleaded guilty. Seimsen pleaded not guilty, but the jury lost no time in finding him guilty, as every statement in the confession was proved to be true. Both were sentenced to be hanged, but an appeal was taken to the Supreme Court, which handed down a decision on April 27, 1908, in which the rulings of the lower court were affirmed.

On July 31, 1908, both men were hanged from the same scaffold at San Quentin. Dabner's father died shortly before the execution, and Pfitzner's father died soon after hearing of his son's tragic death.

It was learned that the third man in the Behrend robbery was Harry Kearney from Sacramento, who is now in prison in Washington for a similar offense.

Dowdall has since been returned to State prison for committing a burglary.

———————

PART II.

CELEBRATED CASES ON PACIFIC COAST.

JOAQUIN "MURIETA," TIBURCIO VASQUEZ AND NUMEROUS OTHER MEXICAN BANDITS WHO OPERATED IN CALIFORNIA.

(From "Ridge's History of Murieta" and "Sawyer's History of Vasquez.")

Joaquin "Murieta," the first and most notorious of the Mexican bandits who operated in California after the close of the Mexican war, was born in the Province of Sonora in 1830. His parents were highly respected and Joaquin, who was very light complexioned for a Mexican, grew up to be an athletic and handsome young man. He was studious, of a mild disposition and had friends galore. "Murieta's" true name was Carrillo.*

* Cincinnatus Heine Miller, generally known as "Joaquin Miller, the poet of the Sierras," is said to have taken the sobriquet "Joaquin" because of his admiration for the daring of this bandit.

At the conclusion of his poem, "Joaquin Murieta," Miller has written the following note:

> "After the cruel conquest of California from Mexico, we poured in upon the simple and hospitable people from all parts of the United States. Strangers in language and religion, let it be honestly admitted, we were often guilty of gross wrong to the conquered Californians. Out of this wrong suddenly sprang Joaquin Murieta, a mere boy, and yet one of the boldest men in history. But he soon degenerated into a robber and a large reward was offered for his head. The splendid daring and unhappy death of this remarkable youth appeal strongly to me; and, bandit as he was, I am bound to say I have a great respect for his memory."

A very pretty sixteen-year-old Mexican girl named Rosita Feliz, also known as Mariana Higuera, lived with her parents near Murieta's home, and the two young folks became lovers. The girl's father became convinced that the relationship between his daughter and the handsome young Murieta was not what it should be. A violent quarrel ensued which resulted in

Murieta and his pretty sweetheart eloping to California in the spring of 1850. At this time Murieta was 19 years of age and Rosita was 17. They proceeded to the mines in Stanislaus County, where Murieta secured work and became a general favorite among his associates.

There was a gang of American ruffians in this camp who pretended to believe that because the Mexicans had been defeated in the war just concluded with the United States, that they had no right to seek employment in American enterprises. They went in a body to Murieta's home and informed him that "no damned Mexican had a right to work in an American mine." Murieta protested against the conduct of this gang in his own home and they then bound and beat him and outraged Rosita in his presence.

Joaquin and Rosita then went to Calaveras County, where they settled on a small piece of land. They were just beginning to get along nicely when they were again visited by a band of men, calling themselves Americans, and informed that their presence was not needed. The couple having a lively recollection of their previous experience with "Americans," decided to move to Murphy's diggings in the same county, where Murieta again worked as a miner. This was in April, 1850. As he had some difficulty with his employer he soon left this position and became a gambler.

About this time his half-brother arrived from Mexico and rented a piece of land near where Joaquin was living. One day the latter visited his half-brother, who loaned him a horse on which to ride back to town. It transpired that this horse had been stolen and then sold to Murieta's half-brother. While riding to town, Joaquin met the rightful owner, who recognized his horse and accused the young Mexican of having stolen it.

Joaquin protested his innocence, but a crowd gathered and it was decided to lynch him then and there. He finally persuaded them to accompany him back to his half-brother, whom he felt confident would be able to give a satisfactory explanation as to how he gained possession of the animal. The half-brother stated that he purchased the horse from a man, but being a stranger in the country he could not give his name. The crowd considered this sufficient evidence to justify them in lynching the man, and after doing so they stripped Murieta and horsewhipped him until his body was covered with blood.

After they departed Joaquin cut down his brother's body, and according to a statement made by Rosita years afterwards, this last outrage caused Murieta to kneel over the body of his murdered brother and with uplifted dagger he swore that he would devote the remainder of his life to slaughtering Americans, whom he regarded as the foremost enemies of his race.

Shortly after this, the terribly mutilated body of an American miner was found near Murphy's diggings, and it proved to be the body of one of the men who participated in the lynching of Joaquin's brother. Joaquin knowing that he would be suspected of this and numerous other murders which he contemplated committing, kept out of sight.

A few weeks later a doctor, who also had a hand in the lynching, was walking along the road one night when a bullet pierced his hat. After the doctor's experience the remainder of the lynching party became panic-stricken, but with the cunning of a fox and the patience of an ox, Murieta succeeded in killing all of those who remained in that part of the country — several having departed between two days.

A band of Mexican desperadoes was then organized, and they committed the most atrocious murders in connection with their robberies. This gang varied in numbers from twenty to fifty, but it was some time before the identity of any of its members was ascertained. Finally it was learned that Murieta, who was then in his twentieth year, was the leader, and Manuel Garcia, alias "Three-fingered Jack," probably the most fiendish cutthroat of all the Mexican bandits, was his lieutenant. Garcia lost one of his fingers while serving as a Mexican guerrilla during the war with Americans. Among the members of the gang were Reyes Feliz, a brother of Joaquin's sweetheart; Joaquin Valencia, who served under the famous Mexican guerrilla chief, Padre Jurata, and Pedro Gonzales. Many of the bandits were accompanied by their mistresses, who frequently wore men's clothing.

This band declared that they would never harm but always protect anyone who befriended them. They also gave warning that death would invariably be the penalty to those who betrayed them, and as they gave abundant evidence of their sincerity, many persons who trembled at the mention of Murieta's name, did all in their power to creep into his favor, and the result was that he had no difficulty in procuring provisions, ammunition and information regarding the movements of the authorities.

It would require a volume to relate the crimes of this band. Travelers were dragged from their horses, their throats cut and pockets rifled. Farm houses were entered and the inmates robbed and murdered and the houses burned.

In the fall of 1851 this gang operated in the country adjacent to Marysville, Cal., and as a result seven murders were committed in twelve days.

One day two men who were traveling along a road by the Feather River, near Honcut, looked ahead and saw four Mexicans dragging a man along the road at the end of a lariat which was around the victim's neck. The two men hastened back and notified the authorities, and a search resulted in the finding of the bodies of four men in the vicinity, all having rope marks around the necks.

Murieta's gang then changed the scene of their operations to the foot of Mt. Shasta; arriving in November, 1851. Here they resumed operations by stealing horses and murdering prospectors.

One day Reyes Feliz, of this gang, rode into the town of Hamilton. He was a handsome fellow, and when he met the voluptuous wife of a packer named Carmelita, she fell in love with him at first sight, and after he confided to her who he was, she agreed to accompany him to the camp of the bandits.

Residing near Hamilton was a hunter and trapper commonly known as "Pete." He was half Indian and half French, and had two pretty daughters aged 16 and 18 years respectively. One day two of Murieta's gang met the youngest daughter while she was out hunting and they bound her with a lariat with the intention of committing an assault upon her, but Murieta was attracted to the scene by the girl's cries and immediately ordered that she be released and permitted to go her way unharmed.

In the spring of 1852, Murieta's band stole 300 head of horses, which they drove from the mountains through the southern part of the State and disposed of them in the Province of Sonora. In a few weeks they returned to the State and made their headquarters at the Arroyo Cantoova, a tract of 8000 acres of rich pasture land lying between the Coast Range and Tulare Lake. The gang now consisted of seventy men.

On April 20, 1852, Murieta divided his band into three parties, and sent them in different directions to steal horses and cattle, while he and Rosita, disguised as a man, went to visit some Mexican friends at Mokelumne Hill, in Calaveras County. Murieta wore a disguise and people in the little town never dreamed that the notorious bandit was in their midst until an incident occurred in a saloon one evening.

Murieta was sitting in the barroom reading, when a man standing at the bar with a party of friends began telling what he would do to Murieta if he met him. The bandit's love for something sensational seemed to outweigh his discretion, and he jumped upon a chair, tore off his false mustache, and drawing two pistols, proclaimed his identity. When he saw the consternation he had brought about, he laughed and strode majestically from the place. That night he and Rosita departed for Arroyo Cantoova. Here they met Reyes Feliz, Rosita's brother, and his sweetheart, Carmelita, also disguised as a man.

They stole twenty horses from Ovis Timbers and drove them down into the country of the Tejon Indians. Timbers trailed them and informed Sapatorra, the Indian chief, of the presence of the Mexican horse thieves on his land, but the identity of the thieves was not known. For the purpose of seizing the horses the chief surrounded Murieta and his party, and being taken unawares, they were forced to surrender without a struggle.

Sapatorra then notified the Los Angeles authorities that he had captured some Mexican horse thieves, but the authorities little thinking that the notorious Murieta was in the party, sent word back to release them. The chief then relieved the entire party of all their clothing, and after whipping the men, turned them all loose.

The next day Feliz was attacked by a bear and almost killed. Carmelita stayed with him while Murieta and Rosita started out in search of food and clothing. Fortunately for them they met an American friend known as Mountain Jim, and after the American had a hearty laugh at their predicament, he took them into his cabin and set out to procure clothing, food and arms, not only for them but for the wounded Feliz and Carmelita, who were still in the woods. As soon as Murieta was clothed, he and Jim started to the rescue of Feliz and his sweetheart, and found them so weak from exposure and hunger that they had to carry them to the cabin on their horses.

After a short rest the party proceeded in the direction of San Gabriel Mission, where they met one of Murieta's gangs. From the numerous depredations recently committed by this gang they were well supplied with money and horses.

They rested in this neighborhood for two weeks, and one day Gonzales and another desperado known as Juan, of this gang, went into Los Angeles and became intoxicated. Gonzales was taken into custody by Deputy Sheriff Love but Juan escaped and returned to the camp to relate the fate of Gonzales. Murieta and several of his band hurriedly saddled up their horses and started for the place of detention. Love saw them approaching and divining their intentions, he shot Gonzales dead, mounted a horse and galloped away.

About this time Deputy Sheriff Wilson of Santa Barbara County was in Los Angeles, and did considerable boasting regarding what he would do to Murieta. The latter heard of this, but as he did not know Wilson, he disguised himself and accompanied by a member of his gang who did know him, he proceeded into Los Angeles to locate the deputy sheriff. When they entered the main Street, Wilson was standing among a group of men who were arguing, and Murieta rode up into the group, leaned over and whispered in Wilson's ear, and before the latter could reply or move, the bandit drew a revolver, shot him through the head and fled to his camp.

A few days after this occurrence Murieta and "Three-fingered Jack" found two Chinamen asleep on the roadside, and after robbing them and turning their pockets inside out, "Jack" cut their throats.

About this time Major-General Joshua H. Bean of the militia began to organize a large posse to exterminate this gang. Murieta and "Jack" heard of it and one night in July, 1852, they waylaid the General, and after dragging him from his horse, stabbed him to death. Immediately after this murder, Murieta collected his whole band and proceeded to Calaveras County, committing' numerous outrages en route.

In August, 1852, Murieta was in the town of Jackson, Amador County, where he was recognized by a man named Joe Lake, who knew the bandit when he was a miner. Lake promised Murieta that he would not reveal the latter's identity, but the bandit's back was scarcely turned before Lake went to the town of Hornitas and notified the authorities. The next day, Murieta, disguised with a beard, rode into Hornitas, and seeing Lake in front of a saloon, he rode up, tore of his disguise, and shot Lake dead. The next day the whole band, with the exception of Carmelita and Feliz, who was still in poor health from exposure and his experience with the bear, departed for the mountains.

Feliz and Carmelita then returned to the neighborhood of Los Angeles. One night they attended a fandango in Los Angeles and Feliz was arrested on the charge of having participated in the murder of General Bean. Although he did not take part in the crime he was hanged, and Carmelita wandered away into the country and shortly afterward died from grief.

Murieta soon became dissatisfied with the quiet life in the mountains and proceeded with his gang to San Luis Obispo. He had been there but a short time when a party of thirty-five Americans was organized for the purpose of capturing the outlaws. One of Murieta's numerous spies informed him of the time that this party would leave the Rancho Los Cozatos and he and his gang concealed themselves in the brush near the road and as the party passed they opened a deadly fire from ambush. About twenty men were killed on each side and the attacking posse retired. Murieta and several of his men who were wounded sought seclusion until they recuperated from their wounds.

On December 1, 1852, Murieta and all that was left of his gang started for Mariposa County. Near the Merced River they met a party consisting of four Frenchmen, six Germans and three Americans. These men were ordered to stop, but on showing resistance six were instantly killed and $15,000.00 in gold dust was taken from the party.

Immediately after this occurrence they met a Chinaman whom they robbed, and after scaring him nearly to death, permitted him to go his way. The next evening they arrived at the ferry of the Tuolumne River and found the ferryman asleep in bed. They rode up to the house, broke in the door and Murieta pointed a pistol at the ferryman's head and ordered him to hand over his money. The ferryman produced about $100.00 but begged the bandits not to take it, as it was all he had in the world and he was growing old and feeble. This plea touched the tender spot in Murieta's heart, for he returned the money and paid the regular fare for his men who were carried across the river.

Two days afterwards the gang was camped near Stockton and Murieta provided himself with a supply of new clothes. On the next Sunday Murieta donned his best clothes, rode into Stockton on a beautiful horse, and at once attracted attention because of his handsome appearance and his exhibition of horsemanship. Finally he saw a notice on a post which read:

"Five thousand dollars will be paid for Joaquin Murieta, dead or alive."

He laughed, dismounted and wrote underneath the notice: "I will pay ten thousand. Joaquin Murieta." He then rode away and those who had been observing him, went to see what he had written. Their astonishment on learning the identity of the dashing horseman can be better imagined than described.

This foolish act made it necessary for Murieta to again change the locality of his camp the next day. But before moving he ascertained that a schooner would go down the slough early on Monday morning and that there would be considerable gold dust aboard. Murieta and four of his men procured a skiff and remained concealed in the tules until the schooner was opposite them. They then went alongside and boarding the vessel, began firing at once. The two men who were managing the vessel were killed instantly, and two miners who were in the hold seized shotguns and came up on deck, and while they were both killed, they succeeded in killing two of Murieta's men. The bandit and his two remaining companions then robbed the vessel of $20,000.00 worth of gold dust, and after setting it on fire, returned to their camp. It was estimated that the gang then had about $50,000.00, with which they returned to Arroyo Cantoova, where they remained until December. At this time there were about ninety desperadoes in the gang, and about twenty-five women, nearly all of whom habitually wore men's attire.

On December 10, 1852, Murieta detailed twenty men under command of Guerra to operate in the country where they were located, and he proceeded to Calaveras County with seventy men, leaving all the women behind.

Three days after the departure of the chief, Guerra was killed by his mistress, Margarita, who immediately took another bandit of the party named Coneja as her mate.

Murieta and his forces reached Calaveras about Christmas. Here he again divided his forces, detailing twenty-five men under command of a bandit named Reis, a like number in charge of Vulvia, and he took the remaining twenty men to a mining camp located near the south fork of the Mokolumne River. Here he was recognized by a man named Jim Boyce, for whose bravery Murieta had great respect. He immediately left the place with his gang and a few days afterwards learned that Boyce had organized a posse of twenty-five men to hunt for Murieta. He at once set spies to work and, locating the posse, the bandits trailed them until they went into camp one night, and then swarmed down upon them when they were preparing to retire and killed twenty-two, Boyce and two others escaping.

After this Murieta's gangs were again divided into small parties of five and six men, and they killed nearly every person who crossed their paths. In the middle of February, 1853, Murieta and "Three-fingered Jack" met two Americans and a German who were en route from Murphy's diggings to San Francisco, and after relieving them of their gold dust, they murdered the three men and threw their bodies into an abandoned shaft. The same day they met six Chinamen, and after relieving them of their valuables, the fiends tied their queues together and killed them all by cutting their throats.

On February 19 a mass meeting was held in Jackson and it was resolved that a posse should be formed immediately under command of Undersheriff Charles A. Clark. The first day out they captured the bandit "Juan" and another member of the gang and hanged them to a tree.

On February 22, Captain Ellis and posse learned that Murieta and six men were at a place called Freeman's Camp, and when they arrived they found the bodies of three Chinese who had just been murdered and five others who were dying. One of these unfortunates was still conscious and informed the posse that Murieta had just robbed them of $3000.00. The Chinese in this neighborhood then became terror-stricken and flocked to the larger towns for protection.

On the night of April 1 it was learned that Murieta and six other Mexicans were asleep in a shack located on the outskirts of the little town of Hornitas. J. Prescott and a posse of fifteen men proceeded to the place and surrounded the shanty. Prescott lighted a candle and entered, but as he did so he received a bullet in the chest. He fell and the light went out. The bandits then fled through different doors. As it was dark and the posse was so stationed that they were afraid of shooting each other, the desperadoes again escaped.

Murieta's ability to gather information was marvelous. It was thought that only a few members of the posse knew who gave the information regarding Murieta's presence in the cabin, yet the next morning the informant's body was found hanging to a tree.

On May 17, 1853, the Legislature passed a bill which was signed by Governor John Bigler, authorizing Captain Harry Love to organize a company of Mounted Rangers. It provided for twenty men at $150.00 per month for three months, and their duty was to kill Murieta.

On July 1, Murieta and seventy of his men reassembled at Arroyo Cantoova with 1500 head of horses, in addition to the gold they had stolen. Captain Love learned of this move and he went to the bandits' camp with his posse, but when he arrived and saw seventy men against his twenty, he stated that he was a government official procuring the names of Mexicans employed in rounding up wild horses. This explanation seemed to satisfy the bandits for the moment, but the posse had only traveled a few miles when Murieta received information which caused him to break camp, and after dividing his gang into several small parties, he sent them in different directions. Love learned of this move and also learned the road that Murieta would probably take with his party.

Shortly after sunrise on July 25, 1853, Love and his posse located Murieta's camp and made a rush at the bandits before they could procure their weapons. Murieta was in the act of washing his beautiful bay mare from a tin basin. Realizing that he was at last cornered, he hesitated a moment to collect his thoughts, and then called to his companions to save themselves, at the same time mounting his mare and attempting to dash through the posse. He had only proceeded a short distance when his mare was killed and Murieta was thrown to the ground. He arose and attempted to run, but was riddled with bullets. He did not fall instantly, but turned toward the posse, threw up his hands and cried, "Don't shoot any more boys, the work is done." A deadly pallor then came over his countenance, but he tried to remain on his feet. His knees began to shake and he fell to the ground and died without uttering another word.

"Three-fingered Jack" succeeded in procuring his pistol and horse and the portion of the posse which followed him had a running battle for five miles, but they finally killed their man, cut off his left hand on which were only three fingers and brought it back to prove that the desperado had not escaped them.

Captain Love desired to offer proof other than his word that he had killed Murieta and as he could not carry the body any distance with his facilities, he cut off the head of the dead bandit, and brought it back as evidence.

Several affidavits were procured from persons who knew Murieta and identified the head, one affidavit being sworn to before Justice of the Peace A. C. Bain by Rev. Father Dominic Blaine on August 11, 1853.

It was subsequently learned that at the time Captain Love disturbed Murieta at Arroyo Cantoova, the bandit had already perfected plans for a raid that would have made all of his previous deeds appear insignificant.

Steps had been taken to increase the gang to five hundred men, many of the new members being then en route from Mexico. When they arrived, the whole gang intended to proceed to Mount Shasta and then sweep down through the State, stealing everything worthwhile and slaughtering all who opposed them or had at any time antagonized them. They would then go into Mexico and disband.

On May 15, 1854, the Legislature passed a bill allowing Captain Love $6000.00 for his services in ridding the State of Murieta.

The bandit's head was afterward placed on exhibition at "King's" saloon on the corner of Sansome and Halleck Streets in San Francisco, but the mere possession of it seemed to bring bad luck to the possessor.

Shortly after obtaining it, King became insolvent and the head was sold at auction by Deputy Sheriff Harrison to one Natchez, a gunsmith. Harrison committed suicide and Natchez was killed by the accidental discharge of a pistol.

The killing of Murieta caused the remainder of his gang to become discouraged and the majority of them returned to Mexico.

When Murieta left Arroyo Cantoova on his last trip north with his force of seventy men, Rosita, whom he left behind, united her fortunes with one Charles Baker. When Murieta returned and learned of her unfaithfulness, he located Baker's cabin and finding his former sweetheart, shot her in the arm and cut her across the face and breast, leaving her for dead. He then burned the cabin.

In 1872, about eighteen years after Murieta's death, Rosita met Sheriff Harry Morse of Alameda and Sheriff Tom Cunningham of Stockton in San Benito County and showed them the scars from the wounds she received on that occasion. Sheriff Morse stated that she was still a fine-looking woman.

After the extermination of this gang, Juan Soto, Noratto Ponce, Narciso Bojorques, Antonio Garcia, Tiburcio Vasquez and Cleovara Chevez were at different times the leader of the gang of bandits which operated throughout the lower half of the State from 1860 to 1875.

After committing a series of crimes in the southern part of the State, Bojorques arrived in Alameda in 1863, and after murdering Mr. and Mrs. Golding and child, he stole their property and burned their cabin.

A few months afterward, he and another Mexican named Quarte, stole a band of cattle, but when the time came to divide the proceeds, Bojorques murdered his partner in crime. He then fled to Los Angeles, but in 1865 Sheriff Harry Morse located him near San Jose and after a pistol duel with the sheriff, during which the bandit was shot in the body, he escaped, only to be killed five months afterward in a saloon at Copperopolis by an

American bandit called "One-eyed Jack."

In 1865, Ponce shot and killed an old man named Joy in the town of Haywards, and then mounting his horse, he escaped.

Sheriff Morse started in pursuit and a few evenings afterward as it was growing dark, the sheriff met Ponce. Both men began firing simultaneously.

Morse shot Ponce's horse and the bandit fell to the ground, but jumped up and escaped in the darkness. The next day Morse found Ponce's coat saturated with blood, and six weeks afterward he learned that the wounded desperado was being nursed back to health at the home of Jose Rojos, in Contra Costa County.

Morse proceeded to the place, and as he came in sight of the house, he saw Ponce slipping off into the brush. Both men then opened fire, but Morse was again victorious, for the bandit fell dead from a bullet through the head.

In 1871, Thomas Scott, an ex-assemblyman, conducted a store at Sunol, Alameda County, and on the evening of January 10, three Mexicans entered the store, shot and killed the clerk, Otto Ludovici, and after ransacking the place, made their escape.

Sheriff Morse ascertained that a veritable Hercules named Juan Soto was the leader of this gang. The very appearance of this bandit would strike terror to the average heart.

He was of Mexican and Indian parentage, and had long black hair, fierce black eyes and a cruel mouth only partially concealed by a stubby mustache and beard. He stood 6 feet 3 inches in height, weighed 220 pounds and had the strength, activity and ferocity of a tiger.

Morse learned that this gang had a rendezvous in the Panoche Mountains, about 50 miles from Gilroy. When the posse approached the house it was agreed that the members should be divided into squads for the purpose of surrounding the building, and Morse and a deputy sheriff named Winchell entered the house where they found Soto surrounded by several companions, but not known thieves.

Morse pointed his revolver at Soto and commanded him to surrender, but the bandit ignored the order, and his friends attempted to overpower Morse.

The "brave" Winchell then ran from the building, leaving the sheriff to fight against this gang, Morse finally freed himself and ran out of the house after Soto, who had in the meantime escaped from the building.

When Morse got outside he indulged in a duel with the bandit. One of the sheriff's bullets struck Soto's pistol, disabling it, and the latter ran back into the house for another weapon.

Presently Morse observed him while attempting to escape from a rear entrance.

The sheriff fired at the fleeing desperado, the bullet striking him in the shoulder. The wounded and enraged bandit then turned like a cornered tiger and started toward Morse, but the latter fired one more shot which crashed through the bandit's brain and he dropped dead.

Tiburcio Vasquez, the most notorious of the Mexican bandits since the days of Murieta, was born in Monterey, Cal., in 1835.

His parents were respectable Mexicans and gave Tiburcio a fair education, but he preferred companions of questionable character, and among them was a notorious bandit named Antonio Garcia.

One evening, Vasquez, Garcia and one Jose Guerra were attending a fandango in Monterey.

A quarrel arose between Garcia and Guerra, during which a constable named Hardimount appeared upon the scene and endeavored to exercise his authority. The combatants immediately turned their attention to him and he was shot through the heart.

A vigilance committee was then operating in Monterey and Guerra was hanged the next day. Garcia fled to Los Angeles, but he was subsequently hanged for this murder.

Although Vasquez was not prosecuted, his downward career began about this time.

He left Monterey and began operating as a horse thief in Santa Clara, Merced and Fresno Counties.

In 1857 he and an old compadre were arrested for horse stealing. His companion turned State's evidence and Vasquez was sent to San Quentin prison for five years on August 26, 1857.

On June 25, 1859, he escaped with several other prisoners, after overpowering the guard and obtaining the keys.

Vasquez made his way to Jackson, Amador County, where he was arrested for stealing two horses, and on August 17 he was again in San Quentin, where he remained until August 13, 1863.

In 1864 an Italian butcher was murdered at a place called Enriquita. Vasquez was in the town at the time, but it was not then suspected that he committed the crime.

As there were several Italian witnesses to be examined and as Vasquez was the only person in the town who could speak both Italian and English fluently, he acted as interpreter.

Vasquez departed immediately after the coroner's investigation, which shed no light on the mystery, but it was subsequently learned that he was the murderer.

Shortly afterward, while riding a horse near Mt. Diablo, the animal stumbled, throwing Vasquez to the ground and breaking his arm.

This accident was witnessed by a wealthy Mexican rancher whose home was nearby, and although Vasquez was unknown to this gentleman, he kindly took him to his home.

The bandit, who had rather pleasing manners and an oily tongue, stated that his name was Rafael Moreno; that he had just arrived from Mexico, and was without funds.

This gentleman invited him to stay at his home until he had recovered, but his recovery was very slow, due to the fact that his host had a pretty young daughter named Anita, who fell in love with the slippery bandit.

One morning Anita and Vasquez were missing and the enraged father mounted his fleetest horse and started in pursuit.

He got close enough to Vasquez to fire a shot, which struck the ingrate's arm, but the daughter was rescued and returned to her home.

On January 18, 1867, Vasquez was again sent to San Quentin for stealing cattle in Sonora County, and was discharged on June 4, 1871.

After being liberated, he became a constant visitor at the home of Abelardo Salazar in San Juan, but it was not until Salazar's buxom young wife disappeared with Vasquez that Salazar understood the object of the bandit's frequent visits. Vasquez soon grew tired of his companion and deserted her.

Shortly afterward he met Salazar in San Juan and after a bitter quarrel both men drew their pistols and fired, but the only damage done was a wound in Vasquez's neck.

As soon as this wound healed, Vasquez with two other Mexicans named Bassinez and Rodriquez, held up a stage at San Felipe. The six passengers were bound and robbed and left helpless on the road. The three bandits then started toward San Juan, but on the road they met Thomas McMahon, the treasurer of San Benito County and robbed him of several hundred dollars.

Rodriquez was captured and sent to San Quentin prison for ten years, where he died.

A posse started in pursuit of Vasquez and Bassinez, and overtook them near Santa Cruz. A desperate battle occurred during which Bassinez was killed and Vasquez and a constable were seriously wounded.

Notwithstanding his injuries, Vasquez mounted his horse and escaped. He remained in seclusion until his wounds healed. In the fall of 1871, his niece, Concepcion Espinosa, was living with one Jose Castro, who conducted a saloon about twenty-five miles from Hollister, California.

Vasquez visited them and induced Castro to assist him to hold up the San Benito stage about ten miles from Castro's place, and a considerable amount of money was stolen. A posse was organized and Castro was captured and lynched, but Vasquez again escaped.

In January, 1873, Vasquez became the guest of Abdon Leiva and wife at their home at Cantua Creek. Here a new gang was organized consisting of Vasquez, Clodovea Chavez, Leiva, Moreno and Gonzalez.

They committed several unimportant holdups, but on August 26, 1873, they planned and executed a raid on Snyder's general merchandise store and saloon at Tres Pinos, San Benito County. Leiva and Gonzalez preceded the gang to the store and spent their time at the bar until their companions arrived — the other three being delayed as they stopped and robbed the New Idria stage, which they chanced to meet on the road.

L. C. Smith, a blacksmith, Andrew Snyder, the proprietor of the store, John Utzerath, a clerk, and three others were in the store at the time the first two bandits arrived, and when the gang was reinforced by the other three, pistols were drawn and the victims ordered to lie down while one of the bandits bound each one.

At this moment, a sheep-herder named Barney Bihury entered the store and Gonzalez pointed a pistol at his head and ordered him to lie down.

He ignored the command and started to run away, but a bullet from Moreno's pistol crashed through his brain, killing him instantly.

The little son of L. C. Smith chanced to pass the store at this time and started to run when he heard the shot. Chavez gave chase, and after knocking the boy down with a blow from his pistol, dragged him back to the store.

As Chavez was about to enter the store with the boy, a teamster named George Redford drove up. Chavez pointed his pistol at him and ordered him to come in the store, but the man was slightly deaf and not hearing the command, started to run, but was shot dead by Chavez.

Leander Davidson and wife who conducted a hotel nearby, came to their front door at the sound of the shots and Leiva ordered them to go inside. They proceeded to do so, but as they were closing the door behind them, Vasquez dashed out of the store and fired a bullet which passed through the door and killed Davidson instantly.

After looting Snyder's store, he was released and taken to his home by Leiva, where several hundred dollars were found.

They then took about eight horses, and after packing provisions on the back of each, they departed, Chavez, Vasquez and Leiva proceeding toward Los Angeles, the latter's wife joining them.

While camping at a place called Elizabeth Lake, Vasquez sent Leiva on an errand, but the latter returned unexpectedly and found his wife and Vasquez in each other's embrace.

Leiva drew his pistol but he was overpowered by Chavez.

Vasquez refused to fight a duel with Leiva and the latter took his wife and decided to surrender to the authorities.

In the meantime, a posse headed by Sheriff J. H. Adams was organized and valuable information was obtained from Leiva. But while the latter was assisting the posse, Vasquez located Leiva's wife, who deserted her two children to go with him.

They traveled through the country together for several months, but realizing the additional risk he ran by having a woman with him, he deserted her in the mountains and when she finally reached the home of a farmer, she was almost dead from exhaustion and starvation.

Moreno was captured, found guilty of the murder of Bihury and sentenced to life imprisonment.

In the meantime, Vasquez, Chavez and Androtio joined forces, and on November 4, 1873, Androtio and Chavez visited the cabin of a sheep-herder in the Cholame valley. After this man had prepared a meal for them, they killed him and took $200.00 which he had saved to enable him to visit his aged mother in the East.

They then mutilated his face and threw his body in a ditch. Two men saw them disposing of the body, and the murderers seeing this, ran for their horses. Chavez mounted his horse and escaped, but Androtio's horse became frightened and ran away. The two men who saw the crime committed gave the alarm and a posse captured Androtio who confessed and was hanged.

On November 13, 1873, Vasquez and Chavez entered a store

conducted by a man named Jones about two miles from Millerton, in Fresno County, and after binding the occupants, obtained six hundred dollars and escaped.

On the night of December 26, 1873, these two bandits with several others, entered the town of Kingston, Fresno County, and dividing into gangs, simultaneously robbed the two principal stores after they had tied the inmates hand and foot. On this occasion they obtained $2000.00 and a supply of clothing and provisions.

Governor Booth became aroused and the legislature passed a bill empowering the governor to expend any part of $15,000.00 in an effort to capture Vasquez.

Afterward, a reward of $8000.00 was offered for Vasquez if captured alive and $6000.00 for his dead body.

On the afternoon of February 26, 1874, Vasquez and Chavez proceeded to Coyote Hole station on the Los Angeles and Owens River stage road. When near the building they met a Mr. Raymond and to prevent him from giving an alarm they bound him to a tree. They then approached the building and ordered everybody out.

Vasquez and Chavez covered them with rifles and forced an old Mexican to do the searching. The party were then placed on a hillside nearby and ordered not to leave the spot or death would be the penalty.

The bandits then waited for the stage and ordered Davis, the driver, to throw up his hands. Mr. Belshaw, one of the owners of the Cerro Gordo mines, and several other passengers were robbed and several hundred dollars were taken from Wells Fargo's box.

On the next day, February 27, they stopped the Los Angeles stage between Mill Station and Soledad and robbed the passengers of about $300.00.

As Vasquez and Chavez knew that Sheriff Morse from Alameda County had a posse in that neighborhood disguised as surveyors, they remained in seclusion during the month of April, but when Morse left they resumed operations.

On May 6, the desperadoes proceeded to the house of Alexander Repetto, near the Old Mission, in Los Angeles, and after tying him to a tree demanded $800.00 as a ransom. Repetto sent a boy to Los Angeles for the money, but the lad notified Sheriff Rowland instead. A posse was formed and arrived at the house in time to see the bandits make their escape.

Within a few hours after this occurrence, they met Charles Miles, John Osborne, Pat Cone and J. Rhodes riding in a buggy and relieved them of their valuables.

On May 14, 1874, it was learned that Vasquez was at the home of a man named "Greek George," near Los Angeles. A posse from Los Angeles, consisting of Sheriff Rowland, Undersheriff Johnson, Major H. M. Mitchell and G. A. Beers, special correspondent for the San Francisco Chronicle, procured a wood wagon and instructed the driver to proceed to George's house. The posse was concealed in the bed of the wagon and when they arrived at the house they jumped out and surrounded the building. A woman opened the door and then gave the alarm to Vasquez, who jumped through a window. He was confronted by several armed men, but instead of surrendering, he attempted to escape and was shot eight times. He then surrendered, but it was thought that he would die from his wounds. He recovered, however, and was indicted for the murders committed at Tres Pinos in San Benito County.

On January 5, 1875, his trial began in the District Court at San Jose. On January 10 he was found guilty and on March 19, 1875, he was hanged.

While Vasquez was in custody, Chavez, who was still enjoying his liberty, addressed a communication to the authorities in which he threatened to kill everyone who in any manner assisted in the prosecution of Vasquez. The condemned man heard of this and caused a message to Chavez to be published, in which he disapproved of the action contemplated and advised his former companion to change his course of life, lest he, too, die on the gallows.

Vasquez' word was the only law which Chavez recognized, and he not only abandoned this plan but proceeded to Arizona, where he procured legitimate employment at Baker's Rancho, sixty miles from Yuma. He was recognized by Louis Raggio, a former cattle-herder in California, who informed C. S. Calvig and Harry Roberts of the bandit's presence. As a reward was offered for Chavez, dead or alive, these two men went to the ranch and on meeting Chavez, ordered him to throw up his hands. Instead of complying with the order, the former bandit started to run, whereupon Calvig poured the contents of a shotgun into his back and he died without uttering a word.

This was the end of the Mexican bandits.

———————

ED. BONNEY, WHO MURDERED HIS PARTNER, G. W.

HIRSCH, AND THEN ATTEMPTED TO SEVER HIS HEAD FROM HIS BODY.

On January 14, 1861, the body of a man was found by a fence, some distance from a road leading into a little town then called San Antonio, but now East Oakland. The head was almost entirely severed from the body, which was somewhat decomposed.

As no one in that neighborhood could identify the corpse, it was brought to San Francisco, where it was recognized by Edward W. Bonney as the remains of G. W. Hirsch, who was, up to the time of his death, his partner in the stationery business in San Francisco.

The murdered man was a native of France, 30 years of age and unmarried. He had only been in this country six weeks and was living at the "What Cheer House" at Sacramento and Leidesdorff Streets, San Francisco. It was at this hotel that he became acquainted with Bonney, who induced him to form a partnership and open a stationery store at the corner of Sacramento and Montgomery Streets. Business at this location proving unsuccessful, they removed to a store on Clay Street, opposite the Plaza.

It was Bonney's conflicting statements which first caused him to be suspected of having murdered his partner. He first stated that on Sunday, January 2, 1861, Hirsch had started for San Jose with $600.00 of the firm's money, for the purpose of opening a branch store in that town.

His next statement was that he had accompanied his partner in a buggy for a short distance in the direction in which the body was found, but that they overtook two Frenchmen, friends of Hirsch, and that he (Bonney) insisted upon getting out of the buggy and returning to Oakland, leaving Hirsch to continue his journey with his two friends.

Bonney was taken into custody by Captain Lees, pending further investigation.

It was afterward proven that Bonney, knowing that Hirsch had this money in his possession, induced him to accompany him on a buggy ride on Sunday, January 2, and while driving along the road, Bonney struck him on the head with some blunt instrument and continued to beat him on top of the head until he was dead. He then took his victim's money but saw no place to dispose of the body without it being observed by the next person who passed. He furthermore feared that because of the teams that were frequently passing, he might be seen dragging the body if he attempted to take it any distance from the road. He could not put the body down by his feet without attracting attention, so he sat the corpse upright in the buggy, and tearing off and using his shirttail, he bandaged almost the entire face, to prevent persons whom he passed on the road from seeing that he had a corpse for a companion on his Sunday afternoon drive.

He passed a great many people who noticed him and what they supposed was an invalid companion. These people were all produced as witnesses for the prosecution. When the body was found some of the bandages were also found.

Bonney continued along this road until he saw a good opportunity to dispose of the body, which he immediately took advantage of. The idea then entered his head that the mystery would be far more difficult to fathom if the body could not be identified, so he attempted to sever the head from the body with his pocket knife, with the intention of depositing it elsewhere. Either his knife or his nerve failed him for he abandoned that part of his plans when the head was almost severed from the body.

Bonney was convicted of murder in the first degree and on May 9, 1862, he was hanged.

THE NOTORIOUS MAJORS FAMILY.

Lloyd L. Majors was born in Ohio in 1837. After receiving a common-school education he attended the Grand River Institute and afterward graduated from the Ann Arbor College in Michigan. In 1870 he was admitted to the bar, and after practicing four years he became a Methodist minister.

Meeting with financial reverses, he came to California, taking up his home in Los Gatos in 1880, where he opened a saloon. The resort was conducted in an orderly manner and Majors became quite popular in the town. He was elected Foreman of a lodge of United Workmen and was at one time appointed Grand Marshal of a Fourth of July procession. On another occasion the clergy and the citizens' committee unanimously agreed upon him as the proper person to deliver the Garfield memorial address.

Majors did not appear to be adapted to the saloon business and he was in a bad way financially. Finally his saloon burned down. At first this was looked upon as a misfortune, but it was subsequently learned that he carried a very heavy insurance.

Almost immediately after he received his insurance money, Majors began the construction of a forty-room hotel. When he had completed the saloon part of the building, work ceased and Majors attempted to raise sufficient money to enable him to proceed. Shortly afterward, in February,

1883, he announced that Joseph Jewell, a painter who had recently arrived in Los Gatos and had become a habitué of Majors' saloon, had entered into partnership with him. Majors furthermore stated that Jewell had just fallen heir to a fortune and would furnish the money necessary to complete the hotel.

About three miles from Los Gatos, and near the village of Lexington, lived an old bachelor named William P. Renowden, who was supposed to be very wealthy. As he deposited no money in the banks, it was generally believed that this old recluse had buried his savings near his isolated cabin.

On March 11, 1883, this cabin was burned to the ground and in the ruins were found the bodies of Renowden and a Canadian named Archibald McIntyre. It was evident that both men had been murdered. It was subsequently learned that Majors had made systematic inquiry regarding Renowden's habits and wealth, even visiting different banks at San Jose in an effort to learn if Renowden had any money on deposit.

As Majors, Jewell and an overgrown boy named John Showers were observed holding mysterious conferences, and as Showers and Jewell were seen acting in a suspicious manner at Lexington the day previous to the double murder, the trio were taken into custody. Showers soon weakened and made a complete confession, which was substantially as follows:

"Jewell approached me several days before the murder and told me that it was definitely known that old man Renowden had a lot of money secreted in or near the cabin, and Jewell suggested that we go to the cabin some night and threaten to kill him if he did not tell where it was concealed. A week before the murder, Lloyd Majors drove Jewell to the cabin for the purpose of looking over the ground, and they had dinner with the old man. On the night of March 10 I met Jewell and we walked to Lexington, where we spent the night in a deserted cabin, drinking whisky. We also spent the greater portion of the next day in this cabin, but at night we proceeded to Renowden's cabin. We knocked at the door and I told the old man we were hunters who had lost our way and asked him to come out and direct us to the road to Los Gatos. When Renowden had accompanied us a short distance, Jewell commanded him to throw up his hands, but instead of doing so the old man sprang at Jewell and called for help. To our surprise, another man, whom I have since learned was McIntyre, ran out of the cabin toward us. I shot and killed McIntyre. I then ran to Jewell's assistance and knocked Renowden senseless by striking him over the head with a gun. We then dragged him to the cabin and restored him to consciousness. As he refused to tell us where his money was hid we poured turpentine over the lower part of his body and set him on fire. Again he became

unconscious and again we restored him. As he still refused to divulge the location of the hidden treasure we shot him to death. We hastened to Majors' saloon in Los Gatos and told him of what had transpired. He gave us some money and a bottle of whiskey, and advised us to get out of the country. I afterward learned from Majors that late on the night of the murder he rode over to the cabin alone and set it on fire."

The three defendants were tried at San Jose for the murder of Renowden. Jewell was found guilty on May 11, 1883, and sentenced to be hanged. Majors was found guilty on May 24, and Showers pleaded guilty on May 28. Majors and Showers were sentenced to penal servitude at San Quentin for life. The latter was used as a witness against Majors and Jewell.

After Majors was sent to State Prison, Jewell made a confession which fully corroborated Showers' statement. He furthermore added that it was part of the conspiracy entered into between Majors and himself that Jewell would kill Showers after finishing the old man, and place the bodies in such a position as to make it appear that they had killed each other, but the unexpected appearance of McIntyre upset this plan.

This confession, voluntarily made by a man within the shadow of the gallows, convinced the authorities that Majors was the chief conspirator and originator of the plot and should also hang.

On July 23, seventeen days after Majors had been sent to State Prison, the Grand Jury indicted him for the murder of McIntyre and the prisoner was returned to San Jose for trial. The date for Jewell's execution had been set for July 27, 1883, but it was postponed until November 30 to enable him to testify against Majors.

The latter was granted a change of venue and his trial began in Oakland on October 31. On November 16 he was found guilty and sentenced to be hanged. He appealed to the Supreme Court, but on March 13, 1884, the higher court refused to grant a new trial and on May 23, 1884, Majors was hanged.*

* Sheriff Hale was compelled by law to execute this man, and as it was to him a most painful duty, he fathered a bill which became a law and which provided that thereafter all executions should take place in the State prisons, under the immediate supervision of the Warden. Shortly after this law became effective, Hale was appointed Warden at San Quentin, where he was compelled, during his term, to supervise the execution of many murderers.

He was sullen and indifferent to the end.

Showers was transferred to Folsom Prison on May 6, 1884, and on May 15, 1899, he was killed by a fellow convict named George Putman, a friend of the Majors family, who was executed on November 19, 1900, for this deed.

Majors left a widow and two little boys named Archie and Abie, who lived in Oakland after the father's execution. The poor woman did all in her power to raise the little fellows to be useful citizens and endeavored to conceal from them the facts regarding the disgraceful end of their father.

A few years after her husband's death, she married a man named J. H. Wagner. After two more children were born, Wagner deserted his wife, leaving her in absolute poverty. Abe Majors went to work and cheerfully gave his earnings to his mother.

One day someone told him of the history of his father. The boy rushed home in a whirlwind of passion, expecting to hear that the story was false. The heart-broken mother admitted it was true, and the boy left home at once, leaving his destitute mother to seek relief from the Humane Society.

Abe finally returned to Oakland, and he and his brother Archie spent much of their time at the home of Bert Willmore, a boy who lived with his mother at 1264 Webster Street.

During the month of January and early part of February, 1896, a series of burglaries was committed in Oakland, Alameda and Berkeley. In three weeks thirty-five burglaries were committed, and in some instances safes were blown open.

The skillful and successful manner in which these bold cracksmen were plying their nefarious vocation, convinced the authorities that the work was being done by experienced Eastern crooks.

At 5:30 a. m., February 6, 1896, Officers M. Powers, George Kyte and Special James Doolan were standing at the corner of Fifth and Washington Streets, Oakland, when two boys approached. As the officers had become suspicious of almost everyone it was suggested that these boys be searched, but Officer Kyte laughed at the idea and said: "They're only a couple of newsboys." The other officers insisted, however, and they were rewarded by finding a coil of fuse and several burglar's instruments. The boys also carried large revolvers, which they afterwards stated would have been used on the arresting officers if an opportunity had presented itself.

When first arrested, Bert Willmore gave his right name, but the other boy said his name was Ralph Ford. That afternoon Sheriff White positively identified the other lad as Abe Majors, who by a singular coincidence occupied the same cell in which his father was confined years before.

The boys then made a complete confession, wherein they related, with the utmost nonchalance, the complete details of all the burglaries they had committed during the preceding three weeks. To corroborate their statement, they led the officers to the Willmore home, where they had deposited their loot.

They were charged with burglarizing the offices of Charles Butler, the grain merchant, and the Girard Piano Company. Both boys were sentenced to serve five years on each charge, but were paroled on December 24, 1898. On that same day C. C. Sullivan, who had served seventeen years of a fifty-year sentence for killing a woodchopper named William Shields in a saloon fight at Kingston, Fresno County, was also paroled.

At 1 a. m., October 9, 1899, H. O. Tenny, who roomed over Gott's jewelry store at Park and Central Avenues, Alameda, heard a noise at the rear of the store and, looking out the window, saw the forms of two men in the back yard. Tenny quietly rushed out and notified Officer Hadley, who entered the yard in the rear of the store on a tour of inspection. He soon saw the burglars and several shots were fired by all concerned, but none were effective. The burglars escaped but were closely pursued by the officer and several citizens who were attracted by the shots. City Marshal Conrad also joined in the hunt and as he approached a fence he saw one of the burglars. Both men opened fire simultaneously, but Conrad's aim was the surest and the result was that he killed his man instantly.

A few moments later the other burglar was found hiding behind some brush. He surrendered but gave an assumed name. The next day he was identified as C. C. Sullivan, a habitué of the Cafe Royal in San Francisco. Up to this time Sullivan refused to divulge the name of his confederate, but when identified he stated that the dead man was Bert Willmore, and that Majors, Willmore and he were paroled on the same day.

On the night of April 29, 1899, two highwaymen held up the town of Brigham, Utah, and after thoroughly terrorizing the citizens they hastily committed several robberies and fled. Sheriff Gordon and a deputy gave chase and engaged the fugitives in a running fight, during which about forty shots were fired, but no one was injured. The robbers then dropped much of their plunder and fled to the mountains. The Sheriff telephoned to Ogden for assistance and a posse, headed by Sheriff Layne and Captain Brown of the Ogden police, responded, leaving Ogden at 4 a. m., April 30, for the mountains. At noon the trail was found and shortly afterward the robbers were sighted. A battle took place, during which one of the robbers was killed. The other fled and Captain Brown, believing he could take him alive, started in pursuit. As the officer was gaining ground, the robber turned and fired one shot which pierced the officer's heart, killing him instantly. The bandit then surrendered. The prisoner stated that his name was George Morgan; that he was 19 years of age and that the dead bandit was his brother James. He added that they hailed from Chicago.

Several days afterwards, however, it was learned that the dead robber was Archie Majors and the prisoner was his brother Abe. By this time Abe had fully developed all of the characteristics of his fiendish father. Without any sign of remorse he discussed his past and apparently was absolutely indifferent as to his future.

He was found guilty of the murder of Captain Brown and was sentenced to be shot on July 7, 1899. A stay was granted and on August 14, 1899, he was granted a new trial, which resulted in his being convicted of murder in the second degree. On October 8, 1901, he was sentenced to life imprisonment at the State Prison at Salt Lake, Utah.

At 6:30 p. m., on October 9, 1903, Guards Wilkins and Jacobs of this prison, were engaged in locking up several of the convicts for the night when they were suddenly overpowered and unmercifully beaten with pistols which had in some mysterious manner been smuggled into the jail. A general jailbreak was attempted, which was led by Abe Majors, Frank Drayton, a burglar serving twelve years, and James Lynch and Nick Haworth, who were awaiting execution for murder. A ladder was procured from the carpenter shop in the jail and the convicts were in the act of scaling the prison wall when a general alarm was sounded. The two murderers awaiting execution escaped, but Drayton was killed and Majors was shot through the arm.

ERLAND H. SODERBURG, MATRICIDE.

In March, 1907, Erland H. Soderburg, who was employed as a pile driver in San Francisco, resided at 463 B Street, Oakland, Cal., with his aged mother.

On the evening of March 23, 1907, he returned home from work somewhat intoxicated, but the next morning he returned to his work in San Francisco as usual. During the day the neighbors heard Mrs. Soderburg cat crying constantly, and as the old lady had failed to make her appearance that day, they decided that she must have gone out without feeding the cat, which would be most unusual.

One lady took some food into Mrs. Soderburg's kitchen for the cat, and noticed that the floor showed evidence of having been washed, evidently on that morning. Ashes of burned rags were also found in the stove. The matter was reported to the Oakland police and Detectives St. Clair Hodgkins and Flynn were assigned to the case. On inspecting the premises they found the badly mutilated body of Mrs. Soderburg crowded into a small closet.

The detectives arrested the son on his return from work that night, and under their skillful questioning, he broke down and confessed that in the heat of passion he slaughtered his mother with a butcher knife, jammed the body into the closet, washed up the floor and burned the blood-stained rags.

He was convicted and on May 17, 1907, was sentenced to State Prison for life.

THE MURDER OF OFFICER FENTON OF OAKLAND AND THE BURGLARY OF THE POST OFFICE AT CAMPBELL, CAL.

On the night of January 2, 1908, a daring burglary was committed in the post office at Campbell, Santa Clara County, Cal., and among other things, $3,000.00 worth of postage stamps were stolen. The thief left no clew as to his identity.

On the afternoon of January 4, 1908, Police Officer James Fenton was patrolling his beat in West Oakland and when he reached the corner of Seventh and Pine Streets he noticed a man approaching who was carrying a suit case. The man acted suspiciously and the officer asked him where he was going. He replied, "To San Francisco."

Fenton demanded that he show the contents of his suit case, whereupon the stranger drew a revolver and shot the officer. Fenton in falling grappled with the man and they both fell to the ground. The man attempted to shoot Fenton again, when a barber named Shields, who was working in a shop across the Street, ran over, and taking the dying officer's revolver from his pocket, shot the officer's assailant. Fenton died immediately and the murderer only lived long enough to utter one or two unintelligible words, but his identity was never learned.

When the valise was opened it was found that it contained the stamps stolen at Campbell.

Shields, the barber, was appointed a special officer for his bravery and was otherwise rewarded by the deceased officer's friends.

THE MYSTERIOUS MURDER OF MRS. DONOHUE, NEAR OAKLAND.

(From Oakland Police Records.)

On June 12, 1908, Daniel H. Donohue, a Street-car motorman residing at 1266 Sixty-second Street, Emeryville, a suburb of Oakland, reported to Chief Wilson of the Oakland police that his wife Alice, a middle-aged woman, was missing, and he requested the Chief to issue circulars announcing that he (Donohue) would pay a reward of $10.00 for information as to her whereabouts.

He claimed that as he left home on the evening of June 11 to attend a lodge meeting, his wife complained of severe pains in her head. When he returned at midnight she had mysteriously disappeared. He furthermore stated that in view of the fact that the woman had left all her money and jewelry at home, he was inclined to believe that she had become suddenly insane and committed suicide.

Three weeks after his visit to Chief Wilson, Donohue met Police Captain Bock and requested him to have the offer of a reward withdrawn as he suspected that his wife had left with another man, but shortly afterward he abandoned this theory as untenable and concluded that his original theory was the correct one.

John Krasky was the manager of the Western Furniture Factory, which was located on Sixty-fourth Street, about six blocks from the Donohue home. On August 28, 1908, his little dog became entrapped under the furniture warehouse and a boy employed there, named Frank Walsh, while attempting to extricate the animal, discovered three shirtwaists, a shawl, a long red coat and a short-handled shovel under the building.

Captain of Detectives Walter Peterson of Oakland and Marshal Cary and Deputy Marshal Pippy of Emeryville were notified, and they took charge of the clothing. Donohue was sent for and he immediately identified the articles as wearing apparel belonging to his wife, and he predicted that her body would be found in that vicinity.

Two days later Frank Walsh and Tony Figone were digging about the premises in search of the body. Within fifty feet from where Walsh found the clothing, they discovered the badly decomposed body of Mrs. Donohue, which had been doubled up and buried about three feet under the ground.

Captain Peterson was present with Donohue when the body was unearthed. The latter jumped down into the hole with the body and made a display of "grief" that was considered almost too great to be genuine and which was not at all consistent with his subsequent conduct.

He was interrogated at great length by Captain Peterson and many of his answers to questions were at variance with those previously given. For instance: When he first reported the disappearance of his wife, he laid great stress on the fact that she had left her money and jewelry at home, but when the body was found he claimed that the purse containing her money, and her pearl earrings, gold watch and wedding-ring were missing.

The spade found with the clothing was positively identified by Mrs. Emma De Verra of 1282 Sixty-first Street as the property of an old Swedish laborer known as Gustave Arkill, who lived directly across the Street from the Donohue home. Mrs. De Verra made a statement substantially as follows:

> "Arkill recently used this spake while digging a well for me. He frequently watched Mrs. Donohue's actions from my home and requested me to do likewise and report the result of my observations to him. He furthermore stated that, at the request of Donohue, he had on one occasion trailed Mrs. Donohue to the Globe Hotel in Oakland, where she met a man. On the day Mrs. Donohue disappeared I saw Arkill, and he was extremely nervous and pale. At that time he had on a pair of striped pants which were covered with mud."

Arkill was arrested the day the body was found. In his pocket was found a black bordered handkerchief which Mrs. De Verra identified as one she had seen Mrs. Donohue use. A comparatively new tortoise shell back comb was found in Arkill's room, which Mrs. De Verra and Mrs. W. E. Green of 1267 Sixty-third Street identified as one worn by Mrs. Donohue just previous to her disappearance.

Donohue came to Arkill's assistance by claiming that the comb and handkerchief were never in his wife's possession. The mud-covered pants referred to by Mrs. De Verra were found in Arkill's room. He claimed the mud got on them years before while he was digging a well. Although the comb was evidently new, he stated that it was the property of his first wife, who had been dead for many years. He denied ever owning a spade similar to the one found near Mrs. Donohue's body.

Captain Peterson then investigated Arkill's record and found as follows: His true name was Gustave Ahlstedt. In 1898 he lived with his first wife at 331 Jessie Street, San Francisco, who charged that her husband attempted to poison her by putting strychnine in her coffee, but as she could not substantiate her charge the case was dismissed. Shortly afterward the couple were divorced in Contra Costa County. Ahlstedt returned to San Francisco, where he married again and resided with his wife at 51 East Park Street, on Bernal Heights, San Francisco.

On January 29, 1902, he came home unexpectedly and found his wife entertaining one Thomas Normile of 3274 Folsom Street. Ahlstedt shot and killed Normile, for which he was arrested, tried by a jury and acquitted.

Mrs. Elizabeth Laumeister of 529 Andover Avenue, San Francisco, swore to a warrant charging that on September 27, 1906, Ahlstedt broke into her home and stole a deed to some land and $40.00. Ahlstedt disappeared and she neither saw nor heard of him again until the Donohue murder brought his name into the papers. This lady identified the short-handled shovel as one she had seen Ahlstedt use in San Francisco, and O. H. Adams subsequently testified that he was with Ahlstedt when he found the shovel shortly after the big fire in 1906.

After Mrs. Donohue's clothing was found, Donohue and Ahlstedt were observed holding long and mysterious conferences.

Donohue claimed that he and Mrs. Donohue were married about ten years previous to her death. He had her life insured for $3,800.00, and immediately after her disappearance he took great care to pay up all her dues and assessments. When the body was found he at once demanded the insurance money on the grounds that he was her lawful husband.

On the morning of September 3, the San Francisco Call published a history of the life of the murdered woman, which was substantially as follows:

The woman's maiden name was Alice Steward. While very young she married a man in Pennsylvania from whom she claimed she obtained a divorce. About one year later she went through a marriage ceremony at Birmington, Pa., with an industrious coal miner named Joseph Barry. They lived together for several years and finally came to San Francisco. Eventually Barry learned that the marriage was illegal because the divorce from the first husband had not been properly obtained. Shortly after this they separated and the woman went to live with Donohue, who was at the time a grip-man on the Powell Street railroad in San Francisco.

This article also exposed the past life of the woman, which showed that she was a dissolute character, who had associated with many men who bore most unenviable reputations.

On the day this article was published the Coroner's inquisition began. Donohue was to be one of the first and most important witnesses examined. At the appointed hour he did not respond to the summons and Deputy Coroner B. H. Sargent and Deputy Public Administrator Flood were dispatched to the Donohue home to ascertain the cause of his absence. The officials knocked loudly at the doors, but receiving no response, it was finally decided to break into the house. There they found the body of Donohue lying on the floor. Nearby was a 38-calibre revolver with which he had shot himself through the mouth, blowing out his brains. By his side was the Morning Call, and it was evident that he had been reading the article regarding the alleged Mrs. Donohue just previous to taking his own life.

A note written by the suicide was also found, in which he protested his innocence and charged that Joseph Barry committed the murder. Captain Peterson finally located Barry at the Midas Coal Mines in Shasta County. But it was proven by numerous reliable witnesses that Barry went to work in the mines on February 22, 1908, and had not been away from that neighborhood for one day since then.

As the body of the so-called Mrs. Donohue was very badly decomposed it was impossible to ascertain definitely the true cause of death, nor did the Coroner's jury charge any person with the murder.

Although Captain Peterson suspected that Donohue murdered his paramour for the life insurance, the evidence was not sufficient to justify him in making a formal charge.

Captain Peterson also suspected that Ahlstedt had a guilty knowledge of the crime.

When Ahlstedt was released he was brought to San Francisco and tried on the burglary charge preferred by Mrs. Laumeister, but he was acquitted on January 19, 1909.

CAREER OF THE HANDSOME BUT NOTORIOUS CRIMINAL, MATHEW KENNEDY, ALIAS KID McMANN, ALIAS JAMES KELLEY, WHO OPERATED THROUGHOUT AMERICA AND AUSTRALIA BUT CAME TO A TRAGIC END IN BERKELEY, CAL.

In March, 1884, a small post office near Windsor, Ontario, was robbed of a considerable sum of money and postage stamps. A few hours later two young men, who acted very mysteriously, attempted to cross on the ferry running from Windsor to Detroit. They were apprehended by the authorities, and after some questioning, it was decided to search them. The result was that most of the stamps and money were recovered. It was ascertained that the prisoners were two Detroit hoodlums named Mathew Kennedy and William Callehan.

While awaiting trial in the jail at Sandwich, near Windsor, they killed Jailor Leech with pistols which had evidently been smuggled into the jail, and then escaped. Callehan procured some women's clothing and in that disguise crossed the river and disappeared, but Kennedy was recaptured a few hours later. He was tried and convicted for this murder and was sentenced to serve twenty years at Kingston, Ontario, but one year later he escaped.

On January 29, 1887, the fur store of Benedict & Ruedy in Cleveland, Ohio, was burglarized and furs valued at $6000.00 were stolen. It was learned that Kennedy committed the theft and he was arrested at Allegheny City three days after the burglary.

Captain Hohne and Detective William Hulligan of the Cleveland police department went to bring the prisoner back to the scene of the crime. They left Allegheny with their prisoner at midnight on February 4. When the train stopped at a town called Ravenna, four men, including one "Blinkey" Morgan, boarded the car and began shooting at the officers and beating them over the heads with the butts of their revolvers, until both were unconscious. Kennedy was handcuffed to Detective Hulligan but the ruffians broke the lock and liberated him. The entire gang then fled.

Detective Hulligan died four days later. These assaults aroused great indignation and rewards aggregating $16,000.00 were offered for the arrest of the gang.

The Pinkerton Detective Agency located "Blinkey" Morgan at Alpena, Michigan, in July, 1887, and he was returned to Ravenna, tried, convicted and hanged. It was subsequently learned that the rest of the gang went to Australia where Kennedy, who was afterward known as James Kelley, became an associate of two men known as Jack Casey and Jimmy Murphy. These men made several trips from Australia to America.

In the early part of 1898, Willard R. Green, a Denver millionaire who had been visiting in San Francisco, charged that Augustus Howard, the owner of the race horse "Yellowtail," had swindled him out of $100,000.00 and then employed Kelley, Casey and Murphy to accompany him (Green) on the boat which left San Francisco on April 20, 1898, for Australia, for the purpose of throwing him overboard, but they did not have an opportunity. (Casey subsequently confessed that this charge was true.)

In May, 1899, the steamer Alameda left Australia for America. At Sydney thirty boxes, each containing 5000 sovereigns (about $25,000.00) were placed on board the vessel. Each box weighed ninety pounds and was checked by Purser T. C. Smith and Third Mate A. M. Smith as it was brought aboard. At the hatch of the specie tank, in which it was deposited, each box was again checked by Second Mate Mekkleson, and Chief Officer Rennie, who was in the tank, also counted the boxes and supervised the stowing of them.

Four days before the vessel reached San Francisco the steward went to the specie tank and found that the seal had been broken. He notified his superiors and a search showed that one of the boxes had been stolen, the thief probably using a skeleton key on the lock to the specie tank.

It was suspected that a fellow giving the name of Frank Wilson, who boarded the vessel at Sydney but left it at Honolulu, stole this money. He was believed to be a member of the Howard-Kelley gang.

In September, 1898, Kelley, Casey and Murphy were arrested on a charge of robbing a warehouse in Melbourne, but were released on October 20.

On November 27, 1898, the National Bank of Auckland was robbed of £235, and these three fellows were suspected of committing the crime, but as the evidence was not conclusive they were released. They then left for San Francisco, arriving in January, 1899. Shortly afterward Captain of Detectives Lees found that the notes stolen from the Auckland bank had been disposed of in San Francisco by two men of the description of Kelley and Casey.

On March 30, 1899, a wagon belonging to the Anglo-California Bank was stopped by the driver in front of Wells, Fargo & Company's office. Just then a handsome, well-dressed young man approached and engaged the driver in conversation. At the same time another man stole a sack containing $10,000.00 out of the wagon. The driver afterward identified a picture of Kelley as the photograph of the man who engaged him in conversation.

The next heard of Kennedy, alias Kelley, was in Mexico, where he was arrested on a charge of stealing a package of notes valued at $10,000.00 from a bank in that city. Again he escaped from jail.

The following is the substance of the statement made by Officer J. LeStrange of Berkeley, Cal., on September 28, 1905:

"At 1 a. m., this date, I was near Ninth Street and University Avenue, when I saw two men a short distance from me. As I approached they disappeared, but a few moments later I saw four men on San Pablo Avenue, two of whom I recognized as the men I had seen a few moments previous. I was in civilian's dress. They approached me, and after asking for information in regard to the car service, they walked down the Street a short distance and then came back. I walked toward them, when they separated. One fellow sprang toward me with an oath, placed his pistol against my stomach and ordered me to hold up my hands. I pulled out my revolver and shot him in the neck, severing his windpipe. He fell in a heap. Just then his companions opened fire at me, but as I tripped and fell, one said, 'I got the ___.' They then rushed to the dying man, but as he was beyond human aid they dropped him and disappeared in the darkness."

City Marshal Vollmer heard the shots and rushed to the scene, but no trace could be found of the three men who fled.

In the pockets of the dead man were found several safecracking tools, also a syringe of the variety used for injecting nitro-glycerin into doors of safes. There was nothing on the body to indicate the identity of the dead man. A picture was taken of the face and reproduced in the Chicago Detective. On October 8, William Pinkerton and Captain Hohne of Cleveland, Ohio, who was almost killed by Kennedy's gang, positively identified the picture as the photograph of the remains of Kennedy, alias Kelley, etc.

———————

JACOB OPPENHEIMER, ALIAS 'THE HYENA."

Jacob Oppenheimer was formerly a messenger boy for the American District Company in San Francisco, and was noted for his depraved habits. After being dismissed from the service in 1889, he engaged in a row with Manager Wehe, during which he attempted to cut Wehe's throat. For this crime he was sent to the House of Correction for eighteen months.

On the night of May 1, 1892, he and a man named Lawless entered the telegraph office on Sutter near Leavenworth Street, and held up the clerk. They both wore masks and were armed with revolvers. After threatening to kill Clerk John Monahan if he made an outcry, they compelled him to open the safe and deliver its contents, and they then disappeared.

On the night of June 11, 1895, Oppenheimer and two brothers named Walter and Charles Ross, held up and robbed John McIntosh, a saloonkeeper at McAllister and Leavenworth Streets, and obtained a small amount of money. Charles Ross was the only one of the trio convicted for this crime, and he was sentenced to serve fifteen years at San Quentin.

In September, 1895, Walter Ross was living with a woman named Grace Walls in a Morton-Street house. Learning that the woman intended to leave him, he went to her den, choked her almost to death, and robbed her of a sealskin sacque, jewelry and $150.00 in coin. He was arrested, found guilty and in November, 1895, was sentenced by Judge Wallace to serve twenty-five years in Folsom.

In June, 1895, Oppenheimer and Berry Harland committed a brutal robbery in the outskirts of Oakland. For this crime Oppenheimer was sentenced in August, 1895, to serve fifty years at Folsom and Harland was sentenced to life imprisonment at the same institution.

Oppenheimer pretended to believe that the Ross boys had betrayed him, and as Walter Ross was in the same prison with him he never missed an opportunity to express his hatred toward him. On September 30, 1898, as the prisoners were standing in line waiting for the door leading to the dining room to open, Oppenheimer caught sight of Walter Ross, who was in the same line. He walked up behind him, threw his arm around his neck and whipping out a knife he had made out of a file, stabbed Ross several times, inflicting wounds which caused him to die within an hour.

He was charged with murder, convicted and sentenced to life imprisonment, which seemed a farce in view of the fact that he was at the time serving a fifty-year sentence. He was then removed to San Quentin.

On May 15, 1899, while working in the jute mill he committed a violation of the rules, for which Guard James McDonald reported him to W. D. Leahy, chief guard of the jute mill. The next day McDonald caught him violating the same rule, and taking him by the arm said: "You denied that I caught you yesterday so I intend to prove that I was right this time."

McDonald was forced to drag Oppenheimer, when suddenly the latter drew a knife with a blade eight inches long, which he had made in the prison, and drove it into the guard's breast to the hilt. He withdrew it and then drove it in again near the heart. McDonald dropped to the floor and when the next assault was made he grasped the blade, but Oppenheimer pulled it away from him and in drawing it through McDonald's hand almost cut several of his fingers off. He continued to butcher the prostrate guard until Guard Samuel Yoho rushed up and knocked Oppenheimer senseless with a cane. McDonald staggered to his feet and made a rush at Oppenheimer but was restrained.

Assisted by two guards McDonald walked to the operating room with the blood rushing from his wounds as he advanced. When he was stripped and the extent of his injuries discovered it was considered a miracle that he did not die instantly. There were seven wounds on his body and the air whistled through one gaping wound in his chest, which had penetrated his lung, every time he drew a breath. But he finally recovered and the only additional punishment which could be inflicted on Oppenheimer was solitary confinement.

His last assault, however, resulted in the Legislature adding section 248 to the Penal Code, which makes it a crime punishable by death for a convict serving a life sentence to assault any person with intent to produce great bodily injury.

Oppenheimer was placed in one of the strongest and most closely-guarded cells in the prison, from which it was thought no human being could escape. Here he remained like a caged tiger until about 4:30 p. m., August 14, 1907, at which time his guard, Manuel Silveira, stepped away a few feet to wash his hands. As if by magic, the bars fell away, Oppenheimer rushed out and fled to the prison kitchen. Here he encountered convict George Wilson, who was in the act of cutting bread. After a struggle, Oppenheimer obtained the knife and stabbed Wilson in the arm and hand. Wilson's cries caused the guards to rush upon Oppenheimer, and after a terrific struggle he was overpowered.

It was then learned that he had in some mysterious manner obtained possession of a sack needle, and with a patience and persistence seldom found outside of fiction, ground it until he had formed it into a saw, and then for months sawed on the bars at every opportunity, until he had cut six bars, each two and one-half inches wide and one-half inch thick. He stated that all this was done for the purpose of killing a convict named Jack O'Neil, who was serving thirty-five years for a burglary committed in Sacramento, Oppenheimer claiming that on one occasion O'Neil betrayed him.

Oppenheimer was the third prisoner tried for the violation of the law passed because of his assault upon Guard McDonald. He was convicted and sentenced to be hanged, but the case was appealed to the Supreme Court on the grounds that the law under which he was convicted was unconstitutional inasmuch as it was an unusual punishment to hang a man for an assault to commit murder.

The Supreme Court, however, declared that the constitutionality of the law had already been determined by that tribunal in the cases of Inijada and Carson, two convicts who committed assaults while attempting to escape from Folsom prison with "Redshirt" Gordan and others.

Oppenheimer's case is now on appeal to the United States Supreme Court. He has addressed a communication to the Legislature in which he attributes his downfall to the fact that as a messenger boy he visited dance halls and rooms where opium smokers were secretly congregated, and he advocated the passage of a law prohibiting "boys" under the age of twenty-one from serving as messenger boys.

THE MURDER OF ALBERT N. McVICAR AT STOCKTON BY

HIS WIFE, WHO WAS KNOWN AS EMMA LEDOUX.

Emma Head was born near Jackson, Amador County, where her parents were in comfortable circumstances.

While quite young she married a man named Barrett, but after living with him a short time in Fresno, Cal., a divorce was granted, and she then married a man named Williams, with whom she went to Arizona.

The woman had his life heavily insured and shortly afterward he died under peculiar circumstances.

In September, 1902, she was married to Albert N. McVicar in Bisbee, Arizona, by Rev. H. W. Studley.

They soon separated and she finally became an inmate of a brothel.

Without being legally separated from McVicar she married one Eugene LeDoux in Woodland, Cal., on August 12, 1905, and the couple resided at her mother's home near Jackson.

In the meantime McVicar had obtained employment at the Rawhide mine in Jamestown, Toulumne County, and on March 11, 1906, he met the so-called "Mrs. LeDoux" in Stockton, Cal., by appointment. Being ignorant of the woman's bigamous relationship with LeDoux, McVicar went to the California Hotel with her and registered as "A. N. McVicar and wife."

The next day the couple purchased considerable furniture from Bruener's store in Stockton and ordered it shipped to Jamestown.

On the following day they came to San Francisco and proceeded to the Lexington Hotel, 212 Eddy Street, from where Mrs. "LeDoux" telephoned to Bruener's requesting that the shipment of the furniture to Jamestown be delayed.

On the evening of their arrival at the Lexington, McVicar became ill and the woman sent for Dr. John Dillon, who diagnosed the ailment as ptomaine poisoning. He administered antidotes and the patient recovered. The next day "Mrs. LeDoux" called upon the doctor and requested him to procure some morphine for her as she claimed she was addicted to the use of the drug.

Dillon provided her with a vial filled with half-grain morphine tablets.

On March 15, the couple went to Jamestown where McVicar was employed.

They registered at a hotel as "McVicar and wife" and in conversing with McVicar's friends the woman stated that they intended to make that town their permanent home.

McVicar went back to his place of employment, but a few days later, on March 21, he quit work and drew from the company all the money due him, amounting to $163.

As a reason for his sudden change of plans, McVicar stated that his wife had persuaded him to accept a position as superintendent of her mother's farming operations, which would be a far more lucrative occupation.

On March 23 the couple went to Stockton, where they called at Brenner's furniture store and purchased additional furniture, which was ordered shipped to the home of her mother; but at the suggestion of the woman it was consigned to Eugene LeDoux, her "brother-in-law."

McVicar and wife then proceeded to the California Hotel. That evening McVicar purchased three flasks of whisky and the couple was seen going to their room at 9:15 p. m.

The next morning "Mrs. LeDoux" went to the store conducted by D.

S. Rosenbaum and purchased a trunk, which she ordered delivered to room 97, California Hotel.

Shortly afterward she met an express man named Charles Berry and requested him to call at her room for the trunk in time for the 1 o'clock train.

The woman then went to G. H. Shaw's hardware store where she purchased some rope to "tie up a trunk filled with dishes" from a salesman named Bee Hart. When he delivered the rope he jokingly said: "Be careful you don't hang yourself," to which she laughingly replied that she would "be careful."

At 12:15 p. m., Mrs. LeDoux notified Berry, the express man, that she would not be ready at 1 o'clock, but for him to call at 2 p. m. and take the trunk to the depot.

She sent a telegram to Joseph Healy, a young plumber, residing at 1152 Florida Street, San Francisco, requesting him to meet her that evening at the Royal House, 126 Eddy Street, San Francisco.*

*Healy first met this woman in San Francisco, in January, 1904, when she represented herself to be a single woman named Emma Williams. He fell madly in love with her and as she promised to marry him he presented her with a diamond engagement ring.

After sending this telegram the woman repaired to her room, where she packed the trunk and bound it with the newly purchased rope, and leaving it for the express man, she went to the depot.

At 2 p. m. Berry called for the trunk, but as it was very heavy he called upon one Joe Dougherty to assist him.

When Berry arrived at the depot he met the woman, who in the meantime had displayed considerable uneasiness because of the non-arrival of the trunk, and was at the moment of its arrival attempting to telephone to the California Hotel concerning it.

The trunk was put on the baggage car of the train leaving at 4 p. m. for San Francisco, but as the baggage master noticed that it bore no check or other identification mark it was placed back on the depot truck.

In the evening it was placed in the baggage room, but in handling it the baggage man's suspicion was aroused by the peculiar thumping sound when he turned the trunk over. Upon investigating further he believed he detected an odor similar to that of a human body.

The police were notified, and when the trunk was broken open the body of a man was found.

This discovery created great excitement and the press all over the

State gave much publicity to the case.

The body, which was entirely dressed with the exception of coat and shoes, was soon identified as the remains of McVicar, and it was found that death was due to morphine poisoning and asphyxiation.

The day after the body was found, Detective Ed. Gibson, of San Francisco, learned that Mrs. LeDoux met Joe Healy in San Francisco. He located the young man, from whom he obtained a statement substantially as follows:

"I received a telegram from the so-called Mrs. LeDoux and I met her at the Royal House as she requested.

"I knew that she had married McVicar, but she told me last night that he had recently died an 'easy' death and she had shipped his body to his brother in Colorado.

"When I read the paper this morning and learned that McVicar's body was found in a trunk last night at Stockton, I showed her the article and she told me that she would go to Stockton immediately. She purchased her ticket and I accompanied her as far as Point Richmond this morning."

Gibson then had all stations on the way to Stockton notified by telegraph and it was learned that the woman left the train at Antioch, Contra Costa County, and proceeded to the Arlington Hotel, where she registered as Mrs. Jones.

She was taken in custody by Constable Whelehan, and McVicar's watch and chain were found in her possession.

When she was returned to Stockton she made a statement substantially as follows:

"McVicar and one Joe Miller were drinking in our room on the night of March 23d, and Miller put poison in the glass from which McVicar drank. The latter soon became unconscious and died.

"Fearing that I might be accused of the murder, I assisted Miller to put the body in the trunk. Miller and I then left for San Francisco and he also accompanied me from that city to Point Richmond."

All the evidence tended to prove that "Mrs. LeDoux" alone committed the murder and that her statement regarding Joe Miller was a myth.

Dr. Dillon, who furnished the morphine; the salesmen who sold the furniture, trunk and rope; the express man, baggage man, hotel attachés and Joe Healy testified before the Grand Jury, and the woman was indicted on April 2d.

As it was evident that the defendant had no intention of taking McVicar to her mother's home, where LeDoux was staying, it was the theory of the prosecution that McVicar was about to discover his wife's bigamous relations with LeDoux and that she decided to gain possession of all of McVicar's money to purchase the furniture which she expected to eventually use in the house she and LeDoux occupied, and then prevent the impending expose by forever sealing McVicar's lips.

On April 17th her trial began before a jury. She was found guilty and sentenced to be hanged, but an appeal was taken to the Supreme Court.

During the empanelment of the jury the court directed an order to the Sheriff for a special venire for 75 men. Upon the return of the venire the panel was challenged by the defendant's attorney on the ground that the Sheriff was prejudiced and had expressed an opinion that the defendant was guilty and was also actively assisting the prosecution.

As the trial judge refused to allow the challenge, the Supreme Court held that he erred and a new trial was granted.

The second trial was set for January 26, 1910, but on that morning the following letter to her attorney, Charles H. Fairall, was made public:

"Dear Sir: Owing to the condition of my health, which has become badly shattered by four years of confinement, I do not feel able to stand the strain of another trial.

"I therefore have decided to plead guilty, and I want you to do what you can to dispose of the matter quickly.

"Yours sincerely,

MRS. EMMA LEDOUX."

Her attorney made an eloquent plea for leniency, and Judge W. B. Nutter sentenced her to life imprisonment.

_____

WILLIAM WELLS, WHO MURDERED MATHIAS WETZELL IN SACRAMENTO, AND WHILE BEING RETURNED A PRISONER TO THE SCENE OF HIS CRIME, MURDERED HIS THREE CUSTODIANS AND ESCAPED — SUBSEQUENTLY KILLED IN WASHINGTON TERRITORY.

In April, 1860, an old man named Mathias Wetzell was murdered in Sacramento and robbed of a large amount of jewelry and precious stones.

On July 3d of the same year, William Wells was arrested in Virginia City, Nev., on suspicion, and some of Wetzell's property was found in his possession. Deputy Sheriff Wharton, of Sutter County, and George Armstrong, a mountaineer of Virginia City, started to take him back to the scene of the crime. They reached Marysville on July 24, 1860, and the next day started by wagon for Sacramento. When they reached the town of Nicholas, Driver Whitney, in charge of the stage which had just left Sacramento, informed the officials in charge of the prisoner that he had passed a group of men on the road, and he suspected that they were friends of Wells, and would endeavor to rescue the prisoner.

As there was another road leading into Sacramento from this place, it was decided to travel by that route, thus avoiding these men.

But as the driver was not familiar with that route, another driver, named W. C. Stoddard, was employed. The party left Nicholas at 10 p. m., Deputy Sheriff Wharton, taking a seat beside the driver and Armstrong being with Wells, who was handcuffed, in the back of the wagon.

About 1:30 a. m. the party was nearing Sacramento. Armstrong, who had the keys of the handcuffs in his pocket, dozed off, and Wells slipped his hand in the sleeping man's pocket and, procuring the key, released his hands. He then took Armstrong's revolver and shot Wharton in the back.

Wharton fell over on the horses, which became unmanageable.

The prisoner then shot Stoddard, who died instantly, and then killed Armstrong.

He then fled, but Wharton, who had in the meantime disengaged himself from the plunging horses, fired at the retreating prisoner, but owing to the darkness the bullet went wide of its mark.

The deputy sheriff, although fatally wounded, crawled into Sacramento and related what had transpired to Officer Grant. A posse immediately repaired to the scene of the tragedy, where the two bodies were found.

It was then seen that Wells had returned and removed all the valuables from the bodies, including the jewelry he had previously stolen from Wetzell, which was in the possession of Armstrong, and was being taken back to Sacramento to be used as evidence against the defendant.

Wharton died the next day.

On May 5, 1874, the Sacramento Union published a letter received from a man named E. Chaney of Placerville, Idaho, in which he stated that Wells had been killed in Washington Territory in 1864 by a member of the party with whom he was traveling.

THE CRIMINAL CAREER OF CHARLES MORTIMER—A

REMARKABLE CASE OF CIRCUMSTANTIAL EVIDENCE.

Charles J. Flinn, alias Charles Mortimer, was born in New Hampshire in 1834, and moved to Sacramento, Cal., in 1861. He gained the reputation of being an honest and industrious man, but evil companions influenced him from the path of rectitude, and he finally became one of the most notorious criminals in the State of California.

He began with a series of petty offenses, but in 1862 he was sent to State Prison from San Francisco for one year for robbing Conrad Phiester of $800.

In 1864 he entered the room of Charles L. Wiggin, on Geary Street, in San Francisco, and after chloroforming him, stole money and jewelry valued at $1500.

While in jail, Mortimer professed to repent, and as an evidence of good faith, he volunteered to accompany Special Officer Rose into Santa

Clara County where he claimed he had buried Wiggin's property, and return it to its rightful owner. Rose accompanied him, and when they reached a desolate spot, Mortimer observed a place on the ground which had the appearance of having recently been disturbed, and he informed Rose that that was the spot where the property was buried.

The officer foolishly knelt down and started to examine the ground, and Mortimer took advantage of his position and kicked him on the head. Before the officer could recover, the prisoner secured his pistol and continued to beat the prostrate man about the head until he thought he was dead, and then made his escape.

In 1865 a prisoner was brought to San Francisco from Trinity County, en route to State's Prison, to serve a seven year term for robbery.

Officer Rose had recovered in the meantime, and when the prisoner was brought into the station he recognized him as Mortimer and would have shot the prisoner, if he had not been overpowered by brother officers.

Mortimer was liberated in 1872, and he then became the consort of a woman named Carrie Spencer, whom he met in a dance hall. He was never prosecuted for the assault on Rose, as that person had in the meantime left San Francisco for parts unknown.

In May, 1872, a woman named Caroline Prenel, an inmate of a den on Waverly Place in San Francisco, was strangled and a man named Henry Beck was arrested for the murder and indicted by the grand jury. In a subsequent confession made in Sacramento, Carrie Spencer stated that Mortimer committed the crime, and to substantiate her confession she handed some of the murdered woman's jewelry to the authorities which Mortimer had given to her. Beck was promptly exonerated but Mortimer was never tried for the crime, for at the time the Spencer woman made her confession, Mortimer was under investigation for the murder of a woman in Sacramento.

In 1851, a Mrs. Mary Shaw, commonly known as Mrs. Gibson, arrived in Sacramento, and gained considerable notoriety because of her strenuous opposition to the railroad company when it was alleged that they sought to appropriate her property for railroad purposes.

She conducted a saloon in Sacramento which was frequented by people of ill repute and also Indians. About 7 a. m., September 20, 1872, a man named Chris Weiderholt was passing her saloon, when a man who frequented her place called to him and said that although the doors of the resort were all open, he could not find the proprietress.

Officer Wentworth was notified and in the woman's bedroom her body was found with her head lying in a pool of blood, caused from a deep knife wound in her neck which severed the jugular vein. She was fully dressed and appearances indicated that she made a desperate battle for her life. In her death grasp she seized a bunch of reddish brown hair, evidently from the beard of her assassin. A glass partially filled with beer was also found in the room. Upon the arrival of a female relative of the deceased it was ascertained that a pocket in her dress had been torn out and $500.00 extracted therefrom.

About 2 a. m. on the morning of the murder Officer Harris met Charles Mortimer. He had a bundle in his possession and his clothes were torn and blood was on his face. Harris interrogated him as to the cause of his condition and when Mortimer stated that he had been beaten by a couple of men, the officer accompanied him to his room at the Mechanics Exchange. When the officer learned of this murder he repaired to Mortimer's room, and although he was absent, Carrie Spencer was in, and she was taken into custody. En route to the station the officer met Mortimer, and although he wore a reddish-brown beard when he met him at 2 a. m., Mortimer was now clean shaven.

One of the employees of the hotel stated that he noticed Mortimer just before he went to the barber shop, and his face appeared as though someone had pulled out a bunch of his whiskers. Several dresses belonging to the murdered woman were found in Mortimer's room.

It was proved that Mortimer and the Spencer woman were drinking in Mrs. Shaw-Gibson's saloon on the day of the murder, and a ring found in Mortimer's possession at the time of his arrest was identified by Henry Jefferson as the property of the murdered woman.

Dr. J. F. Rudolph, a chemist, analyzed the contents of the beer glass found near Mrs. Shaw-Gibson's body and found strychnine present.

On October 10, 1872, the preliminary examination began in the Police Court and Mortimer was held to answer before the District Court, where his trial began on March 12, 1873. At this trial Carrie Spencer testified that on the morning of the murder Mortimer returned to their room, woke her up and showed her a bundle of clothes and some jewelry and about $300.00. She asked him where he got it and he replied that it came from the place where they were drinking that afternoon, and that he "croaked the old woman so that she could not squeal."

The Spencer woman then produced several sheets of paper which were all written upon, and she stated that one day previous to the trial she visited Mortimer at his cell and he handed her this paper, and ordered her to commit its contents to memory and testify accordingly, or he would cut her throat from ear to ear.

On March 15, the case was submitted to the jury, and after deliberating thirty-five minutes they returned a verdict of guilty. On March 29, Mortimer was sentenced to be hanged on May 16.

On April 16, at 1:30 a. m., Deputy Sheriff Manuel Cross was on guard at the jail where Mortimer was awaiting execution. He heard the bell ringing at the gate, and taking his revolver in his hand, proceeded to ascertain the cause of a visit from any one at this unusual hour. When he was passing through the yard and was within ten feet of the gate he saw a man standing perfectly still. This man was without hat or shoes, his coat was turned inside out, and his face was partially masked. Upon drawing nearer the officer observed that the man had a pistol pointed directly at him.

Notwithstanding his disadvantage, Cross suddenly raised his pistol and fired twice, one bullet passing through this mysterious man's chest and the other through his mouth — both fatal wounds. Although fatally wounded the man ran into the jail and directly to Mortimer's cell, and fell dead in front of it without uttering a word.

The jailor then identified the remains as those of a man who had called previously, giving the name of Williams, and inquiring as to Mortimer's welfare. Papers in his possession, however, indicated that his right name was W. M. Flinn, it being recalled that Flinn was Mortimer's right name.

The next day Mortimer was escorted to Wick & Clark's undertaking parlors to view the body. He instantly recognized the remains as those of his 23-year-old brother, whom he had not seen for sixteen years, but he identified him through photographs recently received. The dead man bore an excellent reputation in the East, but risked his life to prevent any member of the family from dying on the gallows.

Mortimer was in absolute ignorance of his brother's presence in Sacramento.

The condemned man took advantage of the tragic death of his brother and used it as an opportunity to feign insanity. He cut a lock of his dead brother's hair from his forehead and, taking it back to his cell, he pretended to believe that it was his brother, and sat watching the hair day and night. He even pretended to be enraged if a fly came near it. He ceased these tactics, however, when he saw they would avail him nothing.

On May 15, 1873, he was executed in the County Jail, and before he mounted the scaffold he stated that his one regret was that he could not lay his hands on Carrie Spencer for one minute, and then he would gladly die.

THE MURDER OF CAPITALIST AARON M. TULLIS BY PUBLIC ADMINISTRATOR TROY DYE AND TWO CONSPIRATORS NEAR SACRAMENTO.

Aaron M. Tullis, an old bachelor, resided on Grand Island on the Sacramento River for many years, and by hard work and judicious investments he accumulated a fortune estimated at $100,000.00, including 667 acres of orchard land which yielded him a handsome income.

At 6 p. m. on August 1, 1878, two men came down the river in a duck boat and landed near Tullis' residence. They asked the Chinaman at the house where Mr. Tullis could be found, and were directed to the orchard where Tullis was budding trees.

About 6:30 p. m. people living across the river heard three shots fired, and the next morning the body of Tullis was found with two bullet wounds, one in the small of the back and one in the neck.

As none of the valuables were removed from the body, and as Tullis led a secluded life and did not interfere with his neighbors, it was hard to find a motive for the crime. The Chinaman gave a very unsatisfactory description of the two visitors, and the prospects of apprehending the murderers did not seem bright.

Immediately after the discovery of the body, Public Administrator Troy Dye applied for letters of administration on the estate, but a Mr. Figel, a friend of Tullis', objected to Dye acting as administrator and telegraphed to Tullis' brother in Texas for instructions. During this time Sheriff Drew and Deputy Harrison were cleverly weaving a case around the conspirators. While they located people who saw the two men in the boat, none of them knew the men, and no further trace could be found of them or the boat. The officers continued their search on the river, and near Clarkville they found a piece of lumber on which someone had been figuring, and among other words and figures was found "64 feet." It was ascertained that this amount of lumber would make the boat described to them, so they took the board back to Sacramento and began a search of the lumber yards. When they arrived at the yard conducted by Walton, at Twelfth and J Streets, L. B. Lusk, the salesman, identified the words and figures as his own writing, and stated that he had sold 64 feet of lumber to Edward Anderson on July 30, who requested that it be sent to the home of Troy Dye on I Street near Twenty-first, where he intended to make a duck boat.

Anderson formerly worked for Dye when the latter was in the butcher business. Dye admitted that the boat was built at his home, but he stated that Anderson intended to use it to carry himself to his place of employment up the river.

On August 12, Troy Dye was arrested, and on the following day Anderson was arrested at his home at L and Nineteenth Streets. Express man Stone stated that he hauled the boat to the river on the early evening of July 31.

On August 14, Dye broke down and made a complete confession to District Attorney G. A. Blanchard, as follows:

"I was born in Iowa and I am now 35 years old. I came to Sacramento in 1866 and I was first employed as a rancher, then as a butcher and afterward I conducted a saloon. On March 4, 1878, I took office as public administrator. A few weeks later, while Forepaugh's circus was in town, I was in company with Ed. Anderson and several friends, and in speaking about the income from my new office I explained that I received no regular salary, only a percentage from the estates that I administered upon.

"This put an idea into Anderson's head and without consulting me, he went that night to the residence of a rich man named Jackson whom he saw down town and laid in wait to murder him with an iron bar as he returned to his home. Fortunately for Jackson he was accompanied by two friends and thus his life was saved.

"The next day Anderson told me of what he had attempted to do and I admonished him to be very careful. He replied that he had already killed two men. He said that six years previously he was working on Patton's ranch and he killed a man who was the cause of his (Anderson) being discharged and threw the body in a well.

"In the second case the victim was a sheep-herder who had a falling out with Anderson and the latter struck him with an iron bar after he had gone to sleep and then burned the cabin.

"I continued to conduct my saloon after being elected to office, and one night Anderson and Tom Lawton, who resided with his mother and sisters in Sacramento, came to my saloon and we had a long talk about my office. Shortly afterward Anderson went to Yuba City in Sutter County to work, and on July 5 I went up after him and discussed the advisability of killing Tullis. Anderson was agreeable to the proposition and agreed to leave his position on July 13 and join Lawton and me in Sacramento. He kept his agreement and on the next day Lawton and Anderson stole a boat and rowed to Tullis' place. The next morning I met the men near Freeport according to agreement, but they stated that they had accomplished nothing, as Tullis was away on a visit to friends.

"Anderson then returned to Yuba City, but came back to Sacramento on the 27th inst. He wanted to go after Tullis again, to which I was agreeable, but I was opposed to his building the boat that they used as I feared it would lead to our arrest. I preferred to steal a boat.

"I loaned my pistol to Lawton and borrowed one from a blacksmith named Way to loan to Anderson. They left Sacramento on the evening of July 31 and took along a basket of provisions. On the evening of August 1 they found Tullis in his orchard and first knocked him down with a sandbag and then shot him twice.

"They then rowed away and broke up the boat in the tules on the Odell ranch, and I met them the next morning with a horse and buggy about a mile below Richland."

When confronted with Dye's confession Anderson weakened and admitted that it was the truth. Lawton escaped before the confession was obtained and was never apprehended.

While Dye claimed that he had never participated in any other crime, it was subsequently learned that his saloon, known as the "Sierra Nevada," had been a rendezvous for thieves. On March 28, 1878, just a few weeks after Dye took office, the body of a young man named George Lawrence, who had been a frequenter of Dye's saloon, was found in Tivoli pond, north of Sacramento. The day before Lawrence disappeared, he delivered his property to a young man, who subsequently delivered it to Dye and then suddenly disappeared.

On October 29, 1878, Dye, Anderson and Lawton were indicted for murder, and on January 7, 1879, the trial began before the Sixth District Court. Creed Raymond entered a plea of guilty for his client Dye.

The prosecution presented its case, and on January 10 the jury returned a verdict of guilty with the death penalty attached.

On January 11, Anderson's case commenced and he also plead guilty and was sentenced to be hanged.

A. F. Clarke was Dye's partner in the saloon business and as the defendants Anderson and Dye stated that he had a full knowledge of the conspiracy, an indictment was found against him, but on motion of the district attorney the case was dismissed.

March 13, 1879, was set as the date for the execution of Dye and Anderson, but a stay was granted, and the cases were appealed to the Supreme Court, which sustained the lower court in a decision rendered on April 22.

The date for the execution was then set for May 29.

Anderson remained indifferent to the last, but Dye nearly collapsed when he bade his little family good-by, and collapsed completely when the cap was placed over his head.

THE SLAUGHTERING OF F. H. L. WEBER AND WIFE IN

SACRAMENTO BY THE ESCAPED RUSSIAN NIHILISTS.

F. H. L. Weber crossed the plains in 1858, and for thirty years prior to his death he conducted a grocery business on L Street, near the Capitol, in Sacramento; residing with his wife on the floor over his store.

On December 29, 1894, at 9:30 p. m., A. A. Jost, a partner in the business, bade Weber "good-night" and left for his home.

At 11 p. m. two neighbors saw Weber moving about his rooms with a candle in his hand.

Shortly afterward they heard the exclamation "Oh!" which was immediately followed by a noise similar to one piece of steel striking another, but as they attached no importance to what they had seen and heard, they gave the incident no further thought at the time.

On the following morning, Mr. Weber's son, Luther, who opened his father's store, was startled when he observed a pool of blood on the floor of the store, and on looking up saw that the ceiling was saturated with the crimson fluid.

He rushed up the back stairs and there a gory spectacle was presented to his view.

On the kitchen floor he found his father's body with the head cleft wide open; his brains having oozed out on to the floor, and in the doorway of the same room lay his mother's body, butchered in the same frightful manner.

The sight paralyzed the son for a moment, but when he realized what had happened, he fled screaming from the building.

It was evident that Weber, Sr., had heard some unusual noise and was in the act of investigating when his neighbors saw him with a candle. When he was attacked in the kitchen his wife evidently started to his assistance when she was also assaulted.

The assassins then ransacked the entire house, and in addition to taking two suits of clothing belonging to Weber, they stole two watches, $200.00, a revolver and some underwear.

An ax belonging to Weber was found covered with blood in the back yard, and on further search some rough clothes covered with blood were also discovered.

It was concluded that at least two men were implicated in the murder and that they wore Weber's clothing in lieu of their own blood-soaked garments.

On New Year's eve the usual round-up of drunks occurred in San Francisco, and as a result the cells at the old California Street station were crowded.

On the following morning, according to custom, the bleary-eyed and foul-smelling drunks were placed in a line, and after solemnly swearing off for the remainder of the year they were released, after being reprimanded by the judge.

The work of scrubbing out the cells then began, and a small gold watch was found behind a toilet in one of the cells.

It was sent to Captain Lees for investigation, and from a description already received, he instantly recognized it as one of the watches taken from Weber's house on the night of the murders.

Luther Weber immediately came to San Francisco and identified the watch as one presented to his father.

In August, 1893, ten prisoners, who were confined in the Russian penal settlements on Saghalien Island, made their escape, and after enduring almost indescribable hardships, finally reached the eastern coast of the island. After procuring an open boat they put to sea, where their sufferings from exposure, thirst and hunger were about to drive them insane, when they were picked up by the American Bark "*Chas. W. Morgan*," bound for San Francisco.

When they arrived in San Francisco they claimed that they were thrown into the Russian prison merely because of their political beliefs. The newspapers published lengthy interviews, in which the Russians described at length the suffering they had endured, and the good people of the city, believing them to be poor, persecuted creatures, showered them with kindness.

Among these refugees were John Koboloff, alias Ivan Kovalov, and two others, named Nikitin and Stcherbakov.

On June 12, 1895, Deputy Sheriff Martin Hughes informed Captain of Detectives Lee that he believed that a man named E. K. Bennett, of 937 Post Street, could impart some valuable information regarding the Weber murder case.

Lees sent for Bennett, but all he knew was that a man named L. Stevens, residing at 715 Howard Street, was supposed to know something concerning the crime.

Stevens was brought forth, and he stated that he had become acquainted with a ship carpenter named Vladislav Zakrewski, who had gained the confidence of Kovalov, one of the Russian refugees.

Zakrewski told Stevens that he could put his finger on the murderer of the Webber's, and after swearing Stevens to secrecy, stated that Kovalov was not only the murderer but that he still had some of Weber's belongings in his possession.

Detective Chas. Cody and Officer Tom Tobin (now lieutenant) located Zakrewski in a shack on the Seventh-Street dumps. He stated that one night Kovalov visited him and they spent the evening drinking. Finally Kovalov became intoxicated and, in a burst of confidence, related to Zakrewski how he and another Russian refugee named Alatthiew Stcherbakov murdered the Webber's. Zakrewski then accompanied the officers to Kovalov's room at the St. David house, on Howard near Fourth Street, where Kovalov and one Arnold Levin were found in bed.

Both men were taken into custody and all of their effects were removed to Captain Lees' office.

The daughter of the murdered couple came from Sacramento and she positively identified a pair of suspenders found in the possession of Kovalov as the property of her father, and pointed to some fancy needle-work she had done on them.

The incident in relation to the watch found in the prison was again a subject for investigation.

It was ascertained that Kovalov was arrested on New Year's Eve, while engaged in a drunken brawl with a young man named Geo. Petelon, in a saloon at Clay and Kearny Streets.

On June 25, 1895, Petelon was located, and upon being brought before Kovalov, immediately identified him as the man with whom he was arrested and sent to the California-Street station.

He furthermore stated that although Kovalov could speak the English language well enough to be understood, he could not read it, and on New Year's eve, when they first met, the prisoner purchased an evening paper and asked Petelon to read to him all it contained in regard to the developments in the Weber murder case.

On the night of March 31, 1895, William Dowdigan was en route from his grocery store to his residence, in San Jose, when he was attacked by three men. Dowdigan had a jackknife in his hand and he stabbed one of his assailants in the side, whereupon all three fled. Dowdigan reported the occurrence to the police, who placed little credence in the story, but the next day the body of a man, which answered the general description of one of the holdup men, was found near the scene of the assault.

In addition to the wound in the side, the man had also been stabbed through the heart.

Zakrewski informed Captain Lees that he accompanied Kovalov, Stcherbakov and Nikitin to San Jose for the purpose of committing a series of robberies, but that he changed his mind and refused to participate in any crime. Kovalov afterward confessed to him that the remainder of the party held up Dowdigan and as Stcherbakov was so seriously wounded by the grocer that they would have to leave him behind, it was feared that he would fall into the hands of the police and tell all he knew, so Kovalov stabbed his companion through the heart for the purpose of sealing his lips.

On June 27, the authorities proceeded to the potter's field in San Jose and dug up the body of the highwayman. Although terribly decomposed, enough remained intact to convince the officers that it was the remains of Stcherbakov.

Levin, who was arrested with Kovalov, confessed that he accompanied Stcherbakov and Kovalov to Sacramento, but when they requested him to aid them in the commission of several burglaries, he refused and returned to San Francisco. He furthermore said:

> *"I saw them again in San Francisco on January 5, and they were both well dressed and Kovalov wore a gold watch and chain.*
>
> *"Kovalov was extremely nervous and when I questioned him as to the cause, he began crying and expressed the fear that he would be hanged, but would not state what crime he had committed to justify such punishment.*
>
> *"On another occasion, Kovalov informed me that he was implicated in the murder of a large family in Russia and that was the true cause of his confinement in the Russian prison."*

On June 28, 1895, Kovalov was surrendered to the Sacramento authorities, and on July 3 he was held to answer before the Superior Court.

On November 4 his trial began, but was continued for the purpose of examining into the prisoner's sanity.

He was declared to be of sound mind and the trial proceeded. After the prisoner saw the amount of evidence which had been introduced against him, he took the stand and admitted he was present at the murder, but stated that Stcherbakov struck the blows with the ax.

Kovalov expressed a desire to be hanged as soon as possible, as he felt that he would go insane from the mental torture he was enduring.

When the case was submitted to the jury, on November 30, Kovalov was found guilty of murder with the death penalty attached. On February 21, 1896, he was hanged.

By virtue of the authority found in Section 1547 of the Penal Code, the Governor offered a reward of one thousand dollars for the apprehension and conviction of the murderers.

Captain Lees claimed this reward, but payment was refused by Controller Colgan on the grounds that Lees was a public officer working for a fixed compensation and that he merely performed his sworn duty.

The matter was taken before Superior Judge Troutt, who decided in favor of Lees.

The case was then appealed to the Supreme Court, and on March 11, 1898, that Court handed down a decision upholding Colgan's contention.

THE REMARKABLE CASE OF BROWNING AND BRADY,

MURDERERS AND TRAIN ROBBERS.

At 9 p. m., October 12, 1894, two young men, one very tall and powerfully built and the other of medium height, halted a track-walker named John Kelly as he was speeding along on a track tricycle about seven miles from Davisville, Cal.

They relieved Kelly of $5.50, some dynamite cartridges used for signaling trains, and his red lantern. Their next move was to bind him hand and foot and render the tricycle useless.

The cartridges were then placed on the track and the robbers awaited the arrival of No. 3 Omaha Overland, which left Sian Francisco at 6 p. m.

Presently it appeared, and in response to the wild waving of the red lantern in the hands of one of the robbers and the explosion of the dynamite cartridges. Engineer Bill Scott lost no time in bringing his train to a standstill.

The bandits then pointed pistols at the engineer and fireman and ordered them to accompany them (the robbers) to the third car back, which was Wells Fargo and Co.'s express car.

The fireman was instructed to uncouple the express car from the cars in the rear.

The engineer and fireman were then ordered to accompany the robbers to the locomotive and pull the three cars about three miles from the remainder of the train, the robbers keeping them covered with revolvers all the while.

When they came to a stop, the fireman and engineer were instructed to accompany the robbers to the express car, and Engineer Scott was told to persuade J. F. Paige, the express messenger, to open the door or he (Scott) would be killed.

In response to Scott's pleadings, Paige finally opened the door, but not before he had fired several shots, none of which did any damage.

The engineer and fireman were then ordered to enter the car and carry the contents of the safe, nearly $53,000.00, back to the locomotive.

The fireman was ordered to uncouple the engine from the cars. The robbers then entered the cab and throwing the throttle wide open they sped away in the darkness, leaving the trainmen standing by the track dumfounded.

After traveling a couple of miles they stopped the engine, and after removing their loot, reversed the lever, opened the throttle and jumped to the ground.

The engine returned to the three cars, but as the steam was then low, the only damage done was to cave in the end of the first car.

When the robbers jumped from the engine they were about two miles from Sacramento, and as their loot was too heavy to carry any distance without attracting attention, it was surmised that the money was cached near the spot where the bandits left the locomotive.

The railroad and express company detectives cooperated with Chief of Police Drew of Sacramento in organizing and sending out Posses after the bandits, but they returned despondent and empty handed.

For several years prior to 1895, the Ingleside roadhouse was conducted in the southwestern suburbs of San Francisco by aged Cornelius Stagg, who was a jovial host and boon companion.

At 9:40 p. m., on March 16, 1895, two men, wearing linen dusters and white masks, entered the side door of this roadhouse.

At the time the bartender and three patrons were in the barroom. The robbers covered the four men with pistols and ordered them to throw up their hands. The taller of the two then left these four in charge of his companion while he proceeded to the rear rooms on a tour of inspection.

In the sitting-room he found Mr. Stagg conversing with Robert Lee, his colored servant.

The robber ordered the two men to hold up their hands, but Stagg, being a practical joker himself, concluded that some of his friends were turning the tables on him and merely laughed at the command.

The infuriated robber then sprang at him and struck him a terrible blow over the head.

The negro took advantage of his opportunity and instantly bolted for the door.

It is presumed that Stagg continued to offer resistance, for immediately afterward two shots were heard. The tall robber then returned to the barroom and after hurriedly removing the contents of the money-till, about $4.00, the two bandits backed out of the place and disappeared.

The men in the barroom then rushed to the sitting-room to ascertain the cause of the shooting, and they found Stagg dying from two bullet wounds.

At 1:45 a. m., March 30, 1895, the Oregon Express train. No. 15, was running at a high rate of speed near Wheatland, a small town twelve miles south of Marysville, Cal., when Engineer A. L. Bowser and Fireman Barney Nethercott were startled by feeling a pointed instrument against their backs and at the same time hearing a command to halt the train. Upon turning around they observed two masked men who had revolvers in their hands. The engineer lost no time in bringing his train to a halt at the next road crossing in accordance with the command of the taller of the two bandits.

The robbers then ordered Bowser and Nethercott to precede them to Wells Fargo and Co.'s car. Upon being informed that his car would be dynamited if he did not open it instantly, the express messenger opened the door and the shorter of the two robbers entered and began a search for money. The through safe containing the valuables was locked with a combination unknown to the messenger, and as the robbers had no equipment for blowing open the safe, they handed Fireman Nethercott a sack made from the leg of an old pair of overalls, and compelled him and the engineer to precede them into the passenger cars. The passengers who had not gone to bed were instructed to keep their seats and place their valuables in the sack which the fireman carried. All the passengers in the first car complied with the request with the exception of a man named Sampson, who positively refused to part with his valuables. For his "obstinacy" the tall robber beat him over the head with his revolver in a most brutal manner. The bandits and their involuntary companions then proceeded to the smoking car, where they began operations in the same manner as in the first car.

In the meantime, a colored porter, knowing that Sheriff J. J. Bogard of Tehama County was in bed in a sleeping car, ran to locate the official and notify him of what was transpiring. The Sheriff dressed hastily and, pistol in hand, he rushed to the smoker. He immediately opened fire on the taller of the two masked robbers and shot him through the breast, killing him instantly. The shorter of the two bandits then began firing, the first shot killing the Sheriff, and the next shot seriously wounding the fireman, who still held the improvised receptacle for the loot.

After firing several shots promiscuously, the lone bandit backed out of the car and disappeared in the darkness without stopping to take the booty from the wounded fireman. The train bearing the dead and wounded was then rushed to Marysville.

Peace officers went to work on the case at once. On the day following the tragedy. Sheriff Sam Inlow of Yuba County and Deputy Sheriff Bogard of Tehama County, a brother of the murdered Sheriff, located a bicycle in the brush near the scene of the holdup, and on the same day they found another bicycle hidden under a small bridge near State Senator Dan Ostrom's home, which was about three miles from the scene of the robbery. It was the theory of the officers that this was the bicycle upon which the short bandit escaped and that the one found in the brush belonged to the bandit who was killed.

As the robbers ordered the train to stop near the spot where the bicycle was concealed in the brush, it was presumed that the machines had been previously hidden there to be used as a means of escape.

The general appearance and modus operandi of these two men convinced the authorities that they were the same men who held up the

Omaha train near Davisville on October 12, 1894, and also murdered old Cornelius Stagg in San Francisco.

Believing that these men procured their bicycles in San Francisco, the machines were brought to the city, where they were positively identified by Perkins & Speiker, bicycle agents, who had rented out the machines to two men about one week previous to the last holdup. When shown a photograph of the dead bandit, the members of the firm at once recognized it as a likeness of the taller of the two men who hired the bicycles. After showing the picture to several people in the neighborhood it was finally ascertained that it was a photograph of the remains of a man known as O. S. Brown, who had resided at 626 Golden Gate Avenue, San Francisco.

A further investigation disclosed the fact that a short man named John Brady, alias John McGuire, alias Henry Williams, an ex-convict who resided at 305 Grove Street, had been Brown's inseparable companion, but had disappeared immediately after the bicycles had been procured. (These men had previously served a term in prison for horse stealing.)

Brady's room was searched and in a trunk Captain of Detectives Lees found photographs of Brady and the man known as Brown, whose right name was Samuel Browning. The newspapers published Brady's likeness, but the bandit remained under cover for many months.

On July 25, 1895, a man entered the grocery store conducted by Phil Reihl in the village called Freeport, a few miles from Sacramento. He purchased a can of oysters and some crackers, and while Reihl was wrapping up the package the stranger picked up the newspaper of that date. He became so absorbed in an article that he became unconscious of his surroundings and the expression on his face as he perused the article attracted Reihl's attention.

After finishing the article the stranger threw down the paper and his suppressed excitement was apparent as he hastily left the store. Through curiosity Reihl picked up the paper and. saw that the article which so affected his strange customer was in relation to a clew which the officers had recently obtained regarding the whereabouts of Brady. The grocer immediately telephoned to the Sheriff, who sent Deputies Alexander McDonald and W. A. Johnson in pursuit.

At 8 a. m, on the following day the deputies saw a man sitting under a bridge near the village of Richland, about 17 miles from Sacramento. They managed to close in on him without being observed, and when they pointed their weapons at him he was so surprised that he had no opportunity to resist.

At first he claimed that he was not Brady and that he had never committed a crime, but a sawed-off shotgun was lying beside him which was subsequently identified as property stolen from Wells-Fargo Express car during the last holdup.

On July 27 the man admitted that he was Brady and made a complete confession, in which he stated that Browning and he robbed Stagg's place and also committed both train robberies. He furthermore took the officers to the spot in the tules near Sacramento where he and Browning had buried $50,000.00 of the money stolen near Davisville. The officers recovered $17,000.00, but what became of the balance remained a mystery until the year following.

On July 29 Brady was taken to Marysville by Sheriff Inlow to be tried for the murder of Sheriff Bogard. On August 13 his preliminary examination was concluded and he was held to answer. On November 27, 1895, Brady was convicted and sentenced to life imprisonment.

On the morning of February 7, 1896, a stranger entered the office of Detective Hume, of Wells, Fargo & Company, and informed him that he suspected that a man known to him as Carl Herman had gained possession of the money stolen by Browning and Brady, When asked the reason for his suspicions he replied:

"I have a friend named Kohler who is a blacksmith and a personal friend of Herman, who until October, 1894, was commonly called 'Carl the tramp.' Up to that time he never had a cent, never worked and was a typical tramp. Suddenly he discarded his rags, arrayed himself in the costliest garments and had diamonds galore. He became a constant visitor at the racetrack, where he met a woman known as May Vaughn. Herman spent money lavishly on her and her female companions, and finally fitted up a flat for the Vaughn woman at 412 Post Street, San Francisco. He then went to Chicago, but becoming lonesome, he telegraphed $1,000.00 to May with instructions to join him immediately. May got the money but did not go to Chicago. Carl then returned to San Francisco but not to May.

"Herman found no difficulty in getting 'friends' to help him spend his money and one night he gave a dinner at Zinkand's which cost him over $300.00."

The stranger also informed Detective Hume that Kohler had an appointment with Herman at Second and Howard Streets that morning. Detectives White and Thacker were detailed to watch the place designated, and at the appointed time a man of Herman's description made his appearance. The detectives took him into custody and using the information obtained from the stranger, they soon had the man so unnerved that he voluntarily made the following confession:

"My right name is John P. Harms. On the night of the Davisville train robbery I slept in the tules near Sacramento, and on the following morning I discovered a spot where the ground had been recently disturbed and covered over with leaves in a very careful manner. I investigated and soon dug up the golden treasure. I could only carry $33,000 conveniently, so I placed that amount in my blankets and beat a hasty retreat."

The detectives learned of deposits in banks and notes which Harms held aggregating $12,000.00. Wells-Fargo gained possession of this money through civil suits and Harms was charged with grand larceny. He was convicted and on May 31, 1896, was sentenced to serve three years in Folsom Prison. On October 8, 1898, he was released.

ADOLPH WEBER, BANK ROBBER AND MURDERER OF

HIS FATHER, MOTHER, SISTER AND BROTHER.

On May 26, 1904, at the noon hour, a masked man entered the Bank of Placer County, located at Auburn, Cal., and drawing a revolver, ordered the employees present to hold up their hands. He then stole $5,000.00 and disappeared.

At that time, many circumstances pointed toward Adolph Weber as the robber. He was the son of Julius Weber, who being in prosperous circumstances, retired from the brewery business, and resided with his family in the suburbs of Auburn. At the time of this robbery, Mr. Weber, Sr., missed a home-made money bag from the house and it was said that the evidence against young Weber became so convincing that a compromise was effected to avoid a prosecution.

The Weber family consisted of Mr. and Mrs. Weber, an eighteen-year-old daughter named Bertha, and two sons, Adolph and Earl, aged twenty and eight years respectively. Earl was an invalid.

On November 10, 1904, about 7 p. m., the Weber home was burned down. At the time the fire was discovered, the son, Adolph, entered a store conducted by one Cohen in Auburn, and purchased a new pair of trousers. He wrapped up his old pants and running to his burning home, broke in the window with his hand and threw the trousers into the flames. In breaking the window, he cut his hand so severely that he became weak from the loss of blood, and spent the remainder of the night at the home of Adrian Wills.

When the fire was first discovered, a man named George Ruth broke in the door and found the bodies of Mrs. Weber and Bertha in a room which had not been reached by the fire at that time. Bullet wounds were found and they had evidently been dragged into this room after being killed and an effort had been made to set their clothing on fire. The little invalid boy, Earl, was not yet dead, but died shortly afterward from the effects of blows delivered on his head by some blunt instrument. The body of the father was not found until the following day, and bullet wounds were also found in his body.

At the conclusion of the coroner's inquest on November 12, 1904, Adolph Weber was placed under arrest on a charge of murder. Mrs. Snowden, the aunt of Julius Weber, testified that after the murders, she told Adolph that she believed that he knew a great deal about the crime, whereupon he flew into a rage and said: "Your turn will come next."

The trousers which Weber threw through the window were subjected to an examination and blood stains were found thereon.

On November 21, 1904, a 32-calibre revolver was found under the flooring of the barn in the rear of Weber's house. All the shells were exploded and on the handle of the revolver was found clots of blood and some of the little boy's hair. The murderer had evidently used all of his cartridges in killing the other three and used the butt of his pistol to finish the invalid child.

Henry Carr, who conducted a pawnshop on DuPont Street, in San Francisco, positively identified this pistol as one he sold to Weber in July, 1904, when he came to Carr's place with a companion, who purchased a pair of brass knuckles and a blackjack.

J. A. Powell, a mining man from Bullion, testified that about 7 p. m. on the evening of the murder, Weber entered the washroom of the American Hotel and began to wash his hands. His actions were so peculiar that Powell watched him very closely, and when Weber observed that he was being watched, he fled from the washroom without drying his hands.

On November 23, Coroner Shepperd and other officers were digging in the yard of the former Weber residence and unearthed a 5-pound lard can full of $20.00 gold pieces, which was evidently the proceeds from the bank robbery.

When the bank robbery was committed, the robber dropped his

pistol, which was afterward identified by a pawnbroker from Sacramento named Lichenstein, as one he had sold to Weber.

His trial for the murder of his mother began on February 6, 1905, and on February 22 the jury brought in a verdict of guilty of murder with the death penalty attached.

Numerous appeals were taken; also a stay of execution was granted pending his examination for insanity, but on September 27, 1906, he was hanged. He maintained the same stoical indifference on the gallows as he had shown throughout his incarceration.

Weber's relatives undoubtedly knew that he committed the bank robbery, and his motive for committing these murders, which have few parallels in the annals of crime, was probably for the double purpose of forever sealing their lips and to gain possession of the Weber fortune.

THE REMARKABLE CRIMINAL CAREER OF THE STAGE ROBBER, CHARLES BOLES, ALIAS "BLACK BART."

On August 12, 1877, the stage running from Fort Ross to Russian River was held up by a lone highwayman wearing a mask and exhibiting a shotgun. There were no passengers on the stage and after obtaining $325.00 from Wells-Fargo's treasure box, the bandit very courteously bid the driver good-day and disappeared.

On July 28, 1878, the stage running between Quincy and Oroville was held up by a robber whose general appearance and conduct indicated that he was the same individual who committed the Russian River robbery. On this occasion he obtained jewels and money valued at $600.00 from Wells-Fargo's treasure box.

After the stage departed, he picked up a Wells-Fargo waybill and dedicated the following verse to the company, which was afterward found at the scene of the holdup:

"Here I lay me down to sleep.

To wait the coming morrow, Perhaps success, perhaps defeat

And everlasting sorrow. Yet come what will — I'll try it on,

My condition can't be worse. And if there's money in that box

'Tis money in my purse.

Black Bart, P. O. 8."

As the mail was also robbed on this last occasion, the Federal government joined Wells, Fargo & Company in offering large rewards, but this did not stop "Black Bart," for he held up two other stages within a few months afterward. The first was the stage running from Covelo to Ukiah and the second was on the road from Weaverville to Shasta.

On November 3, 1883, the twenty-eighth and last stage was held up by this lone and courteous bandit. On this date he stopped the stage running from Milton to Sonora, near Copperopolis. The driver, J. McConnell, was the only occupant, and the highwayman ordered him to unhitch the horses and hand out Wells-Fargo's box, from which the robber took $4,100.00 in amalgam and $550.00 in gold coin.

At this stage of the proceedings, an Italian boy with a rifle carelessly thrown over his shoulder, came down the road. This seemed to alarm the robber, who grabbed his loot and ran. McConnell procured the rifle from the boy and fired several shots at the fleeing highwayman, who, in his haste, dropped a handkerchief on which was a laundry mark, "F. O. X. 7." This was the only clew as to his identity.

Captain Harry Morse took charge of the case. Working on the theory that the robber probably visited the country regions only for the purpose of committing these crimes and then probably enjoyed his ill-gotten gains in the metropolis, a search was made in the laundries in this city to ascertain who received laundry with this mark.

After a search of the entire city it was finally ascertained that T. C. Ware, a laundry agent on Bush Street near Montgomery, used this mark to designate a customer known as "Charles E. Bolton."

Morse then ascertained that Mr. Bolton resided in room 40 at the Webb House, located at 27 Second Street, and that he posed as a mining man whose "interests" required him to make frequent trips to the mining regions. A "shadow" was placed on this building and Captain Morse made frequent visits to the laundry office.

One day while there, Mr. Bolton was seen approaching, and Ware agreed to introduce Morse to him, representing that he (Morse) was a mining man. When Bolton arrived, the introduction took place and Morse stated that he had some ore which he wished to have examined, and as Ware had stated that Bolton was a mining man, the latter agreed to accompany Morse for the purpose of making the examination, but when they reached Wells-Fargo's office, Morse took him into Detective Thacker's private room.

Bolton was about fifty years of age, immaculate in appearance and an extremely interesting conversationalist. When he learned the nature of the investigation he pretended to be indignant and threatened those who were detaining him.

A search was made of his room and a Bible was found in which was written: "To my beloved husband, Charles E. Boles." Handkerchiefs similar to the one dropped were also found.

Boles was then taken to San Andreas, and after a severe examination he made a complete confession of the twenty-eight robberies he had committed.

He stated that his right name was Boles, and that he served in an Illinois regiment during the Civil War. He proudly boasted that he had resolved never to harm a human being, and that the shotgun which he invariably carried was as harmless as a broomstick, as it was never loaded. He then took the officers to the spot in the hills where he had buried the proceeds from the last robbery.

He pleaded guilty to the last robbery and on November 21, 1883, was sent to San Quentin for seven years.

During his visits to San Francisco between robberies, he ate at a restaurant patronized by a number of local detectives and frequently joked with them regarding the inability of the country officers to capture "Black Bart."

In 1899 he was released and stated before leaving prison that he would commit no more crimes.

When asked if he would write any more poetry he replied: "Did you not hear me say I would commit no more crimes?"

Immediately after leaving San Quentin Boles came to San Francisco and, after calling on the officers who were instrumental in his conviction, he disappeared, never to be seen or heard of again.

THE FOUL MURDER OF CAPTAIN AND MRS. WICKERSHAM NEAR CLOVERDALE, CAL., BY A CHINAMAN, WHO WAS ARRESTED AND COMMITTED SUICIDE IN JAIL AT HONG KONG.

Captain J. C. Wickersham was born in New York in 1834 and was a nephew of J. G. Wickersham, the Petaluma, Cal., banker.

Mrs. Wickersham was born in Masonet, Mass., her maiden name being Pickett. She was much younger than the Captain and was a small and very pretty brunette.

The couple were very happy on their well-stocked ranch, which was located about twelve miles from Cloverdale, Cal., and their many charitable deeds endeared them to all who knew them. The only other person on the ranch was their Chinese servant, named Aug Tai Duck.

At this time the Indians were numerous throughout the State and were frequently severely chastised when found prowling around farm houses, as it was believed that they had come only to steal. It therefore became a practice among those whose "intentions were honorable," to stand off a safe distance from a house where they wished to converse with the occupants and call out to attract attention.

On the morning of January 21, 1886, some Indians approached the Wickersham home and called out repeatedly, but received no response and saw no sign of life. Instinct seemed to tell them that something was wrong, but fearing to enter the premises they reported their suspicions to a neighbor named J. E. Jewell. The latter immediately repaired to the Wickersham home, where he beheld a terrible sight.

The frightfully mutilated body of Captain Wickersham was in a sitting posture in a chair drawn up to the dining table, his untouched meal before him. A great gaping wound in the chest showed that a load from a shotgun had been fired into his body at close range, and the top of his head was literally blown off by a similar weapon.

A search was made for Mrs. Wickersham, and her terribly mutilated body was found on the bed. The assailant had struck her over the nose and mouth, breaking the nose and cutting the lips so that the teeth protruded. She was also bound, gagged and foully outraged, and then shot in the breast' with a shotgun.

The terror-stricken Jewell fled from the house and proceeded to Skaggs Springs, from which place Sheriff Bishop, Marshal Blume, Coroner

King and Constable Truitt were notified.

These officers attempted to reach the scene of the tragedy, but the heavy rains had swollen the little brooks to raging torrents and they were forced to turn back.

The next day, January 22, Deputy Sheriff Cook and Constable Truitt headed a party and after many perilous adventures, during which one of their horses was drowned, they reached the scene of the slaughter.

In the kitchen they found an empty shotgun, four empty cartridges, and the Chinaman's apron saturated with blood.

At 3 p. m. on the same day, a Coroner's inquest was held at Cloverdale and the Chinese servant was charged with the crime.

An investigation disclosed the fact that the heathen did not linger long at the ranch after committing these atrocious deeds. That very night, January 18, he ran through the rain and slush to Cloverdale and confessed his crime to his uncle, who advised him to flee to San Francisco and thence to China.

Conductor Mold of the Donohue Railroad stated that on the morning of the 19th, a Chinaman of Aug Tai Duck's description came running down the track like a wild man just as the train was leaving Cloverdale for Tiburon.

The engineer slowed up, but the Chinaman was so completely exhausted that he experienced much difficulty in climbing up the steps of the car.

The murderer's uncle, Ah Kum, fearing that he would be prosecuted if he did not divulge to the authorities the information he received, proceeded at once to San Francisco and sought the advice of Lee Cum Wah, the President of the Ning Yung Association, of which both Ah Kum and the murderer were members. It was decided to notify Chief of Police Crowley, who instructed Ah Kum to be at the wharf the next day when the Steamer Rio de Janeiro left for China.

Either through a misunderstanding of orders or a fear of future consequences, Ah Kum failed to appear at the appointed time, and messengers were sent to Chinatown, but they did not return with Ah Kum until the vessel was well out to sea.

It was then learned that the murderer was on board the vessel and had purchased his ticket from Hop Wo & Co.

Chief Crowley telegraphed to Washington to United States Senator Leland Stanford of California, who was also the President of the

Southern Pacific Railroad and founder of the Stanford University, that the murderer had escaped, and requested him to ask Secretary Bayard to communicate with the Japanese Government for the purpose of having Aug Tai Duck apprehended at Yokohama. This was done and the United States Government was notified. Detective Chris Cox of San Francisco took the next steamer to bring back the murderer. In the meantime it was shown to the Japanese that there was no treaty to justify their actions.

It was therefore decided to turn the fugitive over to the Captain of the "City of New York" with instructions to deliver the prisoner to the British authorities in Hong Kong.

While en route to Hong Kong, the prisoner became extremely melancholy and decided to commit suicide by starvation, but when he was informed that he would probably not have to return to California, he cheered up and ate ravenously.

On March 13, he arrived at Hong Kong and was placed in the Victoria Jail to await the arrival of the detective.

On March 29, at 1:30 a. m. Turnkey Thomas Roolf, in making his rounds, found the murderer hanging by the neck to the bars of his cell. He had defeated justice by hanging himself with a silk sash which he wore around his waist.

It was a most singular coincidence that both vessels carrying this fugitive were subsequently lost at the entrance to San Francisco harbor, and that one of the heroes of the hour was a Chinaman.

On October 26, 1893, the Pacific Mail Steamer City of New York, left the San Francisco Mail dock at 2:35 p. m., bound for China. She was in command of Captain F. H. Johnson and Pilot George Johnson. A dense fog suddenly came in from the ocean and the vessel struck Point Bonita at 4:35 p. m. Although a great number of passengers were on board no lives were lost, but the vessel was eventually pounded to pieces by the great waves.

On the evening of February 21, 1901, the Rio de Janeiro arrived off San Francisco from China, and after taking Pilot Fred Jordan on board, anchored outside for the night on account of the fog. The vessel was in command of Captain W. Ward of San Francisco. The next morning an attempt was made to enter the harbor, but the vessel ran into a fog bank and at 6 a. m. she struck Mile Rock. In less than ten minutes she sank. The water was extremely deep at this point and notwithstanding the numerous efforts made, her exact location has never been ascertained.

One hundred and twenty-seven persons were drowned, including Captain Ward and Rounseville Wildman, United States Consul-General at Hong Kong, and his wife. Although Pilot Jordan went down with the vessel he came to the surface and was saved by a Chinaman. Two Italian fishermen saved twenty-two people whom they found clinging to wreckage. The only body ever recovered was that of Captain Ward, which was found a year later.

THE LYNCHING OF FIVE APPARENTLY INNOCENT PERSONS AT LOOKOUT, MODOC COUNTY.

(From Attorney-General Tirey L. Ford's report to Governor Gage.)

On May 24, 1901, some harness was stolen from a barn belonging to L. W. Leventon, who resided in Lookout, Modoc County, Cal. Several other thefts had been committed and the following residents of the county were suspected of participating therein:

> *Calvin Hall, a seventy-four-year-old Grand Army veteran; James Hall, his son by an Indian wife; Frank Hall, an Indian adopted by Hall when a baby; Martin Wilson, aged thirteen years, son of Hall's former wife, and Daniel Yantis, a white man.*

On May 25 the suspected persons were arrested on a charge of burglary and on May 27, after hearing the evidence, the court dismissed the charge against Calvin Hall and continued the cases against the other defendants.

Immediately upon the dismissal of the burglary charge against Hall, Robinson Dunlap swore to a complaint charging him with petit larceny, but the defendant was released on his own recognizance.

On the afternoon of Thursday, May 30, J. W. Brown, a deputy constable, accompanied by four men, went to Calvin Hall's home, which was a short distance from the village of Lookout, and without authority removed him to Meyers' Hotel at Lookout, where the other four prisoners were held under guard.

About 1:45 a. m. on May 31, all of the prisoners except Calvin Hall, were sleeping on the floor of the barroom in this hotel, and under the guard of Brown and one Sid. Goyette, when they were aroused from their slumber by a mob of nineteen men, whose faces were concealed with barley sacks. The prisoners were bound and gagged and taken to the bridge which spans the Pitt River, about three hundred feet away, and lynched.

The mob returned to the hotel and found Calvin Hall asleep on a sofa in the parlor. He was then subjected to the same treatment the other four received.

On June 3, 1901, Superior Judge J. W. Harrington of Modoc County appealed to Attorney-General Tirey L. Ford to send a representative from his office and a detective to assist in the investigation about to begin before the grand jury. General Ford responded by sending Charles N. Post and George A. Sturtevant, now a judge in the Superior Court of San Francisco.

From the beginning, the authorities were confronted by apparently insurmountable obstacles, as those who were in a position to render assistance were either prejudiced against the victims of the mob or feared that they would meet with a similar fate if they performed their duty as citizens.

After an examination which lasted nearly a month, indictments were found against Robert Leventon, Isom Fades and James W. Brown for the murder of young Wilson.

The defendants filed a petition in the Supreme Court to prevent Judge Harrington from trying the cases, but the petition was denied.

Detective Eugene Thacker, and afterward Detective Tom Gibson of the San Francisco Police Department, were detailed on the case and rendered valuable assistance.

On November 21, 1901, the trial of Brown began at Alturas, and on February 27, 1902, it was concluded.

Notwithstanding the fact that the Attorney-General believed that he had a perfect case against the defendant, which was further strengthened by confessions made by John Hutton and Claude Morris, who participated in the lynching, Brown was acquitted.

As a result of disclosures made by Hutton and Morris, nineteen men were indicted, but as most of the citizens eligible for jury duty had fixed opinions which would prevent them from serving as jurors, the trial judge informed General Ford that it was his opinion that another jury could not be obtained and no further action was taken.

THE MURDER OF DR. A. W. POWERS IN SAN BENITO COUNTY.

Dr. A. W. Powers was born in Vermont, where he studied medicine, and in 1855 moved to Bear Valley, about thirty miles south of Hollister, where he became a practicing physician. At the time of his death he was seventy years of age.

Although it was conceded that Powers was a first-class physician, he was exceedingly unpopular with many of his neighbors, and it was alleged that persons incurring his enmity were almost certain to have their stock poisoned, but in no instance was the proof against him strong enough to justify a prosecution.

On September 10, 1885, an incendiary fire destroyed considerable property belonging to John T. Prewett, a neighbor of Powers' with whom he had had trouble, and many persons were morally certain that Powers started the fire.

To add to his unpopularity, the doctor boasted that he had evidence in his possession which would send some of his neighbors to State Prison for defrauding the United States Land office by proving up falsely on their lands.

On September 17, 1885, Powers spent the day with the family of A. R. Severnean, leaving for his home, some three miles distant, about 5 p. m.

Nothing more was heard or seen of him until the following day, when some boy hunters found his body hanging to the limb of a tree about thirty yards from the Bear Valley road.

Sheriff B. F. Ross proceeded to the scene of the tragedy and found a gunshot wound in the man's back, and an autopsy subsequently performed, showed that the man died from that wound and that the body was hanged after death. On the shirt of the dead man a piece of cardboard was pinned on which was written, "Vigilantes 150." By certain marks on this piece of cardboard. Detective Jerome Deasy, of Harry Morse's San Francisco Detective Agency, ascertained that it was torn from a corset box which came from Freud & Co., on Market Street, San Francisco.

Judging from the footprints near the scene of the hanging it was estimated that about six men participated in the deed.

As it was known that Prewett felt extremely bitter toward Powers, whom he suspected of burning his property, Henry Melindy, a nephew of the murdered man, swore to a complaint charging him and Andrew Irwin with the murder.

It was learned that immediately after the burning of Prewett's property, written invitations were sent out to the neighbors to assemble at Irwin's cabin to discuss ways and means to dispose of Powers. These invitations were in the same handwriting as that on the card pinned to Powers' shirt. The names of all who attended this meeting were obtained and they were arrested. Among them were S. W. Alexander and his son Dick. When Alexander Sr. was arrested he broke down and stated that while he was present at the meeting he did not participate in the hanging, but that his son did. When confronted with this statement, Alexander Jr. made the following confession:

"Although the meeting was held, nothing definite was decided upon, but on September 17 I went to Prewett's house about 7 p. m., when I saw Prewett ride up the road on horseback and he had a shotgun with him.

"After supper Prewett and I rode over to Irwin's cabin where another meeting was to be held that night. On the way he told me that he was riding along the road that day, and coming upon Dr. Powers suddenly and unexpectedly, he ordered the doctor to throw up his hands. Powers was obstinate and Prewett shot him in the back. Powers fell from his horse and Prewett fired another charge into his back as he lay on the ground. He then dragged the body into the brush.

"When we arrived at Irwin's cabin six or seven of our neighbors were there, and a regular meeting was held, Isaac Slavin acting as chairman. As soon as the meeting was called to order, Prewett described the incidents regarding the killing of Powers as already related to me, and then proposed that they go in a body and hang the remains to a tree, so as to give the impression that it was the work of a great number of people, who could no longer tolerate the presence of this troublemaker. All present were agreeable to this plan and they then stood and, holding up their right hands, took a solemn oath of secrecy. It was further agreed that death would be the penalty to anyone who broke faith.

"Slavin then took a piece of cardboard from his pocket and wrote thereon, 'Vigilantes 150.' We then proceeded to the spot where the body was concealed and after Slavin pinned the card on the shirt we hanged it to the limb of a tree."

The detectives visited Freud & Co., the corset makers, and ascertained that the only corsets they had sent to any person in that part of the country was to Miss Slavin in Bear Valley. They identified the mark on the pasteboard as being one of the firm's private marks.

All who were present at the meeting at Irwin's cabin were held without bail, except one Stice, whose bail was fixed at $5,000.00, but on December 1 all of the other persons arrested in connection with the case were released on bail except Irwin and Prewett.

On February 15, 1886, Prewett's trial began. In addition to Alexander, a great many other witnesses were produced. W. T. Smith, special agent of the Government Land Office, testified that Prewett had obtained government land under false representations.

W. T. Garner testified that Prewett had threatened to kill Dr. Powers and his nephew Melindy, and that Prewett stated that he had already killed two men in Colorado.

On March 2, while the trial was still in progress, the charges against all of the alleged conspirators who were out on bail, were dismissed, as it was the intention of the prosecution to use them as witnesses for the State, but when they were placed on the stand they refused to testify, and two of them were fined $500.00 each for contempt of court.

The case was submitted to the jury at 3 p. m. on March 15, but not being able to agree upon a verdict they were discharged on the 19th inst. after being out 90 hours.

It was then learned that when the first ballot was taken in the jury room, Juror W. P. Phillips said as he cast his ballot: "Here goes old Phillips for acquittal, and he won't change his vote till doomsday,"

On April 1, Phillips was arrested on a charge of perjury in connection with answers he gave while being interrogated previous to being selected as a juror, but the charge was dismissed by Judge Hoffman. Four years afterward Phillips was burned to death in a fire at Fresno, Cal.

Prewett's second trial began on June 7, but on July 1 the further hearing of the case was discontinued for the reason as the minutes of the court show "that it is impossible at the present time to procure a jury in this county."

The case was then transferred to Monterey County, where the second trial began on March 5, 1888. The jury again disagreed and the case was dropped from the calendar.

On November 14, 1887, Andrew Irwin was placed on trial and on November 29 he was found guilty of murder in the second degree. On December 19 he was sentenced to San Quentin for life, but an appeal was taken to the Supreme Court and a new trial was granted after Irwin had served about one year in prison. As there seemed to be no disposition to prosecute the case any further, Irwin was liberated.

———————

SONTAG AND EVANS, NOTORIOUS TRAIN ROBBERS, MURDERERS AND JAIL BREAKERS.

(From Police Records and George Sontag's Statement to the Author.)

John Contant was born in Minnesota in 1861 and his brother George was born in the same State in 1864. Shortly after the birth of George, their father died and the mother married a man named Sontag, the boys taking the stepfather's name.

They lived for some time in the town of Mankato, where George was employed as a train brakeman until he procured a position in a grocery store in Nebraska. While thus employed he embezzled his employer's money and was sent to State Prison.

He had only served about a year when he escaped with a fellow convict. As they were wearing their prison garb, they burglarized a store that night and, procuring civilians' clothes, they disappeared, although Sontag voluntarily returned to the prison and served out his sentence, being released in 1887.

John Sontag came to Los Angeles, Cal., in 1878 and eventually became a brakeman on the Southern Pacific Railroad. He was injured while thus employed and became bitter against the company because of alleged ill-treatment accorded him after he became convalescent. About this time he obtained employment from Chris Evans, who had a farm near Visalia, Cal.

Evans, whose long flowing beard gave him the appearance of a typical farmer, was always considered a hard-working and honest man, and his family was highly respected. He had a real or fancied grievance against the railroad company which he did not hesitate to express, and the result was that he and John Sontag decided to seek revenge and incidentally obtain a little "easy" money.

On the night of January 21, 1889, they boarded the train at a station near Goshen, Tulare County, and when they had traveled a short distance, they put on masks, climbed over the tender, ordered the engineer to stop, proceeded to the express car and without any difficulty obtained about $600.00 and then escaped. They had tied a couple of horses in the neighborhood which they rode back to the ranch, returning to Visalia the next day.

On February 22 they boarded the train at Pixley, Cal., and executed another robbery in precisely the same manner as at Goshen. With the $5,000.00 obtained in this holdup they opened a livery stable at Modesto, but the stable was burned down, evidently by an incendiary.

In May, 1891, John Sontag went to Mankato, Minn., to visit his brother George, and in the course of a few days John confided to George that he had robbed a couple of trains.

In June, John started back to California and told George before he left that he and Chris Evans had planned to hold up a train at Ceres, Stanislaus County.

They attempted to rob this train and wrecked the express car with dynamite, but Detective Len Harris of the Southern Pacific Company was on the train, and he stepped out and began firing at Evans, who returned the compliment with buckshot, but no one was seriously injured. The bandits then fled to Modesto without procuring any valuables. John returned to his brother in Mankato and related what had occurred, and asked George to suggest a train that they could hold up in that neighborhood.

After studying the situation, George decided that they would hold up train No. 3, which left Chicago at nighttime and stopped at a station called Western Union Junction. They sent their relatives to Racine, Wis., and then went to Western Union Junction and waited for No. 3 on the night of November 5, 1891.

When the train stopped they secreted themselves near the tender and when they had traveled a few miles they climbed over the tender, thrust pistols in the faces of the engineer and fireman, ordered the train stopped and compelled the engineer and fireman to accompany them to the express car.

They obtained $9,800.00 without any difficulty and returned to their relatives at Racine.

It was then agreed that George should go to Visalia and meet Chris Evans, and that John Sontag would follow. When George arrived he found Chris Evans sitting as one of "twelve good men and true" in judgment in the case of some petty offender. When he beheld Evans in the jury box wearing a sanctimonious expression and long flowing whiskers, he experienced some difficulty in keeping a straight face.

He left the courtroom and went to Evans' home. When the latter arrived at the lunch hour they had a heart-to-heart talk regarding further "enterprises," and George loaned Evans $200.00. As George Sontag became ill he returned to his eastern home on April 24, 1892, before anything could be accomplished. John Sontag had returned to California in the meantime and he wrote to George to ascertain if he knew of any other good opportunity in their line back east.

George arranged to hold up No. 1 from Omaha at a station called Kasota Junction, and Chris Evans went east to participate in the job, which they attempted to execute on the night of July 1, 1892. Although George Sontag gained access to the express car, he could not locate the money and they profited nothing by the venture.

John Sontag remained in California and George wrote to him that he would proceed at once to Fresno, Cal., and that Evans would follow.

The Sontag brothers and Evans assembled at Fresno on August 1, 1892, where it was agreed they should hold up passenger train No. 17, bound from San Francisco to Los Angeles, and that the train should be boarded at Collis, near Fresno. August 3 was the night selected, and according to agreement, Evans walked out on the country road, where George and John Sontag overtook him in a buggy and Evans rode with them to Collis. When the train stopped, Evans and George Sontag boarded it, concealing themselves near the locomotive, and as usual, adjusted their masks. When the train got under way they climbed over the tender and ordered the engineer to stop. John Sontag did not board the train but took the team to a spot agreed upon and there awaited the other two. George Sontag marched the fireman and engineer back to the express car at the point of a gun, and when they arrived there Evans blew the door in with dynamite. The Wells-Fargo messenger threw up his hands, and George Sontag entered the car and seized three sacks of money and ordered the fireman to carry one and the messenger the other two. They started toward the locomotive which Evans crippled with a dynamite cartridge. After taking the two prisoners a short distance up the track, they ordered them to hand over the money and go back to the train. The two bandits then proceeded to the spot where John Sontag was waiting with the buggy. They drove George to the suburbs of Fresno and he went to the depot, where he purchased a ticket for Visalia, taking the same train which he had held up, as it was delayed in making repairs to the locomotive disabled by Evans' dynamite cartridge. While on the trip he eagerly listened to the passengers who described their experience during the holdup.

John and Evans returned to Visalia in the buggy and immediately proceeded to their barn, where they opened the sacks and learned to their sorrow that they had only seized $500.00 in American money, the remainder being Mexican and Peruvian coin.

George Sontag's actions while in Fresno planning this last robbery aroused suspicion and the team which they used was recognized as one belonging to J. Sontag and Evans. It was suspected that George Sontag knew more about this crime than he cared to tell, although the evidence against him was by no means conclusive. Accordingly, Deputy Sheriff Witty and Detective George Smith called at Chris Evans' house and stated to George Sontag that they heard he was a passenger on the train at the time of the holdup, and that they would be pleased to interview him at the Sheriff's office. After interrogating him at length Sontag was detained by the Sheriff and Witty and Smith returned to Evans' house in a buggy. As they approached they saw John Sontag enter the house, and when they arrived they told Evans' daughter that they wished to speak to John. The child, evidently acting under instructions, stated that he was not in, whereupon the two officials stepped inside and, seeing Chris Evans, asked him regarding Sontag's whereabouts. He also said John was not in.

One of the officers then pushed a portiere aside and there stood John Sontag with a shotgun in his hand. The officers reached for their revolvers, but at that instant Evans also produced a shotgun. The officers, seeing that they were taken at a disadvantage, turned and ran. Evans pursued Witty and shot him, inflicting a serious wound, and when Witty fell Evans came up to him and held his pistol at the head of the prostrate man, but did not fire as Witty appealed to him not to shoot again as he was dying. Sontag fired at Smith but the bullet missed its mark.

Evans and Sontag then went into the house and after obtaining a supply of ammunition, took the officers' buggy and escaped. They evidently returned to the Evans' home during the night, and on the next day, August 5, 1892, a posse consisting of Oscar Beaver, Charles Hall, W. H. Fox and Mr. Overall surrounded the house, at 1:30 p. m. Beaver saw the bandits take the horse and buggy out of the stable and he commanded "halt." Each side opened fire; Beaver was completely riddled with buckshot and died instantly.

Sheriff Cunningham and a posse heard the shots from town and hurried to the scene, but the bandits had escaped.

Nothing further of importance occurred until September 13. On this date a posse consisting of two Indian trailers imported from Arizona, Vic. Wilson of El Paso, Texas, Al. Witty, the brother of George Witty, who was the first man wounded by the outlaws, Detective Smith, Constable Warren Hill and Y. McGinnis of Modesto, drove up to Young's cabin, but had no idea that the bandits were in the house, although they knew they were in the vicinity. When they reached the gate, Evans and Sontag opened fire. Wilson and McGinnis fell dead and Witty fell from a shot in the neck; Hill's horse was shot dead and the bandits again escaped.

On October 25, 1892, George Sontag was placed on trial for the Collis train robbery, and on October 29 the case was submitted to the jury, which returned a verdict of guilty after deliberating one and one-half hours. On November 3 he was sentenced to life imprisonment at Folsom.

A period of several months elapsed without anything being accomplished toward the capture of Evans and John Sontag. It was evident that they were receiving food and shelter from sympathizers in the mountains, and a great many people in the valley, who were antagonistic to the railroad and believed that there was some justification in the actions of these desperadoes. They made frequent visits to Evans' home in Visalia and often remained there over night.

On June 11, 1893, a posse consisting of United States Marshal Gard, Deputy Sheriff Rapelje of Fresno, Tom Burns and Fred Jackson were stopping in a vacant house when they observed Evans and Sontag come down a hill and pass to the rear of this house. Evans saw Rapelje and opened fire at him. Jackson then fired, wounding Sontag and Evans. Both bandits got behind a straw stack and in some unaccountable manner they again escaped, although Sontag was wounded unto death.

The next day, E. H. Perkins, who lived nineteen miles northeast of Visalia, called at the Visalia jail and informed the officials that John Sontag was lying helplessly wounded near a straw stack in the neighborhood of Perkins' home. When the officials learned of Sontag's condition, and having in mind the reward, there was a wild race to "capture" the prostrate man, and he was taken without a struggle.

On the following day, June 13, Sheriff William Hall and Deputies Al. Witty and Joe Carroll placed Chris Evans under arrest at Perkins' home. He virtually surrendered, as he was worn out and weak from the loss of blood.

George Sontag had only been in Folsom prison a short time when he began laying plans to escape. He confided his plans to convict Frank Williams, a life termer, who told him that if he (Sontag) could get someone to furnish the weapons to be used in the escape, he (Williams) could have them smuggled into the prison. The friend who Williams believed would smuggle guns in was referred to as "Mr. Johnson," but as a   matter of fact he was William Fredericks, who had just been released after serving a term for robbing the Mariposa stage and was subsequently hanged for murdering Cashier Herrick in the San Francisco Savings Union Bank at Polk and Market Streets while attempting to rob that institution in broad daylight. (For particulars see history of Fredericks.)

It was agreed that Williams should write to "Johnson" requesting him to call on Mrs. Chris Evans, and that Sontag should write to Mrs. Evans, hinting as to the object of "Johnson's" visit.

The Sontag and Evans gang while at Evans' home did not refer to their weapons as guns and pistols, but named a pistol "Betsy" and a sawed-off gun "Mr. Ballard." Sontag prepared a letter which read as follows:

"Dear Mrs. Evans: — A very dear friend of mine named Mr. Johnson will call on you, and it is my wish that you will treat him the same as you would me. I wish you would introduce him to Betsy and Mr. Ballard, as he is a very nice man. Sincerely yours,

George Sontag."

Sontag and Williams then ingratiated themselves with a clergyman who frequently visited the prison and who was greatly impressed by their outward show of penitence. The good man concluded that it was their environments that led them astray and not their natural inclination. So when this brace of penitents "innocently" asked him to mail two letters, he willingly agreed to do so, as he read them and they appeared "perfectly harmless." Mrs. Evans refused to assist them.*

* In a confession made by Fredericks to Detective Seymour on March 24, 1894, he stated that it was he who furnished all the weapons and ammunition used in the attempted jail break, and that he wrapped them in a blanket and left them in the prison quarry. He stated that he stole two rifles in a saloon in Visalia and bought other weapons and ammunition in Sacramento. Before being released from Folsom he promised to assist several of the convicts to escape, and on the day of their attempt he was stationed at a deserted stamp mill near the prison with clothing to be exchanged by the convicts for their prison garb.

At 3:30 p. m., June 27, Lieutenant of the Guards Frank Brairre was sitting in a chair near the quarry, when George Sontag approached him. As Sontag belonged in the stonecutters' shed nearly a quarter of a mile away, the Lieutenant said:

"Well, what do you want here?"

"Rock," replied Sontag sententiously.

At that moment convict Anthony Dalton approached from behind and seizing Brairre said: "We want you."

Convicts Frank Williams, "Buckshot" Smith, Charles Abbott and Hy

Wilson then rushed up, and using the Lieutenant as a shield, attempted to escape. Williams ordered Brairre to signal Guard Prigmore, who was in charge of a Gatling gun, not to shoot, but the signal was not given in a satisfactory manner, and Williams shot over Brairre's head, but it is not probable that he intended to kill him for they would then lose their shield and would be riddled with bullets from the numerous guns already trained on them. All these convicts were armed with rifles and knives. They took the guard up the hill and when they came to the brink of a deep gulch, he jumped over, carrying Smith to the bottom with him. They bounded to their feet about the same time, and Smith seized a stone hammer and struck the guard on the head, but after a desperate struggle the guard overpowered him. When the guard jumped over the cliff the Gatling guns went to work with deadly effect on Sontag, Williams, Abbott, Dalton and Wilson.

The desperate men then sought refuge behind a big rock, but this did not afford protection from all the guns, and in a few moments Williams, Dalton and Wilson were virtually shot to pieces, and Sontag and Abbott, both dripping with blood from their own wounds, piled up the dead bodies of their fellow prisoners and used them as a shield.

Finally they concluded that there was no possible chance for escape and they gave a signal of surrender by placing a hat on the end of a rifle barrel and waving it in the air.

While this battle was raging rumors reached the main prison that the convicts had escaped, and the prisoners cheered and yelled like fiends until the wagons drove up, loaded with the dead and dying prisoners. Like magic a death-like silence came over them when they beheld the gory remains of their associates and realized how completely and tragically the attempt to escape had been frustrated.

It was thought that George Sontag would die from his wounds, but he eventually recovered, although he will be a cripple for life.

A young convict named Thomas Schell, from San Francisco, happened to be within range of the guns when the firing began, and although he did not participate in the attempted jail break, he was killed by a chance bullet.

Dalton was a graduate of Harvard College, but was a criminal at heart and was, at the time of his death, serving a twenty-year sentence for burglarizing Ladd's gun store in San Francisco. While being taken to Folsom to serve this sentence he escaped temporarily by jumping from the car window while the train was running full speed. Williams was serving a life sentence for robbing stages. He held up twelve stages in five months and held up one stage twice on the same day.

On July 3, 1893, John Sontag died at the Fresno jail from the wounds he received while making his last stand with Evans.

On November 28, 1893, Chris Evans was placed on trial for the murder of Vic Wilson, but before the jury had been empaneled, George Sontag sent for Warden Aull at the Folsom prison and made a full confession of all of his crimes. He stated that he had two reasons for so doing.

First: Because Mrs. Evans had ill-treated his mother when she came to Visalia to nurse John, and had given her none of the proceeds of the Collis robbery; and

Second: Because he was crippled for life while attempting to escape from Folsom, and by assisting the prosecuting officers he hoped to secure their assistance when he applied for a pardon later on.

On December 2, George Sontag was brought from Folsom to Fresno and testified against Chris Evans.

On December 14 the jury, after deliberating seventeen hours, returned a verdict of guilty of murder and fixed the punishment at life imprisonment.

While awaiting sentence Evans was incarcerated at the Fresno jail where his wife visited him daily, and he was also permitted to have a waiter from Stock's restaurant bring his meals into the corridor of the jail, where Evans partook of them.

About 6 p. m., December 28, 1893, Mrs. Evans was in the prison with her husband when Morrell, the waiter, called and took Evans' meal into the corridor of the prison. The prisoner was, as usual, permitted to leave his cell and eat in the corridor in company with his wife and the waiter. When Evans had finished, the waiter called to Ben Scott, the jailer, to let him out with his tray of dishes. When Scott opened the door, the waiter drew a long knife and held it near Scott's heart and ordered him to hold up his hands. The jailer thought it was a joke, but was convinced to the contrary when Evans whipped out a revolver, which Morrell had smuggled in to him, and pointed it at Scott's head. Mrs. Evans attempted to grasp the pistol, but Evans pushed her away, and Scott believing that "discretion was the better part of valor," opened the door and Evans and Morrell walked out.

Before leaving, however, Evans said to Scott: "My wife had nothing to do with this and you take good care of her." The desperadoes then made Scott accompany them. They next met ex-Mayor S. H. Cole. "Up with your hands," said Evans to Cole, and proved his earnestness by placing his pistol against Cole's chest, and he was forced to join the party.

When they reached the Adventist Church they met City Marshal John Morgan and William Wyatt. Morrell thrust a pistol up to their faces and commanded them to throw up their hands, and although Morgan was acknowledged to be a brave man, he was so taken by surprise that he complied with the request, but when Morrell began searching him,

Morgan threw his arms around the robber whom he and Wyatt were rapidly overpowering. Morrell called to Evans, who had remained some little distance away with his involuntary companions. Cole and Scott Evans left his prisoners, who then fled, and he ran to Morrell's assistance. He fired two shots into Morgan, who relinquished his hold on Morrell and sank to the ground, seriously wounded, while Wyatt ran for help. Morrell obtained Morgan's pistol and he and Evans ran to a team which was hitched nearby, but the animals became excited because of the shooting and as soon as untied they ran away, leaving the bandits to make their way on foot.

After traveling a few blocks they seized a horse and cart from a newsboy and escaped.

Although these men were seen several times after their escape, nothing of any moment occurred until February 8, 1894, when a posse came upon them, and although several shots were exchanged, no damage was done and they again escaped.

On February 19 the bandits became so bold as to go to Evans' home in Visalia, and the information was at once conveyed to the officers, who formed a cordon of fifty men around his house about 3 a. m. The outlaws knew nothing of their predicament until Sheriff Kay sent a boy named George Morris to the house with a note informing them that further resistance would be foolish. It was now daylight and Evans could see that they were trapped. He finally sent his little son out with a note to Sheriff Kay which read as follows:

> "Sheriff Kay: — Come to my house without arms and you will not be harmed. I want to talk to you.
>
> "Chris Evans."

After an exchange of several notes it was agreed that Sheriff Kay and Will Hall would go into Evans' yard unarmed, and when they did so Evans and Morrell came out, shook hands with the officers and surrendered unconditionally.

Morrell was charged with robbery for forcibly taking Marshal Morgan's pistol and was sentenced to life imprisonment.

On February 20, 1894, Evans was sentenced to serve the remainder of his life in State Prison.

After Evans was sent to State Prison, his wife and daughter Eva appeared throughout the State in a melodrama called "Sontag and Evans," which depicted the bandits as persecuted heroes.

On March 21, 1908, George Sontag was pardoned and obtained employment as a "floor manager" in Tim McGrath's resort on Pacific Street in San Francisco. He soon left this position and wrote a book dealing with his past life, in which he warns others of the folly of wrongdoing.

———————

JAS. C. DUNHAM, MURDERER OF SIX PEOPLE.

Jas. C. Dunham was a native of Santa Clara County, Cal., and at the time of his disappearance he was 32 years old.

His mother died in San Jose in 1893, and it is said that she was possessed of such an ungovernable temper that she was known as "Kate the Terror." Her disposition seems to have been inherited by her son James, who was extremely violent when his temper was aroused.

Ordinarily he was gentlemanly and ambitious to improve his mind. At various times he followed the occupation of nurseryman, drummer, bicycle-agent, confectioner, orchardist, and at the time of the murders he was studying law.

On May 26, 1896, he was stopping at the home of his father-in-law. Col. McGlincy, which was in the country, a short distance from San Jose, Cal.

On that evening, Col. McGlincy, Jas. Wells, Mrs. McGlincy's son by a former husband, and George Schaible, their hired man, drove to a nearby village called Campbell, and returned about 11:30 p. m. They took the horse and buggy to the barn' and after the horse was unhitched McGlincy and Wells crossed over to the house, leaving Schaible in the stable. Soon after these two men entered the house, Schaible heard several pistol shots and immediately after that McGlincy ran from the residence over to a chicken house, pursued by Dunham, who had a pistol in his hand.

Dunham fired several shots into the building and McGlincy, who had been wounded, came out and pleaded for mercy. He then fell and as he lay on the ground, Dunham shot him to death. Schaible concealed himself in the hay and Dunham searched for him, but failing to find him, he saddled up a horse and galloped away, pistol in hand. L. C. Ross, a neighbor of McGlincy's, heard the first shots and after hurriedly dressing, ran to the McGlincy home. Upon seeing McGlincy's body in the yard, he hurried home to procure a shotgun, and while en route he heard a horse galloping up the road.

After arming himself, he aroused another neighbor named Page, and they proceeded to the McGlincy home. There, at the midnight hour, they were confronted by a horrible spectacle. In addition to the body of McGlincy in the yard, they entered the house and found Wells shot to death, Mrs. McGlincy and her daughter, the murderer's wife, were stabbed to death and two employees named Minnie Schessler and Robert Briscol were hacked with a hatchet until their bodies could hardly be recognized.

The only human being within reach of this butcher, who was not slaughtered, was his own little baby, scarcely a month old.

The appearance of the house indicated that a terrible struggle for life was made by some of the victims. Blood was spattered over the walls, and furniture and bric-a-brac was knocked down and broken.

While riding away from the scene of his bloody deeds, Dunham passed Chas. Sterritt on the San Jose road. The murderer, who still had his revolver in his hand, asked Sterritt where he was going and who he was looking for. The next time he was seen was on the following evening at 6:30 p. m., when he conversed with Manager Snell of the Smith's Creek Hotel. Dunham was bloodstained and his horse was hardly able to stand from exhaustion. He then rode off toward the mountains and no further trace was found of him until May 29, when his horse was found abandoned in Indian Gulch, five miles from Mount Hamilton.

The reward offered for the capture of Dunham amounted to $2200.00.

People from all parts of the United States were constantly "locating" the fugitive and the authorities were put to considerable expense in investigating these false clews.

But the most remarkable case of mistaken identity occurred on September 5, 1908, when a woman residing in Sherman, Texas, reported to the authorities of that place that she was well acquainted with Dunham and positively identified a man living in that community under the name of William Hatfield as the much-sought murderer. He was arrested and as he gave a most unsatisfactory account of his movements, both previous and subsequent to the date of the murder, Sheriff Langford of Santa Clara County went to Texas, and after a legal battle, during which considerable jealousy was exhibited, because of the amount of the reward money involved, the suspect was finally extradited.

On October 23, Hatfield arrived in San Jose, where it was proven beyond all doubt that he was not the man wanted, but it was necessary to charge him, and immediately afterward he was legally exonerated.

It is estimated that while he was incarcerated in San Jose, over twenty thousand people visited him.

It was never definitely learned what motive prompted Dunham to commit this foul deed.

There was nothing to indicate that it was premeditated and the general belief is that he had some real or imaginary grievance and that the ungovernable temper which he is said to have inherited changed him for the moment into a fiend.

It seems impossible that Dunham could have escaped or even lived for many days after his horse fell from exhaustion.

His deeds, name and description were on every tongue throughout that part of the country, and every man who answered his description in any respect was detained pending investigation unless his identity was proven beyond all doubt. He had no means to disguise himself and although he had no provisions, he never applied to a living soul for food or shelter, and no human being could have made any progress over that mountainous country without proper nourishment.

Every Avenue of escape was guarded, either by officers or those who were anxious to assist in his apprehension, either in the interest of justice, or to procure the large reward.

The naturally melancholy Dunham, alone and exhausted in the wild mountains, without a friend, hunted like a ferocious animal, and seeing no Avenue of escape, and once captured, no escape from the gallows, probably realized the enormity of his crimes, for he was possessed of more than ordinary intelligence, and then decided to seek some isolated spot where he probably ended his miserable existence.

THE ROBBERY OF THE EUREKA STAGE, NEAR NEVADA CITY, DURING WHICH BANKER WM. CUMMINGS WAS KILLED.

On September 1, 1879, the Eureka stage, carrying Banker William Cummings of Moore's Flat, and about ten other passengers, was held up by two masked men near Nevada City.

All the passengers were ordered to leave the stage and hold up their hands. While one robber kept the passengers covered with a gun, the other searched them and the stage. A valise belonging to Cummings was pulled from under the seat and as it contained a gold bar valued at $6,700 the banker sprang at the robber and both men fell to the ground. Cummings was getting the better of the struggle when the robber called to his companion for help. The second robber responded by shooting Cummings in the neck, killing him almost instantly.

The robbers then took the valise and the loot they had obtained from the other passengers and disappeared.

Nothing further was learned in regard to the identity of the robbers until September, 1882, when Captain of Detectives Lees of San Francisco ascertained that John Patterson, alias John Collins, who was at the time awaiting trial in St. Louis for a burglary he had recently committed in that city, was probably one of the Moore's Flat robbers. Lees and Detective Aull of Wells, Fargo & Co. soon convinced themselves that Patterson participated in the crime, and they proceeded to St. Louis with the necessary requisition papers.

Patterson was brought to California and was tried and convicted. He was hanged at Nevada City on February 1, 1884.

Shortly after Patterson was captured, Lees learned that Charles Dorsey, alias Thorne, alias Moore, a prosperous wood merchant in Union City, Indiana, was the robber who killed Cummings, and had obtained his start in business through his share of the proceeds from the gold bar, which the robbers sold at the mint in New Orleans.

"Moore" was so highly respected in Union City that Lees was .threatened with mob violence when he went to the town and declared his intention to take him to California to be tried for murder.

Dorsey, alias Thorne, alias Moore, was tried, convicted and sentenced to life imprisonment at San Quentin.

There were several old soldiers on the jury, and it is claimed that Dorsey's attorney's reference to his client's brilliant war record saved his neck.

Dorsey escaped from San Quentin on December 1, 1887, but was recaptured in Chicago on October 26, 1890.

ROBBERY OF SELBY SMELTING WORKS BY JOHN WINTERS.

On August 5, 1901, the Selby Smelting Works, located at the edge of the bay, at Vallejo Junction, Cal., was burglarized and $283,005 in gold bullion stolen.

The burglary was committed by digging a tunnel under the building and up to the vault, which was drilled.

Ex-Chief of Police Lees, Captain of Detectives John Seymour, Detective Tom Gibson and Captain Sayers of Pinkerton's Agency began an investigation.

Suspicion fell on a former employee named John Winters, who had a cabin about one-quarter mile from the works, and who was said to have been engaged to be married to Miss Ida Spencer of San Rafael, Cal.

Detective Gibson inspected Winters' cabin, and there shovels, clothing and various articles were found, on which was mud similar to that found in the tunnel, where his cap was found.

He was traced to San Rafael on August 7, 1901, by Gibson and arrested at the hotel where Miss Spencer resided. It was then learned that he had that day offered to purchase for her property worth $5000.

Winters was brought back to San Francisco, and after an extended cross-examination, during which the evidence against him was produced, he broke down, made a confession and volunteered to accompany the officers in a boat and indicate the place in the bay where he had thrown the bullion, which he had calculated on recovering in the future for his personal use.

The tug "Sea Witch" was engaged, and ex-Chief Lees, Captain Sayers, Detectives Tom Gibson, Charlie Crockett and Winters arrived at the place indicated at 4:30 a. m., August 9. This hour was selected because of the low tide.

Gibson and Crockett stripped and eventually recovered every bar that was stolen.

Winters was tried at Martinez, Cal., pleaded guilty and on August 21, 1901, was sentenced to serve fifteen years' imprisonment. He was paroled on November 24, 1908.

THE SENSATIONAL ESCAPE OF MULTI-MURDERER TOM

BLANCK AND SEVERAL OTHER DESPERADOES FROM

THE SEATTLE JAIL, AND THE TRAGIC END OF BLANCK.

On September 30, 1894, Constable William Jeffery of Puyallup, Wash., visited some relatives a short distance from town, and about 5 p. m. he, in company with Thomas Alexander and Tom Bowley, was returning home on foot.

When they reached a little railway station called Meeker Junction the constable observed a young man and sixteen year-old boy run from some box cars into an unoccupied structure nearby. When the pair neared the building one of them dropped a bundle, which Jeffery hastened to inspect. Among other articles he found a 45-calibre Colt's revolver, which he was examining when the two fellows reappeared, and the older of the two exclaimed, "Drop that!" "Is it yours?" asked Jeffrey. "Yes," replied the stranger. The constable then inquired if there were any marks of identification on the weapon, to which the man replied, "Yes, D. P." While Jeffery was looking for the alleged mark, the fellow suddenly drew another revolver and simultaneously with his command, "Hands up!" he fired at the officer, the bullet passing through his heart and killing him almost instantly.

The pair then escaped and a few moments later they held up a farmer driving along a road and seized his horse and wagon.

As Jeffery was a most efficient and popular officer, the indignant citizens formed large posse to assist Sheriff Matthews to apprehend the murderer.

At 2 o'clock on the following morning Deputy Sheriff Harry Moore and John Ball met a suspicious-acting character on the road near McMillan. It was too dark to distinguish his features, but the officer commanded him to halt, whereupon the stranger fired at Moore, the bullet inflicting a serious wound in his breast. This man, whom it was subsequently learned was Blanck, then disappeared in the darkness.

On the next day at noon Frank Murray, a sixteen-year old boy, having respectable relatives residing at Hillsboro, entered a store in South Prairie, Wash., and purchased a large amount of provisions. As he acted suspiciously and answered the description of the youth who accompanied the man who murdered Jeffery, he was arrested and he freely admitted that he was with "Hamilton" when that individual killed the constable, but that they had since parted company.

On October 3, 1894, a robber attempted to hold up the "Mug" Saloon in Seattle, but as the bartender, Charles Bridwell, offered resistance the bandit shot him dead and then disappeared.

A few days later Detective Cudihee of Seattle arrested a suspect after a desperate battle, during which a bullet from the desperado's pistol grazed the detective's neck. The prisoner gave the name of Tom Blanck and subsequently made a confession substantially as follows:

> "I was born in New York and my first crime was at Nelson, B. C, in January, 1891, when my partner and I held up a stage and killed the driver because he resisted. After obtaining $4500 from the treasure-box we escaped.

> "In February, 1891, I committed a burglary at Kalama, Wash., for which I was arrested, but I escaped from jail shortly afterward.

> "I then went to Fairhaven, where I committed a burglary but as I was pursued by Policeman Peter Brugh I shot him twice and then escaped.

> "On August 18, 1894, I robbed several people in the barroom of the Broadwater Hotel at Helena, Montana, and in the following September I killed Steve Gross, a bartender, at Meaderville, Montana, and subsequently killed a deputy sheriff who pursued me.

> "My next victim was Constable Jeffery, and it was I who shot Deputy Sheriff Moore the next morning. I also killed Bridwell, the bartender, in Seattle."

Blanck was tried and convicted for the murder of Bridwell, and was sentenced to be hanged. At this time he was confined in the county jail at Seattle.

At 7:30 p. m. March 17, 1895, Jailer Jerry Yerbury was passing Blanck's cell when the desperado pointed something at him which resembled a black pistol, at the same time commanding the jailer to come close to his cell or be killed instantly.

After some pleading Yerbury finally complied with the request and the bandit then ordered him to open the cell door, which he did.

With the assistance of Frank Hart, a bunko man, Blanck bound Yerbury with a rope, took his pistol and then invited all prisoners who desired their freedom to accompany him.

The following accepted his invitation:

Servius Rutten, convicted of murder; William Holmes, a negro, who murdered his comrade; C. W. Brown, a counterfeiter; R. H. Ford, and Charles Williams, burglars; Frank Clinafelter, horse thief, and William Cosgrove, convicted of petty larceny.

Murderer James Murphy not only refused to accept the invitation but notified the officials of what had transpired.

After the excitement had subsided the weapon which struck terror to the heart of Yerbury was found and proved to be an excellent imitation of a revolver made of wood and blackened.

On the following day Cosgrove, the petty larceny thief, was recaptured near O'Brien Station.

On that night Deputy Sheriffs M. Kelly and Dick Burkman saw two men on a road near Black River Junction. It was too dark to distinguish their features, but when the fellows drew near the officers sprang out and ordered them to throw up their hands. The taller of the two, who proved to be Rutten, the convicted murderer, obeyed the command, but his companion, whom Rutten afterward admitted was Blanck, darted into the brush and escaped.

On March 21, 1895, a man of Blanck's description obtained food at the home of James Nelson, which was located near Orillia, Wash. Deputy Sheriffs Robert Crow and John Shepich were notified and they started in pursuit. Near Kent, a small town near Seattle, they saw a man of Blanck's description. As they drew near they pointed rifles at him and commanded him to throw up his hands. After some hesitation he suddenly drew a revolver and during the general fire which followed Shepich was shot in the breast and seriously wounded. When Blanck had emptied his revolver he darted into the nearby brush, but when commanded to come out he did so. By this time Charles Newell had joined the officers and when the bandit reappeared all three men opened fire, with the result that seven shots entered Blanck's body, killing him instantly.

The officers subsequently testified before the coroner that their reason for firing at Blanck when he obeyed their command and came out of the brush was because they thought he had two revolvers, but the only one found was the one which he stole from Jailer Yerbury.

Holmes, the negro murderer, was recaptured by Sheriff Hagan on the day Blanck was killed.

HARRY TRACY, ONE OF THE MOST FIENDISH

DESPERADOES IN CRIMINAL HISTORY.

In 1892, there lived in the town of Vancouver, Washington, two fifteen-year-old boys, named Harry Tracy and David Merrill. Tracy's conduct was exemplary until he met Merrill, but immediately afterward a change occurred and step by step he waded into crime until his deeds were the talk of the continent. At the outset, Merrill seemed to possess the master mind of the pair, but as Tracy was an apt pupil, this soon changed, and he became the dictator.

Their first depredation consisted of the stealing of three geese from a farmer living on the outskirts of Vancouver and selling them to a poultry market. For this crime they were sentenced by Justice of the Peace M. A. Tuson to serve twenty days in jail.

After being liberated they purchased firearms and practiced almost daily at the Vancouver barracks until they gained reputations as expert shots. Articles were constantly disappearing from the barracks in a mysterious manner, and the army officers, becoming satisfied that these two boys were the thieves, ordered them to keep away from the quarters.

After committing numerous petty offenses, Tracy was arrested for house-breaking in Provo, Utah, and on July 10, 1897, was sent to State prison for one year.

On October 8 of the same year, he and three other prisoners were working on a drain ditch outside of the prison walls, where Tracy secured a pistol which a friend had planted there for him. With this weapon he held up the guard and made his escape.

He then joined the notorious "Robbers Roost" gang, which was operating in Colorado, and of which Dave Lent, Pat Johnson, Dave Merrill and John Bennett were members.

When this band killed a boy named Wm. Strang, the indignant citizens demanded of the authorities that they be immediately exterminated.

A posse was organized and on March 1, 1898, they encountered the outlaws near Craig, Colorado.

A desperate battle was fought, during which several on each side were wounded and Deputy Sheriff Valentine S. Hay was killed.

The desperadoes made their escape, but on March 4, Sheriff C. W. Neiman and posse of Routt County, Colorado, captured Lent, Tracy, Johnson and Bennett.

As the Strang boy was murdered just over the line in Wyoming, Johnson, who was accused of the actual killing, was extradited, but was subsequently acquitted because of insufficiency of evidence.

A mob seized Bennett and lynched him.

Tracy and Lent escaped from jail, but were recaptured the next day. They were then transferred to the more secure jail in Aspen, Colorado, and again escaped.

Lent was never seen again by the authorities.

Tracy joined Merrill, and in December, 1898, they returned to Portland, Oregon, where they soon had the citizens terrorized by the series of depredations they committed.

They held up and robbed a Street-car, and also burglarized several saloons and stores.

On February 6, 1899, Merrill was arrested, and on the next day Detective Dan Weiner arrested Tracy after a desperate battle.

The pair were found guilty of robbery and on March 22, 1899, Tracy was committed to the Salem prison for twenty years and Merrill for fifteen years.

They were employed in the foundry in the prison, and at 7 a. m., June 9, 1902, they were marched in line with the other prisoners to their work. It was the duty of Guard Frank Giard to count the prisoners marched in, and after doing so, Giard announced to Guard Frank Ferrell that 159 prisoners were present.

Ferrell replied "All right." Just then Giard heard a rifle shot and turned in time to see Ferrell fall dead. Tracy then turned his rifle on Giard and shot without hitting him, and Merrill fired at the other shop guard. Ingham, a life prisoner, attempted to disarm Tracy but was immediately shot and mortally wounded by Merrill.

They then fled from the building and directed their attention to the fence guards, where S. R. Jones was guarding one corner of the stockade. They both fired at Jones, one bullet striking him in the abdomen and one in the chest, and he fell dead at his post. Guard B. F. Tiffany then emptied his rifle at the desperadoes, but none of his bullets struck their mark. Tracy fired one shot at him and he fell outside the wall with a wound in his chest.

Tracy and Merrill then procured a ladder, scaled the wall and running to Tiffany, assisted him to his feet and used him as a shield until they got out of range of the other guards. They got in a position where they could be observed from the prison and deliberately blew the top of Tiffany's head off and then disappeared in the timbers.

Posses of peace officers and citizens were at once organized and rewards were offered for the bodies of the convicts. It is said that Tracy and Merrill obtained their sawed-off rifles in the following manner:

On May 20, 1892, Harry Wright was released from the Salem prison and carried with him a letter from Merrill to a relative. It was apparently only a short note, not covering more than one-half of the paper, but underneath it was a note written in invisible chemical ink, in which he requested the relative to provide the bearer with money for reasons which would be explained later.

Wright also stole a horse and buggy in Portland, which he sold to assist in raising funds. He purchased two high-grade rifles with short barrels and a quantity of ammunition, which were smuggled into the prison the night before the break.

On the day following their escape, Tracy and Merrill entered Salem, Oregon, at 10 p. m., and held up a man at the point of a rifle and took his clothes. They then stole an overcoat and two horses and continued on their way north. Their next appearance was in the town of Gervais, twenty mile: north of Salem, where they demanded and procured food and held up two deputy sheriffs and took such wearing apparel from them as they needed. Learning that a posse was en route to Gervais with bloodhounds, they returned toward Salem, remaining in the woods in the daytime and at night they entered the town, and accosted a citizen named J. W. Roberts as he was entering his home. They took his clothes (the object being to change as often as possible), and then ordered him to go in his house and remain there until daylight under pain of death.

Early on June 13, they broke through a cordon of militia and deputy sheriffs near Gervais and a few hours afterward stopped at a farm near Monitor, which was owned by a man named H. Aikus. They ordered the women folks to prepare a breakfast, and supplied themselves liberally with eatables and cooking utensils.

On June 15, the bandits stole a team from G. R. Randall, near Oregon City, and on June 16 they appeared at the farm of Chas. Holtgrieve on the Columbia River and demanded dinner. There were five men in the house at the time and the convicts made them all enter a boat and row them across the Columbia River. On June 17, about 6 a. m., they appeared at the cabin of a rancher named Reedy, about four miles back of Vancouver. They bound and gagged him, took his clothes and left him lying on the ground.

From June 17 to July 2 little was heard of the bandits, but on the last named date Tracy appeared at the Capitol City Oyster Co.'s place at South Bay, near Seattle. He entered the home of Horatio Ailing, while another man named Lattrige was present.

Tracy made known his identity, and ordered them to prepare a meal. In the meantime, a Frank Scott and John Les5inger came in. Tracy then ordered all four men to stand facing the wall with their hands up while he prepared his own breakfast. At this time Captain Clark of the gasoline launch "N. and S." and his son entered the house, and they also joined the "wall flowers." While eating his breakfast, Tracy learned of Clark's launch, and after satisfying his appetite ordered all present to accompany him to the launch. On the way he stated that he had killed his partner in crime, Merrill, because he showed evidence of a faint heart. He said that they had agreed to fight a duel and that it was arranged that they should place back to back and at a signal each should step out ten paces and turn and fire.

At the eighth step, Tracy turned and killed Merrill by shooting him in the back. He claimed that this occurred about four miles south of Chehalis, Washington, on June 28. An investigation proved his statement to be true as the body of Merrill was found thrown head first over a log.

When Tracy and his involuntary companions reached the launch, he ordered them all into the boat and instructed Clark to proceed with the party to Meadows Point, near Seattle. At this place they disembarked, and Tracy ordered one of the party to take a rope from the launch and bind the rest of the party. This done, he compelled this man to accompany him to a place called Ballard, six miles from Seattle, and then ordered him to leave him and to proceed along an isolated path and say nothing of what had transpired.

July 3 proved to be the red-letter day in the career of this arch-criminal. His marvelous luck and cunning remained with him, and, as usual, he escaped unharmed.

At 3:30 p. m. he encountered a posse at a place called Bothell, near Seattle, and by quick maneuvering he gained an advantageous position and opened fire on the posse before they were aware of his presence.

He only fired five shots. With the first he instantly killed Deputy Sheriff Chas. Raymond. Another ball splintered the stock of Deputy Sheriff Jack Williams' rifle, and the ball entered his breast. He then wounded others in the party and escaped.

Later in the day Tracy met an aged farmer who was driving a team along the outskirts of Seattle. He seized the team, made a prisoner of the old man, and then drove up to the residence of Mrs. R. H. Vanhorn, located near Woodland Park, Seattle. He fastened the team and forced his aged prisoner to accompany him into the lady's home and ordered her to cook a meal for him. Tracy did not watch this lady very closely and therefore did not observe that a butcher boy called at her door for orders. Mrs. Vanhorn whispered to the boy that Tracy was there and the boy rushed back to Freemont, a suburb of Seattle, and notified Sheriff Cudihee and Policeman Breese of the fact. These men, accompanied by C. J. Knight and Neil Rawley, armed themselves and, proceeding to Mrs. Vanhorn's house, they secreted themselves within view of the entrance. Presently Tracy stepped out with the old man on one side and another man on the other.

The officers could not shoot without endangering the lives of innocent persons, so Breese called out: "Tracy, drop that gun." Quick as a flash the bandit fired and killed Breese instantly. With the next shot he mortally wounded Rawley. He continued to use his involuntary companions as shields until he reached a place of safety, when he dismissed them and disappeared.

On July 5, he entered the home of a Fisher family, near Pontiac, and acting under his orders, they prepared his breakfast. While he was eating he stationed the family by the door. It is needless to state that he now had the entire country terrorized and a great many amusing stories are told of posses of citizens which boldly started to find him, but on learning of his whereabouts, stampeded in the opposite direction.

On Saturday, July 6, Tracy appeared at Meadow Point, on the water front, three miles north of Seattle. Here he met a Japanese fisher boy whom he forced to row him twelve miles to Madison Point, where the boy was dismissed.

The bandit then proceeded to the home of Farmer John Johnson. By employing the usual tactics of announcing his name and displaying his weapons, Tracy terrorized the family and then requested Mrs. Johnson to prepare his breakfast. There was a large, powerful man named John Anderson employed at this farm, and after breakfast Tracy procured ropes and bound the Johnson family and then ordered Anderson to accompany him. From that time until the following Tuesday, Anderson was a mere slave and beast of burden for the bandit.

Tracy forced his companion to row him down the sound, and on the next day the boat they used was found in a clump of bushes in Miller's Bay. When they reached land, Tracy compelled Anderson to carry the blankets and provisions, and while Tracy slept, or ate, Anderson was bound to a tree.

On Monday, after a long tramp, they entered the woods from which the notorious desperado, Tom Blanck, emerged, only to be killed.

At the Black River bridge, Tracy met four friends, evidently by appointment.

On Monday night Anderson was again bound to a tree, and on Tuesday the pair proceeded to Gerrell's home, two miles from Renton, Wash. Tracy went into the kitchen, and after ordering a meal, began joking with the women folks. Gerrell's home was near the railroad track and presently a train came along bearing one of the numerous posses which were scouring the country for the outlaw. As the train stopped, Tracy took Anderson into the woods and bound him to a tree. The bandit then escaped, and shortly afterward Anderson was found and released.

On July 10, Tracy called at the ranch of M. E. Johnson, near Kent, fifteen miles from Seattle, and ordered him to go to Tacoma and buy him a 45-calibre revolver and 100 cartridges. He told Johnson that if he betrayed him, he would slaughter his entire family, which remained with Tracy at the farmhouse during his absence. Needless to say, Johnson kept faith and at night Tracy appropriated one of Johnson's horses and an ample supply of food and departed.

On the night of July 11 Tracy was surrounded near Covington. Just before daylight he approached the lines in such a careless manner that the guards thought he was one of their party. During the night he had evidently crept up and overheard the name of one of the guards, and on being challenged gave that name, and had succeeded in passing through the lines before the mistake was discovered. Eight charges of buckshot were sent after him and Tracy fired one shot in return, but no one was injured.

On Sunday, August 4, an eighteen-year-old boy named G. E. Goldfinch was riding a horse near the Eddy ranch, about eleven miles from Creston, Wash., when he observed a man who was evidently camping in the woods. The stranger stopped him and after stating that he was Tracy, directed the youth to conduct him to the nearest ranch. Goldfinch escorted him to the Eddy ranch, where Tracy commanded that no person would be permitted to leave the ranch night or day without his permission. So terrorized were the persons addressed that they made no effort to disobey his order.

On Monday, Goldfinch was permitted to go, but was warned to say nothing of what had transpired. The boy paid but slight attention to the admonition and as a result a posse was organized in Creston, which consisted of Deputy Sheriff C. H. Straub, Dr. E. A. Lanter, Attorney Maurice Smith and Joseph Morrison, a track foreman.

On August 6, 1902, they proceeded to the Eddy ranch, where they saw a man come out of a shed whom they suspected was Tracy, but not being positive they refrained from firing. Mr. Eddy was seen working in the field, so one of the posse approached him without being observed by the suspect. Eddy informed him that the man was Tracy. Eddy then arranged to drive his team to the barn.

During his stay on this ranch, Tracy volunteered to do his share of the work, so when Eddy appeared at the barn, Tracy came out to assist in unhitching the horses. While he was thus occupied, the posse appeared in full view. They commanded the outlaw to surrender, but instead of obeying the command, Tracy used Eddy and one of the horses as a shield until he reached the barn, where his rifle was hid.

He then slipped out of a side door and dashed into a wheat field. At every motion of the wheat the posse fired a volley in that direction. Finally Tracy fired one shot and then all was silent.

Shortly after this, Sheriff Gardner of Lincoln County appeared on the scene with his son. After a conference it was decided not to venture into the field that night, so it was surrounded until the following morning. They then made their way through the grain and found that Tracy had committed suicide by blowing off the whole side of his head with his huge revolver.

An inspection of the body showed that one of his legs had been shattered by two rifle balls fired by the posse. He attempted to stop the flow of blood with a bandage, but as further flight was impossible, he realized the hopelessness of further combat with the determined posse, and therefore made good his boast that he would never be taken alive.

His body was taken back to Salem Prison, for the double purpose of having it officially identified and to demonstrate to the convicts, who looked up to Tracy as a hero, the folly of attempting to follow in his footsteps.

The reward for Tracy, dead or alive, was $4,100.00.

———————

PART III.

ALFRED G. PACKER, THE "MAN-EATER," WHO MURDERED HIS FIVE COMPANIONS IN THE MOUNTAINS OF COLORADO, ATE THEIR BODIES AND STOLE THEIR MONEY.

In the fall of 1873 a party of twenty daring men left Salt Lake City, Utah, to prospect in the San Juan country. Having heard glowing accounts of the fortunes to be made, they were light-hearted and full of hope as they started on their journey, but as the weeks rolled by and they beheld nothing but barren wastes and snowy mountains, they grew despondent. The further they proceeded, the less inviting appeared the country, and they finally became desperate when it appeared that their only reward would be starvation and death.

Just as the prospectors were about to give up in despair, they saw an Indian camp in the distance, and while they had no assurance as to what treatment they would receive at the hands of the "Reds," they decided that any death was preferable to starvation, so they agreed to take a chance.

When they approached the camp they were met by an Indian who appeared to be friendly and escorted them to Chief Ouray. To their great surprise, the Indians treated them with every consideration and insisted upon their remaining in the camp until they had fully recuperated from their hardships.

Finally the party decided to make another start, with the Los Pinos Agency as their goal. Ouray attempted to dissuade them from continuing the journey, and did succeed in influencing ten of the party to abandon the trip and return to Salt Lake. The other ten determined to continue, so Ouray supplied them with provisions and admonished them to follow the Gunnison River, which was named after Lieutenant Gunnison, who was murdered in 1852. (See life of Joe Smith, the Mormon.)

Alfred G. Packer, who appeared as the leader of the party which continued the journey, boasted of his knowledge of the topography of the country and expressed confidence in his ability to find his way without difficulty. When his party had traveled a short distance, Packer told them that rich mines had been recently discovered near the headwaters of the Rio

Grande River, and he offered to guide the party to the mines.

Four of the party insisted that they follow Ouray's instructions, but Packer persuaded five men, named Swan, Miller, Noon, Bell and Humphrey, to accompany him to the mines, while the other four proceeded along the river.

Of the party of four, two died from starvation and exposure, but the other two finally reached the Los Pinos Agency in February, 1874, after enduring indescribable hardships. General Adams was in command of this agency, and the unfortunate men were treated with every consideration. When they regained their strength they started back to civilization.

In March, 1874, General Adams was called to Denver on business, and one cold, blizzardy morning, while he was still away, the employees of the agency, who were seated at the breakfast table, were startled by the appearance at the door of a wild-looking man who begged piteously for food and shelter. His face was frightfully bloated but otherwise he appeared to be in fairly good condition, although his stomach would not retain the food given him. He stated that his name was Packer and claimed that his five companions had deserted him while he was ill, but had left a rifle with him which he brought into the Agency.

After partaking of the hospitality of the employees at the Agency for ten days, Packer proceeded to a place called Saquache, claiming that he intended to work his way to Pennsylvania, where he had a brother. At Saquache, Packer drank heavily and appeared to be well supplied with money. While intoxicated, he told many conflicting stories regarding the fate of his companions, and it was suspected that he had disposed of his erstwhile associates by foul means.

At this time General Adams stopped at Saquache on his return from Denver to the Agency, and while at the home of Otto Mears he was advised to arrest Packer and investigate his movements. The General decided to take him back to the Agency, and while en route they stopped at the cabin of Major Downey, where they met the ten men who listened to the Indian chief and abandoned the trip. It was then proven that a great part of Packer's statement was false, so the General decided that the matter required a complete investigation, and Packer was bound and taken to the Agency, where he was held in close confinement.

On April 2, 1874, two wildly excited Indians ran into the Agency, holding strips of flesh in their hands which they called "white man's meat," and which they stated they found just outside the agency. As it had been lying on the snow and the weather had been extremely cold, it was still in good condition.

When Packer caught sight of the exhibits, his face became livid, and with a low moan he sank to the floor. Restoratives were administered and after pleading for mercy, he made a statement substantially as follows:

"When I and five others left Ouray's camp, we estimated that we had sufficient provisions for the long and arduous journey before us, but our food rapidly disappeared and we were soon on the verge of starvation. We dug roots from the ground upon which we subsisted for some days, but as they were not nutritious and as the extreme cold had driven all animals and birds to shelter, the situation became desperate. Strange looks came into the eyes of each of the party and they all became suspicious of each other. One day I went out to gather wood for the fire and when I returned I found that Mr. Swan, the oldest man in the party, had been struck on the head and killed, and the remainder of the party were in the act of cutting up the body preparatory to eating it. His money, amounting to $2,000.00, was divided among the remainder of the party.

"This food only lasted a few days, and I suggested that Miller be the next victim because of the large amount of flesh he carried. His skull was split open with a hatchet as he was in the act of picking up a piece of wood, Humphreys and Noon were the next victims. Bell and I then entered into a solemn compact that as we were the only ones left we would stand by each other whatever befell, and rather than harm each other we would die of starvation. One day Bell said, 'I can stand it no longer,' and he rushed at me like a famished tiger, at the same time attempting to strike me with his gun. I parried the blow and killed him with a hatchet. I then cut his flesh into strips which I carried with me as I pursued my journey. When I espied the Agency from the top of the hill, I threw away the strips I had left, and I confess I did so reluctantly as I had grown fond of human flesh, especially that portion around the breast."

After relating his gruesome story, Packer agreed to guide a party in charge of H. Lauter to the remains of the murdered men. He led them to some high, inaccessible mountains, and as he claimed to be bewildered, it was decided to abandon the search and start back the next day.

That night Packer and Lauter slept side by side, and during the night Packer assaulted him with the intent to commit murder and escape, but he was overpowered, bound, and after the party reached the Agency, he was turned over to the Sheriff.

Early in June of that year, an artist named Reynolds, from Peoria, Ill, while sketching along the shores of Lake Christoval, discovered the remains of the five men lying in a grove of hemlocks. Four of the bodies were lying together in a row, and the fifth, minus the head, was found a short distance away. The bodies of Bell, Swan, Humphreys and Noon had rifle bullet wounds in the back of the head, and when Miller's head was found it was crushed in, evidently by a blow from a rifle which was lying nearby, the stock being broken from the barrel.

The appearance of the bodies clearly indicated that Packet had been guilty of cannibalism as well as murder. He probably spoke the truth when he stated his preference for the breast of man, as in each instance the entire breast was cut away to the ribs.

A beaten path was found leading from the bodies to a near-by cabin, where blankets and other articles belonging to the murdered men were discovered, and everything indicated that Packer lived in this cabin for many days after the murders, and that he made frequent trips to the bodies for his supply of human meat.

After these discoveries the Sheriff procured warrants charging Packer with five murders, but during his absence the prisoner escaped.

Nothing was heard of him again until January 29, 1883, nine years later, when General Adams received a letter from Cheyenne, Wyoming, in which a Salt Lake prospector stated positively that he had met Packer face to face in that locality. The informant stated that the fugitive was known as John Schwartze, and was suspected of being engaged in operations with a gang of outlaws.

Detectives began an investigation, and on March 12, 1883, Sheriff Sharpless of Laramie County arrested Packer, and on the 17th inst. Sheriff Smith of Hinsdale County brought the prisoner back to Lake City, Col.

His trial on the charge of murdering Israel Swan in Hinsdale County on March 1, 1874, was begun on April 3, 1883. It was proven that each member of the party except Packer possessed considerable money. The defendant repeated his former statement, wherein he claimed that he had only killed Bell, and had done so in self-defense.

On April 13, the jury found the defendant guilty with the death penalty attached. A stay of execution was granted to Packer, who immediately appealed to the Supreme Court. In the meantime he was transferred to the Gunnison jail to save him from mob violence.

In October, 1885, the Supreme Court granted a new trial and it was then decided to bring him to trial on five charges of manslaughter. He was found guilty on each charge and was sentenced to serve eight years for each offense, making a total of forty years.

He was pardoned on January 1, 1901, and died on a ranch near Denver on April 24, 1907.

THE DALTON GANG OF MURDERERS, TRAIN AND BANK ROBBERS.

After the extermination of the James-Younger gang, the Dalton brothers stepped in and occupied the place once filled by them in the ranks of bloodthirsty criminals. In the Dalton family were six boys, named Ben, Frank, Grattan, William, Robert and Emmet.

In April, 1889, the Territory of Oklahoma was thrown open. For weeks previous to that time, thousands of people were camped along the frontier so as to be located in the most advantageous position to rush in at the appointed time and stake claims on the most valuable land, which they afterwards purchased from the Government for less than two dollars per acre.

For many months after the rush, lawlessness reigned supreme in this Territory. Bob Dalton was performing the duties of a Deputy United States Marshal at this time, but he began to associate with the outlaws and finally became a leader among them. Emmet and Grattan joined the gang, but in 1890 the Territory became "too warm" for the Daltons, so they went to California, where their brother Bill had rented a ranch in Tulare County.

At 7:50 p. m., January 6, 1891, train No. 17 left Alila, Cal., for Bakersfield, but had scarcely gone one mile on its journey when Engineer Thorn and Fireman Radliff were confronted by two masked men who stood on the tender of the engine. The engineer was ordered to stop the train and the frowning muzzle of a pistol placed against his temple caused an immediate compliance with the command.

The engineer and fireman were then ordered to accompany the robbers to the express car. The express messenger, suspecting what had happened, put out the lights in his car and lay on the floor. He was ordered to open the door, but his reply was a shot from his revolver which was followed by a fusillade, during which Fireman Radliff was mortally wounded. The desperadoes then gave up the struggle and fled. A pursuit was at once begun but all trace of them was lost until March 12. On this date Sheriff O'Neil of Paso Robles arrested William Dalton on the strength of evidence he had gathered, and upon being interrogated Dalton made some damaging admissions, which led to the arrest of his brother Grattan a few days later.

Both were taken to Visalia and charged with this crime, but William was eventually acquitted. On July 7 Grattan was convicted, after having tried to throw the entire blame on his brothers, Robert and Emmet, who were still at large. His sentence was continued until October 6, but on Sunday night, September 26, he in some mysterious manner obtained possession of the keys to the prison kitchen and cell door, and in company with one William Smith, a convicted burglar, and W. R. Beck, a notorious character, escaped.

Services were being conducted in a church nearby, and the team belonging to George McKinley, one of the worshipers, stood awaiting him, but the three desperadoes took possession of it and made good their escape.

On December 24, Sheriff Hensly of Fresno met Grattan Dalton in the mountains, and after an exchange of several shots the bandit again escaped. He then joined Emmet and Bob in the Oklahoma reservation.

Deputy United States Marshal Ransom Payne incurred the displeasure of this gang, because he had the "audacity" to attempt to capture them. Bob and Emmet Dalton and one Charlie Bryant learned that this officer would leave Wichita, Okla. Ter., on the evening of May 9, 1891, for his home in Guthrie, so they decided to rob this train and kill the officer. They went to a little station called Wharton and ordered the station keeper to signal the train to stop. When the train came to a standstill, one bandit took charge of the engineer and fireman, and the remaining two went through the train inquiring for Payne. That official being alone and not knowing the number of bandits in the party, and realizing that he would probably be killed if the Daltons were in the gang and discovered him, decided to evade them and left the train and hid in the brush near the track.

Failing to locate Payne, the two desperadoes proceeded to the express car, where they obtained about $1,500. The bandits then made their escape on horses, and when the train left Payne came out of hiding and ran to the stationhouse, where he found the station keeper bound and gagged. The next day a posse was organized and in August, 1891, Bryant was arrested. One of the posse named Edward Short took charge of him, while the remainder continued in pursuit of the Daltons. Short boarded the train with his prisoner, and when the train stopped at a little station he left Bryant, who was handcuffed, in charge of Wells-Fargo's agent, to whom he loaned a revolver. The agent, believing the prisoner was asleep, laid the pistol down and continued with his work. Just then Bryant jumped up, seized the weapon and attempted to escape. Short saw him leave the car and instantly drew another revolver. A duel followed with the result that both men were killed.

The Dalton gang remained in seclusion until the night of June 2, 1892, when Bob, Grattan and Emmet Dalton, assisted by three or four others, held up the Atchison, Topeka and Santa Fe train at Red Rock Station, Oklahoma. As the passenger train stopped at this station only when signaled to do so, the station keeper was ordered to display the necessary signal. When the train stopped the engineer was overpowered by two robbers and the remainder of the gang proceeded to the express car, where $1,800 was obtained, after which they escaped in the darkness.

In the early part of the following July, the territorial police and railroad officials learned that the Dalton gang were rendezvoused near the Missouri, Kansas and Texas Railroad in Oklahoma, and as they had profited little financially from their recent raids it was suspected that one of the trains on this road would soon be attacked. It was therefore decided to put a heavily armed posse on each train. Thus prepared, the authorities rather welcomed an attack, feeling confident that it would mean the extermination of the gang.

On the evening of July 15, 1892, the three Daltons, reinforced by five others, rode up to Adair station in Indian Territory and after robbing the agent they ordered him to signal the train to stop. Conductor George Scales and Engineer Ewing were immediately taken into custody, and the party then went to the express car which was in charge of Messenger George Williams, who reluctantly opened the safe and several thousand dollars were stolen.

The "guards," who were lounging in the smoker instead of being with the messenger, did not appear very anxious to perform their duty, although some of them ventured out and opened fire in a half-hearted way. A stray bullet struck and mortally wounded a Dr. W. Goff, who was at the time in a nearby drug store. Two of the guards named Kinney and La Flore were also shot, but their wounds were superficial. During the fusillade, a wagon was driven up to the train, the bags of money were thrown in and the bandits again escaped.

The next raid attempted by these bandits occurred at their old home in Coffeyvile, Kansas, on October 5, 1892. The gang on this fatal day consisted of Bob, Grattan and Emmet Dalton, Dick Broadwell and Bill Powers. They rode into town about 9:30 a. m., and were recognized by a merchant named Alexander McKenna, who quickly but quietly rushed about notifying everyone he met.

The five bandits proceeded to C. M. Condon's bank and Grattan Dalton, Powers and Broadwell entered the bank, where they found President Charles Carpenter and Cashier Charles Ball.

As soon as the three men entered this bank, Bob and Emmet Dalton hastened to the First National Bank across the Street, as it was planned to rob both institutions simultaneously. In each bank the bandits were informed that the time lock would not be off for several minutes and the robbers decided to wait.

In the meantime the news of the movements of the gang had spread through the town like wildfire, and the gunsmiths were loaning weapons and ammunition to all who desired them. As a result both banks were soon surrounded by determined men, all heavily armed, and the bullets began to fly through the windows of the bank.

When the vault was opened at the First National, Cashier Thomas Ayers handed out the money, amounting to over $20,000. Bob and Emmet Dalton put this in a sack and escaped out of the back entrance. They ran in the direction of Condon's Bank, but when they observed the crowd of armed men in front of that institution, they began firing, with the result that a young clerk named Lucius Baldwin was instantly killed.

In the general battle that followed, two shoemakers named George Cubine and Charles Brown, were killed by Bob Dalton when he saw them attempting to shoot him. Immediately after killing these men, Bob saw Cashier Ayers of the bank with his rifle raised, and Dalton shot him in the head, inflicting a serious but not fatal wound.

At this time the three robbers in Condon's Bank rushed out into the shower of bullets with about $3,000, and joining Bob and Emmet Dalton, they ran to their horses, but did not have an opportunity to mount.

John Kloehr, a stableman, and City Marshal Charles Connelly, both armed with rifles, then joined in the battle. Grattan Dalton killed Connelly and almost immediately afterwards Kloehr killed Bob Dalton. Bandit Powers was the next to be killed and Grattan Dalton was then killed by Kloehr.

All of the bandits having been killed except Broadwell and Emmet Dalton, these two, realizing the great odds against them, mounted their horses and attempted to escape. They had only gone a short distance, however, when Emmet wheeled about and in the face of a heavy fire, returned to the body of his brother Bob, and as he was in the act of lifting the body with the intention of carrying it away on his horse, a load of buckshot was poured into his back and he fell unconscious,

Broadwell was fatally wounded as he attempted to escape and his body was found a short distance from town. Several horses were also killed and many citizens wounded.

Emmet Dalton finally recovered from what were diagnosed as necessarily fatal wounds, and he was sentenced to serve the remainder of his life at the State Prison at Lansing, but Governor Hock pardoned him in January, 1907.

After the tragic death of his brothers, Bill Dalton reorganized the gang and operations were resumed in Oklahoma Territory. Their rendezvous was in the extreme eastern part of the Cherokee strip, but considerable of their time was spent in a little village called Ingalls. As they purchased their provisions, ammunition and whisky in this village, they were shielded by those who profited from their trade.

On September 1, 1893, Bill Dalton, Bill Doolin, Arkansas Tom, George Newton and Tulca Jack were drinking at the bar in the village hotel when the place was surrounded by a posse consisting of ex-Sheriff Hixon, Deputy Marshals Thomas Houston, Lafe Hadley, Dick Speed and several other officials and civilians. The outlaws ran out of the place and at the beginning of the firing Deputy Speed was killed. Hadley killed Dalton's horse and the bandit fell and laid motionless on the ground. Hadley, believing him to be dead, approached, but as he drew near Dalton jumped up and shot the deputy in the head, killing him instantly. The bandit then mounted the murdered officer's horse, and although severely wounded, he escaped.

During the battle Deputy Houston and a clerk named Simmons were also killed, and S. W. Ransom, N. S. Murray and a twelve-year-old boy named Briggs were seriously wounded. All of the bandits escaped with the exception of Arkansas Tom, who was barricaded in the hotel and who subsequently surrendered on the condition that he would be protected from the mob. The next day it was ascertained that none of the bandits escaped without wounds.

The last raid committed by the Dalton gang occurred at the First National Bank at Longview, Texas, at 3 p. m.. May 23, 1894. At this time two roughly dressed men entered the bank and presented a note to President Clemmons, which read as follows:

"Home, May 23rd.

"This will introduce you to Charles Spreckelmeyers, who wants some money and is going to have it. B. and F."

When Mr. Clemmons read the note and looked up, he was covered by a rifle in the hands of one bandit while the other went behind the counter and secured $2000.00 in ten dollar bills and nine twenty-dollar bills. City Marshal Muckley immediately learned of the raid and hurriedly gathered a posse who gave the robbers a hot battle. One of the bandits, Geo. Bennett, alias Jim Wallace, was killed as was also George Buckingham of the posse. Marshal Muckley and J. W. McQueen, a saloon-keeper, received serious wounds.

On June 7, 1894, a suspicious looking character, giving the name of Wall, came into the town of Ardmore, I. T., with two women who also acted quite mysteriously. They purchased about $200.00 worth of provisions and then called at the express office. The attention of the authorities was attracted by the peculiar actions of the trio, and while they made many conflicting statements, the information was elicited that they were living near a place called Elk. Sheriff Hart immediately organized a posse as he believed the provisions were purchased for some persons who feared to come to town, and as the Dalton gang was uppermost in his mind, he concluded that these three persons were connected with the gang. They were held prisoners and at 8 a. m. the next morning the house where it was suspected that Dalton was hiding was surrounded.

Dalton came to one of the windows and seeing some of the posse he jumped from a window on the opposite side of the building and started to run.

Sheriff Hart called on him to halt, but as he ignored the command, one shot was fired from the sheriff's rifle and Dalton dropped dead without uttering a word.

The house was then searched and conclusive evidence was obtained, not only as to Dalton's identity, but also that he participated in the Longview bank robbery. The officials then returned to Ardmore and when the mysterious trio were informed of the death of Dalton, one of the women became hysterical and said she was Dalton's wife and that they were married at her home in Merced, California, in 1888.

_____

THE REMARKABLE LIFE OF JOE SMITH, FOUNDER OF THE MORMON CHURCH, AND HIS DEATH AT THE HANDS OF A MOB. THE MASSACRE OF 150 EMIGRANTS BY THE MORMON BISHOP JOHN D. LEE AND PARTY AND THE CONVICTION AND EXECUTION OF LEE

TWENTY YEARS LATER.

(From Beaddle's "History of Mormonism" and Rankin's

"History of the Mountain Meadow Massacre.")

Joseph Smith, founder of Mormonism, was born on December 23, 1805, at Sharon, Vermont, but he subsequently moved to Manchester, N. Y.

As a youth Joseph was wild and intemperate, but he claimed that the Lord sent heavenly messengers to tell him that his sins were forgiven.

According to Smith's claim, angels notified him to go to Cumorah Hill, near Manchester, on September 22, 1826, and when he arrived there an angel descended from heaven and delivered to him a Golden Bible. On the leaves, which consisted of thin plates of gold, were hieroglyphics, which Smith claimed he translated "by the gift and power of God." From this translation the Book of Mormon was published, and on April 6, 1830, the Mormon Church was organized near Manchester.

Three men named Cowdery, Whitmer and Harris made affidavits that they were witnesses to the deliverance of the Golden Bible which, according to Smith's claim, the angels took back to heaven when the translation was completed.

In February, 1833, Smith and two others were elected presidents of the church and were at once favored with "visions of the Savior and concourse of Angels."

A few months later the Mormons established their church near Independence, Missouri, where the following, consisting of 1500 members, met with strong opposition from the old residents, who on November 4, 1833, destroyed the Mormons' property by fire and drove them across the river into Clay County.

In 1837, the church had 12,000 members. While a large percentage of the Mormons were quiet and unoffending, others were constantly defying the government and openly declared their independence of all earthly rulers and magistrates.

In May, 1839, they burned and plundered the town of Gallatin, Mo., and as a result Governor Boggs called out the militia. Prophet Joe Smith and many others were arrested, but after being imprisoned a short while they were permitted to go free, provided they would leave Missouri.

They proceeded direct to Hancock County, Ill., where they built a town, which they named Nauvoo.

In April, 1840, Brigham Young, President of the Twelve Apostles, went to Europe for a year, where he established missions.

In 1841, Prophet Joe Smith drew up a charter for the town of Nauvoo, which was adopted by the legislature. Under this charter the mayor was an absolute czar of the town, and Smith was elected to the office.

He claimed that on July 12, 1843, God expressly commanded him to inform the Mormons that it was desirable that each man have more than one wife, so that the earth may be multiplied and replenished.

On June 24, 1844, Governor Ford ordered the "Prophet," Mayor Smith, and his brother Hyrum to consider themselves under arrest on a charge of treason, for declaring martial law in Nauvoo in open resistance to legal process.

Smith and his brother surrendered and were placed in jail at Carthage.

As there were many rumors that the indignant citizens intended to lynch Smith, a company of militia, in command of Captain R. F, Smith, was detailed to guard the jail.

At 6 p. m. on June 27, 1844, a great mob, armed with weapons, rushed upon and overpowered the guard. They then broke into the jail and shot and instantly killed Hyrum Smith in his cell. The "Prophet" jumped out of a second-story window, and as he struck the ground his body was completely riddled with bullets.

During the next year, the College of Twelve Apostles, of which Brigham Young was president, ruled the church.

In 1845, the legislature revoked the charter prepared by Smith.

Thefts were constantly being committed, and the Mormons were nearly always blamed for them, whether there was evidence to justify the accusation or not.

In May, 1846, a mob of Anti-Mormons ordered about 150 Mormon families residing near Nauvoo away from their homes. They refused to go, whereupon their houses were burned to the ground.

At this time public prejudice against the Mormons, especially the polygamists, was rapidly increasing and the leaders realized that they could not remain in this community.

In June, 1846, the majority of them moved and the main body concentrated near Omaha. A few months later those who remained behind were driven out.

On July 24, 1847, Young and the first party of Mormons entered Salt Lake City, Utah, where Brigham Young was given all the power formerly held by Smith.

On September 9, 1850, Congress passed an act to organize the territory of Utah, and President Fillmore appointed Brigham Young governor.

In 1852, Lieutenant Gunnison and a party of eight United States topographical engineers were massacred. It was reported that the outrages were committed by Indians, but apostates who subsequently escaped claimed that the deeds were done by painted Mormons.

In the early part of September, 1857, a company of emigrants from Arkansas, Missouri and Illinois, which was led by Captain William Fancher, entered Salt Lake City, en route to California. This train consisted of 166 people, including men, women and children, who were well supplied with money, horses and cattle and everything necessary to make the trip as comfortable as possible.

Dr. Brewer, of the United States Army, said that it was "probably the finest train that ever started across the plains."

The Mormons claimed that while in Salt Lake City some of the members of this party were very indiscreet in expressing their opinion of the Mormon religion, and it was also alleged that one of this party boasted that he participated in the killing of the founder of the church.

It was furthermore claimed that these emigrants killed an ox by means of poison and fed the meat to the Indians, killing four, but Jacob Hamblin, a Mormon employed as an Indian interpreter, and several other reputable people, who had an opportunity to observe the actions of the emigrants, stated that outside of denouncing polygamy they did nothing to offend the Mormons.

When these emigrants had been at Salt Lake City but a few days they were astounded to find that under no circumstances could they purchase food or anything else from the Mormons, and shortly afterward they were ordered from the city.

According to testimony afterward given by Bishop Klingensmith, President Isaac Haight, his superior in the church, preceded the emigrant train on their journey west and warned his followers not to supply them with provisions.

Among the emigrants was a young man named William A. Aden, who recognized William Laney, a Mormon residing at Parowan, Utah, as the person whose life he had saved from an anti-Mormon mob in Tennessee some years previously. The grateful Laney also recognized his benefactor and after embracing Aden, took him to his home and supplied him with potatoes and onions.

According to a confession subsequently made by John D. Lee, whom Brigham Young appointed Bishop of Harmony, Washington County, and also "Farmer to the Pahute Indians," the Aden-Laney incident was reported to Bishop Dame a few hours after its occurrence and the latter raised his hand and crooked his little finger, whereupon his (Dame's) brother-in-law, Barney Carter, went to Laney and struck him over the head with a picket from a fence, fracturing his skull. Although the man recovered his mind became deranged.

On their way west, Captain Fancher's company of emigrants came upon a beautiful and fertile spot, known as Mountain Meadows. As this spot, which was about 200 miles from Salt Lake City, was an ideal pasture land, it was decided to stop there and recruit their stock preparatory to entering the parched desert.

At daybreak on Monday, September 7, 1857, the emigrants, several of whom were still asleep, were attacked, apparently by Indians, and at the first volley seven were killed and fifteen wounded.

With great rapidity and rare presence of mind the emigrants divided into two parties; one being assigned to give battle to the "Indians" while the remainder wheeled their vehicles around as a protection for the women and children. They then banked dirt up against the wheels and within a few moments were far better fortified than the attacking party, who were forced to remain at a distance. The emigrants held this fort for four days, but the "Indians" killed their stock and members of the party at every opportunity.

As water became scarce, two little girls dressed in white were sent to a near-by spring with a bucket, but as they went forth hand in hand they were riddled with bullets.

On September 11 it was decided to decoy the emigrants from their stronghold.

A flag of truce was then displayed by the attacking "Indians," and in response the emigrants waved a white garment. To their surprise, a white man, who proved to be John D. Lee, marched up with another man and met an envoy from the beleaguered camp. With a great display of indignation Lee denounced the "Indians" for murdering innocent and unoffending emigrants. He explained his position in the Mormon Church and government and told the envoy that if the emigrants would lay down their arms and march out peacefully, his party would protect them from the "Indians."

As their supply of food was gone and they could not obtain water, the emigrants gladly accepted this offer. Under the direction of Lee their arms were loaded in a wagon into which were also placed all babies who were presumed to be too young to talk.

The emigrants were then instructed to form in single file and Lee, who remained with the wagon containing the seventeen babies and numerous weapons, led them along a road, one side of which was lined with brush.

Suddenly he turned around and shot and killed the nearest person to him, a woman. It was subsequently learned that this shot was the prearranged signal for action all along the line. The instant it was fired "Indians" rushed out from behind the brush and opened fire on the emigrants, everyone in the party except the seventeen babies being killed. These babies were subsequently delivered to J. Forney, Superintendent of Indian Affairs.

Some of the young women were frightfully abused, even as they were dying from their wounds.

All jewelry, money, stock and desirable clothing was then seized and the bodies left where they fell.

Eight days later, interpreter Jacob Hamblin visited the scene of the butchery and found that wolves and ravens had torn the bodies to pieces, but he buried what remained of 120 bodies.

On November 20, 1857, Lee made a report of the massacre to Brigham Young, in which he claimed that the Pahute Indians were responsible for the slaughter and he also charged that the outrage was committed because the emigrants fed the Indians poisoned cattle.

On January 6, 1858, Governor Brigham Young made a report to Jas. W. Denver, Commissioner of Indian Affairs, at Washington, D. C, in which he quoted parts of Lee's report, and condemned the emigrants for treating the Indians like ferocious beasts. He also claimed that the massacre of Lieutenant Gunnison and party was due to inhuman treatment of the Indians by a party which preceded Gunnison.

The years rolled by and the story invented by Lee was accepted as true in the absence of proof to the contrary.

But "murder will out," and two of the little children, who were presumed to be too young to remember, subsequently told what they knew, and it finally reached the ears of the federal authorities, who gradually learned more and more of the details of the massacre.

In the summer of 1874, the grand jury of the second Judicial District Court found an indictment against Lee.

In June, 1875, he was tried before a jury composed of two Gentiles, nine regular Saints of the Mormon Church and one renegade Mormon. The jury disagreed and the second trial began in September, 1876. This time the jury was composed entirely of Mormons.

Labin Morrill, a Mormon, testified that there was great excitement over the alleged statement of some of the emigrants that they had participated in the killing of Joseph Smith, and as a consequence a council was held at Cedar City, at which Bishop Klingensmith and President Haight decreed that the emigrants must die.*

* According to Linn's history, there was another motive for this outrage.

A fanatical defender of polygamy named Parley Pratt, while in San Francisco in June, 1855, induced the wife of Hector McLean, a custom house official, to accept the Mormon faith and elope with him to Utah as his ninth wife. McLean traced them to Fort Gibson, Arkansas, where he killed Pratt, but as he was exonerated, it was decided to hold all Arkansans accountable for Pratt's death.

Samuel Knight, another Mormon, swore that Lee accompanied the flag of truce to the emigrants' camp and superintended the forming of the line of emigrants. Knight also swore that he saw Lee kill the first woman in the line.

Samuel McCurdy swore that one Bateman carried the flag of truce and that Lee accompanied him. He also testified that he saw Lee kill the woman, which was the prearranged signal for the general slaughter.

Jephi Johnson corroborated the other witnesses and also testified that he subsequently saw some of the emigrants' stock at Lee's home.

Jacob Hamblin testified to burying 120 bodies, and he furthermore swore that Lee admitted to him that he cut the throat of a seventeen-year-old girl named Dunlap during the massacre.

Hamblin also swore that he informed Brigham Young of what had transpired and that the latter replied:

"As soon as we can get a court of justice we will ferret this thing out; but until then don't say anything about it."

Klingensmith, a former Mormon Bishop, turned State's evidence. He not only corroborated the testimony of Morrill, Johnson and Knight, but testified that the massacre was committed by Indians and Mormons painted as Indians. He also swore that Lee sold much of the emigrants' property at public auction.*

* Klingensmith made his first confession some time previous to the trial, and when Brigham Young obtained positive proof of Lee's guilt the latter was excommunicated from the Church, and Young subsequently

rendered every assistance to the prosecution.

Lee took the witness stand and admitted his guilt but swore that President Haight of the Church promised him a "celestial reward" for his services.

The defendant was found guilty and on April 23, 1877, twenty years after the massacre. United States Marshal Nelson and posse took him to the scene of the crime to be shot to death.

The condemned man sat on the edge of his coffin and his only request was that the five soldiers move closer to him before they fired. The request was complied with and Lee then raised his arms over his head and when the command "Fire" was given the rifle balls pierced his heart.

Shortly after the massacre was committed it was generally suspected among the better class of Mormons that Lee was the instigator of the foul plot and he was ostracized and abhorred for years before his indictment. Towards the last the abject wretch had an unceasing dread of vengeance; he seldom left his home and it is said that he would undoubtedly have gone insane if the merciful bullets had not put an end to his miserable existence.

THE MURDER OF JAMES R. HAY IN SALT LAKE CITY BY PETER MORTENSEN, A PROMINENT CONTRACTOR, AND THE REMARKABLE VISION OF JAMES 'SHARP, THE FATHER-IN-LAW OF THE MURDERED MAN.

(Utah Reports and Salt Lake Police Records.)

Peter Mortensen was a prominent contractor and builder in Salt Lake City, Utah, and purchased considerable material from the Pacific Lumber Company, of which James R. Hay was secretary and treasurer.

As Mortensen owed this company $3,907 and had been requested to immediately liquidate the indebtedness, he called at the office of the company on December 16, 1901, about 6 p. m., for the purpose of arranging for a settlement.

He there met Secretary Hay and Manager Romney, and gave them an order on another person for $107, and stated that he had the balance, $3,800, at his home at Forest Dale, a suburb of the city, and added that if Mr. Hay, who resided in the same neighborhood, would call upon him that night with a receipted bill, the balance would be paid.

It was nearly 8 p. m. when the three men left the office; Mr. Hay and Mortensen proceeded homeward on the Calders Park car. Hay having the receipted bill in his possession. He arrived at his home at 8:45 p. m., and after supper informed his wife and children that he was going over to Mortensen's house to collect some money, and that he would soon return.

At 10:20 p. m. Mrs. Hay and her children retired, but at 1 a. m. she awoke and became alarmed at the long absence of her husband. Mrs. Hay remained awake and at 3 a. m. she went to Mortensen's home, and after arousing him, inquired for her husband. Mortensen appeared extremely nervous and stated that Mr. Hay had left his house hours before and had gone to Mr. Romney's house; adding that he had probably missed the last car home. The next morning Mrs. Hay telephoned to Mr. Romney, who informed her that he had not seen her husband since 8 o'clock the preceding evening. Romney then communicated with Mortensen, who stated that on the preceding evening he had paid $3,800 to Hay in twenty-dollar gold pieces, which he had concealed in glass jars in his cellar, and that Hay then started to his (Romney's) office.

Mr. James Sharp, the father of Mrs. Hay, upon being informed of the disappearance of his son-in-law, went with the police to Mortensen's home. The latter produced the receipt, which he stated Hay gave him for the money, and explained that he and the missing man sat on a small settee while counting the money. The following conversation then took place between the aged Mormon, Sharp, and Mortensen:

Sharp — Where did you last see my son-in-law?

Mortensen — Here (indicating a spot on the walk about ten feet from the house).

Sharp — If that is the last place you saw him, that is where you killed him.

Mortensen — How do you know he is dead?

Sharp — I have had a vision and the proof to you will that within twenty-four hours and within one mile of the spot where you are standing, his dead body will be dug up from the field.

Mortensen appeared dumfounded but made no reply. At this time the ground was covered with snow.

On the next morning, December 18, Frank Torgersen was looking for horses in a field near Mortensen's house and near a fence which ran parallel with the Park City railroad track, he discovered considerable blood. This caused him to make a close inspection of the neighborhood, with the result that he found a snow-covered mound about the size of a grave. Torgersen then proceeded to Mortensen's house, where he asked for a shovel. Mortensen loaned him a shovel, stating it was the only one he possessed, although another shovel was subsequently found which had the appearance of being recently cleaned. Torgersen then returned to the mound and after digging for a few moments, unearthed the body of Hay. A bullet wound was found in the back of his head.

The news of this discovery spread like wildfire and a number of people repaired to the scene, among them being Royal B. Young.

Mr. Romney observed Hay as he put the receipt for Mortensen in his inside coat pocket on the evening of the 16th, and when the body was examined this pocket was found turned inside out, but a watch and other jewelry were left undisturbed.

The body was then placed in a wagon and brought to town, Mortensen accompanying the remains. In front of Hendry's store the wagon was stopped and the father-in-law, Sharp, appeared. Standing beside Mortensen and looking at his dead son-in-law he said: "He murdered you for a receipt that was on your body and he never gave you a dollar." Mortensen made no reply but hung his head.

To men named Penrose, Hilton and Sheets he made conflicting statements as to what kind and number of receptacles were used to store the $3,800 alleged to have been paid to Hay, and also as to where they were concealed. To one he said a sack was used; to another he said two glass fruit jars were necessary, and to the third he stated that three jars were needed. To two of the witnesses he claimed that the money was concealed on a wall in the basement, and to another he stated that a portion of it was hid in the pantry.

Upon indicating the place on the wall where the jars were alleged to have been concealed, an examination was immediately made and it was found that the dust was undisturbed. There were four openings for windows in this basement, thus making it very light, but there were no windows and the basement was accessible to strangers. If the glass jars had been placed in the position indicated, the jars and contents could have been easily seen, and it was furthermore demonstrated that one jar of the size described by Mortensen would have been sufficient to hold this money.

Charles F. Watkins, the brother-in-law of Mortensen, stated that he asked Peter if he could show that he had paid Hay the money and he replied: "I can, but as my books are in bad shape it will be necessary for me to represent that you have loaned me $1,500." Watkins replied that his own bank account would not permit such misrepresentations.

It was shown that the settee upon which Mortensen claimed he and Hay sat while counting the money was too small for two men to sit on.

The moon was shining brightly on the night of this homicide, and John Allen, a motorman, stated that his car passed the spot where the body was found about 10:20 p. m., and he saw a man with a shovel on his shoulder cross the track. With the aid of the moon and the headlight he recognized this man as Mortensen.

On December 18 Mortensen was arrested. During the trial, James Sharp, the father-in-law of the murdered man, testified and on cross-examination counsel for the defendant elicited from the witness the statement that he had received a revelation from God, who told him that Peter Mortensen had murdered his son-in-law for a receipt and buried the body in a nearby field.

As four of the jurors were members of the Mormon Church and believed in the doctrine of revelation, this statement was regarded as most damaging to Mortensen's case.

His business transactions and financial condition were also the subject of much investigation, and evidence was produced tending to show the impossibility of the defendant possessing $3,800 on the night of the tragedy.

Mortensen testified as to his movements on this night, and described in detail the manner in which he claimed he handed one hundred and ninety twenty-dollar pieces to Hay as they sat on the settee, and also described the manner in which he claimed Hay left the house shortly afterward.

Mrs. Mortensen corroborated several of her husband's statements.

The jury then visited the home of Mortensen in charge of Royal B. Young, who was at the grave when the body Hay was exhumed, and who accompanied the authorities in their investigation at Mortensen's home. Mortensen declined to accompany the jury on this tour of inspection.

The defendant was found guilty of murder but the case was appealed to the Supreme Court because of the misconduct of the jury and

Young at the premises.

Alma H. Rock, a juror, averred that Young informed the jurors that the premises had been changed since the day of the murder and that he (Young) indicated a spot near a fence where he found a depression in the snow which was caused, according to his opinion, by the body being thrown over the fence, the head striking the snow. Young admitted that Rock's affidavit was true and a new trial was granted, which resulted in another conviction.

The case was again appealed to the Supreme Court on the grounds of newly discovered evidence, but another trial was denied.

On October 6, 1903, Judge Morse sentenced Mortensen to be executed on November 20, but as the law permitted the condemned man to decide whether he desired to be hanged or shot, the Judge asked:

"What mode of execution do you elect?"

Mortensen stood erect and in a firm voice replied: "I elect to be shot."

On November 14, the State Board of Pardons refused to commute the sentence.

On the night before the execution Governor Wells spent a greater part of the night with Mortensen, who presented a most ingenious defense, but the Governor declined to interfere.

On November 20 Mortensen was led into the prison yard at 10:30 a. m., and maintaining his courage to the last, he said:

"I did not kill Jimmy Hay. Neither here nor in the hereafter will I forgive those who are responsible for my death."

He refused to see a minister of any denomination and also refused stimulants, explaining that he needed neither.

After bidding the guards good-by he was bound in the chair provided for the execution. A physician pinned a piece of white pasteboard over Mortensen's heart, while the executing squad, consisting of five men, were concealed behind a curtain hung in the door of the blacksmith shop about twelve yards distant. These men were handed loaded rifles, but one of the rifles contained a blank cartridge, thus making it impossible for any one of the squad to be positive whether he fired a bullet or a harmless blank cartridge.

At the command "fire" four bullets pierced the cardboard and passed through Mortensen's heart. His head dropped on his breast, his hands quivered a moment and then all was still.

———————

THE REIGN OF TERROR IN THE MINING REGIONS IN IDAHO AND COLORADO AND THE CRIMINAL CAREER OF HARRY ORCHARD, WHO MURDERED EX-GOVERNOR STEUNENBURG, OF IDAHO, AND EIGHTEEN OTHERS.

(From Denver Press, Boise Police and Pinkerton Records.)

From 1892 to 1905 a series of the most cowardly and atrocious crimes were committed in the gold and silver mining regions in Idaho and Colorado.

As these crimes were nearly always committed during the frequent strikes, many of those who were antagonistic to the unions claimed that the union sympathizers were responsible for the outrages; but the friends of the union men claimed that the crimes were committed by agents employed by the enemies of organized labor for the purpose of turning public sympathy from the strikers and as an excuse to keep troops on the grounds during the strikes.

The first disturbance of any magnitude occurred at 4 a. m., on July 11, 1892, when a battle between the union and non-union miners occurred at the Frisco mine at Gem, Idaho.

During the battle, J. Bean, a Theil detective, and four miners named James Hennessy, John Starlick, Gus Carlson and Harry Cummings were killed and fifteen others were seriously wounded. The mill was then blown up.

Governor Willey appealed to President Harrison for Federal troops, and on July 13, General Schofield, Acting Secretary of War, sent troops into the Coeur d'Alenes district, where martial law was declared.

On July 16 President Harrison issued a proclamation in which he commanded the rioters to disperse. After a short time conditions became normal and the troops were withdrawn.

At 10:15 a. m., on April 29, 1899, a gang of armed men from Burke, Idaho, seized the Northern Pacific train at Wallace, and after picking up reinforcements at Gem and Mullen, they proceeded to Wardner, Idaho, where the Bunker Hill-Sullivan mine was located.

This party consisted of several hundred men, and they proceeded directly to the Bunker Hill-Sullivan mill, where they engaged in a battle with the men at work there.

This fight resulted in the death of Jack Smith and Jim Chayne. The mill was then blown up and set on fire.

At the request of Governor Steunenburg, President McKinley sent Federal troops to Wardner, where the so-called "bull pen" was established and martial law was again declared. Hundreds were incarcerated in the "bull pen," but the prisoners were afterward released without being charged, with the exception of P. Corcoran, who was convicted of the Bunker Hill outrage, but he was subsequently pardoned.

After many months the troops were withdrawn.

In August, 1903, nearly all the miners in Colorado and Idaho who were affiliated with the Western Federation of Miners went on a strike because the demand that eight hours should constitute a day's work was not complied with in all cases.

On September 2, 1903, Governor James Peabody, of Colorado, sent Brigadier-General Chase and Attorney-General Miller to Cripple Creek to investigate the alleged lawless conditions, and as a result of their report he sent the National Guard, in command of Adjutant-General Bell, to the Cripple Creek district, on September 4, 1903; but martial law was not declared at that time.

President Moyer, of the Western Federation, protested to the Governor against this action, as he stated that conditions did not warrant it.

On the following day many citizens of Victor, Colo., held a mass meeting, at which they denounced the Governor for sending the troops.

About noon on November 21, 1903, an explosion occurred in the Vindicator mine at Cripple Creek, which killed Superintendent Charles McCormick and Melvin Beck, a shift boss.

At first opinion was divided as to whether the explosion was the result of an accident or a deep-laid plot, but shortly afterward a badly mutilated pistol was found near the scene of the explosion, and it was then generally agreed that this weapon was used in some manner to explode the dynamite.

On December 4, 1903, Governor Peabody declared martial law in the Cripple Creek district, and Provost Marshal Thos. McClelland took possession of the Mayor's office.

On June 6, 1904, twenty-six of the non-union men who were working in a mine at Independence, Colo., finished their day's work at 2 a. m., and, according to custom, repaired at once to the depot to board a suburban train which was due at 2:30 a. m.

While these men were waiting on the platform a terrific explosion occurred which completely demolished the depot and wrecked several houses in the neighborhood.

Fourteen men were killed and the remainder injured, some being made cripples for life.

A convention of the Western Federation of Miners was being held at the time, and on the following day a resolution was unanimously passed in which the perpetrators of the outrage were bitterly denounced.

Mr. Fred Bradley was manager of the Bunker Hill-Sullivan mine at the time the company's mill was blown up in 1899. He subsequently moved to San Francisco and lived with his family at the northwest corner of Washington and Leavenworth Streets, in a building containing several flats which was the property of Attorney Walter Linforth.

At 7:50 a. m., on November 17, 1904, Mr. Bradley was about to leave home to go to his office, and while in the house he lighted a cigar.

When he opened the front door a terrific explosion occurred which could be heard for blocks.

It seemed a miracle that Mr. Bradley was not killed instantly, but he escaped with serious injuries, from which he has since practically recovered.

Experts decided that the explosion was caused by defective gas pipes, and this opinion was approved by members of Mr. Bradley's family, who had frequently detected the odor of illuminating gas in the house.

Mr. Linforth brought suit against the San Francisco Gas Company, and a jury awarded him $10,800 damages.

About 1 a. m. on May 12, 1904, several shotgun reports were heard in front of a residence in Denver, Colo., and shortly afterward the body of a man was found which proved to be the remains of a private detective named Lyte Gregory. The upper part of the body was riddled with buckshot, but at the time no trace of the murderer could be found.

Frank Steunenburg was born in 1861. Early in life he obtained employment in a newspaper office, and in 1887 he moved to Caldwell,

Idaho, where he published the Caldwell Tribune,

In 1890 he was a member of the Idaho Constitutional Convention, and in 1897 he was elected Governor of the State. Before his term of office expired he was a candidate for United States Senator, but was defeated. When he retired to private life he returned to his old home in Caldwell.

At 6:40 p. m., on December 30, 1905, Mr. Steunenburg was walking to his home, which was in the suburbs of the town, and as he opened the gate leading into his yard an explosion occurred which could be heard for miles.

Mrs. Steunenburg rushed out and found her husband lying on the snow, his body being terribly mangled. He died a few moments afterward.

The gate was blown away and the ground was considerably torn up in that vicinity. A careful search was made, and a short piece of fish-line was found.

Governor Gooding was immediately notified, and a reward of $5,000 was at once offered for the apprehension of the perpetrator of this deed. Additional rewards were also offered by others, bringing the total up to $25,000.

Every Avenue of escape from the city was guarded and an inquiry was then instituted regarding the movements of every person in the town who was not known to be above suspicion.

The result was that on January 1, 1906, the authorities learned that a man who was registered at the Saratoga Hotel as M. J. Goglan had acted very mysteriously both before and after the explosion.

He was interrogated at length, but his answers were so evasive and unsatisfactory that it was decided to take him into custody.

His room was searched, and while plaster of Paris, chloride of potash and other articles were found, the presence of which he could not explain, the most damaging evidence was a little piece of fish-line similar to that found near the scene of the explosion. On his person were found some business cards which read:

"Thomas Hogan, Colorado Agent Mutual Life Insurance Company."

When questioned as to his reason for using two names he was unable to explain. He was taken to jail, and within a few days he stated that his right name was Harry Orchard and that he was a miner and a member of Burke Union.

On January 10, 1906, James McParland, the celebrated Pinkerton detective, of "Mollie Maguire" fame, arrived on the ground, and after a long interview with Governor Gooding, went to work on the case.

On January 16, 1906, Orchard was held to answer for the murder of Governor Steunenburg.

On February 17 a great sensation was sprung when Chas. H. Moyer, President of the Western Federation of Miners; Wm. D. Haywood, Secretary-treasurer of the same order, and George Pettibone, formerly a member of the executive board, but then a merchant, were arrested in Denver and charged with being accomplices in the Steunenburg murder.

A special train was chartered and the prisoners were at once taken to Boise, Idaho. Shortly afterward a member of the Federation named Steve Adams was also arrested.

On February 24 a special Grand Jury was empanelled, and indictments were found against Moyer, Haywood, Pettibone, Orchard, Adams and Jack Simkins, also a member of the Federation and said to be a fugitive from justice.

It was then rumored that the indictments were found on confessions made by Orchard and Adams, but the prosecution refused to divulge the nature of the evidence until the trial.

On March 9, 1906, the defendants were arraigned before District Judge Frank Smith at Caldwell. Attorneys E. F. Richardson of Denver and Clarence Darrow of Chicago appeared as the leading counsel for Moyer, Haywood and Pettibone.

They contended that their clients had been illegally removed from Colorado and that the enemies of the Federation had succeeded in causing Orchard to implicate the head officials of the order for the purpose of striking a blow at organized labor.

An application was made to the Supreme Court of Idaho for a release of the prisoners on writs of habeas corpus. This was denied on March 12, but as Moyer, Haywood and Pettibone were being detained in the penitentiary, the court ordered that they be removed to the Canyon County Jail, which was done against the protest of Governor Gooding.

On March 15 the attorneys for these prisoners applied to Judge Beatty, of the United States District Court, for their release on a writ of habeas corpus, but the writ was denied on March 20. The Supreme Court of the United States was then appealed to, and the trials were continued until a decision was rendered by the court of last resort. This court refused to interfere, and on June 4, 1907, the trial of Haywood began.

He was accompanied into court by his invalid wife and aged mother. Attorney James Hawley made the opening statement for the prosecution.

C. F. Wayne testified that he passed through the gate leading to Governor Steunenburg's residence twenty minutes before the explosion and noticed nothing unusual.

Dr. J. W. Gue described the condition of the body of the murdered man, and Julian Steunenburg testified that he met Harry Orchard three days previous to the death of his (Steunenburg's) father, and that Orchard inquired as to when the ex-Governor was expected home.

On June 5, 1907, Orchard was called to the witness stand and in the soft, easy tones that characterized his speech, he testified substantially as follows:

"My right name is Albert E. Horsley, and I was born in Northumberland County, Canada, in 1866. There I spent the most of my life. After working at various occupations, my wife and I conducted a cheese factory. I deserted my wife and seven-months-old baby and ran away to America in 1896, with a married woman named Hattie Simpson, but we soon separated and she returned to her husband.

"Shortly afterward I went to Spokane, Wash. From there I went to Wallace, Idaho, where I drove a milk wagon.

"A year afterward I quit this occupation and went into the wood and coal business.

"In March, 1899, I left this business and went to work in a mine at Burke, Idaho.

"I immediately joined the Burke Union, which was connected with the Western Federation of Miners.

"In April, 1899, there was some labor trouble at the Bunker Hill-Sullivan mine at Wardner, and on the 29th inst. I accompanied a lot of men to the Bunker Hill mill, which we blew up, I personally lighting the fuse. Two men, named Chayne and Smith, were killed during the battle which preceded the explosion.

"I then went away from the mining country.

"About July, 1902, I returned and procured employment at the Vindicator mine in Colorado. I worked in this mine until the general strike in August, 1903.

"I did well in this mine, as I made considerable side money by 'high grading' (a term 'applied to stealing high grade ore and selling it). I met a widow named Mrs. Ida Toney, who had three children, and *shortly afterward I married her, thus adding bigamy to my other crimes.*

"Some months after the strike, when the Vindicator mine was being operated by non-union men, I used to sneak down a shaft at night time and continued 'high grading.' While down there in November, 1903, I set some dynamite by a guard rail at the sixth level, and attached a pistol near the guard rail in such a position that moving the rail would cause it to be discharged and the bullet would strike the dynamite, causing it to explode.

"On the 21st inst. this was exploded and Superintendent McCormick and Shift Boss Melvin Beck were killed.

"In May, 1904, I met Steve Adams, also a Federation man, and we began to lay plans to kill Governor James H. Peabody of Colorado. We located his residence in Denver and ascertained that he frequently came home late at night in a hack.

"One night we hid across the Street under some trees with our pump guns, but instead of the Governor, three women got out of the hack.

"A few nights after this Adams and I located a private detective named Lyte Gregory in a saloon in Denver. We always considered this man an enemy of the Federation, so when he left the saloon we followed him on to a dark Street and I shot him three times with my pump gun. He died shortly afterward.

"On June 5, 1904, Johnnie Neville (who has since died) and I left Independence, Colo., to go on a hunting trip, but I returned to Independence that night and met Steve Adams according to agreement.

"We then took about one hundred pounds of dynamite and placed it under the depot. I then arranged a little windlass on which was fastened a small bottle of sulphuric acid. This was placed over some giant caps which were placed on the dynamite. Spilling the acid on the caps would explode them and the concussion caused by that explosion would explode the dynamite. I then fastened a long wire to the windlass. We took the other end of the wire and remained in a secluded spot until the non-union miners came on to the platform about 2:30 a. m. We then pulled the wire and the whole depot was blown up and of the thirty men on the platform, fourteen were killed and the remainder wounded, some being made cripples for life.

"I immediately left Adams and returned on horseback to Neville. I remained in seclusion for a couple of months.

"In August, 1904, I went to San Francisco for the purpose of killing

Fred. Bradley. I located his home, but I learned that he was out of the city and would not return for two months, so I went into the country. When I returned I rented a room from Mrs. Soward on Washington Street, near Bradley's home.

"I frequently patronized the corner saloon and grocery store conducted by one Guibbini, and there met Miss Sadie Bell, one of Bradley's servant girls. I was introduced as Mr. Berry and took her to the theater. When Bradley returned home in the latter part of October I decided to poison him by putting strychnine in the milk bottles left by the milkman in the morning.

"My attempt to poison him proved unsuccessful, as the family detected that the milk was bitter and had it analyzed.

"This failing, I decided to blow him up with a bomb, which I arranged somewhat similarly to the one used at Independence depot, only I used gelatin instead of dynamite, and had the string fastened to the windlass attached to the front door so that the acid would be poured on the caps when the door was opened.

"I did considerable experimenting in my room, and one day I went out and forgot to put the different articles away, and the landlady saw them.

"On the early morning of November 17, I set the bomb which blew out the front of the house and inflicted serious injuries to Mr. Bradley. I returned to Denver in December, 1904, and lived with Steve Adams.

"A few weeks later Adams and I attempted to assassinate Chief Justice Gabbert, of the Colorado Supreme Court, but as we never had an opportunity to carry out our plans we finally decided to start after Governor Peabody again.

"We carried the guns that we had the night I killed Lyte Gregory the detective, but after trailing Peabody for weeks we decided that we could not safely kill him in that manner, so early one morning we buried a bomb in the snow on the sidewalk near his home and stood off some distance, having hold of one end of a fine wire, the other end being attached to the acid bottle suspended over the giant caps.

"Just as the Governor passed by the bomb several people were near us, so we did not dare pull the wire. We then dug the bomb out of the snow and left.

"In January, 1905, I moved to a little place near Denver, called Globeville.

"The union men there were out on a strike, and as they belonged to the Western Federation I wanted to blow up a lodging-house in which were domiciled three hundred nonunion men. Haywood and Moyer heard of my plans and ordered me not to carry them into execution.

"About April, 1905, I procured a contract to write insurance for the Mutual Life Insurance Company, using the name of Thomas Hogan, the object being to show that I had a legitimate occupation if called to account for my movements.

"I then proceeded to Canon City, Colo., where Governor Peabody then lived. I prepared a bomb with the intention of blowing up his home while he was there, but I did not have an opportunity.

"About June 1 I returned to Denver and I decided to kill Judge Gabbert, of the Supreme Court. I studied his movements and I buried a bomb, something similar to the one I used at Bradley's, near a short cut through a lot that he usually used to go down town in the morning. I had a wire attached to it which just reached to the top of the ground, and when I saw him coming I intended to fasten a purse to the wire, expecting he would stop to pick up the purse.

"Just as he appeared another man came near from another direction, and as he would see me if I attached the purse, I had to abandon my plans for the time being.

"In a few days, however, I decided to make another bomb and set it near the first one, as I was afraid to touch the first one. I did so, but instead of killing Judge Gabbert a stranger was blown to pieces. I then determined to blow up Judge Goddard. I buried a bomb by his gate and attached the string fastened to an acid bottle to the gate so that the acid would spill when the gate was opened. This bomb failed to work and I left it there.

"In the latter part of October, 1905, Jack Simpkins and I went to Caldwell, Idaho, for the purpose of assassinating ex-Governor Steunenburg.

"One day we ascertained that he was down town, and by our own observations we knew that he habitually traveled over a certain path in reaching his home.

"We buried a bomb in this path and attached a wire to it which we figured would come in contact with his feet as he passed along, but it did not work.

"I then returned and removed the bomb.

"I did not make any further attempt to kill him until Christmas night, *when I hid near his house with my shotgun, intending to shoot through the window at him, but again I was disappointed.*

"I left Caldwell, but returned in a couple of days and stopped at the Saratoga Hotel.

"I saw Steunenburg on the Streets of Caldwell on Saturday, so I went to my room and took a bomb I had already prepared and buried it in the snow near his gate post and fastened the wire attached to the acid bottle to the gate. I then hurried away and passed Steunenburg while he was on his way home.

"Before I arrived at the hotel I heard the bomb explode."

Orchard furthermore claimed that he had committed all these crimes because it was believed that the persons he assassinated or attempted to assassinate were antagonistic to the Federation.

He testified that Moyer, Haywood and Pettibone had encouraged him in much of his work and that Haywood had supplied him with money.

Orchard was then turned over to Attorney Richardson for cross-examination.

It appears that some years before, Orchard and several others purchased the Hercules mine when the value of the property was unknown.

Orchard sold out for comparatively nothing, but subsequently it was discovered that the property was very valuable, and as a consequence the owners, including August Paulson, became very wealthy.

Mr. Richardson brought out the fact that Orchard visited Paulson's home at Wallace, Idaho, where he was cordially received by the entire family, and that while partaking of Paulson's hospitality he was arranging plans to kidnap his host's little boy and hold him for a $50,000 ransom. Confronted with the proof, Orchard reluctantly confessed that the charge was true and that inclement weather was all that prevented him from consummating the deed.

After being on the witness stand several days, Orchard gave way to a great number of witnesses by whom it was proven by circumstantial evidence that Orchard had committed all the crimes he had confessed to, but there was very little evidence produced to corroborate his claim that the officers of the Federation had aided and encouraged him in his fiendish work.

Mrs. Sadie Swan, who as Miss Bell worked for Mr. Bradley in San Francisco, identified Orchard as a man she had often met at the corner grocery just previous to the explosion in the Bradley home.

She also recalled the occasion when the "bitter milk" was sent to the chemist to be analyzed.

O. Crook, the milkman, testified that the Bradley family had complained to him about the bitter milk and that he took it to the city chemist to have it analyzed.

P. L. McCleary, assistant city chemist of San Francisco, testified that he analyzed the milk and found between 40 and 60 grains of strychnine in one bottle.

Mrs. Soward, who conducted the rooming-house where Orchard had lodgings while laying his plans to assassinate Bradley, testified that one day when Orchard was out she went to his room and found a screw-eye in his door to which was attached a piece of fish line. She also found several other articles which led her to believe her roomer was an inventor. He was known to her as Berry.

Judge L. M. Goddard, of the Colorado Supreme Court, testified that on February 13, 1906, Detective McParland informed him of Orchard's confession and that the next day General Wells dug up the bomb which Orchard had planted at his (Goddard's) gate. As this bomb was dug up on St. Valentine's Day, the Judge humorously referred to it as a "Valentine." It contained forty sticks of dynamite, thirty-seven of which were exploded in the presence of witnesses in the suburbs of Denver.

On June 24 the prosecution closed and the defense began.

On July 3 David C. Coates, former Lieutenant-Governor of Colorado, testified that Orchard asked him to act as a go-between in taking a ransom, as he intended to kidnap Paulson's child. When Coates threatened to expose Orchard, the latter tried to pass it off as a joke.

On July 10 Moyer took the witness stand. He denied all of Orchard's allegations so far as they connected him with wrongdoing.

Moyer testified that he was arrested at Ouray on December 14, 1903, on a charge of desecrating the American flag by using it for advertising purposes. He was released on $7,000 bonds, but was immediately taken into custody by General Wells as a military prisoner and placed in the "bull pen," but was released a couple of months later.

On July 11 Haywood took the stand in his own defense.

He denied all of the charges made by Orchard so far as they referred to him.

The evidence was concluded on July 23, and after several days of argument the case was finally submitted to the jury on Saturday, July 27.

On Sunday morning the jury came into court with the following verdict:

"State of Idaho vs. William D. Haywood: "We, the jury in the above entitled cause, find the defendant not guilty.

THOS. B. GESS, Foreman."

Pettibone's trial began at Boise on November 27, 1907, and the evidence was very similar to that produced in the Haywood case.

On December 12 Orchard testified substantially the same as at the previous trial. On cross-examination, in reply to Attorney Darrow's question, he stated that the reason he had made a confession to Detective McParland was because he realized the enormity of his crimes and had decided to confess all of his sins and then ask God for forgiveness.

It might be stated that some doubt Orchard's sincerity and are of the opinion that he confessed to all the crimes he committed only when he realized that McParland had a complete case against him for the murder of Governor Steunenburg and that his reasons for so doing was because .he expected that consideration would be shown him if he appeared as a witness for the prosecution.

On December 21 Mrs. Ida Toney, the unfortunate widow who married Orchard believing him to be a single man, testified for the prosecution and corroborated Orchard's testimony regarding a visit Pettibone made to Orchard's home on one occasion.

Charlie Neville testified that he and his father accompanied Orchard from Independence on a hunting trip on the day preceding the explosion at the depot, and on that night Orchard left their camp in a mysterious manner, returning about 3 a. m. the following day.

On January 3, 1908, the cause was submitted to the jury, the attorneys for the defense having refused to argue the case. On the following day Pettibone was acquitted.

The charge against Moyer was immediately taken up by Judge Wood, and Attorney Hawley for the prosecution signified the desire of the State to have an order of dismissal entered. Judge Wood complied with the request, at the same time remarking that he considered it the proper course to pursue.

On March 10, 1908, the case of Harry Orchard was called before Judge Wood in the District Court at Caldwell.

He pleaded guilty and March 18 was the date set for sentence. On that date he was sentenced to be hanged on May 15.

In passing sentence Judge Wood recommended that the State Board of Pardons commute the sentence to life imprisonment. Shortly afterward a reprieve was granted until July 5.

On July 1 the Pardon Board, consisting of Governor Gooding, Secretary of State Lansdon and Attorney-General Gukeen, commuted the death sentence to imprisonment for life.

Shortly after Orchard's confession, Steve Adams made a statement to Detective McParland in which he not only corroborated Orchard's confession, but added that he had committed other murders in which Orchard did not participate.

Fred Tyler, who was alleged to have jumped Jack Simkins' lumber claim in the wilds of St. Joe County, Idaho, and whose body was found in the woods on August 11, 1904, was murdered by Adams, according to his statement. In addition to this, he claimed that he killed Arthur Collins and a man named Boule.

Afterward Adams repudiated the entire "confession," and claimed that persons interested in the prosecution promised him immunity if he would make a "confession" implicating the Western Federation.

This "confession" was not admitted as evidence, either in the trials of Haywood or Pettibone, nor was Adams used as a witness.

On February 11, 1907, Adams was brought to trial at Wallace, Idaho, for the murder of Tyler.

On March 6 the case was submitted to the jurors, who were unable to agree on a verdict, after deliberating thirty-one hours.

In December he was again tried on the same charge at Rathdrum, Idaho, and again the jury disagreed.

Adams was then removed to Telluride, Colo., to be tried for the murder of Arthur Collins, but a change of venue was granted and the trial began at Grand Junction, Colo., in June, 19Q8. The defendant was acquitted and discharged from custody.

When Orchard's confession regarding the explosion at the Bradley home became known, the San Francisco Gas Company moved for a new trial on the grounds of newly discovered evidence, but this was refused.

The case was then appealed to the Supreme Court, which decided that the granting of a new trial, on the grounds of newly discovered evidence, is largely discretionary with the trial court. It was furthermore decided that the affidavits relative to the new found evidence were not properly presented.

On August 19, 1909, the Gas Company paid Linforth $13,904.50, being the original amount of damage, plus interest and costs.

On July 21, 1909, Orchard was baptized by Elder Steward, of the Seventh Day Adventist Church, and the prisoner now takes a leading part in conducting the religious services at the Penitentiary each Sabbath,

---

THE HIDEOUS MURDERS COMMITTED BY THE BENDER

FAMILY IN KANSAS.

On March 9, 1873, Dr. William H. York left Fort Scott, Kansas, on horseback for his home in Independence, Kansas, and although the days and weeks rolled by, he did not appear at his home. Dr. York was in comfortable circumstances; possessed of a cheerful disposition, and had friends galore who decided that he had not voluntarily disappeared, and they concluded that he had become the victim of foul play, as it was known that he had considerable money on his person.

Senator and Colonel York employed detectives and joined them in the search for their missing brother. Excitement ran high throughout the State, and volunteer searching parties inspected nearly every foot of ground and dragged the rivers throughout the surrounding country.

There was a little town called Cherryvale, about fifty miles from the south line of the State, and Dr. York was traced to this place. About two miles south of this town, on the main wagon road, stood a small frame tavern, having a room in front where meals were served to wayfarers by William Bender and his family, who moved into the house in March, 1871.

Bender was sixty-three years of age and Mrs. Bender was about sixty years old. The son was twenty-seven, and the daughter Katie was twenty-four years of age. The father and son were large, coarse appearing men, and the daughter was a large, masculine, red-faced woman who bore an exceedingly bad reputation.

The family professed to be spiritualists and the daughter claimed that she possessed supernatural powers, as will be seen by the following advertisement inserted in the Kansas papers:

"Professor Miss Kate Bender can heal disease, cure blindness, fits and deafness.

"Residence, 14 miles east of Independence, on the road to Osage Mission. June 18, 1872."

On April 3, 1873, a party of men rode up to this roadside tavern and asked the Bender family if they had heard or seen anything of the missing Dr. York, but they claimed to be ignorant of his whereabouts. A few days afterward, another party called and made the same inquiry. The Bender family, fearing that they were suspected, hitched up their team and, without touching the household effects, drove away.

On May 9, another searching party, while passing Bender's tavern, noticed its deserted appearance. This impressed them as being rather singular, and when they went to the rear of the house, they found that some hogs and calves had died there, evidently from thirst or hunger. This aroused suspicion and the authorities instituted an investigation.

In a small one-half acre orchard adjoining the house, the surface of the ground had been carefully plowed and harrowed, but there had just been a heavy rainfall and in a certain place the ground had settled very noticeably and the settled portion was about the size of a grave. The ground was then dug up and the badly decomposed body of Dr. York was found. The skull had been crushed and the throat cut. Before nightfall seven more bodies were exhumed and were subsequently identified as follows:

No. 1, W. F. McCrotty, a resident of Cedarville, who was contesting a case before the land office in Independence and who probably stopped at Bender's for refreshments.

No. 2. D. Brown, a resident of Cedarville, who had been trading horses in the neighborhood with a man named Johnson. Brown's body was decomposed beyond recognition, but it was identified through a silver ring which Brown wore and which he had shown to Johnson.

No. 3. Henry F. McKenzie of Hamilton County, Indiana, who had been missing since December 5, 1872. He was en route to Independence for the purpose of locating there. His sister, Mrs. J. Thompson, identified his wearing apparel.

Nos. 4 and 5. Mr. Longoer and his baby girl. This gentleman had buried his wife in 1872 and was about to leave for Iowa

Nos. 6 and 7 were the unidentified bodies of two men.

In each instance the skull was battered to a pulp and the throat cut from ear to ear, with the exception of Mr. Longoer's eighteen-months-old girl, who died from suffocation. As there were no marks on the child's throat, and as she was lying under her father's body in the grave, it is probable that she was thrown in alive and was suffocated when her father's body was thrown in on top of her.

The next day another body of a child was found, but it was so badly decomposed that it was impossible to ascertain its sex. Judging from the length of its golden hair and the size of the body, it was evidently the remains of an eight-year old girl. This body was evidently butchered by a fiend. The breast bone was driven in; the right knee was wrenched from its socket and the leg doubled up under the body.

When the officers entered the deserted house they were met by an unbearable stench. It was then revealed how the whole series of crimes was committed.

A little booth was formed by cloth partitions, in which the guests partook of their meals. The table was purposely set back so near this partition that when they sat in an upright position in their chairs, the back of their heads would be against and indent this cloth. If the guests had the appearance of having money in their possession, one or both of the male members of the family would patiently wait on the opposite side of the curtain with heavy stone-breaker's hammers, two of which were found by the officers, and when the guests sat upright and the impression of the back of their heads appeared on the cloth partition, the assassin, or assassins in case two guests were to be disposed of at once, would swing the hammers and crush in the victims' skulls.

As people were constantly passing on the road who might stop at Bender's, it was necessary to get the bodies out of sight as quickly as possible, and for this purpose a trapdoor was made in the floor, which was directly over a pit about six feet deep, which had been dug in the ground. After the body was thrown in the pit, the throat was cut from ear to ear, for fear there might be a spark of life yet remaining. It was the accumulation of congealed blood in the pit which caused the terrible stench.

After it became dark, the grave would be dug and the body buried. The reason for keeping the ground in the orchard constantly plowed and harrowed was to prevent the new graves from being noticed.

When the neighbors learned of this series of atrocious murders, they became almost insane in their desire for vengeance, and they immediately organized vigilance committees and scoured the country in the hopes of apprehending this family of fiends.

About a mile from Bender's tavern was a grocery store conducted by a man named Brockman, who had been a partner of Bender's from 1869 to 1871. As both men were Germans and close friends, it was suspected that Brockman was an accomplice in some of the murders, or at least could impart valuable information, both as regards the crimes and as to Bender's whereabouts. A posse therefore seized him and after taking him to the woods, some eight miles distant, they placed a rope around his neck and told him to confess all that he knew or be hanged.

He begged for mercy and swore that Bender had never made a confidant of him. The frenzied posse then hanged him to a tree, but when he was on the point of death, they let him down to the ground and after restoratives were administered, he finally regained his speech. Again he was ordered to confess and again he swore that he was ignorant of Bender's doings.

He was hanged again and this method of torture was repeated three times, but it availed the posse nothing, and they finally left Brockman lying on the ground in a semiconscious condition, but he eventually recovered.

Sometime previous to the discovery that Bender's tavern was a human slaughter-house, the body of a man named Jones was found in Drum Creek. The back of the head was completely crushed and almost severed from the body. The only clew obtainable was a wagon track through the snow, which led down to the creek near where the body was found. But there was a peculiarity about this track because of the fact that one of the wheels was evidently considerable out of plumb, therefore, in revolving it made a zigzag track through the snow. In view of the discoveries at Bender's tavern, an experiment was subsequently made with the wagon in which the family temporarily escaped, and it was found that their wagon left tracks similar to those found in the snow.

This deviation from the usual method of disposing of the bodies of the victims, was due to the fact that at the time of this murder the ground was frozen, thus making grave-digging slow work and hard to conceal. Upon arriving at the frozen creek, it became necessary to cut a hole in the ice and push the body underneath, in order to conceal it for the time being.

There is no doubt but that the methods above described were those employed by these butchers, as two prospective victims unconsciously escaped from their clutches after all the preliminaries were arranged, and it was not until the expose that they realized their hair-breadth escape from being "planted" in "Old Man Bender's" orchard.

Mr. Wetzell of Independence, Kansas, read Kate Bender's advertisement of her remarkable ability as a healer of the afflicted, and being constantly tortured with neuralgia in the face, he induced a friend named Gordan to accompany him to her home. Upon examining his face, Kate expressed confidence in her ability to effect a permanent cure, but as it was about dinner time she invited both men to dine first. She set the chairs for the guests so that their heads were in close proximity to the cloth partition, and eatables were then placed on the table.

When they first arrived they observed that Old Bender and his son scrutinized them closely, but assuming that it was done merely through curiosity, they gave the incident no further thought at the time.

When the visitors took their position at the table the father and son disappeared. For some reason, which Wetzell and Gordan could not explain, they immediately arose from the table and stood at the counter to eat their meals.

Up to this time Miss Bender was most affable toward her guests, but at this unexpected turn of affairs, she became caustic and almost abusive in her language toward them.

The two male Benders then reappeared from behind the partition, and after casting a glance at the two strangers, they repaired to the barn, a few rods from the house. The guests became suspicious at this sudden change of demeanor on the part of their hostess and immediately left the building and went out on the road.

Providentially two wagons were being driven past at this moment, and Gordan and Wetzell jumped into their buggy and drove away ahead of them, but on reflection they concluded that perhaps they were unnecessarily alarmed and dismissed the incident from their minds.

As there has been much speculation as to the fate of the Bender family the following letters from the Chiefs of Police of Independence and Cherryvale, Kansas, to the author are published in part:

"Cherryvale, Kansas, June 14, 1910.

"Dear Sir: — Yours just received. It so happened that my father-in-law's farm joins the Bender farm and he helped to locate the bodies of the victims. I often tried to find out from him what became of the Benders, but he only gave me a knowing look and said he guessed they would not bother anyone else.

"There was a vigilance committee organized to locate the Benders, and shortly afterward old man Bender's wagon was found by the roadside riddled with bullets. You will have to guess the rest. I am respectfully yours,

(Box 11.) J. N. Kramer,

"Chief of Police."

"Independence, Kansas, June 14, 1910. "Dear Sir: — In regard to the Bender family I will say that I have lived here forty years, and it is my opinion that they never got away.

"A vigilance committee was formed and some of them are still here, but they will not talk except to say that it would be useless to look for them, and they smile at the reports of some of the family having been recently located.

"The family nearly got my father. He intended to stay there one night, but he became suspicious, and although they tried to coax him to stay he hitched up his team and left.

"Regretting that I cannot give you more information,

"I am yours respectfully,

"D. M. Van Cleve,

"Chief of Police." 12

DR. B. C. HYDE'S DIABOLICAL PLOT TO GAIN POSSESSION OF COL. SWOPE'S MILLIONS.

(From Kansas City Star, Times and Journal.)

Thomas Hunton Swope, afterward known as Colonel Swope, was born in Kentucky in 1829. After accumulating a few thousand dollars in his native State, he proceeded to Kansas City, Mo., in 1860, where he invested a large portion of his savings in suburban lands which were practically worthless then but which subsequently enhanced in value until Swope became a multi-millionaire. He conceived a plan of devoting to public benefactions a large part of his wealth and as a part of this philanthropic plan he gave to Kansas City a magnificent tract of territory embracing 1354 acres, which is now known as Swope Park, the second largest park in America. In his later years Swope became extremely eccentric and seldom appeared in public. He had two sisters and two brothers. One brother, Logan Swope, died in February, 1900, leaving a widow and seven children, named Chrisman, Frances, Thomas, Lucy, Margaret, Stella and Sarah. In 1909, Chrisman, the eldest, was 31 years of age, and Sarah, the youngest, was 14 years of age. Mrs. Logan Swope resided with her family in a large mansion near Independence, Mo., which is a short distance from Kansas City. Colonel Swope, who never married, and his cousin, J. Moss Hunton, resided in the same house.

Colonel Swope's property was valued at $3,600,000 and he made a will which provided that Mrs. Logan Swope's children should each receive about $200,000, with the exception of Francis, who was to receive but $135,000. There was also a residuary fund amounting to $1,405,595 which was to be equally divided among these seven children, but Swope had about decided to change his will and leave the residuary to charity. The entire Swope family knew the contents of this will and also knew of Swope's determination to change it. The executors of this will were J. Moss Hunton, Attorney John Paxton and Steward Fleming, Colonel Swope's nephew.

Bennett Clarke Hyde was born in Cowper County, Missouri, in 1872, but spent his boyhood days in Lexington, Mo., where his father was a Baptist preacher. Young Hyde received a college education and afterward graduated from the University Medical College in Kansas City, Mo. In 1898-99 Dr. Hyde was demonstrator of anatomy at this college and during this time several graves were robbed. Finally two negroes named Sam McClain and Charley Perry were arrested for robbing the grave of Michael Kelly at St. Mary's Cemetery in Independence, Mo. They subsequently confessed to this crime and several others of a similar nature, and swore that they sold the bodies to Dr. Hyde. The doctor was arrested but the case never came to trial and was dropped from the calendar on March 4, 1899.

On May 4, 1905, Dr. Hyde was appointed police surgeon of Kansas City, but on September 10, 1907, he was suspended by Mayor Jones on a charge of cruelty to Mrs. Annie Clement, a negress who had attempted to commit suicide by morphine poisoning and to whom Hyde administered oil of mustard for the purpose of arousing her from her sleepy condition.

On June 21, 1905, Dr. Hyde and Frances Swope were clandestinely married at Fayetteville, Ark. Mrs. Logan Swope was bitterly opposed to this marriage, as she stated that she felt certain that Hyde married Frances for money alone, and she furthermore stated that Hyde had made love to two other wealthy women and after obtaining $4,000 from one and $2,000 from the other, he "threw them over." Following the public announcement of Dr. Hyde's marriage, Mrs. Sarah Frank, of Kansas City, a widow, brought suit against Hyde asking damages for breach of promise, but the case was settled out of court.

As a result of this marriage, Hyde and his wife's relatives were estranged for over a year, but in August, 1906, a reconciliation was effected and shortly afterward Colonel Swope paid $7,500 for a home at 3516 Forest Avenue, Kansas City, and presented it to Hyde and his wife.

On September 5, 1909, Colonel Swope, who was then 81 years of age, fell to the floor in the Swope mansion and while he was not seriously injured, he imagined that he was about to die and insisted upon being put to bed. Dr. Hyde engaged a nurse named Pearl Keller to care for him.

On the evening of October 1, 1909, Moss Hunton was eating his dinner in the Swope home when he collapsed. Dr. George T. Twyman, the regular family physician, and Dr. Hyde, were summoned and they diagnosed the case as apoplexy. Dr. Hyde suggested that the patient be bled, to which Dr. Twyman acquiesced; Hyde then began to draw blood from the patient's arm. When one pint had been drawn Dr. Twyman stated that that was sufficient, but Dr. Hyde continued until two quarts were drawn. Dr. Twyman again insisted that no more be drawn and called Dr. Hyde's attention to a recent case where a physician had bled a patient to death. Miss Keller, the nurse, and Mrs. Hyde were in the room at the time, and when Hyde continued to ignore Dr. Twyman's advice, Mrs. Hyde, according to the statements subsequently made by Dr. Twyman and Miss Keller, said to her husband, "Dear, I believe I would quit. Dr. Twyman thinks you have bled him enough." Hyde then quit but almost immediately afterward Hunton gave a spasmodic gasp and died.

About twenty minutes later. Dr. Hyde said to Miss Keller: "I want to have a private talk with you after a while." About an hour afterward Miss Keller saw Dr. Hyde alone in the sitting room and the doctor said: "Miss Keller, I am not a business man but I can be one. This man Hunton was one of the executors of the Swope estate and in a few days the old man will make a new will and appoint new executors, and I wish you would suggest that I take Hunton's place." Miss Keller replied that she was engaged to perform professional services only and that she could not interfere in private affairs.

Although Colonel Swope insisted upon remaining in bed, he was feeling unusually well on the second day following the death of Hunton. Notwithstanding his favorable condition, Dr. Hyde gave Miss Keller a "digestive tablet" with instructions to give it to her patient. After much persuasion the nurse finally induced the old man to swallow it and twenty minutes later he was seized with violent convulsions. During his conscious moments he said: "Oh, God, I wish I hadn't taken that damned medicine."

Upon noting the sudden change in Swope's condition, Miss Keller called Dr. Hyde from another room and after making a hasty examination of the patient, he stated that Swope was also a victim of apoplexy, probably brought on by the shock of Hunton's death, but the nurse subsequently stated that the symptoms and Dr. Hyde's treatment of Swope and Hunton were entirely different.

Although Dr. Twyman was Colonel Swope's regular physician and could easily have attended the patient, Dr. Hyde did not notify him of the changed condition of Swope.

On the evening of October 3 Colonel Swope died, and shortly afterward Hyde called Miss Keller to one side and advised her to charge $35 per week instead of $25, the regular rate.

Prior to October 1, 1909, Dr. Hyde drank the cistern water in the Swope home which was used by the entire family, but about this time he notified the Swope's that if they continued to use this water without boiling it they would have typhoid fever.

On Thanksgiving Day, November 25, 1909, Hyde and his wife dined at the Swope home, and they brought bottled water, which they only drank.

Three days later Mrs. Swope went to Chicago, but was called home on December 5.

Within two weeks after the Thanksgiving dinner the following persons, who were either members of the Swope family, visitors or servants, were stricken with typhoid fever:

December 1 — Leonora Copridge, the colored servant girl.

December 2 — Chrisman and Margaret Swope, aged 31 and 21, respectively, and Miss Georgie Compton, a seamstress.

December 4 — Miss Nora Dickson, a visitor and former governess in the house.

December 5 — Steward Fleming, a visiting relative.

December 10 — Sarah Swope, aged 14 years.

December 11 — Stella Swope, aged 16 years, and Mildred Fox, a 14-year-old girl, residing in Kansas City, who had only spent one day at the Swope mansion and was taken ill in her own home.

This epidemic resulted in four other nurses being called, namely: Misses Churchill, Gordan, Houlehan and Van Nuys.

On December 5 Dr. Hyde told Miss Houlehan, the nurse, that he had just given Chrisman Swope a capsule and instructed her to bathe him. While she was sponging the sick man he had a convulsion. Dr. Hyde was called and he declared that the patient was suffering from cerebral meningitis. He sank into a coma, but the next day he was evidently improving, until Dr. Hyde gave him another capsule, when he almost immediately became so restless that morphine was administered. A few moments later he died. Dr. Hyde then felt his pulse, and after throwing the dead man's feet around in a rough manner, said: "He's gone, prepare him for the undertaker."

The night his brother-in-law died, Dr. Hyde attended a banquet given in celebration of his election as president of the Jackson County Medical Society.

Miss Lucy Swope left her home for a trip through Europe on September 26, 1909, and on the day her brother Chrisman died a cable was sent requesting her to return at once, without giving the true reason for the request. She was due to arrive in New York on December 15, and her mother desired that some lady friend go to New York for the purpose of breaking the news and to be her companion on the homeward trip. A friend named Miss Mary Hickman was selected, and Mrs. Swope gave her daughter, Mrs. Hyde, sufficient money to purchase a ticket for Miss Hickman, when Dr. Hyde, who had never shown any particular interest in Lucy up to this time, insisted upon going himself, and he went, against the wishes of Mrs. Swope.

Hyde left Kansas City on December 13, but on the preceding evening he went to Margaret Swope's room, which was in semi-darkness at the time. Margaret was Dr. Twyman's patient, and Dr. Hyde had never treated her up to this time. Without making any examination of the young lady's pulse or inquiring into her condition or even admitting enough light into the room to note her appearance, Hyde at once administered a hypodermic injection into her arm. This injection caused great pain and the arm was disabled for months afterward.

Just as Hyde was leaving the room, Margaret's nurse, Miss Churchill, entered, and Hyde said: "I have just given Margaret an injection of camphorated oil, as I found that she had an intermittent pulse." Miss Churchill was much surprised at this unusual proceeding. She immediately felt Margaret's pulse, which she found to be perfectly regular, and she tried to detect the odor of the camphorated oil, alleged to have been injected, but failed.

On December 15, Hyde met Lucy Swope in New York, and they left that night for Kansas City. At this time Lucy was in good health. On the second day of the trip she started to get a drink of water, but Hyde stopped her and said: "Wait a minute, I have a folding cup that Frances sent you. I will get the water in that." Lucy subsequently stated that it seemed to take Hyde a long time to get the water. During the trip Lucy told Hyde that she intended to take some pills, and Hyde tried to persuade her to take some powders he had, but she declined.

When Miss Lucy reached her home she remained only a few hours, and did not drink any water in the Swope home. She then went to the home of Miss Elinor Minor, where she remained for two days, at the expiration of which time she became feverish and was taken home, A few days later Drs. Twyman and Sloan found that she was suffering from typhoid fever.

During Hyde's trip to New York the typhoid patients improved, especially Margaret, and when Hyde returned and visited this young lady on December 18, she was laughing and talking with Miss Houlehan, Hyde asked if Margaret was still taking the capsules, and upon receiving an affirmative answer, he examined the capsules, but the nurse did not observe just what he did. Shortly after Hyde left the room Miss Houlehan gave Margaret a capsule, and a few moments later   Margaret was seized with convulsions. Fortunately, Dr. Twyman arrived on the scene at this time. Margaret vomited freely, and fortunately for the interests of justice the ejecta was placed in a bottle and saved.

A few moments later the five nurses held a conference, at which they agreed that Dr. Hyde was responsible for the conditions in the Swope home, and they decided that either Hyde or they must leave that night.

They then called upon Dr. Twyman, and after explaining their reasons for accusing Hyde they stated that either Hyde or they must leave at once.

Dr. Twyman then sought Mrs. Swope and informed her of the nurses' accusations and their ultimatum. Mrs. Swope replied: "Oh, God, do you think so; then it must be true. The burden has been on my heart and I tried to cast it off, but I cannot do it."

It was then decided that Dr. Twyman should leave word for Dr. Hyde to call at his (Twyman's) office in Independence that evening, and at 8:30 p. m, Hyde left the Swope mansion for that purpose. When Hyde arrived at the office, Dr. Twyman said: "Dr. Hyde, I have a very serious and delicate matter to discuss with you, but my duty compels me to speak plainly. The fact is that the nurses believe that you are entirely responsible for the conditions in the Swope home, and they have decided that you or they must leave the house at once." Hyde replied: "Well, that's pretty bad. Tell me all they said." Dr. Twyman then repeated the substance of his conversation with the nurses. Hyde then threatened to sue the nurses for libel, but Dr. Twyman advised him to do nothing of the kind, but to leave the Swope home as quietly as possible.

Hyde acted on this advice, and returning to the Swope mansion he informed his wife of what had transpired, and at 11 o'clock that night Hyde and his wife left for their home in Kansas City.

Although Dr. Twyman endeavored to convince the nurses that they were wrong in their conclusions, he gave instructions the next day to destroy all medicine in the Swope home, and in his testimony before the Grand Jury said: "I fully believe that someone is responsible for the poisoning and administering of typhoid germs in the Swope home."

On the same evening that Dr. Hyde was called to Dr. Twyman's office, Tom Swope escorted his sister Lucy back to Elinor Minor's home, and was returning to his mother's home about 8:30 p. m., when, within about two blocks of his mother's home, he observed another man about one block in front of him who was coming toward him. When the two men were about one block apart, the man coming from the direction of the Swope home crossed the Street and when he drew near a Street lamp he searched his pockets and then throwing something to the ground he proceeded to stamp it into the snow. Swope continued to walk toward his home on the opposite side of the Street from this man, and when the man drew nearer to the Street lamp Swope saw it was Dr. Hyde, who was then en route to Dr. Twyman's office. Swope made no sign of recognition, but passed by on the opposite side of the Street, evidently without being observed by Hyde.

When the doctor passed out of sight, Swope, whose curiosity was fully aroused, hastened to where his brother-in-law dropped the article, and found a piece of a capsule. Swope was formerly engaged in testing ores in Tonopah, Nevada, and having used the cyanide process he was familiar with the odor of the drug, and he concluded that this portion of a capsule had the odor of cyanide of potassium. He took the broken capsule home and Miss Van Nuys, the nurse, who had also used this drug in cleaning jewelry, agreed that the particle of the capsule smelled like cyanide.

Attorney John Paxton was then communicated with by telephone, and he accompanied Tom Swope to the spot where the capsule was found, and they found several other particles of capsules. These were placed in an envelope and sealed, and three days later Mr. Paxton and Tom Swope took this envelope and the bottle containing the ejecta from Margaret Swope's stomach, to the celebrated Professor Ludvig Hecktoen, of the Rush Medical College, Chicago. He turned the packages over to two men of international repute, Professor Haines, of Rush Medical College, and Professor Vaughan, of the University of Michigan. These men made an analysis and found unmistakable traces of cyanide in the stains on the envelope containing the pieces of capsules, and they found strychnine in the ejecta from Margaret Swope's stomach.

When the typhoid epidemic in the Swope home became the talk of Kansas City, Dr. E. E. Stewart, of that city, recalled the fact that on November

10, Dr. Hyde had procured from him five tubes containing typhoid, diphtheria and other germs for the alleged purpose of taking up the study of bacteriology. His suspicions being aroused, Dr. Stewart proceeded to Dr. Hyde's office while Hyde was making his trip to New York after Lucy Swope. Stewart found Miss Bessie Coughlin in charge of the office, and he told the young lady that his germs were dead and he desired to borrow Dr. Hyde's.

A short time before this Hyde had told Dr. Stewart that he had done very little with the germs, but Stewart afterward stated that when he examined the typhoid tube he found enough germs gone to inoculate the whole of Kansas City. He also discovered that the tube which was presumed to contain diphtheria germs had been opened, but through some mistake it contained pus germs.

It was afterward claimed that Hyde injected pus germs into Margaret Swope's arm, believing that they were diphtheria germs.

When Hyde returned from New York and learned that Dr. Stewart had obtained the germ tubes from Miss Coughlin, he reprimanded her, and on New Year's Day she was discharged.

Dr. Stewart and Dr. Frank Hall made a close examination of the Swope home, but could find no cause for the typhoid epidemic.

On September 3, 1909, Hyde purchased several five-grain capsules of cyanide of potassium from Hugo Brecklein, a Kansas City druggist, who stated positively that Hyde claimed he wanted to use them on some dogs which were bothering him, but Hyde stated that he did not say "dogs," but "bugs," referring to cockroaches in his office.

On December 30, 1909, an autopsy was performed on the body of Chrisman Swope, and although Dr. Hyde's death certificate showed that he died from cerebral meningitis, the brain was found to be perfectly normal.

Professors Vaughan and Haines found traces of strychnine and cyanide in the liver, and while it was evident that Chrisman was suffering from typhoid at the time of his death, the disease had not reached such a stage as to make death possible.

On January 12, 1910, an autopsy was held on the body of Colonel Swope. In this case Dr. Hyde certified that death was due to cerebral hemorrhage, but the brain was found to be absolutely free from the blood clots which would accompany such a condition. From what Professor Hecktoen learned of the symptoms in the death of Colonel Swope, he testified before the coroner that he believed death to be due to cyanide and strychnine poisoning.

Professors Vaughan and Haines testified that they analyzed one-seventh of Colonel Swope's liver and found one sixth of a grain of strychnine, indicating that the entire liver contained about one grain, or almost twice as much as was necessary for a fatal dose. Dr. Hyde refused to testify before the coroner.

On December 29, while the investigation of the mysteries of the Swope mansion was in progress, Mrs. Hyde telephoned to Dr. Stewart, who supplied Hyde with the germs, to call on Dr. Hyde at his home. When he arrived Hyde claimed that he was also a victim of typhoid, and requested Dr. Stewart to draw some blood from his (Hyde's) ear, for the purpose of making a test. It was found that Hyde had the symptoms of typhoid, but it was Dr. Stewart's opinion that Hyde had been inoculated with dead bacteria, which would bring about the symptoms of a genuine case. Dr. Stewart stated that Hyde appeared to be anxious to have it generally believed that he was a victim of typhoid.

During this alleged illness, Lenora Von Bocher acted as Hyde's nurse, and she subsequently testified that Hyde took her chart prepared during his "illness,", and although it was her personal property, he never returned it to her, notwithstanding the fact that she repeatedly requested him to do so.

On January 10, 1910, John Paxton swore to a warrant charging Hyde with the murder of Colonel Swope. The doctor was arrested on the following day and released on $50,000 bond.

On January 12, Mr. Paxton wrote a letter in which he charged that Hyde was guilty of three murders and numerous attempts to commit murder. This letter was subsequently published, and as a result Hyde sued Paxton for libel and demanded $100,000 damages.

On February 15, 1910, the Grand Jury began an investigation of the mysteries of the Swope home, and on March 5 the following indictments were found against Hyde:

For carelessly bleeding Moss Hunton to death — charged with manslaughter.

Charged with murder for poisoning Colonel Swope.

Charged with murder for poisoning Chrisman Swope.

For attempting to murder Margaret Swope, three indictments were found; one for administering typhoid germs; one for injecting pus germs, and one for administering strychnine.

Seven other indictments were found, charging him with attempting to murder Lucy, Sarah and Stella Swope, Mildred Fox, Georgie Campton,

Nora Dickson and Leonora Copridge.

Hyde was again arrested and released on $100,000 bond.

It was decided to try him for the murder of Colonel Swope, but as it was the theory of the prosecution that Hyde's motive was to eventually gain control of the Swope millions by killing the greater part of the family, the evidence regarding all the cases was admitted. The trial began before Judge Ralph Latshaw in Kansas City on April 16, 1910.

Mrs. Hyde, who was in a delicate condition at the time, remained loyal to her husband and refused to recognize her mother, brother and sisters. She expressed the belief that her husband was innocent, and it is claimed that she mortgaged property to defray the enormous expenses of the defense. She engaged Frank Walsh and four other attorneys and also several experts.

The prosecution was represented by District Attorney Virgil Conkling and four special prosecutors engaged by Mrs. Swope, who was firmly convinced of her son-in-law's guilt. Hyde pleaded not guilty.

On April 19 Dr. G. W. Twyman, one of the most important witnesses for the prosecution, died before his testimony could be obtained.

At irregular intervals up to within a week of his death Colonel Swope took a tonic of iron, quinine and strychnine, which was recommended by Dr. Hyde and sold by Overton Gentry, an Independence druggist. It was shown, however, that this tonic contained such a small percentage of strychnine that it was absolutely harmless.

Nearly fifty witnesses testified for the prosecution, and on April 27 the evidence against Hyde became so strong that Judge Latshaw ordered him into custody.

On May 4 the prosecution rested and the defense began. In referring to the cause of Chrisman Swope's death, Dr. Froehling testified that meningitis might be present and no evidence of it seen even with a microscope. He further testified that the appearance of Margaret Swope's arm was such that Dr. Hyde might have injected camphorated oil as he claimed.

On cross-examination Attorney Reed asked: "When strychnine and cyanide are administered together, does not one tend to neutralize the other's effect?"

Dr. Froehling replied that he could not answer that question. As several physicians testified for the prosecution to the effect that they had never used cyanide as a medicine, Dr. J. W. Allen testified for the defense that he frequently used cyanide for spasmodic coughs, but confessed that he never used five-grain capsules — the quantities which Hyde purchased.

Dr. W. M. Cross, although called as a witness for the defense, testified that he could find no cause for the typhoid epidemic in the Swope home. He also testified that it was possible for embalming fluid and the ammonia naturally in the body to form hydrocyanic acid in sufficient quantities to show tests for cyanide, but Professor Paul Schweitzer testified in rebuttal that this acid could only be formed in the presence of red-hot heat, and Professor H. P. Cady testified that he had recently made an experiment and that the lowest temperature that the tests would show hydrocyanic acid was 358 degrees Fahrenheit.

In examining some of the physicians the defense attempted to show that it was possible for flies to have carried the typhoid germs into the Swope home, but the prosecution called attention to the fact that the epidemic occurred in the winter, when flies are scarce.

Professor E. E. Smith testified that it was possible that Professor Vaughan mistook cinchonadyne, an integral part of the quinine in Colonel Swope's tonic, for strychnine, but C. H. Briggs, a chemist in the employ of the firm which prepared this tonic, testified in rebuttal that the quinine used in this tonic contained less than one per cent, of cinchonadyne.

On May 9 Mrs. Hyde testified that up to within two days of her brother Chrisman's death he took pills prepared by Charles Hatred Jordan, a Chilean yarb doctor, but it was not shown that any of this doctor's medicines contained anything of a harmful nature.

In her testimony Mrs. Hyde contradicted the nurses, Dr. Twyman and nearly all the members of her own family. She testified that her mother requested Dr. Hyde to go to New York after Lucy, and furthermore swore that Tom Swope was at home when he claimed he saw Dr. Hyde stamp the capsules into the snow. She swore that she did not request her husband to stop bleeding Moss Hunton, as claimed by Dr. Twyman and Miss Keller, the nurse.

On May 9 Dr. Hyde took the stand in his own behalf. He testified that the missing germs had been used by him in making tests, and claimed that he had been using cyanide for ten years to remove nitrate of silver stains from his fingers. He swore that the cyanide which he had recently purchased from Brecklein was used to kill cockroaches in his office.

When turned over for cross-examination Hyde became almost hopelessly tangled.

Although he claimed he had used cyanide for ten years he could not recall one place where he had procured it previous to the purchase of the five-grain capsules from Brecklein, who was produced as a witness by the State.

He claimed that he purchased it in capsules because it would retain its strength better in that form.

When asked if it would not have been more convenient to have it put in a small bottle with a glass stopper, instead of opening the small capsules when he sprinkled it around his office for the purpose of killing cockroaches, he replied that the first method suggested had not occurred to him.

He furthermore admitted that he had not informed either Miss Coughlin, his clerk, or the janitor, of the fact that this poison had been sprinkled around the office.

At the conclusion of Hyde's testimony the defense rested, and several witnesses were called in rebuttal.

Margaret Swope testified that it was true that Chrisman asked for some of Dr. Jordan's medicine two days before his death, but Mrs. Hyde could not find it, and she said to Margaret: "I'll give him some aspirin tablets. He'll never know the difference."

Other members of the family then testified as to Tom Swope's movements on the night the capsules were found in the snow, and much additional evidence was produced tending to show that he was not home, but was probably just where he claimed to have been when the capsules were smashed in the snow.

Mrs. James Clinton testified that Tom stopped at her house to use her telephone while on his way home that evening.

No surrebuttal testimony was offered and the case was finally submitted to the jury on Friday, May 13, 1910.

After deliberating for three days the defendant was found guilty as charged and sentenced to life imprisonment.

Juror W. C. Crone's son Albert had recently been convicted on circumstantial evidence for killing his sweetheart, Bertha Bowler, and Juror Crone held out for Hyde's acquittal until after sixty hours deliberation, when he also voted for conviction.

When the jury was discharged he said: "Hyde's own testimony finally convinced me of his guilt."

On July 5, 1910, Hyde was sentenced to life imprisonment at hard labor, but an appeal to the Supreme Court was immediately filed.

QUANTRILL AND THE JESSE JAMES AND YOUNGER

BROTHERS' GANG.

William Clarke Quantrill, afterward known as Charlie Quantrell and Charlie Hart, was born in Canal Dover, Ohio, on July 31, 1837.

At the age of sixteen he became a school teacher and followed that vocation until March 30, 1860, when his school at Stanton, Kansas, closed.

According to William E. Connelley's history of the Border Wars, it was Mrs. Mary Quantrill, a sister-in-law of Charlie Quantrill, and not Barbara Freitchie, who waved the American flag in the faces of the Confederate soldiers when they passed through Frederick in September, 1862.

Connelley stated that Quantrill was cruel, treacherous and ungrateful; that while he was a school teacher he was leading a Dr. Jekyll and Mr. Hyde life, and was even then a murderer, cattle-thief and kidnaper of slaves.

When his school closed, Quantrill moved to Lawrence, Kansas, where he soon became a member of a gang of border ruffians who committed all the crimes on the calendar.

About December 15, 1860, Quantrill and three companions named Morrison, Lipsey and Dean, planned to rob the home of Morgan Walker, a prosperous farmer residing in Jackson County, Missouri. Quantrill notified Walker's son of the proposed raid, and the two men then made arrangements to conceal guards about the premises and Quantrill agreed to inveigle his "accomplices" into a position where the guards could shoot them down. The looters arrived at the appointed time and Quantrill entered the house, but sent his companions around to a side porch where the heavily armed neighbors were concealed behind a loom. They opened fire, killing Morrison instantly and wounding the other two, who escaped temporarily. Quantrill remained at Walker's house and the next day a negro located the wounded men in the woods and notified Walker. Quantrill accompanied the posse and when they located Dean and Lipsey, Quantrill and the entire posse opened fire. Both fugitives were mortally wounded but Quantrill rushed up to them and fired several additional shots into their bodies. He gave the following reason for this treacherous act:

"In 1855, my brother and I were traveling overland to California when a gang of thirty Kansas Jayhawkers attacked us, and after killing my

brother and wounding me, they stole all we possessed. I learned their identity and swore that I would kill every member of the gang. Assuming the name of Charlie Hart and professing great admiration for the gang, I joined them and was received with open arms, as they did not recognize me. Whenever I had an opportunity to kill any of them without being suspected, I took advantage of it. Eventually they were all dead but three, and that trio accompanied me on the Morgan Walker raid."

Connelley states that this story is false throughout and was invented by Quantrill for the purpose of winning the friendship of certain Missourians who despised the so-called "Jayhawkers."

After this occurrence it is said that the feeling against Quantrill in Lawrence was so bitter that he would have been lynched had he returned.

Shortly after the Civil War began, Quantrill organized a band of Southern guerrillas, consisting of Cole Younger, Frank James, Oll Shepherd, Bill Anderson, George Todd and others, the command finally having 450 members.

Henry Washington Younger settled in Jackson County, Missouri, in 1825, and three years later he married Miss Bursheba Fristo, a very estimable young lady of Jackson County. Mr. Younger represented Jackson County for three successive terms in the Legislature and was subsequently elected County Judge. Fourteen children were born to this couple, among them being Thomas Coleman, commonly called "Cole," who was born January 15, 1844; James, who was born on January 15, 1848; John, in 1851, and Robert or "Bob," on December 12, 1853.

At the outbreak of the Civil War, Mr. Younger, Sr., went to Kansas City to complain of the manner in which some of his property had been destroyed, and he charged the Kansas "Jayhawkers" with committing the depredations. After registering his complaint, he started to drive home, but had only proceeded a short distance from Kansas City when he was shot to death.

It was known that the Younger family was in sympathy with the South, and as Cole was accused of being a spy in communication with Quantrill, a demand was made for his surrender, but he escaped and joined Quantrill's company.

In October, 1862, Stephen Elkins, afterward a United States Senator, was arrested by Quantrill's men on a charge of being a Union spy, and was about to be killed when Cole Younger, who was formerly a pupil of Elkins', interceded in behalf of the prisoner and procured his release.

In 1864, James Younger also joined the guerrillas, but was shortly afterward taken a prisoner and was not released until the conclusion of the war.

Toward the close of the war Cole Younger came to the Pacific Coast, being in Seattle when the war ended.

Frank James was born in Scott County, Kentucky, in 1845, his father being a Baptist preacher. Four years later his brother Jesse was born in Clay County, Missouri, and a few months afterward his father came to California, where he died. Seven years later the widow, from whom the boys probably inherited their aggressive nature, married Dr. Reuben Samuels.

When the war broke out Frank joined Quantrill's company, and in 1863 Jesse joined another company of guerrillas.

Shortly after the war began, Colonel Jennison of the Federal Army lost control of his men, some of whom committed so many outrages in Missouri that the Federal government ordered Jennison out of the service.

To wreak vengeance for the crimes committed by Jennison's men, Quantrill's gang committed a series of deeds as brutal and inhuman as could have been conceived by savages, although they frequently displayed great bravery in open battle.

On April 21, 1862, the Federal government declared this gang to be outlaws, and the Confederate government also disapproved of many of their acts.

Because of depredations alleged to have been committed by the Kansas Jayhawkers, Quantrill and his company, which then consisted of 448 men, rode into Lawrence, Kansas, at daybreak on the morning of August 21, 1863, and began to shoot down every male person in sight, most of whom were non-combatants. In referring to this massacre in the history of his life, Cole Younger, who participated in the raid, said:

"It was a day of butchery. Bill Anderson, whose sister was arrested as a Confederate spy and was killed by the collapsing of the building in which she was confined, claimed he killed fourteen and the count was allowed. The death list that day is variously estimated at from 143 to 216, and the property loss by the firing of the town and the sacking of the bank, etc., at $1,500,000. No guerrillas were killed."

According to Connelley's complete history of this raid, Younger's estimate is very conservative.

After the raid at Lawrence, Quantrill gradually lost control of his men and his company rapidly became demoralized. Many deserted him, and in the early part of 1864 he took the remnant of his company to Texas. While there two of his men killed two Confederate officers, but as these men claimed they acted under Quantrill's orders, General McCulloch placed Quantrill under arrest, although subsequently he escaped.

Shortly after this he relinquished his command to George Todd and, assuming the name of Captain Clarke, he, Oll Shepherd, Frank James and twenty others began operations in Kentucky.

On February 28, 1865, they plundered the town of Hickmail, Kentucky, and killed several people, for which they were pursued by Federal troops and several guerrillas were killed.

On May 10, 1865, Captain Edward Terrill and thirty Federal soldiers located Quantrill and several of his men in a barn near Bloomfield, Kentucky. They attempted to escape but Quantrill received a bullet wound near the spine, which partially paralyzed him, and two of his men were killed. Quantrill was taken to Louisville, where he died twenty-seven days later.

In the summer of 1866, after the war was ended, the Governor of Kansas made a requisition on the Governor of Missouri for those who participated in the Lawrence raid, as it was decided to institute criminal proceedings against them. Cole Younger, Frank James and several other guerrillas met, but after a discussion they decided not to surrender.

Shortly after this, a series of the most atrocious crimes were committed. Banks were robbed in broad daylight, trains were wrecked, citizens offering the slightest resistance were shot down like dogs, and officers were brutally murdered while in the discharge of their duty.

It was finally learned that a gang consisting of Jesse and Frank James, Cole, Bob, Jim and John Younger, Clell Miller, Charley Pitts, Oll and George Shepherd and several others who fought under Quantrill, were engaged in similar depredations, but as the modus operandi was uniform in nearly all these events, the James gang was accused of committing many crimes of which they were innocent. Many books have been written and melodramas produced in which these criminals have been pictured as heroes, but most of their crimes were most cowardly and despicable.

The Allen Pinkerton Detective Agency was employed to capture them, and from information obtained from Mr. William Pinkerton and officials who investigated the movements of these bandits, the following is set forth as the criminal record of the James-Younger gang:

On March 12, 1868, a man giving the name of Colburn called at the bank in Russellville, Kentucky, and asked for change for a $100 bill.

On the 20th inst., "Colburn" returned with a companion and found two employees of the bank, named Long and Barclay, in conversation with a farmer named T. H. Simmons. "Colburn," or more properly speaking, Cole Younger, drew a pistol and ordered the three men to surrender. After a narrow escape from being shot, Long escaped through a side door and gave the alarm, but the other two men complied with the order to remain still.

Other members of the gang remained on their horses outside, and when Younger and his accomplice had gathered about $9,000 in currency and about $5,000 in gold and silver, the outside guard became alarmed at the approach of an armed posse and called to the robbers in the bank, who hurried out with their loot and the gang rode away, several shots being fired after them. George and Oll Shepherd were identified and the former was arrested, convicted and served three years. Oll Shepherd escaped into Jackson County, Missouri, where he was killed by a sheriff's posse, while attempting to escape. It was subsequently learned that the others of the gang participating in this raid were Jesse and Frank James and Jim Younger.

On December 8, 1869, Cole Younger, Frank and Jesse James rode into the town of Gallatin, Missouri, and proceeded to the Daviess County Savings Bank. On entering they commanded the cashier, Captain John W, Sheets, to open the vault, and upon his refusal to do so Jesse James shot him dead. They then gathered up the few hundred dollars in sight and escaped, but Jesse James' horse became unmanageable and ran away as the bandit was about to mount, and he was forced to ride behind his brother until they met a man named Smoot, who was ordered to turn over his horse to Jesse. The horse which ran away from Jesse was afterward identified as his property.

One day in January, 1865, John Younger, who was then a large, fine looking fourteen-year-old boy, went into Independence, Mo., for the purpose of having Cole's revolver repaired. The boy became engaged in a quarrel with a young man named Gillcreas, and the latter struck the youth over the face with a piece of mackerel and otherwise abused Younger, until he drew his brother's pistol and instantly killed Gillcreas. The coroner's jury acquitted the boy, who shortly afterward left for Texas, where he secured employment in a store at Dallas.

On January 16, 1871, he was drinking in a saloon and offered to wager that he could shoot the pipe out of the mouth of a man named Russell, who was sitting on a chair. The bullet grazed the man's nose and he ran from the place. The next day Russell procured a warrant for Younger's arrest, and it was given to the Sheriff, Captain S. W. Nichols, formerly of the Confederate Army, for service.

The Sheriff, accompanied by John McMahon, proceeded to Younger's home, and served the warrant. Younger requested permission to finish his breakfast, which was granted, but the Sheriff, who remained on guard outside, observed his prisoner attempting to escape out the back way. A pistol duel followed during which the Sheriff was shot through the heart and McMahon was seriously injured. Younger escaped and returned to his brothers in Missouri.

On June 3, 1871, the James and Younger brothers, accompanied by Clell Miller, went into the town of Corydon, Iowa, for the purpose of robbing the County Treasurer of recently collected taxes. Jesse James entered the office and requested change for a $100 bill, but the clerk stated that the safe was locked and that no one but the Treasurer, who was out, was familiar with the combination. The clerk suggested, however, that the Obocock Bank, which had just opened that day, might accommodate him. Jesse withdrew and after a consultation with his associates it was decided to celebrate the opening of the new bank by robbing it.

The gang then proceeded to the bank, Jesse James entering and asking for change for his $100 bill. While the clerk turned and opened the safe, two of the James gang entered, the remainder being stationed as guards outside, and when the clerk turned around he was looking into the muzzle of a pistol. He and the president of the bank were then ordered into a back room and about $15,000 was stolen. A colored preacher who entered the bank at this moment was also relieved of his savings.

The robbers then mounted their horses and rode out of town, but they had only traveled a short distance when they saw a gathering of citizens who were assembled at a proposed school site — the Treasurer of the county being among them. The bandits masked their faces with handkerchiefs and, riding up to the gathering, one of the robbers advised them to return to town and start another new bank.

In September, 1872, the Kansas City Fair was held, and on the 26th inst., an enormous crowd gathered to watch a racehorse called Ethan Allen perform. After the receipts of the day had been counted, Secretary Hall, of the association, according to custom, sent a trusted employee to deposit the money, about $10,000, with the First National Bank. The employee had hardly left the grounds when a gang of not more than five mounted men surrounded him, and pointing pistols at his head, relieved him of the box and dashed out of town.

The James and Younger gang were at once accused of committing this crime, but they denied all knowledge of it, although Cole Younger admitted that he and his brother John were in Kansas City on the following day. It is the general belief of the authorities that the James gang were the robbers.

In July, 1873, this gang received information that a large amount of money would be transferred on the Chicago, Rock Island & Pacific Railroad on the 21st inst. They therefore concealed their horses about two and one-half miles west of Adair Station, Iowa. Near this point was a bridge crossing Turkey Creek, and near this bridge the gang waited until nearly 9 p. m., when the train was due, and then removed a rail and awaited results. Engineer John Rafferty and Conductor William A. Smith were in charge of the train, and as it approached this spot the engineer could see that the rail had been removed and immediately set his brakes, but the train was wrecked, Rafferty being instantly killed and numerous passengers seriously injured. Among the passengers were L. and W. Slessinger and A. Goodman of San Francisco.

The robbers then terrorized train hands and passengers alike by frequently firing shots, and they robbed everyone in sight. But they had miscalculated in regard to the amount of money the express messenger had in his possession, as the entire proceeds did not exceed $3,000.

On the next day this gang, consisting of seven men, stopped at the residence of Mr. and Mrs. Stuckey in Ringold County for dinner, and from the description given there is little doubt but what it was the James-Younger gang — minus Cole Younger, who is said to have been opposed to taking human life except in self-defense. The railroad company and Governor Carpenter offered a reward of $5,500 for the conviction of these fiends.

At 4:30 p. m., January 31, 1874, the Little Rock express train was due at a station called Gadshill, in Missouri. Just a few moments previous to this time a gang of five masked men appeared, and after putting the station agent under guard, they set the switch, placed a signal in the middle of the track, and awaited the arrival of the train. The engineer, observing the signal, brought his train to a standstill, and when the conductor came forward to ascertain the cause of this unusual and sudden stop, a pistol was pointed at his head and he was placed under guard with the engineer, fireman and express messenger. The robbers procured $10,000 from the Adams Express car, and money and jewelry valued at $3,400 from the passengers. One of the gang wrote the following note before the train arrived and left it in one of the cars:

"The Most Daring Robbery on Record.

"The southbound train on the Iron Mountain railroad was stopped here this evening by five heavily armed men and robbed of _____ dollars. The robbers arrived at the station a few minutes before the arrival of the train, arrested the agent, and put him under guard, and then threw the train on the switch.

"The robbers were all large men, none of them being under six feet tall. After robbing the train, they started in a southerly direction, all mounted on fine horses.

"There's a H___ of an excitement in this part of the country.

The Pinkerton Detective Agency began an investigation and among the detectives engaged on the case was Joseph W. Witcher, connected with the Chicago branch of the agency. On March 10, 1874, this brave man started alone to the home of the James brothers, but en route, he stopped at the little town of Liberty, in Clay County, which was full of people who, either from motives of policy or sympathy, befriended this gang at every opportunity. It is surmised that Witcher's actions aroused the suspicion of some of these people, and that the James brothers were not only notified of his presence, but also that the mysterious man had started in the direction of their home. At any rate, when he approached the James-Samuels home, he was intercepted by Jesse James and two other men, who interrogated him as to his business. The detective, who was roughly dressed, stated that he was a fugitive from justice, but the trio searched him, and finding a pistol in his possession, became convinced that he was a detective. They bound him and took him from Clay County across the river to a spot near Independence, in Jackson County, and there killed him, leaving the body on the road.

Notwithstanding the fact that Jesse James and Cole Younger were comrades in crime, the latter had no admiration for the former, and he claimed that James took Witcher to Independence, Younger's home, and murdered him there so that the Younger brothers would be accused of the crime.

Among other detectives and officials working on the Gadshill train robbery was Louis Lull, a former Captain of Police in Chicago, but at the time in the employ of Pinkerton's agency, and James Wright. These men received information that some of the Younger brothers were in the neighborhood of Montegaw Springs, Mo. At Osceola, Mo., an ex-deputy sheriff named Edward Daniels, joined the two men. When the trio reached the home of Theodore Sniffer on March 16, 1874, Lull and Daniels stopped to make inquiry regarding the roads, but Wright continued on his journey.

After obtaining the desired information, the two men proceeded along the road, but they did not go according to directions. By a singular coincidence, John and Jim Younger were in an adjoining room in Sniffer's house while the detectives were there and, suspecting the mission of the strangers, they followed on horseback. When they overtook the detectives, the Youngers stated their suspicions, and after a few words firing became general, with the result that John Younger and Daniels were almost instantly killed by gunshot wounds in the neck, and Lull was shot through the abdomen and died six weeks later, Jim Younger escaped.

After the murder of these detectives, the indignation of the citizens in that part of the country against this gang knew no bounds, and they resolved to exterminate the outlaws at any cost. A watch was set on the James-Samuels home and it was finally reported that the two bandits were there. At midnight on January 25, 1875, a posse said to have been led by a neighboring farmer named Daniel Askew, surrounded the house, and set it on fire with the expectation of driving the two bandits out in the open. While the building was on fire, one of the posse threw an explosive through a window and the result was that James' mother, Mrs. Samuels, was seriously injured, and her eight-year-old son by her second husband was killed, but the James boys were not in the house at all. This unjustifiable act turned the tide of sympathy back to the outlaws, as no excuse could be found for the wanton slaughter of this innocent child.

Two months afterward. General Jeff Jones, a member of the State Legislature from Callaway County, Missouri, introduced what was known as the Outlaw Amnesty Bill, which read in part as follows:

"Whereas, by the 4th section of the 11th article of the Constitution of Missouri, all persons in the military service of the United States, or who acted under the authority thereof in this State, are relieved from all civil liability and all criminal punishment for all acts done by them since the 1st day of January, A. D., 1861; and,

"Whereas, By the 12th section of the said 11th article of said Constitution provision is made by which, under certain circumstances, may be seized, transported to, indicted, tried and punished in distant counties, any Confederate under ban of despotic displeasure, thereby contravening the Constitution of the United States and every principle of enlightened humanity; therefore be it

"Resolved, By the House of Representatives, the Senate concurring therein, that the Governor of the State be, and he is hereby requested to issue his proclamation notifying Jesse W. James, Frank James, Coleman Younger, James Younger and others, that full and complete amnesty and pardon will be granted them for all acts charged or committed by them during the late Civil War, and inviting them peacefully to return to their respective homes in this State and there quietly to remain, submitting themselves to such proceedings as may be instituted against them by the courts for all offenses charged to have been committed since said war, promising and guaranteeing to each of them full protection and a fair trial therein, and that full protection shall be given them from the time of their entrance into the State and his notice thereof under said proclamation and invitation."

This bill was approved by Attorney-General Hockaday and favorably reported by a majority of the committee on criminal jurisprudence, but while it was pending, Mr. Askew, the man who was suspected of having led the gang that burned the James-Samuels home, was shot and killed one night in front of his own home by two men. Suspicion naturally fell on the James brothers, but it was never proved who committed the crime.

Evidence was then produced tending to show that it was quite possible that Askew did not participate in the attack on the James-Samuels home, and believing that another innocent person had fallen by the hand of the James brothers, the tide of sympathy which swept toward them, now as swiftly swept away, and the result was that the Amnesty Bill was defeated.

In the early part of December, 1875, this gang learned that a large amount of money would be shipped on the Union Pacific Railroad on the 12th inst. It is the theory of many that they obtained this information through one Bud McDaniels, who participated in the robbery.

On December 12 this gang assembled at a little station called Muncie, which is about five miles from Kansas City, Kansas, and where the trains stop for water. The train arrived at this point at 5 p. m., just as it was growing dark. The masked bandits boarded it and adopted their usual methods of intimidation. The messenger seeing that it would be folly to resist, opened the safe and $55,000 was obtained.

When McDaniels received his share of the loot it turned his head and he proceeded to celebrate by indulging too freely in intoxicants while in Kansas City, two days later. His drunken condition caused his arrest, and when searched over $1,000 was found in his possession. As he could not give a satisfactory account either as to where he obtained the money or of his movements on the day of the train robbery, an investigation was instituted and sufficient evidence was gathered to justify the authorities in charging him with being implicated in the robbery. While being taken to court he escaped from his guard, but after enjoying his liberty for a week, he was discovered by an officer and as the fugitive again attempted to escape he was shot dead.

About 10 p. m., July 7, 1876, this gang, reinforced by one Hobbs Kerry and Bill Chadwell, a horse thief from Minnesota, approached Henry Chateau, the watchman at Rocky Cut, near Otterville, on the Missouri Pacific Railroad, an after procuring his red lantern, they placed railroad ties on the track and waved the lantern as the train approached. The engineer saw the signal and applied the air brakes, but the locomotive ran into the ties before it came to a standstill. The masked bandits then began to yell like Indians and discharged their pistols.

J. B. Bushnell, the express messenger, realizing the meaning of the commotion, mingled with the passengers before the bandits reached the

Adams Express car and attempted to conceal his identity, but the baggage man was threatened with death if he refused to point out the messenger. He lost no time in complying with the request, and the messenger lost no time in providing the desired keys, but as there was a through safe to which he had no keys, the robbers broke it open with a sledge hammer and obtained $17,000 from the two safes. They then disappeared, but Kerry was subsequently captured and confessed that he accompanied the James-Younger gang on this expedition.

The next raid attempted by these bandits resulted in the extermination of most of its members. In the middle of August, 1876, they decided to raid the bank in Northfield, Minnesota.

There are two theories as to why this bank was selected. One was that Chadwell, who hailed from Minnesota, suggested it, but Cole Younger claimed that this particular bank was selected because they had received information that General Benjamin Butler and his son-in-law, Governor J. T. Ames of Mississippi, both of whom had incurred the displeasure of the Southerners during the war, were the principal stockholders.

September 7 was the day set for the raid, and the gang consisted of Cole, Bob and Jim Younger, Jesse and Frank James, Bill Chadwell, Clell Miller and Charley Pitts. It was agreed that Jesse James, Bob Younger and Pitts should enter the bank; Miller and Cole Younger to remain on guard outside, and the remainder of the gang to be stationed at a bridge a short distance away, and in case they were needed at the bank a pistol shot would be the signal. They had planned to wreck the telegraph office immediately after the raid.

When the three bandits entered the bank they found the cashier, Joseph Heywards, and Clerks A. E. Bunker and Frank Wilcox behind the counter. They ordered Heywards to open the safe, but he insisted that he could not do so because of the time lock. Bunker then tried to grasp a revolver that lay near him, but Pitts observed the move and put the pistol in his own pocket. Bunker then escaped through a window, but was shot in the shoulder while so doing. The robbers gathered what money was in sight and as they were leaving the bank, Pitts shot Heywards through the head, killing him instantly.

While this scene occurred in the bank, a hardware merchant named J. S. Allen attempted to enter the bank on business, but was obstructed by Miller. Allen then realized what was afoot, and running up the Street he cried: "Get your guns, boys; they're robbing the bank." It was at this moment that Pitts killed the cashier and Chadwell, Frank James and Bob Younger, hearing the shot, rode up to the bank from the bridge.

In the meantime, Dr. H. M. Wheeler, Elias Stacy, J. Manning and two other citizens procured weapons and began firing from windows at the bandits. The shooting now became general, with the result that Clell Miller and Bill Chadwell were instantly killed. Cole, Bob and Jim Younger were wounded, and Nicholas Gustafson, a non-combatant, was killed.

Realizing that they were being worsted, the James' and the Younger brothers and Pitts mounted their horses and fled. But as all of the Younger brothers were bleeding profusely they did not make rapid progress.

They had failed to wreck the telegraph office, and as Chadwell, the only man in the gang who was familiar with the country, was dead, they were practically lost. The news was telegraphed to all neighboring towns and posses came from all directions. For days the hunted criminals had little opportunity to sleep or eat. It was raining most of the time and they suffered excruciating pain from their wounds.

At the expiration of a week it was decided that the James brothers should leave the Youngers and Pitts, and they crossed the Missouri River and escaped.

On September 21, a Norwegian boy named Oscar Suborn saw the Younger brothers and Pitts approaching Madelia, Col., and the alarm was immediately given. A posse headed by Captain W. W. Murphy, Colonel Vought and Sheriff Glispin started in pursuit and cornered the bandits in some brush in the river bottom. Six of the posse volunteered to go into the brush after the bandits, and as they drew near, firing between the volunteers and the outlaws became general, with the result that Pitts was killed. Cole and Jim Younger fell from their wounds and Bob, believing the rest had been killed, called out, "They're all down but me. I surrender." On Pitts' body the revolver belonging to the Northfield bank was found.

On November 9, 1876, the Younger brothers were placed on trial for the Northfield murders. As the law stood at that time, if the accused pleaded guilty to a murder charge, he escaped the death penalty and was sentenced to life imprisonment as an inducement to save the county the expense of a trial. The three brothers took advantage of this and a few days afterward they began their sentence in Stillwater Prison, Minnesota. On September 16, 1889, Bob died from consumption, supposed to have been caused by the bullet which pierced his lung during his last fight at Madelia.

Contrary to expectations, these men were model prisoners, and when they had served twenty years, many influential persons became interested in their case, and as a result Cole and Jim were conditionally paroled on July 14, 1901, three of the conditions being that they should not leave the State of Minnesota, that they should give a full account of themselves monthly, and should not exhibit themselves at any place where a charge was made for admission.

Jim Younger never fully recovered from his wounds and after being released he became extremely melancholy and constantly remained in his room reading socialistic literature. He was stopping at the Hotel Reardon, located at Seventh and Minnesota Streets, in St. Paul, and on Sunday afternoon, October 19, 1901, he committed suicide by shooting himself in the head.

When the James brothers left the Youngers after the Northfield raid, they went to Mexico, where they remained for some time, and then proceeded to Paso Robles Springs in California. They remained in seclusion until about 6 p. m. on October 7, 1879, when they and four others, all wearing masks, rode into the little village of Glendale, on the line of the Chicago, Alton & St. Louis Railroad, about twenty miles from Kansas City, Mo.

They went directly to the railroad station, and after placing the three men at the station under arrest, they ordered the station man to display the signal for the train to stop. When the train arrived and came to a standstill, the engineer was covered with a revolver and the remainder of the gang proceeded to the express car. The messenger, William Grimes, realizing the cause of the stop, attempted to conceal the contents of the safe, some $35,000, but was caught in the act and badly beaten. After taking this money the bandits disappeared. One Tucker Bassham was arrested in June, 1880, and charged with being implicated in this crime. He subsequently made a confession, in which he implicated the James brothers. He was convicted and sent to prison for ten years.

On the afternoon of September 3, 1880, Frank James and Jim Cummings held up the stage en route to Mammouth Cave in Kentucky. As the eight passengers were wealthy tourists, the holdup netted the robbers about $1,500 in money and jewelry. After procuring the names of the victims, the bandits permitted them to proceed on their journey.

On Friday evening, July 15, 1881, the Chicago, Rock Island & Pacific train left Kansas City, Mo., in charge of Conductor William Westfall. Shortly after passing the little town of Winston, two masked men crawled over the coal on the tender and ordered the engineer to stop the train, which he did. At the same time two of the bandits, who probably boarded the train at either Cameron or Winston, put on masks and without any provocation, deliberately killed Conductor Westfall because he attempted to escape. For the purpose of intimidating the passengers, several shots were fired, one of which struck a stonemason named McMillan, killing him instantly.

A demand was then made on Charles Murray, the express messenger, for the keys of the safe, but as the loot fell far short of expectations, only $1,500 being taken, one of the bandits struck Murray over the head with a revolver, knocking him down.

Investigations subsequently instituted showed that the James gang committed this crime, James' step-brother, young Samuels, being in the gang.

On September 7, 1881, at 9 p. m., the Chicago & Alton train was held up at a point called Blue Cut, near Independence, Mo. The train usually slowed down at this point and Engineer Foote, seeing obstructions on the track ahead, came to a full stop. Just then he was surrounded by masked men, two of whom remained by the engine and the remainder proceeded to the express car, where about $2,000 was obtained from Express Messenger Fox. The leader of this gang loudly proclaimed himself to be Jesse James., and afterward James told the Ford brothers that he led the gang.

The magnitude of the numerous crimes committed by these ruffians and the impudence and audacity with which they were perpetrated, had by this time aroused the indignation of the whole State of Missouri, and Governor Crittenden determined that the gang which had given his State so much unenviable notoriety, must be either captured or annihilated at any cost. After a consultation with the railroad and express officials, a reward of $30,000 was offered for the capture of these bandits, dead or alive.

The feeling against these outlaws had become so intense that several members of the gang began to lose courage, and as a result a mysterious woman called on Governor Crittenden on February 16, 1882, and desired to know under what conditions an outlaw could surrender. She was informed that if either of the James brothers desired to surrender it would have to be unconditional, but if any minor member of the gang would surrender and faithfully assist the authorities in apprehending and punishing the leaders, his services would be amply rewarded. Three days later Dick Little of the gang surrendered to Sheriff Timberlake of Clay County and made a voluminous confession.

During the preceding November, Jesse James and his wife and two children moved to a cottage at 1318 Lafayette Street, St. Joseph, Mo., where they lived under the name of Howard, that being the name by which Cole Younger referred to James when speaking of the two bandits who escaped after the Northfield raid.

A very young man named Robert Ford, alias Johnson, who enjoyed James' confidence, also resided in this house. This man entered into an agreement with Governor Crittenden and Sheriff Timberlake to rid the community of James, the reward, of course, being uppermost in his mind.

On April 4, 1882, the Burgess murder trial was to begin in Platte City, and as the case was attracting a great deal of interest in that part of the country, James concluded that everyone, especially peace officers, would be at the trial. He therefore decided that this would be a good day to rob the Platte City Bank. For the purpose of perfecting plans for the robbery Charley, a brother of Robert Ford, came to James' home on Sunday, March 26. The Ford brothers pretended to enter enthusiastically into the scheme.

From this time until Monday, April 3, the Ford brothers remained as guests of James, who contemplated executing the robbery of the Platte City Bank on the following day.

On the morning of the 3rd, the weather was so warm that a coat could not be comfortably worn, so James, who was doing chores about the house which necessitated frequent trips to the yard, decided to remove his pistols lest some passerby should see them hanging to his belt. While thus unarmed, James picked up a duster, and mounting a chair, he proceeded to dust a picture on the wall. Robert Ford instantly took advantage of the opportunity and drawing his own revolver, shot the bandit twice in the back. James fell to the floor without uttering a word, and died within a few moments.

The Ford brothers immediately surrendered to Marshal Craig, who charged them with murder. On April 17 they were arraigned, and pleading guilty to the charge, they were sentenced to be hanged on May 9, 1882.

On April 18, Governor Crittenden granted the brothers an unconditional pardon. Immediately after their release, Sheriff Trigg placed Bob Ford under arrest on the charge of murdering a man named Wood Hite, whose body was found about a week previously in a well on the Ford farm. After some delay Ford was tried on this charge, and on October 26, 1882, the jury returned a verdict of not guilty, after being out forty-one hours.

Frank James, believing that he was dying from consumption and being out of funds, surrendered to Governor Crittenden on October 5, 1882, Indictments were found against him on three charges:

First: For the murder of John McMillan, the stonemason, who was shot and killed on the train near Winston.

Second: For the murder of Conductor Westfall on the same night; and

Third: For murdering Captain John Sheets, the cashier of the Gallatin Bank, on December 7, 1869.

As the murder at the Gallatin Bank appeared to be the strongest case, James was tried on that charge, but was acquitted, as these bandits habitually wore masks when making raids and therefore it was almost impossible to identify them, although the horse which ran away from one of the robbers was identified as Jesse James' property. As Governor Crittenden refused to surrender James to the Minnesota authorities, who were anxious to try him for the Northfield raid, the ex-bandit, then a physical wreck, was given his freedom.

In September, 1875, James married a Miss Annie Ralston, the daughter of a highly respected and prosperous farmer living near Independence, Mo. After his release James proceeded to his father-in-law's farm, where he eventually regained his health and has ever since led an exemplary life.

The Ford brothers soon spent their reward in riotous living and Bob was forced to go on the stage in a blood-and thunder drama. While "acting" he met a woman named Nellie Watterson, who afterward accompanied him to a mining camp in Colorado named South Creede, where they opened a dive. This resort was located in a tent opposite the Foretone Hotel.

Deputy Sheriff Edward Kelly, formerly City Marshal of Batchelor, Col., objected to the manner in which the dive was conducted, but as Ford maintained a defiant attitude, the two men became deadly enemies. On February 17, 1892, they had a fight at the Creede Exchange, in which it is claimed that Kelly came out second best.

At 3:40 p. m., on June 8, 1892, Kelly approached Ford's saloon and, without warning, fired the contents of a shotgun into Ford, killing him instantly. Had the victim of this cowardly crime been any one but the much-despised Ford, summary justice would probably have been meted out. Kelly was immediately arrested, turned over to Sheriff Gardner, charged with murder and convicted. He was sentenced to life imprisonment but was liberated in 1900.

Shortly afterward he went to Oklahoma, where Police Officer Joseph Burnett attempted to arrest him on January 13, 1903. As Kelly attacked and was overpowering the officer, the latter drew his revolver and killed him.

In later years the terms of Cole Younger's parole were modified so that he was permitted to travel about the country and deliver a prepared lecture, in which he observed that "the man who chooses the career of outlawry is either a natural fool or an innocent madman."

THE OUTRAGES COMMITTED BY THE SIOUX INDIANS

AND THE SUBSEQUENT CONVICTION AND EXECUTION

(From Judge Buck's History of Indian Outbreaks.)

By virtue of a treaty with two tribes of the Sioux (also known as Dakota) Indians on July 23, 1851, and with the remaining two tribes on August 5, of the same year, there was set apart for them by the American Government a tract of land in the Minnesota Valley about one hundred miles long by twenty miles in width. For this reservation the Indians agreed to sell to the Government all other lands in their possession in Iowa and Minnesota for the sum of $2,709,010.

It was furthermore agreed that $275,000 should be paid to the Indians as soon as they settled upon the reservation and $30,000 additional to be used for the establishment of schools and the erection of mills, shops, etc. The balance was to remain in trust with the United States Government and 5 per cent, interest to be paid thereon annually to the Indians.

On November 12, 1852, when the first payment was to be made, the Indians refused to accept the money, as they claimed that they did not fully understand the treaty when they signed it, and intimated that they had been made the victims of sharp practice. While they eventually accepted the money, they continually expressed dissatisfaction with the manner in which they were treated.

On March 8, 1857, a former Chief named Inkpaduta, who had been outlawed some years previously for killing another Chief named Tasagi, and a band of about twelve followers, were hunting near Spirit Lake, which is located on the boundary line of Iowa and Minnesota, when a dog belonging to a white man bit one of the band. The injured Indian killed the dog, whereupon the owner administered a beating to the Indian. As there were many white men present the Indian offered no violent resistance, but the entire band hastened to a nearby settlement, where they killed every white man, woman and child in sight, excepting three married ladies named Noble, Marble and Thatcher, and a Miss Gardner. These women were taken prisoners, and after being frightfully outraged were compelled to carry the loot seized by the Indians. Mrs. Noble and Mrs. Thatcher finally became exhausted, and as they could proceed no further the Indians killed them. Mrs. Marble and Miss Gardner were subsequently released for a monetary consideration.

On March 26, some of this gang went to Springfield, where they butchered seventeen people, including women and children.

Colonel Alexander, in command of Fort Ridgley, was informed of these massacres and he dispatched a company of infantry to the scene of slaughter. As the Indians had long since disappeared and the soldiers were not properly equipped to pursue them further through the snow, they buried the dead and then returned to the fort.

In 1861 there was, according to the census, 7,737 Indians on this reservation. Crops were very poor and it was said that some of the Indians died from starvation. It was furthermore claimed by the Indians that there was corruption in the Indian Department having the distribution of government annuities; that the traders charged exorbitant prices; that white men debauched their women, and that they had not been paid for their lands as provided by the treaty.

In answer to this charge the Government officials claimed that the hostility arose out of the fact that the majority of the Indians were opposed to the efforts made to transform them from barbarians to civilized beings and to compel them to subsist by industry.

Some of the Indians adopted the white man's customs and lived by the sweat of their brows, and as a reward for their good behavior the Government extended to them special privileges, which caused those who were too "proud" to work to become more dissatisfied than ever.

In the summer of 1862 a great number of the white men living near the reservation left their homes to participate in the Civil War, and as a consequence the Indians became more bold and defiant.

On August 16, 1862, four Indians were on their way to hunt deer when they stopped at the home of Robinson Jones, near Acton, Meeker County, Minnesota, and demanded whisky, but were abruptly refused and ordered out of the house. They then proceeded to the home of Howard Baker, Jones' stepson. At this house, which was within view of Jones' home and one-quarter mile from it, were Mr. and Mrs. Baker and Mr. and Mrs. Webster. Seeing the Indians stop at his stepson's house, Jones and his wife followed. A quarrel ensued between Jones and an Indian whom he accused of stealing a gun, during which Jones referred to the Indians as "black devils." The Indians then withdrew from the house about fifty feet, and while they were conferring Jones and his wife and Webster and Baker came out in the yard. Suddenly the Indians turned and opened fire, killing all four peopled The Indians then fled, and Mrs. Webster and Mrs. Baker, who were in the house at the time of the shooting, spread the alarm through the neighborhood.

The four assassins ran to the home of a Mr. Eckland, where they stole two horses. Two Indians mounted each animal, and they escaped to the reservation, where they related their experience.

When Chief Little Crow was informed of what had transpired he sounded a general alarm and warned the Indians to prepare for the trouble which he felt certain the whites would make for them. The Indians then decided to make the attack themselves. The next day they entered the store conducted by Andrew Myrick and demanded food. Myrick replied: "Go and eat grass," and for this reply he was shot and instantly killed. The Indians then got a handful of grass, and after stuffing it in the dead man's mouth, laughed and said: "Myrick is now eating grass himself."

They then killed every man, woman and child they could catch with the exception of two young ladies named Mary Schwandt and Maltie Williams, who were frightfully outraged and taken prisoners, but were subsequently released to General Sibley's expedition.

At 5 o'clock on the morning of August 20, about twenty Indians rode up to a little settlement beside Lake Shetek, where fifteen families resided. Although these people had always treated the Indians kindly, they killed every man, woman and child who did not escape by crawling into the high grass in the fields. A Mrs. Alomina Hurd, whose husband was the first to fall, was permitted to leave the village with her two babies, provided she took the road the Indians designated. She lost her way and traveled for five days through the storm then raging with nothing to eat but a piece of decayed ham.

The hero of the day was an eleven-year-old boy named Mertin Eastlick, who carried his fifteen-months-old brother Johnny on his back for fifty miles, but he died shortly afterward from exposure, over-exertion and lack of nourishment. Mr. Eastlick had been killed and Mrs. Eastlick was lying helpless on the ground from a bullet wound. Her two little boys named Freddie and Frank, aged five and seven respectively, were with her. Two squaws saw them, and catching the children they beat them to death with bludgeons before the helpless mother's eyes. Many other children were only beaten until they became helpless and then left to die from hunger and exposure to the storm.

Three days after the massacre a mail man drove by with a wagon and took Mrs. Eastlick with him. When they had traveled fifty miles they overtook little Mertin Eastlick, whom the mother had lost and had given up for dead, trudging along the road with his little brother still on his back.

On August 19, another band of Indians attacked the little town of New Ulm, which is located on the Minnesota River. The citizens had been forewarned of their approach and they put up such a strong defense that the Indians were repulsed, but not before many people of both sexes were killed and five houses burned.

The next day Chief Little Crow personally led 600 Indians to the town, and although fourteen men were killed and the greater portion of the town burned, the Indians were finally forced to retreat.

Little Crow and his men next attacked Fort Ridgley, but he lost about 100 men while only three soldiers were killed.

While Little Crow and his men were engaged at New Ulm and Fort Ridgley, other members of the tribe were scouring the country and torturing and killing nearly every white person they met. A young woman named Mrs. Waltz, *enceinte*, was seized and, in the presence of her young brother, who was also tortured but finally recovered, she was cut open and the child removed and nailed to a tree. This baby was afterward found in this position by the soldiers who were sent out to bury the dead. They also found the body of a little girl laid beside its mother's body. The child was killed by being pulled asunder by the legs.

On August 26, arrangements were completed to capture the fiercest warriors of Little Crow's band by means of strategy. The officials pretended to be ignorant of the identity of the leaders of the numerous outbreaks and they notified about 300 of the most desperate men to report at the Government warehouse to receive their annuities. About fifty of these fellows, including Little Crow, were evidently suspicious, for they did not respond, but 234 reported on the following morning as requested. For obvious reasons they were never permitted to carry their weapons into the building where the annuities were paid, so their suspicions were not aroused on this morning when soldiers stationed outside took their weapons before they entered. It was arranged to get them all inside at once and then the signal was given to some soldiers concealed nearby, who took the Indians into custody without difficulty. For many days previous to this capture the Indians seized men, women and children, until they had 270 prisoners.

Simultaneous with the capture of the Indians, General Sibley gained such an advantageous position with his artillery that the Indians left in charge of the white prisoners were at his mercy, and when they were commanded to surrender the captives they did so immediately. Many of the women prisoners had been subjected to most inhuman barbarities.

On September 3, 1862, General Sibley and 2,000 soldiers were encamped at Wood Lake, Minnesota. On the morning of this day several wagons loaded with soldiers left the camp to go to the agency, and when they were about a mile away from the camp, twenty-five Indians who were concealed in the grass, jumped up and opened fire. The soldiers responded, and several on each side were killed. The firing attracted the attention of the soldiers in camp and also Little Crow and about 800 Indians who were in the woods nearby. The result was a general battle, which proved to be Little Crow's Waterloo. Nearly 300 Indians were taken prisoners, and as a result Little Crow was deposed as Chief.

Shortly after these Indians were captured a Military Commission was appointed to investigate the various charges. The first person arraigned was O-ta-kle (man who kills many), a mulatto commonly known as Godfrey. The charges against him read as follows:

"Charge, Murder.

"Specification First: In this, that the said O-ta-kle, or Godfrey, did, at or near New Ulm, Minnesota, on or about the 19th day of August, 1862, join a war party of the Sioux tribe of Indians against the citizens of the United States, and did with his own hand murder seven white men, women and children, peaceful citizens of the United States.

"Specification Second: In this, that the said O-ta-kle, or Godfrey, did at various times and places, between the 19th of August and the 28th of September, 1862, join and participate in the murder and massacres committed by the Sioux Indians on the Minnesota frontier.

"By order of Col. H. H. Sibley,

"Com. Mil, Expedition.

"Witnesses: Mary Woodbury, David Faribault, Mary Swan, Bernard La Batle."

He was found guilty and sentenced to be hanged, but he subsequently turned state's evidence, and in consideration of assistance rendered to the prosecution. President Lincoln commuted his sentence to ten years' imprisonment.

Of the entire number convicted, thirty-eight were executed simultaneously on December 26, 1862, from a large square scaffold constructed in Mankato, Minn., by the father of John and George Sontag, who with Chris Evans, became notorious as desperadoes in California.

The Indians who were convicted but escaped the death penalty were imprisoned at the Military Prison at Davenport, Iowa, but all were liberated in 1866.

Former Chief Little Crow, who was accused of being the principal instigator of the war on the whites, was picking strawberries with his sixteen-year-old son near Scattered Lake on July 3, 1863, when he was recognized by a man named Nathan Lampson, who immediately fired upon the former Chief, inflicting a wound in the chest from which he died a few minutes later.

————————

THE HAYMARKET RIOT IN CHICAGO, IN WHICH EIGHT POLICE OFFICERS WERE KILLED AND SIXTY-EIGHT WOUNDED. THE TRAGIC SUICIDE OF THE BOMBMAKER AND EXECUTION OF FOUR OF THE CONSPIRATORS.

(From Captain Schaack's History of the Case.)

The first symptoms of an anarchistic movement in the United States appeared in 1878, at which time the leaders openly advocated the destruction of all forms of society, religion and government.

On Thanksgiving Day, 1884, they paraded in Chicago, and for the first time in America, exhibited their black flag. At this time, A. R. Parsons, the editor of a sheet called the "Alarm," Samuel Fielden, Oscar Neebe and August Spies, the editor of the "Arbeitzer Zeitung," were the recognized leaders in Chicago.

Spies hated the police because Officer Tamillo had found it necessary to kill his brother, a young tough, who was raising a disturbance at a picnic.

While Parsons was cautious as to the manner in which he expressed himself in the "Alarm," he threw caution to the winds while addressing a mob, when he believed none of the authorities were present.

On the evening of January 12, 1885, a secret meeting was held at Mueller's Hall, at Sedgwick Street and North Avenue, during which Officer M. Hoffman was present in disguise. Parsons opened the meeting, but before addressing the assembly, he asked his brethren to scrutinize those present and if they saw any enemy in the hall, to strangle him and throw him out the window.

After becoming satisfied that he was addressing none but anarchists, he discussed the merits of a new invention which he exhibited and stated that they were for the purpose of burning buildings.

He called them "little darlings," and informed his hearers that instructions as to their use would be cheerfully given at 107 Fifth Avenue, where the office of their leading paper, the "Alarm," was located.

On February 16, 1886, differences arose between the McCormick Harvester Co. and their employees, and the anarchists, through one Louis Lingg, endeavored in every conceivable manner to convince the employees that the only way they could accomplish their object would be by the use of violence. On March 2, 1886, Parsons, Spies and Michael Schwab, an assistant editor under Spies, called a mass meeting, and their incendiary speeches caused E. E. Sanderson, representing the strikers, to denounce the proceeding as being injurious to their cause.

On May 3, the anarchists made an attack on McCormick's place for the purpose of bringing about a conflict between the police and the strikers, believing that it would then be easier to persuade the latter to become anarchists. After a terrific battle, the police repulsed this mob. Editor Spies also tried to persuade the strikers to commit acts of violence, but not meeting with success, he, Parsons, Feilden, Neebe, George Engel, who conducted the paper called the "Anarchist," and an employee of his named Adolph Fischer, arranged for a secret conference at Greif's Hall, No. 54 West Lake Street, on the evening following the day of this battle.

One Gottfried Waller presided at this meeting and he subsequently informed the authorities of all that transpired on that occasion. At this meeting it was decided that the German word "Ruhe," meaning "peace," would be the signal to summon their brethren to action.

On the next day, May 4, 1886, the signal word "Ruhe" appeared in the anarchists' papers, and a circular was printed which read as follows:

"ATTENTION!

"Great Mass Meeting to-night at 7:30 o'clock, at the Haymarket, Randolph Street, between Desplaines and Halsted.

"Good speakers will be present to denounce the latest atrocious act of the police, the shooting of our fellow workmen yesterday afternoon."

"Haymarket square" is a continuation of Randolph Street. It is paved and about two hundred feet wide for a distance of two blocks. It was given this name by reason of the fact that in years gone by farmers congregated at this point to sell their hay, etc.

Anticipating trouble, one hundred and seventy-six police officers were assigned to this place under command of Inspector John Bonfield, Capt. Wm. Ward and Lieut, (later Chief) G. W. Hubbard, but they were instructed not to interfere unless inflammatory language was used or some unlawful act committed.

At 8 p. m. a crowd of 3000 people had assembled.

Spies mounted a wagon and urged workingmen to arm themselves for defense if they wished to cope with the "Government hirelings."

Parsons then made a speech, during which Mayor Harrison mingled with the crowd of listeners, and after referring to Parsons' speech as harmless he left the scene.

Fielden then took the stand (or wagon) and he began by advising his followers to "Kill the law, exterminate the capitalists, and do it to-night."

As the crowd was becoming excited, Inspector Bonfield decided that the time for action had arrived. He marched his men up to the gathering and as Fielden saw them approaching, he cried: "Here come the bloodhounds. You do your duty and I'll do mine."

Captain Ward then ordered the gathering to disperse.

At this moment Fielden jumped from the wagon and when he reached the sidewalk he cried out so all could hear him: "We are 'peaceable.'"

The word "Ruhe" (peace) was to be the signal for action and the instant Fielden made this remark, a bomb, lighted and hissing like a skyrocket, was hurled in the midst of the police. The explosion, which immediately followed, could be heard for blocks.

This was instantly followed by hundreds of pistol shots, both from the police and anarchists.

Officers and rioters were falling in all directions, but by a magnificent display of bravery, the officers remaining on their feet rallied, and in the face of the heavy fire, they swept all before them. The dead and dying were then conveyed to the Desplaines Street station. As the anarchists who escaped uninjured returned and removed many of the bodies of their fallen comrades and escorted the wounded to their homes, the total number of those killed or wounded during the riot was never learned, but the following officers were killed: M. J. Degan, M. Sheehan, George Muller, John Barrett, Thomas Redden, Timothy Flavin, Nels Hansen and Timothy Sullivan. In addition to this, sixty-eight officers were wounded, many becoming cripples for life.

As it was evident that the throwing of this bomb was not the work of one crank, but the result of a deep-laid conspiracy, the officers bent their energies to apprehend and procure legal evidence against the chief conspirators.

As the office of the "Arbeitzer Zeitung" was the headquarters of the leaders of the organization, a raid was made on the place on the following morning and manuscript was found which subsequently proved valuable to the authorities. Among others arrested at this place was Adolph Fischer.

When arrested, this man had a revolver and a dagger made out of a file in his possession.

An examination showed that the dagger had been dipped in a deadly poison.

August Spies, Chris. Spies, Michael Schwab, Oscar Neebe and Samuel Fielden were arrested on May 5. Rudolph Schnaubelt, who was a close friend of those already arrested, was taken into custody on May 6, but unfortunately was released almost immediately afterward. (The seriousness of this mistake on the part of the officials will appear later.)

A search was made for Parsons but he escaped, although he subsequently surrendered under the most sensational circumstances.

As there seemed to be considerable dissension in the detective office, little progress was made toward making a case against the prisoners until Capt. M. Schaack informed Chief Ebersold that he had valuable information, and asked for and obtained permission to handle the case.

The captain then detailed six of his best detectives, noted for their bravery, ability and integrity, to assist him. (Among them was Hermann F. Schuettler, now assistant superintendent of police, who has acquired a national reputation because of the great ability he displayed in handling the Cronin, Luetgert, Car Bam and numerous other famous murder cases, and who is now justly regarded as one of the most capable and conscientious police officials in America.)

A few days afterward, the officers located a bomb factory at 442 Sedgwick Street, the residence of an anarchist named Wm. Seliger, a carpenter by trade. He was placed under arrest and subsequently admitted that Louis Lingg lived there and made the bombs.

On May 12, John Thielen, a carpenter, residing at 509 North Halsted Street, was arrested, and after a severe cross-examination, admitted that he assisted Lingg and Seliger to make twenty-two bombs on Sunday, May 2. He claimed that Lingg volunteered to make bombs for anybody who would throw them, and on the evening of the riot, Lingg, according to Thielen's confession, carried a satchel-full of bombs to 58 Clybourn Avenue, and told the anarchists there assembled to help themselves.

Thielen also stated that he attended the meeting on May 3, when George Engel instructed those present as to the plans for the following evening.

It was presumed that the circular would cause the police to hold a large reserve force of officers at the different stations in the suburbs, and details of anarchists armed with bombs, were instructed to remain near the different stations, until they saw an illumination near the Haymarket, to be caused by burning a building immediately after the bomb was thrown.

They were then to blow up the stations. As the reserve forces at several of these stations consisted of from fifty to one hundred and twenty men, it can be imagined what would have happened if this plan had not miscarried.

The anarchists had so much faith in their bombs that they figured there would be no officers left at the Haymarket after they finished their work, and that they would have ample opportunity to start a conflagration. But when the brave officers rallied and charged them, they scattered in all directions and their desire to illuminate the heavens was immediately overcome by a greater desire to save their heads from the officers' batons.

Mrs. Seliger, at whose home the bombs were made, stated that she had an idea of the fiendish work Lingg had on hand, and she got down on her knees and begged her husband to accompany him that night and to prevent him from committing any depredation.

Seliger promised his wife that he would do her bidding and then kissed her good-by.

Lingg was with the gang detailed to destroy one of the police stations, and Seliger remained by his side constantly. Lingg requested him to keep his cigar lighted so that he could ignite his fuse at a second's notice.

Suddenly the patrol wagon loaded with officers dashed out of the station, en route to the Haymarket. Lingg asked for the lighted cigar, but the light had gone out and Seliger pretended to be searching his pockets for matches until the patrol wagon had passed. Lingg became furious when he saw the wagon load of officers disappear down the Street.

On May 14, Detective Schuettler traced Lingg to the home of Gustave Klein, at 80 Ambrose Street.

Lingg was as ferocious as a tiger, as cunning as a fox and as strong as a lion.

Mr. Schuettler, who is a man of magnificent physique, and noted for his bravery, burst in the door, whereupon Lingg sprang at him and fought like a demon. He attempted to shoot the officer but was finally overpowered and taken to jail. Among Lingg's effects was a letter from his mother, informing him that he was her illegitimate son.

On May 18, Ernst Hubner, a carpenter, residing at 11 Mohawk Street, was arrested, and he subsequently confessed that he assisted Lingg to make bombs on May 4.

Hubner also substantiated the statement made by Thielen regarding the instructions given by Engel on May 3.

On May 19, Engel, who then conducted a toy store at 286 Milwaukee Avenue, was arrested, but he denied all the accusations made against him.

On May 20, Gottfried Waller, who acted as chairman of the meeting on May 3, was arrested and on May 24 he was brought before Engel and corroborated the statements previously made by Hubner and Thielen regarding Engel's instructions.

On May 20, Otto Lehman, a carpenter, was arrested, and he admitted that he attended the meeting on May 3 and heard Lingg and Schwab advise those present to arm themselves and seek revenge on the police on the following evening. He also stated that Fischer agreed to have the circulars printed, announcing the Haymarket meeting.

A great number of well-known anarchists were then arrested and in nearly every instance they told the police all they knew to save themselves.

A young man named Chas. Brown called upon Captain Schaack and stated that he was in sympathy with some of the teachings of the anarchists, but that he was bitterly opposed to violence.

As he attended the meetings, he was well posted and volunteered to assist the authorities. His offer was promptly accepted, but in the latter part of July, 1887, he suddenly disappeared.

Captain Schaack claimed that a young woman, who was in sympathy with the anarchists, entered into a conspiracy with them to drown the informer.

It was agreed that she would ask Brown to take her boat riding in Cedar Lake, just over the State line in Indiana. It was arranged that she should tip the boat over and that a party of anarchists, which would be close at hand in a boat, would rescue her but let the informer sink. Brown consented to take the ride, but when the woman tipped the boat over the rescuing party was too far away, and they both drowned. On August 3, Coroner Van De Walker of Lake County, Ind., informed the Chicago authorities that he had recovered both bodies.

The identity of the anarchists who followed this couple in another boat was never learned by the authorities.

The Haymarket case was presented to the Grand Jury, and on May

28 fifteen indictments were returned for murder, conspiracy and riot against Spies, Parsons, Fischer, Engel, Lingg, Fielden, Schwab, Neebe and Schnaubelt.

Evidence was produced which proved that the latter, who had been taken into custody and released, was the man who threw the bomb at the Haymarket.

After being liberated Schnaubelt disappeared, and it was claimed that he subsequently died in Germany, but Theodore Kytka, who was employed as a handwriting expert in the Haymarket case, and who knew Schnaubelt well, informed the author that he saw the fugitive in Arizona in 1899, but before he could locate an officer Schnaubelt disappeared. His sister resided in San Rafael, Cal., until recently and she stated that her brother died from consumption in Arizona in 1901.

Parsons, who had been working as a carpenter and painter in Wisconsin after he fled from Chicago, received information that the police had no evidence against the conspirators, so he decided to create a sensation. On June 21, he returned to Chicago, and while Judge Gary was considering a motion for separate trials. Parsons suddenly appeared in the courtroom and took a seat among the defendants.

At the trial, the original manuscript of the circular calling for the Haymarket meeting was introduced and proven to be in Spies' handwriting.

A grocer named M. M. Thompson, who conducted a store at 108 South Desplaines Street, testified that just before the bomb was thrown he heard Spies say: "Is one enough?"

The latter then disappeared but returned presently and secretly handed something to Schnaubelt, who placed it in his pocket and then sat on the wagon from which the speakers addressed the gathering.

Harry Gilmer, a painter, residing at 50 North Ann Street, testified that he saw Schnaubelt throw the bomb and that Spies lighted it.

The particles of the shell of the bomb removed from bodies of the officers were found to be similar to the shells of the bombs made by Lingg, which were about the size of a baseball.

On August 19, 1886, the case was submitted to the jurors, and on the following day they returned a verdict of guilty against the defendants, Spies, Schwab, Fielden, Parsons, Fischer, Engel and Lingg, and fixed the penalty at death. Neebe's punishment was fixed at imprisonment in the penitentiary for fifteen years.

A motion for a new trial was entered on the grounds that some of the jurors were prejudiced and on the further grounds of newly discovered evidence. The motion was denied on October 7.

Before passing sentence, the court asked the defendants if they had anything to say, whereupon all of the defendants made long speeches in which they expressed their contempt for the law.

Lingg was the most vicious in his expressions, and among other things said: "Perhaps you think 'you'll throw no more bombs,' but let me assure you that I die happy on the gallows, so confident am I that the thousands to whom I have spoken will remember my words; and when you shall have hanged us, then mark my words, they will do the bomb throwing."

The cases were then appealed to the State Supreme Court and on September 14, 1887, Justice Benjamin Magruder handed down a decision, in which all of his associates concurred, sustaining the findings of the lower court. The condemned men's followers then engaged Gen. Ben Butler as attorney, and on October 27, 1887, the case was brought before the United States Supreme Court, the contention being that the Illinois Jury law was in contravention of the Fourteenth Amendment of the Constitution of the United States. This court refused to interfere.

Appeals were then made to Governor Oglesby for executive clemency, especially in the cases of Schwab and Fielden.

It was claimed that the former was not present at the meeting and that there was no proof that he knew that violence would be resorted to. Regarding Fielden, it was argued that he became intoxicated with the applause of his audience, and did not realize the effect his words had on his hearers.

On November 6, while the Governor had these appeals under consideration, the authorities decided to search Cook County jail. A starch box was lying on the floor and one of the deputies, named O. E. Hogan, put the box on a platform for the moment and shortly afterward kicked it off and it fell on the floor and broke.

It was then discovered that it contained a false bottom, similar to that found in Lingg's trunk, and four dynamite bombs were concealed there. These instruments of destruction were made out of pieces of inch gas-pipe and were about six inches long.

On November 10, at 8:45 a. m., a loud explosion was heard in Lingg's cell. The officials found that the desperate man had gained possession of a dynamite bomb, which he placed in his mouth and lighted it with a candle which was flickering in a corner of his cell. Although most of his face had been blown away he lived until 2:45 p, m. that day. It is the general opinion that Lingg's sweetheart smuggled the bomb into his cell.

On the day of Lingg's suicide. Governor Oglesby commuted the sentence of Fielden and Schwab to life imprisonment.

On November 11, Spies, Parsons, Fischer and Engel were hanged. They remained defiant to the last.

During the trial of these anarchists, a beautiful young woman named Miss Nina Van Zandt made the acquaintance of Spies, and finally she publicly announced that she loved the anarchist.

The woman attended each session of the court, and when she became conscious of the notoriety she had achieved, she concluded that it was a good opportunity, not only to exhibit herself but her extensive wardrobe.

She expressed a desire to marry Spies, and the prisoner, believing that he might gain sympathy if he could point to this beautiful woman as his wife, consented to have the ceremony performed, but the authorities objected.

It was then decided that a proxy marriage should be performed between the young woman and Chris. Spies, the brother of the prisoner. A justice was found who performed the ceremony on January 29, 1887, but the marriage was generally regarded as illegal.

When Spies' body was taken to his home, Miss Van Zandt, dressed in deep mourning, was there to receive it.

The funeral services were set for Sunday, November 13, and the anarchists intended to carry a red flag at the head of their procession, but the permit was denied. The coffins of Engel and Lingg were draped with red flags.

A Civil War veteran, named Howell Trogden, preceded the procession, carrying an American flag, greatly to the chagrin of the anarchists, none of whom dared to interfere with him.

In December, 1888, the citizens of Chicago contributed $10,000.00, which was used to erect a monument where the brave officers fell at the Haymarket. On top of the pedestal was the figure of a police officer in full uniform with his right hand uplifted.

This monument was subsequently removed to another part of the city.

On June 26, 1893, Fielden, Neebe and Schwab were pardoned by Governor Altgeld.

THE CELEBRATED MURDER OF DR. CRONIN IN CHICAGO.

(From Chicago Police Records and Hunt's "Crime of the Century.")

The United Brotherhood or "Clan-na-gael" was an organization composed of Irishmen who were in sympathy with the movement to free Ireland from its dependence upon the British Government.

It was organized in 1869 and with a few exceptions its great membership consisted of men who affiliated with the order from motives of the purest patriotism.

Subordinate lodges or camps were instituted throughout the United States, but the order was particularly strong in Chicago.

The affairs of the organization were handled by an executive committee which, at a national convention held in Chicago in 1881, was reduced to five members.

On that executive board were Alexander Sullivan, a prominent Chicago lawyer; Michael Boland of Louisville, and D. S. Feeley of Rochester, N. Y.

It was alleged that these three men combined against the other two and were thereafter referred to as the "Triangle," who ruled the order with an iron hand.

The members made liberal contributions toward the assistance of their brethren in Ireland and eventually dissatisfaction arose as to the manner in which this money was handled.

In 1885, Dr. Patrick Cronin, a prominent Chicago physician, having offices in the Chicago Opera House building and also at 486 North Clark Street, where he resided with T. Conklin and wife, became the leader of the opposition to the methods of the Triangle and demanded that a detailed account be furnished of the disposition of all contributions, which were variously estimated at between $100,000 and $250,000.

Shortly after Cronin assumed this attitude he was charged with treason and brought to trial before a committee composed of members said to have been in sympathy with the Triangle, among them being Dan Coughlin, a detective in the Chicago police department.

Cronin was found guilty and expelled from the order, but he had a large following and the result was that thousands withdrew from the organization and formed new camps which soon grew to be as powerful as the original body.

Realizing that the object of the order could only be accomplished by working harmoniously together, influential leaders of both factions held a conference in 1888 and the result was that Dr. Cronin's following agreed to "bury the hatchet" and return to the original order, providing that all actions of the Triangle since 1881 be fully and fairly investigated.

This being agreed to, a committee headed by Dr. Cronin was appointed and the sessions began in New York in August, 1888.

The "Triangle" made a vigorous protest against Dr. Cronin remaining on this committee but the protest was overruled.

The doctor made copious notes throughout the trial and at its conclusion, four of the six investigators decided that the charges against the "Triangle" had not been proven, Cronin voting with the minority.

The physician then publicly announced that he would save his notes and that when the Irish National League assembled in Philadelphia in 1889, he would read a full report of the secret proceedings just concluded so that the members of the Clan-na-gael throughout the world would know the treachery of the Triangle.

When it became known that the Triangle had been exonerated, or "whitewashed" as Cronin put it, his followers became more dissatisfied than ever.

At this time Patrick O'Sullivan, who had an ice house at Lake View, a suburb of Chicago, and Detective Coughlin took an active part in the affairs of Camp 20. They were bitterly opposed to Dr. Cronin and his followers, although Cronin was not aware of the attitude of O'Sullivan.

In April, 1889, the latter persuaded Justice of the Peace John Mahoney to introduce him to Dr. Cronin.

O'Sullivan then informed the doctor that he had heard of his (Cronin's) ability as a physician and he desired to enter into a contract whereby the doctor would attend to any of O'Sullivan's employees who were sick or disabled.

Notwithstanding the fact that other reliable physicians were far more accessible in case of emergency; that the iceman had only four men in his employ and their work was not at all hazardous, Dr. Cronin's suspicions were not aroused by this peculiar proposition, although he had prophesied that his enemies would attempt to permanently seal his lips before he could make his report public.

He contracted to perform this service for $8 per month and agreed to respond whenever anyone called and presented one of O'Sullivan's cards.

At 8 p. m. Saturday, May 4, 1889, a very unprepossessing appearing man rushed into Dr. Cronin's office on North Clark Street and excitedly announced that one of O'Sullivan's men had just been injured in the region of the abdomen and that the doctor should render immediate assistance or the man would die.

Hastily placing his surgical instruments in a case and picking up a package of absorbent cotton, the doctor rushed down to the Street where the stranger had a white horse and buggy in waiting. Mrs. Conklin saw this horse and buggy and just as the doctor was being driven away, a friend of his named Frank Scanlan passed and saluted him.

Dr. Cronin did not return that night or the next day and as he was ordinarily most methodical in his habits, the Conklin's became alarmed.

The police department was notified and Acting Captain Herman Scheuttler was assigned to the case.

O'Sullivan, whose home was adjacent to his ice house, was immediately interrogated, and he stated that he had not sent for Dr. Cronin and furthermore had not seen him for many days. He admitted having entered into the agreement heretofore referred to, but could not explain why he had selected a doctor six miles away to attend to emergency cases.

On the Sunday morning after the disappearance of Cronin a cheap trunk was found in a ditch near Evanston Avenue and the Catholic cemetery.

Upon closer inspection it was found that the interior of the trunk was bespattered with blood and partially filled with absorbent cotton which was saturated with gore.

Human hair similar to Dr. Cronin's was also found in the trunk.

Five days after the disappearance of the doctor, a stable owner named Foley informed the police that a young man had offered to sell, him a horse and wagon for $10 and that he believed the fellow had stolen the rig. The man was apprehended and gave the name of Frank Woodruff.

He was evidently anxious to gain some cheap notoriety, even if it placed him in an unenviable position, for he invented several weird and conflicting stories to make it appear that he had used this wagon for the purpose of carrying the mysterious trunk to the place where it was found, and stated that it was used as a receptacle to convey the body of a woman who had been the victim of a criminal operation, and that a man of Dr. Cronin's description superintended the removal.

He afterward changed his story at intervals to correspond with the new evidence produced.

To add to the confusion, several apparently responsible persons claimed that they had met Dr. Cronin after his disappearance.

A newspaper reporter in Toronto even published a long interview which he claimed he had had with the missing man in Toronto, in which the doctor was alleged to have stated that fear for his personal safety drove him from Chicago.

On May 22, three sewer men, acting on complaints to the effect that the sewer at Evanston Avenue and North Fifty-Ninth Street was obstructed, proceeded to that locality. Being attracted by the terrible stench that pervaded the atmosphere in the neighborhood of the catch basin, an investigation was instituted and they found that the nude body of a man had been thrown head first into the basin.

With considerable difficulty it was brought to the surface. A towel saturated with blood was wrapped around the neck, underneath which was found an Agnus Dei.

Although decomposition had reached an advanced stage and the body was terribly swollen, Dr. Cronin's friends were positive it was his remains and Dr. Lewis, a dentist, positively identified some dental work as that which he had done for Dr. Cronin.

Although there were five scalp wounds, there was no fracture of the skull and the immediate cause of death was never satisfactorily proven.

After it became known that Dr. Cronin had been murdered, the Clan-na-gael and numerous other Irish societies passed resolutions denouncing those who participated in the murder and expressing the hope that the assassins would be brought to justice.

On the day following the finding of Cronin's body, Captain Schuettler had an interview with O'Sullivan, the ice man, who stated that a man had rented a cottage on Ashland Avenue, which was within 150 feet of his (O'Sullivan's) home, and that his actions had been most mysterious.

Captain Schuettler proceeded to the cottage and a casual glance convinced him that this was the scene of the murder. Considerable blood was found on the front steps and about the rooms, and the floor had just received a coat of yellow paint in a clumsy effort to hide the blood.

The small amount of furniture in the house bore the brand of the A. H. Revell Furniture Co. of Chicago.

A key was found which belonged to the blood-stained trunk found on the morning following Dr. Cronin's disappearance.

Captain Schuettler then interrogated Jonas Carlson and wife who owned the cottage and lived in a smaller cottage in the rear.

Carlson's statement was as follows:

"About noon on March 20 a man of medium size with dark mustache, hair and eyes called at my home and asked how much rent I wanted for the cottage in front. I replied $12 a month.

"He finally agreed to take it and stated that his sister and brothers would move in shortly. He paid the rent in advance and gave the name of Frank Williams.

"My son and daughter-in-law were present at the time.

"The next morning a Swedish express man brought a few articles of furniture to the house which Williams helped him to unload.

"A whole month passed, and Williams again paid the rent but stated that the reason the family had not moved in was because his sister was very ill.

"Up to May 18 the cottage was still unoccupied, although occasionally at nighttime lights were seen inside, and it became known as 'the house of mystery.'

"On May 18, I received a note from Hammond, Ind., which read as follows:

"'Mr. Carlson. Dear Sir: My sister is low at present and my business calls me out of town. If you will please put the furniture in your cellar for a few days I will pay you for your trouble. I am sorry that I lost the key to the cottage door, but I will pay you for all trouble. My sister told me to paint the floor for her so that it would not be hard to keep clean. I am now sorry I gave the front room one coat.

"'F. W.'"

That afternoon Carlson's son inspected the cottage and was horror-stricken at finding it in the condition already described, but dreading notoriety, the family hesitated about notifying the police. Notwithstanding the fact that O'Sullivan informed Captain Schuettler that the conduct of the tenant in Carlson's cottage should be investigated, it was proven by the Carlson family that the minute Williams rented the cottage he proceeded directly to O'Sullivan's house, and addressing O'Sullivan, said, within the hearing of Carlson, "Well, the cottage is rented."

Afterward, when the Carlson's became suspicious of their strange tenant, O'Sullivan assured them that he was all right and even offered to pay the rent if Williams did not.

Captain Schuettler then proceeded to Revell's furniture store, where he learned that the blood-stained trunk and all of the furniture found in the Carlson cottage had been purchased at their place on February 17, by a man giving the name of J. B. Simonds, and at his request it was delivered to rooms 12 and 15 at 117 South Clark Street, which was across the Street from Dr. Cronin's office.

It was the theory of Captain Schuettler that it was the original intention to inveigle the doctor into these rooms and murder him there, but that the Carlson cottage was afterward chosen because of its isolated location.

The description given by the real estate agents of the man who rented the rooms tallied with that of the mysterious Simonds who purchased the furniture. Simonds was never apprehended, but it was suspected that he was none other than Pat Cooney, alias "the Fox," who was a companion of O'Sullivan and Coughlin and a bitter enemy of Cronin's.

The next important information came from a milk dealer named William Mertes.

On the night that Dr. Cronin disappeared, Mertes passed the Carlson cottage at 8:30 p. m.

He saw a buggy drawn by a white horse stop in front of the cottage and observed a man of Dr. Cronin's general appearance alight and go up the steps.

He knocked at the door which was opened and as soon as the man entered and the door was closed, he heard angry voices, but believing it was an ordinary quarrel he passed on.

As soon as the man entered the door the man in the buggy drove off.

The next important witness located by Captain Schuettler was the Swedish express man Martinsen, who stated that in the latter part of March a man whose description tallied with that of Frank Williams, engaged him to haul the furniture from 117 Clark Street to the Carlson cottage.

Every effort was made to trace the white horse and buggy which carried Dr. Cronin to his doom.

Detective Dan Coughlin, who was one of the committee which found Dr. Cronin guilty on the treason charge, was connected with a police station near Patrick Dinan's livery stable, located at 260 North Clark Street.

On the day of Dr. Cronin's disappearance, Coughlin instructed Dinan to have a horse and buggy in readiness for a friend of his who would call that night at 7 p. m., and he furthermore cautioned him to say nothing about it.

Believing that the rig was to be used in detective work, Dinan kept his word for a time, but as it answered the description of the horse and buggy used on the night of the murder, he finally decided to have a talk with Captain Schaack of Haymarket riot fame, who was then in command of the police station near his stable. When he reached the station Dinan was met by Coughlin, who asked him what he wanted. Dinan told him and Coughlin replied:

"Now, look here, there's no use making a fuss about this thing. You keep quiet or you'll get me into trouble as everybody knows Cronin and I were enemies."

Dinan pretended to acquiesce in the suggestion, but at the earliest opportunity the matter was reported to headquarters.

Frank Scanlan, who saluted Dr. Cronin as he was being driven away in the buggy, and Mrs. Conklin, Cronin's landlady, were shown this horse and buggy and they declared it was the same one in which the doctor left his office, and the description of the driver, as given by Dinan and Mrs. Conklin, was identically the same.

Coughlin was then called upon to explain his conduct. He admitted that Dinan's statement was true and claimed that the man who used the rig introduced himself as Thomas Smith, a friend of his (Coughlin's) brother, in Hancock, Michigan. He said that Smith stated that he wanted to use a horse and buggy that evening and asked Coughlin to engage one for him at Dinan's.

As Coughlin could not produce Smith and as his conduct convinced the investigating authorities that he had a guilty knowledge of the murder, he was taken into custody.

The next day, a William Smith, who knew Coughlin in Hancock, called on the authorities to convince them that he knew nothing of the conspiracy.

On May 26, Dr. Cronin was buried, the funeral being extremely spectacular.

There were nearly 8000 men in line, representing the Hibernians, Clan-na-gaels, Foresters, Catholic benevolent societies and other orders of which the deceased was a prominent member. There was also a band and several drum corps.

On the day following the funeral, the authorities made a careful analysis of the evidence against O'Sullivan, the ice man, and it was decided to take him into custody.

It was also learned that prior to May 4, O'Sullivan and Coughlin were in daily communication over the telephone while Coughlin was in the police station.

At the coroner's inquest, Luke Dillon, the great Irish leader, gave testimony in which he denounced Alexander Sullivan of the Triangle as a rogue.

After receiving all the evidence gathered at that time, the coroner's jury rendered a verdict on June 11, in which it was recommended that Alexander Sullivan, Patrick O'Sullivan, Coughlin and Woodruff be held to answer before the grand jury for the murder.

Sullivan was immediately taken into custody, but there was really no legal evidence to justify his arrest and he promptly procured his release on $20,000 bail.

Some months afterward a demand was made that the bondsmen be released and Sullivan discharged, and the application was granted.

This was not the first time that Sullivan was arrested.

On August 7, 1876, at a meeting of the Chicago City Council, a communication from Principal Frank Hanford of one of the high schools was read, in which he charged that Sullivan's wife, who was also a prominent educator, was creating dissension in the board of education.

That same night Sullivan and his wife called on Hanford and demanded a retraction. A squabble followed, during which Sullivan claimed that Hanford struck Mrs. Sullivan, whereupon Sullivan shot and killed him.

After two trials Sullivan was acquitted on March 10, 1877.

Before the disappearance of Dr. Cronin, one Martin Burke, alias Delaney, hung around the Market Street saloons and spent money so freely as to attract attention. He was a member of the same camp as Coughlin and O' Sullivan and boasted that these men were his friends. He also expressed the opinion that Cronin was a British spy and should be killed.

It was known that he made frequent and mysterious visits to the neighborhood of O'Sullivan's home and after the disappearance of Cronin, Burke also suddenly disappeared.

Officer John Collins informed Captain Schuettler of these facts, and after some clever work a photograph was obtained of a group of men which included Burke. This picture was shown to the three Carlson's and the Swedish express man Martinson, who at once picked out the photograph of

Burke as the likeness of the much-wanted "Frank Williams," who moved the furniture from 117 Clark Street and rented the Carlson cottage.

It was learned that Burke had left the city, so Captain Schuettler had a complete description and photograph sent to the police of all Eastern and Canadian cities.

On June 16, Chief McRae, of Winnipeg, saw a man of Burke's description at the Winnipeg depot, and observing that the man became extremely nervous when he noticed that he was being scrutinized, the chief finally became so positive that the man was Burke that he approached him and said: "What is your name?"

The man replied "W. J. Cooper," but he almost immediately afterward admitted that he was Martin Burke, alias Delaney.

Chief Hubbard of Chicago was notified and the necessary steps were taken to extradite the prisoner.

Express man Martinson was sent to Winnipeg and he picked Burke out of a line of fifty-two prisoners. Prominent attorneys were employed to prevent the extradition of Burke, but after a long and bitter legal battle he was returned to Chicago.

The feeling throughout the country was so strong against him that it was feared that he would be taken away from the officers and lynched at some of the stations.

On June 12, the grand jury began their investigation

Attorney John Beggs was Senior Guardian of Camp 20; and when testifying before the grand jury it was claimed that his statements were inconsistent and contradictory regarding the allegation that, at the request of Dan Coughlin, he selected a secret committee to investigate the charge that Dr. Cronin was a spy.

It was therefore concluded that he had a guilty knowledge of the murder.

Mertes, the milk man who saw the buggy driven up to the Carlson cottage on the night of the murder, identified a little German named Kunze, a friend of Coughlin's, as the man who drove the buggy away, and another man claimed to have seen Kunze at 117 Clark Street, where the furniture was first moved in.

On June 29, the grand jury indicted Beggs, Coughlin, Burke, O'Sullivan, Woodruff, Kunze and Cooney on the charge of murder.

The trials of all the defendants, except Woodruff and Cooney, began on August 26.

While prospective jurymen were being examined it was charged that at least two court bailiffs were parties to a conspiracy to bribe jurymen in the interests of the defendant and as a result several indictments were found.

In addition to the witnesses who appeared before the coroner and grand jury, several others testified before the trial jury.

John Garrity testified that Coughlin had once asked him if a man named Sampson could be hired to "slug" Dr. Cronin and disfigure him for life.

Mrs. Addie Farrar testified that O'Sullivan told her that Cronin was a British spy and should be killed.

On November 8, while the trial was in progress, a com plaint was made that the sewer at Evanston and Buena Avenue was obstructed. This was about a mile from the catch basin: where Cronin's body was found.

Laborers were dispatched to the scene and within a short time they found all of Dr. Cronin's clothes, which had been cut from his body, his leather satchel and prescription book on which his name was written.

Mrs. Paulina Hoertel corroborated the statement of Milkman Mertes in regard to the white horse and buggy driven up to the Carlson cottage. She also saw a man of Dr. Cronin's general appearance enter the house and then heard someone cry "Jesus."

William Neiman testified that O'Sullivan and two men who resembled Kunze and Coughlin drank wine in his saloon, which was a block from the Carlson cottage, at 11 p. m. on the night of the murder, although O'Sullivan denied having left his home at all that night.

Detective B. Flynn of the regular department testified that he searched Detective Coughlin when the arrest was made and that he had found two knives in the prisoner's pocket which were afterward identified as being similar to knives which belonged to Dr. Cronin.

Coughlin produced witnesses who swore that they had seen both knives in the possession of the detective long before the disappearance of the doctor.

The defendants then put on several witnesses, principally for the purpose of proving an alibi.

On November 30, both sides had completed their case and fourteen days more were consumed in argument.

On December 16, the cause was finally submitted to the jury. After deliberating seventy hours the jury returned the following verdict:

"We, the jury, find the defendant John F. Beggs not guilty.

"We, the jury, find the defendant John Kunze guilty of manslaughter as charged in the indictment and fix his punishment at imprisonment in the penitentiary for a term of three years.

"We, the jury, find the defendants Daniel Coughlin, Patrick O'Sullivan and Martin Burke guilty of murder in the manner and form as charged in the indictment and fix the penalty at imprisonment in the penitentiary for the term of their natural lives."

Shortly afterward, Kunze was granted a new trial, which resulted in his acquittal.

On January 19, 1893, the Court of Appeals granted a new trial to Coughlin on the ground that two of the jurors were prejudiced against him. The second trial resulted in his acquittal.

O'Sullivan and Burke died in the penitentiary.

As there was no evidence against Woodruff except his own conflicting statements, none of which could be corroborated, his case was stricken from the docket on April 21, 1890.

After Coughlin was released he opened a saloon in Clark Street, Chicago, but it was subsequently charged that while employed in the Illinois Central Railway Company's claims department he attempted to bribe jurors in damage suit cases.

Several indictments were found against him and he fled to Honduras.

On August 21, 1910, John Tyrell, attorney for Frank B. Harriman and others, who were formerly high officials on this road, but whose trials on charges of graft were then pending, charged that considerable of the money alleged to have been lost through car repairing frauds, was really expended in supporting Coughlin's family and keeping the fugitive in affluence in his Central American exile.

President J. H. Harahan of this road states that the charges are false.

THE MURDER OF MAYOR CARTER H. HARRISON OF CHICAGO BY EUGENE PRENDERGAST.

Carter Henry Harrison was born in Lafayette County, Kentucky, on February 25, 1825, and graduated from Yale College in 1845.

He lived in Chicago many years, and accumulated a vast fortune. Harrison was a Democrat and was elected by that party to the office of Mayor of Chicago, taking his seat on April 18, 1893. He was a grand character and had friends and admirers galore.

Mr. Harrison was a widower and had two grown sons, named Preston and Carter, the latter subsequently serving as Mayor of Chicago for several terms.

On October 28, 1893, Harrison, Sr., visited the World's Fair, then being held in Chicago, and returned to his home at No. 231 Ashland Boulevard at 5 p. m. After dinner he retired to his room to rest. At 8 p. m. the doorbell rang and was answered by a domestic named Mary Hansen who was confronted by a small man about 25 years old, with a wizened, smooth-shaven face. He stated that his name was Prendergast and that he had urgent business with the Mayor.

The servant proceeded to Mr. Harrison's room to deliver the message, but was surprised to see that the caller had followed her through the hall. The Mayor then stepped out of his room and engaged the stranger in conversation, while the servant went downstairs.

After a brief conversation, the Mayor was heard to say: "I tell you I won't do it," Immediately afterward three shots rang out.

W. J. Chalmers, who lived across the Street, heard the shots and after rushing into his own house to notify his wife, he hurried over to the Harrison home. Just as he was leaving his own home he saw the assassin run out of the Harrison residence, pistol in hand, closely pursued by Harrison's hired man, who stopped when the murderer turned and fired at him.

Chalmers found the Mayor lying in the hall near his room.

An examination showed that one bullet had pierced the abdomen, a second had struck over the heart and the third had passed through the dying man's hand,

Preston Harrison was soon by his father's side, but the Mayor was rapidly sinking and in a feeble voice requested that Miss Annie Howard, his fiancée, be sent for, but he died before her arrival.

Sergeant of Police Frank McDonald was in command of the

Desplaines Street station at the time of the tragedy and was in the act of receiving the news of the assassination over the telephone when he was interrupted by a man who suddenly appeared in the station and remarked: "I did the shooting and this is the gun I did it with."

Turning around the sergeant beheld a small man with a revolver in his hand, and after disarming him the prisoner voluntarily made the following statement:

"My name is Patrick Eugene Joseph Prendergast, and I was born in Ireland in April, 1868, but I came to this country with my mother when I was two years old.

"I have been a messenger boy for the Western Union Telegraph Co., but recently I have been employed as a distributor for the 'Inter Ocean' and 'Evening Post.'

"I worked hard for the election of Mayor Harrison during his campaign and he promised to give me a position, but as he refused to keep his word I killed him."

On October 30, Prendergast was indicted by the grand jury and on November 2 he was arraigned.

He pleaded "Not guilty;" it having been decided to attempt to prove he was insane. A great deal of time was consumed in examining into his mental condition, but he was adjudged sane and on December 29 was found guilty of murder with the death penalty attached.

Motions were made for a new trial which were overruled and his execution was set for March 23, 1894. Prendergast was held in contempt by all classes for his cowardly crime.

One Thomas Higgins was sentenced to be executed with Prendergast, and he stated that he did not fear the execution but hated to think of going to his death with Prendergast.

At the eleventh hour Prendergast obtained a reprieve until April 6, and Higgins expressed gratification when he learned that he would not be subjected to the disgrace of hanging with Prendergast.

The latter was granted a new trial; was again found guilty and hanged on July 13, 1894.

ADOLPH L. LEUTGERT, A PROMINENT SAUSAGE MANUFACTURER IN CHICAGO, WHO KILLED HIS WIFE AND DISSOLVED HER BODY IN A VAT IN HIS FACTORY.

In the latter part of April, 1897, Adolph Leutgert, a powerfully built, coarse appearing man, who conducted a sausage factory at the comer of Hermitage Avenue and Diversey Boulevard, in Chicago, failed in business. He had been married twice. By his first wife he had a grown son named Arnold, and by his second wife, Louise, he had two boys named Elmer and Louis. The family lived on Hermitage Avenue, next door to the factory, and a young woman named Mary Seimmering was employed as a servant in their house.

On May 1, Mrs. Leutgert suddenly disappeared, but her husband was apparently unconcerned regarding her absence and advanced the theory that she had committed suicide because of his failure in business.

On May 4, Deidrich Bicknesse, Mrs. Leutgert's brother, called to see her, and Leutgert informed him that she had been missing for three days, but admitted that he had not notified the police of the singular incident nor had he taken any steps to locate her.

Bicknesse, observing Leutgert's utter indifference, had the police notified and Captain Herman Schuettler instituted an investigation.

The press gave much publicity to the mysterious disappearance and the police began a general search, even going to the extent of dragging the river for a considerable distance, but nothing was discovered.

Finally Captain Schuettler decided to confine his investigation to the factory in general but to a large vat therein in particular, and a rapid solution of the mystery followed.

In the sediment in the bottom of the vat, two gold rings, one having the initials "L. L." engraved inside, a tooth, and two corset steels were found.

The rings were positively identified as the property of Mrs. Louise Leutgert, and in the yard where the bones from the animals were thrown, a part of a skull and other pieces of human bones were found.

It was learned that during the period between May 2 and May 17 Leutgert made many efforts to gain an entrance to the factory, but was always refused admission by the sheriff's deputies who were in charge.

On May 18, Leutgert was arrested and four days later was indicted by the grand jury.

He attempted to gain his freedom on a writ of habeas corpus but failed.

On August 7, the prosecution obtained a corpse, and placing it in the identical vat where Mrs. Leutgert's body was destroyed, boiled it in caustic potash for two hours. At the expiration of that time, nothing remained of the fleshy parts of the body but a fluid and all of the bones, except the larger ones, were completely destroyed.

This proved that their theory was correct.

On August 24, Leutgert's trial began before Judge Tuthill. The attorney for Leutgert claimed that he had also made a test with a corpse, but that the boiling process did not dissolve it. The contention of the defense was that no crime had been committed and that Mrs. Leutgert was not dead, but was remaining in seclusion. A letter was received by Alderman Schlake signed by "Loisa Leutgert," in which the missing woman was represented as saying that she was then living with friends in Chicago, but it was shown that the handwriting in no manner resembled that of the missing woman and the missive was evidently sent for the purpose of confusing the authorities.

Nicholas Faber and Emma and Gottliebe Schimpke testified that they saw Leutgert enter his factory about 10 p. m. on the night of May 1 with a woman about the size of Mrs. Leutgert.

Frank Bialk, a watchman in the factory, which had been shut down since the failure, testified that on this night, Leutgert instructed him to bring down two barrels of caustic potash and place them in the boiler room, and that Leutgert then poured the contents of both barrels in one of the vats. The watchman was instructed to keep up steam all night and at 10 p. m. he was sent by Leutgert to the drug store after some nerve medicine.

When he returned, Leutgert was in the room where the vats were located and had the door locked.

Bialk furthermore testified that he resided at the home of Police Officer Klinger and that on May 6 Leutgert called on him. After concealing the officer under the bed in Bialk's room, Leutgert was admitted to the room and in suppressed excitement asked if the officers had discovered anything at the factory, Bialk answered "No," and Leutgert, with a show of relief, remarked: "That's good."

He then admonished the watchman to tell the police nothing

and promised that when the factory re-opened, good positions would be provided for Bialk and his son.

Frank Odorfsky, an employee of the factory, who assisted Leutgert to put the caustic potash in the vat, testified that in all his experience in the factory he had never seen caustic potash used there before.

Mrs. Agatha Tosch, whose husband conducted a saloon opposite the factory, testified that she saw smoke coming from the factory chimney on the night of May 1, although the factory was supposed to have been shut down at the time.

She also stated that Leutgert visited her on the following day and requested her to say nothing about the smoke as it would get him in trouble.

Chas. Hengst stated that he was passing the factory about 10 p. m. on May 1, and heard a noise similar to that made by a person screaming.

Chemist Carl Voelker testified that there was no occasion for caustic potash in a sausage factory.

Mrs. Christina Feldt, a widow with whom the defendant had at one time been infatuated, testified that Leutgert often expressed his hatred for his wife and intimated that he would get rid of her.

Dr. Chas. Gibson and Professor De la Fontaine testified that the masses of soft substance which had presumably boiled over the vat was flesh that had undergone burning by potash.

Particles removed from the drain pipes leading from the vat were then produced and proven to be portions of human bones.

Leutgert handled these exhibits in the most cold-blooded manner, and demonstrated that he was devoid of all feeling.

Professor Geo. Dorsey of the Field Columbian Museum, testified that one of the bones found in the pile of animal bones was the upper portion of the left thigh bone of a woman.

During the trial, Chas. Winthers of 250 Orleans Street, was arrested for attempting to intimidate Mrs. Tosch, the witness who saw the smoke coming from the chimney in the sausage factory on the night of May 1.

Captain Schuettler testified regarding the indifference exhibited by Leutgert as to the fate of his wife, and as to the result of his official investigations.

The defense began on September 24, and several persons testified that since May 1 they had at different places seen a woman who resembled Mrs. Leutgert.

It was the theory of the prosecution that Leutgert, tiring of his second wife, was anxious to get her out of the way so that he might marry Mary Seimmering, the family servant. On September 25, this girl testified for the defense and described Leutgert's "kind treatment" toward his wife.

She denied having been on intimate terms with Leutgert, although members of the grand jury were subsequently produced who swore that she had told them of her improper relations with the defendant.

The defense then produced a number of experts for the purpose of offsetting the testimony given by experts for the prosecution.

William Charles, Leutgert's business partner, testified that the caustic potash was bought for the purpose of making soft soap, as they intended to clean the factory prior to turning it over to an English syndicate.

To rebut this testimony, Deputy Sheriff Frank Moan swore that when he took possession of the place there were over 100 boxes of soap in stock, thus showing that there was sufficient on hand for cleaning purposes.

On October 18, the case was submitted to the jury and after deliberating for sixty-six hours they failed to agree, nine favoring a conviction and three voting in favor of an acquittal.

On November 29, 1897, the second trial began and Leutgert made an appeal to the public for financial assistance, but few people responded.

On January 19, 1898, the defendant took the stand in his own behalf for the first time and the police experienced great difficulty in handling the crowd.

The trial resulted in a conviction and on May 5 Leutgert was sent to the Joliet State prison for life.

At 6 a. m. on the morning of July 27, 1899, Leutgert left his cell and returned shortly afterward with his breakfast in a pail, but just as he was about to eat it, he dropped dead from heart disease.

After his death, Frank Pratt, a member of the Chicago bar, stated that he visited Joliet in February, 1898, to consult a client named Chris Merry, and being somewhat of a palmist he asked Leutgert if he wanted his "hand read."

The latter consented and Pratt told Leutgert that he possessed a violent temper and at times was not responsible for his actions.

Pratt stated that Leutgert then virtually admitted that he killed his wife when he was possessed of the devil.

Pratt is quoted as saying that he regarded this admission as a professional secret and therefore did not feel at liberty to divulge it until after the death of Leutgert.

It is said that Leutgert also made similar admissions to a fellow prisoner.

THE YOUTHFUL BUT MURDEROUS CHICAGO BANDITS,

MARX, VAN DINE, NEIDEMEYER AND ROESKI.

During the months of July and August, 1903, a reign of terror prevailed in Chicago similar to that which prevailed in San Francisco shortly after the great earthquake when Seimsen and Dabner, the "gas pipe" thugs, were plying their vocation. The gang responsible for this condition consisted of four very young men named Gustave Marx, Harvey Van Dine, Peter Neidemeyer and Emil Roeski.

While this gang consisted of four members, there was no instance where less than two or more than three participated in any one crime.

Their criminal career began in 1901, when Neidemeyer, Van Dine and Marx stole some lead pipe from the Audubon School in Chicago, for which they were sent to the "Bridewell" jail for three months.

On the night of July 3, 1903, Neidemeyer and Roeski held up L. W. Lathrop and Martin Doherty while they were engaged in their duties at the Clybourn Junction station of the Chicago and Northwestern Railroad in Chicago. Lathrop offered resistance and was shot, but not fatally wounded. After obtaining $70 the bandits escaped.

On July 9, Marx, Van Dine and Roeski held up the saloon conducted by Ernest Spires at 1820 North Ashland Avenue. Roeski went into the saloon and ordered a glass of beer. At that time the proprietor and a young man named Otto Bauder were the only other persons in the place. Van Dine and Marx then entered and ordered them to throw up their hands. Bauder tried to escape but Roeski shot him in the back, inflicting a fatal wound. Less than $50 was taken from the proprietor and the bandits departed.

On the following night, Van Dine and Roeski entered Greenberg's saloon at Robey and Addison Streets, and after forcing the bartender, Louis Cohen, who was the only one in the saloon, into the large ice chest, they took $25 from the cash register and disappeared.

On the night of July 12, the same pair entered Charles Alvin's saloon at Sheffield Avenue and Roscoe Street, and after drawing their automatic revolvers, which they habitually displayed on such occasions, ordered the proprietor and four patrons to hold up their hands while one of the robbers searched them. About $125 was obtained and again the pair escaped.

On July 20, the same two entered Peter Gorski's saloon, located at 2611 Milwaukee Avenue. The proprietor, who was alone at the time of their entry, attempted to hide behind the bar, but was shot in the head, a serious but not fatal wound being inflicted. The robbers obtained less than $5 from the cash register and fled.

On the night of August 1, Van Dine and Neidemeyer entered the saloon conducted by Benjamin La Cross, located at 2120 West North Avenue, where the proprietor and Adolph Jennsen were playing a game of cards. Without the slightest provocation the blood-thirsty bandits opened fire, inflicting wounds from which both men died within twenty-four hours. Sixty-four dollars was obtained on this occasion.

About 3 a. m. on August 30, 1903, Marx, Van Dine and Neidemeyer approached the car barn of the Chicago Street Railroad Company at Sixty-first and State Streets. In the office of the company, William Edmund, Frank Stewart and Henry Biehl were engaged in balancing up the day's receipts, and J. Johnson, a motorman, was asleep in a chair in an adjoining room. Neidemeyer stopped at a side window of the office where he could observe all that transpired inside, while Marx and Van Dine, who carried a sledge hammer, proceeded to the entrance. The former pointed his automatic revolver through the receiving window at the occupants of the office and commanded them to throw up their hands, while Van Dine broke in the door with his sledge hammer, which was left in the office.

As the clerks attempted to defend the company's money, a fusillade of bullets was fired, both from the bandits in the office and from Neidemeyer, who fired through the window from the outside. On hearing the shots, motorman Johnson came into the room, the final result of the firing being that Stewart and Johnson were killed and Edmund and Biehl were seriously wounded. The bandits then gathered $2,250 and went to Jackson Park, where the money was divided.

In the early part of November, 1903, Assistant Chief Schuettler learned that Marx was a frequenter of numerous resorts on the west side, and although out of employment, he was spending money recklessly. It was also ascertained that while under the influence of liquor he exhibited an automatic revolver. Detectives John Quinn and William Blaul of the 42nd Precinct were detailed to locate and arrest this fellow.

On the night of November 21, 1903, he was located in Greenberg's saloon, the same place which Van Dine and Roeski held up on July 10. It was arranged that Blaul should enter the side door at the same instant Quinn entered the front door of the saloon. Marx saw them as they entered, and like a flash he fired at Quinn, killing him instantly. Blaul fired and slightly wounded Marx. The officer then leaped forward and overpowered the bandit before he had an opportunity to fire again. Marx was manacled and taken to jail, where Assistant Chief Schuettler subjected him to a severe examination. At first the thug was non-committal, but when he realized that he would probably hang for the murder of Quinn and believing that his companions had deserted him, he finally made a complete confession of the crimes committed by the gang, as heretofore related in this narrative.

In addition, it was learned that the sledge hammer used in the car barn robbery, which had a letter "N" burned in the handle, was stolen by Van Dine from the Northwestern railroad shops, where he was formerly employed.

Shortly after the confession was made, it became public property and the pictures of the missing bandits were obtained by the police and published in the papers.

Van Dine, Roeski and Neidemeyer then boarded a train and rode out into Indiana, where they took refuge in an abandoned cellar over which a house once stood. After spending a day and night in this cellar they proceeded to a country store conducted by Julius Scheurer at Clarks Station, on Thanksgiving Day, November 26, to replenish their supply of provisions. At this store was a school-teacher named Henry Reichers, who had seen the newspaper pictures of the bandits, and immediately recognized this trio as the men wanted by the authorities. This information was at once conveyed to the Chicago police, and Assistant Chief Schuettler detailed a posse, consisting of Detectives Joseph Driscoll, Mat. Zimmer and six others, to repair to the scene.

That night the officers located the abandoned cellar, but the bandits had fled. As it was dark the officers decided to rest until daylight at John Haynes' farmhouse, when they again took up the trail, which they had no difficulty in following through the snow. It led them to an old dugout made by railroad laborers near Miller Station.

The officers formed a semi-circle around the cave and called out to the bandits to surrender, but instead of doing so, Neidemeyer and Van Dine stuck their heads out of the hole and began a deadly fire with their automatic revolvers, Driscoll being mortally wounded and Zimmer receiving two serious wounds. As the detectives were entirely exposed to these expert shots, they were forced to retreat.

At this moment the bandits rushed out of the cave, firing as they ran; Neidemeyer and Roeski being wounded as they fled. They had only traveled a short distance when Roeski became exhausted and, leaving his companions, he cut across a field.

Van Dine and Neidemeyer then ran along the railroad track to a little station, where a locomotive was coupled to some cars. They climbed into the cab, where they found Engineer Coffey and Brakeman L. Scovia. With a display of revolvers, the bandits commanded them to uncouple the locomotive from the train and carry them down the track as fast as possible. Scovia attempted to grapple with Neidemeyer, who shot him in the head, killing him instantly. Seeing the folly of resisting, the engineer promptly obeyed their commands.

In the meantime the movements of the desperadoes had been telegraphed to all the way stations for miles around, and rapidly formed posses were prepared to give them a warm reception.

The locomotive bearing these bandits had only traveled a few miles when a locked switch compelled them to stop and return over the same track. When they had gone back a short distance they ordered Coffey to stop, and after admonishing him to render no assistance to their pursuers under pain of death, they started across the country.

A party of hunters, upon learning of what had transpired, took up the trail and chased the thugs into some marsh land. When the desperate pair saw that they could proceed no further, they turned and had about decided to fight to the end when the contents of a shotgun poured into Van Dine's face, blinded him with his own blood, and he proposed to Neidemeyer that they surrender. The latter acquiesced and the pair then informed the hunters of their decision, and after throwing up their hands, walked out to their captors.

In the meantime Chief O'Neil sent out heavy reinforcements in command of Assistant Chief Schuettler, who divided his men into squads and dispatched them in different directions. It was to one of these squads that the bandits were delivered by the hunters.

When Roeski left his two companions, he went to a railroad station named Aetna. His bravado having completely deserted him, he threw his pistol away and lay down on a bench in the station, where the officers finally located him and he surrendered without a struggle.

No effort was made by the Governor of Indiana to enforce the extradition laws and the trio were immediately taken back to Chicago, where they freely discussed their crimes, thereby corroborating the confession previously made by Marx.

The grand jury found indictments against the four men for their numerous crimes, and in the early part of January, 1904, Van Dine, Neidemeyer and Marx were tried for the car barn murders. They were found guilty and hanged on April 22, 1904.

On April 19 Neidemeyer attempted to commit suicide by severing the arteries in his arm with a lead pencil and swallowing the sulphurated ends of a quantity of matches. On the morning of the executions, his helpless condition made it necessary for the officials to carry him to the scaffold in a chair.

As Roeski did not participate in the car barn tragedy, he was tried for the murder of Otto Bauder during the saloon holdup on July 9, 1903. He was found guilty, but as some of the jurors had some doubt as to which bandit fired the fatal shot, he was sentenced to serve the remainder of his life at Joliet prison.

JOHANN HOCH, NOTORIOUS BIGAMIST AND MURDERER.

(From Chicago Police Records and Illinois Supreme Court decisions.)

Johann Hoch was born in Strasburg, Germany, in 1860. His father and two brothers were ministers in Strasburg, and Johann was educated for the ministry, but he abandoned the idea and came to the United States.

Under the name of John Schmidt, Hoch married a middle-aged woman named Caroline Streicher, in Philadelphia, on October 20, 1904, but eleven days later he disappeared, and on November 9 he registered at Mrs. Kate Bowers' hotel, 674 East Sixty-third Street, Chicago.

On November 16, he went to the Chicago City Bank to see Mr. Vail, the owner of a vacant cottage at 6225 Union Avenue, which Hoch desired to rent. Representing himself as holding a responsible position with Armour & Co., he succeeded in procuring the cottage in which he claimed he and his wife intended to reside.

On December 3, he published an advertisement in the Chicago Abend Post, a German paper, which read as follows:

"Matrimonial — German; own home; wishes acquaintance of widow without children; object, matrimony. Address M 422, Abend Post."

Marie Walcker, a hard-working woman about forty-six years of age, who had obtained a divorce from her first husband and was conducting a little candy store at 12 Willow Street, saw this advertisement and requested her sister, Mrs. Bertha Sohn, to prepare and forward a letter which read as follows:

"Dear Sir: — In answer to your honorable advertisement I hereby inform you that I am a lady standing alone. I am forty-six years and have a small business, also a few hundred dollars.

"If you are in earnest. I tell you I shall be. I may be seen at 12 Willow Street.

"Marie Walcker."

In response to the letter, Hoch called at the candy store on December 6, and during an extended conversation which followed he represented to Mrs. Walcker that his wife had been dead for two years; that he possessed $8,000, the cottage which he rented from Vail, and several vacant lots in the neighborhood of the cottage. He also claimed that his father, who lived in Germany, was 81 years of age and that when the old man died he would inherit $15,000.

It was .soon agreed by the couple that they were intended for each other, and Hoch became a constant visitor at the store for the next four days, at the expiration of which time the couple decided to marry at once. The license was therefore procured and the marriage ceremony performed.

The "bride" sold her store for $75, which she gave to Hoch along with her entire savings, amounting to $350, which he claimed he needed to prepare his home for occupancy, as his money was tied up at that time.

Mrs. Walcker-Hoch had a widowed sister named Mrs. Fischer, whom Hoch met shortly after his latest marriage, and whom he learned had $893 deposited in a savings bank.

A week after the marriage, Mrs. Walcker-Hoch became very ill, and on December 20 Dr. John Reese was called in. The woman complained of excruciating pains in the abdominal regions; she vomited freely; had a violent thirst and a tingling sensation in the extremities, which she described as similar to ants crawling through her flesh. The doctor diagnosed the trouble as nephritis and cystitis (Bright's disease and inflammation of the bladder).

Hoch sent for the sick woman's sister, Mrs. Fischer, who frequently assisted about the house. She mailed her picture to her sick sister, which Hoch received, and he wrote a letter acknowledging the receipt of it, in which he stated that he intended to keep the picture himself and carry it on his breast.

Shortly afterward he accompanied Mrs. Fischer from the sick chamber to a car, and en route he told her that if he had met her four weeks sooner he would have married her. Finally Hoch and Mrs. Fischer appeared to be so friendly that the sick woman became jealous, and Mrs. Fischer left the house in a rage but she soon returned.

On January 12, 1905, Mrs. "Hoch" died, and Dr. Reese certified that death was due to nephritis and cystitis.

Mrs. Fischer was at the house at the time, and a few moments after the death occurred Hoch proposed marriage to her. She protested that the proposal was a trifle too sudden, although she accompanied him to Joliet three days after the funeral, where they were clandestinely "married."

Hoch then suggested that the "honeymoon" be spent in Germany, reminding his "bride" of the advisability of visiting his "aged and wealthy father," but he added that before they took the trip he would need $1,000 to straighten out his business affairs in Chicago. The "bride" volunteered to come to his assistance and she drew $750 from the bank and delivered it to Hoch.

They then proceeded to 372 Wells Street, where the "bride" rented a flat and kept roomers previous to her marriage. At the door they were met by Mrs. Sauerbruch, who stated in an undertone that Mrs. Sohn, the sister who prepared the letter Mrs. Walcker sent to Hoch in answer to his advertisement, was in the rear of the house and had been denouncing Hoch as a murderer and swindler. The bigamist became greatly agitated and requested that he be left alone in the parlor while the two women went to the rear of the house to pacify Mrs. Sohn.

The women returned in a few moments but Hoch had disappeared. This move convinced the latest Mrs. Hoch that her sister's suspicions were well founded, and Inspector of Police George Shippy was notified.

The body of Mrs. Walcker-Hoch was exhumed and a post-mortem examination held, which resulted in the discovery of 7.6 grains of arsenic in the stomach and 1.25 grains in the liver. As there was no arsenic in any of the medicines prescribed by Dr. Reese nor in the embalming fluid, the authorities became convinced, in view of Hoch's conduct, that it was he who administered the poison. His picture was published in the papers and great publicity was given to the case.

On January 30, 1905, Mrs. Catherine Kimmerle, who conducted a boarding-house at 546 West Forty-seventh Street, New York, notified the police that a man giving the name of Henry Bartells, but whose actions and appearance tallied with Hoch's, was stopping at her place. Twenty minutes after he entered the house he volunteered to assist her in the kitchen by peeling potatoes, and the next day he proposed marriage, but the lady became frightened at his ardent manner of proposal.

The man was taken into custody, and after admitting that he was Hoch, claimed that he assumed the name of Bartells because of trouble he had with his sister-in-law regarding property.

When searched a fountain pen was found in his possession but there was no pen in the holder. A closer inspection revealed the fact that the reservoir contained fifty-eight grains of a powdered substance which the prisoner claimed was tooth powder, but when informed that the substance would be analyzed, he replied: "Well, it's no use; its arsenic which I bought with the intention of committing suicide."

He insisted that he did not have the arsenic in Chicago and gave the location of a drug store in New York where he purchased the pen and arsenic. The police visited the store and found that fountain pens were not sold there and that no arsenic had been sold to Hoch.

By the time the prisoner was returned to Chicago, Inspector Shippy had learned of the following women who were among Hoch's victims:

Mrs. Martha Steinbucher; married to Hoch in 1895 and died four months later. When this lady was dying she declared that she had been poisoned, but it was thought that she was delirious when she made the statement and no credence was placed in it. Hoch sold her property for $4,000 and disappeared.

Mary Rankin married Hoch in November, 1895, in Chicago, and he disappeared with her money on the following day.

Martha Hertzfield married him in April, 1896, and four months later Hoch disappeared with $600 of her money.

Mary Hoch married her namesake in August, 1896, at Wheeling, W. Va., and died shortly afterward.

Barbara Brossert married him on September 22, 1896, in San

Francisco, after a three days' courtship. This lady was a widow living at 108 Langton Street. Hoch married her under the name of Schmitt and disappeared two days afterward with $1,465 of her money. As this was Mrs. Brossert's life savings the loss so affected her that she died shortly afterward.

Hoch then took up lodgings at 30 Turk Street, in the same city, and immediately attempted to creep into favor with the landlady, Mrs. H. Tannert. After a few hours' acquaintance, he proposed marriage, but the lady refused the offer and Hoch left San Francisco.

Clara Bartel married Hoch in November, 1896, at Cincinnati, Ohio, and died three months later.

Julia Dose married this man in January, 1897, in Hamilton, Ohio, and on the day of her marriage Hoch disappeared with $700 of her money.

In April, 1898, he was arrested in Chicago for selling mortgaged furniture, and was sent to the house of correction for two years. After being liberated he began operations again as follows:

He married Anna Goehrke in November, 1901, and deserted her immediately.

Mrs. Mary Becker married Hoch on April 8, 1902, in St. Louis, and died in 1903.

Mrs. Anna Hendrickson married him on January 2, 1904, in Chicago, and eighteen days later the bridegroom disappeared with $500 of her money.

He married Lena Hoch in June, 1904, in Milwaukee, and she died three weeks later, leaving Hoch $1,500.

Then came the marriage to Caroline Streicker in Philadelphia and Mrs. Walcker and her sister, Mrs. Fischer, in Chicago, as previously related.

In addition to this list he had another wife in Germany.

On his return to Chicago from New York, Hoch was interrogated at length by Inspector Shippy and then five of his former "wives" were admitted to the room for the purpose of identifying the prisoner. When they caught sight of Hoch, it required considerable effort on the part of the officials to quiet them, as they were collectively expressing their opinion of the prisoner in most vigorous terms.

On February 23, the coroner's jury returned a verdict accusing Hoch of murdering Mrs. Walcker by means of arsenic poisoning. The case was then taken before the grand jury, where Hoch was indicted, and on May 5, 1905, he was placed on trial.

During the trial, Inspector Shippy testified that Hoch admitted to him that he had no love for any of his wives, and that when he advertised for them, he mentioned his preference for middle-aged women because it was easier to separate them from their money than younger women.

On May 19, Hoch was found guilty, and on June 3, the date for his execution was set for June 23.

He appealed to the Governor, who refused to interfere. On the day set for his execution, a Miss Cora Wilson, who conducted a furrier's store at 66 Wabash Avenue, Chicago, came to the rescue by advancing sufficient money to make it possible for an appeal to be taken to the Supreme Court, and the Governor consented to a postponement of the execution.

Miss Wilson claimed that she had never seen Hoch, but that she desired that he be given every opportunity to prove his innocence.

After reviewing the case the Supreme Court sustained the lower court, and the execution was then set for August 25, 1905. On August 24, he obtained another lease of life until the October session of the Supreme Court, but on December 16, this court again refused to interfere and the execution occurred on February 23, 1906.

MRS. BELLE GUNNESS, THE ARCHFIEND WHO REQUIRED A PRIVATE GRAVEYARD FOR HER NUMEROUS VICTIMS, BUT WHO WAS SUBSEQUENTLY MURDERED AND CREMATED WITH HER THREE CHILDREN.

Belle Paulsen was born in the little town of Christiania, Norway. Her father, Peter Paulsen, was a traveling conjurer and magician, and when Belle was a mere child she participated in the exhibitions by dancing on the tightrope.

They prospered and through their frugality they were enabled to retire when Belle was still in her teens, and the father purchased a little farm in their native land.

Belle then came to the United States, and about two years later she married a Swede named Albert Sorenson. They resided in Chicago, and in 1900 Sorenson died under most suspicious circumstances. While it was said that he died from heart failure, his relatives were positive that he was poisoned, and as a motive for the deed, pointed to the fact that the widow collected the life insurance of $8,500 as soon as possible after his death. It is stated that an inquest was ordered, but for some reason the body was never exhumed.

Mrs. Sorenson then moved to Austin, Ill., and a short time afterward her home there was burned. A question arose as to the origin of the fire, but in the absence of proof of fraud the insurance companies were forced to pay the insurance.

She then returned to Chicago, where she conducted a confectionery store at Grand Avenue and Elizabeth Street, which was subsequently gutted by fire. This mysterious fire resulted in another investigation by the insurance officials, but they were forced to pay her claim.

Shortly afterward she purchased a farm about six miles from La Porte, Indiana, and married Peter Gunness a few months later.

In 1904, a meat chopper is said to have fallen off a shelf and split his head open, thus ending his existence. The weeping widow described to the coroner's jury how it fell from a shelf and struck her "poor husband's head," and in the absence of proof to the contrary, the statement was accepted as true.

At the time of the death of Gunness, she had three small children, named Philip, Myrtle and Lucy. She also had an adopted daughter named Jennie Olsen, who was fourteen years of age.

In September, 1906, this girl disappeared, and Mrs. Gunness accounted for her absence by stating that she had sent her to Los Angeles to complete her education.

The woman then employed a man named Ray Lamphere to do the chores about the place. In 1906 she inserted an advertisement in the matrimonial columns of the leading papers of Chicago and other large cities, which read as follows:

> "Personal — Comely widow who owns a large farm in one of the finest districts in La Porte County, Indiana, desires to make acquaintance of a gentleman equally well provided, with view of joining fortunes. No replies by letter considered unless sender is

In May, 1907, Ole B. Budsburg, a rather elderly widower residing in Iolo, Wisconsin, saw the advertisement, and as it looked good to him he decided to make a nice, quiet investigation without telling his grown up sons, Oscar and Mathew, a word about it.

The poor old gentleman left his home but never returned, and the last seen of him was when he negotiated the sale of a mortgage at the La Porte Savings Bank and drew the money on April 6, 1907.

In December, 1907, Andrew Hegelein, a thrifty bachelor from Aberdeen, South Dakota, also corresponded with Mrs. Gunness. She replied that it would be advisable for him to come to the farm, and she suggested that he might sell out his business interests in South Dakota, as she was very favorably impressed with his letters.

As far as was convenient to do so, Hegelein, delighted with the headway he was making, complied with her request and repaired to her farm, arriving in January, 1908. He had been at Mrs. Gunness' place about two weeks when he accompanied her to the Savings Bank in La Porte and presented a check for $2,900, but as he was unknown there and as the bankers would not accept the endorsement of Mrs. Gunness for this amount, they left the check there for collection. In a few days the draft came and the money was delivered to him, which she must have obtained, for almost immediately afterward she deposited $500 in that bank, $700 in the State Bank, and also paid numerous large bills.

A few days later Hegelein disappeared, and Mrs. Gunness stated that he had drawn the money for the purpose of going to Norway. He had a brother named A. K. Hegelein in Aberdeen, South Dakota, and as the weeks rolled by and he heard nothing from his brother, he became alarmed and wrote to Mrs. Gunness regarding his whereabouts.

In her reply she stated that all the information she could impart was the missing man's own statement to the effect that he drew his money with the intention of going to Norway, but she expressed some apprehension over his failure to confide his plans to his brother, and she suggested in her letter that he sell out the remainder of his brother's stock along with his own, and come to her farm, so that she might join him in an extensive search.

At 3:30 a. m. on April 28, 1908, Mrs. Gunness' home was burned to the ground and in the ruins the charred remains of a woman and three children were found. The bodies of the little ones were at once identified as the remains of Mrs. Gunness' children, but as the woman's head was burned or cut off, there was some question as to whose remains they were.

Ray Lamphere, the farm hand, left her employ on February 3, 1908, because of a quarrel with Mrs. Gunness, and procured employment on a farm owned by John Wheatbrook, a short distance from the Gunness place.

After Lamphere left Mrs. Gunness, he frequently intimated that he could make it interesting for her if he wanted to talk, but her only response to this was that Lamphere was crazy.

As it was proven conclusively that he was on the ground at the time the fire started, he was taken into custody by Sheriff Smulzer.

The mysterious remarks made by Lamphere in regard to making trouble for Mrs. Gunness were recalled, and a most thorough investigation was instituted, with the result that five more mutilated and decomposed bodies were found buried in the back yard on May 5.

One was identified as the body of Jennie Olsen Gunness, the sixteen-year-old adopted daughter of Mrs. Gunness, who was supposed to be in Los Angeles completing her education. It is presumed that she was murdered because she knew too much regarding the death of Peter Gunness in 1904.

The second body was that of Andrew Hegelein from South Dakota. The third was the unidentified body of a man, and the fourth and fifth were the bodies of two eight-year-old girls. On May 6, four additional bodies of men were unearthed in the back yard.

In most instances the limbs were removed from the bodies in such a manner as to indicate that the amputations were performed by someone familiar with anatomy. The theory is that some of the bodies were too heavy for the woman to handle as a whole.

On May 9, two more bundles of bones, decayed flesh and clothing were found in the private graveyard, but the ravages of decomposition made identification impossible. On May 14, a few bones of one more victim were found in the ashes in the cellar.

In view of these discoveries a serious doubt arose as to the actual fate of Mrs. Gunness. It was suspected that in addition to murdering her children and several others, she had inveigled some unsuspecting woman into her home, and after killing her, disfigured her remains in such a manner that they could not be recognized, and after setting fire to the house, escaped; believing it would be taken for granted that the charred remains of the woman were those of herself and that no further search would be made for her. This theory proved incorrect, for on May 16 a lower jawbone was found in the ashes and was taken to Dr. Morton, a dentist in La Porte, for examination. Some dentistry work was plainly visible on the teeth which still adhered to the jawbone, which he positively identified as work done for Mrs. Gunness a year previously. Rings found on the fingers of the dead woman were also identified as the property of Mrs. Gunness.

There was a difference of opinion as to how Mrs. Gunness met her death. The theory of the prosecution was that she was burned to death, but Dr. J. Meyers gave it as his opinion that death was caused by contraction of the heart, probably due to strychnine poisoning, which was the poison used in killing Hegelein and several other victims.

Shortly after Mrs. Gunness' private graveyard was discovered, Oscar and Mathew Budsburg came to La Porte, as they suspected that their aged father, who had mysteriously disappeared from his home in Iolo. Wis., in May, 1907, might have fallen into this woman's trap. Their suspicions proved to be well founded, for they identified one of the bodies as that of their missing father,

Olof Lindboe of Chicago stated that his brother, Thomas, had worked for Mrs. Gunness three years previously, and the last letter he had received from him contained the information that Thomas intended to marry his employer. As Olof heard nothing more from his brother he wrote to Mrs. Gunness, who replied that Thomas had gone to St. Louis, but Olof never heard from him again.

On May 12, the surgical instruments with which the bodies were probably dismembered, were found in the ashes.

On May 19, Miss Jennie Graham of Waukesha, Wis., arrived in La Porte to inquire regarding her brother, who had left home to marry a rich widow in La Porte, but who was never heard from after that. As most of the bodies were badly mutilated and decomposed, it was impossible to ascertain if her brother's remains were among them.

Henry Gurholdt of Scandinavia, Wis., corresponded with Mrs. Gunness, and then took $1,500 with him to La Porte and was never seen again, but a watch found with one of the bodies was exactly the same in appearance as the one he wore.

Mrs. Marie Svenherud of Christiania, Norway, made inquiry through Acting Consul Faye of Chicago for her son Olof, who had written her that he was about to leave Chicago for La Porte to marry a rich Norwegian widow with whom he had become acquainted through the agency of the matrimonial advertisement column of a newspaper. The mother added that she never heard from her son again.

After the disappearance of Hegelein, Lamphere was seen wearing an overcoat which belonged to the former, and on May 18 a watch which was in the possession of Lamphere at the time of his arrest was identified by J. G. Ramden of Manfred, N. D. as the property of his half-brother, John Moe of Elbow Lake, Minn., who left his home in 1907, ostensibly to marry a widow in La Porte, but was never heard from afterward. Lamphere stated that Mrs.

Gunness had presented him with the watch.

When first interrogated as to his whereabouts on the night of the fire, Lamphere claimed that he was in the company of a negress named Mrs. Elizabeth Smith until 4 a. m., or one-half hour after the fire started, but he subsequently confessed that he burned the Gunness home but denied that he had committed murder.

Lamphere and a neighbor named Fred Brickman stated that they dug trenches for Mrs. Gunness at different times, but that they had no knowledge as to for what purpose they were used.

On May 22, 1908, Lamphere was indicted for the murder of the Gunness family by means of arson, and also on the charge of accessory in the murder of Hegelein. He pleaded guilty of arson and was sentenced to imprisonment for an indeterminate period of from two to twenty years. Immediately after his conviction Lamphere's health failed rapidly and he died from consumption on December 30, 1909.

On January 14, 1910, Rev. E. A. Schell made public a confession made by Lamphere shortly after his arrest, in which he admitted that he helped Mrs. Gunness to bury one of the victims and saw her chloroform another after felling him with a hatchet. He also confessed that he chloroformed the Gunness family, but claimed that Mrs. Smith, a negress with whom he had spent a portion of the night, assisted him, and that it was she who set the house on fire.

As there was no evidence to substantiate the charge against the negress she was never prosecuted. It is the opinion of Attorney Ralph Smith that the negress did not accompany Lamphere on this night.

———

THE MURDER OF CHIEF OF POLICE HENNESSEY IN NEW ORLEANS AND THE SUBSEQUENT KILLING OF ELEVEN SUSPECTS IN THE PRISON BY INDIGNANT CITIZENS OF NEW ORLEANS. — INTERNATIONAL COMPLICATIONS

PREVENTED BY THE PAYMENT OF AN INDEMNITY BY

THE UNITED STATES GOVERNMENT.

In the early part of 1890, an Italian named Provenzano, enjoyed a monopoly of the unloading of fruit and other profitable dock work in New Orleans. Another Italian named Matranga, who conducted a saloon, became envious of Provenzano and decided to procure a portion of this profitable business. He therefore gathered about him numerous adherents and it was decided to begin operations on a large scale.

The bitterest feeling arose between the two factions. One morning in July, Provenzano's men were en route to the dock in a wagon shortly before daybreak, when several assassins, armed with shotguns loaded with buckshot, waylaid them as they passed through a dark alley. Two men were killed and several were seriously wounded.

Chief of Police David C. Hennessey began a rigorous fight against those suspected of being implicated in this assassination, and in an interview stated that their arrest would occur shortly and that he had an abundance of evidence to convict them, not only of this outrage, but of numerous other depredations which had recently been committed.

About midnight on October 15, 1890, the Chief started to walk to his home on Girod Street, and when he turned into this Street from Basin Street, three men, who had been concealed in a doorway, jumped out and began firing at him. He was virtually riddled with bullets, but he succeeded in drawing his own pistol from, which he fired four shots, none of which took effect as far as is known.

The Chief died shortly after being wounded and as a result of the assassination the feeling against the lower class of Italians became so intense that they feared to venture out upon the Streets.

Among the eleven men arrested on suspicion of having participated in the murder was Antone Scaffide. On October 17, a young man named Joseph Duffy called at the jail and asked to see Scaffide. When the prisoner was brought before him, Duffy whipped out a revolver and fired at Scaffide, the bullet inflicting a painful but not serious wound in the neck. When asked his reason for committing the assault, he stated that he only wished there were more men like himself in New Orleans.

On December 22, several of the accused Italians were placed on trial and they pleaded not guilty. It was claimed that several of the jurors were either intimidated or corrupted. At any rate none of the defendants were convicted — much to the disgust of many of the citizens of New Orleans.

Believing that the trials throughout were a travesty of justice, several of the most prominent citizens concluded that the people must assume the authority which had been delegated to the courts. They therefore issued a call for a mass meeting at Clay Square at 10 a. m., on March 14, 1891, and it was suggested that those who responded should come prepared for action. At the appointed time several thousand persons congregated, and addresses were made by three of the leading lawyers of the city, who stated that the time had arrived when the people must administer justice themselves. They then proceeded to the arsenal, where shotguns and rifles were furnished. They then went to the prison. After sweeping the small force of police and deputy sheriffs aside, they commanded Captain Davis to open the door, but as he ignored the order the door was broken open by the use of axes and battering rams. The turnkey was relieved of his keys and the crowd then had access to the whole prison. The Italians who were confined in the prison awaiting a new trial, had been secreted in the female ward, but the crowd soon located them, and the prisoners crouched in the corners of the cells begging for mercy. Their cries fell on deaf ears, for they were riddled with bullets. One man named Pollize, after being killed was hanged from a window, as a warning to others.

The following is the list of those killed: Joseph Macheca, Manuel Pollize, Antonio Scaffidi, Antonio Bagnetto, Frank Romero, Lorenzo Comitz, Vincent Caruso, Antonio Marchesi, Charles Trahina, Rocca Geracci and Pietro Monasterio.

After these eleven men were killed, Attorney W. S. Parkerson advised the crowd to disperse, which they did, after carrying him on their shoulders to Clay Square.

Mayor Shakespeare of New Orleans, when asked if he regretted the killing of the Italians, is said to have replied as follows:

"No, sir; I am an American citizen and I am not afraid of the devil. These men deserved killing and they were punished by peaceable and law-abiding citizens. They took the law in their hands and we were forced to do the same."

For several days after the wholesale killing, Italians held indignation meetings throughout the country, and it was thought for a time that international complications would arise.

On April 3, the grand jury of New Orleans indicted two of the trial jurors in the Hennessey murder case on the charge of accepting bribes, and Dominick O'Malley, a private detective, Thomas McCrystal and four others were indicted for attempting to bribe jurymen. McCrystal made a confession in which he implicated O'Malley, but as his statement could not be corroborated, the charge against O'Malley was dismissed. McCrystal pleaded guilty.

No action was ever taken against those who participated in the killing of the Italian prisoners, but President Harrison's attention was called to the occurrence by representatives of the Italian government, and after a complete investigation of the matter, 125,000 francs was offered as an indemnity by the American government and accepted by the Italian government. This money was paid from a special fund carried in the Diplomatic Appropriation Bill, and was delivered to the heirs of the men killed.

―――――――

HISTORY OF THE CRIMINAL OF THE CENTURY, HERMAN W. MUDGETT, ALIAS . H. H. HOLMES, WHO MURDERED NUMEROUS PEOPLE, INCLUDING WOMEN AND CHILDRIN.

(From Detective Frank Geyer's History.)

Herman W. Mudgett was born in Gilmantown, N. H., on May 16, 1860, but spent his boyhood days on a farm near Burlington, Vt.

He was extremely bright, ambitious and studious, and at the age of sixteen years he became a school teacher.

On July 4, 1878, at the age of eighteen, he married Clara A. Lovering at Alton, N. H., and about this time he gave up his position as a school teacher to enable him to take a course in a medical school at Burlington, Vt.

A year later he finished his course at this school and then went to Ann Arbor College, Michigan, to complete his education.

In 1881, Mudgett gained possession of a body that bore a remarkable resemblance to a fellow student who was his closest friend and who had taken out a life insurance policy for $1,000 a short time previously, in which Mudgett was named as beneficiary.

This put an idea into the heads of the two students. They surreptitiously placed this body in the bed of Mudgett's friend, who immediately disappeared.

There was evidently little or no investigation made regarding the case, as Mudgett collected the insurance without trouble, and presumably divided it with his "dead" chum.

Shortly after this Mudgett left college, and under the name of Holmes procured a position at an insane asylum in Norristown, Pa.

After six months he left this position and proceeded to Philadelphia, where he procured employment as a drug clerk.

He next went to Chicago, where he opened a drug store of his own. Continuing to use the name of Holmes he married Miss Myrta Belknap, in Chicago, on January 28, 1887, thus committing bigamy.

On January 17, 1894, under the name of Howard, he again married in Denver, Miss Georgie Yoke, of St. Louis, being the victim.

Before marrying Miss Yoke, Holmes traveled about the country under numerous assumed names, engaging in various enterprises, none of which would bear investigation. He accumulated considerable money and constructed a four-story building at the corner of Sixty-third and Wallace Streets in Chicago, which was known as "Holmes Castle."

About 1889 Holmes met Benjamin F. Pitezel in Chicago, who was afterward suspected of being Holmes' partner in many crimes.

At that time Pitezel's family, consisting of a wife and four small children, named Dessie, Alice, Nellie and Howard, lived in St. Louis.

Holmes was a man of medium height and build. He was immaculate in appearance, suave in manners and as this narrative will show, fiendish in disposition.

Pitezel was a mesmeric subject, and Holmes, being possessed of hypnotic powers, discovered this fact, and thereafter Pitezel was so much clay in his hands.

On November 9, 1893, Pitezel took out a $10,000 life insurance policy from the Fidelity Mutual Life Association of Philadelphia, which was made payable to his wife.

Holmes, knowing this, suggested to Pitezel and his wife that Pitezel go to Philadelphia, and under the assumed name of B. F. Perry, open up an office and put up a sign "Patents Bought and Sold."

Holmes stated that he would then institute a search among

hospitals or medical colleges and find a body having features and physique similar to Pitezel. The body would be surreptitiously placed in the establishment and laid in such a position as to so clearly indicate that death had resulted from an accidental explosion that no questions would be asked. Pitezel would disappear and Mrs. Pitezel's fourteen-year-old daughter, Alice, would journey to Philadelphia and identify the remains as those of her father. The insurance money would be paid without question, and then Pitezel would quietly return to his family. Mrs. Pitezel offered strenuous objections to the plan, but Holmes commanded Pitezel to do his bidding, and the result was that on August 17, 1894, Pitezel opened his office at 1316 Callowhill Street and put out his sign as directed.

On June 15, 1894, while Holmes, then known as Howard, was in St. Louis arranging details for his latest scheme, he purchased a drug store, upon which he gave a mortgage. Shortly afterward he sold this mortgaged property, and on July 19 he was arrested on a charge of obtaining money by false pretenses in connection with this sale.

While in jail he met Marion Hedgspeth, who, with three others, robbed a train near St. Louis in 1891, and was captured in San Francisco. (See history of Marion Hedgspeth.) Holmes asked Hedgspeth if he knew of any slick lawyer.

The train robber recommended him to J. D. Howe, of St. Louis, and Holmes then foolishly unfolded his whole scheme in regard to Pitezel, to Hedgspeth, and told him that he would give him $500 for his services if the plan worked.

On July 31 Holmes was released on bail furnished by his third "wife." A few days after being released he proceeded to Philadelphia, where he met Pitezel, alias Perry, and on August 17, the day on which the latter opened his office in Callowhill Street. Holmes accompanied him to a secondhand furniture store located at 1037 Buttonwood Street, and assisted him in selecting furniture.

On August 22 a carpenter named Eugene Smith, who was of an inventive turn of mind, passed this office, and being attracted by the sign, stepped in to discuss the merits of a set-saw he had invented and desired to put on the market. "Perry" listened attentively to his description of the invention and asked him to bring a model the next day. Smith complied with the request, and after an examination of it. Perry predicted heavy sales.

On Monday, September 3, Smith called to ascertain how his device was selling. "Perry" was not in the office, but his hat and coat were there, and Smith, believing he had stepped out for a few moments, waited until he became impatient and left. He returned the next day and again saw no one, but observed that the coat and hat were in the same position. He then made inquiry in the neighborhood and learned that "Perry" had not been seen since Saturday.

His suspicions being aroused he decided to investigate. As "Perry" occupied both floors of the small two-story building, Smith proceeded upstairs, and in a back room he found the mutilated body of Perry. The breast and side of the face were badly burned; fragments of a large bottle were found near the corpse, and a tobacco pipe and burned match were also found.

The body was removed to the morgue, and after lying there until September 13 without being claimed, it was buried in the potter's field.

On September 19 Attorney Howe called on Mrs. Pitezel in St. Louis and informed her that her husband was dead, and requested that the fourteen-year-old daughter Alice accompany him to Philadelphia for the purpose of identifying the remains. Mrs. Pitezel then signed a paper prepared by Howe, which gave him power of attorney to collect the money, and he left with Alice, Mrs. Pitezel believing that the child would be instructed to identify the body of a stranger and that her husband was alive and well.

On September 21 Howe, Alice, Holmes and Smith, who discovered the body, called at the Philadelphia office of the insurance company, and after Smith was interrogated the party proceeded with the insurance officials to disinter the remains. Holmes explained that he was a close friend of the Pitezel family and knew that Pitezel was located at 1316 Callowhill Street, under the assumed name of Perry, because of financial troubles in Fort Worth.

When the body was exposed, Alice Pitezel and Holmes immediately identified the remains as those of Pitezel. While the cause of Pitezel's death was not perfectly clear to the insurance officials, they concluded that the large bottle which was found broken by his side contained some inflammable substance which exploded as the victim was evidently in the act of lighting his pipe.

Against this theory it was argued that the body reclined in a peaceful attitude and the stomach when opened gave forth a distinct odor of chloroform.

At any rate, the insurance money was paid to Howe, who proceeded to St. Louis and paid Mrs. Pitezel the $10,000, less $2,800 deducted for expenses.

As Alice did not accompany Howe, Mrs. Pitezel anxiously inquired as to her whereabouts, but the attorney assured her that Holmes would see that she was well provided for. A few days after this Holmes visited Mrs. Pitezel, who begged piteously to be taken forthwith to her husband and child.

Holmes told her that she must be patient, as the insurance officials were suspicious of the entire transaction and that he considered it advisable for the family to remain separated for the present; in fact, he stated that he had come to get the two smaller children, Nellie and Howard, and take them to Covington, Ky., where a nice old lady was caring for Alice.

Mrs. Pitezel made strenuous objections to this plan, but after some argument Holmes persuaded her to consent to their going.

The monster then produced a note on which he stated that he and Mr. Pitezel had obtained $16,000 from Attorney Samuels in Fort Worth, and in order to save their property there a portion of the amount must be forwarded immediately.

In this manner he obtained $7,000 from her, and after instructing her to proceed to the home of her parents in Galva, Ill., he departed on September 28 with the two children, after promising that the entire family would be reunited at the earliest possible moment.

At this time Alice was in the keeping of a lady in Covington, Ky., and at Holmes' request she wrote a cheerful letter to her mother in which she spoke of the kind treatment accorded her. This greatly increased Mrs. Pitezel's confidence in Holmes, and she ceased to regret parting with the other two children.

Immediately after the letter was forwarded, Holmes had Alice meet him and the other two children in Indianapolis, and from thence they journeyed to Cincinnati.

He left Cincinnati on October 1 with the three children and proceeded to Indianapolis, where he put the children in the Circle Hotel and then met Miss Yoke and stopped with her at another hotel in the neighborhood. This lady believed herself to be Holmes' lawful wife and knew nothing of his misdeeds.

He represented that he was endeavoring to place a patent copier on the market with which he expected to make a fortune, and that his mysterious journeys were in connection with this business. He planned so that Miss Yoke never met the children.

The next day Holmes took Alice and Nellie to Detroit, but little Howard had mysteriously disappeared. Holmes wrote for Mrs. Pitezel to bring the baby and Dessie to Detroit, where they were to meet Mr. Pitezel. Holmes and his "wife" stopped at one hotel, the two girls at another, and when Mrs. Pitezel arrived she stopped at Geis's hotel, a very short distance from the New Western, where Alice and Nellie were staying, under the name of Canning, that being the name of their grandparents.

Holmes instructed the children to remain in their room, and when he met Mrs. Pitezel he stated that an investigation had been instituted and he deemed it necessary to delay the reunion of the family. As to the investigation, Holmes unconsciously spoke the truth.

It will be recalled that he promised to pay Marion Hedgspeth $500 if the insurance swindle was consummated, but as time rolled by and Marion saw nothing of the money, he decided to turn informer for two reasons: First, to get revenge, and second, to gain the good will of those who might be able to assist him. So on October 9 he wrote a letter to Chief of Police Harrigan, of St. Louis, wherein he exposed the entire scheme, but of course he did not believe that Pitezel was dead.

On October 18 Holmes took his "wife" and Nellie and Alice Pitezel to Toronto, Canada, he and his wife stopping at the Walker House under the name of Howell, and the children were registered at the Albion under the name of Canning, as in Detroit.

Mrs. Pitezel was instructed by Holmes to leave on October 19 for Toronto, with Dessie and the baby, and if he deemed it safe she could there join the remainder of the family. By this time the poor woman was almost insane from grief, as she began to fear the worst. She asked Holmes to allow her husband to write to her, but he stated that the authorities might intercept the letters.

Holmes called on Mrs. Pitezel in Toronto and told her it was impossible to reunite the family at that time, and he sent her with Dessie and the baby, Wharton, to Ogdensburg, N. Y., and thence to Burlington, Vt., where Holmes rented a house at 26 Winooski Avenue, where he intended to murder the remainder of the family, but fortunately the opportunity did not present itself. (After the family left this house a large bottle of chloroform was found in the cellar, where it had been left by Holmes.)

The mother now began to lose hope of ever seeing her husband and three children again, and she finally returned to her relatives in Galva, Ill.

Pleading urgent business, Holmes left Miss Yoke about November 1 and went to Gilmantown, where he remained with his legal wife until November 17, when he went to Boston. The detectives got on his trail while he was at his old home and traced him to Boston, where he was arrested on November 19. His effects were searched, and several letters were found which had been written by the Pitezel children to their mother.

Holmes believed that the authorities either suspected him of having substituted a body, falsely claiming it was Pitezel's, or wanted him for horse stealing in Texas.

Having in mind the manner in which horse thieves were frequently punished in Texas he immediately stated that he had defrauded the insurance company by swearing the body found in Callowhill Street was

Pitezel's, when, as a matter of fact, he stated, Pitezel had left America with his three children.

He expressed a willingness to return to Philadelphia and plead guilty to the insurance swindle charge, providing he was not turned over to the Texas authorities. As he made a statement in which he claimed Mrs. Pitezel was a party to the fraud, she was arrested and brought to Boston with Dessie and the baby. Mrs. Pitezel was subjected to a severe cross-examination, but at its conclusion the authorities were convinced that she was innocent. However, on November 19 Mrs. Pitezel and Holmes were taken to Philadelphia as prisoners, the two children and Miss Yoke accompanying the party. It was June 3, 1895, before Holmes was brought to trial for defrauding the insurance company. He willingly pleaded guilty.

At this time several months had elapsed since either Pitezel or his three children had been heard from, and the authorities were becoming convinced that Holmes was guilty of far worse crimes than defrauding an insurance company by substituting a body. They strongly suspected that he was guilty of at least four murders.

As Pitezel was suspected of having an intimate knowledge of Holmes' criminal career, it can be seen that his desire to permanently seal Pitezel's lips was only equaled by his desire to obtain the bulk of his life insurance. Mrs. Pitezel would eventually realize this, and if her husband was not returned to her she would inform the authorities, with the result that the body in the potter's field would be subjected to a closer examination, which would mean that Holmes would probably be charged with the murder of Pitezel.

The older children were probably informed by their mother of the insurance swindle and were assured that their father would return, and of course children talk. The officers assumed that Holmes realized all this and that he decided that his safety was assured only after the entire family was disposed of. He could not hope to kill six people at once without being detected, so he decided to separate them and murder them one by one.

On December 27, 1894, Holmes made another statement substantially as follows:

"I regret that I have made false statements in the past, but the following are the facts:

"While Pitezel was at 1316 Callowhill Street he drank very heavily, and I took him to task about it. He appeared to be despondent and said that he had better drink enough to kill himself and have done with it all. The next morning I visited his place, and using a key I entered the building. I found a letter addressed to me, which

I destroyed, in which he said I would find his body upstairs. I went upstairs and found him lying dead on the floor. There was a rubber tube in his mouth which was attached to a quill run through a cork in a large bottle containing chloroform.

"I had arranged with Pitezel that the body substituted for his should be burned about the face and hands by pouring a mixture of benzene, chloroform and ammonia on it and then setting it on fire; that a large bottle was then to be broken and a smoking pipe and burned match placed nearby; the object being to show that the person supposed to be Pitezel or Perry, had actually ignited the mixture in the bottle while lighting the pipe, and that the bottle exploded and death was caused by the burns. Seeing Pitezel's body, I decided to carry out this plan in all its details. The three children are now in Europe in the custody of Miss Minnie Williams, formerly of Fort Worth, Texas."

It was easily proved that Holmes told the truth regarding the identity of the dead man found in Callowhill Street, but the remainder of the statement was not believed.

It was now clear that Holmes was not guilty of substituting a body, and action regarding that case was postponed, pending a further search for the missing children.

The District Attorney then looked about for a detective possessed of sufficient ability and determination to undertake this gigantic task, and he decided upon Frank Geyer, of the Philadelphia Police Department.

As eight months had elapsed since the children were last seen, and as it was probable that persons who had seen them had forgotten their faces, it can be readily understood that the obstacles confronting this officer were apparently insurmountable.

On June 26, 1895, he started out with photographs of Holmes and the three children.

He proceeded to Cincinnati and began visiting the hotels. When he reached the Hotel Bristol at Sixth and Vine Streets, the clerk identified the pictures as those of a man and three children who registered under the name of Cook.

It was the detective's theory that Holmes had murdered the children in some house in the suburbs of some city, so he began to make rounds of the real estate offices, both in the city and in the suburbs. When he arrived at the office of J. C. Thomas, at 15 East Third Street, the clerk recognized the picture of Holmes and Howard Pitezel, and it was learned that Holmes had rented a house at 305 Poplar Street, where he only remained two days. Geyer proceeded there and interviewed a Miss Hill who resided next door.

She saw Holmes moving an immense stove into the house, but no furniture.

The singular incident so impressed her that she unconsciously watched the proceeding very closely. Holmes observed this and decided to change his plans, but before leaving the house with Howard he offered the stove to the "inquisitive" lady.

Geyer then proceeded to Indianapolis and visited the hotels and real estate offices. He gathered valuable information as to the route taken by the children from the letters which they wrote to their mother, but which Holmes withheld and foolishly kept in his possession.

Here Mr. Herman Ackelow was located, and he at once identified the pictures of the children as those of guests who stopped with him when he conducted the Circle House. He also stated that the children were held in their room practically as prisoners, and although they were constantly crying, they refused to state the cause of their grief. In a letter written by Alice to her mother just after they left Indianapolis, and which was found in Holmes' pocket when arrested, the girl innocently remarked that "Howard" (meaning her brother) "is not with us now."

This convinced Geyer that the child had been murdered in or near Indianapolis, but he failed to obtain any clew at that time upon which to work.

The detective then proceeded to "Holmes Castle" in Chicago, but he learned nothing there regarding the Pitezel children. He then proceeded to Detroit and found that on October 12 Nellie and Alice Pitezel were registered at the New Western Hotel, but neither Howard nor the trunk were seen there.

Thinking that Holmes might have had Howard and the trunk with him, Geyer proceeded to learn where Holmes stopped, and found that he and Miss Yoke were registered as "G. Howell and wife" at the Normandie, but as neither the boy nor the trunk were seen at this place the detective became more convinced than ever as to where little Howard met his fate. But intent on tracing the girls first, Geyer proceeded to Toronto, Canada, where Mrs. Pitezel next met Holmes.

He arrived on Monday, July 8, and found that Holmes and Miss Yoke registered on October 18, 1894, at the Walker House, under the name of Howell and wife, and that the children were registered at the Albion Hotel under the name of Canning. Herbert Jones, the chief clerk of this hotel, stated that on October 25 Holmes called for the children, paid their bill and they were never seen again.

As it was known that Holmes went to his first wife in Gilmantown a few days after this, Geyer became convinced that the fiend had rented a house in Toronto for the purpose of murdering the two girls.

He prepared a list of all real estate agents and had the newspapers publish the pictures of the children and print his theories.

He then began a canvas of the real estate offices, which lasted for days, but nothing was accomplished. Finally Greyer learned that a Mrs. Frank Nudel had rented a house at No. 16 Vincent Street, in October, 1894, to a man who only remained there a few days and acted quite mysteriously. He immediately proceeded to the house, but when he reached the house located at No. 18 Vincent Street he showed the pictures of Holmes and Alice to Mr. Thomas Ryves, who resided there, and that gentleman instantly recognized them as the photographs of a man and girl who were at the house next door for a day and then disappeared.

Mr. Ryves furthermore stated that this man borrowed a spade from him, saying he wanted to plant some potatoes.

On receiving this information Geyer hurried to the home of Mrs. Nudel, and when he showed the lady and her daughter Holmes' picture and asked them if they had ever seen the man, they instantly replied that it was the picture of the man who rented their Vincent Street property. Geyer's enthusiasm now knew no bounds. He rushed back to No. 18 Vincent Street and borrowing the same shovel Holmes had used, proceeded to the next house. No. 16, where a family named Armbrust was then living.

After hurriedly making known his mission the lady told him to proceed with his investigation.

He examined the house, and on raising the linoleum in the kitchen he discovered a trap door which led to a dark cellar.

He procured a light, and after examining the ground he found a spot which appeared to have been recently disturbed. He had only been digging a minute or two when a terrible odor arose which became more horrible with each shovelful of dirt removed. He finally unearthed what was apparently the arm of a child, but as the flesh fell from the bones he decided that great caution would be necessary or the bodies would fall to pieces. So Undertaker Humphreys was called in and the digging proceeded, with the result that the terribly decomposed bodies of Nellie and Alice Pitezel were found.

While the features of the children could not be recognized, the clothing and hair were readily identified by the heartbroken mother, who started for Toronto as soon as she was advised of the discovery. To make "assurance doubly sure," Geyer located a family named McDonald, who moved into the house after Holmes left, and they found a wooden egg, from which, when parted in the middle, a little "snake" would spring out, Mrs. Pitezel recognized this as a toy she had purchased for her little girls.

These bodies were entirely nude when found, and the clothing spoken of above was taken from the dead children by Holmes and stuffed up in the chimney in the parlor with some straw and set on fire, but as they did not burn, the chimney was left in a clogged condition, and Mrs. Armbrust on examining it found the clothes and fortunately did not dispose of them.

It is perhaps needless to say that Holmes' object in removing and destroying the clothes was to prevent the bodies from being identified.

On July 19, after the burial of the Pitezel children in Toronto, Geyer proceeded to Detroit, where he learned that Holmes had rented a house at 241 East Forest Avenue, and an investigation showed that he had dug a grave in the cellar, but before he had an opportunity to complete his work information reached him that detectives were on his trail, and he abandoned his plans for the time being.

Geyer left Detroit on July 23 and returned to Indianapolis to search for little Howard Pitezel's body.

For days and days he made a tireless round of the real estate offices both in the city and for miles out into the suburbs.

On August 1 he went to Chicago, as a child's skeleton had been found at "Holmes Castle," but Geyer became convinced that this was the remains of some other unfortunate child, and in a few days he returned to Indianapolis. The search now included all the small towns within a radius of several miles from the city. After nearly a month's work no place remained unsearched but the pretty little town of Irvington, about six miles from Indianapolis. In this town Mr. Geyer, who was now almost exhausted, wearily made his way to the real estate office of an elderly man named Brown. After relating his story and showing his pictures hundreds of times, after weeks of fruitless labor and nights of restless sleep, Geyer again related his story and showed his pictures of Holmes.

The old man adjusted his glasses and finally remarked that it was the picture of a man who rented a house from him in October, 1894.

As the house belonged to a Dr. Thompson, who had seen the tenant, Geyer, who had now taken a new lease of life, hurried to him, and the doctor not only identified the picture as a likeness of his tenant, but told the detective that a boy in his employ named Elvet Moorman had seen this man with a boy at the house.

When interviewed Elvet immediately identified the pictures of Holmes and little Howard.

He stated that his duty compelled him to go and milk a cow every afternoon, which was kept in a lot in the rear of the house Holmes rented, and that while so engaged Holmes asked him to help him put up a stove when he had finished milking.

The boy complied with the request, and while assisting Holmes he asked him why he did not use a gas stove instead of a coal stove, and Holmes replied that "gas was not healthy for children." Little Howard was present when this remark was made.

Geyer then proceeded to the vacant cottage, which was across the Street from a Methodist church. He searched the house from cellar to roof and discovered nothing. He then looked through the lattice work between the piazza floor and the ground and saw some pieces of an old trunk.

He broke in after this and found that in one place on the remains of the trunk a piece of blue calico had been pasted, and on this calico was the figure of a flower. As the earth appeared to have been disturbed Geyer began digging with a vengeance, but all in vain.

He then proceeded to the barn, and there found an immense coal stove. As it was growing late Geyer quit for the night, with the intention of resuming the search in the morning. Mrs. Pitezel was then with her folks in Galva, Ill, and Geyer telegraphed this query: "Did missing trunk have blue calico with white flower over seam on bottom?" and the answer was, "Yes."

When Geyer left the cottage, two boys named Walter Jenny and Oscar Kettenbach, who knew of Geyer's mission, decided to "play detective." They began looking for evidence in the cottage and ran their busy hands into a stovepipe hole in the chimney in the basement. They brought out a handful of ashes, but in those ashes were several teeth and small pieces of bone. While Geyer was still in the telegraph office at Irvington he was informed of this discovery, and rushed back to the cottage.

Procuring a hammer and chisel he tore down the lower part of the chimney and found almost a full set of child's teeth, several pieces of human bone and a large charred mass which proved to be a portion of a child's stomach, liver and spleen, baked hard.

The corner grocer then came forward and announced that the boy, whose picture Geyer showed him, came to his store in October and left his coat there, saying that he would call for it, but never returned.

Mrs. Pitezel was again sent for and she identified the coat as one belonging to little Howard.

Geyer then located Albert Schiffling, who conducted a shop at 48 Virginia Avenue, Indianapolis, and he stated that on October 3 Holmes, accompanied by little Howard, called on him and left some surgical instruments to be sharpened. But the child little realized that they were being sharpened for the purpose of dismembering his body so that it could be cremated in the stove afterward set up.

A coroner's jury, after hearing the evidence, had no hesitancy in rendering a verdict to the effect that Howard Pitezel was murdered by Holmes.

On September 1, 1895, Detective Geyer returned to Philadelphia, and after being congratulated on all sides for unraveling one of the greatest mysteries in criminal history in America, he proceeded to bring the archfiend to justice.

Holmes having been indicted for the murder of Benjamin Pitezel, the trial was set for October 28. While Detective Geyer was engaged in locating missing members of the Pitezel family, the authorities in Chicago, Fort Worth, Texas, and numerous other cities were investigating Holmes' career previous to the death of Pitezel.

When the officials inspected "Holmes Castle" at Sixty-third and Wallace Streets in Chicago, they were astounded at the elaborate preparations made by this criminal to trap his victims and dispose of their remains right in the heart of a great city.

This structure was a four-story brick building covering a lot about 50x120 feet. The lower floor was occupied by stores, a drug store being on the corner; the outside rooms of the three upper stories having square bay windows and were arranged into apartments and offices, with the exception of that part used by Holmes in connection with his human slaughter-house. His rooms were on the second floor, and in his office was a vault from which neither air nor sound could escape when the door was closed.

From his bathroom, which had no windows and no means of lighting, unless an artificial light was brought in, was a secret stairway leading to the basement, and in order to reach this stairway the rug in the bathroom was raised, and there was found a trap door. The laboratory on the third floor was connected with the cellar in a similar manner. There was no other means of reaching this particular part of the cellar except by these secret stairs.

In this cellar was a large grate with a removable iron covering in front, and under this grate was a large firebox. In an ash pile in the corner several small pieces of burned human bone were found, and in the center of the room was a long dissecting table, upon which was found blood and indentures from surgical instruments.

On July 24, 1895, Detectives Fitzpatrick and Norton, of the Chicago police, began a systematic search for evidence of crime committed by Holmes in this building. They dug up the cellar, and buried in quicklime they found seventeen ribs, three sections of vertebrae of the spinal column and several teeth attached to the upper portion of a jaw bone. A part of a child's cape coat, which was decayed and lime-eaten, and a woman's garment thoroughly saturated with blood and brown with age were also found. These discoveries were all taken to Dr. C. P. Stingfield, and after a microscopical examination he declared that the stains on the woman's garment were human blood and that the bones were portions of the anatomy of children from eight to fourteen years of age. In one of his numerous statements Holmes claimed that the Pitezel children had gone to Europe in care of a Miss Minnie Williams. This resulted in an investigation as to the identity of Miss Williams, and also resulted in two more murders being charged to Holmes.

Miss Williams entered Holmes' employ as a stenographer in 1893. At this time he was at the head of the so-called "Campbell Yates Manufacturing Company," with "offices" in the castle.

Learning that she and her sister, Nettie, owned a valuable piece of land in Fort Worth, Texas, he professed love to Miss Minnie, and it is said that they lived as man and wife in the castle. In the later part of 1893 Minnie, at Holmes' request, wrote to Nettie that she was about to be married, and requested Nettie, who was a teacher in an academy at Fort Worth, to proceed to Chicago at once to attend the wedding.

Nettie arrived in Chicago shortly afterward, but within a short time both girls mysteriously disappeared and were never seen again.

In February, 1894, Pitezel, under the name of Lyman, proceeded to Fort Worth from Chicago and placed a deed on record from one Bond to Lyman for a valuable piece of ground at Second and Rusk Streets.

"Bond" was supposed to have obtained the title from Minnie Williams. On this property "Lyman" began erecting a building, and shortly afterward, Holmes alias "Pratt," appeared on the scene.

Their business affairs became badly muddled and they left town before the building was completed, but not before Holmes stole a horse and engaged in numerous other shady transactions.

On July 19, 1895, the police made another search of the Castle and found more charred bones, several metal buttons and part of a watch chain. C. E. Davis, who formerly conducted a jewelry store in the Castle, identified the watch chain as belonging to Minnie Williams, and also stated that he repaired it on two occasions. He furthermore stated that he had seen Minnie Williams wearing a dress on which were buttons similar to those found.

On August 4 Detective Fitzpatrick found Minnie Williams' trunk in Janitor Pat. Quinlan's room in the Castle, a clumsy effort having been made to paint over her initials on the trunk.

When confronted with this evidence Holmes denied having killed the Williams girls, but he related a weird tale about Minnie attacking and killing her sister Nettie, and to protect Minnie, whom he claimed to love, he advised her to go to Europe, and he carried Nettie's body to the lake and sank it.

In 1880 I. L. Connor, a jeweler, married a beautiful eighteen-year-old girl named Smythe, in Davenport, Iowa. About one year afterward a little daughter was born. This child was named Gertrude. In 1889 Connor moved with his family to Chicago and he obtained employment in Holmes' drug store, which was located in the Castle.

Mrs. Connor was still a beautiful woman, and being possessed of considerable business ability, Holmes consulted with her about several of his schemes, and they became quite confidential. Differences arose between Connor and his wife, with the result that he left, but Mrs. Connor and Gertrude remained at Holmes Castle.

In 1892 both Mrs. Connor and Gertrude disappeared. While in prison in Philadelphia, Holmes was interrogated as to their fate, and he stated that Mrs. Connor died from an operation, but that he did not know what became of Gertrude.

On August 2, 1895, some of Mrs. Connor's wearing apparel was found in the castle and identified by her husband. On this same day Janitor Pat. Quinlan and his wife confessed that they saw the dead body of Mrs. Connor in the Castle. On July 22, 1895, A. Minier, a nephew of Mrs. Connor, swore to a warrant charging Holmes with her murder.

Her father, A. Smythe, produced a letter supposed to have been written by her in November, 1892, wherein she stated that she contemplated going to St. Louis. Smythe stated that the writing was a poor imitation of his daughter's penmanship.

In 1892 Holmes was president of the A. B. C. Copying Company, which also had offices in the Castle, and Miss Emily Cigrand was employed by him as a stenographer. She was formerly employed in a similar capacity at the hospital at Dwight, Ill., where Pitezel, under the name of Phelps, was being treated for a time. She was dismissed from this position and Pitezel recommended her to Holmes.

She and Holmes became very intimate, and were known as Mr. and Mrs. Gordon where they had apartments near the corner of Ashland Avenue and West Madison Street. Miss Cigrand made a practice of writing several times a week to her parents, who resided in Oxford, Ind., but after December 6, 1892, they never heard from her again.

Holmes was suspected of having murdered several other persons with whom he had business dealings and who suddenly disappeared, but as the evidence against him in these cases is by no means conclusive, no details are given.

On July 28 Charles M. Chappell, of 100 Twenty-ninth Street, Chicago, reported to Lieutenant Thomas, of the Cottage Grove Station, that he worked for Holmes as a "handy man" during the summer of 1892. On October 1 Holmes asked him if he could mount a skeleton. Chappell said he thought he could, and Holmes gave him the skeleton of a man to mount, and when the work was completed Holmes paid him $36.

In January, 1893, Chappell was given another skeleton of a man to mount. When Holmes first showed him the body it was in the laboratory and there was considerable flesh on it. As Holmes had a set of surgical instruments and a tank filled with fluid for removing the flesh and apparently made no attempt to conceal anything from him, Chappell thought he was doing the work for some medical college.

In June, 1893, Holmes gave Chappell another skeleton to mount, but as he never called for it Chappell turned it over to the police on the day he made these disclosures.

On October 28, 1895, the trial of Holmes for the murder of Benjamin Pitezel began in Philadelphia. The work of selecting jurors had hardly begun when Holmes had a misunderstanding with his attorneys and they temporarily withdrew from the case. Holmes personally conducted the examination during their absence.

It was the theory of the prosecution that Holmes chloroformed Pitezel while the latter was either asleep or intoxicated. Three physicians testified that the death was caused by chloroform poisoning.

Mrs. Pitezel, who had become a physical wreck, identified a photograph as the picture of her deceased husband, and also identified the clothing removed from the body in the potter's field as having belonged to Mr. Pitezel. She then testified at length regarding the insurance swindle conspiracy, and repeated the many conversations she had with Holmes regarding the whereabouts of her husband. To show that Pitezel was not contemplating suicide, as claimed by Holmes, Mrs. Pitezel produced a letter written by her husband some days previous to his demise, in which he expressed his intention to have his family join him in Philadelphia at an early date.

Several persons who knew Pitezel as "Perry" when he kept the place at 1316 Callowhill Street, identified the picture of Pitezel as the photograph of Perry. Many of them saw the corpse and stated that the remains were those of the man they knew as Perry. Several of these witnesses also testified that "Perry" was last seen alive at 10:30 p. m. on Saturday,

September 1, 1894, when he visited a neighboring saloon to purchase a supply of whisky to last him over Sunday, the Excise law preventing the sale of liquor on Sunday.

Eugene Smith, who placed the patent set-saw with Perry, testified to finding the body on the following Tuesday, and experts testified that the condition of the body indicated that the man was dead at least two days. This would mean that he died on Sunday.

Miss Yoke, who had believed she was Holmes' (or Howard's) legal wife, testified that she and Holmes were at this time living at 1905 North Eleventh Street. That on Saturday evening a man called to see Mr. Holmes and that Holmes informed her that he was a prominent railroad man who was about to leave a large order for his patent copier, but that Holmes afterward admitted the man was Pitezel. She also stated that Holmes left their apartments at 10:30 a. m. Sunday, and did not return until 4:30 p. m., at which time his excited and overheated condition attracted her attention.

They hurriedly packed their belongings and left that night for Indianapolis, remaining there but a few days and then proceeding to St. Louis, where Holmes called on Mrs. Pitezel. It was proved that on August 9, 1894, Holmes telegraphed $157.50 to the Chicago office of the Fidelity Mutual Life Association, to pay the half-yearly premium on Pitezel's policy. No witnesses were called for the defense.

In charging the jury, Judge Arnold, in commenting on Holmes' absolute power over Pitezel, said:

> "Truth is stranger than fiction, and if Mrs. Pitezel's story is true it is the most wonderful exhibition of the power of mind over mind I have ever seen, and stranger than any novel I ever read."

On November 2, 1895, the case was submitted to the jury, and after deliberating a short time a verdict of guilty was returned.

On May 7, 1896, Holmes was hanged in Moyammensing prison, Philadelphia. He assumed an air of utter indifference to the end. Some days before his death, when it was evident that all hope had vanished, Holmes made a "confession," wherein he admitted that he had killed twenty-seven persons, but on the scaffold he contradicted this statement and claimed that the only persons for whose death he was either directly or indirectly responsible, were two women upon whom he performed criminal operations.

MARION HEDGSPETH, TRAIN ROBBER, WHO WAS CLEVERLY TRAPPED IN SAN FRANCISCO, AND WHO SUBSEQUENTLY INFORMED ON HOLMES, THE "CRIMINAL OF THE CENTURY."

On the night of November 30, 1891, two masked men boarded the "Frisco" Express train as it was leaving St. Louis, Mo. They remained in seclusion until they had traveled a few miles, and then crawling over the tender, they presented pistols at the heads of the engineer and fireman and ordered them to stop a few miles from St. Louis, where two accomplices of the highwaymen were stationed.

The engineer and fireman were then ordered from the cab and kept covered while the party proceeded to the express car, where the robbers demanded admission, but were refused by the messenger. The robbers then set off a stick of dynamite and blew in the side of the car, seriously injuring the messenger. They then entered, blew open the safe, and after taking $10,000, made their escape.

The Pinkerton Detective Agency and Chief of Detectives Desmond of St. Louis investigated the case and gathered evidence which convinced them that the robbers were Marion Hedgspeth, James Francis, Dink Wilson and Adelbert Sly. The latter was traced to Los Angeles and arrested by Robert Pinkerton.

Hedgspeth was traced to San Francisco and was arrested at the general post office. It was learned that he was traveling under the name of H. B. Swanson, and a decoy letter was mailed and finally advertised. On January 14, 1892, a watch was set, consisting of Detectives Bryam, Whitaker and Silvey, and on February 10 Hedgspeth called for his mail. He was heavily armed and made a desperate struggle, but was overpowered by the officers.

Sly and Hedgspeth were returned to St. Louis and were sentenced to twenty years' imprisonment.

Francis was killed in Kansas while resisting arrest, and Wilson shot and killed Detective Harvey of Syracuse, N. Y., for which he was electrocuted at Sing Sing, N. Y.

While in jail in St. Louis, Hedgspeth gained the confidence of Holmes, the "criminal of the century," and subsequently rendered great assistance to the authorities. (See Holmes' case.)

A BRIEF HISTORY OF THE LIFE AND ASSASSINATION OF PRESIDENT LINCOLN.

(From Nicolay 's History of Lincoln's life and De Witt's history of the assassination.)

Abraham Lincoln was born in a log cabin in the backwoods of Kentucky on February 12, 1809. His father, who was extremely poor, could not sign his own name until his wife taught him to do so.

From his boyhood until he became of age, Abe spent most of his time at muscular labor; the aggregate of his schooling up to this time hardly amounting to one year. But the hours his companions devoted to amusement, he devoted to his efforts at mental improvement.

At the age of twenty-one he left home to become a clerk in a general merchandise store in a little village in Illinois called New Salem.

In August, 1832, he was a candidate for Assemblyman but was defeated. From May 7, 1833, to May 30, 1836, he served as postmaster of New Salem; at the same time acting as deputy surveyor. In addition to these occupations, he was elected Assemblyman in 1834 and was reelected in 1836, in 1838 and in 1840.

In 1837, while serving as an Assemblyman, Lincoln moved to Springfield, Ill., where he studied law, and at the expiration of his fourth successive term in the Legislature, he opened a law office in Springfield.

In August, 1846, he was elected to Congress, where he served two years and then resumed his law practice in Springfield.

As is well known, Lincoln was always opposed to slavery, and his debates with Senator Douglas on that subject in 1854 and 1858 made him a power in American politics.

In 1856, the first national convention of the Republican Party was held in Philadelphia and John Fremont of California was nominated for President. Lincoln was sent as a delegate to the convention from Illinois, and without any solicitation on his part, one hundred and ten of the three hundred and sixty-five delegates cast their votes for him for Vice-president. He was a candidate for United States Senator but was defeated.

At the Republican National Convention held in Chicago in May, 1860, Lincoln was nominated for President and on November 6 he was elected. He was inaugurated on March 4, 1861, and United States Senator William H. Seward was appointed Secretary of State.

As is well known, Lincoln had been President but a few months when the nation was plunged into one of the most terrible wars in history; and although nearly a million lives were lost and an expenditure of nearly thirty-five hundred million dollars was entailed, it had at length its happy consummation, not only in reuniting the Union, but in abolishing slavery forever from the country.

On June 7, 1864, Lincoln was again nominated for President. He received 484 votes, while U. S. Grant, who had been promoted to the rank of Lieutenant-General on March 12, 1864, and was bitterly opposed to the efforts made to array him in political opposition to the President, received twenty-two votes.

In November, 1864, Lincoln was re-elected and Andrew Johnson was elected Vice-President. The inauguration occurred on March 4, 1865, and ex-Senator Seward was retained as Secretary of State.

Lincoln's re-election seemed to have thoroughly disheartened a great majority of the Confederate soldiers and on April 9, 1865, General Lee surrendered his command, which was the flower of the Confederate army, to General Grant.

While General Johnson still had a large army in the field, the President construed Lee's surrender as the termination of the war, as he felt confident that Johnson would see the folly of continuing after he learned of Lee's action, and that he would soon surrender to General Sherman.

Junius Booth was born in England in 1796, and by the time he reached majority he was one of England's foremost tragedians. He was married in London in 1821 and immediately sailed with his bride to America, where he afterward resided. He made his first public appearance in America on July 6, 1821, at Richmond, Virginia.

Although a great actor, Booth was extremely eccentric and in later years his mind became unbalanced by his intemperate habits. In his history of the New York Tombs, Warden Sutton states that his predecessor, Warden Malachi Fallon, who was the first City Marshal of San Francisco, was a personal friend of Booth and that frequently, when the actor became intoxicated while in New York, friends would inveigle him into a carriage and take him to the Tombs, where Fallon would take charge of him until the evening performance.

Booth died in 1852, leaving a large family; three of his sons, Edwin, Junius and John Wilkes Booth, becoming celebrated actors. The latter was a strikingly handsome young man and was generous to a fault with his friends but it was soon evident that he inherited much of his father's eccentricity. He spent his boyhood days in Virginia and became known as a fanatical secessionist. He often boasted of the fact that he participated in the hanging of the aged John Brown, who attempted to free the slaves in 1859.

In April, 1864, the new commander of the Federal army, General Grant, issued orders that no more Confederate prisoners would be exchanged. As there were then 23,000 of these prisoners, the idea entered the head of John Wilkes Booth that President Lincoln could be kidnaped and delivered to the Confederates, who would then be in a position to demand either the termination of the war or the exchange of all the Confederate prisoners for the Commander-in-Chief of the Federal army.

In September, 1864, Booth went to Baltimore, where he had a conference with Michael O'Laughlin and Sam Arnold, two of his old schoolmates who had served two years in the Confederate army. He explained that Lincoln detested having guards around him and that as he frequently walked the Streets of Washington alone, several able-bodied men could overpower him, place him in a waiting closed carriage, drive him out of the city and land him in Richmond.

Arnold and O'Laughlin entered enthusiastically into the scheme and Lincoln's re-election in November made Booth more determined than ever to consummate the deed.

About November 15 he visited Charles County, Maryland, for the purpose of purchasing a horse, and while there he met Dr. Samuel Mudd, who assisted him in buying a one-eyed horse from a neighbor. This animal was afterward placed in a livery-stable in Washington.

On December 23, Booth met Dr. Mudd in Washington and requested the doctor to introduce him to a former Confederate spy named John Surratt, whose mother formerly conducted a tavern in Surrattsville, Maryland, but had recently leased the same to a man named Lloyd, and she was then conducting a boarding and lodging-house at 541 H Street, in Washington. By a singular coincidence, Surratt, accompanied by his roommate, Louis Weichmann, appeared on the scene at this moment and introductions followed. After a general conversation the men parted and Booth went to New York. He returned to Washington in January and calling at Mrs. Surratt's lodging-house, he unfolded his scheme to young Surratt, who not only agreed to assist but also induced David Herold, a young drug clerk in Washington, and George Atzerodt, a carriage-painter, to participate in the enterprise.

Edwin Forrest began an engagement at Ford's Theater on January 2, 1865, and it was reported that the President would attend the performance on the evening of January 18. This put another idea into Booth's head. One of the conspirators would put out the lights in the theater on that night; another would have a closed carriage at the rear entrance, which Booth was well acquainted with, and the remainder would be stationed near Lincoln's box and when the lights were extinguished they would rush upon the President, gag and bind him, carry him out to the carriage and then to Richmond.

The plans were discussed, but as a storm was raging on the 18th inst., the President did not attend the performance, so it was decided to arrange some other plan, as some of the conspirators regarded this scheme as impracticable.

While waiting for an opportunity to present itself, Booth went to Baltimore and on March 1, while in that city, he met an old acquaintance, a big, powerful young fellow named Lewis Powell, alias Payne. Booth learned from this fellow that he had not only been wounded while serving as a Confederate soldier, but that his two brothers had been killed. As Payne was extremely bitter against the President, Booth decided to invite him to assist in the work at hand, and he took Payne to Washington, where he was entertained at Mrs. Surratt's home.

On March 16, the President was expected to attend an entertainment at the Soldiers' Home, which was located in the suburbs of Washington. The conspirators, Arnold, Herold, O'Laughlin, Atzerodt, Payne, Surratt and Booth, decided that this was the day to seize the President, so they rode out to a secluded spot near the road, but again they were doomed to disappointment, as Lincoln abandoned the trip at the last moment.

The chagrined plotters, fearing that they had been betrayed, scattered in all directions, but that night Booth and Payne had a conference in the room occupied by Surratt and Weichmann. After a lengthy discussion, it was decided that the kidnaping plan was impracticable, and the next day this decision was made known to the remainder of the plotters, who decided to disband, although Payne, Atzerodt and Herold remained at the beck and call of Booth.

Young Surratt was employed as a clerk for the Adams Express Company up to the time that the conspirators intended to drag Lincoln from the theater, but for the purpose of carrying out this plan, he asked for a leave of absence. This being refused, his mother interceded in his behalf and when she was refused he resigned his position. The kidnaping plot having been abandoned and Surratt being out of employment, he left Washington and went to Canada.

Weichmann was a clerk in the War Office, and about the time the conspirators disbanded, he informed Captain D. H. Gleeson, U. S. A., that while he did not have the entire confidence of this gang he knew enough to convince him that there was a conspiracy afoot to kidnap the President. Gleeson evidently placed little credence in the story, as he merely told Weichmann to "keep his eye on them." Surratt subsequently claimed that Weichmann turned informer because he was refused permission to be a party to the enterprise.

After the surrender of Lee, Booth became desperate and, after hearing the President make a speech which was not to his liking, he decided that Lincoln must die.

On Good Friday, April 14, 1865, Booth made his customary daily call at Ford's Theater in Washington for his mail, and young Ford informed him that Lincoln and General Grant would occupy the President's box that night to witness a performance of "Our American Cousin."

Booth at once decided that the time for action had arrived. His first move was to transfer the one-eyed horse which he had purchased with the assistance of Dr. Mudd to a stable in the rear of Ford's Theater. He next called on Mrs. Surratt and handed her a pair of field-glasses, which he requested her to deliver to Lloyd, who was conducting her old tavern at Surrattsville, which was ten miles from Washington.*

* Lloyd afterward swore that in addition to delivering the field-glasses Mrs. Surratt said: "Have those shooting-irons ready, as parties will call for them to-night." The "shooting-irons" referred to were carbines left with Lloyd by Surratt, Atzerodt and Herold about five weeks before.

Booth's next move was to summon Payne, Atzerodt and Herold for a conference. It was then decided that in order to paralyze the government, Lincoln, Vice-President Johnson, Secretary of State Seward and General Grant must be assassinated simultaneously.

For the purpose of making their escape all of the conspirators were supplied with horses. Atzerodt was detailed to kill Johnson, and he at once engaged a room in the Kirkwood Hotel, where the Vice-President was a guest.

A few days before, Secretary Seward was thrown from his carriage and as a result he was confined to his bed. Herold was instructed to point out Seward's residence to Payne, who, upon some pretext, was to gain admission to the mansion and kill the Secretary. Herold was then to proceed to the assistance of Atzerodt, while Booth was to kill Grant and Lincoln as they sat in the theater. All of Booth's tools accepted their orders cheerfully except Atzerodt, who showed but little liking for his part of the plot.

Ten o'clock was the time set for the slaughtering, and as that hour approached, Atzerodt rode to the Kirkwood House, but his courage fled when he reached the hotel bar and he proceeded no further with the business. After partaking of a few drinks he went into seclusion for the night and at sunrise he departed for the home of his boyhood.

Payne and Herold proceeded to the Seward mansion about 10 p. m. Herold remaining outside, while Payne, after much argument with the servant who opened the door, finally gained admission by representing that Dr. Verdi had sent him with a bottle of medicine for the Secretary and had instructed him to personally explain the directions to the patient. Upon reaching the top of the stairs, Payne encountered the Secretary's son, who stated that his father was asleep and could not be disturbed. After some dispute, Payne suddenly drew a revolver and struck Young Seward over the head, knocking him down. The soldier nurse, hearing the noise, rushed out of the sick chamber and Payne stabbed him with a knife. The desperate man then rushed to the bed where the prostrate Secretary was asleep and stabbed him several times about the face and neck, inflicting serious but not fatal wounds.

The commotion had aroused the entire household and an attempt was made to overpower Payne, but he broke away and, dashing down the stairs to the Street, mounted his horse and rode away bareheaded, he having lost his hat in the struggle. At the first cry for help from Seward's house, Herold became alarmed and deserted Payne.

Mr. and Mrs. Lincoln, Major Rathbone and Miss Harris entered the President's box in Ford's Theater about 8:30 p. m., while the play was in progress. General Grant changed his plans during the day and instead of attending the performance, went to visit his daughter Nellie.

About 9:30 p. m. Booth appeared at the rear entrance to the theater with a saddle-horse. He sent for Edward Spangler, a scene-shifter, to hold the horse, but as Spangler was busy, he instructed another stage-hand to hold Booth's horse. The conspirator hovered about the rear of the theater until 10:10 p. m., when he proceeded to the President's box, suddenly opened the door and drawing a derringer pistol shot Lincoln in the back of the head. Major Rathbone sprang at the assassin, who dropped his pistol and stabbed the Major in the arm. Booth then sprang from the box to the stage, but his spur caught in the American flag with which the box was draped and he fell on the stage, breaking a small bone near his left ankle. He arose immediately and brandishing a dagger and crying "Sic semper tyrannis," fled out the back entrance, mounted his horse and dashed away before the stupefied audience realized what had transpired.

The President lost consciousness immediately and died at 7:22 a. m. the following day.

It was agreed in advance that Booth and Herold should proceed to Surrattsville immediately after the assassination, and they met on the road that night and hurried to Lloyd's tavern to procure the field-glasses left there by Mrs. Surratt. They then repaired to Dr. Mudd's home for the purpose of getting medical attention for Booth, arriving about 3 a. m. and remaining until daylight. Mudd admitted that he treated a man, but claimed that he did not recognize him as Booth.

Shortly after leaving Mudd, the two fugitives appeared at the home of Colonel Samuel Cox, formerly of the Confederate army. He turned them over to his foster-brother, Thomas Jones, who secreted them in a pine forest and supplied them with food for several days. During this time Booth suffered intense pain from his injury, which had been greatly aggravated by hard riding and exposure. The leg became useless and he was compelled to use a crutch when he walked.

Secretary of War Stanton detailed La Fayette C. Baker, Chief of the Federal Secret Service, to take personal charge of the investigation. On April 20 Stanton issued a proclamation announcing that $100,000 reward would be paid for information leading to the arrest and conviction of the conspirators and warning all persons who aided or harbored the assassins that they would be executed if convicted of this offense.

On April 24 Booth and Herold stopped at the residence of Richard H. Garratt and represented that they were former Confederate soldiers who had just had some trouble with Federal soldiers, who were looking for them. They were given food and permitted to sleep in the tobacco warehouse. They remained at Garratt's all day on the 25th inst., and slept there again that night. Before reaching Garratt's they met a former Confederate Captain named Jett, to whom they confided their deeds and their plans for the immediate future. The next day Jett was interrogated by a party of Federal soldiers. He told them all that the fugitives had said and accompanied them to Garratt's place, where they arrived about 2 a. m., on April 26.

After some questioning, the Garratt's admitted that two strangers were asleep in the warehouse. This building was then surrounded and the occupants were ordered to surrender. Herold obeyed the order and stepped out, but Booth was defiant. For the purpose of driving him out the building was set on fire, but before the fire had gained much headway. First Sergeant Boston Corbett, an eccentric individual who was afterward confined in an insane asylum, fired a shot through a crack in the building, the bullet lodging in Booth's neck and inflicting a wound which caused his death a few hours later. His last words were: "Tell mother I die for my country."

Two hours after the assault on Seward, Booth's one-eyed horse, which Payne rode, was found wandering about the Streets about one mile from the capitol.

It will be recalled that Surratt's roommate, Weichmann, informed Captain Gleeson of the kidnaping conspiracy about the time it was abandoned. While it was apparent that no credence was placed in the story at that time, immediately after the assassination Gleeson advised Secretary of War Stanton to send for Weichmann, and as a result of the interview, a series of investigations were made at the Surratt lodging-house. On the third night after the murder, the officers, who had spent several hours interrogating the occupants of the house, were about to leave when the doorbell rang.

One of the detectives responded and observed that the caller answered the description of Payne. He was without a hat and clearly showed the effects of exposure. He was ushered into the house and stated that he called to see Mrs. Surratt about digging a gutter. Mrs. Surratt was called and asked if she knew the man, who in reality was Payne, and although she had frequently entertained him, she swore that she had never seen him before. She and Payne were both taken into custody.

Sam Arnold was arrested at Fortress Monroe on the preceding day and O'Laughlin virtually surrendered at Baltimore about the same time.

It developed that Spangler, the scene-shifter who instructed a young fellow to hold Booth's horse, also tried to persuade a fellow scene-shifter named Jake Ritterspaugh to withhold valuable information from the authorities, and it was further shown that while Spangler was preparing the President's box he cursed Lincoln because "he got so many men killed." This information resulted in Spangler's arrest.

Atzerodt was arrested at Barnsville, Maryland, on April 20, and Dr. Mudd was arrested on the following day.

It was the theory of the authorities that the murder of Lincoln was committed in the execution of a gigantic conspiracy planned by Jefferson Davis, the President of the Confederacy. This theory was based on testimony given by Stanford Conover, a former Confederate spy who had a grievance against Davis, and three others, all of whom bore unenviable reputations and probably committed perjury. It was subsequently proven that Conover committed perjury and he was sentenced to serve ten years at Albany prison.

President Johnson ordered that nine army officers be detailed as a military commission to try the defendants, and the trials of Mrs. Surratt, Arnold, Mudd, Spangler, O'Laughlin, Atzerodt, Payne and Herold began on May 10, 1865.*

* John Surratt was still a fugitive from justice.

The trials were concluded on June 14, and all of the defendants were found guilty. Mrs. Surratt, Herold, Atzerodt and Payne were sentenced to be hanged, while O'Laughlin, Arnold and Mudd were sentenced to life imprisonment and Spangler was sentenced to six years' imprisonment.

It was the general opinion that Herold, Payne and Atzerodt received their just deserts, but much surprise and indignation was expressed at the findings in the cases of Mrs. Surratt, Arnold and O'Laughlin. A determined effort was made to save Mrs. Surratt from the gallows, but all in vain, as she was hanged on the same scaffold with Herold, Atzerodt and Payne on Friday, July 7, 1865.

While John Surratt was in Canada at the time of the assassination, the authorities were strongly convinced that he was one of the chief conspirators and that he was in Canada acting as one of Jeff Davis's agents. A large reward was offered for his apprehension, but when it developed that there was no evidence to prove that Davis was in any way implicated in the crime the reward was publicly withdrawn.

While the excitement was at its height young Surratt escaped to Europe and finally enlisted in the Papal Zouaves at Rome, where he was recognized nearly two years later by a former associate. The American authorities were notified and after much hesitation Surratt was arrested and returned to Washington on February 23, 1867. His case, which was tried in the Civil Court, dragged along from June to August 7, when it was submitted to the jury. After deliberating for three days the jury stood 8 to 4 for acquittal and they were discharged. Surratt remained in prison until June 22, 1868, when he was released.

O'Laughlin died in prison on August 18, 1867, during a yellow fever epidemic.

Dr. Mudd, Spangler and Arnold were pardoned by President Johnson on February 13, 1869. Spangler died on August 9, 1870, at Dr. Mudd's home, and Mudd died on January 10, 1883.

THE ASSASSINATION OF PRESIDENT GARFIELD.

(From McCabe's "Life of Garfield" and Washington, D. C.,

Police Records.)

James Abraham Garfield was born in the village of Orange, twelve miles from Cleveland, Ohio, on November 19, 1831.

When he was two years old his father died, leaving the family in straitened circumstances. By the time James reached the age of seventeen years he had worked as a farm hand, carpenter's helper and boatman.

Realizing the advantage of an education, which had up to this time been sadly neglected, the young man devoted all of his spare time to study, with the result that he was admitted to Williams College in 1854, where he paid his tuition from his savings. Two years later he was graduated with the highest honors.

He was then made Professor of Latin at the Hiram Institute. At the age of twenty-six he was appointed President of this college. In 1859 he was elected State Senator.

He was appointed Lieutenant-Colonel of the Forty-second Ohio Regiment on September 25, 1861, and on December 17 he was placed in command of the Seventeenth Brigade.

On January 10, 1862, he was promoted to the rank of brigadier-general because of his gallant conduct in battle, and on October 18, 1863, he was made Major-General of Volunteers for gallant conduct at the battle of Chickamauga.

In 1862, while he was still in the army, the people of his home district elected him to Congress, and on December 5, 1863, he reluctantly resigned his commission to accept his seat in the House of Representatives.

While still serving as Congressman, Garfield was elected to the United States Senate on January 15, 1880, to succeed Allen G. Thurman, whose term would expire on March 3, 1881. At the national convention held in Chicago on June 2, 1880, Garfield attended as the leader of the delegation from Ohio, and made the nominating speech for Sherman, although the real battle was between Blaine and Grant until the thirty-sixth ballot.

When the result of the thirty-fourth ballot was announced and it was learned that seventeen votes had been cast for Garfield, he protested against anyone voting for him without his consent. When the next ballot was finished, Garfield had fifty votes. The next ballot gave him three hundred and ninety-nine votes and the nomination.

He was elected President on November 2, 1880, and inaugurated on March 4, 1881.

Shortly afterward a faction of the Republican Party, known as the "Stalwarts," became opposed to some of the President's policies.

On the morning of July 2, 1881, President Garfield, accompanied by Secretary Blaine, was waiting at the Baltimore and Potomac depot in Washington for a train, upon which the President was going on a visit to New England.

As the President and Blaine were walking through the main corridor of the depot, a man walked up and fired two shots at Garfield, the first making a harmless wound in the upper left arm, and as the President turned suddenly the next bullet entered near the back bone. '

Mr. Garfield fell heavily and his wounds bled profusely. Shortly afterward he was removed to the White House.

The assassin was immediately captured by Officers Parks and Kearney. When the officers dragged him through the crowd he shouted in a dramatic manner:

"Arthur is President now; I am a Stalwart."

When the prisoner arrived at the jail he made a statement substantially as follows:

"My name is Charles J. Guiteau and I was born in Freeport, Ill., in June, 1841. My father, who died recently, was cashier of the Second National Bank in that town. I have a college education and I am a lawyer, theologian and politician. I speak French and German fluently. For the past two years I have traveled throughout New England delivering lectures.

"I came to Washington on March 6, 1881, and I was an applicant for the Consulship at Marseilles, France.

"About the latter part of May I determined to kill the President for the purpose of reuniting the Republican Party. His death was a political necessity. On June 8 I purchased the pistol in Washington and immediately began target practice.

"On Sunday, June 12, I intended to kill him at the Christian Church, but feared I might kill someone else. I then learned that he would leave the city on June 18 with his wife, so I waited at the depot to kill him, but Mrs. Garfield looked so frail I did not have the heart to shoot the President in her presence.

"This morning I paid a colored hack driver $2 to have his hack at

my disposal at the depot after I shot the President, but the police intercepted me."

It was subsequently learned that Guiteau had long been regarded as an eccentric but harmless person.

Several efforts were made to find the exact location of the bullet in the President's body, but without success, although the physicians knew about where it was lodged.

Owing to the excessive heat in Washington the President was removed to Long Branch on September 6, where he died at 10:35 p. m., September 19, 1881, over two and one-half months after the assault.

Guiteau was immediately charged with murder. He was convicted on January 25, 1882, and was hanged at the United States Jail in the District of Columbia on June 30, 1882.

THE ASSASSINATION OF PRESIDENT McKINLEY.

(From Fallows' "Life of McKinley.")

William McKinley was born in Niles, Ohio, on January 29, 1843. His parents being poor, William was compelled as a boy to procure employment to assist him in purchasing school books. At the age of seventeen he became a country school teacher.

On June 11, 1861, he enlisted with the Twenty-third Ohio Regiment, under command of Colonel Rutherford B. Hayes.

On April 15, 1862, McKinley was promoted to Commissary Sergeant, and on September 23, 1862, he was advanced to Second Lieutenant. On July 25, 1864, he was promoted to Captain and on March 13, 1865, he was brevetted Major. He was mustered out of service on July 26, 1865, and began to study law in Poland, Ohio.

In 1867, he began the practice of law in Canton, Ohio, and afterward served for several years as District Attorney.

In 1876 he was elected to Congress, and was continuously re-elected thereafter until 1890, when he was defeated. He rounded out his congressional career with the passage of the protective tariff law known as the McKinley Bill.

He was subsequently elected Governor of Ohio, which office he held for two terms.

At the Republican National Convention held in St. Louis in June, 1896, McKinley received the nomination for President of the United States. He was elected and on March 4, 1897, was inaugurated.

In 1900 he was again nominated at the convention held in Philadelphia, and in the following November he was reelected.

September 5, 1901, was set apart as "President's Day" at the Pan-American Exposition at Buffalo, N, Y., in honor of President McKinley, who delivered an address to the assembled thousands.

On the following day the President attended the exposition as a guest, and arrangements were made for a public reception at the Temple of Music, which was to take place at 4 p. m. At the appointed hour the President arrived, accompanied by John C. Milburn, the President of the Exposition, Secretary Cortelyou and Secret Service Detectives Ireland and Foster.

It was arranged for the visitors to pass in single file and greet the President. When about one hundred persons had shaken hands with McKinley a negro named Parker was next in line, and after receiving a pleasant word from the President, he gave way to the next man in line, who was a quietly dressed, intelligent appearing young man with reddish hair and smooth-shaven cheeks. His right hand was thrust beneath the lapel of his coat and a handkerchief was wrapped about it in such a manner as to indicate that the hand had been injured. He offered his left hand to the President, who grasped it. Like a flash the stranger withdrew the right hand from the coat and pressing it against the President's abdomen fired two shots from the pistol hid in the handkerchief; both bullets entering the body.

The President fell back in a chair and his first words were: "May God forgive him."

The detectives and the negro sprang upon the assassin, and after disarming him he was finally taken to jail, after a narrow escape from mob violence.

After rendering first aid to the President at the Fair Grounds he was removed to the home of President Milburn.

On September 11 the physicians announced that the President was out of danger, although one of the bullets, which had passed through the stomach and lodged in the back, had not been definitely located.

On the 13th, however, a change occurred. At 10 p. m. he sank into unconsciousness and died the following morning at 2:15 o'clock.

When the assassin was lodged in jail it was ascertained that his name was Leon Czolgosz. He stated that he was born in Detroit and was twenty-eight years of age. He added that he was a disciple of Emma Goldman, but that he alone was responsible for his actions, and he believed that he had done his duty.

On September 23, his trial began before Justice Truman White. The prisoner pleaded guilty and assumed an air of indifference. No witnesses were examined for the defense and on the following day the case was submitted to the jurors, who, after thirty minutes' deliberation, found the defendant guilty.

On October 29, he was electrocuted in the State Prison at Auburn. He walked quietly to the chair and seated himself. He was then given permission to speak, which he took advantage of by saying:

"I killed the President because he was the enemy of the good people; of the working class of people. I am not sorry for the crime, that's all there is about it."

At that moment the current was turned on; his body bounded against the back of the chair and the anarchist was dead.

Several celebrated specialists then held an autopsy and found all the organs, including the brain, in a perfectly normal condition.

A grave had been prepared in the prison yard, into which was emptied six barrels of quicklime and a carboy of sulphuric acid, and into this seething mass the body of Czolgosz was placed.

THE CELEBRATED TRUNK MURDER CASE IN ST. LOUIS

IN WHICH THE SAN FRANCISCO POLICE TOOK A PROMINENT PART.

On January 28th, 1885, the Steamer Cephalonia left Liverpool for Boston. On board were two highly educated and refined appearing young Englishmen named Charles Arthur Preller and a man known as Walter Lennox Maxwell, M. D. They were strangers to each other when they boarded the vessel, but as they were both Englishmen bound for a foreign land, they immediately became quite friendly, and by the time they reached Boston, on February 3, they had become inseparable companions.

They went to the same hotel, where they discussed a trip to Auckland, New Zealand, but as Preller, who was a commercial traveler, was forced to make a business trip to Canada and thence to Philadelphia, they agreed to meet in St. Louis a few weeks later and arrange the details. Preller left for Canada on February 6, but Maxwell remained in Boston until March 28, during which time he became financially embarrassed and was forced to pawn a watch.

He arrived in St. Louis on March 30 and proceeded direct to the Southern Hotel, where he was assigned to room 184.

Almost immediately after his arrival the manager of the hotel received a telegram signed by Preller asking if Maxwell had arrived. Upon receiving an affirmative answer Preller started for St. Louis and arrived at the hotel on Friday, April 3.

Maxwell had but $60 at this time, so he endeavored to sell some stereopticon apparatus to raise money.

The two men spent most of their time in Maxwell's room. The latter was very effeminate in his manner and a letter subsequently found, but which was not fit for publication, indicated that a peculiar relationship existed between the two.

On different occasions Preller displayed considerable money, mostly in $100 bills. He was last seen shortly after dinner on Easter Sunday, April 5. On that evening Maxwell told different persons about the hotel that Preller had gone to the country but would return in a few days.

At 10:15 o'clock that night Maxwell showed the effects of excessive drinking and talked in an incoherent manner. In the presence of Henry Arlington, the head waiter, he displayed a pistol and a roll of $100 bills. He also asked: "If a man committed murder in this country and had $600 could he beat the case?"

On the next morning (Monday) Maxwell went to Hickman's barber shop at Fifth and Chestnut Streets, where a barber named Armo shaved off his beard. After the work was completed he asked the barber, "Could anyone recognize me now?"

He then went to a trunk dealer named Frederick Beiger and purchased a canvas trunk and two trunk straps. A hotel porter named William Train took these to Maxwell's room the same day and there saw a zinc trunk in the room, which he moved to one side and which he afterward recalled was very heavy. This trunk was the one which Maxwell brought to the hotel when he first arrived.

On this day Maxwell paid his bill and disappeared. As the room he vacated was not needed and as he had left the zinc trunk and the one he had just purchased there, it was presumed that he or Preller would return in a few days, and they were not disturbed.

About six days later a peculiar odor was noticed in this room, but on the 14th inst. it became so unbearable that an investigation was instituted. The zinc trunk, which was securely bound with ropes and the two straps purchased from Beiger, was opened, and the body of Preller was found cramped up in it. With the exception of a pair of drawers, upon the waistband of which was the name "H. M, Brooks," the body was nude. For the purpose of preventing identification the mustache had been cut off with scissors. On the breast were two gashes, skin deep, in the form of a cross. On a paper placard was the inscription, "So perish all traitors to the great cause." The writing on this card was compared with Maxwell's signature on the register and proved to be the same style of writing. It was the theory of the police that this placard was placed in the trunk for the purpose of misleading and conveying the impression that the murder was a political assassination.

Among Preller's effects was found the following telegram:

"Boston, Mass., Mar. 19, 1885. "C. A. Preller, Belvedere Hotel:

"Yes, could go direct to Auckland from here. Will write to Philadelphia to-morrow.

W. H. Lennox Maxwell."

This caused the police to suspect that Maxwell might have started on this trip with Preller's money. They therefore made inquiry at the depot and ascertained that a man of Maxwell's appearance had purchased an unlimited ticket to San Francisco and had given the name of "H. M. Brooks."

In Maxwell's trunk were found several prescription blanks from

Femon's drug store, located at Fifth and Chestnut Streets, St. Louis. The detectives called on Femon, who stated that he knew Maxwell, and that on April 5 he sold him four ounces of chloroform at 2 p. m., and two ounces at 4 p. m. Professor Ludeking immediately performed an autopsy and declared that Preller died from chloroform poisoning.

Great publicity was given to the case by the press and two St. Louisans who had seen Maxwell at the Southern Hotel notified the police that on May 6 they took westbound train No. 23 and rode as far as Pierce City, Mo. They stated positively that Maxwell was on the train and had his beard shaved off.

A telegram was immediately sent to Captain of Detectives I. W. Lees of San Francisco, in which a complete description of Maxwell was given.

At that time it was Captain Lees' custom to spend much of his time in the evenings around the corridors of the Palace and Grand Hotels, and he recalled that some evenings previously, while he and Detective Dan Coffey were at the Palace Hotel, they saw a man who in a general way answered the description of the much-wanted Maxwell. The two officers proceeded at once to the hotel and ascertained that the man they referred to was registered as T. C. D'Auguier of Paris, and was evidently a Frenchman as he spoke with a strong French accent.

The records at the hotel showed that T. C. D'Auguier had only stayed at the hotel one day and while he was assigned to room 692, the chambermaid stated that he had not slept in his bed that night.

It was recalled that when D'Auguier registered another man named Robbins registered at the same time and probably came in on the same train. This man was still stopping at the hotel, and when located by Lees he made the following interesting and important statement:

"I came from Chicago, but when we reached some small station, a car from St. Louis was attached to our train. There was but one passenger on that car and that was the man who came through to San Francisco and registered the name 'D'Auguier' at the Palace Hotel in my presence. When his car joined our train he came into the car I was in and began conversing, speaking with a strong French accent. He said that he was a French brigadier, and as I speak French fluently I addressed him in that language. He was completely nonplused and was forced to admit that he did not speak the language, although he continued to use the French accent.

"As he joined us from another train, the conductor, desiring to keep his records straight, asked him for his name. This seemed to excite him greatly, and he asked me, 'What for does he want ze name, eh ?'

When I explained the matter he breathed a sigh of relief."

Captain Lees then questioned Robbins closely and the description he gave of the man tallied exactly with that given by the St. Louis officials. Robbins also stated that this man carried a pistol and an open-faced watch, which he dropped to the floor on one occasion.

Almost immediately after interviewing Mr. Robbins, Lees learned from the St. Louis police that Maxwell checked three pieces of baggage to San Francisco, and that the checks were numbered 2006, 2069 and 2046. Captain Lees and Detective Coffey went to room 692 and under the bureau they found a crumpled receipt from the transportation company which delivered the baggage, and these three numbers were on the receipt.

As Lees next learned that the St. Louis officials suspected that Maxwell was en route to Auckland, he and Detective Coffey visited the ticket agent and ascertained that on April 12 a man of Maxwell's description paid $90 for a steerage passage and sailed on that day. This man spoke with such a strong accent that the agent could not understand his name so the man wrote the word "D'Auguier" on a card. Fortunately the agent saved the card, which he handed to Captain Lees, and it was obvious that it was written by the same person who registered at the Palace Hotel.

The next important information came from a woman who was an inmate of a brothel on Eddy Street.

She told Captain Lees that on the night of April 11 a man of Maxwell's appearance came to her resort where he spent the night.

He had been drinking heavily and spoke with a French accent, but on one occasion he was looking at an album containing photographs of celebrities and when he saw the picture of Henry Irving, the celebrated English tragedian, he exclaimed in perfect English: "Why, there's Irving's picture."

The woman laughingly said: "Why, I thought you were French." The man replied: "Oh, yes, Madam, I am ze Frenchman but I know ze Irving."

This woman furthermore stated that on one occasion she left the room occupied by the "Frenchman" and herself and when she returned and opened the door suddenly, he was sitting on the edge of the bed with a pistol in his hand. He put the pistol under his pillow, braced a chair against the door and lay awake all night.

In describing the man's jewelry she stated positively that he had a new closed-case watch and a peculiar looking chain, one link being gold and the next silver. Lees telegraphed to St. Louis and learned that the murdered man had such a chain in his lifetime.

As Mr. Robbins stated positively that the "Frenchman" had dropped an open-faced watch and as this woman was just as positive that she saw a closed-face watch in the possession of the "Frenchman," Captain Lees concluded that a new watch had been purchased and the old one disposed of. He therefore detailed Detective Coffey to visit the pawnshops. After a long search he finally located a pawnbroker on Market Street who had purchased an open-faced watch from a man of Maxwell's appearance. The watch was still in stock and when the dealer opened it the name "Hugh M. Brooks" was engraved inside the case.

Immediately after this discovery a Market Street secondhand book-dealer called on Captain Lees and stated that on the morning of April 12 a man of Maxwell's appearance entered his store and said: "Monsieur, I take ze long ride and I like ze book so lively as to keep up ze spirit." The seller then offered him a spicy novel written in French, but the "Frenchman" said: "No, no; I like ze translation ze best." He finally purchased "Peck's Bad Boy."

As Captain Lees had become firmly convinced that D'Auguier was Maxwell, he telegraphed to Chief Harrigan that there was no doubt but that the man wanted left San Francisco on April 12 for New Zealand.

Harrigan had the Auckland officials notified and Maxwell was apprehended as the vessel came into the harbor.

He denied that his name was Maxwell and although he claimed he had never been in St. Louis, he had a diary in his pocket which contained a memorandum in his own handwriting showing that he arrived at St. Louis on March 30, and left on April 6.

He also had Preller's watch-chain and some of his clothing in his possession.

On May 25, President Cleveland signed the extradition warrant which was served by Detectives Tracy and Badger of St. Louis.

The prisoner engaged an attorney with the $125 he had left and an attempt was made to prevent the extradition.

After a delay of seventy-seven days the prisoner was turned over to the detectives, who arrived in San Francisco on August 11, 1885. By this time the prisoner refused to discuss his case.

He was returned to St. Louis and an investigation was at once begun by the grand jury.

The prisoner was identified as Maxwell by the druggist who sold the chloroform; by the trunk-dealer who sold the canvas-covered trunk and also the straps bound around the zinc trunk which contained the body; by the barber who shaved him, and about six attaches of the hotel, including a porter named William Train, who carried the trunk to Maxwell's room.

An indictment was found against the prisoner on a charge of murder. He pleaded not guilty and his trial began in May, 1886.

After Arlington, the head-waiter at the hotel; Armo, the barber; Beiger, the trunk-dealer; Fernon, the druggist; Professor Ludeking and numerous attaches of the hotel testified to the facts heretofore related in this narrative, Detective John F. McCullough was called and his testimony created a sensation.

Circuit Attorney Clover believed that if some shrewd person representing the prosecution, but apparently a criminal, could be stationed in Maxwell's cell, he could gradually ingratiate himself into the confidence of the prisoner and obtain damaging admissions, or possibly a confession.

He therefore arranged to have Detective McCullough "forge" the name of one Morris to a check. A prosecution was then instituted; witnesses who honestly believed the name was signed with intent to commit forgery testified before the grand jury, and that body, knowing nothing of the prearrangement, indicted McCullough, who had for the occasion assumed the name of "Dingfelder."

The detective was confined in jail awaiting trial and was placed in Maxwell's cell, where he remained forty-seven days and nights.

The following is the substance of the detective's testimony as to what transpired during that time:

"I represented that I was friendly with people who would testify falsely to help me out of trouble and the defendant said: 'I wish I could get witnesses to do that for me, I might go free also.'

"I told him I expected to get cut on bail soon and when I did I would help him, but I must know what he wanted the witness to testify to and also the circumstances of the case.

"He said that he wanted to prove that he had had $100 bills while he was in Boston, as the prosecution claimed he had exhibited money only after the death of Preller.

"The defendant then told me that he became enraged at Preller on May 3, the day he arrived in St. Louis, because he refused to pay his (Maxwell's) passage to Auckland, and he decided to get even with him. He said that on Sunday Preller complained of a pain in the side.

The defendant said he could fix that so he injected a large amount of morphine into his arm, rendering him unconscious. He then tied a cloth about his face and kept it saturated with chloroform until he was dead. The body was then stripped and placed in the trunk.

"I told the defendant that I expected to be released on a bond in a few days and that when I sent the witnesses to him there would have to be some means of identification. The defendant then wrote 'Dingfelder, 2.W' on a card, the '2.W' meaning two witnesses. This card was torn in half, the defendant taking one-half and I the other. (The detective here produced his half.) It was then agreed that I would give my piece of the card to the witnesses and when they called they would produce this piece of card, and if it matched the piece the defendant had he would feel safe in talking to them. I was released on bonds shortly after this card incident and I went to New York, from where I wrote to the prisoner regarding the witnesses and received an answer."

(Here the witness produced the letter and envelope.)

Upon cross-examination the detective testified that he believed he was justified in such deceptions if done for the purpose of ascertaining the truth where a murder had been committed.

On May 26, the defendant took the stand and testified substantially as follows:

"My true name is Hugh M. Brooks. I am 25 years of age and I was born in Hyde, Chester, England. I studied law in Slockport from 1878 to 1882 and was admitted to the bar. I also studied medicine and surgery at Manchester, but I am not a licensed physician, I first saw Mr. Preller at the Northwestern Hotel at Liverpool, but was not introduced to him until we met on board the steamer Cephalonia bound for Boston.

"I had then assumed the name of Maxwell. When we separated in Boston it was with the understanding that we should meet again in St. Louis.

"I treated Mr. Preller several times and he acknowledged having been benefited.

"On the Sunday after the arrival of Mr. Preller in St. Louis he complained that he was not well and when he described the symptoms, I concluded he was suffering from a stricture and that a

catheter should be inserted in the urethra.

"I discussed the administering of chloroform with Preller and looked up authorities to refresh my mind as to the precautions necessary.

"I then went to the drug store and procured four ounces of chloroform and a quantity of absorbent cotton. Preller removed all his clothing, except an undershirt, and lay on the bed.

"I poured out a fluid gramme of chloroform on some lint and left the bottle on the washstand, but it fell into the basin and spilled so I was forced to make a second purchase.

"When I returned I proceeded to administer the anesthetic and Preller lost consciousness.

"I was proceeding with my work when he winced as though in pain, so I administered more chloroform. Almost immediately the breathing became labored and I at once resorted to all means of resuscitation with which I was familiar until I was completely exhausted. I then saw that my efforts were all in vain as my friend was dead.

"When I realized what I had done I became almost insane with grief and I drank heavily. The cutting of Preller's mustache, the cross on the breast and placing the placard bearing the inscription in the trunk with the body was done by me when I was in a fear-crazed condition.

"At first I intended to notify the authorities but as I understand the law in England, a man cannot make a statement in his own behalf, and as I thought it was the same here I did not think I could escape punishment.

"I therefore took Preller's money, clothing and jewelry and attempted to escape."

Affidavits from prominent Englishmen were then produced tending to show the good character of the defendant.

On May 30, Morgue Superintendent Ryan, Drs. Hewett and Midlet and Prosecuting Attorney Clover had the body of Preller exhumed and after an examination of the organ referred to, which was in a wonderful state of preservation, it was unanimously agreed that the organ was in good condition and that there had never been any occasion for the treatment described by Maxwell.

On the night of June 4, the case was submitted to the jury and on the following morning a verdict of guilty was returned.

The defendant appealed to the Supreme Court for a new trial, claiming among other things that the trial judge erred in permitting the introduction of the confession against the objection of the defense, as it was claimed that the confession was not voluntarily made, as required by law, but was obtained by fraud and artifice.

On this point the Supreme Court decided that while artifice and deceit were resorted to in obtaining the confession, it did not render the person obtaining it incompetent to testify regarding it, but the circumstances might properly be considered as affecting the credibility of the witness.

The Supreme Court declined to grant a new trial and Brooks was hanged on August 10, 1888.

THE CELEBRATED MURDER OF THE AGED CAPITALIST, CAPTAIN JOSEPH WHITE, AND PARTS OF DANIEL WEBSTER'S FAMOUS ARGUMENT TO THE TRIAL JURY.

(From Benjamin Merrill's history of the case.)

In the year 1830 there lived in Salem, Mass., a very wealthy retired merchant named Joseph White. He was eighty-two years of age and had never married. His niece, Mrs. Beckford, acted as his housekeeper and was assisted by a man servant and a maid servant.

Mrs. Bickford's daughter was married to a young man named Joseph J. Knapp, Jr., and resided with her husband in Wenham, Mass., which was seven miles from Salem. The Knapp family, consisting of the father, Joseph Knapp, Sr., and his sons, Joseph Knapp, Jr., and John Francis Knapp, was well known and highly respected.

On April 5, 1830, Mrs. Beckford went to Wenham, to spend a few days with her daughter, Mrs. Joseph Knapp, Jr.

At 6 A. M., April 7, 1830, Mr. White's man servant arose, and upon opening the shutters of the kitchen window observed that the back window of the parlor was open and that a plank was raised to the window from the back yard. He informed the maid servant of his observations and the two proceeded on a tour of inspection.

When they approached Mr. White's bedroom they were surprised at finding the door open, but their surprise gave way to horror as they approached the bed and found the bed clothing turned down and the sheets and Mr. White's night clothes saturated with blood. Mr. White was dead and his body was cold and stiff.

The authorities were notified and a closer inspection of the body revealed the fact that the skull had been fractured by some implement which had not broken the skin, and thirteen deep wounds were found on the body, which had evidently been inflicted with a long dagger.

There was nothing to indicate that the mansion had been ransacked. Valuable articles were left undisturbed, and as Mr. White was a most amiable character who had no enemies, the authorities were at a loss to understand what motive could have prompted any one to perpetrate this most atrocious crime.

The mystery became all the deeper when it was observed that the window through which the assassin probably entered, was evidently not locked on this particular night, which was a most unusual circumstance.

Some were inclined to look upon the servants with suspicion but it was argued that they were old and trusted employees, and since absolutely nothing of value was disturbed, it was difficult to show what motive either one could have had in committing the murder.

Footprints found in the garden near the board in no manner resembled the prints made by either of the servants.

Great excitement prevailed throughout the community; large rewards were offered for the apprehension and conviction of the assassin, and a Committee of Vigilance was appointed to institute an investigation. Business was almost entirely suspended in Salem on the day of Mr. White's funeral, and during the funeral services none of the mourners exhibited more outward signs of grief than Joseph Knapp, Jr.

On April 27, while the excitement was still at its height, Joseph J. Knapp, Jr., and his brother John went before the Vigilance Committee and testified that on the preceding evening they were returning in a chaise from Salem to their home in Wenham and that as they approached Wenham Pond three robbers came suddenly upon them. One seized the horse's bridle while the other two seized a small trunk in the bottom of the chaise.

The brothers stated that they resisted and that the robbers finally retreated and were lost in the darkness.

This statement caused many to believe that a gang of assassins were operating in the neighborhood and it was suspected that this gang was responsible for the murder of White.

The weeks rolled by and the discouraged citizens concluded that the mystery surrounding the death of Captain White would never be penetrated. Finally a rumor was circulated that some person confined in the jail at New Bedford, seventy miles from Salem, could shed some light on the mystery if he so desired.

No one seemed to know where the rumor started, but a representative of the Vigilance Committee proceeded to the jail at New Bedford and learned that a prisoner named Hatch, who had been arrested for shoplifting before the murder of White, had intimated that he could make important disclosures, but he had not been taken seriously. Hatch was then interrogated and, after some hesitancy, stated that some months before the murder, while he was at large, he was an associate of one Richard Crowninshield, who bore a most unenviable reputation in Danvers and Salem, and he had often heard Crowninshield express his intention to kill White.

Hatch was immediately taken before the Grand Jury and on his testimony an indictment was found against Crowninshield.

Other witnesses testified that on the night of the murder, George Crowninshield, a brother of Richard, and two men named Selman and Chase were with Richard in a Salem gambling-house. On this testimony these three men were also indicted and all four were arrested on May 2, but Selman and Chase were subsequently discharged without a trial.

On May 15, Captain Joseph J. Knapp, Sr., a prominent shipmaster and merchant, and father of Joseph J. Knapp, Jr., received the following letter:

Charles Grant, Jr., to Joseph J. Knapp.

"Belfast, May 12, 1830.

"Dear Sir: — I have taken the pen at this time to address an utter stranger, and strange as it may seem to you, it is for the purpose of requesting the loan of three hundred and fifty dollars, for which I can give you no security but my word, and in this case consider this to be sufficient. My call for money at this time is pressing, or I would not trouble you; but with that sum, I have the prospect of turning it to so much advantage, as to be able to refund it with interest in the course of six months. At all events, I think it will be for your interest to comply with my request, and that immediately — that is,

not to put off any longer than you receive this. Then set down and inclose me the money with as much despatch as possible, for your own interest. This, Sir, is my advice; and if you do not comply with it, the short period between now and November will convince you that you have denied a request, the granting of which will never injure you, the refusal of which will ruin you. Are you surprised at this assertion? — rest assured that I make it reserving to myself the reasons and a series of facts which are founded on such a bottom as will bid defiance to property or quality. It is useless for me to enter into a discussion of facts which must inevitably harrow up your soul. No, I will merely tell you that I am acquainted with your brother Frank, and also the business that he was transacting for you on the 2nd of April last; and that I think that you was very extravagant in giving one thousand dollars to the person that would execute the business for you. But you know best about that, you see that such things will leak out. To conclude, Sir, I will inform you that there is a gentleman of my acquaintance in Salem that will observe that you do not leave town before the first of June, giving you sufficient time between now and then to comply with my request; and if I do not receive a line from you, together with the above sum, before the 22d of this month, I shall wait upon you with an assistant. I have said enough to convince you of my knowledge, and merely inform you that you can, when you answer, be as brief as possible.

"Direct yours to

"CHARLES GRANT, JR.,

"of Prospect, Maine."

This letter was an unintelligible enigma to Captain Knapp, who knew no man by the name of Charles Grant and had no acquaintance in Belfast, Maine.

Receiving this threatening message at a time when the entire community was terrorized, Mr. Knapp became alarmed and proceeded at once to Wenham to consult with his sons, Joseph and John.

After perusing the letter, Joseph Knapp, Jr., stated to his father that it contained "a lot of trash" and suggested that it be delivered to the Vigilance Committee. The father acted on his son's advice. After giving his father this foolish advice, Joseph Knapp, Jr., made a series of stupid blunders. He knew that the letter received by Joseph Knapp, Sr., was intended for Joseph Knapp, Jr., and either for the purpose of directing the investigation into another channel, or to convey the impression that Grant was some crank or joker whose statements were unworthy of investigation, he drove into Salem the next day and requested a friend to mail two letters, at the same time saying that his father had received an anonymous letter and he wanted to "nip the silly affair in the bud."

One letter was addressed to Hon. Gideon Barstow, Chairman of the Vigilance Committee, and read as follows:

"May 13, 1830.

"Gentlemen of the Committee of Vigilance: — Hearing that you have taken up four young men on suspicion of being concerned in the murder of Mr. White, I think it time to inform you that Steven White came to me one night and told me, if I would remove the old gentleman, he would give me five thousand dollars; he said he was afraid he would alter his will if he lived any longer. I told him I would do it, but I was afeared to go into the house, so he said he would go with me, that he would try to get into the house in the evening and open the window, would then go home and go to bed and meet me again about eleven. I found him, and we both went into his chamber. I struck him on the head with a heavy piece of lead, and then stabbed him with a dirk; he made the finishing strokes with another. He promised to send me the money next evening, and has not sent it yet, which is the reason that I mention this.

"Yours, etc.,

"GRANT."

The second letter was addressed to Hon. Stephen White, a nephew of the murdered man and the principal heir. It read as follows:

"Lynn, May 12, 1830.

"Mr. White will send the $5000, or a part of it, before to-morrow night, or suffer the painful consequences.

"GRANT."

Immediately after Mr. Knapp, Sr., delivered the letter sent from Belfast to the Vigilance Committee, a letter was mailed to Chas. Grant, Jr., Prospect, Maine, by the Vigilance Committee and a trusted agent proceeded to that point. He at once took the postmaster of the town into his confidence and remained in hiding in the office.

The same day a man called for the letter and stated that his name was Charles Grant, Jr. He was taken into custody and proved to be an ex-convict named Palmer who resided in the adjoining town of Belfast.

Seeing the advisability of proving that he did not participate in the White murder, Palmer made a statement as follows:

> "I have been an associate of George and Richard Crowninshield and on April 2, 1830, I was sitting by a window in their house and saw Frank Knapp and Charles Allen drive up. The Crowninshield brothers, Knapp and Allen, then went for a walk. Upon their return, George and Richard informed me that Frank Knapp had asked them to kill Mr. White and that Joseph Knapp, Jr., would pay $1000 for the job. Several different modes of executing it were discussed but it was finally decided to kill him at night when Mrs. Beckford was not home."

Palmer was detained as a witness and warrants were at once procured for the arrest of John and Joseph Knapp.

The arrest of these two young men created a great sensation. Fearing that he might have unconsciously assisted the assassin, the young man who mailed the two letters for Knapp went before the Vigilance Committee and testified to all he knew regarding the incident.

It was then proven that the letters were in the handwriting of Joseph Knapp, Jr.

On the third day of his imprisonment, Joseph Knapp made a complete confession as follows:

> "I knew that Mr. White had made out a will in which he gave my mother-in-law, Mrs. Beckford, a legacy of $15,000. According to my understanding of the law, which I have since learned was erroneous, I believed she would get $200,000 if no will was found. I therefore decided to steal the will and have Mr. White assassinated. Four days before the murder I was in Mr. White's chamber and procuring the key to his iron chest, I took his will and carried it home, burning it several days later. My brother Frank negotiated with Richard Crowninshield who agreed to do the deed for $1000.
>
> "The night of April 6th was finally decided upon and I persuaded my mother-in-law to spend a few days with my wife at Wenham.
>
> "On the 6th instant I visited Mr. White's home, to which I always

had access, and unfastened the window at the back of the rear parlor. That day Crowninshield showed me the bludgeon and dagger with which the murder was to be committed. Crowninshield and my brother Frank met at 10 o'clock that night by appointment and proceeded to a spot where they could observe the movements in White's mansion. It was a beautiful moonlight night.

"Crowninshield requested Frank to go home. He left, but soon returned. During his absence the lights in the mansion were extinguished and shortly afterward the hired assassin placed a plank against the house, entered the window and crept upstairs to White's sleeping chamber. The moon was shining through the window on to the old man's face. Crowninshield swung his bludgeon and struck White on the left temple, probably killing him instantly. But, to be certain, he lowered the bed clothes and stabbed him repeatedly in the region of the heart.

"He then felt his pulse and being satisfied that the job was well done, he departed. He met Frank on a side Street and explained in detail what he had done. After hiding the bludgeon under the steps of a meeting-house on Howard Street, he returned to Danvers.

"I was at home in Wenham on this night. A few days later, Crowninshield, accompanied by my brother Frank, called on me at my home in Wenham and demanded his money. I was only able to pay him one hundred five-franc pieces. He related to me all the details of the assassination and I informed him that our work had been all in vain; that the will I stole was not the last one, and even if it had been, my object would not have been accomplished because of my misunderstanding of the law.

"The story my brother and I told the Vigilance Committee on April 27th in regard to the alleged robbery was a sheer fabrication. It was I who wrote the two anonymous letters."

Richard Crowninshield, who had assumed an air of indifference ever since his arrest, collapsed when informed of Knapp's confession.

The officers proceeded to the meeting-house and found the bludgeon described by Knapp, under the steps.

When Palmer was brought to Salem he gave the authorities additional information regarding Crowninshield's criminal career which enabled them to recover a quantity of stolen property concealed in Crowninshield's barn.

On June 15, Crowninshield committed suicide by hanging himself to the bars of his cell with a handkerchief.

Indictments for the murder were shortly afterward found against John Knapp as principal and Joseph J. Knapp, Jr., and George Crowninshield as accessories.

As the law stood at that time it was necessary to convict the principal before an accessory could be tried.

John Knapp's trial began before the Supreme Court in Salem on August 20th, 1830, and the great lawyer and statesman, Daniel Webster, was engaged to conduct the prosecution. Joseph Knapp, Jr., was promised immunity if he would testify to the facts for the prosecution, but when called to the stand he refused to testify against his brother. A strong case was made, however, without his assistance.

Before entering into a discussion of the evidence, Mr. Webster, in addressing the jury, spoke as follows:

> "I am little accustomed, gentlemen, to the part which I am now attempting to perform. Hardly more than once or twice has it happened to me to be concerned on the side of the government in any criminal prosecution whatever; and never, until the present occasion, in any case affecting life.

> "But I very much regret that it should have been thought necessary to suggest to you that I am brought here to 'hurry you against the law and beyond the evidence.' I hope I have too much regard for justice, and too much respect for my own character, to attempt either; and were I to make such attempt, I am sure that in this court nothing can be carried against the law, and that gentlemen intelligent and just as you are, are not, by any power, to be hurried beyond the evidence. Though I could well have wished to shun this occasion, I have not felt at liberty to withhold my professional assistance, when it is supposed that I may be in some degree useful in investigating and discovering the truth respecting this most extraordinary murder.

> "It has seemed to be a duty incumbent on me, as on every other citizen, to do my best and my utmost to bring to light the perpetrators of this crime. Against the prisoner at the bar, as an individual, I cannot have the slightest prejudice. I would not do him the smallest injury or injustice. But I do not affect to be indifferent to the discovery and the punishment of this deep guilt. I cheerfully share in the opprobrium, how great soever it may be, which is cast on those who feel and manifest an anxious concern that all who had a part in planning, or a hand in executing, this deed of midnight assassination may be brought to answer for their enormous crime at

the bar of public justice.

"Gentlemen, it is a most extraordinary case. In some respects, it has hardly a precedent anywhere; certainly none in our New England history. This bloody drama exhibited no suddenly excited, ungovernable rage. The actors in it were not surprised by any lion-like temptation springing upon their virtue, and overcoming it, before resistance could begin. Nor did they do the deed to glut savage vengeance, or satiate long-settled and deadly hate. It was a cool, calculating, money-making murder. It was all 'hire and salary, not revenge.' It was the weighing of money against life; the counting out of so many pieces of silver against so many ounces of blood.

"An aged man, without an enemy in the world, in his own house, and in his own bed, is made the victim of a butchery murder, for mere pay. Truly, here is a new lesson for painters and poets. Whoever shall hereafter draw the portrait of murder, if he will show it as it has been exhibited, where such example was last to have been looked for, in the very bosom of our New England society, let him not give it the grim visage of Moloch, the brow knitted by revenge, the face black with settled hate, and the bloodshot eye emitting livid fires of malice. Let him draw, rather, a decorous, smooth-faced, bloodless demon; a picture in repose, rather than in action; not so much an example of human nature in its depravity, and in its paroxysms of crime, as an infernal being, a fiend, in the ordinary display and development of his character.

"The deed was executed with a degree of self-possession and steadiness equal to the wickedness with which it was planned. The circumstances now clearly in evidence spread out the whole scene before us. Deep sleep had fallen on the destined victim, and on all beneath his roof. A healthful old man, to whom sleep was sweet, the first sound slumbers of the night held him in their soft but strong embrace. The assassin enters, through the window already prepared, into an unoccupied apartment. With noiseless foot he paces the lonely hall, half lighted by the moon; he winds up the ascent of the stairs, and reaches the door of the chamber. Of this, he moves the lock, by soft and continued pressure, till it turns on its hinges without noise; and he enters, and beholds his victim before him. The room is uncommonly open to the admission of light. The face of the innocent sleeper is turned from the murderer, and the beams of the moon, resting on the gray locks of his aged temple, show him where to strike. The fatal blow is given, and the victim passes, without a struggle or a motion, from the repose of sleep to the repose of death! It is the assassin's purpose to make sure work; and he plies the dagger, though it is obvious that life has been destroyed by the blow of the bludgeon. He even raises the aged arm, that he may not fail in his aim at the heart, and replaces it again over the wounds of the poinard! To finish the picture, he explores the wrist for the pulse! He feels for it, and ascertains that it beats no longer! It is accomplished. The deed is done. He retreats, retraces his steps to the window, passes out through it as he came in, and escapes. He has done the murder. No eye has seen him, no ear has heard him. The secret is his own, and it is safe!

"Ah, gentlemen, that was a dreadful mistake! Such a secret can be safe nowhere. The whole creation of God has neither nook nor corner where guilt can bestow it, and say it is safe. Not to speak of that Eye which pierces through all disguises and beholds everything as in the splendor of noon, such secrets of guilt are never safe from detection, even by men. True it is, generally speaking, that 'murder will out.' True it is, that Providence hath so ordained, and doth so govern things, that those who break the great law of Heaven by shedding man's blood seldom succeed in avoiding discovery.

"Especially, in a case exciting so much attention as this, discovery must come, and will come, sooner or later. A thousand eyes turn at once to explore every man, everything, every circumstance, connected with the time and place; a thousand ears catch every whisper; a thousand excited minds intensely dwell on the scene, shedding all their light, and ready to kindle the slightest circumstance into a blaze of discovery. Meantime the guilty soul cannot keep its own secret. It is false to itself; or rather it feels an irresistible impulse of conscience to be true to itself. It labors under its guilty possession, and knows not what to do with it. The human heart was not made for the residence of such an inhabitant. It finds itself preyed on by a torment, which it dares not acknowledge to God or man. A vulture is devouring it, and it can ask no sympathy or assistance, either from heaven or earth. The secret which the murderer possesses soon comes to possess him, and leads him whithersoever it will. He feels it beating at his heart, rising to his throat, and demanding disclosure. He thinks the whole world sees it in his face, reads it in his eyes, and almost hears its workings in the very silence of his thoughts. It has become his master. It betrays his discretion, it breaks down his courage, it conquers his prudence. When suspicions from without begin to embarrass him, and the net of circumstance to entangle him, the fatal secret struggles with still greater violence to burst forth. It must be confessed, it will be confessed; there is no refuge from confession but suicide, and suicide is confession.

"It is said, that 'laws are made, not for the punishment of the guilty, but for the protection of the innocent.' This is not quite accurate, perhaps, but if so, we hope they will be so administered as to give that protection. But who are the innocent whom the law would protect? Gentlemen, Joseph White was innocent. They are innocent who, having lived in the fear of God through the day, wish to sleep in His peace through the night, in their own beds. The law is established that those who live quietly may sleep quietly; that they who do no harm may feel none. The gentleman can think of none that are innocent except the prisoner at the bar, not yet convicted. Is a proved conspirator to murder innocent?

"Are the Crowninshields and the Knapps innocent? What is innocence? How deep stained with blood, how reckless in crime, how deep in depravity may it be, and yet retain innocence? The law is made, if we would speak with entire accuracy, to protect the innocent by punishing the guilty. But there are those innocent out of court, as well as innocent prisoners at the bar.

"The criminal law is not founded in a principle of vengeance. It does not punish that it may inflict suffering. The humanity of the law feels and regrets every pain it causes, every hour of restraint it imposes, and more deeply still very life it forfeits. But it uses evil as the means of preventing greater evil. It seeks to deter from crime by the example of punishment. This is its true, and only true, main object. It restrains the liberty of the few offenders, that the many who do not offend may enjoy their liberty. It takes the life of the murderer that other murders may not be committed. The law might open the jails and at once set free all persons accused of offenses, and it ought to do so if it could be made certain that no other offenses would hereafter be committed; because it punishes, not to satisfy any desire to inflict pain, but simply to prevent the repetition of crimes. When the guilty, therefore, are not punished, the law has so far failed of its purpose; the safety of the innocent is so far endangered. Every unpunished murder takes away something from the security of every man's life. Whenever a jury, through whimsical and ill-founded scruples, suffer the guilty to escape, they make themselves answerable for the augmented danger of the innocent.

"We wish nothing to be strained against this defendant. Why, then, all this alarm? Why all this complaint against the manner in which the crime is discovered? The prisoner's counsel catch at supposed flaws of evidence, or bad character of witnesses, without meeting the case. Do they mean to deny the conspiracy? Do they mean to deny that the two Crowninshields and the two Knapps were conspirators? Why do they rail against Palmer, while they do not disprove, and hardly dispute, the truth of any one fact sworn to by him? Instead of this, it is made matter of sentimentality that Palmer has been prevailed upon to betray his bosom companions and to violate the sanctity of friendship."

After a lengthy discussion of the evidence, Mr. Webster closed his argument with the following impressive appeal to the jury:

"Gentlemen, your whole concern should be to do your duty, and leave consequences to take care of themselves. You will receive the law from the Court. Your verdict, it is true, may endanger the prisoner's life; but then, it is to save other lives. If the prisoner's guilt has been shown and proved, beyond all reasonable doubt, you will convict him.

If such reasonable doubts of guilt still remain, you will acquit him. You are the judges of the whole case. You owe a duty to the public as well as to the prisoner at the bar. You cannot presume to be wiser than the law. Your duty is a plain, straightforward one. Doubtless, we would all judge him in mercy. Towards him, as an individual, the law inculcates no hostility; but towards him, if proved to be a murderer, the law and the oaths you have taken, and public justice, demand that you do your duty.

"With consciences satisfied with the discharge of duty, no consequences can harm you. There is no evil that we cannot face or fly from but the consciousness of duty disregarded.

"A sense of duty pursues us ever. It is omnipresent, like the Deity. If we take to ourselves the wings of the morning and dwell in the utmost parts of the seas, duty performed, or duty violated, is still with us, for our happiness, or our misery. If we say the darkness shall cover us, in the darkness as in the light our obligations are yet with us. We cannot escape their power nor fly from their presence. They are with us in this life, will be with us at its close; and in that scene of inconceivable solemnity which lies yet farther onward, we shall still find ourselves surrounded by the consciousness of duty, to pain us wherever it has been violated, and to console us so far as God may have given us grace to perform it."

The defendant was found guilty as charged. Joseph Knapp was then tried and convicted and the two brothers were hanged from the same scaffold.

George Crowninshield proved an alibi and was acquitted.

THE MURDER OF GOVERNOR WILLIAM GOEBEL

IN FRONT OF THE STATE HOUSE IN FRANKFORT,

KENTUCKY.

State Senator William E. Goebel was the candidate of the Democratic party of Kentucky for Governor in the election of 1899 and his principal opponent was W. S. Taylor, the Republican nominee.

The State Board of Election Commissioners canvassed the returns and issued a certificate of election to Taylor, who was duly inaugurated and took possession of the archives and records appertaining to the office.

Shortly afterward a contest was instituted by Goebel before the Legislature at Frankfort and was pending on January 30, 1900.

At 11 a. m. on this date, Goebel left his hotel in Frankfort in company with Colonel Jack Chinn and Captain E. Lillard, warden of the penitentiary.

When they reached the State House gate, a shot was fired from the direction of a three-story building in which a number of State officials, including Governor Taylor and Secretary of State Caleb Powers, had offices.

Simultaneously with the first shot, Goebel uttered an involuntary exclamation of pain and looking in the direction of this building he attempted to draw his revolver, but his strength failed him and he sank to the sidewalk, mortally wounded.

Several other shots were fired from the same direction with great rapidity but no other wounds were inflicted.

When informed of the cowardly assault, Taylor appeared to be horror-stricken and bitterly denounced the act.

He at once ordered out the militia for the purpose of "preserving order," but the rapidity with which the armed forces responded, caused many to suspect that the soldiers had been held in waiting for some reason not generally known.

The Democratic majority of the Legislature immediately made several attempts to meet, but were forcibly dispersed by order of Governor Taylor.

Despite this opposition, the meeting was held on January 31, and William Goebel was declared Governor and John C. Beckham, Lieutenant Governor.

Ignoring the protests of his physicians, Goebel, by a superhuman effort, sat up in bed and took the oath of office administered by Chief Justice Hazelrig.

His first official act was to issue a proclamation ordering the militia to withdraw from the capitol, but the order was ignored.

On February 1, "Governor" Taylor signed vouchers on the Farmers' Bank in favor of the militia officers who needed money for their men, but President Rodman refused payment on the ground that Taylor had usurped the office.

Taylor then issued a pardon for a convict named Douglas Hayes, but Warden Lillard, who was with Goebel when he was shot, refused to liberate the prisoner.

As Taylor ordered the militia to prevent the Legislature from convening, an order restraining him from interfering was issued by the court, and one Alonzo Walker was deputized to serve the order on Taylor. The latter would not permit Walker to enter his office, so he tacked the notice on the door, whereupon Taylor rushed out and ordered the soldiers to take him into custody.

On February 3, 1900, Goebel died, and almost immediately afterward J. C. W. Beckham was sworn in as his successor, and he opened an office in the Capitol Hotel.

The feeling was so intense that the soldiers were frequently compelled to fire over the heads of mobs which were constantly gathering and hooting at them.

On February 6, Judge Moore issued a writ of habeas corpus ordering the release of Walker, and although Taylor ignored the order at first he subsequently obeyed it.

On February 8, Governor Goebel was buried with the greatest pomp and ceremony ever witnessed in Kentucky.

On February 10, Taylor withdrew the troops, and two days later the Legislature met unmolested for the first time since the assault on Goebel. The first act was to offer an enormous reward for information leading to the conviction of the assassin.

The bullet which probably passed through Goebel was found embedded in a tree and was a 38-calibre steel jacket rifle bullet. Taking into consideration the position in which Goebel stood when shot, the angle at which the bullet passed through the body, and its position in the tree, surveyors decided that it was probably fired from the window of Caleb Powers' office.

Much other evidence was also obtained tending to show that the shots were fired from Powers' office, and, as a result, warrants were issued for Powers and John Davis, a policeman of the State Capitol square. "Governor" Taylor protected these men and instructed the soldiers not to permit Sheriff Sutter to enter the Capitol for the purpose of serving the warrants.

Powers and Davis subsequently escaped from Frankfort, but it was learned that they were disguised as soldiers and were accompanied by twenty-five soldiers on a train en route to Barboursville, the stronghold of the Taylor faction.

Chief of Police Ross of Lexington gathered his entire force, and when the train pulled into the depot they made a rush into the car, and after a desperate battle Powers and Davis were arrested.

It was learned that on January 18 a meeting was held, in which Caleb Powers was an active participant, for the purpose of bringing fifteen hundred armed men from the eastern section of the state to Frankfort for the purpose of influencing legislative action by their presence. Powers personally arranged the details for their coming and pledged them to secrecy.

Evidence was obtained tending to show that, on January 19, the Militia Company of Frankfort was secretly assembled.

The members were drilled daily, but secretly, inside of the arsenal, where board was provided for them.

While at Barboursville, on January 22, 1900, Caleb Powers addressed to Adjutant General Collier a letter which read as follows:

"My Dear Sir: — There are two companies at this end of the state that refuse to go unless they are called out regularly.

"The London company under Captain E. Parker and the Williamsburg company under Captain Watkins are the ones.

"We must have these men and guns as we are undertaking a serious matter and win we must. Send orders to have these companies join us Wednesday night. Don't fail. Wire tomorrow.

"Will be there Thursday with 1200 men. Arrange board and lodging.

"Sincerely yours,

Caleb Powers."

Powers also ordered printed badges bearing the picture and autograph of Taylor which were to be distributed among the men at the train.

On January 25, twelve hundred men arrived at Frankfort, including several members of the militia, who kept their uniforms concealed. They were accompanied by Powers.

Of the twelve hundred, all were immediately sent home with the exception of 200 picked men.

Just previous to the shooting, Caleb Powers, his brother John, who was a captain in the militia, and F. Wharton Golden, a sergeant in the same organization, boarded a train for Louisville, but Caleb returned almost immediately after arriving at his destination.

On March 23, Powers' trial began. He immediately filed a pardon signed by "Governor" Taylor, but the court adjudged it invalid on the ground that the judgment of the Legislature was conclusive, and therefore Taylor was a mere usurper and intruder.

An appeal was immediately taken to the Court of Appeals, which upheld the trial judge.

The Supreme Court of the United States was then appealed to, with the result that on May 21, 1900, a decision was handed down which sustained the lower courts, and Taylor was ousted after the mandate from this court was issued.

Powers' case was transferred to Scott Circuit Court by change of venue upon indictment charging him as accessory before the fact to the murder of Goebel.

At the trial, Sergeant F. Wharton Golden of the State Militia testified that Powers had instructed him to procure a number of men to enter the executive halls and kill enough Democrats to have the contest decided in favor of Taylor. Golden then related how he met John Powers, a brother of Caleb, and John said: "Goebel is to be killed to-day;" and almost immediately afterward John gave a tall man with a black mustache a key to Caleb's office. Golden also asserted that "Governor" Taylor was implicated in the conspiracy.

Golden furthermore testified that John Powers had informed him that two negroes, "Tallow Dick" Combs and "Hocker" Smith had been hired to assassinate Goebel.

On March 26, during the trial, a colloquy arose between Col. T. C. Campbell, counsel for the prosecution, and Judge Geo. Denny, attorney for Powers, and the lie was passed. Instantly the enormous crowd stampeded. Doors and windows were broken in the mad flight, but, to the wonderment of all, the expected fusillade did not occur.

On March 27, Henry E. Youtsey, a clerk in the State Auditor's office, was arrested and charged with being one of the conspirators. Two days later "Tallow Dick" Combs, the negro mentioned by Golden, was also arrested.

About this time, Youtsey made a confession, in which he charged "Governor" Taylor and Caleb Powers with hatching the plot, and he also implicated ex-Secretary of State Charles Finley.

Youtsey declared that a gun-fighter named Jim Howard fired the fatal shot from a 38-calibre rifle which he, Youtsey, had delivered to him with a box of cartridges for that purpose. He stated that Howard received $1600 for the job.

Following the disclosures made by Youtsey, the grand jury indicted "Governor" Taylor, Caleb Powers, Charles Finley, Jas. B. Howard, Dick Combs, W. H. Culton, a clerk in the State Auditor's office, and several others on April 17, but Taylor was not arrested until May 31.

In the meantime, the trial of Caleb Powers was continued.

On July 18, the co-defendant, Culton, was called as a witness for the prosecution and gave very damaging testimony against Powers.

Ed. Steffel, a messenger boy, swore that he saw the barrel of the rifle sticking out of Powers' window when the shots were fired; that the window was open a few inches at the bottom and the curtain was drawn down.

He stated that the reason he paid particular attention to the partially opened window was because it was unusual to see a window in that condition on a cold, raw day in midwinter.

On July 30, Caleb Powers testified in his own behalf. He protested his innocence, but admitted that he was instrumental in bringing mountaineers into Frankfort, claiming that it was done for the purpose of protecting Taylor.

On August 18, the case was finally submitted to the jury, and after deliberating forty-five minutes, a verdict of guilty was rendered, which was received with prolonged applause.

On October 2, the trial of Henry Youtsey began in Georgetown.

McKenzie Todd, former private secretary to "Governor" Taylor, testified that three days previous to the shooting, he entered Caleb Powers' office and saw Youtsey experimenting with a rifle at the same window from which it was alleged the shots were fired.

On October 9, Arthur Goebel, a brother of the murdered Governor, was about to take the witness stand, but Youtsey sprang at him and was only overpowered after a desperate struggle. Youtsey was then on the verge of a mental collapse and his condition was such that several days elapsed before the trial was resumed. Arthur Goebel then testified that he visited Youtsey in his cell shortly after his confession and that he stated that it had been arranged to have the negro, Dick Combs, do the shooting, but that Taylor objected on the ground that the negro could not be trusted.

Evidence was produced showing that just previous to the shooting, Youtsey went to the office of the commissioner of agriculture, where he met a squad of armed men and brought them back to the foot of the stairway in the hall near the door leading from Powers' office.

He then told them that a man would soon come out of the office and join them and at that instant they should all go off together and scatter.

On October 20, Youtsey was found guilty and sentenced to life imprisonment.

Jim Howard, who was charged with firing the fatal shot, was subsequently tried, convicted and sentenced to life imprisonment, but was pardoned on June 13, 1908.

Caleb Powers obtained a new trial and was again convicted.

Again he appealed the case and again obtained a new trial, which resulted in the jury disagreeing.

On June 13, 1908, he was pardoned while he was confined in the Georgetown jail awaiting his fourth trial.

In March, 1909, Taylor, ex-Secretary of State Finley and the remainder of those charged with the murder (excepting Youtsey) were pardoned by the Governor.

On February 3, 1910, the tenth anniversary of the death of Governor Goebel was observed at Frankfort by the unveiling of a $15,000 monument above the grave in the State Cemetery, in the presence of a great throng.

Coincident with this ceremony, the body of Arthur Goebel, who died three days previous to the unveiling, was laid to rest beside his brother.

At the conclusion of the ceremony, the only living brother, Justus Goebel, bitterly denounced Governor A. E. Wilson for pardoning Powers and

Howard.

In conclusion he said: "To-day another brother, Arthur, you have just buried. The shot that killed William broke Arthur's heart, and the pen that pardoned Powers and Howard pierced that broken heart and killed him."

THE MURDER OF THE BEAUTIFUL AND ACCOMPLISHED MRS. WOODILL, WARD OF LYMAN GAGE, SECRETARY OF THE UNITED STATES TREASURY, AND THE TRAGIC SUICIDE OF SUSPECTED MURDERER.

In the year 1893, Col. Charles A. Thompson and wife took up their residence on a farm near McDaniel in Talbot County, Maryland. The couple had several children and a pretty little adopted daughter known as Edith May Thompson.

The records in Minneapolis show that this child was born in Asoton, Washington, on November 30, 1886; that she was the daughter of Mathew and Zetella Witz and was adopted by Charles and Laura Thompson in Minneapolis on October 13, 1890.

Notwithstanding the fact that both Witz and Thompson were comparatively poor men, this little girl was always provided with plenty of money, and in addition to receiving a fine literary and musical education, she traveled extensively in Europe.

The child claimed that a rich "Uncle" furnished the money, but her closest friends stated that she never knew the circumstances surrounding her birth.

Edith was a very pretty girl and possessed a fascinating personality. When she was twelve years of age she visited Washington, D. C, where she met Secretary of the United States Treasury Lyman Gage. Her beauty, sweet disposition and accomplishments at once attracted his attention and she was thereafter known as his ward. At the age of seventeen years, Edith married Dr. W. W. Caswell of Boston. They lived together but a short time, and eighteen months later the marriage was annulled.

In 1908, Gilbert Woodill, a young Los Angeles automobile dealer, visited New York, where he met the former Mrs. Caswell for the first time. He fell in love with her at first sight and as his business compelled him to return to Los Angeles immediately, he married her after five days' acquaintance. The couple then left for Los Angeles, where they resided at 1204 Orange Street.

In May, 1909, Woodill was compelled to go east on business and his wife accompanied him. After he had transacted his business in New York, he accompanied his wife to McDaniel, Maryland, to visit Mrs. Woodill's foster parents, Colonel and Mrs. Thompson. Woodill only remained a few days, but during that time he met a middle-aged man known as "Roberts," who had purchased a farm adjacent to the Thompson estate, several months prior to the visit of the Woodill's. "Roberts," who appeared to be a highly educated man who had evidently traveled extensively, became very friendly with the Thompson family before the arrival of the Woodill's.

Business compelled Woodill to return to Los Angeles, but his wife remained with her foster-parents.

On Saturday, June 19, Mrs. Woodill informed the Thompsons that she intended to go to Baltimore for a couple of days. On the following Monday Thompson met "Roberts" and told him that he feared all was not well with Edith, but "Roberts" laughed at the idea. Two days later a letter mailed at Baltimore and presumed to have been written by Mrs. Woodill, was received by Thompson.

On the afternoon of June 24, the nude body of a young woman was found floating in Rose Creek not far from the bungalow recently built by "Roberts" on his property.

The left side of the face and head had been crushed in; a cord was tied around the body and at the other end of the cord was tied a kettle filled with stones; it evidently being the belief of the assassin that this weight would keep the body submerged. As the body was terribly swollen and the face beaten to a pulp, it was not identified at once, but Dr. Smithers, who had recently done some dental work for Mrs. Woodill, examined the teeth and at once declared the corpse to be her remains.

It was subsequently learned that instead of going to Baltimore on the preceding Saturday, Mrs. Woodill left the train at a little station called Royal Oak, where she met "Roberts" who had a team and driver in waiting. They were then drive to a point on the river where they boarded a gasoline launch belonging to Roberts.

Later in the evening the launch was grounded opposite the residence of Dr. Seth, but "Roberts" refused assistance. He waded to the shore and procuring a rowboat, he rowed Mrs. Woodill down the river. When this information had been gathered, a search was made for "Roberts" at his bungalow.

He had disappeared but blood stains were found on the floor and fragments of burned cloth were discovered in the fireplace.

Near midnight, on June 25, John McQuay, a farmer residing on the bank of a little wandering stream called Harris Creek, heard the splash of oars, and looking out saw the dark figure of a man pulling up the stream. He called to the oarsman, but received no response. Suspecting that he was the much wanted "Roberts," McQuay telephoned to Deputy Sheriff Mortimer, who formed a posse and started in pursuit. About three hours later the posse heard faint splashes from oars and presently they saw the dark shadow of the lone boatmen. Members of the posse called out: "Roberts, throw up your hands." His reply was a pistol shot. Believing they were being fired upon, the posse fired a volley, but there was no response and the man had disappeared from view. As the posse feared that he might have laid down in the boat and would shoot if they came closer, they merely kept the boat in sight until daylight, when they approached and found the dead body in the boat. It was "Roberts' " remains, and he had committed suicide by shooting himself in the heart, powder burns being found around the wound.

The dead man's clothing was then searched. One hundred and sixty dollars was found and also letters showing that "Roberts" was in reality Robert Eastman, called "Lame Bob" because of his crippled foot. He was formerly a New York broker and had offices at 33 Wall Street, but at the time of his suicide he was a fugitive from justice, having swindled various persons out of sums aggregating many thousands of dollars.

On January 26, 1908, he married Vinnie Bradcome, a young actress from New York, who was then playing with the Rogers Brothers, but he deserted her shortly after their child was born.

Eastman had evidently planned to commit suicide if cornered, as will be seen by the following letter addressed to his wife, which was found in his pocket:

"Vinnie — Take this money and go at once to McDaniel, Talbot County, Md., and claim my body and all my property. The property consists of twenty-two acres of land and a bungalow. There is also a motor boat. Have a sale and convert the whole thing into cash.

"Little girl, I had no hand in the tragedy. I was there and removed the evidence after the other two couples fled. I did this for self-protection and am haunted. The victim was my particular friend and we were well mated. Have only known her three weeks.

"We all, that is, two men and two other women from Annapolis, went *to the bungalow for a time. Everyone got full excepting Edith and myself. Edith tried to win one of the girl's fellows and was hit three times on the head with a full bottle of champagne and hit the fellow once. She fell over on the floor and died. The man did not come too for an hour. I was left with the corpse and cannot take a chance for a trial.*

"Life to me is very bitter, so I will pull down the shades and say good-by. You can claim my property and say as little as possible, but get it. I'm awfully sorry for you and our boy. I have been hustling madly to make your path clear, but fate is against me. Bob."

The officials made a complete investigation and at its conclusion they agreed that Eastman alone murdered Mrs. Woodill. Several letters were found in the bungalow which indicated that the pair were exceedingly friendly, but absolutely nothing was found to substantiate Eastman's statement that he had entertained a party of guests just previous to the murder. The unfinished bungalow was scarcely habitable and the furniture and accommodations were hardly sufficient for one person. No wine bottles were found.

Two days after the murder, which occurred on June 19th, Eastman visited Baltimore, where he probably mailed the letter supposed to have been sent to Col. Thompson by Mrs. Woodill. He also pawned her jewelry for $200 at the store conducted by Benjamin & Co. in Baltimore, which Thompson afterward redeemed.

Despite prolonged investigation, the authorities have never penetrated the motive for the atrocious murder of this beautiful young woman, whose life, from the cradle to the grave, has been shrouded in so much mystery.

On August 15, 1910, a story was published intimating that Mary Scott Castle Charlton,* whose body was found in Lake Como, Italy, in June, 1910, and her husband, Porter Charlton, who was formerly employed in a bank in Baltimore and had made frequent visits to St. Michaels, were members of the party referred to by Eastman and possibly participated in the murder, but there was no evidence produced to connect this couple with the crime.

* Mary Scott was born in Elko, Nevada, in 1872. Shortly afterward the family moved to San Francisco, where Mary eventually became very popular in the smart set, of which her aunt, Mrs. Monroe Salisbury, was a dictator for years.

Miss Scott was distantly related to the late President Harrison and the Breckenridges of Kentucky, and her brother. Captain Henry Scott, U. S. A., married Admiral Sampson's daughter.

Mary Scott's marriage to Attorney Neville Castle of San Jose, in 1897, was one of the social events of the year. As Mrs. Castle was a beautiful woman and possessed of considerable histrionic ability she decided to go on the stage, and two years after her marriage she made her debut at the California Theater with the Frawley Company.

Soon after domestic tranquility departed from the Castle home and the couple separated, Mrs. Castle going East, where she played on the Keith Circuit for some time, and Castle eventually going to Nome, Alaska.

On August 3, 1909, Mrs. Castle fired a shot at Attorney William Craig in a corridor of the Waldorf-Astoria Hotel in New York, because she claimed he had on a previous occasion made an offensive remark which he refused to retract. Captain Scott came to his sister's rescue and finally persuaded Craig not to prosecute the woman.

On January 10, 1910, Castle obtained a divorce from his wife.

On March 12, Mary Castle and Porter Charlton, the 21-yearold son of Judge Paul Charlton of the Bureau of Insular Affairs at Washington, were clandestinely married at Wilmington, Del. Shortly afterward the couple left for Italy, where they rented a cottage at Moltrasio on Lake Como.

On June 10, the woman's body was found in a trunk partially submerged in the lake. It was evident that she had been struck on the head with some blunt instrument, and as it was known that she and her husband had drank heavily and quarreled frequently, it was suspected that he was the assassin. A search was instituted but he had disappeared.

Feeling certain that Charlton would return to America at once, Captain Scott decided to watch the incoming steamers, with the result that on June 23 he saw the suspect come ashore from the Princess Irene. He was arrested and subsequently confessed that he struck his wife with a mallet after a violent quarrel, and after placing the body in a trunk threw it in the lake.

As there is some doubt as to Charlton's sanity, it is probable that he will not be returned to Italy for trial.

THE MOLLIE MAGUIRE'S.

(From Pinkerton's Archives and Detective McParland's

statement to the author.)

From 1860 to 1875, the secret organization known as the Mollie Maguire's was very powerful in Pennsylvania, especially in the coal mining regions of Schuylkill, Carbon, Columbia and Luzerne Counties.

This order as a whole was composed chiefly of reputable citizens who were unanimous in their abhorrence of the thieves, incendiaries and assassins who appeared to be in control of the order in the counties above mentioned, and who terrorized the community and laughed at justice as they murdered fellow miners, mine superintendents and others because of real or fancied grievances.

On the evening of November 5, 1863, G. W. Ulrich, a clerk in George K. Smith's store at Audenried, Carbon County, was at the home of his employer when someone knocked at the door, Ulrich opened the door and was confronted by a large, rough-appearing man who stated that he had a letter to deliver to Mr. Smith personally. Ulrich replied that Mr. Smith was sick and could not be seen, whereupon the stranger struck the clerk over the head with a revolver while a gang, which up to this time had remained out of sight, rushed into the house. Mr. Smith came into the hall, where he was immediately surrounded and one of the gang shot him in the back of the head, killing him instantly. The assassins then escaped.

On August 25, 1865, David Muhr, superintendent of a colliery, was shot and killed in broad daylight on a public highway in Foster Township. There were several involuntary witnesses to this murder but when questioned they were afraid to speak.

On January 10, 1866, Henry H. Dunne, another mining superintendent, was killed while driving along a road near Pottsville.

On October 17, 1868, Alexander Rae, a very popular mining superintendent, was shot six times and instantly killed while driving along a road near Centralia in Columbia County.

On March 15, 1869, Superintendent William H. Littlehales of the Glen Carbon Coal Company, was shot to death on a road in Cass township, Schuylkill County, in the presence of several witnesses, who were at the time afraid to tell what transpired.

At 7 p. m. on December 2, 1871, Morgan Powell, assistant Superintendent of the Lehigh and Wilkesbarre Coal and Iron Company, was shot and killed on the public Street at Summit Hill, Carbon County. Rev. Allen

Morton saw the assassins run away but could not distinguish their features.

In addition to these crimes, F. W. S. Langdon, C. Burns and Graham Powell, all prominent mining men, were killed in Carbon County, but in no instance was the assassin brought to justice — at least not at that time.

The community became paralyzed with fear and the mining industry was seriously injured.

Finally F. B. Gowen, president of the Philadelphia and Reading Railway, Coal and Iron Companies, called upon Allen Pinkerton in October, 1873, and after relating the history of the case, asked that the famous detective bring the leaders to the bar of justice. Pinkerton decided that the only way to proceed would be to detail one of his men to disguise himself as a laborer, procure employment in the mines, learn the identity of the leaders of the Mollie Maguire's, gain their confidence and eventually gain admission to the order. It can be readily seen that this was a task for no ordinary man.

After carefully considering all of his available operators, Pinkerton finally decided upon James McParland, but he had no assurance that McParland would accept this hazardous detail. At best it meant indescribable hardships; months and probably years away from friends and kindred; the constant fear of being suspected, which would mean certain death, and continual association and dissipation with the thieves and murderers in their vile resorts.

Pinkerton realized all this but when he laid his plans before McParland, the young detective was not only willing but anxious to begin operations immediately.

The result was that on October 27, 1873, James McParland, the detective, became Jim McKenna from Denver, a vagabond and fugitive from justice, who was presumed to have killed a man in Buffalo. On this day he took the train for the mining regions, where he immediately made himself a favorite in the saloons because of his ability to sing and dance and tell stories in an entertaining manner.

One of his greatest punishments and which probably had much to do with temporarily undermining his health, was the necessity of being a "good fellow" and seldom refusing an invitation to partake of the "choice" brands of liquor dispensed at these resorts.

It was McKenna's plan to take soundings in different places and finally settle in the locality most desirable for the work at hand. After seeking "work" at Tower and Mahoney cities, he arrived at Pottsville on November 17, 1873. He took lodgings at a Mrs. O'Regan's boarding-house, where he met an agreeable young fellow named Jennings, who volunteered to show him the town that night.

They stopped at several resorts, and as they passed a saloon conducted by one Patrick Dormer, in the Sheridan House, McKenna suggested that they go in and get a drink. In a most mysterious manner Jennings drew him to one side and warned him against visiting that resort. When pressed for a reason Jennings confided to McKenna that Dormer was a "Captain of the Sleepers" or Mollie Maguire's, and his resort was their rendezvous.

As soon as McKenna could get rid of Jennings that night he returned to Dormer's, apparently in a slightly intoxicated condition. The place was crowded and an old fiddler was perched on a whisky barrel scratching away at his instrument for the entertainment of the patrons.

After purchasing a drink, McKenna began to jig to the music. He did so well that Dormer and his patrons applauded long and loudly, and the Captain of the Sleepers treated him and asked his name. McKenna then volunteered to sing a song, which added greatly to his popularity. He was bid to make himself at home and later in the evening he engaged in a card game with Dormer, Dan Kelly and one Frazer. McKenna and Dormer were partners, and during the game the detective caught Frazer cheating and exposed him. This resulted in a challenge to fight, and the bar-room floor was cleared for the occasion. Although smaller than Frazer, McKenna won the battle. After that Dormer was his best friend and told him to be sure and come around the next day.

McKenna became "confidential" and told Dormer that he had killed a man in Buffalo and was a fugitive from justice. Dormer then confided to McKenna his position in the Mollies and introduced the detective to several other shining lights in the order.

Desiring to familiarize himself with more of the country, McKenna began to bemoan his hard luck in failing to procure employment, and expressed his determination to proceed elsewhere. Dormer gave him a letter to Mike, alias "Muff," Lawler, a leader of the Mollies at Shenandoah, in which he requested that McKenna be provided with employment.

On December 15, 1873, McKenna left for Shenandoah, but made a short stop at Girardville, where he learned through a school teacher named Patrick Birmingham that Jack Kehoe, who conducted a tavern in the town, was a leading Mollie.

By employing somewhat similar methods to those used at Dormer's, McKenna became well acquainted with Kehoe.

Having procured a letter of introduction from "Bushy" Deenan, a prominent Mollie at Pottsville, to Alexander Campbell, a tavern keeper near Tamaqua, McKenna proceeded to that town, ostensibly for the purpose of procuring employment, but in reality to familiarize himself with the surroundings and become acquainted with Campbell, who was a power among the Sleepers.

McKenna then went to Shenandoah, where he took lodgings at "Muff" Lawler's tavern, and eventually became like one of the family. As this was the hotbed of the Mollies the detective made this town his headquarters.

In February, 1874, Lawler procured a position for McKenna in the mines, but the first day that he worked he wore all the skin off his hands.

On February 17, he met with an accident in the mines which disabled him for some time. On the next day Mrs. Lawler was taken sick and could not attend to her boarders, so McKenna moved to the home of Fenton Cooney.

On April 14, 1874, McKenna was initiated into the order of Mollie Maguire's through the influence of Lawler, who was then Body Master, or chief officer of the Shenandoah Division, but was about to seek promotion to the office of County Delegate and wanted McKenna's support.

After kneeling and taking the obligation, in which there was nothing objectionable, McKenna paid his fee and was instructed in the pass words, etc., commonly called "the goods," which were changed every three months.

As McKenna's duty compelled him to constantly mingle with the roughest element, he was frequently forced to participate in many free-for-all bar-room fights, where the weapons consisted of anything the combatants could lay their hands on, and although he had many hairbreadth escapes, the detective was never seriously injured.

In May, 1874, McKenna's health began to fail, and as work was scarce in the mines, he took advantage of the opportunity to recuperate. Desiring to visit and become familiar with the entire mining district, he procured a traveling card signed by Mike Lawler, the Body Master, and Barney Dolan, the County Delegate, and left Shenandoah on May 15, 1874. When he returned in July he was well received, and as "Muff" Lawler was about to resign his position as Body Master,* County Delegate Barney Dolan requested McKenna to be a candidate for the position, but he declined.

* On the night of August 3, 1873, a miner named Tom Jones was knocked down and beaten on a Street in Shenandoah by Edward Cosgrove, a prominent Mollie. Gomer James, a friend of Jones, ran to his rescue and in the general fight which followed, Cosgrove was killed. James was arrested but exonerated. This made Cosgrove's friends in the order furious and they swore vengeance. They demanded that Body Master Lawler should make a requisition on another county for some Mollies unknown in that neighborhood to come and assassinate James, but as he took no action, he was forced to resign.

On July 18, the election was held and Frank McAndrews, who afterwards saved McKenna's life, was elected Body Master and McKenna was elected Secretary. In addition to giving him a better opportunity to learn what was going on, this position gave the detective much writing to do, thus giving him an opportunity to make out his numerous and voluminous reports to his superiors without arousing suspicion.

Shortly after McAndrews was elected, a county convention of Body Masters was held at Mahoney City, and by the order of State Delegate Gallagher, County Delegate Dolan was expelled from the order because of irregularities in his accounts, and John Kehoe of Girardville was elected in his stead. At this same convention the lawless element in the order were bitterly denounced by Gallagher for the odium they had cast on an order which was organized for the purpose of assisting the widow and orphan and relieving the distressed.

In October, 1874, Gallagher wrote a scorching letter to Kehoe, in which he declared that if lawlessness did not cease the Mollies in Schuylkill County would be severed from the order. These denunciations only caused the criminals to intimate that they knew their own business.

There was another notorious organization in this locality called the "Sheet Irons," and they frequently indulged in open warfare with the Mollies.

On August 14, 1874, a schoolmaster named O'Hare was brutally beaten and his house burned to the ground because he had denounced the Mollies.

On October 31, 1874, the firemen belonging to the Citizens' Fire Company in Mahoney City were returning from a fire when a general fight occurred between them and another company of firemen, which was composed entirely of Mollies, during which George Major, Chief Burgess, or Mayor, of the town, was shot and killed. Major's brother, Jesse, believing a prominent Mollie named Daniel Doherty, killed his brother, fired several shots that severely wounded that person. Doherty was subsequently taken to Pottsville, where he was tried for the murder of Major and acquitted.

On November 18, 1874, a man named Patrick Padden was shot and killed at Carbonville. About the same time and in the same locality Michael McNally was found dead on the Street with his head almost severed from his body, and in the same county a mining boss connected with the Erie Breaker was beaten and left for dead.

One Michael Kenny of Scranton was brutally murdered and his body thrown down a steep embankment, where it was accidentally discovered.

Shortly after this three Mollies named Charles Hayes, Daniel Kelley and Edward Lawler, were out on a spree one night and entered a saloon kept by an old woman named Downey. They stole her money and helped themselves to liquor, but as she offered violent resistance, Kelley grabbed her and held her face against the hot stove until Hayes, his companion, knocked him down. This resulted in a fist fight between Kelley and Hayes, and the former was badly beaten.

By this time the clergymen of all denominations were constantly denouncing the Mollies from the pulpit.

Because of labor troubles work was practically at a standstill in the mines in the early part of 1875.

During the latter part of March the telegraph office at Summit Station was burned and shortly afterward a coal train was wrecked.

On May 6, Captain Robert Linden of the Pinkerton Agency was sent to these regions with six men to assist in preserving order and to co-operate with General Pleasants, who was in command of the coal and iron police. As it was desirable that Linden and McParland (or McKenna) have frequent conferences, it was agreed that they would "accidentally" meet in Mike Cuff's saloon in the presence of several Mollies, where Linden would recognize McKenna as the man wanted in Buffalo for "murder." After much pleading on the part of McKenna and any other Mollies who chanced to be near, Linden would finally promise not to turn him over to the authorities. The plan worked perfectly and made Linden very popular with the order. As he was then on intimate terms with the other Mollies, no suspicion was aroused when he was seen talking to McKenna.

As Frank McAndrews, the Body Master of Shenandoah Division, was out of work, he went to Wilkesbarre on May 18, 1875, and left McKenna in command of the division.

At the annual election in Girardville in 1875, Jack Kehoe, the County Delegate and recognized Czar of the Mollies in Schuylkill County, was elected Chief of Police.

On Sunday, June 1, 1875, the Mollies held a remarkable convention in the Emerald House in Mahoney City. Czar Kehoe, after offering up a prayer, instructed that Dan Doherty be brought into the room.* When Doherty entered the room he wore the same coat he had on the day he was shot.

* This was the individual who was shot at the time Mayor Major was killed.

Kehoe said: "Dan, take off your coat and show it to us." Doherty complied with the request and then pointed out the different bullet holes.

Kehoe then asked: "Who do you think did it?"

Doherty replied that it was either Jesse Major or "Bully-Bill" Thomas.

It was then decided that Jesse Major and Thomas must be killed and Kehoe instructed McKenna to assign four men to assassinate Thomas. As the militia had been called out to preserve order, McKenna argued that it would be foolish to attempt the assassination then, and he succeeded in having it indefinitely postponed.

In the meantime McAndrews returned to Shenandoah and relieved McKenna of his position of Acting Body Master. But the sentence of death passed upon Thomas was not to be forgotten.

On June 27, Kehoe issued imperative orders for Tom Hurley, John Morris, Mike Doyle and John Gibbons to proceed immediately to Mahoney City and kill Thomas as he went to work on the following morning. McKenna heard of this and attempted to see Captain Linden and have Thomas warned, but he did not have an opportunity as one Mike Carey remained by his side all that evening and slept in the same bed with him that night.

In the morning McKenna was about to start out to locate Linden when he saw Doyle coming toward the house with the news that he and the other three had finished Thomas. He explained that they lay in wait for their intended victim and when he left his house and entered the colliery stable, they walked up to the stable and began shooting, and that Thomas, after being wounded, ran behind the horses and fell. They were confident that Thomas was dead when they left him. Subsequently the remainder of the gang made substantially the same statement to McKenna. But "Bully Bill" Thomas was not dead, and although somewhat shot to pieces he was soon up and around looking for the scalps of his assailants, whose identity was then unknown to him.

In July, the detective learned of a plot to kill a mine superintendent named Forsythe, but McKenna had him warned of his danger and he moved away.

In the little town of Tamaqua, in Schuylkill County, were two policemen named B. F. Yost and B. McCarron, who had had considerable trouble with James Kerrigan, the Body Master of Tamaqua Division, and one Tom Duffy. In addition to performing police duty on the night watch, these officers were required to put out the Street lights at specified times.

At 2 a, m. on July 6, 1875, they dropped into James Carrol's saloon and then went to Officer Yost's home, where they partook of some light refreshments. Shortly afterward they left the house and went in opposite directions, Yost proceeding to put out a Street light near his home. As he was reaching for the lamp, two men suddenly appeared and Yost was shot, receiving a wound from which he died shortly afterward. Hearing the shots, Officer McCarron rushed back and fired at the fleeing men, who returned the fire, but none of the bullets took effect. In his dying statement Yost said that he had seen the men who shot him in Carrol's saloon that night.

On July 15, 1875, McKenna went to Tamaqua and within a few days learned that Hugh McGehan and James Boyle of Summit Hill had killed Yost for Alex Campbell, the prominent Mollie who conducted the tavern at Storm Hill, and that Campbell had asked these men to do the work because Body Master Kerrigan, who had been arrested by Yost, requested him to do so.

In company with one McNellis, McKenna visited Kerrigan, who admitted being in the background at the scene of the murder. He then produced the pistol the crime was committed with, and asked McNellis to return it to James Roarty of Storm Hill, who loaned it for the occasion. Kerrigan stated that Campbell furnished the two men, with the understanding that he (Kerrigan) would furnish a like number for Campbell when the latter was ready to kill Superintendent Jones of Summit Hill.* Kerrigan then took McKenna to the scene of the murder and proudly explained how it was done.

* The object of having men from other localities do the killing was to prevent the assassins from being recognized.

Carrol, the saloon man who was also Secretary of the Tamaqua Division, admitted to McKenna that McGehan fired the fatal shot, and that he (Carrol) loaned his own single barrel pistol to Boyle for the occasion.

Alex Campbell also admitted to McKenna that McGehan fired the shot, and Roarty admitted that he loaned his pistol to McGehan.

Notwithstanding the fact that Gomer James had been repeatedly warned that his life was in danger, he acted as bartender at a picnic given at Shenandoah on August 14, 1875. At 11 p. m. four men came to the bar and asked for beer. As he had his back turned while drawing the beer, James was shot and killed. McKenna afterward learned that the murder occurred while the Shenandoah Division of Mollies was in session, and that Mike Carey rushed in excitedly and interrupted the meeting by saying in a loud tone of voice, "Tom Hurley has just shot Gomer James." Body Master McAndrews reprimanded him for making this statement in the presence of all the members present.

Hurley was particularly proud of this job and demanded a reward from County Delegate Kehoe. That "worthy" appointed a committee, consisting of McKenna and Pat Butler, to listen to the evidence submitted by Hurley, and as the latter proved conclusively that he committed the deed, Kehoe suggested that he receive $500 reward.

Owing to the crowded condition of Cooney's lodging house, on August 28, 1875, Mike Doyle and McKenna were compelled to occupy the same room. Doyle placed a new pistol on the bureau and McKenna asked him what he intended to do with that. Doyle replied that it was to be used in killing Tom Sanger, a mining boss at Raven Run.

At this particular time Body Master McAndrews of Shenandoah decided that a local boss named Reece must be killed.

At the same time Body Master James Kerrigan of Tamaqua, who participated in the killing of Policeman Yost, was called upon by Alex Campbell for two men to kill John P. Jones at Summit Hill. It was arranged that McAndrews should furnish the two men needed for the Summit Hill job to Kerrigan and that in return Kerrigan should furnish the men to kill Reece. McKenna was sent with the men for Kerrigan and was to bring back the men to kill Reece.

As soon as he reached Tamaqua, McKenna sent a message to his superiors at Philadelphia notifying them of what was contemplated and requesting that the intended victims be warned through Captain Linden. As he could not find Kerrigan immediately McKenna felt that this would be a good excuse to send his two men back home and he took advantage of it. Shortly afterward he returned to Shenandoah and went to Muff Lawler's tavern, where he was informed that Sanger and his friend William Uren had been killed on the morning of September 1, while on their way to work at Heaton & Company's colliery. The gang who executed the job, namely, Mike Doyle, Friday and Charles O'Donnell, Thomas, Munley and Charles McAllister, were at Lawler's house at the time, and in the presence of McKenna they explained all the little details in connection with the double murder, and exhibited the pistols they used.

Although Superintendent John P. Jones had been warned of the plot against his life, he left his home in Langsford on September 3, 1875, on his way to work, and took the route he had been especially urged not to take. The result was that he was riddled with bullets. Some workmen heard the shots and saw three assassins run over the hill, but they were not at that time apprehended.

McKenna ascertained that Mike Doyle and Edward Kelly fired the shots, and that Body Master James Kerrigan was on the scene, but supervised the work from a distance, the same as he did when Policeman Yost was murdered.

There had been considerable talk of forming a vigilance committee to administer summary justice to the leaders of the Mollies and the assassination of Sanger, Uren and Jones, all of whom were most honorable men, aroused the community to the verge of madness.

As it was part of McKenna's plan to create the impression, both in and outside the order, that none were more desperate than he, it was commonly reported that he was in danger of being lynched at any moment. It was McKenna alone who saved the life of Foreman Reece, yet that very man, not knowing the true facts, never missed an opportunity to denounce him. A few days later Doyle, Kelly and Kerrigan were arrested for the murder of Jones.

At 3 a. m. on December 10, 1875, a gang of masked men entered the home of Friday O'Donnell, who participated in the murder of Sanger and Uren. This gang killed Mrs. McAllister, and after dragging Charlie O'Donnell into the Street, riddled his body with bullets.

On January 18, 1876, the trial of Doyle for the murder of John P. Jones began. The Mollies received another staggering blow when Body Master Kerrigan made a complete confession and testified against his accomplices. All three of the murderers of Jones were convicted. In his confession Kerrigan implicated Alex Campbell and stated that Jones was murdered because he had blacklisted McGehan and other Mollies.

In addition to having all the evidence against those who committed murder while he was detailed in the mining region, McKenna had complete cases against John Kehoe, John Campbell and Neil Doherty for the murder of F, W. S. Langdon on July 14, 1862.

In the case of Morgan Powell, murdered at Summit Hill on December 2, 1871, the detective learned that "Yellow Jack" Donohue, Thomas Fisher, Patrick McKenna, Alex Campbell and Patrick O'Donnell were the guilty men.

In the case of the murder of Alexander Rae on October 17, 1868, McKenna learned that Pat Tully, Peter McHugh and Dan Kelly, alias "The Bum," were the assassins, and that Pat Hester originated the job and loaned Kelly his pistol for the occasion. It was believed that Rae would have about $18,000 with him and it was the original intention only to rob him as he came along the road, but as he had but $60 and some jewelry, and as McHugh feared that Rae would prosecute them, Tully shot him back of the ear and then the others fired, riddling his body with bullets.

Finally it became apparent to the Mollies that the prosecution knew every move they had made for years, and they began to look for the "traitor." McKenna was openly accused by Jack Kehoe and others of being a "spy," but the detective expressed great indignation and. demanded that he be tried before a convention.

Some days later Body Master McAndrews told McKenna that there was a gang of Mollies, operating under instructions from Kehoe, who intended to kill him at the first opportunity. Shortly after this Jim McKenna left the coal regions and went to Philadelphia. When he returned with bodyguards to give his testimony at the trials, he was James McParland, the detective.

The Pinkertons had their evidence prepared and their forces swept down on the criminals, making the arrests almost simultaneously.

Mr. F. B. Gowen, President of the Railroad, Iron and Coal Companies, which engaged Pinkerton, acted as leading prosecuting attorney, and his closing argument in the case of Thomas Munley for the murder of Sanger attracted so much attention that it was printed in pamphlet form and widely circulated.

As if by magic, this bold and defiant band of assassins became a trembling, shrinking lot of wretches, each begging for mercy and many pleading for an opportunity to save their own necks by turning informer on their associates in crime. At the same time the law-abiding citizens, who had been terror-stricken by this gang for years, breathed a sigh of relief and rejoiced when they realized that law and order again reigned supreme.

In his address to the jury, President Gowen, in referring to the changed conditions, said: "And to whom are we indebted for this security which we now boast? Under the Divine Providence of God, to whom be all the honor and all the glory, we owe this safety to James McParland, and if there ever was a man to whom the people of this county should erect a monument, it is James McParland, the detective."

The following was the final outcome of the numerous trials:

Convicted of murder and executed — Jack Kehoe, Thomas Munley, Buck Donnelly, James Roarty, James Boyle, Hugh McGeehan, James Carroll, Thomas Duffy, James McDonald, James Bergen, Michael Doyle, Edward Kelly, Thomas Fisher, Alexander Campbell, "Yellow Jack" Donohue, Pat Hester, Pat Tully, Peter McHugh.

The following were also convicted of murder but as they testified and otherwise rendered valuable assistance to the prosecution, they were granted immunity:

James Kerrigan, Dan Kelly, "the bum," Charles Mulherrin, Patsy Butler, Frank McHugh.

The following were convicted of conspiracy to murder: Frank O'Neill, Mike O'Brien, Chris Donnelly, Jack Morris, John Gibbons, Cornelius Cannon.

The following were convicted of accessory after the fact: Thomas Donohue, "Muff" Lawler and Pat McKenna.

After those sentenced to imprisonment had served a few years it was unanimously agreed that justice had been satisfied, and they were pardoned, Detective McParland being an active worker in their behalf.

John Gibbons, one of the conspirators, escaped from jail and was never recaptured.

THE KIDNAPING OF LITTLE CHARLEY ROSS AND THE TRAGIC END OF THE KIDNAPERS.

(From history written by boy's father.)

In 1874, Christian K. Ross, a wealthy and highly respected gentleman, lived with his family in their large stone mansion on East Washington lane, in Germantown, a suburb of Philadelphia, and within its corporate limits.

At this time his family consisted of his wife and seven children, named Stroughton, Harry, Sophia, Walter, Charley, Marian and Annie.

Charley Ross, who was four years of age, was a chubby little fellow with long flaxen curls, and his appearance, intelligence, and disposition made him a favorite with all who met him.

His brother, Walter, was six years old, and the two were constant companions.

On June 27, 1874, two men drove by the Ross mansion in a buggy, and seeing Charley and Walter playing on the sidewalk nearby, they stopped, and after giving the children candy, engaged them in conversation.

These men drove by each day thereafter, always conversing with the children if they were in sight.

On the afternoon of July 1, they again stopped, and Charley Ross asked them for a ride and also asked them to purchase him candy and firecrackers with which to properly celebrate the approaching "Fourth of July." The two strangers readily agreed to comply with his requests, and Charley and Walter were taken into the wagon.

When they had proceeded some distance Charley asked why they did not stop at some store to buy the candy, but the men told him that they would go to "Aunt Susie's," where they could procure a whole pocketful for 5 cents. When they reached Palmer and Richmond Streets, Walter was handed 25 cents and directed to the comer store, where firecrackers were sold. While he was making his purchases, the kidnapers drove off with Charley. When Walter came out of the store he cried loudly when he realized that he was left alone. Among the sympathizers who gathered about him was a Mr. Henry Peacock, who finally restored him to his father.

Several persons were found who had seen the wagon pass when

both boys were in it, but none could be found who observed it after Walter left it, nor could any trace be found of the horse or wagon.

The motive for the abduction was not apparent at first and numerous theories were advanced. Some claimed that family troubles had caused some relative to kidnap the favorite child. Others stated that he had fallen into the hands of gypsies, while some expressed the opinion that the child was merely being concealed by Mr. Ross for the purpose of gaining notoriety.

On July 3, Mr. Ross received a letter which had been mailed in Philadelphia.

It read as follows:

"July 3 — Mr. Ros: be not uneasy you son charly be all writ we is got him and no powers on earth can deliver out of our hand, you wil hav two pay us befor you git him from us, and pay us a big cent to. if you put the cops hunting for him you is only defecting yu own end. we is got him put so no living power can gets him from us a live, if any aproch is made to his hidin place that is the signil for his instant anihilation. if you regard his lif puts no one to search for him yu money can fetch him out alive an no other existin powers, dont deceve yuself an think the detectives can git him from us for that is imposebel. you here from us in few days."

When the contents of this letter became public the officials decided that strenuous methods must be employed. Not only in Philadelphia, but throughout the country within a radius of many miles of that city, a search was instituted, the like of which, both as regards magnitude and thoroughness, has seldom been made by American police officials. The indignation of the people in that vicinity had become so great that the officers felt safe in putting aside the technicalities of the law in reference to searching private property and unless they knew that the occupants of buildings were above suspicion, the premises were searched and any protest caused officials and neighbors to look upon the protestor with suspicion.

In like manner were vessels in the stream inspected, but no trace was found of the missing child, although the thorough search resulted in an enormous amount of stolen property being recovered, and the thieves were subsequently prosecuted.

In the meantime, parents, especially of the wealthy class, had become so terrorized that they practically made prisoners of their children.

On July 6, Mr. Ross received a second letter, also mailed in Philadelphia, in which the kidnapers demanded a ransom of $20,000 and threatened to kill Charley if the detectives were put on their trail or their demand was not complied with.

The letter further stated that if Mr. Ross desired to communicate with the custodians of his child to enter a personal in the Philadelphia Ledger as follows: "Ros. we are ready to negotiate."

On July 7, Ross replied as directed and on the same day another letter was mailed to him in which he was directed to state in a personal whether or not he would come to terms.

It was then decided to continue answering the letters and to frame the answers so as to necessitate further correspondence, as it was hoped that eventually something would be revealed by which the child could be traced, or that a blunder would be committed which would lead to the detection of the writer.

Accordingly, the answer to the last letter was: "Ros will come to terms to the best of his ability,"

On July 9, another letter was written in answer to the last personal, in which the kidnapers stated that they were growing impatient and that the reason for the evasive answer was obvious to them.

Notwithstanding the tenor of the last letter from the kidnapers, Ross continued to publish ambiguous answers, and afterwards he announced that he would not compound a felony by paying money to the monsters who committed this atrocious crime.

But when Ross noted the mental and physical condition of his wife he regretted the stand he had taken, and through the personal columns of the Ledger he expressed a desire to reopen negotiations, which brought a reply from the kidnapers, in which they chided him for his impulsive and indiscreet actions.

On July 22, Mayor Stokley, of Philadelphia, on behalf of several fellow citizens, offered a reward of $20,000 for the arrest of the kidnapers.

On the same day Ross informed the kidnapers, through the usual channels, that he would comply with their request in every particular.

In reply to this the abductors expressed their reluctance to enter into any further negotiations at that time, as they claimed the moon was not at a phase for the propitious transaction of business. (The reason for this statement will appear presently.)

On July 30 the abductors instructed Ross to procure a valise and, after painting it white, to put $20,000 in small bills inside and take the train leaving at midnight for New York. He was instructed to stand on the rear platform of the last car. This train was due to arrive in New York about one hour after sunrise. He was cautioned to be on the alert from the moment the train left the depot, and if he saw a torch and a white flag waved at night time near the track or a white flag alone in the day time, he should throw the valise instantly, and if it was found to contain the money demanded, the child would be restored to its home within ten hours.

Ross procured the valise and proceeded on the journey, but instead of $20,000, the valise contained a letter in which Ross stated that he would not pay the money until he saw his child before him.

He took his position on the rear car and made the entire nerve-racking journey, but seeing no signal he returned home, where he found a letter from the kidnapers censuring him for not making the trip.

It appears that a newspaper erroneously stated that Ross had gone in another direction with some officers to follow up a clew, and believing this information came through an authentic source to the papers, the kidnapers abandoned their plans.

As the moon was not shining on the night selected, it is probable that they were waiting for a dark night so that they could not be followed, and their reason for having the valise painted white was so that it could be easily found on such a night.

Communications again passed back and forth, but Ross stated positively that the payment of the money and the delivery of the child must be simultaneous.

The response to this ultimatum was mailed in New York. The kidnapers stated that the simultaneous exchange was impossible, and they again threatened to kill the child.

On August 2, Chief of Police George Walling, of New York, telegraphed to Philadelphia for the original letters from the kidnapers, adding that he had reliable information as to their identity.

Captain Heins, of the Philadelphia police, proceeded to New York with the necessary papers, and Chief Walling's informant identified the writing as that of William Mosher, alias Johnson.

The informant then stated that in April, 1874, Mosher and Joseph Douglas, alias Clark, endeavored to persuade him to participate in the kidnaping of one of the Vanderbilt children while the child was playing on the lawn surrounding the family residence at Throgsneck, Long Island. The child was to be held until a ransom of $50,000 was obtained, and the informant's part of the plot would be to take the child on a small launch and keep it in seclusion until the money was received, but he declined to enter into the conspiracy.

He gave a minute description of the two men, and as he described little peculiarities about them which had not been published, but which Walter Ross readily recalled when questioned more closely, it was agreed that the information was most valuable.

It was then learned that Mosher was a boat builder by trade and a fugitive from justice at that time.

In 1871 he was arrested for burglary at Freehold, New Jersey, but escaped from jail before his trial.

After his escape, he and Douglas manufactured a moth preventive called "Mothee," and they traveled about the country with a horse and wagon while placing the article on the market. At the time of the kidnaping, Mosher resided with his wife and four children at 235 Monroe Street, Philadelphia, and Douglas resided in the same house.

They kept their horse and wagon in a stable on Marriot lane, but the stable was torn down and the horse and wagon, which was undoubtedly the one in which Charley Ross was carried away, disappeared about the time of the kidnaping.

On August 19, Douglas, and Mosher and his family, moved to New York, where Mosher had a brother-in-law named William Westervelt, who was formerly a police officer in that city.

About this time the Pinkerton Detective Agency was called into the case and every effort was made to apprehend these two men, but as nothing had been accomplished by November 6, Mr. Ross, who had been in constant communication with the kidnapers, answered their twenty-third and last letter, which instructed him to send two relatives to New York with the necessary money and to announce two days in advance, through the personal column of the New York Herald, when they were coming, the personal to read: "Saul of Tarsus. Fifth Ave. Hotel — instant." They also warned Ross to instruct his relatives not to leave their room in the hotel for an instant on that day.

They explained that the person calling for the package of money would be in absolute ignorance of its contents or for what purpose it was to be used, and under no conditions should the relatives converse with the messenger.

They furthermore stated that the route which the messenger would take with the money had been carefully planned so that it would be impossible for him to be followed without them knowing it, and if he was followed they would kill the child and escape. If Ross kept faith they agreed to return the child within ten hours.

Ross had finally decided to act in good faith with them, and on November 15 the following personal appeared in the New York Herald:

"Saul of Tarsus: Fifth Avenue Hotel, Wednesday, eighteenth, all day."

On the seventeenth instant Mrs. Ross' brother and nephew left with the money and carried out instructions, but no one appeared to claim it.

This was the last move made to negotiate with the kidnapers, and Mr. and Mrs. Ross, who had been physical wrecks for months, were on the verge of becoming mental wrecks when they learned the result of the journey.

Notwithstanding their bold front, subsequent events proved that the kidnapers knew that the police were virtually at their heels and they did not dare to come out of hiding, even for $20,000, although at the time they were on the verge of starvation.

About this time, a great many wealthy New Yorkers had their summer homes at Bay Ridge, which is on the east side of the upper bay of New York. In this locality I. H. Van Brunt occupied his permanent home, and next door his brother. Judge Van Brunt, of the New York Supreme Court, had his summer home. During the winter season the Judge closed this house, which was connected by a burglar alarm system with his brothers' home.

At 2 o'clock on the morning of December 14, 1874, the alarm bells began to ring violently, arousing the family of the Judge's brother.

Mr. Van Brunt, thinking that the wind might have blown open a blind, which would have caused an alarm, directed his son, Albert, to investigate. The son had proceeded but a few feet when he observed someone moving about his uncle's mansion with a lighted candle. He hastened back to his father with this information, who immediately dressed. In the meantime, two hired men named William Scott and Herman Frank were aroused. The four men procured shotguns and revolvers and went to the house, two men being stationed at the front entrance and two at the rear. It was a cold, dark, rainy night, but the men waited patiently for nearly an hour. Finally the dark forms of two men were seen as they quietly crept up out of the cellar at the rear.

Van Brunt, Sr., called "Halt," but the response was two pistol shots, which fortunately did no damage. Van Brunt then poured the contents of his shotgun into the foremost man, who fell with a cry of agony. The second man then fired at Van Brunt, but again fortune smiled on him. Burglar No. 2 then attempted to escape by running to the front, where he encountered Van Brunt, Jr. Here a battle ensued with the result that Burglar No. 2 dropped dead from a bullet through the body.

The burglar at the rear, although virtually torn to pieces, continued to fire as long as his ammunition lasted. The shooting aroused the entire neighborhood, and when Burglar No. 1 realized that he had but a few moments to live, he called for a drink of water, and between gasps he made the following statement:

"Men, I won't lie to you. My name is Joseph Douglas and the man over there is William Mosher. He lives in New York, and I have no home. I am a single man and have no relatives except a brother and sister whom I have not seen for twelve years. Mosher is married and has four children. (Here he waited a moment to regain his strength, and then continued.) I have forty dollars in my pocket that I made honestly. Bury me with that." After another pause he continued:

"Men, I am dying now and it's no use lying. Mosher and I stole Charley Ross."

He was then asked why he stole the child and he replied: "To make money." He was then asked who had charge of Charley Ross, and he replied: "Mosher knows all about the boy, ask him." They then informed him that Mosher was dead, and to prove it the latter's body was dragged over to where Douglas was lying and a light placed near the dead man's face. Douglas, who was growing more feeble each minute, barely whispered, "God help his poor wife and family." He then added: "Chief Walling knows all about us and was after us, and now he has us. The child will be returned home safe and sound in a few days."

Although the rain was falling in torrents and the dying man was drenched to the skin, he begged them not to move him or force him to talk, so an umbrella was procured and held over him. For over an hour he lay writhing in agony.

Finally he became unconscious, and fifteen minutes afterward he was dead.

Chief Walling was notified, and he sent Detective Silleck, who had known Mosher and Douglas since childhood, to identify the bodies.

Silleck immediately recognized them, and as there was a glove on one of Mosher's hands, he said: "Take that off and you will find a withered finger caused by the removal of a felon years before." The glove was removed and there was the finger withered away to skin and bone.

So that young Walter Ross could not be influenced in any way, he was not informed of the tragedy, but was taken to New York for a purpose unknown to him.

When he was shown the bodies he at once recognized Mosher's remains as those of the man who drove the wagon, and when shown the remains of Douglas, he stated he was the man who gave them candy.

Peter Callahan, who saw the children in the wagon with the men, also identified the remains. Mrs. Mosher was then located, and while she admitted that she was aware of the fact that her husband kidnaped Charley Ross, she insisted that she did not know where he was concealed.

Mr. Ross then issued a circular wherein he stated that as he was positive that the leaders in the kidnaping conspiracy had been killed, he had no desire to prosecute the parties who then had his child in custody, and that he would give $5,000 as a reward to any person who would restore his boy and no questions would be asked.

On February 25, 1875, the Legislature of Pennsylvania passed a law defining the offense of kidnaping and fixed the punishment at a fine not to exceed $10,000 and solitary confinement not to exceed 25 years, but it was specially provided that if any persons then having any kidnaped child in their possession returned such child to the most accessible sheriff or magistrate previous to March 25, 1875, such persons would be immune from punishment.

Notwithstanding the fact that the law guaranteed protection to anyone who returned this child, and as an extra inducement the father offered a reward of $5000, the child was never seen again.

Mr. Ross believed that his boy was still alive, but his principal reason for arriving at this conclusion was because Westervelt, Mosher's brother-in-law, informed him that he (Westervelt) conversed with Douglas the day before the latter's death, and Douglas stated that Mosher was then arranging plans for the simultaneous exchange of the child and the ransom.

Mr. Ross laid great stress on Westervelt's statement, although Chief Walling had repeatedly declared that he had conclusive evidence that the ex-policeman was aiding the kidnapers rather than the authorities.

As the lad could converse intelligently regarding his home surroundings, and, according to the kidnapers' letters to Mr. Ross, he constantly begged them to take him home so that he could accompany his mother to the country, it was considered probable that if the lad was still alive, he would eventually have had an opportunity to make known his identity to someone who would have restored him to his home, as the case attracted world-wide attention.

KIDNAPING OF WILLIE WHITLA IN SHARON, PA.

At 9:20 on the morning of March 18, 1909, a man drove up in a buggy to the East Ward School in the little town of Sharon, Pa., and told the janitor, William Sloss, to notify Billie Whitla, the eight-year-old son of the prominent attorney, James Whitla, that his father wanted him at his office immediately.

The janitor notified Anna Lewis, the boy's teacher, and the lad was permitted to accompany the stranger in the buggy.

Shortly after the boy was driven away, a schoolmate of his, named Morris, saw him get out of the buggy and mail a letter at the corner of Hull and Sharpsville Streets, and then get back in the buggy with the man.

That afternoon Mrs. Whitla received a letter which read as follows:

"We have your boy, and no harm will come to him if you comply with our instructions. If you give this letter to the newspapers or divulge any of its contents, you will never see your boy again. We demand $10,000 in $20, $10 and $5 bills. If you mark the money or attempt to place counterfeit money you will be sorry. Dead men tell no tales. Neither do dead boys. You may answer at the following addresses: Cleveland Press, Youngstown Vindicator, Indianapolis News and Pittsburg Dispatch in the personal columns. Answer: 'A. A. — Will do as you requested. J. P. W.' "

As Mr. Whitla was quite wealthy and his brother-in-law, Frank H. Buhl, was one of the wealthiest men in that section of the country, they immediately expressed a willingness to follow the instructions.

The horse and buggy which was used by the kidnapers was rented from Thompson's livery stable, in South Sharon, and was found at 5 p. m. the same evening on East Market Street, in Warren, Ohio, the horse being almost exhausted.

As Mr. Whitla feared that if the authorities got on the trail of the kidnapers his son might be killed, he rendered them no assistance and requested that no investigation be made until his boy was returned.

On March 20 Whitla received a letter which was directed in three hand writings. One was that of a woman, another of a man and the third by Billy Whitla.

This letter directed Whitla to proceed to the Flat Iron Park, in Ashtabula, O., designating the route for him to take, and to deposit the money in a certain spot.

Whitla proceeded to the park, but as he did not follow instructions as to the route, no one appeared for the money.

On March 22 Mr. Whitla received another letter, which read as follows:

"A mistake was made at Ashtabula Saturday night. You come to Cleveland on the Erie train leaving Youngstown at 11:10 a. m. Leave the train at Wilson Avenue. Take a car to Wilson and St. Clair. At Dunbar's drug store you will find a letter addressed to William Williams.

"We will not write you again on this matter. If you attempt to catch us you will never see your boy again."

The letter at the drug store instructed Whitla to proceed to a confectionery store conducted by a Mrs. Hendricks at 1386 East Fifty-Third Street, and deliver the package of bills to the woman in charge and inform her it was for Mr. Hayes.

This woman would then give him a note instructing him as to his next move. Whitla did as directed. Mrs. Hendricks received the package of bills, but in complete ignorance of its contents. She then handed Whitla the note which "Hayes" had previously given her with instructions to hand it to the party who delivered the package.

This note instructed Whitla to proceed at once to the Hollenden Hotel and await his son, which he did.

At 8 o'clock that night two young men named Edward Mahoney and Thomas Rumsey saw a boy of Willie Whitla's description on a Payne Avenue Street car, who, upon being interrogated, stated that he was going to meet his father at the Hollenden Hotel.

The boy acted as though he was under the influence of some opiate, and although he stated that his name was Jones, he was turned over to Policeman Dewar, who took him to the hotel and delivered him to Mr. Whitla, who had become hysterical after three hours' of nerve-racking waiting.

It was some moments before the boy recognized his father. After his mind cleared he stated that he had been in the custody of "Mr. and Mrs. Jones," who informed him that he was in their charge because his father feared he would catch the smallpox if he was not taken away. He said it was "Mr. Jones" who called at the school for him.

In the house where the boy was detained he was told to hide under the sink whenever anyone knocked at the door, as it might be the doctor, who would take him to the pest house if he saw him. The boy took great delight in "fooling the doctor."

He furthermore stated that "Mr. and Mrs. Jones" escorted him to the car on the night he returned to his father.

When Billie returned to Sharon with his father the town became the scene of a carnival. A military organization known as the "Buhl Rifles," named after the lad's millionaire uncle, paraded the Streets, followed by a large portion of the population, and bands serenaded at the Buhl and Whitla homes.

Notwithstanding the fact that Chief Kohler, the "Golden Rule chief," of the Cleveland police, whom ex-President Roosevelt regards as one of the leading police officials in America, had been ignored and misled by those who were in a position to assist him to recover the boy and apprehend the criminals, he proceeded with his investigation on the day following the recovery of Billie, and ascertained that the kidnapers had been holding him a prisoner at the Granger Apartment House, at 2022 Prospect Avenue, S. E., nearly all the time he was in their custody.

But the child had been so closely confined that Miss Mills and Mr. Hears, who conducted the house, believed that the man and woman, who gave the names of Mr. and Mrs. J, H. Walters, were alone in the apartments.

Pat O'Reilly, who conducted a saloon on Ontario Street, informed the police that shortly after the ransom was paid a young man and a very pretty dark-complexioned young woman were in his place and that they spent $30 in a very short time. But the most significant circumstance was that the man always produced five-dollar bills when paying for drinks, which he at times purchased for everyone in the house.

On Wednesday, March 24, Captain Shattuck and Detective Woods, of the Cleveland police, arrested a man and woman who answered the descriptions given by O'Reilly, and when they arrived in front of the police station, the man broke away from the officers and attempted to escape.

Captain Shattuck fired a shot at the fleeing man, who stumbled and fell and he was recaptured before he could rise to his feet. When the woman was searched $9,848 was found concealed on her person. The money was of the same denomination as that paid by Whitla and was in packages, just as he had delivered it.

The couple finally gave the names James H. Boyle and wife, and virtually admitted their guilt.

Billie Whitla was brought back to Cleveland, and he at once identified the couple as the Mr. and Mrs. Jones who had "protected" him from the doctor and gave him candy that made him "sleepy."

Mrs. Hendricks identified Boyle as the man who left the note to be delivered to the man who left a package for "Hayes" and who subsequently returned for the package.

As it was feared that Boyle and his wife might be lynched if they were taken to Sharon, it was decided to detain them in the Pittsburg jail until their trial began at Mercer, Pa.

On May 6 Boyle's trial took place in Mercer, Pa. The movements of the defendant and Mrs. Boyle were traced by different witnesses from the time Billie was kidnaped until their arrest.

The evidence produced by the prosecution was so overwhelming that the defense realized the folly of attempting to disprove it, and offered no testimony.

The lad testified that at the request of Boyle he wrote his mother's name and address on the envelope which was mailed in Sharon immediately after the kidnaping. He also stated that Boyle "had whiskers here" (indicating the upper lip) when he called at the school. Abner Hancock, of Niles, Ohio, testified that he shaved Boyle shortly afterward.

After a brief argument the case was submitted to the jury and after a few moments' deliberation the defendant was found guilty.

Mrs. Boyle's case began the same day, and as she was leaving the court a mob of men and women threatened to lynch her, but she defied them and shouted that she would make them all "climb trees" if the officers would release her.

Her trial was resumed on the following day, the evidence against her being similar to that which convicted her husband, with the exception that Billie identified the nurse's suit which Mrs. Boyle wore in the Granger Apartments for the purpose of adding weight to the tale she related to him, which was to the effect that he was being detained in a hospital.

Like her husband, Mrs. Boyle offered no defense, and was promptly found guilty of aiding and abetting in the kidnaping.

On May 11 Mrs. Boyle was sentenced to 25 years' imprisonment, while Boyle was sentenced to penal servitude for life.

Boyle then stated that Harry Forker, Mrs. Whitla's brother, originated and participated in the kidnaping conspiracy.

Boyle claimed that on the night of June 8, 1895, he and Dan Shay, a saloonkeeper, who died in 1907, discovered Forker removing letters from the dead body of Dan Reeble, Jr., which was lying on the sidewalk' on Federal Street in Youngstown. As a price for his silence, Boyle claimed that he had since extorted various amounts of money from Forker, but when he demanded $5,000 in November, 1908, Forker claimed he could not pay the amount, but in a letter suggested that Billie Whitla be kidnaped and held for ransom.

Boyle claimed that he delivered this letter to Whitla after the kidnaping, but before his arrest, with the understanding that he would not be prosecuted.

Mr. Whitla and Mr. Forker branded Boyle's statement as preposterous.

Policeman Michael Donnelly, of the Youngstown police, stated that he was talking to Reeble in front of the building where the latter lived on the early morning of his death. The two men parted, Reeble going upstairs, and when the officer had walked about 200 feet he heard a noise in the direction of the Mauser building, and on returning he found Reeble lying unconscious on the sidewalk. As the dying man made a practice of sitting on his window sill before retiring, he probably lost his balance and fell. According to Donnelly, neither Forker, Shay nor Boyle was present.

THE MURDER OF THE PROMINENT AND WEALTHY PHYSICIAN, DR. PARKMAN, OF BOSTON, BY PROFESSOR WEBSTER, OF HARVARD COLLEGE.

On Friday, November 23, 1849, one of the most prominent physicians in Boston, Dr. George Parkman, mysteriously disappeared. Being very methodical in his habits, his family immediately suspected foul play.

He was the owner of many tenement houses and was rather exacting in his attitude toward his tenants, many of whom were of the rougher class. As he collected the rents himself, the authorities proceeded on the theory that he had antagonized some of these tenants to such an extent that they murdered him for the double purpose of revenge and robbery, and then concealed his body.

The river was dredged and the doctor's tenements and the buildings adjacent thereto were thoroughly searched, but no trace was found of the missing man, although large rewards were offered.

When the doctor left home, about noon on November 23, he stated that he had an appointment with a person at 2:30 p. m., but did not divulge the name of the person.

About 1:30 p. m. he entered the grocery store conducted by Paul Holland, at Vine and Blossom Streets, and after leaving an order, he asked permission to leave a paper bag containing a head of lettuce at the store for a few moments, but he never returned for it. This grocery store was but a short distance from one of the leading medical colleges in Boston, the college being located on Grove Street. Ellas Fuller, who conducted an iron foundry adjacent to the medical college, and his brother, Albert, saw Dr. Parkman in front of the college about 2 p. m. on the date of his disappearance.

Dr. John Webster was the professor of chemistry at this college and also at Harvard College. His standing in the social and professional world was equal to that of Dr. Parkman, and their families were on terms of considerable intimacy.

Notwithstanding the fact that Dr. Parkman called on Dr. Webster at the college at 2 p. m. on Friday, the 23rd instant, and his subsequent disappearance was the principal topic of conversation in Boston the next day and for some time afterward. Dr. Webster did not inform the almost distracted members of the Parkman family of this visit until the Sunday evening following, although it was proven that he saw an account of the doctor's disappearance in the Boston Transcript on Saturday afternoon.

Dr. Webster then stated that Dr. Parkman called on him for the purpose of collecting $450 which Webster had previously borrowed, giving as security a mortgage on a piece of real estate.

He claimed that he paid Dr. Parkman the full amount due, from the proceeds of the sale of tickets to his course of lectures in the college.

Dr. Parkman held a note for this amount, which he had in his possession when he called on Dr. Webster and which the latter subsequently produced to prove that he had paid the money. He added that Dr. Parkman stated that he would proceed forthwith to Cambridge and cancel the mortgage.

Dr. Webster also claimed that he saw Dr. Parkman go down stairs and leave the college after this transaction.

Webster made many conflicting statements as to the denomination of the money paid and as to the circumstances under which it was paid, but his standing in the community was such that it was difficult to believe him guilty of any wrongdoing and it would have been considered preposterous at that time to even suspect him of being implicated in the murder of his friend and benefactor.

Merely as a matter of form, the authorities decided to search the medical college, but before proceeding with the formal search an apology was made to Dr. Webster for the intrusion.

When Ephraim Littlefield, the janitor of the building, observed the farcical search, he looked on with disapproving eyes, and intimated that a more thorough search would result in sensational discoveries.

The authorities then questioned Littlefield closely, and he made the following statement:

"I have known Dr. Parkman for many years. On Monday evening, November 19, 1849, I was assisting Dr. Webster when Dr. Parkman entered the room. He appeared to be angry at Dr. Webster and without any preliminary conversation, abruptly said: "Dr. Webster, are you ready for me tonight?"

"Webster replied, 'No, I am not, doctor.'

"I then moved away, but I heard Dr. Parkman reprimand him for selling mortgaged property, and in a final burst of anger said: 'Something must be done to-morrow,' and he then left.

"On the morning of Friday, November 23, I saw a sledge hammer which belonged in the laboratory, behind Dr. Webster's door. I had never seen it there before and have been unable to find it since.

"At 2:15 p. m. I was at the front door and saw Dr. Parkman approaching the college, but I went inside and did not see him enter the building. About one hour afterward I went to Dr. Webster's laboratory to clean up, but found the door bolted from the inside.

"I knocked loudly but received no response, although I heard someone walking inside who, I supposed, was Dr. Webster. I then tried all the different doors leading to his laboratory, but they were all locked from the inside — a most unusual occurrence.

"At 4 o'clock I tried the doors again, with the same result. At 5 p. m. I saw Dr. Webster leave the building from the back exit.

"I went to a party that night, and at 11 p. m. returned to the college, where my wife and I are domiciled. I again tried Dr. Webster's door and again found it locked.

"On the next day, Saturday, Dr. Webster was in his laboratory all day, but I did not go near him. That evening I met him on the Street, and we discussed the article in the evening paper about the disappearance of Dr. Parkman.

"Formerly he would look me in the face when talking, but on this occasion he hung his head and was pale and agitated. On Sunday and Monday the doors to the laboratory were still locked. On Tuesday I found the doctor's room open and mentioned the fact to my wife.

"On this day he was exceptionally friendly toward me and gave me an order for a Thanksgiving turkey. This was remarkable, as I had known him for eight years, and it was the first time I ever knew of him giving anything away.

"On Wednesday, Dr. Webster came to the college early and again locked the door.

"The flue from his furnace is between the walls near the stairs leading to the demonstrator's room, and when I passed up the stairs the wall was extremely hot."

The janitor's statement in regard to the door to the laboratory being constantly locked for several days subsequent to the disappearance of Dr. Parkman was corroborated by several persons who had called during that period.

These disclosures were made on Thursday, November 29, and the officers proceeded at once to Dr. Webster's laboratory, and after vigorous knocking, the door was unbolted from the inside and the officers were admitted by Dr. Webster, but nothing was said regarding the janitor's statement.

At this time a bright fire was burning in the furnace. Nothing was found on this date, and the search was resumed on Friday in the absence of Dr. Webster.

In the meantime the furnace had become cool enough to permit of an examination, which resulted in the finding of a fractured skull containing a full set of mineral teeth.

By means of a trap door, the officers descended to the cellar, where they found a right leg.

In a tea chest they found the upper part of a man's body and the left leg. The shape of the body corresponded with that of Dr. Parkman.

Dr. Winslow Lewis and two other reputable surgeons stated that the manner in which the body was separated indicated that it was done by someone having knowledge of anatomy.

The fact that these remains were found concealed in the chemical laboratory where no such subjects were required, made it apparent that they were the remains of some victim of foul play, and Dr. Ainsworth, the demonstrator of anatomy at the college, stated that they were not parts of any subject used in the college for dissection.

Dr. N. C. Keep, who had made a full set of false teeth for Dr. Parkman, inspected the plate and teeth and identified them as work he had done for Dr. Parkman, because of a peculiarity of the lower jaw, which caused him much trouble. But to be positive, he produced the model, which fitted the plates exactly.

The result of the police investigations were not made public until it was proven beyond all doubt that the remains of Dr. Parkman had been found. Police Officer Clapp was then sent to Dr. Webster's home at Cambridge to arrest him for murder.

When the public learned of the arrest of the eminent professor, it was at once concluded that a grave mistake had been made and that too much credence had been given to the statement of the janitor, who possibly was attempting to shield himself.

At the trial it was proven that notwithstanding his outward show of prosperity. Dr. Webster was financially embarrassed. It was proven that he had committed a felony by selling the property upon which Dr. Parkman held a mortgage for $450 and that the latter threatened to prosecute him for this offense if he did not immediately pay the principal and interest, amounting to $483.60.

It was proven that it was utterly impossible for Dr. Webster, who saw the state prison and ruin staring him in the face, to raise this small amount of money.

It was proven that he lied when he stated that he paid this amount from the proceeds of the sale of tickets to his course of lectures at the college, as he had received no such amount, and a large portion of what he did receive was paid to others.

It was proven that Dr. Webster called at Dr. Parkman's house and requested the latter to call at the college at 2:30 p. m. on November 23 for the purpose of making a final settlement.

Dr. Webster could give no reason for keeping a roaring fire in the furnace for several days after Dr. Parkman's disappearance, and during the Thanksgiving holidays, when all of the other professors were enjoying a week of recreation.

While it was the duty of the janitor to build the fires, the latter was barred from Dr. Webster's apartments, who personally attended to the building and feeding of the fire.

It was proven that the upper part of the body and left leg found in the tea chest were tied together by a peculiar kind of twine and that Dr. Webster had, on November 27, purchased similar twine and several fish hooks which were found in his apartments.

It was proven that when the officers approached the room in which the tea chest containing a greater part of the body was found. Dr. Webster endeavored to discourage them from searching that room by stating that highly explosive chemicals were stored there.

A pair of trousers belonging to Dr. Webster was found in a closet and subjected to a microscopical examination with the result that human blood was found.

While the search was being made for Dr. Parkman, the City Marshal of Boston received three anonymous letters.

One, supposed to have been written by an illiterate person, suggested that a search be made on "Brooklyn heights," another stated that Dr. Parkman had gone to sea on the ship "Herculian," and a third, signed "Civis," stated positively that the missing doctor had been seen at Cambridge.

Handwriting experts swore positively that all three letters were written by Dr. Webster.

The defense produced witnesses to prove the previous good character of Dr. Webster and also introduced testimony to the effect that Dr. Parkman had been seen after the defendant claimed he left the college. After producing medical experts to contradict the medical testimony introduced by the prosecution, the case was submitted.

Chief Justice Shaw then delivered his charge to the jury, and his instructions regarding circumstantial evidence were so able, comprehensive, and discriminating that they have since been regarded as a model by many of the leading jurists of America. When the cause was finally submitted to the jurors, they almost immediately agreed that the defendant was guilty.

As Justice Shaw was also officially connected with Harvard College and had been friendly with Dr. Webster for years, he almost collapsed while pronouncing the death penalty on his erstwhile friend.

The date of execution was set for August 30, 1850. Notwithstanding efforts made to obtain executive clemency, Dr. Webster went to the gallows on that day, publicly protesting his innocence, although it was claimed that he confessed his guilt to a clergyman.

JESSE POMEROY, OF BOSTON, MASS., THE FOURTEEN-YEAR OLD BOY WHO MURDERED TWO CHILDREN AND FRIGHTFULLY TORTURED SEVEN OTHERS.

On December 22, 1871, the little son of Mrs. Paine, of Chelsea, a suburb of Boston, was inveigled by an unknown boy, evidently about twelve years of age, to Powder Horn Hill, near Boston, where he was stripped naked, tied to a beam and beaten with a rope until he become unconscious. The larger boy then disappeared.

On February 21, 1872, little Tracy Hay den was taken to the same place by a boy of the same description, and in addition to undergoing torture similar to that inflicted upon the Paine boy, he was struck across the face with a board, the blow breaking his nose and knocking out several of his teeth.

On July 4, 1872, this same mysterious youth enticed a boy named Johnny Balch to the same scene of torture, where he received treatment similar to that administered to the other victims, but when the child had regained enough strength to enable him to walk, his companion forced him to accompany him to a salt water creek nearby, where his wounds were washed with salt water.

In September, 1872, another child named Robert Gould was persuaded by this same boy to accompany him to the Hartford and Erie Railroad track, where he was tied to a telegraph pole, stripped, beaten and cut about the head with a knife.

A few days after this, a little chap named Harry Austin met this mysterious young fiend at South Boston, and he was stripped, bound and punctured with pins until he became unconscious.

Within a few days after this, the sixth child, named George Pratt, was enticed into the cabin of a yacht at South Boston, and after being bound, was stripped, beaten and stabbed in the back and groin with a penknife.

Scarcely another week elapsed before little Joseph Kennedy was inveigled to a secluded spot in the Old Colony road in South Boston, where he was maltreated in identically the same manner as was the Pratt child.

A great number of boys were arrested on suspicion, but were discharged.

Finally suspicion fell upon a boy named Jesse Pomeroy, a twelve-year-old youth who lived with his widowed mother, a poor dressmaker, on Broadway Street, between D and E Streets, South Boston.

He was positively identified by several of the children he had tortured, and as it was proven beyond all doubt that he was the much-sought youth, he was sentenced to serve the remainder of his minority at the West Borough Reform School. According to the custom, if the boys confined at this school were exemplary in their behavior and the authorities felt confident that the good conduct would continue after their release, they were often released on probation, providing they had a good home to go to.

Unfortunately this was done in Pomeroy's case on February 6, 1874.

On March 8, 1874, John Curran, whose residence was in the neighborhood of the Pomeroy home, notified the police that his ten-year-old daughter had mysteriously disappeared. The only clew obtainable was the statement of a child who saw a little girl of the same description as Curran's daughter enter a buggy with a strange man. As the missing girl was very pretty and well developed, it was suspected that it was a case of abduction, and the investigation was made along those lines.

On April 22, 1874, the body of a four-year-old boy named Horace Mullen was found in a marsh near Dorchester, a suburb of Boston, Mass.

The body was horribly mutilated; the head being nearly severed from the body, upon which there were thirty-one knife wounds.

Having in mind the past record of Jesse Pomeroy, the officials naturally suspected him, and he was taken into custody on the following day. A knife was found in his possession, upon the blade of which some blood was found near the handle, but the remainder of the blade was clean. Upon his shoes was found mud similar to that found only on marsh lands.

Footprints could be very easily traced through this marshy land to the spot where the body was found. Plaster casts were made and it was found that they not only fitted Pomeroy's shoes in every respect, but it was seen that the tracks were made by a person, who in walking, planted his foot in the same manner as Pomeroy.

In addition to this, other circumstantial evidence was procured and then Pomeroy was taken into the room where the body of the child lay. The following conversation occurred between the officer and Pomeroy:

Officer: Do you know this boy?

Pomeroy: Yes, sir.

Officer: Did you kill him?

Pomeroy: I suppose I did.

Officer: How did you get the blood off the knife?

Pomeroy: I stuck it in the mud.

An examination was then made, and it was found that the boy was perfectly sane, but was naturally a fiend and derived pleasure from torturing others.

He selected children only because he had the physical ability to force them to do his will.

In July of the same year Mrs. Pomeroy's landlord sold the property where she resided, and the new owner proceeded at once to make extensive improvements. Laborers began to excavate the cellar and about 5 p. m. on July 18 they found the badly decomposed remains of a little girl buried under a pile of ashes and stones.

Among those who viewed the remains were Mr. and Mrs. Curran, and while the features were not recognizable, they readily identified the wearing apparel as that of their lost child. Pomeroy had been seen with the child, and he finally confessed that it was he who murdered her and buried the remains.

On December 10, 1874, Pomeroy was convicted on the charge of murdering the Mullen child and was sentenced to be hanged.

An appeal was taken to the Supreme Court, which sustained the lower court on February 12, 1875. Governor Gaston refused to sign the death warrant because of the extreme youth of the murderer.

His successor, Governor Rice, also refused for the same reason, and on August 31, 1876, Pomeroy's sentence was commuted to solitary confinement for the remainder of his life. He has made frequent attempts to escape, but always failed. In some mysterious manner he obtained an explosive, which he placed near the door of his cell, but when the explosion occurred it did more damage to him than it did to the door.

Notwithstanding the fact that Pomeroy has been in solitary confinement for thirty-three years, he has developed into a powerful man, and in 1909 was enjoying perfect health.

As he is seldom permitted to receive visitors he devotes nearly all of his time to reading and study and has become a highly educated man.

THE CELEBRATED MANSLAUGHTER CASE OF SAILOR HOLMES, WHO THREW SEVERAL SHIPWRECKED PERSONS FROM AN OVERCROWDED LIFEBOAT.

(From U. S. Circuit Court Reports.)

On March 13, 1841, the American ship *William Brown* left Liverpool for Philadelphia.

In addition to a large cargo, the vessel carried sixty-five passengers and a crew of seventeen men.

At 10 p. m. on Monday, April 19, when two hundred and fifty miles from Cape Race, Newfoundland, the vessel struck an iceberg and began to fill so rapidly that it was evident she would soon go down.

The "long boat" and "jolly boat" were then cleared away and lowered. The captain, second mate, seven of the crew and one passenger entered the jolly boat, and the first mate, thirty-two passengers and the remainder of the crew entered the long boat.

Thirty-one passengers were left on the ship, and they all begged the captain and mate to take them into the lifeboats, but the first mate replied: "Poor souls! You're only going down a short time before we do."

One hour later the ship went to the bottom and thus thirty-one passengers perished.

The two lifeboats remained together during the night, but at daybreak the captain decided to take his boat in another direction, but before leaving the long boat he instructed all on board to obey the first mate's orders.

The first mate then informed the captain that his boat was leaking badly, and that it would soon be necessary to cast lots to determine who should be thrown overboard.

The captain replied: "Let that be the last resort."

During Tuesday the rain came down in torrents; the long boat was in constant danger of being struck by floating ice; the sea grew heavier and the passengers, many of whom were attired in their nightclothes, suffered intensely from the cold weather.

The men took turns at rowing and baling out the boat, while the terror-stricken women huddled together in an effort to keep warm.

At 10 o'clock Tuesday night the men were completely exhausted from exposure, exertion and lack of nourishment. Finally the mate, who observed that the boat was slowly filling with water, cried out in despair: "This work won't do. Help me, God! Men, go to work, the boat is sinking."

The women passengers became hysterical and many were down on their knees offering up prayers.

The first mate then said: "Men, you must go to work or we shall all perish."

They "went to work" and threw fourteen passengers overboard, but the crew, one of whom was a negro, was not molested.

The first four men to be thrown overboard were named Riley, Duffy, Chas. Conlin and Frank Askin. The latter's two sisters were in the boat, and they pleaded for their brother's life, but all in vain.

The next two to go overboard were Askin's sisters, but the evidence is conflicting as to whether they were thrown overboard or whether their sacrifice was an act of self-devotion to their brother. It was admitted that when Sailor Holmes seized their brother, the sisters expressed a wish to follow him.

Askin struggled violently, and the fact that the boat was not upset in the struggle was used against Holmes afterward to prove the improbability of its capsizing.

The "work" continued until fourteen men were forced into a watery grave. Many asked for and were granted time to offer up a prayer before being cast into the sea.

On Wednesday morning the weather cleared up and the ship Crescent was sighted by the occupants of the long boat. The shipwrecked people were rescued and brought to Philadelphia.

After six days of indescribable suffering, the captain and his party were picked up by a French fishing lugger.

When the Crescent reached Philadelphia, Sailor Holmes was arrested and prosecuted under an act of April 30, 1790, which provided:

"Any seaman who shall commit manslaughter upon the high seas, on conviction shall be imprisoned not exceeding three years and a fine not exceeding one thousand dollars." Holmes was charged with the unlawful, but not malicious, killing of Askin.

During the trial, which began in Philadelphia on April 13, 1842, Holmes' appearance, and the account of his actions just previous to his apparently heartless conduct, commanded admiration.

His physique and countenance would have made an artist's model for decision and strength.

It was proven that he was the last man to leave the wrecked ship, and, when he entered the long boat, he found a widowed mother crying for her sick daughter, Isabelle, who had been inadvertently left on the doomed ship. Holmes immediately climbed up the ship's side and, at great peril to his life, ran astern, located the sick girl, and placing her over his shoulder climbed down the ship's side and restored her to her mother.

With the exception of a shirt and trousers, he gave all of his clothing to the women in the boat and uttered words of encouragement to the remainder of the passengers and crew.

It was proven that the first mate lost courage and turned the command of the boat over to Holmes, who immediately changed the course, thus enabling him to sight the ship Crescent.

Holmes' defense was that the homicide was necessary for self-protection and for the protection of the lives that were spared.

The prosecution claimed that the circumstances did not justify the action taken; that many of the persons thrown overboard struggled violently and, as the boat did not capsize then, there was little chance of it occurring under any of the other conditions then existing.

The court ruled that: "Extreme peril is not enough to justify a sacrifice such as this was, nor would even the certainty of death be enough, if death were yet prospective. It must be instant.

"The sailor is bound to undergo whatever hazard is necessary to preserve the boat and passengers, even to the extent of sacrificing his life.

"While it is admitted that sailor and sailor may lawfully struggle with each other for the plank which can save but one, we think that, if the passenger is on the plank, even 'the law of necessity' justifies not the sailor who takes it from him."

The jury deliberated sixteen hours and then returned a verdict of guilty with a recommendation for mercy.

The defendant was sentenced to six months in the Eastern Pennsylvania Penitentiary and a fine of $20, but the penalty was subsequently remitted.

CAREER OF THE NOTORIOUS BIDDLE BROTHERS, WHO COMMITTED TWENTY-SEVEN BURGLARIES AND TWO MURDERS. THEIR SENSATIONAL ESCAPE FROM JAIL IN COMPANY WITH WARDEN SOFFEL'S WIFE, AND THEIR TRAGIC END.

During the early months of 1901, twenty-seven burglaries were committed in Pittsburg, and the modus operandi of these bold thieves convinced the authorities that the crimes were all committed by the same persons.

In the early morning of April 12 an effort was made to burglarize the grocery-store conducted by Thomas Kahney, who discovered them in the act and was shot dead by one of the thieves.

On the same morning Inspector of Police Robert Gray and Detective Patrick Fitzgerald received information that the movements of a gang of men and women living at 34 Fulton Street should be investigated.

The officers proceeded to the house, and upon being refused admission they began to force an entry. As they did so, a shot was fired which killed Fitzgerald.

A posse then surrounded the house and two brothers, named Ed and Jack Biddle, Frank Dorman and two women, known as Jennie Wilcox and Jessie Wright, were arrested.

It was then learned that the men of this gang committed many and probably all of the twenty-seven burglaries above referred to and also the murder of Kahney, the grocer.

The entire gang was charged with murder, the two brothers being convicted and sentenced to be hanged on December 12, 1901.

Dorman was sentenced to life imprisonment and the two women were acquitted.

The Governor granted the Biddle brothers a respite of sixty days, during which time they were confined in the Alleghany County Jail in Pittsburg.

At 4 a. m. January 30, 1902, Ed Biddle called from his cell to Guard James McGeary and announced that his brother had been taken suddenly ill and requested that the guard procure some cramp medicine immediately.

McGeary hastened to comply with the request, and when he returned with the medicine the Biddies broke through the bars which they had sawed almost in two. They then grappled with McGeary and threw him over a railing down to a cement floor sixteen feet below. The guard struck on his head and for some time it was believed he would die.

The desperate men then produced revolvers which had been smuggled in to them and they shot another guard named Reynolds, inflicting a serious but not fatal wound.

As only one other guard was present, they covered him with a revolver and threw him into the dungeon where his outcries could not be heard.

As these two men then became complete masters of the prison, they took the keys from McGeary's person and walked out of the prison into Ross Street.

When Warden Peter Soffel was informed of what had transpired he almost collapsed, but when he recovered himself he stated that his wife, the mother of his four children, had disappeared and that circumstances convinced him that her infatuation for Ed Biddle, who was a handsome fellow, caused her to surreptitiously supply the brothers with the saws and weapons and that she had probably accompanied them in their flight.

At this time the ground was completely covered with snow and a posse, consisting of three Pittsburg detectives and five other officers, started in pursuit in sleighs.

On the next day, January 31st, the officers learned that the Biddle brothers and Mrs. Soffel had dinner at J. J. Stevens home at Mount Chestnut, five miles east of Butler, Pa.

The officers started in pursuit, and upon nearing McClure's barn, two miles from Mount Prospect, they saw the two brothers and Mrs. Soffel attempting to escape in a sleigh. When the officers got within sixty yards of the trio they commanded them to halt, but as the order was ignored the officers opened fire with their rifles.

The brothers responded, and during the fusillade they received fatal wounds and rolled off the sleigh on to the snow. Mrs. Soffel was also wounded in the breast and fell on to the snow, but by a miracle none of the officers was injured.

The three injured persons were taken to the hospital at Butler, Pa., where Ed Biddle admitted that Mrs. Soffel had rendered the only assistance they had received.

He stated that her reason for so doing was because she believed they were innocent men about to be hanged.

John Biddle died at the Butler hospital at 7:35 p. m. on February 1 and Ed died three hours later.

Mrs. Soffel was seriously but not fatally wounded. When she realized what she had done she expressed the wish that she would also die. She added that the brothers were forced to leave the jail earlier than intended, as she had learned that the cells were to be inspected in a few days and she feared that the officials would discover where the bars had been sawed.

When Mrs. Soffel fell from the sleigh she dropped a long letter written by Ed Biddle to her, which showed that she fell in love with the desperado in November, 1901, and on December 2 she began preparations to liberate him.

It was she who purchased the saws and weapons and smuggled them in to the prisoners.

Mrs. Soffel was prosecuted for her part in the jail break and sent to State Prison for two years. After her release she tried the theatrical business, but the performance was stopped by the authorities. She then went into seclusion, changed her name and earned her living as a dressmaker, fully repentant for her mad infatuation for Biddle.

On August 30, 1909, she died at the West Pennsylvania Hospital in

Pittsburg from a complication of diseases.

THE SENSATIONAL MURDER OF THE BEAUTIFUL AND ACCOMPLISHED BUT WAYWARD HELEN JEWETT IN NEW YORK.

(From Inspector Byrnes' and Warden Sutton's histories of crime in New York.)

Doras Doyen, afterward known as Helen Jewett, was born in Augusta, Maine, in 1813. Her father died when she had reached her thirteenth year. Shortly afterward a prominent judge was attracted by the girl's pretty face, remarkable aptitude for learning and sweet disposition, and as a result he adopted her and spared no expense in educating and providing her with every luxury. Two years later the girl's beauty began to attract general attention, as did also some of her indiscretions.

When she reached the age of seventeen she and a young banker from Portland, Maine, were the principals in an escapade which created such a sensation that her guardian turned her from his home.

She proceeded to Portland, where the young banker provided her with a mansion of palatial splendor, where champagne suppers and midnight carousals were common occurrences.

But the pair soon quarreled and separated, the girl going to New York, where she assumed the name of Helen Jewett, and where her appearance attracted general attention as she promenaded the thoroughfares.

In describing her, Warden Sutton, in his history of the New York Tombs, says:

"She was beautifully formed; had large black eyes which snapped

with mischievousness, and one of the most fascinating faces that ever imperiled a susceptible observer.

"Her disposition was as beautiful as her face and figure and she was charitable to a fault with all who required assistance."

Richard Robinson was born in Durham, Conn., in 1818, where he was carefully raised and educated by his esteemed parents. He developed into a large, handsome boy, and was always immaculate in appearance. He finally objected to being watched over by his parents and ran away from home to New York, where he procured employment in Joseph Hoxie's dry goods store in Maiden Lane.

Being free from restraint the boy began to associate with evil companions and finally became a habitué of questionable resorts where he assumed the name of "Frank Rivers."

One evening in 1834, when he was but seventeen years of age, Robinson was about to enter a theater when he observed a ruffian insulting a beautiful young woman, who was also en route to the same place of amusement.

The youth's athletic physique enabled him to make short work of the hoodlum, which instantly made him a hero in the eyes of the young woman. She handed him a card and extended to him a pressing invitation to call on her at the conclusion of the performance. This card read, "Helen Jewett, Palais de la Duchesse Berri."*

*This place was a magnificently furnished resort conducted by one Madame Berri in Duane Street.

Noting the girl's attractive manners and appearance, Robinson gladly accepted the invitation, and when he arrived at the house he was ushered into the girl's elegantly furnished apartment.

Thereafter Robinson became a constant visitor and within a few weeks Helen's passing fancy ripened into a mad infatuation. Finally she began to fear that her handsome young lover was not devoting as much time to her as was possible and she concluded that she was receiving but a small share of his affections.

Determining to ascertain whether or not the suspicion was well founded, she disguised herself as a boy and followed him about town in the evenings. One night she saw him enter a house in Broome Street, and, gaining admission, she found him in the company of a rival siren. Like a tigress Helen sprang upon the woman and struck her in the face repeatedly, her numerous diamond rings drawing blood with each blow.

This sudden and unexpected occurrence paralyzed Robinson for the moment, but when he recovered he restrained Helen from doing further violence. The unfortunate girl then became hysterical, but when she became calm she repented her actions and on her knees implored Robinson to forgive her. He turned a deaf ear to her pleadings, but several days later, after Helen had written numerous letters in which she begged for forgiveness, a reconciliation was effected.

As generally occurs in such cases, Robinson began to grow tired of the girl's company, and he looked about for an excuse to discontinue the relationship entirely. He therefore decided to set a trap, and in a disguised hand wrote the following letter:

"New York, July 7, 1835. "Dear Miss:

"The author of the following epistle is a stranger to you, and common courtesy demands a perusal of his sentiments. I should have spoken freely what I here remark to your private ear, were it not I was of opinion you would suppose me guilty of trifling with your credulity and insulting your misfortune. I am not ignorant of your present mode of life and your degraded situation, and you will excuse the plainness of both the language and remarks. Acting with the impulse of nobler sentiments than those who have heretofore addressed you, I would present for your reflection the following proposal:

"If the gifted and fascinating Helen will forsake the rough road on which she has previously been a traveler, and adopt one more in unison with her enlightened mind, with no other security than her own word, he who now presents this petition will greet her, not as heretofore she has been, as a mistress, but as one whom the laws of the land bid him protect, cherish and love. I am sensible that the world would chide me for what they term folly, but the purity of my feelings, the genuine motives that inspire me, and the knowledge of your disposition and excellent qualifications that I have gleaned from the information of others, as well as my own observations, have instigated this request, which I solicit may be granted to your suitor, who respectfully subscribes himself, "Yours in esteem,

"Reuben Jarvis.

"To Miss Helen Jewett,

"No. 3 Franklin St., N. Y."

Helen believed that some admirer had written the letter in good faith, but her infatuation for Robinson was so great that she had no hesitation in forwarding the following:

"New York, July 9, 1835. "Dear Sir:

"It would be of little use for me to deny to a person who seems to know me as well as you do that an acceptance of your offer would be one of the most desirable things, as a social advantage, that my imagination could conceive. I do not attempt to conceal that it would; but, sir, I at the same time perceive that its acceptance would inevitably lead to the most unbounded actual misery to both of us hereafter. You could never substantially respect me, and, after the first season of your fancy, your fondness would give place to mistrust, and I would be suspected at a greater disadvantage than the numerous unblemished women who, notwithstanding the blamelessness of their early lives, are rendered miserable by the unfounded jealousy of their husbands every day. Give me leave to speak, sir, on this subject as if I knew something of it. Woman is the bauble of man's passions — always so when he has no deep respect for her purity of character or sentiment. You would be troubled with many unpleasant reflections after the first season of your liking was over, and the check which you would continually find me to your intercourse with society would first manufacture regrets and then turn them into hate. Knowing this from the experience which I have personally had of the evanescent ardor of mere passion, it would be unjust in me not to undeceive you, or not to reject a bond of ultimate misery for both. There are other reasons, less magnanimous than those which I stated, that induce me to respectfully refer your offer back to your reflections, but of those I need not speak. I find no fault with you for your frank estimation of the present degradation I am living under, but I am in a whirlpool from which I cannot rise by means of your proffer, and all I can do is to trim my bark to sail as decently as possible till I am eventually swallowed in its vortex.

"For the compliments which you pay my qualities of heart and mind I feel grateful, of course; but I commend you, if you are sincere, to think as little of them as possible hereafter. What destiny I am reserved for I do not know, but I do know that I cannot eke it out in the current you propose. If, therefore, you see me again — for I have no doubt that you have been acquainted with me more intimately than you pretend — maintain your incognito, and do not encourage yourself that an appeal in person, under any circumstances, will alter the resolution which I have here set down. That you may not hope that this determination was founded in caprice, I repeat there are circumstances of a private and selfish nature which, apart from any conclusion of philosophy, would oblige me to decide definitely

against you.

"Yours with respect,

"H. J.

"To Reuben Jarvis,

"New York Post office."

Shortly after this incident the pair had a serious quarrel, and Robinson left the girl and swore he would never return.

Helen grew despondent and left New York, but returned in October, 1835.

By the merest chance Robinson met her at the wharf, and after considerable pleading on her part another reconciliation was effected.

At this time a woman named Rosina Townsend conducted a house of ill-repute at 41 Thomas Street, which was widely known because of the magnificence of its appointments. Helen became an inmate at this resort and Robinson, under the name of "Frank Rivers," was a frequent caller.

A few months later Helen was informed that during her absence from New York Robinson had wronged a young girl, who subsequently died from poison alleged to have been administered by her betrayer.

Helen accused him of this crime, and although the accusation seemed to strike terror to his heart, he evidently convinced the trusting girl that he was innocent, and it was shortly afterward agreed that Helen should abandon her life of shame and the couple would become man and wife. She became very happy, but on April 10, 1836, she was told that Robinson had no intention of marrying her, as he was at that time engaged to a young lady of wealth and position. The girl became frantic, and immediately wrote to Robinson imploring him to come to her immediately and deny the charge.

She concluded the letter by saying: "You know how I have loved, but for God's sake don't compel me to show how I can hate."

On the next day Robinson forwarded an unsigned letter, written in a disguised hand, in which he stated that he would call at 9 p. m. Saturday, April 11, and requested that she personally receive him at the door.

At the appointed hour Robinson, alias Frank Rivers, called, but the landlady chanced to be near the door and she admitted him. According to his usual custom, he wore a long Spanish cloak on this evening. Hearing his voice, Helen rushed out of the parlor and in the presence of the landlady embraced her lover and joyously exclaimed: "Oh, my dear Frank, how glad I am that you have come."

The pair then retired to the girl's apartments.

At one o'clock Sunday morning all of the inmates of the house had retired; the building was in darkness and all was silent as a grave.

Suddenly Marie Stevens, who occupied apartments on the second floor directly across the hall from Helen Jewett's room, heard a noise which sounded like a heavy blow being struck, which was immediately followed by a long moan.

She heard Helen's door open gently, and then cautiously opening her own door, she observed a tall figure, wrapped in a long cloak and holding a dimly lighted lamp, glide through the hall.

The terror-stricken woman hastily closed her door and a few moments later loud knocking at the front door was heard. The landlady responded and admitted a male guest. She then noticed that a lamp was lighted in the parlor, which was a most unusual occurrence. She inspected the lamp and saw that it belonged to Helen Jewett. Her suspicions being aroused, the landlady began a tour of inspection. Finding the rear door ajar, she called out, "Who's there," but receiving no response she barricaded the door and proceeded to the next floor with Helen's lamp. She knocked at the girl's door, but hearing no answer, she opened the door and was immediately confronted by a dense volume of smoke which almost overpowered her. Her screams aroused the inmates of the house, who rushed to the room and extinguished the fire.

This room was filled with antique furniture, mirrors, valuable paintings and many rare books which had been presented to the beautiful Helen by her different admirers.

The scantily clad body of the unfortunate girl was lying on the bed; her forehead having been split wide open by a powerful blow, evidently from a hatchet, and the upper portion of her body was burned brown by the fire.

The police were notified and the search for the assassin began. In the back yard of the premises was found a bloodstained hatchet which was subsequently identified as the property of Robinson's employer, and near the hatchet was found the long cloak which Robinson habitually wore. The murderer was compelled to scale a whitewashed fence, and as he fled down the side Street a negress saw him, and while she could not recognize his features, she stated that his general physique was similar to Robinson's.

The police went to the suspect's room and found him in bed, where he claimed he had been for hours.

Upon examining his trousers, whitewash was found on one of the knees.

He protested his innocence but was arrested and taken to jail.

A few days later Frederick Gourgas, a clerk in Dr. Chabert's apothecary shop, stated that Robinson, under the name of Douglass, attempted to purchase arsenic from him.

Wealthy relatives came to the prisoner's assistance and employed able attorneys.

It was the theory of the prosecution that Robinson was determined to marry the young woman of wealth and position, but feared that if he did so, Helen would divulge what she had learned regarding the death of the young woman he had ruined.

He therefore determined to kill her with the hatchet which he had concealed under his cloak when Helen embraced him. The fact that he requested that she receive him at the door indicated that he wanted to enter the house unobserved by others, and he probably started the fire with the expectation that it would destroy the building and hide the evidence of his crime.

The trial was set for June 2, 1836.

In the meantime the colored woman, who observed the assassin as he ran away, mysteriously disappeared, and Marie Stevens, who saw him leave Helen's room, was found dead in her bed. It was never definitely determined whether she committed suicide or was murdered.

But without these witnesses the testimony was overwhelmingly against the defendant.

The most important witness for the defense was one Robert Furlong,* who conducted a grocery store at Cedar and Nassau Streets. He swore that Robinson was in his store the greater part of Saturday evening and did not leave until 10:15 p. m.

* Two weeks later Furlong committed suicide by leaping from the deck of a vessel into the North River.

To the great surprise and disgust of all, except a certain class who lived from earnings of fallen women and regarded the defendant as a hero, the jury returned a verdict of not guilty.

It was openly charged that members of the jury were corrupted and the court adjourned amid the wildest confusion.

After his acquittal Robinson became extremely morose. He soon departed for Texas, where he died shortly afterward.

James Gordon Bennett, of the New York Herald, visited the scene of the murder and in the issue of April 13, 1836, said in part:

> "This extraordinary murder has created a sensation in this city never before felt or known,
>
> "This queen of the demi-monde was the most beautiful of her degraded caste and had seduced by her beauty and blandishments more young men than any known in police records."

THE TRUE HISTORY OF THE MYSTERIOUS MURDER OF THE BEAUTIFUL NEW YORK "CIGAR GIRL," MARY CECELIA ROGERS, UPON WHICH WAS FOUNDED EDGAR ALLEN FOE'S STORY, "THE MYSTERY OF MARIE ROGET."

(From Inspector Byrnes' "Mysterious Murders in New York.")

Mary Cecelia Rogers was born in New York in 1820. Her father died when she was five years of age, and as Mrs. Rogers was left in straitened circumstances, she earned a living for herself and her pretty little daughter by conducting a boarding and lodging house in Nassau Street. As Mary grew older she assisted her mother about the house.

She developed into an extremely beautiful young woman of the brunette type. She was rather tall; her form was exquisitely symmetrical; her features were regular; her complexion beautiful and she had a wealth of jet black hair. Added to these physical charms, she possessed a pleasing manner which made her a host of friends and admirers.

She attracted attention wherever she went and finally John

Anderson, who conducted a large retail cigar store on Broadway near Thomas Street, heard of her marvelous beauty and conceived the idea of employing her both as a clerk and as an attraction. This was in the early spring of 1840, and Mary was 20 years of age at the time.

Anderson made his proposition to Mrs. Rogers, but as Mary had never worked away from home, the mother felt reluctant to permit her to accept this position, especially as many young men of unenviable reputations made this store their rendezvous. As Anderson's proposal was very liberal, Mary finally persuaded her mother to permit her to accept the position.

The cigar merchant's fondest anticipations were soon realized, as customers flocked to the store. The girl's conduct was apparently a model of modest decorum, and while she was lavish in her smiles, she did not hesitate to repel all undue advances.

After having worked at this store for ten months, Mary failed to appear one morning in the latter part of January, 1841. Anderson was unable to account for her absence and Mrs. Rogers was frantic. The matter was reported to the authorities and the press gave great publicity to the mysterious disappearance of the now famous "cigar girl."

Six days later the girl returned to the store, and while she appeared to be in good health, the cheery smile was gone and in its stead appeared a sad, thoughtful expression.

To all inquirers she rather abruptly explained that she had been visiting relatives in the country. Her mother and employer gave the same explanation, but as it was evident that it was a subject that those most interested disliked to discuss, no further details were learned.

A few days after Mary returned, a widely circulated rumor had it that she was seen in New York with a tall, handsome naval officer during the time she was supposed to be in the country. These rumors evidently reached Mary's ears, for a week had scarcely passed after her return when she suddenly resigned her position and sought the shelter of her mother's home.

A month later it was announced that she was engaged to be married to Daniel Payne, a young clerk who resided in her mother's house.

At 10 a. m. on the beautiful morning of Sunday, July 25, 1841, Mary knocked at the door of her betrothed and informed him that she intended to spend the day with her aunt, Mrs. Downing, in Bleecker Street. Payne replied: "All right! I'll call for you to-night." As the evening approached, a furious thunderstorm arose and the rain fell in torrents.

Payne spent the day away from home, but believing that Miss

Rogers would not desire to go home in such a storm, he did not call for her but proceeded home alone. When Payne informed Mrs. Rogers why he had not called for Mary, the mother expressed pleasure because he had not brought Mary home through such a storm.

The next day the storm subsided and Mrs. Rogers confidently expected her daughter to return during the day, but as she failed to put in an appearance the mother became greatly alarmed.

When Payne came home to dinner, Mrs. Rogers informed him of Mary's non-appearance, and, without waiting for his meal, the young man repaired at once to the home of Mrs. Downing. To his amazement, he learned that Mary had not been there at all. The anxious mother well remembered Mary's disappearance some months previous, but on this last occasion the girl wore very light clothing and a light bonnet when she left home, so it did not seem reasonable that she would willingly remain away after the storm abated.

Under the circumstances, the second disappearance created a greater sensation than the first. For several days no trace was found of her, but on Wednesday morning some fishermen setting their nets off Castle Point, Hoboken, found her terribly mutilated body floating near the shore, not far from a refreshment saloon known as "Sybil's Cave."

The once beautiful face was beaten to a pulp and terribly swollen. Around the waist was fastened a stout cord, to the other end of which a heavy stone was attached. Encircling her neck was a piece of lace torn from her dress, tied tightly enough to produce strangulation. Sunk deeply into the flesh of both wrists were marks of cords. Light kid gloves were upon the hands and the little bonnet hung by its ribbons around the neck. Her clothing was badly torn and subsequent investigations made by the physicians revealed the fact that she had been brutally outraged before her death.

Payne was immediately interrogated by the authorities, but he gave a satisfactory account of his movements and was at once discharged. A week passed by without any indication of a solution of the mystery and the press began to criticize the police severely.

The authorities then issued a proclamation announcing that a large reward would be paid for the arrest and conviction of the perpetrator of the murder, and it was furthermore announced that in addition to the reward, complete immunity and protection would be given to anyone having a guilty knowledge of the crime (except the real assassin), if such person or persons should be, responsible for the arrest and conviction of the assassin.

The next day the Coroner received an anonymous letter from a young man in Hoboken, who declared that he had seen Mary in Hoboken on Sunday, but had not come forward before owing to what he termed "motives of perhaps criminal prudence." The writer stated that while walking in the Elysian Fields, then a famous summer resort on Sunday afternoons, he had seen a boat pull out from the New York side containing six rough-looking men and a well-dressed girl, whom he recognized as Mary Rogers. She and her companions left the boat on the beach and went into the woods. The writer was surprised to see her in the company of such rough looking characters, and noticed that she evidently went with them willingly, laughing merrily as she walked away from the shore. They had scarcely disappeared in the woods when a second boat put out from New York and was pulled rapidly across the river by three handsomely-dressed gentlemen. One of them leaped ashore, and meeting two other gentlemen who were waiting on the beach, excitedly asked them if they had seen a young woman and six men land from a boat a few minutes before. On being told that they had, and on the direction they had taken being pointed out to him, he asked whether the men had used any violence towards the girl. He was told that she had apparently gone with them willingly, and he then, without making any further remark, returned to his boat, which was at once headed for New York.

The author of this letter was never discovered, but the letter was printed in the newspapers, and the next day the two gentlemen who had been walking on the beach came forward and corroborated the story. They both knew Mary Rogers by sight, and said that the girl who entered the woods with the six roughs resembled her closely, but they were not sufficiently near to be able to positively affirm that it was she.

The next important piece of evidence came from a stage driver named Adams, who, after allowing several weeks to elapse, stated that on the fatal Sunday he had seen Mary arrive in Hoboken, at the Bull's Ferry, accompanied by a tall, well-dressed man of dark complexion, and go with him to a roadhouse near the Elysian Fields known as "Nick Mullen's." Mrs. Loss, the keeper of the house, remembered that such a man had come to her place with a young woman on the day in question, and had gone into the adjoining woods after partaking of refreshments. Soon after their departure she heard a woman's scream coming from the woods, but as the place was the resort of questionable characters, and such sounds were of frequent occurrence, she gave no further thought to the matter.

The exact spot where the hapless girl was brutally ill-treated and then butchered, was discovered by Mrs. Loss's little children on September 25, exactly two months after the murder. While playing in the woods, they found in a dense thicket a white petticoat, a silk scarf, a parasol, and a linen handkerchief marked with the initials "M. R." The ground around was torn up and the shrubbery trampled as if the spot had been the scene of a terrific struggle. Leading out of the thicket was a broad track, such as might have been made by dragging a body through the bushes. It led in the direction of the river, but was soon lost in the woods. All the articles were identified as having been worn by Mary on the day of her disappearance.

Every effort was made to trace the "tall, dark-complexioned man," who answered the description of the naval officer said to have been seen with Mary during her first disappearance, but without success.

It was generally believed at the time that the murdered girl's mother knew more about her daughter's mysterious admirer than she chose to tell.

Daniel Payne never recovered from the shock caused by the awful death of his betrothed. The blow evidently affected his mind, and within a few weeks after the murder he committed suicide and his body was found at the spot in the woods where his sweetheart was probably slain.

The crime was the subject of prolonged investigation, but the veil of mystery has never been penetrated that shrouded the fate of the pretty "cigar girl."

It was upon this case that Edgar Allen Poe founded his tale, "The Mystery of Marie Roget."

THE MURDER OF SAMUEL ADAMS IN NEW YORK BY JOHN COLT, A PERSONAL FRIEND OF THE AUTHOR OF "HOME, SWEET HOME."— THE MARRIAGE AND SUICIDE OF THE CONDEMNED MAN, AND BURNING OF THE TOMBS WITHIN TWO HOURS OF THE TIME SET FOR THE EXECUTION.

(From Warden Sutton's History of New York Tombs.)

On Saturday morning, September 18, 1841, an express man appeared at the foot of Maiden Lane, New York, with a large box to be shipped to New Orleans on a vessel lying at a nearby wharf.

A few moments afterward a very refined appearing man arrived and made the final arrangements for the shipping. It was expected that the vessel would sail within a few hours, but it was delayed a week.

The day before it left one of the crew reported to the Captain that a terrible stench was coming from the hold. An investigation was made and the odor was traced to this box. It was placed on deck and, upon being opened, the badly decomposed body of a man was found.

Some days before this discovery, the press began to give considerable publicity to the mysterious disappearance of Samuel Adams, a well-known printer, and when this body was found, relatives of the missing man were immediately sent for and they at once identified the remains as the body of Adams.

A search was then instituted for the express man who delivered the box. He was soon located and without hesitation stated he had removed the box from an office in a building at Chambers Street and Broadway.*

* In after years this building was occupied by Delmonico's restaurant.

The express man then proceeded with the authorities to this office and identified Mr. John C. Colt, a professional bookkeeper and teacher of penmanship, as the man who ordered the box removed. Colt was also identified as the man who arranged for the shipping. He was then taken into custody and shortly afterward made a confession substantially as follows:

"Adams called at my office at 4 p. m., Friday, September 17, and we had a heated argument regarding the exact amount of a trivial sum of money I owed him. The 'lie' was passed and we came to blows. We then grappled and as he was overpowering me, I reached for a hammer, which was on my desk, and I struck him over the head until he released his hold and fell unconscious. He expired shortly afterward.

"Blood flowed in torrents from the wounds and after washing it up, I decided to notify the authorities. But when I thought of the public censure and the disgrace I would bring upon my esteemed relatives, I concluded to hide my crime by disposing of the body. My first idea was to consume it by burning the building, but when I recalled that many innocent persons slept there who might be burned to death, I abandoned that plan. I then definitely decided to ship the body to some other city on the day following."

Colt's wealthy relatives procured the brightest legal talent to defend him, and they contended that Colt acted in self-defense. The trial lasted ten days and the jury found Colt guilty of murder in the first degree.

The case was appealed, but all in vain. The condemned man was sentenced to be hanged on November 18, 1842.

For some time before the commission of this crime, Colt lived with a beautiful young woman named Caroline Henshaw, and she remained loyal to him to the end. As she and Colt both expressed the wish that they be made man and wife before he paid his penalty, the arrangements were made for the marriage, which occurred a few hours before the time set for the execution. The witnesses to the ceremony were Colt's brother and John Howard Payne, the author of "Home, Sweet Home."

After the ceremony was performed, Colt asked for and was granted permission to remain alone for a short time.

As the hour for the execution was drawing near, the excitement about the Tombs became intense. Shortly before the dread moment was at hand, a fire broke out in the prison and for the time being the execution was forgotten, as it appeared that the prison was doomed. The firemen soon got the fire under control and the authorities proceeded with all haste to prepare for the execution.

Rev. Mr. Anthon went to Colt's cell to console him, but he had barely entered the door when he staggered back with a cry of horror, for Colt was lying dead upon his bed with a dagger in his heart.

THE BLOODY RIOT IN ASTOR PLACE, NEW YORK, WHICH GREW OUT OF THE RIVALRY BETWEEN THE CELEBRATED TRAGEDIANS, FORREST AND MACREADY.

(From Headley's History of New York Riots and Sutton's History of New York Tombs.)

Edwin Forrest, the American tragedian, achieved his first success at the Drury Lane Theatre in London in 1827. Shortly afterward he returned to his native land, where he received continual ovations and became recognized as the foremost American tragedian.

William C. Macready, who occupied a similar position on the English stage, toured America about this time. As he and Forrest frequently appeared in the same city at the same time, there was considerable feeling of friendly rivalry, but Forrest's tour was a great success financially while Macready's tour was just the opposite.

Macready again toured in America in 1844. As before, Forrest and he appeared simultaneously in many cities, with the same results as on the previous tour.

Macready returned to England, and shortly afterward, Forrest, having a lively recollection of his early success at Drury Lane, made arrangements for a return engagement. When he appeared he met with a cold reception and the engagement was a financial failure.

Forrest indignantly charged that Macready's jealousy was responsible for the change of feeling, while others claimed that Charles Dickens's ludicrous criticisms on American customs and manners had instilled in the hearts of the English an antipathy for all Americans.

It was claimed that Macready sat in a box and hissed Forrest during a performance in England, but this was denied by Macready's friends, who charged that while Macready was playing "Hamlet" in Edinburgh, Forrest, who was seated in a box, hissed at a portion of the performance in a most offensive manner.

Forrest soon returned to America, and in published statements bitterly denounced Macready.

The cordial welcome Forrest received on his return to America more than compensated him for the abuse he received abroad, and nightly he appeared to crowded houses.

While Forrest was in the zenith of his popularity Macready returned to America, and on Monday, May 7, 1849, he began an engagement at the Astor Place Opera House. "Macbeth" was to be played on the opening night, and Forrest, who was then playing at the Broadway, put on the same play.

The audience that greeted Forrest on this night was composed of the elite of the city, but with the exception of those occupying boxes, the scum of the city filled the Astor Place Opera House. Some were in their shirt sleeves; others were dirty and ragged, and all wore their hats. Their appearance and sullen demeanor caused the managers and players alike to become apprehensive, and after a conference it was decided to delay the raising of the curtain until Chief of Police Matsell could send a detail of officers.

The terror-stricken players then reluctantly agreed to proceed. All was comparatively quiet until Macready appeared as Macbeth during the third scene of the first act. He was greeted by a deafening and prolonged outburst of groans and hisses. As his voice was completely drowned in the uproar, he defiantly strode to the footlights and, folding his arms, he stood glaring into the faces of the ruffians, whose rage was increased by the actor's display of contempt for them.

Finally they began to hurl ancient eggs and potatoes at the actor.

Realizing that the police detail was entirely inadequate to cope with the situation and that he would not be permitted to proceed with the performance, Macready left the stage and hastily entering a carriage which was stationed at the rear of the theater, he was driven to his hotel.

Considering that they had achieved a great victory, the mob tumbled out into the Street, cheering for "Ned Forrest" as they left the theater.

This outrage was denounced by the press, and the tragedian's calm demeanor in the face of great danger challenged the admiration of many who had previously disliked him.

Determined that Macready should not yield to this lawless element, a petition was prepared and signed by Washington Irving, Ogden Hoffman and many others, in which they guaranteed the actor protection if he would appear on Thursday evening, May 10. Macready finally consented and his ultimatum was published in the press along with a voluminous communication in which he denied that he had ever been inimical to Mr. Forrest while he was in England.

When the ruffians learned of Macready's decision to appear again they attempted by an organized movement to prevent it. A few hours before the performance that portion of the city where the rough element congregated was flooded with circulars which read as follows:

"SHALL AMERICANS OR ENGLISH RULE IN THIS CITY?

"THE CREW OF A BRITISH STEAMER HAVE THREATENED ALL AMERICANS WHO SHALL DARE TO OFFER THEIR OPINIONS THIS NIGHT AT THE ENGLISH ARISTOCRATIC OPERA HOUSE!

"WORKINGMEN! FREEMEN! STAND UP TO YOUR LAWFUL RIGHTS."

As this circular was designed to stir up the hatred of the poor against the rich, and the Americans against the English, it was feared that serious results would follow. A heavy detail of police in civilian dress was distributed throughout the theater, and a large force of uniformed officers was detailed to preserve order outside. The militia was also held in readiness at the Armory.

For the purpose of keeping undesirables out of the theater, prominent citizens purchased great numbers of tickets and distributed them among their friends. Notwithstanding these precautions, many of the ruffians, who were well dressed for the occasion, procured tickets, and when Macready appeared they began to hiss and groan, but the officers sprang up in all directions and promptly dragged the hoodlums into a room provided for the purpose, amid the thunderous applause of the better element. The play then proceeded to the end without interruption.

But a very different condition existed on the Streets in the vicinity. The mob had gradually increased to thousands. They began to throw stones at the police, who were so greatly outnumbered that they became powerless and the militia were ordered to the scene. When they arrived the great mob became more demonstrative. Finally they located a pile of Street cobble stones, which they began to hurl at the militia, some of whom sustained serious injury.

After firing into the air without any effect, except to make the ruffians more ugly, the command was given to fire at the mob, and it was promptly obeyed. Rioters fell in all directions and some who were wounded were trampled to death by the hoodlums who stampeded for shelter. In a very short while the Streets were deserted by all but the troops and the police.

Twenty-two dead bodies were removed and thirty of those wounded were conveyed to the hospitals, but as many of the dead and dying were carried away by their friends, it was never definitely known how many were killed or wounded.

It was learned that the chief instigator of the riot was E. C. Judson, alias Ned Buntline, who edited a sheet called "Buntline's Own." Of the sixty rioters arrested ten were indicted.

On September 29, 1849, Buntline was sentenced by Judge Daly of the Court of General Sessions to one year's imprisonment at Blackwell's Island and $250 fine.

———————

THE MYSTERIOUS MURDER OF DR. BURDELL IN NEW YORK AND THE REMARKABLE SCHEMES TO PROCURE HIS ESTATE RESORTED TO BY MRS. CUNNINGHAM, WHO WAS TRIED FOR THE MURDER.

(From Inspector Byrnes's "Mysterious Murders in New York.")

Harvey Burdell was born in Herkimer County, New York, in 1811. As a young man he first obtained employment as a compositor and later took up the study of dentistry in his brother John's office in New York. After mastering the profession he opened an office adjacent to his brother's.

While Dr. Harvey Burdell prospered, he was very penurious and was continually being sued by his relatives and others for non-payment of just debts.

In 1835, he was engaged to be married to a young lady whose foster parents were quite wealthy. After the clergyman and the entire wedding party had assembled, Burdell announced to the father of the prospective bride that the ceremony could not be performed unless a check for $20,000 was immediately forthcoming. The indignant old man informed the guests of the demand and Burdell was ordered from the house.

As the years rolled by Burdell amassed a fortune estimated at $100,000, among his possessions being a building at 31 Bond Street. New York.

Emma Hempstead was born in New York in 1816. She grew to be a very attractive young woman and was presumed to have married a George Cunningham in 1835. Four children were born to the couple. In 1852, Cunningham died and left $10,000 insurance to the widow.

In 1855 she leased Dr. Burdell's Bond Street property, the dentist reserving a suite for offices on the second floor.

Living with Mrs. Cunningham were her four children, Hannah Conlan, the cook, and three roomers named George Snodgrass, Daniel Ulman and John J. Eckel, the latter apparently being extremely friendly with his comely landlady.

At 10:30 o'clock on the night of January 30, 1857, a gentleman residing at No. 36 Bond Street, was about to retire, when, above the noise of the rain beating against his windows, he heard the cry of "Murder!" After the one shriek, all was silent. He could not tell from whence the sound came and he finally retired.

At 8 a. m. the next day a boy proceeded to Dr. Burdell's office to sweep the floor and light the fire, according to his usual custom. When he opened the door he beheld the butchered body of the doctor on the floor. He ran screaming from the room and notified the remainder of the occupants of the house, who were composedly eating their breakfast.

Apparently Mrs. Cunningham became grief-stricken, but Eckel did not appear particularly disconcerted.

An inspection of the body showed fifteen different wounds, evidently made by a long, narrow dagger.

As the appearance of the room indicated that the doctor, who was a powerful man, had given his assailant a terrific struggle, it was concluded that a strong man had participated in the murder, although a subsequent investigation convinced the authorities that Mrs. Cunningham had probably instigated it.

On the day preceding the murder, a woman visited Burdell's office, and shortly afterward he took her on a tour of inspection through the house in company with the cook. Mrs. Cunningham was not at home at the time, but when she returned that evening she heard of the incident, and the following conversation occurred between her and Hannah Conlan, the cook:

Mrs. C. — Who was that woman, Hannah, you were showing through the house to-day?

Cook — That was the lady who is going to take the house.

Mrs. C. — And when does she take possession?

Cook — The first of May.

Mrs. C. — He better be careful; he may not live to sign the papers!

Medical experts expressed the opinion that the dagger was wielded by a left-handed person. Mrs. Cunningham was left-handed. She and Eckel were taken into custody.

Shortly after her incarceration Mrs. Cunningham produced a marriage license showing that she and Burdell were married October 28, 1856, by Rev. Dr. Marvin.

It was the opinion of the authorities that she had someone bearing a striking resemblance to Burdell personate the doctor on this occasion, the object being that if the doctor should die suddenly, she, as his "wife" would demand her share of the property.

While in the Tombs awaiting trial, this woman conceived a remarkable idea. As the widow of Burdell she expected to be able to procure one-third of the estate, but if she had a child she believed she could get the entire estate. She therefore informed Mrs. Foster, the matron of the prison, that she was in a delicate condition.

She was brought to trial but as the evidence was insufficient, she was acquitted. Eckel's case was dropped without a trial.

After being released, Mrs. Cunningham continued her fight for the estate and continued to grow more "rotund." As it was necessary to get some doctor into the conspiracy, she told Dr. Uhl that she would give him $1000 if he would procure a new-born child at the proper time, and make an affidavit that he attended her (Mrs. C.) during her confinement, and that she was the mother of the infant. The doctor pretended to enter into the conspiracy but he kept District Attorney Hall advised of all his movements.

Dr. Uhl then ascertained that a married woman expected to be confined about July 28, 1857, and he made arrangements to borrow the baby for a short time. Apartments were engaged at 190 Elm Street, where the child was born, and as soon as possible after its birth Mrs. Cunningham called, disguised as a Sister of Charity, and took the baby in a basket to her Bond-Street home.

She then became "very ill" and Dr. Uhl was sent for. After moaning and shrieking for some hours, the announcement was solemnly made that the child was born and that the mother was doing as well as could be expected.

But District Attorney Hall rudely interrupted the little play by appearing upon the scene with a policeman. Shortly afterward Mrs. Cunningham was truly confined — in jail, but was subsequently liberated without a trial.

P. T. Barnum engaged the true mother and child and placed them on exhibition in his New York Museum.

In 1859, Mrs. Cunningham moved to San Francisco, where she married a retired sea captain. They resided on Geary Street near Kearny, next to the residence of Police Captain Douglass.

THE MURDER OF PUGILIST BILL POOLE IN NEW YORK.

(From Sutton's History of New York Tombs.)

In 1855, the secret political party known as the "Know Nothings" was very powerful in New York City.

Bill Poole, a physical giant and champion rough and tumble fighter, and Tom Hyer, who was regarded as the champion of the American prize ring, were the recognized leaders of the sporting element in this party, while John Morrisey, who afterward defeated John C. Heenen in the arena, Louis Baker, James Turner and Patrick McLaughlin, alias Paudeen, led the same element in the Democratic party. Between these two factions of the sporting fraternity a most bitter animosity existed.

One night in January, 1855, Hyer was in Piatt's Hall, under Wallack's Theater, when Turner and Baker entered and began calling the fighter vile names. Hyer expostulated, whereupon Turner drew a pistol and fired, inflicting a flesh wound in the pugilist's neck. Hyer then drew his pistol, turned around and fired at the wall, and placing the weapon back in his pocket he knocked down both Turner and Baker with his fists and then dragged the latter out into the Street. As an officer appeared on the scene at this time the disturbance ceased but no arrests were made.

The occurrence created great excitement and the adherents of both factions armed themselves in anticipation of further trouble.

Poole challenged Morrisey to participate in a rough-and tumble fight at Christopher-Street pier. Morrisey accepted, but when he arrived at the spot selected a gang knocked him down and beat him unmercifully.

He nursed his wrath until the evening of February 24, 1855, at which time he was drinking with some friends in a rear room in Stanwix Hall. Hearing Poole's voice in the main bar room he rushed out, and after pouring out a torrent of abuse, he drew a revolver and pointing it at Poole's head, snapped it three times. Poole then drew a pistol but refrained from using it after being reminded that Morrisey's weapon was useless. Officers were summoned and both men were arrested but bailed out at once.

Morrisey went home but Poole returned to Stanwix Hall, where he remained until midnight. At that hour, Baker, Turner and Paudeen entered the place, and Paudeen walked up to Poole, and after saying, "What are you looking at, you black _____," spat in the fighter's face. Poole then offered to bet that he could whip any one of the gang. Baker cried out,

"Sail in" at the same time drawing a pistol. With the first shot he accidently shot himself in the arm and for some reason fell to the floor. While in that position he fired again, the bullet passing through Poole's leg. The fighter fell and then Baker shot him through the heart. Baker then jumped up and he and his gang fled. Notwithstanding the nature of his wound, Poole staggered to his feet and, seizing a knife, he pursued his assailant a few feet, but fell at the entrance to the hall. His vitality was so great that he lived for fourteen days with a bullet wound in his heart. He died believing that Morrisey was responsible for his assassination.

Morrisey, Baker, Turner and Paudeen were indicted for this crime and the trial of Baker took place in Judge Roosevelt's court. As the indignant law-abiding citizens complained bitterly of the lawless conditions then prevailing, which they attributed largely to lack of diligent prosecution, Attorney General Ogden Hoffman personally represented the State.

Baker's first trial lasted fifteen days and resulted in the jury disagreeing. As he was tried twice again with the same result, the cases of all the defendants were dropped from the calendar.

Paudeen, who spat in Poole's face, entered Butt Allen's dance hall on the early morning of March 20, 1858, where he assaulted one Cunningham, who drew a pistol and killed him. The jury disagreed in Cunningham's case and he was liberated.

THE FAMOUS DRAFT RIOTS IN NEW YORK IN WHICH

OVER FIVE HUNDRED RIOTERS WERE KILLED.

(From the records of the Metropolitan Police and Headley's History of New York Riots.)

In July, 1863, a general Provost Marshal was appointed in New York and the city was subdivided into various districts with an assistant Marshal in charge of each district, for the purpose of drafting men to serve with the Federal army.

Although some of the enrolling officers had previously been subjected to abusive language while taking the names of those subject to draft, it was not anticipated that there would be any violence until the conscripts were required to take their, place in the ranks.

The draft began on Saturday, July 11, and order was maintained throughout the day. As the law exempted every man drawn who would pay $300 toward a substitute, those who were not able to pay this amount became all the more exasperated.

On Monday, July 13, it became evident that mischief was afoot, and J. A. Kennedy, Superintendent of Police, called in all the reserves so as to be prepared for an emergency.

Mobs began to assemble in different parts of the city and in many instances factories closed down because the employees had joined the ruffians, who were armed with sticks and stones. These men were all moving toward a place of rendezvous near Central Park, where at least 20,000 were soon assembled. One mob made an attack on a building on Third Avenue, where the drafting was in progress, and drove the drafting officers into the Street and destroyed all the furniture and records. They then set the building on fire, and it was almost a miracle that women and children on the upper floors were not burned to death.

While this fire was burning, Superintendent of Police Kennedy approached, and although in civilian dress, he was recognized and unmercifully beaten and left lying on the Street. A friend of his, named John Egan, recognized him and induced a man driving a wagon to carry him to police headquarters, but his condition was so serious that Commissioner Thomas C. Acton assumed command of the department.

At this time there were thirty-two precincts in the limits of the Metropolitan Police which were reached by a system of telegraph wires, and in many instances hoodlums cut down the poles.

In the meantime the mob that stood watching the spreading of the conflagration on Third Avenue was attacked by about twenty-five soldiers, who believed they could disperse the unlawful assembly by firing into the air. The firing, instead of intimidating the mob, roused it into a greater fury, and before the soldiers could reload, the ruffians rushed upon them, snatched away their muskets and chased them away, beating them during their flight, one soldier being left for dead on the sidewalk.

Police Sergeant McCredie was dispatched to the scene of the conflagration in command of fourteen men, and they arrived in time to see the terrorized soldiers fleeing from the mob. With his small force McCredie attacked this mob, and succeeded in driving them back a short distance, but the ruffians finally surrounded the officers and beat them so unmercifully that several were believed to be dead. Officer Bennett was removed to the dead house at St. Luke's hospital, where his own wife discovered that he was still alive. Officer Travis was also believed to be dead, and the infuriated men, after jumping on his body, removed every particle of his clothing and left him on the sidewalk.

Officer Kiernan would have been killed if Mrs. Egan, the wife of John Egan, who came to Superintendent Kennedy's rescue, had not thrown herself over the prostrate form of the officer and begged the fiends to desist.

By this time it was estimated that the mob had increased to 50,000. The fire apparatus was on the ground prepared to fight the fire, but it was only after Chief Engineer Decker addressed the mob that the firemen were permitted to extinguish the flames, which had consumed four buildings.

Detectives, in every conceivable disguise, were sent out to mingle with the mobs for the purpose of learning their plans. They soon reported that one of the mobs intended to raid a large gun factory at Second Avenue and Twentieth Street, and the Broadway squad, consisting of thirty-five officers, was dispatched to guard the building.

The mob soon approached and began to batter down the door. When a small opening had been made, a leader attempted to squeeze through it, but was killed by the officers inside. The mob then threatened to burn the building, and the officers, fearing that they would start another conflagration, decided to withdraw through a back entrance. Shortly afterward the mob entered the building and helped themselves to weapons and ammunition.

About this time depredations were being committed simultaneously in different parts of the city. Many thieves, who had no interest in the draft, joined the mobs for the purpose of plundering. They entered houses on Lexington Avenue near Forty-Seventh Street, and after helping themselves, applied the torch. Several stores on Broadway, between Twenty-eighth and Twenty-ninth Streets, were also plundered, and the whole block was burned.

At 4 p. m. another howling mob proceeded to the Colored Orphan Asylum, which occupied an entire block on Fifth Avenue, from Forty-third to Forty-fourth Streets, but while they were breaking in the front entrance Superintendent Davis and about 200 little orphans escaped through the rear exit and fled to the Twentieth Precinct Police Station. They were subsequently transferred to Blackwell's Island.

When the armed multitude entered the asylum they stole everything worthwhile and set the building on fire. Chief Engineer Decker and his firemen appeared upon the scene, but were beaten off and the massive structure soon became a sheet of flames.

A mob of about 5,000, now maddened by liquor, attempted to attack police, headquarters on Mulberry Street. Inspector Daniel Carpenter, in command of 200 officers, met them with such a furious charge that the Street resembled a slaughterhouse by the time the officers had finished their charge, and the pavements were strewn with bleeding and prostrate forms.*

*Among the superior officers especially mentioned in the Metropolitan police records for heroic conduct during this charge is Sergeant William Groat, father of Officer Charles Groat of San Francisco.

Toward evening another mob attempted to destroy the New York Tribune building, but they were handled by Inspector Carpenter about the same as the mob he dispersed in the afternoon.

The last act of the mob on the night of July 13 was the burning of Postmaster Wakeman's home in Eighty-Sixth Street. The police station nearby was also destroyed by this fire, most of the officers being away at the time.

On the following day, July 14, General Brown, U. S. A., had increased his force to 700 soldiers, and they were instructed to co-operate with the police.

At 5 a, m. Inspector Carpenter learned that a mob had gathered on Thirty-Second Street. He proceeded to the spot with about 200 men, and as he was about to attack the mob, his forces were assaulted by men on the roof of a four-story building, who threw paving stones at his officers, some of whom were knocked down. The Inspector then ordered several officers to break into the house and attack the assailants. During the battle on the roof, one rioter was knocked off and fell to the sidewalk below, where his mangled body was picked up and carried away by his companions.

Colonel O'Brien, of the Eleventh New York Volunteers, came upon the scene about this time with fifty soldiers. He ordered his men to fire into the mob, with the result that a great number were killed outright. That afternoon O'Brien was caught away from his soldiers and the mob tortured him frightfully, and after beating him to death, they mutilated his remains.

Near the scene of the murder of Colonel O'Brien was a factory where several thousand carbines were stored. The rioters learned of this and laid their plans to procure the weapons. The police, through their detectives, learned of these plans, and 200 officers were dispatched to the carbine repository in time to meet 1000 rioters. A most bloody battle followed. One of the leaders of the mob, a large muscular man, fought like a demon until an officer struck him a powerful blow with his club and the ruffian stumbled toward an iron fence. He fell heavily on a sharp-pointed iron picket, which entered his mouth and pierced his brain. He died almost instantly, but his body hung in this position until the police returned some hours later and laid it on the sidewalk. The police finally succeeded in dispersing this mob, but it was impossible to learn how many were killed or wounded.

Negroes were afraid to venture out on the Streets, and in many instances their houses were entered, the occupants tortured and slain and the buildings burned.

As mobs bent on violence and devastation were operating in every part of the city, it is impossible to give a detailed account of all that transpired. Stores were closed, business was suspended, Street cars stopped running, and apparently the great city was doomed to destruction.

In one instance a squad of police was fighting a mob when a company of confused soldiers rushed up and opened fire. While they killed several of the mob they also killed Officer Dipple and wounded five other officers. Nothing further of importance occurred on the second day.

The police stations were crowded with colored refugees, all of whom were fed by the police department during the four days of rioting.

On Wednesday, July 15, the first outrage reported was the hanging of three negroes at Eighth Avenue and Thirty-second Street by a mob of about five thousand. The soldiers proceeded to the scene, but upon being assaulted with stones and clubs the command was given to fire. It was necessary to fire six volleys before the mob dispersed, leaving the Street covered with dead and dying rioters.

On this day the rioters planned to destroy the gas and water mains, but the detective's notified headquarters and the mob was repulsed by the soldiers when the attempt was made.

In addition to the depredations already enumerated the mobs continued to enter houses occupied by negroes and after torturing and killing the occupants or beating them unmercifully the houses were either burned or wrecked.

On Thursday, the fourth day of the riot, the City Council passed an ordinance appropriating $2,500,000 toward paying $300 exemption money to poor people who might be drafted, but as this did not stop the depredations it was evident that the leaders were thieves and rowdies who had taken advantage of the original disturbances and organized for the purpose of plying their vocations.

The outrages on the three preceding days were repeated on Thursday, and in every instance the police or soldiers eventually succeeded in permanently dispersing the mobs operating in the different parts of the city, the last battle being fought on Thursday night.

It was impossible to ascertain the number of rioters killed by the police and soldiers, as in many instances the bodies were taken out of the city or privately buried. It was also known that many rioters died subsequently from wounds received from soldiers and police, but relatives attributed their deaths to other causes.

It was estimated that between 500 and 1200 rioters were killed. The only soldiers killed were Colonel O'Brien and a sergeant who was beaten to death in Twenty-Ninth Street. The only police officer killed outright was Dipple, who was probably killed by the confused soldiers. Two other officers died afterward, either from their wounds or their disobedience of their physicians' orders in regard to unnecessary exposure to the hot sun.

Fifty-one buildings were burned, including the Colored Orphan Asylum, three Provost Marshal's Offices and two Police Stations.

Many of the property owners who suffered the greatest loss through these riots, instituted damage suits against the city and it is estimated that the entire cost of the riots to the city approximated $3,000,000.

Twenty of the leading rioters were arrested and nineteen were convicted and sent to prison, the aggregate time of imprisonment being nearly one hundred years.

In most instances the leaders were arrested by the detectives who mingled with the mobs and constantly trailed the leaders during the day and until they returned to their homes alone at night time. The detectives would then pounce upon them and take them into custody.

The following is a list of colored people who were murdered by the mobs in a particularly atrocious manner:

William H. Nichols of 147 East Twenty-eighth Street, struck over head with crowbar and killed in his own home, and his three-day-old baby was killed by being thrown from the second-story window into a back-yard.

James Costello of 97 West Thirty-third Street, stoned to death on Street after killing a rioter in self-defense.

Abraham Franklin, a crippled young man, hanged in the presence of his parents at Twenty-seventh Street and Seventh Avenue.

Augustus Stuart died at Blackwell Island on July 22, from beating received during riot at Seventh Avenue and Thirty-seventh Street.

Peter Heuston, Mohawk Indian, 63 years old, mistaken for negro, died at Bellevue Hospital on July 17, from beating received four days previously.

Jeremiah Robinson, aged negro, attempted to escape in disguise of woman, but wore a hood which did not thoroughly conceal his beard. Before killing this man, the mob, in the presence of Robinson's aged wife, perpetrated atrocities so revolting that they are unfit for publication.

William Jones, while returning to home in Clarkson Street with a loaf of bread, was beaten into unconsciousness, hanged to a lamppost and with a fire built under his feet was roasted alive.

On July 15, a mob set fire to a house located at 147 Twenty-Eighth Street. All colored inmates fled but a seven year-old boy named Joseph Reed, who was convalescing, and who fell on the Street from exhaustion. He was attacked and finally received his death blow from a fiend who struck him on the head with the butt of a revolver.

Joseph Jackson, a nineteen-year-old youth, residing on West Fifty-third Street near Sixth Avenue, was beaten to death at the foot of Thirty-fourth Street on July 15 and his body was thrown in East River.

Samuel Johnson was attacked near Fulton Ferry on July 14 and died the next day.

Williams was beaten and stabbed at the corner of Le Roy and Washington Streets on the morning of July 14. The mob fled at the approach of Police Captain Dickson and posse. The victim was conveyed to the New York Hospital, and in response to a question as to his identity, he feebly articulated the word "Williams" and then died.

Ann Derrickson was a white woman who resided with her colored husband at 11 York Street. On the morning of July 15, her twelve-year-old son was seized by a mob, a rope was placed about his neck and his clothes and hair were saturated with turpentine. Just as the mob was about to hang him to a lamppost preparatory to roasting him alive, the police appeared and the ruffians fled. Mrs. Derrickson fought like a fiend to save her son, but she was rendered unconscious with a blow from a club and died three weeks later.

———————

CAPTAIN GORDON, THE SLAVE-TRADER, WHO SEIZED AND SHIPPED 897 AFRICANS FROM THE CONGO RIVER, AND WAS CAPTURED AND SUBSEQUENTLY EXECUTED IN NEW YORK. EIGHTEEN VICTIMS DIE FROM

SUFFOCATION.

(From Warden Sutton's "History of New York Tombs,")

Nathaniel Gordon was born in Portland, Maine, in 1832, When a mere child, Nathaniel began to go to sea, serving as a cabin-boy and gradually advancing until, at the age of 28 years, he became a captain of a small 500-ton vessel named "*Erie.*"

On April 17, 1860, he left Havana, bound for Africa, and among his crew were four sailors named Martin, Green, Alexander and Hetenburg.

As the cargo consisted of 150 bog-heads of liquor and a great many barrels of pork, beef, bread, rice, etc., the four sailors above mentioned suspected that the cargo was to be exchanged for African slaves. After a conference, which occurred when they were thirty days at sea, the sailors proceeded in a body to the captain and disclosed their suspicions. Gordon disclaimed any such purpose and after rebuking the sailors, ordered them back to work.

The vessel arrived at the mouth of the Congo River on the west coast of Africa in the latter part of July, 1860, and after disposing of the cargo, proceeded a few miles up the river on August 7,

It was then docked and 897 Africans, consisting of men, women and children, who were being held in bondage, were driven aboard and packed between decks.

With all possible haste the vessel was then navigated down the river and put to sea, bound for Cuba.

The captain of the American war-vessel Michigan, which was in the Congo River at the time, was informed of what had transpired, and he immediately started in pursuit.

On the next day he overtook the *Erie*, and went on board.

Upon making an inspection of the boat he found that eighteen of the unfortunates had died from suffocation. Many others were in a precarious condition and none were able to walk.

The crew was placed under arrest and the vessel was towed to Monrovia, where the Africans were taken ashore and given medical attention. The Michigan then brought the *Erie* and her entire crew to New York.

Gordon was indicted under the Fifth Section of the Act of May 15, 1820, United States Statutes, which provides that: "If any citizen of the

United States, being of a ship's crew of any foreign vessel, owned wholly or in part or navigated for any citizen or citizens of the United States, shall forcibly confine or detain or aid and abet in forcibly confining or detaining on board such vessel, any negro or mulatto not held in service by the laws of either the States or Territories of the United States, with intent to make him a slave, such person shall be adjudged a pirate and on conviction shall suffer death."

Most of the crew were detained as witnesses against the captain, and to complete the case, witnesses were brought from Africa.

It was shown that when the vessel started to sea with the slaves, several of the sailors protested and the captain offered them a dollar for each slave landed in Cuba.

On the first trial the jury disagreed, but on the second trial, ending November 8, 1861, Gordon was convicted.

An appeal was taken to the United States Circuit Court, but on November 30 a new trial was denied.

Judge Shipman then sentenced Gordon to be hanged on February 22, 1862. Before pronouncing the sentence, the judge, in addressing the prisoner, said in part:

"Think of the cruelty and wickedness of seizing nearly a thousand human beings, who never did you any harm, and thrusting them between the decks of a small ship, beneath a burning tropical sun, to die of disease or suffocation, or be transported to distant lands, and consigned, they and their posterity, to a fate far more cruel than death.

"Think of the sufferings of the unhappy beings whom you crowded on the Erie; of their helpless agony and terror as you took them from their native land, and especially think of those who perished under the weight of their miseries on the passage from the place of your capture to Monrovia. Remember that you showed mercy to none — carrying off, as you did, not only those of your own sex, but women and helpless children."

On February 20, two days before the execution, Gordon's mother and wife went to Washington to plead with President Lincoln to save the condemned man's life, but the President's twelve-year-old son Willie died on that day, and they failed to obtain the desired, interview.

On the night preceding the day of the execution, relatives of Gordon gave him several cigars, and at 3 o'clock the next morning he was seized with convulsions. Dr. Simmons, the prison physician, diagnosed the case as strychnine poisoning, and after working for several hours, he pronounced Gordon out of danger. The condemned man then stated that he had attempted suicide rather than suffer the ignominy of a public execution.

He declined to state how he obtained the poison, but it was suspected that it was concealed in the cigars.

He was hanged at 1 p. m. that day.

This is the only case in the criminal history of America where capital punishment was inflicted for the violation of this law.

THE CELEBRATED McFARLAND-RICHARDSON MURDER TRIAL IN NEW YORK.

(From Sutton's "History of New York Tombs.")

Daniel McFarland was born in Ireland in 1820, but came to America with his parents at the age of four years.

At the age of twelve he became an orphan and began to earn his living by working in a harness shop. He was studious and frugal and before he reached his majority he began a course in Dartmouth College.

He studied law and was admitted to the bar, and was afterward appointed professor of elocution at Brandywine College in Delaware.

In 1853, while passing through Manchester, New Hampshire, he met a beautiful and intelligent fifteen-year-old factory girl named Abby Sage, whose father was a poor weaver.

McFarland was then 32 years of age, and four years later, on December 14, 1857, he married this girl.

With reference to the married life of this couple, Mrs. McFarland subsequently made an affidavit substantially as follows:

"At the time of our marriage, Mr. McFarland represented to me that he had a flourishing law practice, brilliant political prospects and property worth $30,000, but while on our bridal tour he was forced to borrow money in New York to enable us to proceed to Madison, Wis., which was decided upon as our future home.

"We had resided in this town but a short time when he confessed that he had no law practice of any consequence, and that he had devoted himself solely to land speculations, some of which had resulted disastrously.

"In February, 1858, we moved to New York. Three weeks later he pawned my jewelry to pay the board bill and shortly afterward sent me to my father's home in New Hampshire.

"A few months later I returned to him, and we rented a cottage in Brooklyn, where our first child was born in December, 1858.

"At first Mr. McFarland professed for me the most extravagant and passionate devotion, but he soon began to drink heavily and before we were married a year, his breath and body were steaming with vile liquor.

"I implored him to reform, but he cried out: 'My brain is on fire and liquor makes me sleep.'

"On the day the Southern guns were opened on Fort Sumter, we returned to Madison, but in June, 1861, Mr. McFarland decided that I should become an actress, so he took me to New York to prepare me for that profession.

"By this time he had become a demon. He would rise in bed, tear the bed clothing into shreds and threaten to kill me. When he became exhausted he would tearfully beg my pardon and go to sleep.

"Through the influence of Hon. Horace Greeley, founder of the New York Tribune, I procured for him a position with one of the Provost marshals.

"In 1864 my third and last child was born.

"In 1865 my husband lost his position and I was forced to make money by giving public readings.

"Through the influence of Mrs. L. G. Calhoun I procured an engagement from Edwin Booth at the Winter Garden, where I made my debut as Nerissa in the 'Merchant of Venice.' I also wrote for the Riverside Magazine.

"In January, 1867, we moved to 72 Amity Street, New York.

"At the homes of Mrs. Sinclair and Mrs. Calhoun I met Mr. Albert N. Richardson, who was prominently connected with the New York Tribune, and who was noted for his literary attainments.

"On January 20, he called on me and stated that he was compelled to move from his lodgings, which were almost across the Street from ours, and I suggested that he procure apartments from Mrs. Mason, my landlady. I gave him an introduction to her and he moved into the apartments adjoining ours.

"One day Mr. McFarland came into the house just as Mr. Richardson handed me some manuscript in front of his door. When we entered our apartments my husband flew into a rage and insisted that an improper intimacy existed between Mr. Richardson and I.

"On February 20, 1867, Mr. McFarland became so violent that I feared he would murder me. The next day I left him permanently and sought shelter at Mrs. Sinclair's home.

"Mr. Richardson was there when I entered, and he proved to be a friend in need.

"A few days later he called again and told me that I was the one woman in the world to whom he would entrust the care of his motherless children and concluded by saying that as soon as I was free to marry he would be proud to call me his wife.

"As I considered that the formal separation from Mr. McFarland had the moral effect of a divorce I felt free, and as Mr. Richardson was in every respect the very opposite to the miserable man who had so long tormented me, it was absolutely impossible for me not to love him.

"I was still engaged at the theatre, and on the night of March 13, Mr. Richardson accompanied me toward my home. When we had walked but a short distance, Mr. McFarland crept up behind us and fired several shots, one bullet penetrating Mr. Richardson's thigh.

"In Indiana, on October 31, 1869, I obtained a divorce from Mr. McFarland, and then proceeded to my mother's home at Medway, Mass.

"On Thanksgiving Day Mr. Richardson had dinner with us and then returned to New York."

At 5:15 p. m. on November 25, 1869, McFarland, who was then

assistant assessor of New York City, entered the counting-room of the New York Tribune, situated at Spruce and Nassau Streets, and took a seat on a stool where he was within full view of several clerks.

Ten minutes later Richardson entered the office, where upon McFarland instantly arose, whipped out a pistol, shot Richardson in the breast and then fled from the building.

After receiving first aid the wounded man was removed to the Astor House.

McFarland was arrested at 10 p. m. that night in room 31, Westmoreland Hotel, corner Seventeenth Street and Fourth Avenue.

When the arresting officer, Captain A. J. Allaire, informed him of the charge, the prisoner displayed great agitation. After protesting his innocence he said: "It must have been me."

He was immediately taken before Richardson, who identified him as his assailant.

The former Mrs. McFarland was notified of the tragedy and hastened to the side of her dying lover.

Realizing that his end was near, Richardson expressed a wish that he be married to the woman of his choice, and Mrs. McFarland consenting, the ceremony was performed on November 30, 1869, by Rev. Henry Ward Beecher, Hon. Horace Greeley being one of the witnesses to the solemn proceeding.

Three days later Richardson died and McFarland was immediately charged with murder.

His trial began on April 4, 1870.

Hon. John Graham appeared as leading attorney for the defendant, and in his argument before the jury said in part:

"So sensitive and tender was the defendant's mental organization that he was incapable of grappling with and bearing the deep sorrows and misfortunes which awaited him.

"His speculations were disastrous, and then it was that the seeds of dissatisfaction first began to be sown. On one occasion this woman said: 'All I need to make me an elegant lady and popular with the elite of New York is money,'

"When she first met the defendant she was but a poor factory girl,

and the brilliant mind which she possesses today has been the fruit of the careful, affectionate and assiduous attentions of my client.

"Through the instrumentality of Richardson an engagement was procured for her at the Winter Garden.

"On February 21, 1867, the defendant came home unexpectedly at 3 p. m., and met her coming out of Richardson's room. This beautiful woman was then thoroughly corrupted. She had placed before her as temptations the honors of the stage and the society of great men.

"She was then too elegant and too popular for her humble lot and the demon that placed her before all these temptations for which she must pay the price with her soul was Richardson.

"It is claimed that there was something in my client's actions to justify her conduct. I have shown there was not. But even if there had been it would have been no excuse. Woman never better fulfills her office as a guardian angel than when she is watching over an erring and failing husband. It is at this hour, when he first begins to totter, that her influence should be extended to the uttermost, and her arms be wound around him in a tighter and more affectionate embrace to win him back. Many thousands of husbands have thus in the past been saved, and by the neglect of this, many thousands of husbands have in the past been lost.

"Finally the separation comes. McFarland, now having no home, no child, no hope, no joy, occasionally goes to the Tribune office to see Sam Sinclair, and while there a boy enters and hands him a letter addressed to Mrs. McFarland, which he thought was addressed to Mr. McFarland. He opens it; peruses its contents and finds it is a love letter written by Richardson, who was in Boston, to Mrs. McFarland.

"Finally Richardson openly proclaims his intention to marry this woman if he can obtain a divorce from McFarland for her."

After discussing the evidence at length, Mr. Graham concluded his argument as follows:

"The evidence produced proves the insanity under which the defendant was laboring at the time of the shooting, a condition of mind superinduced by the agony he endured at the thought of the loss of his home, his wife and his children,

"Upon you, gentlemen of the jury, are riveted the eyes of an anxious

public. You are to reflect in your actions the value you place upon your own hearths and the affection with which you regard your own firesides.

"Let those who dare dishonor the husband and the father, who wickedly presume to sap the foundations of his happiness, be admonished in good season of the perilousness of the work in which they are engaged. As a result of your deliberations, may they realize and acknowledge the never-failing justice of the Divine edict that jealousy is the rage of a man and that he will not, cannot and must not spare in the day of his vengeance."

After deliberating for one hour and fifty-five minutes, the jury returned with a verdict of not guilty.

———————————

MURDERER WILLIAM SHARKEY'S SENSATIONAL ESCAPE FROM THE NEW YORK TOMBS WEARING HIS SWEETHEART'S CLOTHING, HE DECEIVES THE GUARDS AND IS NEVER RECAPTURED.

(From Warden Sutton's "History of New York Tombs.")

William J. Sharkey was born in New York in 1845. Although his parents were highly respected, William, while he was still in his teens, had a penchant for associating with gamblers, and naturally he soon became one of them.

He also became very prominent as a ward politician. Among his associates were many pickpockets, and it was suspected that Sharkey had a "touching way" himself.

In 1872, he loaned $600 to a gambler named Bob Dunn to enable that worthy to open a faro bank in Buffalo. Dunn soon lost the money and returned to New York.

On the afternoon of September 1, 1872, Sharkey met Dunn in a saloon located at 228 Hudson Street and demanded the $600 due him. Dunn stated that he could not pay it, and Sharkey drew a pistol and killed him almost instantly.

Sharkey escaped temporarily, but was soon located and apprehended.

He was tried, convicted and sentenced to be hanged on August 15, 1873.

On August 7 a stay of proceedings was granted pending a Supreme Court decision.

While Sharkey was confined in the Tombs, his sweetheart, a rather good-looking young woman named Maggie Jourdan, was a daily visitor, and brought him books, flowers and cigars. Owing to her apparently exemplary conduct, she made a favorable impression upon the prison officials, who rather admired her for her loyalty.

All visitors to the Tombs were provided with tickets upon entering, which were collected when they passed out through the gate.

On November 19, 1873, Miss Jourdan called on Sharkey at 10 a. m., as had been her daily custom since her lover's incarceration, and spent several hours with him as usual.

At noon a Mrs. Wesley Allen called to visit her husband, also a prisoner. Mrs. Allen was seen to stop in front of Sharkey's cell and converse with the prisoner and his sweetheart.

Miss Jourdan left the Tombs at 1 p. m., and shortly afterward a "woman," dressed in black and heavily veiled, passed out, after delivering "her" card to the turnkey.

Officer Dolan, who was near the Tombs at the time, noticed "her" particularly as "she" very handily boarded a passing car going at full speed.

At 1:55 p. m., Mrs. Wesley Allen approached the turnkey and proceeded to pass out with the utmost nonchalance.

Keeper Kennedy stopped her and asked for her ticket. After fumbling in her dress for some time she stated that she must have lost it.

A search was made of the prison, but the only thing unusual found was Sharkey's empty cell. Some of his prison garb was there and the authorities also found the condemned man's black mustache, which was still wet with lather.

Mrs. Allen was detained pending further investigation and Miss

Jourdan was arrested that evening.

Two thousand dollars reward was offered for the body of the escaped felon, but Sharkey was never seen again.

Mrs. Allen was released from custody without being charged. Miss Jourdan was charged with assisting a felon to escape, but was never convicted, although it was generally believed that these two women smuggled into the prison the disguise worn by Sharkey, and that he used Mrs. Allen's pass.

The manner in which his cell door was opened always remained a mystery.

HICKS, THE PIRATE WHO SLAUGHTERED THE ENTIRE CREW OF THE SLOOP E. A. JOHNSON.

(From Sutton's "History of New York Tombs.")

On March 16, 1860, the oyster sloop *E. A. Johnson* left New York for Deep Creek, Va., to procure a cargo of oysters.

The crew consisted of Captain Burr, a man known as William Johnson, and two boys named Oliver and Smith Watts.

At 6 o'clock on the morning of March 21, this sloop, which had been deserted, was picked up by the schooner Telegraph and was subsequently towed back to New York by the steam tug *Ceres*.

The deck and interior of the cabin was virtually covered with blood, indicating that several persons had probably been murdered aboard, but none of the bodies could be found.

The press devoted much space to the mystery, and on the next day two men named John Burke and Andrew Kelly, of 129 Cedar Street. New York, called at police headquarters and stated that a man known as Johnson, who also resided at 129 Cedar Street, with his family, was a member of the crew on this sloop, and that he had returned home the day before the deserted sloop was found, and after hastily packing his effects, moved his family to Providence, R. I.

Officer Nevins located the suspect near Providence and conveyed him back to New York.

The man denied that he had ever been connected with the deserted sloop, but his statement was proved to be false by numerous witnesses.

On his person was found a watch belonging to the captain and a picture which a young lady had presented to young Oliver Watts of the crew.

He was charged with the murder of Captain Burr and his trial occurred in the United States Circuit Court in May, 1860. After deliberating for seven minutes the jury found him guilty, and he was sentenced to be hanged on July 13.

While confined in the Tombs awaiting execution, the condemned man made a confession as follows:

"My true name is Albert Hicks.

"At about 10 p. m. on the second night at sea, Captain Burr and one of the Watts boys were asleep in the cabin, while I was steering, and the other Watts boy was on the lookout at the bow.

"Suddenly the devil took possession of me, and I determined to murder the remainder of the crew and steal everything on board worthwhile.

"Procuring an ax, I crept up behind the boy on deck and I struck him one blow, dashing out his brains. The noise attracted his brother, who came on deck, and I also struck him on the head, knocking him senseless. I then proceeded to the cabin, but the captain made a desperate struggle for his life until I felled him with a blow from the ax, which killed him.

"I then returned to the deck, where I observed that the second boy I struck was not dead, but had recovered consciousness and was struggling to his feet.

"I picked him up with the intention of throwing him overboard. I got his body over the side of the boat, but with a death grip he clung to the taff-rail. Reaching for my ax I cut his hands off and he fell into the water and sank immediately.

"After throwing the other bodies overboard I rifled the captain's money bags and, taking all other valuables I could find, I headed the sloop for the shore.

"When I got close in I used the small boat to effect a landing."

On the morning of the execution, which occurred at Bedloe's Island the condemned man was taken on board the boat Red Jacket, along with 1500 others, who were invited to witness the execution.

As the hour for the hanging had been changed, the captain of the boat gave his passengers a little excursion trip to enable them to view the Great Eastern,* the monster ship which had just made her first voyage to America and was then lying near the foot of Hammond Street.

The party then proceeded to the island, where Hicks was hanged at 10:45 a. m.

*As the first cable, which was laid across the Atlantic in 1858 by the American frigate Niagara and the British warship Agamemnon, became useless shortly after it was laid, the Great Eastern, which had previously made several unremunerative trips to America, again started to America in 1865 with the second cable. When 1065 miles of cable had been paid out, it broke and was abandoned after a vain attempt to grapple the lost end.

During the next year this ship's crew found the lost end of the cable, and splicing if to the remainder of the cable on board, the laying of the second cable was completed, and on July 28, 1866, Queen Victoria sent the first message to President Johnson.

As the propelling machinery was weak in proportion to the vessel's dimensions, the ship was never a success, and she was broken up in 1888. — Harper's Book of Facts.

———————

THE GREAT BANK OF ENGLAND FORGERY AND CAREER

OF GEORGE BIDWELL, ONE OF THE MOST SUCCESSFUL

FORGERS THE WORLD HAS KNOWN, BUT WHO DIED IN

POVERTY.

(From G. Bidwell's history of his life.)

George Bidwell was born in New York State about 1835. His .parents were very strict Methodists and the children were not permitted to play on Sundays. Bidwell, Sr., met with financial reverses, and when George reached the age of 12 years, he conducted a small Street stand, from which he sold various articles and supported the family. He saved enough money to enable him to take his father into partnership with him in Grand Rapids in 1849, and they gradually became prosperous merchants. Through mismanagement they failed in 1854, and young Bidwell even disposed of his jewelry to pay his debts. At the age of 23 he went to New York and gradually became very successful as a drummer for different grocery concerns. In 1858 he married an estimable young lady and supported his family beside.

He left his place of employment shortly after his marriage, and almost immediately afterward received a letter from a former customer in which he was informed that the customer had been asked to pay a balance of $10, which he had already paid to Bidwell, who gave him a receipt at the time. The customer also informed Bidwell's former employers that he had paid the money, and they at once became suspicious and refused to accept Bidwell's explanation that it was an oversight.

They refused to accept the money from Bidwell, but had him arrested for embezzlement. When the circumstances were explained to the magistrate, he was discharged. This experience, however, injured Bidwell's standing in the business community, and although he made several attempts to establish himself in New York, he met with no success. In 1864, he invented a steam kettle from which he made several thousand dollars. With this money he opened a wholesale confectionery business in Toronto, but failed in this. As his family was not with him, he spent his evenings around billiard parlors, where he became acquainted with a man who gave the name of Frank Kibbe, and who confided to Bidwell that $1000 was due him through a business transaction; but as he feared to call for it through fear of being arrested by his creditors, he agreed to give Bidwell $500 if he would get the money, which he did.

Kibbe, seeing that he could trust Bidwell, finally persuaded him to go to Providence, R. I., where they opened a swindling commission house, and by gradually gaining the confidence of the wholesalers they accumulated a large stock. Finally Kibbe persuaded Bidwell to go to New York in the "interest" of the firm, and when he returned he found that Kibbe had sold the entire stock at a discount and departed with the $20,000 he had obtained. Bidwell traced him to Buffalo, where he forced Kibbe to disgorge $10,500.

Bidwell then returned to New York and was attracted by a sign, "Partner wanted with $5000." He made inquiry and a man who called himself Dr. S. Bolivar stated that he had $5000 and was looking for a reliable partner with a like amount so that they might purchase a prosperous grocery business.

Bidwell expressed a willingness to provide the money if the facts were as represented. He sent a friend to the store who learned that the entire business was for sale for $5000 and that the doctor was evidently trying to swindle him out of his money. He then confided to the doctor that he had been engaged in the same "graft" himself, and they had a hearty laugh.

These men evidently concluded that they were well matched, for they formed a partnership and opened up another swindling commercial house in Wheeling, W. Va., under assumed names, but business became so good that they regretted they had not used their own names and operated a legitimate business. Their operations at this place, in July, 1865, caused their arrest and conviction on a charge of conspiracy to defraud. While incarcerated, a jailbreak occurred and four escaped, but one prisoner, named Morgan, was killed by the guards while making the attempt.

Bidwell was sentenced to serve two years, and as it was his first conviction he longed for his liberty and regretted that he had not escaped with his fellow criminals. He and another prisoner procured a knife and after notching the edges, used it as a saw and were about to escape when they were betrayed. They were not discouraged, and on the following Christmas they made good their escape while the guards were full of "Yuletide cheer."

Bidwell then went to New York, and although he attempted to pass some paper which had been forged by one Wilkes, he was unsuccessful.

He then met a forger named George Engle, who was known as the 'Terror of Wall Street," and after gathering in a few thousand dollars from forged paper, they left for England in 1872, accompanied by Bidwell's brother, Austin, and George McDonald. McDonald was a Harvard graduate and his mother, a most estimable lady, accompanied him to the dock, believing that he was going abroad to become a cotton merchant.

Arriving in London, George Bidwell purchased a letter of credit from the London and Westminster Bank under the name of Hooker, and procuring some of the bank's letterheads, he sent forged letters of introduction, purporting to be signed by the manager of the bank, to several of the leading banks in Europe. He also mailed letters to himself which were enclosed in the London bank's envelopes and addressed to him in care of the banks he intended to swindle. He then left for Bordeaux, France, and proceeded at once to the bank, asked for his mail, and on the strength of the letter of introduction already in the bank's possession, he was accorded every courtesy. He presented a forged check for 50,000 francs, which was paid after a slight delay, and he departed. He proceeded immediately to Marseilles, and visited the bank of Brune & Co., where the same modus operandi was employed which proved so successful on the preceding day; the only difference being that on this occasion 62,000 francs were obtained. The next day found him at Lyons, where he obtained 60,000 francs in identically the same manner. He then returned to his confederates in London.

As all of this money was in French notes, they immediately changed it to English gold before the fraud was discovered.

It was then determined to send Bidwell to South America and Engle prepared a forged letter of credit, but as the name of the sub-manager of the bank was omitted, the trip was a failure from a financial standpoint, as Bidwell only obtained £10,000, Brazilian currency, on a forged check. He then returned to Paris, where he joined his companions. Shortly afterward, George Bidwell went to Amsterdam, and while learning the banking system in vogue there, gained possession of a bill on Baring Bros., which he forwarded to his confederate, McDonald, who was in London.

Shortly afterward Bidwell received a dispatch from McDonald as follows:

"London, November 2, 1872. "George Bidwell, Amsterdam:

"Have made a great discovery. Come immediately.

"MAC."

Bidwell returned to London at once, but the "great discovery" did not appeal to him, although it suggested a plan which eventually resulted in the great Bank of England forgery.

When the party first reached London from America, Austin Bidwell deposited about £1500 in the Bank of England under the name of "Warren," and did not draw on it until December 2, 1873.

On this date he deposited £1300 with the Continental Bank under the name of C. J. Horton and transferred his ⊠Warren⊠ account in the Bank of England to this bank, and then began to draw or deposit almost daily to create the impression that he was a business man. He then purchased several bills of exchange, which were also taken to this bank, and it was while handling these bills that it was discovered that the Bank of England was careless in investigating the genuineness of the signatures thereon.

Bidwell then cabled for one Noyes in New York, whom he intended to use in the work at hand. Noyes went to London, and without being taken into the details of the conspiracy, blindly obeyed orders and remained loyal to the end.

On December 28, 1872, Bidwell sent genuine bills of exchange amounting to £4307 to the Bank of England for discount, and as it was done without hesitation, he became thoroughly convinced that the signatures were not properly investigated.

On January 21, 1873, George Bidwell began operating on the Bank of England by forwarding £4250 in false exchange bills to be placed to the credit of ⍰Warren,⍰ which was the name under which his brother Austin had opened his account. In a few days a courteous note addressed to ⍰Mr. Warren⍰ was received which stated that the request had been complied with.

George Bidwell then sent Noyes to the Continental Bank with a ⍰Warren⍰ check for £4000 to be placed to Horton⍰s credit, and in a few days Noyes presented Horton checks for £3000 and purchased United States bonds with the money.

This completed the operation, which was repeated at intervals until they feared that the frequent purchase of United States bonds by Noyes would attract attention. He therefore changed his practice by presenting the checks as before, but instead of purchasing bonds, he drew the money.

Neither McDonald nor Bidwell ever appeared near the banks, and as their success had been phenomenal, they now having $300,000 in bonds and several thousand in cash, they decided that they would make a final scoop and quit.

Accordingly, on February 27, Bidwell sent about £25,000 in false bills to the Bank of England in the usual manner and received the usual courteous note in acknowledgement. Through carelessness, Bidwell neglected to put the date of acceptance on two of the bills, and this proved to be his fatal error. The bank clerk looked upon this as a mere oversight, and on March 1, 1873, the bills were sent to B. W. Blydenstein, the supposed acceptor, who at once declared them to be forgeries. This discovery was kept quiet, and a few days afterward Bidwell sent Noyes to the Continental Bank with the usual style of check, but for the unusual amount of £20,000.

Noyes was placed under arrest at the bank and taken to the Bow Street Station. He passed Bidwell while en route, but pretended not to recognize him.

During the operations, McDonald and Bidwell occupied quarters at aristocratic St. James Place, Piccadilly, where the bills were made. When the arrest was made Bidwell burned up the blocks and, as he thought, all incriminating evidence, but as McDonald was in the act of writing a letter at the time, he told Bidwell to save a piece of blotting paper.

The arrest and expose created a great sensation. McDonald and Bidwell became alarmed and made a fatal mistake by suddenly moving to other quarters before their rent was due. The landlady then recalled the mysterious actions of these men while under her observations, and as it was published that Noyes came from America and the landlady knew her two gentlemen-of-leisure boarders came from the same country, she went to their former lodgings, but all she found was the little piece of blotting paper, which she took to the police station. McDonald fled to New York and Bidwell fled to Ireland, but was thunderstruck, when in Cork, he picked up a paper announcing a large reward for the arrest of George Bidwell. The circular stated that all out-going ships and railroad stations were under surveillance and that Bidwell had been traced to Ireland. This fact was given great publicity, and as every man, woman and child had the reward in mind, he was kept constantly on the alert and was eyed with suspicion at every turn.

He then fled to Edinburgh, Scotland, arriving on March 10, 1873, and remaining until April 3, at which time he was arrested because of a clew given the police by a news dealer where Bidwell bought papers daily. This dealer noted that this man had an American accent and his description tallied with that of the one published of Bidwell.

The police trailed the man to his lodgings, where the landlady referred to him as "mysterious acting." Upon refusing to give an account of himself he was arrested, and taken to the Bow Street Station in London.

Austin Bidwell, instead of going to America, as previously agreed upon, went to Havana. He was brought back to London on May 28. It was claimed that a woman whom McDonald had associated with, gave the police valuable information as to the direction in which the fugitives fled.

McDonald was arrested when his steamer reached New York Harbor and his United States bonds, $10,000 in gold and precious stones of an equal value were taken from him. McDonald employed able counsel and a great effort was made to prevent his extradition on the ground of insufficiency of evidence. His points were not well taken and he was returned to London. After considerable delay the trial on one of sixteen indictments was set for August, 1873.

During the trial it developed that while these men had demonstrated that as cunning criminals they had few equals, yet they did what the commonest criminal nearly always does, that is, leave a trail behind upon which a shrewd detective could pile up a mountain of evidence.

To begin with, it will be recalled that while George Bidwell was destroying the evidence of their crimes in their rooms just previous to their flight, McDonald, who was writing a letter at the time, asked him not to destroy the blotter, as he desired to blot his letter and envelope. It was supposed that Austin Bidwell had gone to New York, and this letter was addressed to him there and the impression of the name and address was left on the blotter, which could be plainly read by holding it to the mirror. They even used this blotter while preparing their forged bills and the forged names could also be plainly discerned.

They sent a box to New York addressed to Major George Matthews, which contained $220,920 worth of United States bonds which were purchased at the Continental Bank by Noyes. This box was seized by the New York police. It was proved that this box was shipped by McDonald on March 5 under the name of Charles Lossing. Attorney Charles DaCosta of New York testified that he was present when the box was opened in New York and that it also contained some of George Bidwell's jewelry. In addition to this evidence, the man who gave the box to McDonald was produced. The detectives also found a London directory in the defendant's room from which a part of a page had been torn, and on obtaining a similar directory it was found that the portion of the page missing contained the names of London engravers.

Five of these engravers identified George Bidwell as the man for whom they had engraved the blocks which were used in printing the bills.

While being chased through Ireland, Bidwell boastfully wrote to McDonald, addressing the mail to New York, of his success in outwitting the Irish police, and enclosed the newspaper clipping announcing the reward for his capture. This letter was addressed to general delivery and was recovered and used against him. Noyes and Bidwell planned to keep their acquaintance a secret, but several witnesses were produced who had seen them holding mysterious conferences.

Mrs. Ann Thomas testified that Austin Bidwell roomed in her home, located at 21 Enfield Road, and that George Bidwell and McDonald frequently called, giving assumed names. She furthermore stated that Austin received packages which were addressed to a "Mr. Warren."

A jeweler also testified that he sold jewelry to Austin under that name.

Before the case was submitted, McDonald made an eloquent plea in behalf of Austin Bidwell, and called attention to alleged extenuating circumstances in his case.

The jury, after deliberating fifteen minutes, returned a verdict of guilty against the four prisoners, and the judge forthwith fixed their punishment at life imprisonment.

While imprisoned, George Bidwell's health failed, and in a fit of despondency, he attempted to commit suicide by cutting his throat. He lost consciousness through loss of blood, but recovered.

On July 18, 1887, George was released from prison because of ill health. He immediately returned to America and wrote a book called "Forging His Chains," which dealt with his life. Later he took his sister to London, where, by constant effort, they succeeded in procuring Austin's pardon in 1892.

In March, 1899, the two brothers went to Butte, Mont. Austin was taken sick and died on March 7. George delivered a lecture on his life in an effort to obtain enough money to bury his brother.

As he only sold fifty tickets, he became extremely melancholy, but resolved to raise the necessary money by making personal appeals to different citizens.

From lack of nourishment, due to poverty, he was now a tottering wreck of his former self, and while begging for money he slipped and fell, injuring his leg so that he was confined to his bed in his lodging-house. On March 25 the clerk found him dead in the same bed in which Austin had died a few weeks before.

An autopsy showed that he died from natural causes, but there is no doubt but that his brother's death, and his own failure to procure sufficient money to properly inter the remains, contributed materially toward shortening the life of this remarkable character, who had fraudulently obtained over $1,000,000 during his career.

While in the English prison he composed the following verse:

" 'Tis fourteen years since on me freedom smiled,

While banished far from country, wife and child;

Misfortune's arrows sharp have pierced my heart, My spirit, too, with most envenomed dart.

In solitude wild fancies thronging.

The heart for home is ever longing.

Then heed the captive's cry and set me free, Almighty God of Grace — if God there be,"

———————

CRIMINAL CAREER OF JIMMY HOPE, THE MOST SUCCESSFUL BANK ROBBER IN AMERICA, INCLUDING THE HISTORY OF THE GREAT MANHATTAN BANK ROBBERY IN NEW YORK, THE SENSATIONAL ROBBERY OF THE KENSINGTON BANK IN PHILADELPHIA AND HIS ATTEMPT TO BURGLARIZE THE SATHER BANK IN SAN FRANCISCO.

(From Inspector Byrnes' "History of Celebrated Criminals.")

Jimmy Hope was born in Philadelphia in J 836, where he married and raised a family.

On April 6, 1869, a well-dressed man went into the Kensington Savings Bank in Philadelphia and asked for a private interview with the president of the bank, which was immediately granted.

The stranger then informed the president that he was a detective and had been sent by the Chief of Police to inform the president that reliable information had been received to the effect that a gang would attempt to rob the bank that night and that three or four policemen in uniform would be secreted in the banking rooms before the bank closed. After pledging the president to secrecy, the "detective" left.

About 2:50 p. m. the uniformed "policemen" appeared and the two porters were instructed to stand guard with them. Early in the evening one of the porters was sent after beer, and as soon as he left, the "policemen," who in reality were Jimmy Hope's gang of safe robbers in disguise, overpowered and gagged the lone porter. When the other porter returned he received the same treatment, and the robbers then proceeded to open the safe. They secured between $80,000 and $100,000 and escaped, but a bitter quarrel occurred when the loot was being divided, which resulted in the killing of three of the robbers.

In this gang were Jimmy Hope, Jim Casey, Tom McCormick, George Howard and three others. Casey was killed by McCormick in New York, and on June 4, 1878, Howard's body was found near Yonkers on the Hudson River, N. Y.

According to an admission made by Jimmy Hope when he was arrested in San Francisco in later years, one of the gang, who was dissatisfied with the manner in which the loot was divided, swore that he would kill Howard, and Hope expressed the belief that Howard's death was due to this dispute. In 1860, Howard, who had several aliases, resided in San Francisco and was interested in the "Ocean House."

In August, 1869, Hope, Ned Lyons and two others hired a basement underneath the Ocean Bank, located at Fulton and Greenwich Streets. New York. A partition was erected to obstruct a view from the Street and they then proceeded to cut through the stone floor directly under the vault. The entrance into the vault was made on a Saturday night. Over $1,000,000 in money and bonds were removed from the vault, but the bonds were thrown away and they took what gold and silver they could carry without attracting attention, which only amounted to a few thousand dollars.

In 1870, Hope participated in the burglary of the paymaster's safe in the Philadelphia Navy Yard, but the admissible evidence was not strong enough to justify a trial.

He next assisted in the robbery of Smith's Bank, at Perry, N. Y. For this crime he was arrested, convicted and sentenced on November 28, 1870, to serve five years at Auburn Prison, New York.

On January 3, 1873, he escaped with three other prisoners.

In November, 1873, Hope and three others rented a house next to the First National Bank of Wilmington, Delaware, and on the morning of November 7 the gang captured the cashier of the bank, who lived nearby, and his entire family; the object being to force that official to open the safe. The servant girl escaped, however, and gave the alarm to the authorities, the result being that Hope and his three confederates, McCoy, Brady and Bliss, were captured, convicted, and on November 25, 1873, they were sentenced to forty lashes and ten years' imprisonment.

When they had served one year of their term the entire gang escaped.

After participating in numerous other bank robberies of more or less importance, Hope began laying his plans for what proved to be his most conspicuous, and in some respects, his most successful robbery, namely the Manhattan Bank robbery in New York City.

In 1878, Dan Kelley was employed as night watchman at the Manhattan Savings Bank in New York City, which was regarded as one of the strongest banking-houses in America.

At 6 a. m. Sunday, October 27, 1878, Kelley, according to custom, awakened Janitor Wertel, who lived with his family in the bank building. Kelley then went home and Wertel began to put on his clothes.

While dressing, several men rushed in upon him and at once overpowered and handcuffed him. Wertel's wife and mother-in-law began to scream, but the robbers displayed revolvers and threatened to kill them if they did not desist. While some of the robbers stood guard over the women, others led Wertel into the bank and threatened to kill him if he did not reveal the combination of the safes to them. He complied with their request, and after opening the outer door, the robbers opened the others by means of the safe-cracking tools they carried.

They then stole securities and money to the amount of $2,757,700. Of this amount $73,000 was in coupon bonds and $11,000 in cash.

The robbers then quietly departed, leaving all their tools behind them. As there were no marks on the doors or windows, it was concluded that they gained an entrance to the bank by means of a pass key. It was therefore believed that someone connected with the bank was implicated in the robbery and several attaches were placed under surveillance by Captain Thomas Byrnes, who afterward gained an international reputation as Inspector Byrnes.

Among those shadowed was one Patrick Shevlin, who had been employed as a watchman at the bank, but who, after the robbery, spent much time and money at a resort where known thieves congregated.

Feeling confident that this watchman had a guilty knowledge of the crime, Byrnes finally took him into custody, and after several days of cross-examination by the shrewd detective, the watchman made one or two fatal slips of the tongue, and then, realizing that he was cornered, admitted that a gang headed by Jimmy Hope had, after much persuasion, influenced him to enable them to procure duplicate keys to the bank and furnish such information as they desired.

They represented that Shevlin would never be suspected, and that he would be given his share of the money obtained.

Police Officer John Nugent was also charged with complicity in the robbery, but was finally acquitted.

Ten men were arrested in different parts of the United States on charges of having participated in this robbery. Most of them were captured while attempting to dispose of the stolen bonds.

On July 18, 1879, John Hope, Jimmy Hope's son, was convicted and sentenced to twenty years' imprisonment, and on December 12, 1879, Billy Kelly was sentenced to ten years' imprisonment. Jimmy Hope was sent to Auburn prison, but subsequently escaped. John Dobbs, Sam Ferris, John Nugent, Abe Coakley, Patrick Shevlin, Pete Emerson and Ed Goodrich were discharged from custody, Shevlin having been granted immunity for his assistance to the prosecution.

As a result of this theft the bank was closed temporarily.

The officials immediately appealed to Congress and succeeded in having the stolen bonds canceled and duplicates issued.

On June 26, 1881, the janitor of the Sather Bank, southeast corner of Commercial and Montgomery Streets, San Francisco, noticed some dirt near the vault which had evidently fallen from the top of the vault. Suspicion was immediately aroused, and Captain of Detectives I. W. Lees was notified.

On investigation he found that on the second floor, in a dark corner where the janitor kept his brooms, etc., an opening sufficiently large to admit a man, had been deftly cut in the floor and through the lower ceiling over the vault. The next night Lees, with a squad of detectives, kept watch, and during the night their vigilance was rewarded when they observed two men enter a hallway leading upstairs. After allowing time for the robbers to resume operations, Lees and his men entered the building and proceeded at once to the hole in the floor, where they observed one of the burglars in the act of lowering himself to the next floor. Upon realizing that he had been discovered, he whipped out a large revolver, but the detectives covered him with sawed-off shotguns and he surrendered. His accomplice, who had gone up to the next floor, escaped, but it was subsequently learned that his name was Dave Cummings, a notorious burglar, who was afterwards sent to an eastern prison for a long term.

The man arrested proved to be Jimmy Hope. He was found guilty of attempting to burglarize the Sather Bank, and on October 15, 1881, was sentenced to serve seven years' imprisonment. Upon his discharge he was returned to Auburn Prison to serve out his unexpired term.

He died in New York on June 2, 1905.

———————

THE SENSATIONAL KILLING OF JAY GOULD'S BUSINESS ASSOCIATE, COLONEL "JIM" FISK, BY THE ARISTOCRATIC EDWARD S. STOKES— FISK'S PHENOMENAL RISE FROM THE POSITION OF A

COUNTRY PEDDLER— THE PROMINENT PART PLAYED IN THE TRAGEDY BY THE BEAUTIFUL JOSIE MANSFIELD FROM CALIFORNIA.

(From Warden Sutton's "History of New York Tombs.")

James Fisk, Jr., was born in the hamlet of Pownal, Vermont, on September 12, 1835.

Being of a roving disposition, he left home at the age of 14 years and worked for Van Amburgh's circus for eight years.

He then returned to his native town and assisted his father, who was a peddler. Fisk, Jr., displayed much business ability and soon quit peddling to go into the dry goods business. He rapidly built up such a trade that the Boston firm, Jordan, Marsh & Co., deemed it advisable to purchase Fisk's stock and engage him as a salesman.

About this time the Civil War broke out. Fisk's employers had an immense supply of blankets at the time and Fisk suggested that if he were permitted to go to Washington he could sell them at a fabulous price to the War Department. He went and not only sold the entire stock of blankets, but procured such a large order for others that the firm found it advisable to purchase the only woolen mill in that part of the country which produced the particular blanket specified in the contract. This mill was in Vermont.

In two years the firm, in which Fisk then had an interest, cleared over $200,000.

In 1865 Fisk left the firm and went to Boston. Remaining there but a short time, he moved to New York, where he entered into the brokerage business.

Shortly afterward Daniel Drew gave the sale of the Bristol line of steamers into Fisk's hands. He made enough money out of this sale to begin operations on a large scale, and so successful was he that he soon possessed a $1,000,000 bank account.

In 1867 he and Jay Gould became directors of the Erie Railroad.

It was said that in February, 1868, Fisk and one or two others so manipulated the stock of this road that they cleared over $1,250,000.

It was also claimed that Fisk was at the head of the ring which attempted to "corner" all salable gold in Wall Street on Friday, September 24, 1869, the day thereafter being referred to as "Black Friday" because of the panic created. He was also Colonel of the Ninth regiment, N. G, N. Y, and became a great power in politics.

Edward S. Stokes was born in Philadelphia on April 27, 1841, his family being one of the oldest and most aristocratic in Pennsylvania. He was schooled in the best academies and enjoyed every comfort that wealth could provide.

Leaving college in 1860, he went to New York, where he became a member of the firm known as Budlong & Stokes, which was located at 25 Water Street.

The operations of this firm amounted to millions and they were highly successful.

In 1865 Stokes withdrew from the firm and at once began the erection of the Brooklyn Oil Refinery, which was completed at a cost of $250,000.

Stokes also invested heavily in numerous petroleum companies which were then organizing in Pennsylvania and bought his stock when the oil fever was at its height. In less than one year the panic came, and with the bursting of the bubble Stokes was financially ruined.

At this time, his refinery, upon which he had no insurance, was completely destroyed by fire. His friends came to his assistance, however, and the refinery was immediately rebuilt, and during the following three years Stokes made enough money to liquidate his indebtedness.

In 1870 Fisk determined to get control of Stokes's refinery in the interest of the Erie Railroad, and a co-partnership was entered into. The two men were then fast friends.

Helen Josephine Mansfield was born in California and developed into a young woman of such beautiful face and form that she attracted attention wherever she went.

She married an actor named Frank Lawler and shortly afterward they drifted East, where Mrs. Lawler obtained a divorce. On the day the divorce was granted, Fisk called at the home of Anna Woods, the actress, who then resided in New York, and on that occasion he met Josie Mansfield Lawler for the first time.

He became infatuated with this beautiful girl at first sight and shortly afterward he established her in a palatial home in New York, although he was at the time living with his wife in the same city.

Stokes frequently dined at the Mansfield house as the guest of Fisk. After a while, Fisk began to pay a great deal of attention to a very pretty

French opera singer, and it is claimed that while he was with the singer, Miss Mansfield was entertaining Stokes.

This rumor reached Fisk's ears, and he ordered Stokes never to enter the house again. As Stokes ignored the command, Fisk, in a fit of passion, wrote a farewell letter to Josie, but repented shortly afterward and a temporary reconciliation was effected.

But this was the beginning of the end. Fisk and Stokes began to quarrel over their business transactions, and on Saturday, January 4, 1871, Fisk swore to a warrant charging Stokes with embezzling $50,000 of the company's funds, but he delayed having the warrant served until late at night. The result was that Stokes, not being able to raise the required bail at that hour, was compelled to stay in jail over Sunday.

On Monday he was brought before Judge Dowling, who released him on $50,000 bail, but the case was subsequently dismissed and Stokes then had Fisk arrested on a charge of false imprisonment.

Josie Mansfield, who had ceased her intimate relationship with Fisk, extended all her sympathy to Stokes, and shortly afterward claimed that Fisk owed her $40,000, for the recovery of which she expressed her determination to sue him.

In reply Fisk charged that the woman and Stokes, who had severed all business relations with Fisk on January 8, 1871, were attempting to blackmail him.

Josie Mansfield's answer to this was a libel suit, and Stokes was her principal witness.

The case was being tried on Saturday, January 6, 1872, and Stokes was present at the trial. After court adjourned in the early afternoon, Stokes drove to Delmonico's for dinner.

After dinner he proceeded toward the Grand Central Hotel, arriving in that neighborhood about 4 p. m.

According to Stokes' statement, he was on his way to purchase theatre tickets, and as he passed the hotel he saw a lady sitting by the parlor window on the second floor that he thought he knew.

At this moment he met a merchant named George Bailey, to whom he excused himself while he went to speak to the lady.

He then went into the hotel and proceeded up the stairs to the parlor. Seeing that he had mistaken a strange lady for his friend, he started down stairs, where he met Fisk, who was coming up stairs. Both men stopped and glared at each other.

Stokes claimed that Fisk drew a pistol and that he (Stokes) believing that Fisk intended to kill him, drew his own pistol and shot Fisk twice. One bullet passed through the arm and the other penetrated the abdomen, causing a wound from which Fisk died at 10:45 a. m. the following day.

Fisk was immediately removed to room 213, where he was visited by Captain of Police, afterwards Inspector, Thomas Byrnes and Coroner Young.

To these officials he made the following statement:

"This afternoon at about 4 o'clock I rode up to the Grand Central Hotel. I entered by the private entrance, and, when I entered the first door I met the boy, of whom I inquired if Mrs. Morse was in. He told me that Mrs. Morse and her youngest daughter had gone out, but he thought the other daughter was in her grandmother's room. I asked him to go up and tell the daughter that I was there. I came through the other door, and was going upstairs and had gone up about two steps, and on looking up I saw Edward S. Stokes at the head of the stairs.

As soon as I saw him I noticed that he had something in his hand, and a second after I saw the flash, heard the report, and felt the ball enter my abdomen on the right side. A second after I heard another shot, and the bullet entered my left arm. When I received the first shot I staggered and ran toward the door, but noticing a crowd gathering in front, I ran back on the stairs again. I was then brought upstairs in the hotel. I saw nothing more of Stokes until he was brought before me by an officer for identification. I fully identified Edward S. Stokes as the person who shot me.

"JAMES FISK, JR."

Stokes surrendered immediately after the shots were fired and on June 19, 1872, his trial began.

It was the theory of the prosecution that Stokes visited the hotel and laid in wait for his victim, but the defense claimed that Stokes acted solely in self-defense, and that the reason no weapon was found near Fisk was because someone had concealed it.

On July 13, 1872, the case was submitted to the jury, and after deliberating for forty hours they stood seven for conviction and five for acquittal. The jury was then discharged.

On December 18, 1872, the case again came to trial, and on January 2, 1873, Stokes was found guilty of murder.

On January 6, one year after the assault, he was sentenced to be hanged on February 28, and was placed in the condemned cell in the Tombs.

An appeal was taken and a stay of execution granted.

On June 10, 1873, the Court of Appeals granted a new trial, which began on October 17.

Several new witnesses were introduced by the defense.

John Moore, an attaché of the Grand Central Hotel, testified that he was standing in front of the hotel when the shots were fired and that he immediately ran inside. Seeing Fisk leaning on the banisters on the stairs, he approached and said to Fisk: "What's the matter ?" Fisk is alleged to have replied: "He was too quick for me this time."

Moore also testified that the bellboy, Redmond, who was one of the principal witnesses for the prosecution, informed him immediately after the tragedy that he knew nothing about the shooting except what he had heard.

Evidence was also produced tending to show that Stokes entered the hotel five minutes before Fisk, and that it was impossible for him to have known that Fisk intended to visit the place at all.

Robert Stobo testified that he saw Stokes meet Bailey in front of the hotel and also observed Stokes when he bowed to a lady sitting by a window, and that he immediately afterward left Bailey and entered the hotel.

For the purpose of proving that Fisk probably carried a revolver on the day of the tragedy, his tailor testified that he made the trousers which Fisk wore when he was shot and that in ordering the pants Fisk left instructions to have a pistol pocket put in them, something he had never done before.

Patrick Logan, a former policeman, but a court officer during Stokes' first trial, testified that while Hart and Redmond, the Grand Central Hotel bellboys, who claimed to have been eye-witnesses to the shooting and gave the most damaging evidence against Stokes, were in his custody, detained as witnesses, they informed him (Logan) that they had been told what to testify to. According to Logan, these boys claimed that Mr. Powers, the proprietor of the hotel, had promised them $1000 each for their testimony.

When asked why he had not testified at the previous trials, Logan answered: "I did not want to get mixed up in the case, but before I would let Stokes hang, I would have told Governor Dix what I knew."

On October 28, 1873, the case was submitted to the jury and the defendant was found guilty of manslaughter in the third degree.

On the following day, the defendant appeared before Judge Davis for sentence.

After criticizing the jury for the mercy extended the prisoner, the judge said to Stokes:

"The sentence of the court is that you be imprisoned in the State Prison at Sing Sing at hard labor for the term of four years,"

Stokes was removed to Sing Sing four days later, where he remained until his discharge, on October 28, 1876.

THE MURDER OF MULTI-MILLIONAIRE WILLIAM M. RICE IN NEW YORK BY HIS SECRETARY, CHARLES F. JONES, AND ATTORNEY ALBERT T. PATRICK.

William Marsh Rice resided in Houston, Texas, for many years, and accumulated a fortune of $7,000,000.

His wife died in Waukesha, Wis., in 1896 under peculiar circumstances.

Just previous to her death, she drew up a will disposing of $2,500,000 worth of community property. A man named Holt was executor of this will, which Rice contested bitterly.

On September 16, 1896, after the death of his wife, Rice made a will leaving the bulk of his wealth to the "William M. Rice Institute for the Advancement of Literature, Science and Art," which he had founded in Texas in 1891.

This will was drawn up by Captain James A. Baker, a prominent Texas attorney.

About the time of his wife's death, Rice, accompanied by his Secretary, Charles T. Jones, left Texas to take up his residence in New York City, where he engaged apartments at the Berkshire, No. 500 Madison

Avenue. Jones was then 23 years of age, while Rice had passed his 81st year and was extremely eccentric.

Attorney Albert T. Patrick of New York formerly resided in Houston, Texas, and he transacted some legal business in relation to Mrs. Rice's will for Attorney Holt, the executor. At this time neither Rice nor Jones had met Patrick, but the former despised him because he had been informed that Patrick had done some "dirty work" in regard to the will for Holt.

One evening in November, 1899, Patrick called at Rice's apartments in New York and was met at the door by Jones.

Patrick gave an assumed name and stated that he desired to see Mr. Rice regarding a deal in cotton. Jones stated that Rice had retired for the night and Patrick agreed to return a few evenings later.

He did so and again Rice was in bed. After some hesitancy, Patrick disclosed his identity to Jones and stated that he was the New York representative of Holt, the executor of the will, and that he was authorized to effect a compromise, which he felt confident would be entirely satisfactory to all concerned. Jones informed Patrick of Rice's prejudice against him, and expressed the opinion that Rice would refuse to meet him. Patrick then requested Jones not to inform Rice of his visit.

After that Patrick called frequently after Rice had retired for the night, and he and Jones became quite confidential.

In the course of conversation, Rice's last will was discussed and Patrick slyly remarked that it was unfortunate for Jones that the bulk of the vast property would go to the Rice Institute and that Jones would receive comparatively nothing. Patrick then intimated that a "will" could be drawn up in which Jones would receive adequate compensation for faithful services rendered to Rice.

Observing that Jones was apparently impressed with this suggestion, Patrick became more bold and stated that he would draw up such a will, but as peculiarities in typewriting machines frequently make it easy to prove whether or not the work was done on a certain machine, he proposed that Jones write it on his own machine, as he attended to all of Rice's correspondence, and it might attract attention if it could be proven that some other machine was used to write this document.

Jones expressed dissatisfaction with the provisions of the first will drawn up by Patrick, but eventually a document was prepared which was dated June 30, 1900, and which was satisfactory to both conspirators.

In this will Patrick substituted himself for the Rice Institute and to prevent Rice's relatives from contesting the forged document he ingeniously provided them with a greater portion of the estate than was bequeathed them in the will of 1896.

Patrick convinced Jones that it might arouse suspicion if he (Jones) received a large part of the estate, but if no provision was made for him, he could have no apparent motive for being a party to a fraud and it would be taken for granted that the document was genuine. With the understanding that Patrick would pay him $10,000 per year Jones typewrote the will, which covered four pages. At the bottom of each page Rice's signature was traced, evidently from the same model, as each was exactly the same size and shape.

At this stage of the proceedings, the thought occurred to Patrick that it might seem singular that Rice should leave him, a stranger, the bulk of his property, so he persuaded Jones to typewrite and send several letters to him (Patrick), which would furnish evidence that Rice was Patrick's warm personal friend and in whom he reposed the greatest confidence. These letters, to which Patrick forged Rice's name, were sent through the mail, and at Patrick's suggestion Jones placed a copy of each in Rice's letter file. Patrick also forged Rice's name to numerous checks, which Jones sent out in his capacity as private secretary — the object being to gather these checks afterward if necessary and show by them that the signatures on them and on the will was in the same handwriting,

Jones also gave Patrick a typewritten order for securities and cash in different safe deposit vaults, to which Patrick forged Rice's name.

In the early part of August, 1900, Jones informed Patrick that Rice seemed to be improving in health. Patrick then gave Jones a very significant glance and asked:

"Don't you think he is living too long for our interests?"

After some hesitation he remarked that if Jones would let him in some night he would soon put Rice out of the way.

Dr. Curry, a friend of Jones, but who had no connection with this conspiracy, prescribed mercury for Jones, and Patrick suggested that Rice be given a dose of it at frequent intervals to weaken his system preparatory to administering chloroform.

Patrick stated that a physician's prescription was necessary to procure chloroform in New York, so Jones communicated with his brother in Texas, who innocently forwarded the amount requested.

The mercurial pills caused a severe diarrhea, and Dr. Curry was called in and prescribed for Rice, but in ignorance of the cause of the disorder.

It was intended to continue administering mercury to Rice for many days before chloroforming him, but Rice, for some reason unknown to Jones, sent a telegram to Captain Baker, his attorney in Texas, requesting him to come to New York at once. Rice also informed Jones that he intended to expend $2,500,000 in reconstructing a mill in Texas. Jones communicated this information to Patrick, and it was then decided to act at once.

At 8 p. m., on Saturday, September 22, while Rice was sleeping soundly, Jones saturated a small sponge with chloroform, and putting it in a towel shaped into a cone, he placed it on Rice's face. At the expiration of thirty minutes, Rice appeared lifeless. Jones then removed the cone and, after burning it in the stove, he opened the windows and notified Patrick and Dr. Curry that Rice was very low. The doctor and lawyer arrived together, and after a brief examination it was found that Rice was dead, and the doctor signed a death certificate, assigning old age, a weak heart and collocratel diarrhea as the cause of Rice's demise.

In the early part of September, Jones, acting under Patrick's instructions, typewrote a letter, purporting to be from Rice to Patrick, in which Rice instructed Patrick to have his body cremated.

Acting in accordance with these "instructions," Patrick took charge of the body and ordered an undertaker to have it cremated immediately, but when informed that the cremation could not take place the next day, he requested that the remains be embalmed at once.

Immediately after the undertaker left, Patrick searched Rice's room and took $450 in bills, valuable securities and jewelry.

On the following Monday, Patrick instructed Jones to fill out checks from Rice's check book, aggregating $250,000, on the Fifth Avenue Trust Co. and on Swenson & Sons' bank, made payable to Albert Patrick, to which the latter forged Rice's signature.

Through an oversight on Jones' part, he misspelled Patrick's first name on one of the checks on Swenson's bank. Patrick also overlooked this defect, and when he went to the bank to draw the money, he signed his correct name "Albert Patrick" on the back of the check.

The clerk then called his attention to the fact that the check was made payable to A-b-e-r-t Patrick, and refused to pay the money until he had communicated with Rice. The clerk then telephoned to Rice's apartments, and Jones assured him that Patrick was all right.

The clerk expressed a desire to speak to Rice personally, whereupon Jones, after a slight hesitation, stated that Rice was dead. The entire transaction aroused the suspicion of the bankers, and Max Gumpel, the San Francisco handwriting expert, who was then in New York, was consulted, and he immediately pronounced the signature of Rice a forgery.

In the meantime, Patrick made arrangements to have Rice's body cremated on Tuesday, and he telegraphed to Holt, the executor of Mrs. Rice's will, that he had an agreement signed by Rice which would end the litigation.

The authorities decided to perform an autopsy on Rice's body, and at the inquest physicians testified that all the organs were normal except the lungs, which were congested.

They also testified that nothing could have caused that congestion but the inhalation of some gaseous irritant. Chemist Witthaus testified that his analysis revealed the presence of mercury, but not in quantities sufficient to cause death.

On October 4, Patrick and Jones were arrested on a charge of forgery.

In some manner Patrick, who feared Jones would testify for the State, passed a knife into his cell and suggested that they jointly commit suicide. Jones made the attempt by cutting his throat, but the wound was not fatal.

In January, 1901, Jones made a complete confession of the facts as related above, and Patrick was then charged with murder.

When Jones became a witness for the State he was removed from the prison, furnished with comfortable quarters in an apartment house, and permitted to go to places of amusement.

At the trial numerous experts were produced who testified that the will and checks were forgeries, and Jones' brother from Texas and the express agents testified regarding the sending of the chloroform with which Rice was murdered.

Patrick was found guilty and sentenced to be electrocuted but the Governor commuted the sentence to life imprisonment.

The case was appealed to the Court of Appeals, but a new trial was denied. Judge Denis O'Brien rendered a dissenting opinion, in which he severely criticized the authorities who granted Jones immunity and permitted him to live in luxury during the trial.

On March 5, 1909, Patrick applied to the Appellate Court for his freedom on a writ of habeas corpus. He acted as his own attorney, and stated that he had never asked to have his penalty commuted to life imprisonment. After again protesting his innocence, he cried: "Give me liberty or give me death."

The writ was denied.

THE FIENDISH MURDER OF WILLIAM GULDENSUPPE IN

WOODSIDE, NEW YORK.

On June 26, 1897, the upper part of the body (minus the head) of a powerfully built man was found wrapped in red oilcloth in the East River, off Eleventh Street. New York City. It was severed above the diaphragm by someone who was evidently proficient in anatomy.

On the following day the lower part of the body (minus the legs) was found in the woods near 176th Street and Under Cliff Avenue, nearly eight miles distant from the gruesome discovery of the preceding day.

This portion of the body was also wrapped in red oilcloth. Shortly afterward, two boys, while swimming near the Brooklyn Navy yard, found two human legs wrapped in canvas.

The New York press gave a great deal of space to the mystery and as William Guldensuppe, a masseur at the Murray Hill Baths, New York, had mysteriously disappeared a few days previously, Frank Gartner, an attendant at the same baths, called at the morgue to view the remains.

He had seen the missing man in seminude condition almost daily, and without hesitancy he identified the remains as those of Guldensuppe, because of a small mark on the body.

Several other attaches of the baths were then called in and they were equally as positive as Gartner.

Dr. J. S. Cosby of 215 Forty-Fourth Street examined the index finger of the left hand and recognized a scar he had caused by lancing Guldensuppe's finger in treating a felon.

It was learned that Guldensuppe had lived with a midwife named Mrs. Augusta Nack at 339 Fifth Avenue.

The woman was taken into custody, and when interrogated as to the whereabouts of Guldensuppe, she stated that she neither knew nor cared where he was.

Acting Inspector O'Brien then obtained a statement from a barber named John Gotha who repeated a confession made to him by another barber named Martin Thorn, which was substantially as follows:

"I roomed in Mrs. Nack's house and when Guldensuppe was absent she made love to me.

"One night Guldensuppe came home and found me in her room. We had a fight and I was so badly punished I had to go to the hospital.

"I then moved to Third Avenue and Twenty-First Street where Mrs. Nack used to visit me clandestinely. She often gave me money and expressed a desire to leave Guldensuppe and live with me.

"On June 22, I saw an advertisement in the paper announcing that a cottage was for rent at 346 Second Street, Woodside, Long Island; so Mrs. Nack and I inspected it on June 24, and after deciding to rent it, we paid $15 down to a Mr. and Mrs. Braun.

"I was determined to get even with Guldensuppe, and I purchased a pistol and stiletto for that purpose.

"The next day, June 25, Mrs. Nack persuaded Guldensuppe to look at the 'new house,' and when he entered the building I was hid behind the door. At the first opportunity I shot him in the back of the head. We then threw him in the bath-tub, and while he was breathing heavily I cut off his head with a razor, and stripped his body.

"I then went to a store and purchased some plaster of Paris and Mrs. Nack went to another store and purchased some red oilcloth. The head was covered with plaster of Paris and bandages and thrown in the river and the other parts of the body were deposited in the places where they were subsequently found."

This statement caused the authorities to take Thorn into custody. After considerable questioning, he stated that Mrs. Nack and he rented the house on Long Island, and that when he entered the house on June 25, Mrs. Nack had already killed Guldensuppe and that his only part in the crime was to assist her in disposing of the remains.

Max Riger and wife, who conducted a store near the scene of the murder, positively identified Mrs. Nack as the woman to whom they had sold red oilcloth similar to that in which the body was wrapped.

Several witnesses identified Mrs. Nack and Thorn as the couple who occupied the cottage.

A carving knife, saw and revolver were found in the cottage, and human blood was found on each.

Constantine Keehn, a barber, of 836 Eighth Avenue, and a confident of Thorn, stated that Thorn told him that he had taken a course in surgery in Germany. Thorn formerly worked for a barber named Hepp on Seventy-Fifth Street, but was discharged when he reported for duty with a pair of black eyes caused by blows from Guldensuppe's fists.

On July 2, Mrs. Nack was charged with murder and a similar charge was entered against Thorn a few days later. Both were found guilty and appealed to the Supreme Court, but the judgment of the lower court was affirmed by that tribunal.

Mrs. Nack was sentenced to serve fifteen years in prison and Thorn was electrocuted at Sing Sing on August 1, 1898.

SYNOPSIS OF THE CASE OF HARRY THAW, WHO KILLED STANFORD WHITE AT MADISON SQUARE GARDEN, NEW YORK.

(From San Francisco Press and New York Police Records.)

Stanford White was born in 1852, and after receiving a college education in America, his father sent him to Europe to study architecture.

When he returned to New York he became a member of the firm known as McKim, Meade & White. He advanced rapidly in his profession, until he was considered one of the greatest architects in America. He drew the plans for the famous Madison Square Garden in New York, where he subsequently came to a tragic end.

Although he had an estimable wife residing in Cambridge, Mass., and a grown son who was at the time attending Harvard College, White had a suite of rooms in the tower of the Madison Square Garden, which he called his studio, but where he gave a great variety of spicy entertainments.

Frequently his guests were girls of tender years. One of the "events" in the tower was a stag dinner, and when the time for dessert arrived an immense pie was brought into the room. Suddenly a beautiful 15-year-old girl, scantily attired, burst through the crust, and after posing for an instant, she joined the guests.

It was claimed that this girl afterward became one of White's victims.

Evelyn Nesbit was born near Pittsburg on Christmas Day, 1884. Her father died when she was 12 years of age, and about three years later her mother, who has been referred to as a frivolous and extravagant woman, married a Pittsburg broker named Charles Holman.

As Evelyn was a remarkably beautiful child she earned considerable money by posing for artists in Pittsburg and afterward in New York. She subsequently became a chorus girl.

In the spring of 1901 Evelyn met a wealthy married man named James Garland, and shortly afterward she and her mother were his guests on a yachting trip.

Later Mrs. Garland sued her husband for a divorce and Evelyn Nesbit was said to have been mentioned as correspondent.

According to Evelyn's own statement a young woman friend invited her to dinner in New York in August, 1901, and without having the slightest idea as to where she was going to dine, Evelyn was inveigled by this girl into the studio in the tower where she met Stanford White for the first time.

About one month after the first meeting. White invited her to the tower at the conclusion of the Florodora performance in which she was a chorus girl.

She claimed that White represented that three other girls would be in the party. When Evelyn arrived at the studio White stated that the other girls had disappointed him, but he invited Evelyn to remove her hat and take a glass of champagne.

She reluctantly accepted the invitation, and after partaking of the wine she immediately lost consciousness. When her mind again cleared she found herself in the bedroom of the suite, the walls and ceiling of which were covered with mirrors.

Realizing that an assault had been committed upon her, she became hysterical, but White finally succeeding in pacifying her and then exacted a promise that she would never tell her mother of what had just transpired.

For several months afterward White met Evelyn clandestinely and the intimate relationship continued. In the meantime he was introduced to Evelyn's mother and won his way into her confidence. Posing as the protector of the family he rendered financial assistance to Evelyn with the mother's knowledge and consent.

William Thaw was one of the most prominent men in Pittsburg, and when he died he left an estate valued at $35,000,000, to be distributed among his family, consisting of Mrs. Thaw and several children.

Among these children was Alice Thaw, who married the Earl of Yarmouth, but was subsequently divorced; and Harry Kendall Thaw.

The latter was a wild, eccentric youth with such extravagant habits that his father provided in his will that Harry should receive only a monthly allowance. He had a penchant for chorus girls, and in that manner met Evelyn Nesbit some months after her first experience with White in the tower. They became very friendly, and Thaw showered her with tokens of his regard.

About this time White gave a dinner to which several guests were invited, including Jack Barrymore the actor, and Evelyn Nesbit. According to Evelyn's statement, Barrymore afterward proposed marriage to her, and as White was apparently jealous of the young man, he suggested to Evelyn's mother that the girl be sent to Mrs. De Mille's private school in New Jersey.

As the mother was also opposed to Barrymore she readily agreed to White's suggestions.

While at this school Thaw and White were such frequent visitors that there was considerable gossip among the pupils regarding their relations with Evelyn. About this time she underwent an operation for appendicitis, but as soon as she recovered she returned to New York, where she resumed the improper relationship with White, the meetings usually taking place in the tower after her night's work at the theater. During this time White was contributing liberally toward her support.

In the early part of 1902 she discontinued her intimate relationship with White, according to her statement, but when she and her mother left for Paris a few months later as the guests of Thaw the girl had in her possession a letter of credit from White.

After Evelyn and her mother traveled in Europe a few months with Thaw, the mother and daughter had a violent quarrel, which resulted in the former returning to America, leaving Thaw and the daughter alone. The pair then traveled under assumed names as man and wife.

According to Evelyn's statement she and Thaw were in Paris in June, 1903, when Thaw proposed marriage to her. She claimed that she hesitated and finally answered "No."

When pressed for a reason for her refusal, she stated that she then confided to Thaw all of her relations with White.

Evelyn returned to New York on October 25, 1903, and was followed by Thaw in November.

On October 27 Evelyn met White by appointment and went with him to the law office of Abe Hummel. *

* Attorneys "Big Bill" Howe and "Little Abe" Hummel were partners and had an immense practice in New York City.

In 1877, Chas. Dodge, then manager of the Palace Hotel in San Francisco, married Miss Clemence Cowles, but in March, 1897, Mrs. Dodge engaged Attorney W. Sweetzer of New York to obtain a divorce for her. Sweetzer served the summons on Dodge and the latter engaged Attorney M. Ruger, who died shortly afterward, to appear for him, but as the evidence was not controverted, the divorce was granted.

In June, 1901, Mrs. Dodge married the wealthy Charles Morse of New York.

Morse's uncle was bitterly opposed to this marriage and in August, 1903, he engaged Abe Hummel to ascertain if the marriage was legal.

On September 3, E. Bracken, who was in Hummel's employ, gave Dodge $500 with the understanding that the latter would call on Hummel at once, which he did. After some conversation the lawyer prepared a false affidavit, which Dodge swore to, in which it was claimed that he was never served with a summons in the divorce case. Hummel subsequently procured a court order requiring Mrs. Morse to show cause why her divorce from Dodge should not be set aside.

Before the referee, who was appointed to take testimony, Attorney Sweetzer swore that he had served the summons on Dodge, but he fell into Hummel's trap by identifying one Herpich, a dummy who had been substituted for Dodge before the referee. This blunder discredited Sweetzer. The Dodge divorce was annulled and the Dodge-Morse marriage dissolved. Sweetzer then made a search of the late Attorney Ruger's effects, where he found two letters from Dodge to Ruger in which Dodge admitted the service of the summons and authorized Ruger to represent him. With this new evidence the Dodge divorce was restored and Dodge was indicted for perjury and arrested. He was admitted to bail and fled, but was recaptured and made a confession involving Hummel, who was indicted for conspiracy, convicted and served about two years at Blackwell's Island.

In this office a lengthy affidavit was prepared in which it was charged that while on the trip through Europe Thaw frequently beat Miss Nesbit until she became unconscious, and that his reason for so doing was because Evelyn had refused to make an affidavit to the effect that White had drugged and outraged her, she, according to the affidavit, stating that such a statement would be false. The affidavit further alleged that Thaw was a cocaine fiend and that the affiant, Miss Nesbit, found a hypodermic syringe in Thaw's bureau and saw him swallow cocaine pills.

Although Evelyn Nesbit signed this statement she afterward claimed that she had been willfully misquoted and that while she signed a paper some days later at the tower, she did not know its contents at the time. A. S. Snydecker afterward swore that Miss Nesbit read the paper carefully before signing it.

When Thaw returned from Europe Evelyn told him of this incident, and at Thaw's request the affidavit was subsequently burned in Hummel's office in Evelyn's presence, but Hummel took the precaution to have it photographed first, and this photograph afterward became one of the principal exhibits in one of the most sensational murder trials in the criminal history of America.

After the affidavit was burned Evelyn ceased to associate with White and devoted most of her time to Thaw. They registered at several hotels in New York, but were requested to leave.

According to a statement made by Ben. Bowman, an employee at the Madison Square Garden, White called after the performance on December 28, 1903, and inquired if Evelyn Nesbit had gone home.

When informed that she had, White pulled out a revolver and swore that he would kill Thaw at once. Bowman related this alleged occurrence to Thaw shortly afterward.

After much persuasion Mrs. Thaw consented to her son's marriage, and he and Evelyn became man and wife in Pittsburg on April 4, 1905.

A few months later Thaw visited Anthony Comstock, Superintendent of the Society for the Prevention of Vice in New York, and reported that White was using his suite in the, tower as a trap for young girls.

An investigation was instituted, but no tangible evidence was obtained. Thaw did not mention his own wife's experience.

Mrs. Harry Thaw claimed that after she was married she saw White a couple of times and he attempted to annoy her by his attentions. She related these incidents to her husband and also told him that a Miss Mabel MacKenzie had informed her that White had openly boasted that he would get her (Mrs. Thaw) back from Thaw.

On the evening of June 25, 1905, Thaw and his wife and Truxtun Beale, formerly of San Francisco, had dinner at the Cafe Martin in New York. While they were dining, White and his son passed through the cafe, and Mrs. Thaw called her husband's attention to the occurrence.

After dinner the Thaw party proceeded to the Madison Square Roof Garden, where the play "Mam'zelle Champagne" was being produced.

Presently White entered alone and took a seat within view of the Thaw party. Harry became very restless and began walking about the place. Finally Mrs. Thaw suggested that they leave and the party proceeded to do so. Thaw apparently following the remainder of the party.

When he reached the table where White was seated Thaw suddenly turned, and facing White he drew a revolver and fired three shots, the first bullet passing through White's eye into the brain, causing instant death; the other two producing superficial wounds.

Thaw immediately surrendered to an officer, to whom he stated: "I killed him because he ruined my wife." Mrs. Thaw rushed up and after embracing her husband asked him why he did it. He replied: "It's all right, I probably saved your life."

Three days later Thaw was indicted for murder. January 23, 1907, was the date set for the trial in Justice Fitzgerald's court. District Attorney William T. Jerome personally prosecuted the case, and D. M. Delmas, the celebrated San Francisco attorney, appeared as chief counsel for the defense.

Nothing of importance which has not already been briefly related in this narrative was brought out by either side. Mrs. Harry Thaw testified in accordance with the statements previously made by her.

It was the contention of the defense that Thaw was insane when he killed White but that he became rational afterward.

During the trial District Attorney Jerome asked that the jury be excused. He then requested that a commission be appointed to ascertain the condition of the defendant's mind. His request was finally complied with, and after a lengthy examination the commission reported that Thaw was sane at the time of the examination. The trial was then continued.

On April 6 the arguments began. Delmas charged that Evelyn Thaw's mother received the wages of her child's downfall, with which she bedecked herself with diamonds and finery and afterward assisted the prosecutor of the girl's husband.

Jerome referred to the tragedy as a mere, sordid, Tenderloin homicide, and referred to Mrs. Thaw's testimony as a tissue of lies invented to prevent a deliberate, cold-blooded murderer from being put under ground.

The case was finally submitted to the jury on April 10, 1907, but after deliberating for forty-seven hours the jurors decided they could not agree and were discharged.

Seven jurors believed the defendant guilty as charged, while five voted for an acquittal on the ground of insanity.

On January 6, 1908, the second trial began before Justice Dowling. On this occasion M. W. Littleton represented Thaw, and produced evidence tending to show that Thaw had inherited insanity.

On February 1 Thaw was found not guilty on the ground that he was insane when he killed White. He was immediately transferred to the asylum for the criminal insane at Matteawan.

In July, 1909, Thaw attempted to procure his release on a writ of habeas corpus. The case was heard before Justice Isaac Mills, at White Plains, New York, and Jerome again represented the State.

Several alienists testified that Thaw was a degenerate paranoiac and would never recover.

Mrs. Susan Merrill testified that between 1902 and 1905 she conducted in succession two lodging-houses in New York where Thaw rented rooms under assumed names and to which he brought at various times over one hundred girls. Thaw represented that he was a theatrical agent, and Mrs. Merrill stated that on several occasions she caught him lashing the girls on the bare arms and bodies with a whip. Mrs. Merrill further testified that Thaw had subsequently provided her with money to purchase the girls' silence, one of them receiving $7,000.

Clifford Hartridge, former counsel for Thaw, then took the stand and produced a whip which he testified had been delivered to him by Mrs. Merrill and a woman named Wallace.

On August 7, 1909, Thaw's attorney, in his closing argument, accused Evelyn Thaw of secretly assisting Attorney Jerome during the case then drawing to a close.

On August 12 Justice Mills dismissed the writ of habeas corpus and declared that the release of the petitioner would be dangerous to public peace and safety and that he was afflicted with chronic delusion insanity. Thaw was then returned to the asylum.

In a suit to recover $92,000 from the Thaws for services alleged to have been rendered, Attorney Clifford Hartridge testified on April 1, 1910, that he paid hush money amounting to $30,000 to feminine acquaintances of Harry Thaw. He further testified that a woman named Mrs. Reed, whom Thaw met at Mrs. Merrill's, received $5,000.

THE MURDER OF ELSIE SIGEL, GRANDDAUGHTER OF THE CIVIL WAR HERO, GENERAL FRANZ SIGEL, BY HER CHINESE ASSOCIATE.

Franz Sigel was born in Germany and as a young man he made a brilliant record as a soldier in the Baden revolution. Shortly afterward he came to New York where he soon became very popular, especially with the German-Americans. When the Civil War broke out, he was appointed Colonel, and many of the Germans who volunteered to fight, expressed a desire to fight with Sigel. In recognition of his distinguished services, he was promoted to the rank of Major General.

After the war he became a prominent factor in New York politics, because of the high veneration the German citizens had for him. He served as Collector of Internal Revenue and later as a pension agent. He had four sons, named Rudolph, Robert, Franz and Paul. Rudolph was committed to the insane asylum in Washington in 1904. Robert was convicted of forgery while serving in the pension office under his father, but subsequently was pardoned by President Harrison.

General Sigel died several years ago and a large statue of him was unveiled on Riverside Drive on October 19, 1907. Many of the leading citizens of New York attended the ceremony to do honor to one of the unique figures in American history.

Paul Sigel married a lady who afterward took an active interest in missionary work in the Chinatown of New York. Mrs. Sigel frequently took her daughter Elsie into the Chinese quarters and as the girl grew older she became greatly interested in the work.

On June 9, 1909, Elsie, who was then 19 years of age, disappeared from her father's home at 209 Wadsworth Avenue. Three days later, Mr. Sigel received a telegram from Washington, D. C, which read:

"I'll be home by end of week. Don't worry.

"ELSIE."

On the afternoon of June 19, 1909, Sun Leung, the proprietor of a chop-suey restaurant located at 782 Eighth Avenue, went to the West Forty-seventh Street police station and informed the officers that he was worried about his cousin, a young Chinese named Leong Lung, alias William Leon, who had been missing for six days.

He explained that his cousin occupied a room on the top or fourth floor in the same building where the restaurant was located; that the door was locked and that after knocking repeatedly he received no response.

Policeman John Riordan was detailed to accompany the Chinese to the room and institute an investigation.

With the exception of a bed and a trunk bound with rope and evidently prepared for shipping, the room was vacant. After removing the rope the officer opened the trunk, where he found the almost nude body of a well-formed young woman. The body was doubled up and wrapped in a sheet. The woman had evidently been dead at least a week. Around the neck was a light cord similar to those attached to window shades. The body bore no marks of violence. Suspended from a thin gold chain, which was about the girl's neck, was a bangle, upon which was inscribed the letters "E. C. S." After a further search in the room a bracelet bearing the initials "E. L. S." was found.

A cousin of William Leon, named Joe Leon, stated that Elsie Sigel was William's sweetheart, and that he had seen them together at the theatre.

Captain Carey of the Homicide Bureau was then notified of the discovery. He learned that this room and the one with which it communicated were occupied by William Leon and his friend Chong Sing, both of whom were known as "Americanized" and "Christianized" Chinese. Both men disappeared about the same time, and both could speak English fluently except when "no sabe talk" served their purpose better. Leon was a promoter of Chinese restaurants.

A detective was sent to the Sigel residence. At first the family denied that Elsie was missing, but finally stated that she was out of the city. Mr. Sigel was induced to view the remains. The police say that he acted rather indifferently and that after looking at the remains and jewelry he failed to identify either.

Mrs. Sigel, however, immediately identified the body as the remains of her daughter. She also identified the jewelry.

The photographs of the two missing Chinese were published in the papers, and the press all over America devoted much space to the tragedy.

On June 19, Mr. Harvey Kennedy of Amsterdam applied at an employment agency located at 38 West Twenty-Ninth Street for a cook, and he engaged a Chinaman giving the name of Ah Sing. The next day Kennedy saw the picture of Chong Sing in the paper, and he at once recognized it as the photograph of his new cook. The police were notified, and when the Chinese was taken into custody he reluctantly admitted that he was the party wanted although he denied being implicated in the murder.

For several months, William Leon lived at Sigel's house, when the family resided at No. 550 West One Hundred and Eighty-Eighth Street.

On the evening of June 1, 1909, eight days before Elsie's disappearance, Leon called at the West One Hundred and Fifty-second Street police station and told Lieutenant McGrath that while living at Sigel's he had loaned Mrs. Sigel $300. He also stated that there had been a misunderstanding regarding the debt and as he wanted to go to the house for the sole purpose of getting some of his clothing, he desired an officer to accompany him, so that he would not be accused of going to create trouble.

The request was complied with, and the Chinese obtained his clothes and left the house in a peaceable manner.

A few days after the discovery of the body, Mr. Sigel made the following statement:

"I know that William Leon and Chu Gain, who conducts the Port Arthur Restaurant, were in love with my daughter, and that Leon was insanely jealous.

"On the evening of June 8, there was a party at my house during my absence, and several Chinese were present. Leon came to the party drunk. He called Elsie to one side and told her that if she had anything to do with Chu Gain he would kill them both."

When interrogated, Chu Gain stated that Leon had threatened to kill him and Elsie because of his attentions to her.

He furthermore stated that about noon on June 9, Chong Sing called on him and stated that Leon would leave the city permanently if furnished with sufficient money for transportation. Believing that he could thus save his life, Chu Gain offered Chong Sing $260, all the money in the place, and the latter, who appeared to be greatly agitated, accepted the amount and hurried away.

Chu Gain was arrested pending further investigation, but was subsequently released.

The following letter, which was evidently written after the party on the night of June 8, was found in Chu Gain's room:

> "June 8, 1909. "Mr. Chu Gain, Nos. 7-9 Mott Street:
>
> "My Dear Friend — I don't want you to feel badly because Willie was here to-night. You know that I love you, and you only, and always will. Don't mind Willie. Although he is nothing to me now, I had to see him last night. I did not send for him. Your ever loving
>
> "ELSIE."

In the room where the murdered girl's body was found, the following letter was also discovered:

> "My Dear Willie — I am writing this letter while mother is away from home. She would not let me if she knew about it. Don't think, Willie, that I will ever give you up. I will always remember the good times we have had together. Please let me know if I can see you soon and how. With love,
>
> "ELSIE."

Chong Sing made several statements to Captain Carey, giving a little additional information each time.

The following is the substance of his different statements:

> "About 10:30 on the morning of June 9, Elsie Sigel called to see Leon for the purpose of reprimanding him for his conduct at the party on the previous evening and also to notify him not to call at the house any more.
>
> "I was downstairs and she went up to the rooms.
>
> "After a while I went upstairs and when I went into one of our rooms I heard a noise in the other room. The door was slightly ajar and I looked through and saw Leon and Elsie struggling. I saw blood on her face and I also saw a handkerchief up to her mouth.
>
> "Elsie was thrown on the bed and lay motionless while 'I Leon ripped off her clothing. He then covered her body with bed clothing and went to the closet and pulled out a trunk. I went into the room at

this time and felt the girl's hand, and Leon said she was dead. I said it was dirty work and that I was going away. I gave him $200 of my money and I then extorted $260 from Chu Gain which I also gave him. I saw him put the body in the trunk. I stayed at my cousin's house after the murder."

At the conclusion of the examination of Chong Sing he was held as a material witness under $10,000 bail.

It was ascertained that a Chinese of Leon's description sent the telegram from Washington to Mr. Sigel on June 11.

Within an hour after the murder, Leon began to make frantic efforts to dispose of the trunk. About 1 p. m. he appeared at the office of the Constitution Express Company, located at 717 Eighth Avenue, and engaged Driver Arthur Logan to remove the trunk to a laundry at No. 370 West One Hundred and Twenty-sixth Street, where a Chinese named Wah Kee signed for the trunk and paid the expressage.

At midnight Leon engaged Martin Lauria, a chauffeur, residing at 310 East Fourth Street, to convey him to the laundry in a taxicab.

Leon then had two other Chinamen bring the trunk out and after it was tied to the seat by the driver, Leon instructed Lauria to convey him and the trunk to a Chinese restaurant conducted by Li Sing at 64 Market Street, Newark.

They arrived at the restaurant about 1 a. m. Leon asked that the trunk be left there indefinitely, but as Li Sing refused, Leon returned that afternoon with James Halstead, a cabman, residing at 18 Plum Street, Newark, and the trunk was returned to the room where the murder was committed and where it remained until opened by the police.

It was the theory of Inspector McCafferty that Elsie's clothing was burned in the stove in Leon's room.

On September 24, 1909, the Coroner's jury rendered the following verdict:

"That the said Elsie J. Sigel came to her death on the 9th day of June, 1909, at 782 Eighth Avenue, by asphyxiation, inflicted at the time and place aforesaid at the hands of Leong Lung, alias William Leon."

As there was not sufficient evidence produced to justify the holding of Chong Sing, he was released after the verdict was rendered.

Notwithstanding the fact that all the leading papers in America and Canada published good pictures of Leon and for many days devoted columns to the case; that the police from the Atlantic to the Pacific made extraordinary efforts to apprehend him, and all ships upon which he could possibly have sailed were carefully searched, no trace of the murderer was ever found.

Images

FIRST CITY MARSHAL
MALACHI FALLON

CITY MARSHAL
BRANDT SEGUINE

CITY MARSHAL
JOHN W. McKENZIE

FIRST CHIEF OF POLICE
JAMES CURTIS

COL. JOHN W. GEARY
LAST ALCALDE AND FIRST MAYOR
ORGANIZER OF S. F. POLICE DEPT.

CHIEF OF POLICE
MARTIN BURKE
ELECTED CHIEF IN 1858
HELD OFFICE UNTIL 1866

CHIEF OF POLICE
PATRICK CROWLEY

CHIEF OF POLICE
THEODORE COCKRILL

CHIEF OF POLICE
H. H. ELLIS

CHIEF OF POLICE
JOHN KIRKPATRICK

CHIEF OF POLICE
I. W. LEES

CHIEF OF POLICE
WILLIAM P. SULLIVAN

CHIEF OF POLICE
GEORGE W. WITTMAN

POLICE COMMISSIONERS AND CHIEF
1878 — 1900

CHIEF OF POLICE
WM. J. BIGGY

CHIEF OF POLICE
JESSE B. COOK

CHIEF OF POLICE
JOHN B. MARTIN

CHIEF OF POLICE
JERRY DINAN

UNITED STATES SENATOR
DAVID BRODERICK
KILLED IN DUEL WITH JUDGE TERRY.

CHIEF JUSTICE D.S.TERRY OF SUPREME
COURT OF CALIFORNIA, KILLED WHILE ASSAULT-
ING JUSTICE FIELD OF U.S. SUPREME COURT.

WILLIAM T. COLEMAN
HEAD OF FAMOUS VIGILANCE COMMITTEE

DENNIS KEARNEY

HERMAN F. SCHUETTLER
ASSIST. SUPT. OF POLICE—CHICAGO—

INSPECTOR THOMAS BYRNES
CHIEF OF NEW YORK POLICE—

ALLAN PINKERTON
ORGANIZER and FIRST CHIEF of U.S. SECRET SERVICE

WILLIAM PINKERTON
CHIEF OF CELEBRATED PINKERTON AGENCY

CHIEF OF POLICE I. W. LEES
FAMOUS SAN FRANCISCO DETECTIVE

JAMES McPARLAND WHO INVESTIGATED
MOLLIE MAGUIRE & HARRY ORCHARD CASES —

FAMOUS DETECTIVES WHO INVESTIGATED MOST of THE CELEBRATED CRIMES IN AMERICA

THEODORE DURRANT,
THE "BELFREY MURDERER"
HANGED.

JOHN SEIMSEN "THE GASPIPE THUGS" LOUIS DABNER
HANGED.   HANGED.

LEON SOEDER,
MURDERER — HANGED.

CORDELIA BOTKIN,
MURDERESS — DIED IN JAIL.

WHEELER
"THE STRANGLER — HANGED.

"HOFF"
MURDERER OF
MRS. CLUTE.
LIFE INPRISONMENT

"LITTLE PETE"
NOTORIOUS "HIGHBINDER"
KILLED IN
CHINATOWN"

MILTON F. ANDREWS,
MURDERER & THIEF,
KILLED HIS PARAMOUR
& COMMITTED SUICIDE
WHEN CORNERED BY
POLICE

SYDNEY BELL,
MURDERER AND THIEF
PAROLED

NOTORIOUS SAN FRANCISCO CRIMINALS

CHARLES BECKER
"PRINCE" OF FORGERS –

ALONZA WHITEMAN
FORMER BANKER, MAYOR OF DULUTH,
STATE SENATOR AND CANDIDATE
FOR CONGRESS; AFTERWARDS A
PROFESSIONAL FORGER.

JOHN WINTER,
WHO STOLE BULLION
VALUED AT $ 280,000
FROM SELBY'S SMELTER.

JIMMY HOPE
NOTORIOUS BANK ROBBER

CHARLES HADLEY,
ACCUSED OF MURDERING NORA
FULLER IN SAN FRANCISCO.

JOHN BYRNE,
FOUND GUILTY OF
MURDERING OFFICER
GEO. O'CONNELL OF
SAN FRANCISCO.

EMMA LADOUX,
MURDERED McVICAR
AT STOCTON CAL.
LIFE IMPRISONMENT

JOSEPH BLANTHER,
MURDERED MRS. LANGFELDT
IN SAN FRANCISCO AND
COMMITTED SUICIDE.

· NOTORIOUS CALIFORNIA BANDITS ·

TIBURCIO VASQUEZ,
HANGED AT SAN JOSE.

JUAN SOTA,
KILLED IN DUEL WITH CAPTAIN
HARRY MORSE.

"BLACK BART"
THE "GENTLEMAN" STAGE
ROBBER–CAPTURED BY
CAPT. HARRY MORSE.

BRADY,
THE TRAIN ROBBER
WHO KILLED SHERIFF
BOGARD

"CARL the BUM",
WHO FOUND BROWNING
AND BRADY'S LOOT

BROWNING,
THE TRAIN ROBBER
KILLED BY SHERIFF
BOGARD

LLOYD MAJORS,
MURDERER,
HANGED IN OAKLAND

ABE MAJORS,
"A CHIP OF THE OLD BLOCK"

WEBER,
OF AUBURN CAL.
HANGED FOR KILLING HIS
FATHER, MOTHER, SISTER
& BROTHER

FRANK MILLER,
BUTLER IN S.F. CHARGED WITH
ENTICING A TRAMP INTO A RESI-
DENCE & KILLING HIM TO OBTAIN
A REWARD

ATTORNEY LE ROY,
HANGED FOR KILLING
N. SKERRETT
IN SAN FRANCISCO

DUNHAM,
WHO MURDERED HIS WIFE
AND FIVE OTHERS NEAR
SAN JOSE

GEORGE SONTAG

CHRIS EVANS

JOHN SONTAG

WM FREDERICKS

BOB DALTON

GRATTON DALTON

DAVE MERRILL

HARRY TRACEY

JAKE OPPENHEIMER

ALFRED PACKER,
KILLED AND ATE FIVE
FELLOW PROSPECTORS.

ORCHARD,
MURDERER OF
GOV. STUENENBERG
AND 18 OTHERS.

GEORGE BIDWELL,
BANK OF ENGLAND
FORGER.

DR. HYDE,
CONVICTED OF MURDER
OF COL. SWOPE ~
KANSAS CITY.

MAT. KENNEDY,
THIEF AND MURDERER,
KILLED IN BERKELEY, CAL.

BUTLER,
AUSTRALIAN MURDERER,
CAPTURED IN
SAN FRANCISCO.

LEON LING,
MURDERER OF ELSIE
SIEGEL, NEW YORK.

CZOLGOSZ
MURDERER OF McKINLEY,

KOVOLOV,
MURDERER OF MR.& MRS.
WEBER, SACRAMENTO, CAL.

CHARLES QUANTRILL

JESSE JAMES in 1860

JIM YOUNGER in 1889

FRANK JAMES in 1889

QUANTRILL
and
JESSE JAMES
and
YOUNGER BROTHERS
GANG of BANDITS

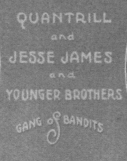

JOHN YOUNGER

COLE YOUNGER in 1889

COLE YOUNGER,
IMMEDIATELY AFTER CAPTURE

BOB YOUNGER
2 WEEKS BEFORE DEATH

LINGG
THE BOMB MAKER

EDITOR A. R. PARSONS

ADOLPH FISCHER

AUGUST SPIES

SCHNAUBELT
THE BOMB THROWER

SAMUEL FIELDEN

MICHAEL SCHWAB

GEORGE ENGEL

OSCAR NEEBE

THE CHICAGO HAYMARKET RIOT CONSPIRATORS

MARTIN BURKE
CONVICTED AND DIED IN JAIL

PATRICK O'SULLIVAN
CONVICTED AND DIED IN JAIL

DR. CRONIN
A LEADER OF THE CLAN-NA-GAEL, WHOSE BODY WAS
FOUND IN A SEWER IN CHICAGO AND THE FOUR MEN
TRIED FOR THE MURDER

DETECTIVE DAN COUGHLAN
CONVICTED BUT OBTAINED
NEW TRIAL AND ACQUITTED

JOHN KUNZE
CONVICTED OF MANSLAUGHTER BUT
OBTAINED NEW TRIAL AND ACQUITTED

EMEL ROESKI   PETE NEIDEMEYER   HARVEY VAN DINE   GUS MARX

~ BANDITS WHO TERRORIZED CHICAGO ~

MUDGETT, alias HOLMES,   HEDGEPETH,   LEUTGERT of CHICAGO,   A. BECKER of CHICAGO,
"THE CRIMINAL OF THE   THE TRAIN ROBBER, WHO   WHO BOILED HIS WIFE'S   WHO FOLLOWED
CENTURY"   INFORMED ON HOLMES.   BODY IN A VAT ~   LEUTGERT'S EXAMPLE.

JOHANN HOCK,   RAY LAMPHERE,
BIGAMIST AND MURDERER   SUSPECTED OF KILLING
OF HIS "WIFES"   THE GUNNESS FAMILY.
                             DIED IN JAIL.

BELLE GUNNESS,
WHO CONDUCTED THE MURDER FARM
NEAR LA PORTE IND., & HER FAMILY.

LEWIS PAYNE
HANGED

JOHN WILKES BOOTH,
KILLED BY SERGEANT
BOSTON CORBETT U.S.A.

DAVID E. HEROLD
HANGED

GEORGE A. ATZERODT
HANGED

MICHAEL O. LOUGHLIN,
CONVICTED AND DIED IN
PRISON

MRS. MARY SURRATT
HANGED

DR. SAMUEL MUDD,
CONVICTED BUT
PARDONED IN
1869

JOHN SURRATT,
IN UNIFORM OF
PAPAL ZOUAVES,
TRIED & DISCHARGED

SAMUEL ARNOLD,
CONVICTED AND
PARDONED IN 1869

EDWARD SPANGLER,
CONVICTED AND
PARDONED IN 1869

CONSPIRATORS IN THE PRESIDENT LINCOLN CASE

Made in the USA
Lexington, KY
11 September 2015